continued on back

Basic Statistics with
Business Applications

Basic Statistics with Business Applications

SECOND EDITION

Richard C. Clelland

Professor of Statistics and Operations Research
The Wharton School
University of Pennsylvania

John S. deCani

Professor of Statistics and Operations Research
The Wharton School
University of Pennsylvania

Francis E. Brown

Professor of Marketing and Statistics
The Wharton School
University of Pennsylvania

JOHN WILEY & SONS, INC. New York · London · Sydney · Toronto

Library of Congress Cataloging in Publication Data:

Clelland, Richard C.
  Basic statistics with business applications.

  (Wiley series in probability and mathematical statistics)

  Bibliography: p.
  1. Statistics. I. DeCani, John S., joint author.
II. Brown, Francis E., joint author. III. Title.
HA29.C63 1973   519.5′02′4338   72–8057

ISBN 0-471-16051-2

Printed in the United States of America

10 9 8 7 6 5 4 3 2

Preface

This edition of *Basic Statistics with Business Applications* is a consolidation of the first edition. The topics covered are the same, but we have edited and reorganized the material and have used a more consistent mathematical level from chapter to chapter than was done previously. We have made the following major changes.

1. Introductory material has been written that presents classical inference in the context of decision theory. The two decision theory chapters of the first edition have been moved up to follow classical inference. Thus the first eight chapters are now followed by a four-chapter section on inference and decision theory. The last four chapters cover regression, time series, and econometrics. They again form a well-integrated section.

2. In several places in the probability chapters, sections involving non-essential mathematics have been eliminated or reduced. In particular, the sampling chapter (Chapter 8) has been extensively reworked, and the amount of multiple integration employed has been greatly reduced. Similar changes have occurred in Chapters 4 to 6. As a result, the presentation of various topics has been simplified, although the mathematical level needed to use the book remains the same.

3. In other places the mathematical level has been raised to remove un-evenness. A satisfactory treatment of the random variable concept has been included in Chapters 4 and 5, the time series chapter has been extensively rewritten, and the previous treatment of the preposterior distribution of the mean in the normal case has been replaced by a complete derivation.

4. Finally, we think you will find this edition less verbose.

We have not, of course, adopted all of the suggestions made by readers and reviewers of the first edition. In particular, we have resisted the sort of approach represented by the question, "Why don't you cut out the moment-generating functions and write chapters on chi-square and the analysis of variance?" We think that a college student should not be asked to accept on faith any more material than is absolutely necessary. If moment-generating functions are not included, then the student must take all inference on faith. We feel that such an approach is unnecessary and unfair to students having a year of college mathematics including calculus. Chi-square and the analysis of variance are quite another matter. The distribution theory involved is far beyond the ability of students who have had a single year of college mathematics. We, therefore, do not feel that such topics are appropriate as part of a first course of this type despite their usefulness in practice.

Why then did we include the *t* distribution? Because, despite the impossibility of including distribution theory on *t*, we found that we could not do without it. It is too important a part of classical inference and regression to be omitted in any worthwhile discussion of these topics.

We are grateful for the many useful suggestions from reviewers, teachers, and students that have helped us create a stronger second edition. Finally, we thank Anne B. Clelland for her loyal and zealous production of indices, problem solutions, and teacher's manuals.

Richard C. Clelland
John S. deCani
Francis E. Brown

Preface to the First Edition

There was a time when the typical course in business statistics could always be cited as an example of academic cultural lag. While teachers in mathematics and engineering departments were deriving the t distribution for college sophomores who knew some calculus, teachers of business statistics were hard pressed to explain to reluctant college seniors who knew only high school algebra just why it was that the t distribution had wider "skirts" than the normal distribution. Catalog descriptions of courses in business statistics used such smug phrases as "emphasizes the logic rather than the mathematics" of statistical methods, and teachers of business statistics were mildly apologetic in the presence of their more fortunate colleagues in engineering and mathematics. We speak from experience; we have long been painfully aware of the need for a change, but the change could not occur in the teaching of statistics without a concomitant change in the mathematics requirements for business students. Unfortunately, in business schools, cultural lag was not restricted to the teaching of statistics.

"There *was* a time," we have said. Happily, that time has passed.

Prompted by an intensive self-survey and by the Ford Foundation and Carnegie Foundation reports on undergraduate business education, the Wharton School of the University of Pennsylvania in 1959 and 1960 began a drastic revision of its undergraduate curriculum. Many courses, long on tradition but short on intellectually challenging content, were dropped; new courses were added; and old courses were modernized. Among other things, the new curriculum required a one-year course in mathematics of all freshmen. (This course produces students who have some technical proficiency in elementary calculus and linear algebra and can look a simple mathematical expression in the eye without flinching.) At the same time, the existing one-year course in elementary business statistics was revised to take advantage of the freshman course in mathematics, and was given at the sophomore level instead of the junior-senior level. This new program went into effect in September 1961, and the revised statistics course was taught for the first time beginning in September 1962.

This brings us to our reason for writing this text: there was no suitable text available. We wanted a text that used calculus, linear algebra, and set theory to present statistical ideas at a somewhat simpler level than did the usual course in statistics given by engineering or mathematics departments. While desiring to emphasize that statistics can be used in many different areas of application, we realized that our students are undergraduate business students. Therefore, our illustrative examples come primarily from business, and we have included chapters on the analysis of economic time series, index numbers, and econometric models.

To be more specific as to presuppositions and content, this text assumes that the reader is familiar with set-theoretic notation and such set operations as union, intersection, and complementation, that he can integrate and differentiate simple polynomial and exponential functions of one variable, and that he is familiar with the addition, multiplication, and inversion of matrices. In three years of teaching from the text in mimeographed form, we have found that this is not too much to expect of students who have had the one-year course in mathematics required of our freshmen. Certain new mathematical ideas are used in the text, but these are explained either at the points where they arise or in the appendices.

We have attempted to write a book that balances theory and application. New topics are usually introduced in a problem context, and a large number of examples is employed throughout. On the other hand, our presuppositions regarding the reader's mathematical background have made it possible to discuss the reasoning underlying many statistical procedures which, otherwise, would have to be taken on faith. We feel strongly that students who have attained the presupposed mathematical level are entitled to a more thorough explanation of the subject matter than can be given using algebra alone. Hence, this text places great emphasis upon probability, and develops the idea of probability distributions at some length before introducing the concepts of inference and correlation.

The text provides material for a three-semester course. By omitting chapters in the last half of the book, a two-semester course can easily be arranged. In fact, the required course at the Wharton School is of this type. Sections marked with an asterisk are theoretical developments which can be omitted without interrupting the sequence of the unstarred sections.

Nearly every preface ends by expressing thanks to the various people and institutions that have helped to make the book possible. This should, in no way, detract from the sincerity with which those thanks are meant. No book is possible without the help of many people whose names do not appear on the title page. Many of our colleagues have read and used the text in mimeographed form, and their suggestions have made the book a better one than it would have been otherwise. We are also grateful to Mr. George Green, Mr. Abed-Alla Malki, and Mr. David Alberts for their work in checking calculations in the text and solving exercises and to Mrs. Sidney Balis, Mrs. William Busch, Mrs. Walter Koenig, and Mrs. Lawrence Hopkins for their patience in reading handwritten and edited manuscript, which was often illegible, and for managing somehow to type it neatly and accurately. The Ford Foundation provided partial support for the writing of the text. We also very much appreciate the competence and courtesy of the editorial staff of John Wiley and Sons. Of course, we owe a great debt to the subject of this experiment: our students. Whether they liked it or not, the text was written for them. They reacted to it, sometimes violently but always helpfully, and we reacted to their reactions. They made the course fun to teach, and we hope that they learned as much from us as we have from them.

While the book has five authors, only four can sign the preface. The fifth, J. Parker Bursk, died in the spring of 1963. We are sure that we speak for him in expressing our thanks to others who have helped with the book, but we speak for ourselves and for many generations of students at the Wharton School in expressing our thanks to him. Parker Bursk taught statistics at the Wharton School—and taught it extremely well—for more than 40 years. As chairman of the department, he insisted on first rate teaching and set the best example of this himself. In our discussions of the material for this text, he tended to look at things from the student-reader's point of view, arguing for simplicity and clarity of expression. While we can point to some of his contributions to this book, we cannot point to them all, for he was our teacher as well as our colleague and friend. No chapter in the book was written without our wondering to ourselves, "How's Parker going to react to this?" He usually did react, and when he did the text improved as a result.

RICHARD C. CLELLAND
JOHN S. DECANI
FRANCIS E. BROWN
DONALD S. MURRAY

Table of Contents

1 Research and Statistics

1.1 INTRODUCTION

Civilization today is research-minded. On every side, in every discipline, from every age come questions. How can we increase the thrust for missiles? What is the cause of cancer? What is the effect of the interest rate on economic growth? Why do people buy from a particular retail outlet? What are the distinctive qualities of a good executive? It is the task of statistics to supply methods that will be useful in answering these and other questions. Statistics, as a field of study, is concerned primarily with the method or procedure for obtaining answers, not with the numerical results of investigations. In this respect, statistics may seem similar to "scientific method" or, as other authors might say, "research" or simply "science." All three terms carry connotations of care, planning, and objectivity, as well as purposive and efficient study; as normally employed, these terms are broader in coverage than statistics. We shall use the term "research" (although the others would be equally appropriate), and discuss some of its features before returning to statistics and its role in research.

Research is questioning. The word has, however, implications beyond those of asking or inquiring. The posing and answering of a question is a necessary but not a sufficient condition. Importance and complexity are often attributes of research, but they are neither necessary nor sufficient. The term research becomes appropriate (or inappropriate) only after one considers the *way* in which the problem is attacked.

All of the questions posed above are under current study, but should the studies be classified as "research?" Various groups within our society have decided that these problems are of sufficient importance to warrant the expenditure of time and money. However, the importance of the problem is not enough. In order to secure insights into the nature of research, let us consider the question: "What are the distinctive qualities of a good executive?"

Given below are several possible approaches to the problem. Which, if any, of these approaches illustrate the research method?

1. List the first three personality traits that the investigator associates with executives of his acquaintance.

2. Ascertain the color of hair of 50 executives of large corporations.

3. Administer a standardized personality test to five "good executives" chosen by the staff of the research project.

4. Appoint a committee of five competent psychologists to prepare a list of N possible qualities (N to be determined by the committee). Assign numbers 1 through N to these qualities. Select one of these numbers by a random process. Accept the quality corresponding to that number as the dominant quality of a good executive.

5. Collect all the data that relate to the question.

All too frequently the fifth procedure is accepted as the proper research approach, but it ignores a vital point: planning. Which data relate to the question? How can they be analyzed so as to yield an answer to the problem? We shall return to these questions throughout the text, but answers to them are needed before one can proceed with a specific study. Research work must be planned. All aspects of a study must be considered and meshed early in the project. Thus, possible procedural errors can be identified and avoided.

Planning or design is a characteristic of research, but a brief consideration of the fourth approach should convince the student that planning alone is not sufficient. No doubt the precise manner in which the steps are to be performed in this procedure could be stipulated in greater detail, yet the plan has been specified at least as well as those of the other approaches. Despite the planning, this tack would hardly be accepted as a good design. The final choice is based on chance rather than on evidence concerning the distinctive qualities of good executives. Selection of the answer should be based on evidence relevant to the question.

Although there are also obvious weaknesses in the first three approaches, the phraseology of the question under consideration is too vague to permit appraisal of any research design. It is impossible to construct a good design until the question has been carefully phrased and well defined. The other questions mentioned in the opening paragraph are also too vague. However, one cannot improve on them in a vacuum. One must know the environment in which they arose and the alternatives[1] facing the man who asked each of them. The object of research is to aid in the selection among these alternatives.

---

[1] The "alternatives" in statistics consist of the complete list of possible answers or courses of action, whether the number available be two or more.

"How can we increase the thrust for missiles?" Totally different research designs would be appropriate for a physicist and a personnel officer asking this question. For the physicist, the problem would be a technical one with alternatives in the area of fuel systems. The personnel officer might consider it in terms of reducing duplication of effort. Both approaches may be a part of one broad problem, but they would be extremely cumbersome to handle simultaneously. This is frequently the situation; as the vagueness of a problem disappears, it becomes necessary to break it into parts and investigate its various aspects separately. A more precise statement of the problem often permits identification of the most crucial aspects. The more relevant features of a problem are often obscured by a vague question, whereas explicit statements of the various terms frequently reveal them to the knowledgeable investigator.

The terms of a problem fall into two general classes: those that identify items within the scope of the study and those that indicate the kind of information to be sought concerning those items. The items within the scope of the problem constitute the "population" (or "universe"); individually they are called the "elements" of the population. As we shall see, in a well-defined problem, a clear delineation of the universe is a necessity. Whether the total population or only a sample of it is to be studied, the research worker must be able to distinguish between items that are members of the set under investigation and those that are not. If sampling is to be employed, not all elements will be studied, although all are members of the universe.

The various properties of the elements are referred to as "characteristics." The characteristics pertinent to the problem should be clearly defined before data are collected. As most terms have optional definitions, it is desirable to employ the same one throughout any study. In addition, the specification of pertinent characteristics aids in establishing direction and purpose for the study.

In dealing with the distinctive qualities of good executives, the characteristics are the "distinctive qualities," and the elements are "good executives." Project yourself to the completion of the study. The research might show that 70 percent of the good executives classify as X or that the average score of good executives on a certain test is 18.3. Such information would not be very informative unless there were standards against which to compare results. The wording of the question implies that one wishes to differentiate between good and poor executives. If this be the case, the population should consist of executives divided into the two groups rather than one group of only "good" executives. Granted that the elements for the study are executives, how does one distinguish an executive from a nonexecutive? Is the distinction based on job title? Are both sexes included? Is there a minimum size for the organization? Is the study limited to corporate or business executives? After selecting an appropriate definition for "executive," the research worker must decide on the time and space coordinates of the problem. The study might be limited to a specific city, or it could be international in scope. It might be restricted to the current period, or the coverage could be extended either into the past or the future. The choice among this vast array of possibilities must be based on the purpose of the research. Who posed the problem, and how is he going to use the results? If a decision must be made by him, what alternative actions are available? A large manufacturing company might be satisfied to limit its study to the present and very recent past, and consider only business executives. A group of psychologists might wish to cover a longer period and include executives from the political and military scene as well. In either case, the purpose and decisions should be enumerated, and the universe specified in a manner consistent with the enumeration.

What are the relevant characteristics in this illustration? Color of hair was suggested in one procedure. Personality traits and the results of a personality test were proposed in others. Here, we have an example of the necessity of delimiting the problem to manageable proportions. How about age, education, intelligence, height, etc.? The investigator would be hesitant to rule out a huge list of characteristics as nonrelevant, but he may be forced to restrict the current study to a few of them. By delimiting his problem he can make some contribution, and hope that others will fill in gaps that he cannot consider.

The posing of a well-defined problem aids the research worker in his plan and design and also accomplishes another desirable end. The results of an investigation should depend neither on the disposition of the investigator at the time of the study nor on his identity. The laboratory scientist has stressed this point for years. All experimentation must be objective, and the experiment repeatable. If we find that an experiment yields different results on a series of trials, we would be unwilling to have any one of the results guide our actions. Careful planning and precise instructions should give a research design repeatability. In the laboratory, the research worker normally repeats his experiment and seeks verification from other competent scientists. The social scientist frequently does not have laboratory conditions and the controls associated with them. Consequently, his experiment may not be strictly repeatable. In this situation he should be even more careful to assure himself that the research is conceptually "repeatable"—that the experiment is conducted in such a way that the results do not depend on the identity of the investigator nor on his disposition at the time. By specifying precise definitions and enumerating each step of the research, all parties will know something much more important than the answer. They will know which question has been answered.

Any specific research problem must rely on a substantive field for definitions of terms, alternative courses of action, relevance of material, and a conceptual framework. The field of statistics can aid in establishing a more precise statement of these aspects of the problem, but in general they are provided by another discipline. Statistics takes them as given, and attempts to establish an efficient method of obtaining the necessary data, analyzing them, and, subject to certain risks, choosing an answer.

To the statistician, the key is an "efficient" method of making observations and using them as a basis for decision. What is known already? How much additional information is needed? What are the various sources of data, their respective costs, and the accuracy of each? What are the dangers associated with incorrect decisions? Each of these questions plus many others is reflected in the method that would be recommended for a specific problem. But what if the problem has no quantitative aspects? Frequently statistics is viewed as solely concerned with numbers. To an extent this is true, but it is not very restrictive. As long as one employs a classification system and attempts to place the various observations in one or more of the categories, the methods of statistics may be useful in solving the problem. This then is the role of statistics in research: *to aid in constructing a statement of the problem in relevant and unambiguous terms and to provide an efficient method of collecting and analyzing the pertinent information, all phases coordinated toward the goal of choosing an appropriate course of action.*

The statistical approach, if this name is considered appropriate for the procedure described, is employed in all research. A list of alternative answers is composed for the problem. These are possible answers only because the investigator does not have sufficient information. If he had complete knowledge, he would choose one from among them and reject the others. He should specify which alternative would be the proper answer for each possible "state of nature." These states of nature correspond to all of the possible answers for the question under study. An alternative that is not the proper answer in at least one of the possible states is not really an alternative.

Consider the plight of one of the authors of this book. His automobile had been involved in an accident 1200 miles from home, and several hundred dollars worth of damage had been done. Initially he viewed his alternatives as having the repair work done within a few miles of the accident, driving the vehicle home in its present condition and then having the work done, or trading for a new car at either location. He quickly dismissed driving home for either repair or trade-in, since he was unwilling to undertake a trip of that distance in an automobile in need of major repair. He planned to shop around for several estimates on both repairs and trade-ins, but regardless of the offers, he would not drive the vehicle home as it was.

Within this setting of alternative actions and possible states of nature, the statistician establishes a method for obtaining some relevant information, acquires that information, and compares it with the various possible states that have been previously constructed. It is tempting to say that the selection among the alternatives is then based on the evidence, but that is not quite correct. The selection is based on the predisposition of the research worker *as modified by* the evidence and the comparisons based on it. The research worker must enumerate the possible states of nature and the alternatives corresponding to each, plus his opinions concerning the likelihood of these states occurring and the degree of conformity that he will require in the comparisons. We shall consider these items, particularly the latter, in a more formal way, but in an informal and subjective way we have been doing this all our lives.

What shall I wear? Where should I live? How shall I provide for my material needs? Whom shall I marry? These questions are of a more personal nature than those posed at the beginning of this chapter, and are not usually approached in what we have identified as a "research" manner. But on an informal, more subjective, and sometimes inefficient level, each of us goes through the same stages. What are the permissible answers?—If there be only one, it is not a problem at all. Under what conditions would I be advised to choose each alternative, and with which of these conditions is the evidence more consistent? Consider the first of these questions, "What shall I wear?" A girl helping her mother clean the house views this as a mundane question, not worth much attention. An old blouse and blue jeans may be accepted immediately without considering the relative merits of any alternative. The same girl selecting her bridal gown and accessories deems the same question as one of the more important of her life. She makes an intelligent investigation of all relevant material. The research design will not be formal in nature, but it will be executed with both planning and care. Try to imagine, if you can, the young lady saying as she awakens on her wedding day, "Mother, I'm getting married today. What shall I wear?" Hardly! The complicated interrelationships among such factors as complexion, height, weight, season, time of day, flowers, and (unfortunately) cost will have been carefully analyzed; and the results will be ready for the camera, her groom, and invited relatives and friends. Is this research? It is not the type of research that we shall be primarily concerned with, to be sure, but the ingredients are the same: a problem, alternative choices, and the collection and appraisal of information to guide in the selection among those alternatives. The difference is in the formal structure, the explicit statement of alternatives, the identification of the required information, and an indication of how such information will be collected and used in choosing among the alternatives.

1.2   PREVALENCE OF RESEARCH

We have identified the basic difference between the problem of choosing wearing apparel and the research problems that we shall consider as the absence of a formal structure. The ingredients of personal questions are the same as those of the typical research problem, but the approach in the personal situation is normally more intuitive and subjective. Of course, vocational guidance, marriage counseling, and other relatively new fields have tried to introduce a more objective and scientific approach to their problems. The authors simply state that any question can be formulated as a research problem. This is not to say that the relevant data and correct conclusions can always be obtained, but the first step of formulation is always possible.

The adoption of a research approach has been a major part of the quest for better answers. It has been pervasive throughout various disciplines. This adoption has been accompanied by the use of some form of statistics in the majority of cases. Neither the research approach nor the use of statistics is new, but their prevalence is. Governments have collected data for years, going back at least to Moses who took a census when the children of Israel came out of Egypt. Even at this early date, Moses was conscious of the necessity of defining his problem and specifying the population under study: "from twenty years old and upward, all that are able to go forth to war." The universe was defined, and by implication the purpose of the research was identified.

Today, research activities have been expanded greatly within the government and extended to practically the whole spectrum of knowledge. The United States Government has a Bureau of the Census in constant operation. In contrast to the earlier definition used by Moses, this Bureau's definition of the population for the decennial census includes all human beings, and data are collected for many characteristics of that population. The duties of the Bureau have been expanded to include studies of several other populations in such work as the Census of Housing, Census of Manufacturing, Census of Agriculture, etc. Virtually every government agency does research work, using results obtained by the Bureau of the Census to some extent, but frequently collecting additional data itself. Such matters as price levels, employment and unemployment, defense capabilities and requirements, immigration, circulation of money, radio broadcasting, and educational facilities are studied in order to assess the needs and potentials of the nation. As the United States has grown and the economy has become more complex, the government has assumed a more dominant role in every phase of our lives. In this position it has been necessary for the government to seek information upon which to base its decisions.

Government-sponsored research is important, but a tremendous amount of research is done by nongovernmental groups. Indeed, research permeates every sector of our society. Every field of knowledge progresses by research and usually by statistically oriented research. For example, physics and chemistry come quickly to mind with the law of falling bodies, states of equilibrium, and the formation of compounds. Medical research is becoming more and more prominent as exemplified by studies of cancer and heart disease. Agricultural as well as industrial production has been subjected to study by statistically designed experiments. Psychologists have investigated learning laws, thresholds of perception, and many other topics. Linguistics has recently employed statistics in translation and vocabulary studies, and the results of different fund-raising techniques have been compared by statistical analysis. The only fields that cannot use a statistical and research approach are those that have not developed sufficiently. Such fields are characterized by one of two conditions: the questions are still too vague, or the pertinent information is unobtainable. This statement may seem obvious, but it explains the rapid adoption of statistical research by a wide range of fields. Knowledgeable persons have stated their questions more precisely—the first step in research—and, in so doing, have clarified their concepts. This clarification often contributes to the location of pertinent data.

The focus of this text is on business, and most of the illustrations will come from business, but statistical methods are not dependent on the substantive field. The type of data that is relevant and available is dependent on the substantive field, and the significance of the results must be interpreted in its context. The characteristics of the substantive field make some statistical techniques particularly useful for business, and limit the utility of others; the techniques themselves are neither business nor nonbusiness. Although our study will stress those that have been most used in business, the student should note their appropriateness in other areas.

1.3 PROBLEMS HANDLED BY STATISTICS

It is difficult to establish a list of the types of problems handled by statistics. A few examples may be informative. We shall not define all of the terms of the questions, although such definitions would be necessary in a complete study. Our purpose is to indicate some of the general types of problems considered in statistics.

Many questions require measures of central tendency and measures of dispersion. What is your academic point average? What is the average income of clerical workers within a certain company? Both questions seek one number that will somehow summarize many numbers. How consistent has your academic performance been? How great are the differences in the incomes of clerical workers? These questions are quite different from the first two, although the same data are relevant for each. The second set of questions is concerned with the extent of similarity or dissimilarity rather than with the magnitude of the figures. Statistics considers both types of question and we shall discuss them in detail in Chapter 6.

There are many cases in which the information does not permit the presentation of a single number as *the* answer. What is the average amount of time required to complete a specific task in an assembly plant? What percentage of the voters is in favor of the president's farm program? These questions are quite similar to those posed in the preceding paragraph, but differ in the nature of the information available. A research worker might be dubious about presenting a single number as the answer even if he made a complete census. This would certainly be the case if he had only sample data. In such a situation he would probably present a range or interval. The range that he cites would not be that found in the original data but one based on techniques that will be developed in Chapter 9.

Another series of problems concerns prediction. What will be the population of India in 1980? What will be the gross national product of the United States in 1975? Statistics has attempted to answer such questions (with limited success) by developing models and extending them in time. Somewhat similar approaches have been attempted for shorter time periods in problems dealing with stock-market fluctuations and business cycles in general (also with rather limited success). These problems will be discussed in Chapter 15.

Somewhat greater success has been enjoyed in attempts to estimate one characteristic, given data for one (or more) other characteristic(s). Boyle's and Charles' laws of gases are physical examples of this approach. Given that a man is 6 ft 1 in. in height, what do you estimate his weight to be? If you should respond with different answers depending on the height of the man, you are using this approach. In Chapter 14 we shall formalize the estimating procedure to be employed, but the method, not the idea, will be new.

Another type of problem, which we shall discuss in Chapter 10, is the testing of hypotheses. Should a hospital clinic continue to X ray for lung cancer or should it employ a new test? The statistician is interested in a wide variety of problems similar to this, problems in which the answer consists of accepting or rejecting an hypothesis. Based on the evidence, the clinic will adopt the new test or continue to use the X ray. In either case, an error may be made. Many statistical problems are of this type: making decisions under uncertainty. We consider which of two errors is more serious and do our best to keep its probability at a very low level. In the preceding example the clinic must decide which is the more serious mistake: adopting the new test when it should not, or failing to adopt it when it should. The consequences of the two possible errors are the determining factors. In this situation the clinic would be guided by how satisfactory the X ray has been, the costs in time and money for both techniques, and any pain or possible injury associated with them. If the X ray has been quite satisfactory on all counts, the clinic would probably require very conclusive evidence that the new test is superior. If, on the other hand, the experience with the X ray has not been very satisfactory, the clinic might be willing to shift on somewhat less conclusive evidence.

The student has been choosing among alternatives and evaluating the risks associated with possible errors most of his life. Should a doctor be consulted in case of injury? Most people think the more serious error is failing to consult a doctor when he should be consulted. The possibility of medical complications is considered much more serious than the cost in time and money that accompanies the visit to the physician. This theme of types of errors—their identification, evaluation, and reduction—is pervasive in statistics. We shall return to it throughout the text.

The business enterprise of today uses statistics as a vital part of its decision process. Intuition still plays a part, but even the most skeptical manager mixes data with impressions in his formula for success. The amount of statistics used in business varies from rough calculations based on trade journal figures to elaborate mathematical models based on original data. The variability in the amount invested in research and in the degree of sophistication in analyses results partially from the variability in the potential gains of research. This is particularly true where companies differ in size. It is also a function of the risks and uncertainties in the problems subjected to research. Despite these differences, some knowledge of statistics is necessary for any person who wishes to pursue a business career. The demand for such knowledge is greater today than it was a decade ago, and it is constantly increasing.

The role of statistics extends from the genesis of an enterprise to its dissolution, and from the details of its operation to broad policy decisions. Organizational and financial structure, plant location, market areas, and even basic economic activities can be the objects of statistical investigation. Indeed, without these studies, the organization starts at a decided disadvantage. The basic supply-and-demand structure prior to the entry of the new concern must be analyzed. This analysis should include the geographic distributions of supply and demand plus a variety of factors that will indicate how the new company can best enter the industry. What is an optimum size? What is a minimum size for profitable operation? What are the capital requirements for each? What are the potential sources and costs of that capital? What is the expected ratio of profit to investment? What is the expected ratio of profit to sales? These and many other statistical questions should be considered before launching the enterprise.

Once established, the concern has operational questions to consider. Personnel policies, channels of distribution, and production schedules are examples of timely problem areas. Tentative answers must be arrived at for many separate detailed questions in each of these areas. Recruitment is only a part of personnel policies, but the company must establish its quantity and quality requirements and determine the inducements that it can offer. Production schedules and personnel policies must be related. Statistical techniques can be quite helpful in this process. Production, too, must consider both quantity and quality. With respect to quantity, total demand, its seasonality, and inventory policy must be coordinated with production. Statistical theory has been applied to this question quite successfully, and statistical quality control has addressed itself to the quality aspect of production. The list could be extended to include most other phases of business operations.

1.4   DESCRIPTIVE STATISTICS AND INDUCTIVE STATISTICS

In research of any type, it is necessary to distinguish between those cases in which all elements of the population are studied and those in which the study is based on a sample. The findings of a research project are presented either as descriptions of the elements examined or as a basis from which to generalize about other elements. In the first instance the study is a census of the population and, subject to the relevance and accuracy of the data, the findings are correct. In the second instance it is again necessary to cite relevance and accuracy as limiting factors, but the problem of going from the sample to the population is also introduced. We shall employ the term *descriptive statistics* when no attempt is made to infer conditions beyond the elements examined, and the term *inductive statistics* when the study serves as a basis for inferences regarding other elements.

Let us examine some of the differences between the two types of statistics by considering ten invoices of a record distributor. These invoices range in value from $18.65 to $131.10 and have an arithmetic mean value of $42.71. These numerical results are examples of descriptive statistics. Assuming the data are correct, the investigator could employ these figures as "descriptive" of these ten invoices. Frequently an investigator would not be satisfied with statements about these ten invoices, but would require statements about "invoices of the record distributor." One must then consider the relationship between the ten and the population of invoices in general.

The relationship between the sample and the population depends on how these ten invoices are selected. If this sample is composed of the ten largest or the ten smallest invoices for a particular time period, the sample results will be a poor base for generalization. Likewise the sample would be inappropriate if it were selected at a time period when the invoices were unusually large or small in value. Pre-Christmas orders may be unusually large, and midsummer orders may be abnormally small. There may be differences by day of the week or by hour within the day. A person thoroughly familiar with the operation may select ten invoices that seem representative to him. This can be done by picking the orders from certain days which he believes are more representative, or from certain customers whom he thinks are typical, or in any other manner that he chooses. The results will be as good as his judgment. If he exercises good judgment the results will be good, but if he exercises poor judgment they will be poor. Unfortunately, this is the only answer we can give; the results of a sample selected in this manner cannot be objectively appraised.

Selection of the ten invoices by probability methods would permit an objective appraisal of the sample results. This is accomplished by permitting chance rather than personal judgment to determine the individual elements of the sample. A sample in which the individual elements are determined by chance is called a *probability sample*. This does not mean that one must ignore everything one knows about the phenomenon under investigation. There are many ways in which a probability sample can employ existing information and still yield a measure of reliability for the sample results. Some of these sampling plans will be discussed in Chapter 2 and in more detail in Chapter 8.

In our example, the statements concerning the ten invoices are based on ten observations. Simple arithmetical operations were performed, but in each case they were reports concerning the properties of those ten observations. The range was from $18.65 to $131.10, meaning that the invoice with the lowest value was $18.65 and the one with the highest value was $131.10. The arithmetic mean was $42.71, indicating that the sum of the values on all ten invoices divided by 10 was equal to $42.71. Other statements could be made, but each would be an example of descriptive statistics as long as those statements merely described characteristics of the ten invoices. But what about invoices in general for this distributor? The office manager might estimate that the arithmetic mean is $42.71 for all invoices, but he would probably be wrong. How far wrong? Is a sample of ten large enough? Provided that it is a probability sample, we can answer these questions, and we shall consider them in Chapter 9.

Our purpose at this point is not to discuss the ways of selecting samples or appropriate measures of sample reliability, but to indicate the nature of the problem as one moves from descriptive to inductive statistics. Basically, one must recognize that the sample may not be a faithful representation of the population. Although the uncertainties and risks associated with inductive statistics can be appraised, they are introduced by incomplete enumeration and are not to be found in descriptive statistics.

1.5   RELIABILITY AND ACCURACY

The induction from sample results to the population is a potential source of error. This error occurs because a sample rather than a census is employed. It is referred to as *experimental error*. If the particular method were applied in precisely the same way to another sample (or in another experiment), different results would eventuate. The measure of experimental error is really a measure of the differences resulting from different trials (or experiments or samples) of the same procedure on the same population. Every student who has taken a laboratory science course is familiar with the fact that slightly different results occur in different trials. The extent of these differences is an indication of repeatability or reliability. On the other hand, a procedure could have a very small measure of experimental error, yet yield very inaccurate results. Such a procedure would give similar results in repeated trials, but all would be misleading. The student in the laboratory who has an improperly calibrated scale might obtain approximately the same readings from a series of weighings. All would still be in error. This inaccuracy is a second source of error and is not restricted to inductive statistics.

Careless measurements, misunderstood questions, faulty memory, outright lies, incorrect calculations, missing data, and miscopied figures are additional possible sources of inaccuracies. These kinds of errors, in contrast to experimental error, are classified as *systematic error*. They do not disappear when one studies the entire population and, in the typical case, they cannot be measured. They are associated with the procedure employed in defining, collecting, and processing the data, and may be present in either a sample or census. Systematic error, or *bias* as it is often called, can best be viewed as a difference between the "average value"[2] obtained by a definite procedure and the true value in the population. If there is no difference between the two values, the procedure is *unbiased*. It is the procedure, not the specific result, that is appraised. Even though a particular procedure be unbiased, a specific sample result would probably differ from the true population value because of the presence of experimental error. In the case of a census, of course, an unbiased method would yield the true value. Unfortunately, one practically never knows if one's method is biased. To know this, one must know the true state of nature and the various results to be obtained from using a particular method. The only practical way of assessing a method for bias is to give careful consideration to the various phases of the project. Revisions where the procedures seem dubious will decrease the magnitude of the bias, but these revisions cannot be based on rigorously derived formulas.

[2] The term "average value" is used here in an intuitive fashion. An exact term for the idea involved is "expected value," which will be defined in Chapter 6 and used thereafter.

A method can be unbiased although many responses are in error. A method can be biased although almost all of the answers are accurate. The concept of systematic error involves the total study, not specific individual responses.[3] It is also possible for a method to be unbiased with respect to some characteristics but biased for others. Consider a survey of income. If persons with high incomes understate them and persons with low incomes overstate them, there will be some offsetting of these inaccuracies. If the total dollar amount of overstatement in the population would precisely equal the total dollar amount of understatement, the method would be unbiased for estimates of the arithmetic mean income. An estimate of the dispersion (extent of differences) would tend to be too low, however, and the procedure would be biased for that estimate. The method would also be biased for an estimate of the arithmetic mean if the understatement and overstatement were not equal. The method could be biased even though all persons answered honestly. In this situation the source of difficulty might lie in the definition of income. If the research worker requests income after taxes but many respondents supply data on income before taxes, the results will be inaccurate for the problem posed.

Improper sampling procedures are another source of systematic error. Judgment samples always raise the question of possible bias and never answer it. A sample of this type might yield good results, but one never knows. Sampling can be a source of bias even when a probability sample is employed. The most frequent form of this difficulty is the selection of a sample from the wrong universe. A simple random sample of shareholders is not a simple random sample of shares. The investigator must be extremely careful, or he can unwittingly make inferences about populations other than the one sampled.

The preceding discussion has distinguished between accuracy and reliability. *Accuracy*, as used in statistics, is measured by systematic error, and is associated with the total method apart from consideration of the particular sample selected. *Reliability* is measured by experimental error, and is associated with differences introduced because only one of the many possible samples is selected. A third term, sometimes confused with accuracy and reliability, is precision. *Precision* refers to the refinement of the measurement: 7.581 is more precise than 7.58. When results are rounded, they become less precise, but there is no loss in accuracy provided that the method of rounding is unbiased. A method that always raises or lowers halves is biased, but one in which halves are rounded to the nearest even (or nearest odd) figure is unbiased.

---

[3] The terms *experimental error* and *systematic error* both refer to the results of the total study. No specific term will be employed to designate an error for a specific element.

1.6 CONCLUSION

This chapter has attempted to indicate the place of statistics in our society, in general, and in research problems, in particular. No definition was suggested for the term "research," but a definition consistent with the discussion might be "planned and organized investigation of all relevant information." The field of statistics can contribute to research at all stages, but the usual concept of statistics stresses description and analysis of quantitative material. In this approach, the data are taken as given, and their relevance and accuracy are assumed. Experimental error is of prime interest in analysis, and consequently of prime interest in this concept of statistics. Systematic error, except for some of the more technical aspects, is viewed more as a part of the substantive area in which statistics is applied. Much of this book will take this approach, since its focus is on analysis, but the relevance and accuracy of data are obviously critical features in a research project.

Chapter 2 will consider the formulation of a research project in some detail. The nature of the data is of vital concern, and various aspects of definition and collection will assume major roles in this discussion. Descriptive measures and analysis should be an integral part of the research design, but calculations and technical aspects of description and analysis will be postponed. Only general aspects of statistical research will be discussed in the next chapter.

IMPORTANT TERMS AND CONCEPTS

Accuracy
Bias
Census
Characteristic
Error
 Experimental
 Systematic
Formulation of question
Population
Precision

Reliability
Research
Sample
Science
Scientific Method
Statistics
 Descriptive
 Inductive
Universe

EXERCISES

1. Distinguish among science, research, and statistics.
2. Distinguish among accuracy, precision, and reliability.

3. a. Distinguish between descriptive and inductive statistics.
   b. Give an original example of the use of descriptive statistics and an original example of the use of inductive statistics.
   c. Which of the following belong to the realm of inductive statistics? Which belong to the realm of descriptive statistics? Explain.
      (1) A generalization about habits of all corporate presidents from a survey of the presidents of the ten largest corporations in the United States.
      (2) A statement by a physician about the habits of cancer patients.
      (3) "During the period from 1950 to 1960, real GNP in the United States rose at the rate of 2.9 percent."
      (4) "All Ironclad undergraduates are male. Therefore, all undergraduates of all colleges in the United States are male."
      (5) "The boiling point of water is 212°F."

4. Discuss and criticize the following statements:
   a. "A census always gives better information than a random sample."
   b. "A census is always more reliable than a sample."
   c. "A census is always more precise than a sample."
   d. "A census is always more accurate than a sample."
   e. "A judgment (nonprobability) sample is sometimes preferable to a probability sample."

5. a. Distinguish between a probability sample and a judgment sample.
   b. What is the advantage (or advantages) of probability sampling?

6. The Hubertus Corporation is interested in studying the financial effects of pension plans for persons whom it has employed over a long period of time. Define three populations that might be made the subject of relevant research studies.

7. The Robertson Sporting Goods Company wishes to test two different types of golf ball core to see which is best.
   a. What population should it study?
   b. Should it employ a sample or a census?
   c. What might "best" mean in this situation?
   d. If the characteristic of interest is distance off the tee with a driver, what are two possible sources of bias in the study?
   e. What do accuracy, reliability, and precision mean in the context of part *d*?

2 Formulation of a Research Project

2.1 DEFINING A RESEARCH PROBLEM

" 'Twould be trivial to state the obvious were it not for the universal neglect thereof."[1] A research project has two principal parts: the question posed and its answer. These two should be the centers of attention; all else is introduced as a bridge between them.

We have already mentioned the importance of a well-defined question which identifies the pertinent universe, the relevant characteristics, and the admissible answers. The investigator must translate a vague inquiry (his own or someone else's) into a well-defined question. This is his first task. His second is the establishment of ordered pairs relating all possible states of nature to the various admissible alternatives. He must enumerate all of his alternatives and all possible states of nature. The ordered pairs establish the relation between these two sets, specifying the answer that corresponds to each possible state. If the investigator possessed complete knowledge of the universe, the selection of the proper answer would be automatic. In the usual situation he does not have such perfect information, and both the methods by which he obtains relevant, although imperfect, information and the way in which this information is used in the selection among answers are of considerable importance. Temporarily, let us place ourselves in the novel position of complete knowledge. In this world of make-believe we need concern ourselves only with the formulation of the question and the construction of the ordered pairs which relate states of the universe to the alternative answers. Later we shall discuss the compromises introduced into research, some because complete knowledge is unachievable and others because it is too expensive. Starting with the ideal often permits a better

---

[1] Anonymous.

perspective of the problem, since we are forced to appraise, before the fact, the relevance of various characteristics and the precision required.

Consider the problem of the purchasing agent for the Jones Manufacturing Company. Two suppliers have submitted bids on condensers. Prices, terms, and delivery are similar, and the decision is to be based on quality. Two universes are involved: one for each supplier. Each universe consists of the condensers to be supplied to the Jones Company during the year covered by the contract. The relevant characteristic is quality, and the purchasing agent is willing to judge quality by the average (arithmetic mean) length of life under a severe test.

The question can be stated quite simply: "Which potential supplier will supply condensers with the higher average length of life under the designated test?" Using μ as the symbol for the arithmetic mean, the ordered pairs for decision making become: if $\mu_A \geq \mu_B$, choose A; if $\mu_B > \mu_A$, choose B.[2] The purchasing agent cannot actually investigate either of the specified universes before making the choice, since both lie in the future. Furthermore, he would not subject the entire universe to the test even if he could. He would then know which supplied the higher quality condenser, but he would have none to use in his products. The analysis has focused attention on the relevant points, however, and the purchasing agent should consider how he can best approximate the perfect information. The answer to this question centers on how many condensers from each supplier are to be tested and how they are to be selected. Generally, the number should be large enough to give a reliable estimate, and the manner of selection should yield an accurate one. This is not a very adequate answer, since it is not operational, but we shall return to these concepts after considering a more complex problem.

Let us turn to the problem of relieving economically depressed areas. The first step is to identify the areas that are "economically depressed." The second is to institute measures that will alleviate depressed conditions in the identified areas. The federal government is concerned with this problem for many areas, but we shall limit our consideration to one: Philadelphia. We shall also restrict ourselves to the first problem: Is Philadelphia an econom- ically depressed area? Before considering the definition of an "economically depressed" area, let us determine the time and space limits of the universe. If we are contemplating remedial action, the time factor should correspond to the period in which such action would be instituted and have an effect. Herein lies a difficulty that is almost always present in research: one investi- gates the present, the near past, or the not so near past, but introduces measures for a future time, assuming that the characteristics determined for

---

[2] A is to receive the contract in case the means are equal because, on net balance, he has more minor considerations in his favor.

the time coordinate of the study will approximate those at which the action is to be taken. Sometimes this assumption is a close approximation, but in other situations it is unrealistic. The student must evaluate how critical the assumption is for each problem. Observe, in this particular problem, the rapidity with which we slipped from the first stage (identification) into the second (selection of appropriate action), even though we were concerned only with the first. This demonstrates the central role that we shall give to applied research as distinct from pure research. The former is concerned with the implications of, and actions resulting from, the answer to the question, while the latter stops at the answer. For this particular problem, one might select the appropriate time coordinate as the final date of the most recent quarter, for example, June 30, 1973.

Turning now to the geographical boundaries of the universe, what do we mean by Philadelphia? Is it the city proper, or does it encompass all or part of the suburbs? The Bureau of the Census has defined the Philadelphia Standard Metropolitan Statistical Area (SMSA) as the eight-county area including Philadelphia, Delaware, Chester, Montgomery, and Bucks counties of Pennsylvania and Camden, Burlington, and Gloucester counties of New Jersey. The appropriate geographical limits depend on the problem and the actions contemplated. If the federal government were considering specific public works as measures to combat depressed conditions, the universe to study would be the area that would be affected by those public works. But this is reversing the proper procedure. The basic question concerns the economic well-being of a specific area. If the contemplated actions will influence the universe, the problem has been changed. We are then asking "Which, if any, of the proposed actions should be adopted?" The goal is not to adopt an action, but to alleviate economic distress that might be present. The question should be framed in terms of the goal, and the universe should be determined by the question so phrased. The goal is the economic well-being of the nation and its components, here Philadelphia.

One approach is to consider an area that is closely interrelated in an economic sense. Using this approach, the universe should be defined to encompass an area that is an economic unit. The Bureau of the Census defines an SMSA in terms somewhat similar to this, but it is obvious that there are varying degrees of economic interrelationship. The area could be extended to cover the world, or it could be restricted to a small portion of the city. One might argue in favor of various specific geographical areas as appropriate for study, but we shall accept the SMSA as a meaningful economic unit. Our problem, then, is the classification of the Philadelphia SMSA as either (a) economically depressed, or (b) not economically depressed. The time and space coordinates for the universe have thus been adopted: June 30, 1973, and the eight-county region previously specified.

The pertinent characteristic is the economic condition of the area, but what is the appropriate way of measuring economic condition? Income, production, and employment come quickly to mind. The first two are output measures, and the third is an important input item. Either output, input, or some combination might be appropriate. As an alternative, one could single out a certain part of output or input as particularly significant; for example, capital expenditures or some form of construction. We might take a complementary approach and look for the absence of economic well-being. Unemployment could be adopted as an appropriate measure; and we shall adopt it, based principally on two assumptions: (1) it is a fairly good indicator of the impact of economic depression on individuals, and (2) together with employment it is a reasonably satisfactory indicator of potential overall economic activity; separately they show the realized and unrealized portions of that potential.

Unemployment, however, is an elusive concept. Who is unemployed? How about a housewife who lost her part-time job? A housewife who started looking for work when her husband lost his job? A housewife who performs the same household duties as the first two, but who is not looking for work? A full-time student seeking part-time work? A student looking for a summer job? A student enjoying his summer vacation and not looking for work? A person absent from work but on sick leave? A permanently disabled individual? All of these decisions depend on the basic question: Are we interested in classifying all persons or a subset of persons? The two assumptions of the preceding paragraph indicate that our attention centers on the reduction of activity below some "potential" output and the impact of such a reduction on the individuals affected. With this in mind, we shall include only those persons who are both willing and able to work and shall use the term *labor force* to designate the set of persons who possess both characteristics.

Are those seeking or holding part-time employment also members of the labor force? If so, should they be considered members to the same extent as those seeking or holding full-time employment? If we possessed complete information, we might wish to classify individuals as fractional members of the labor force, dependent on the portion of a full work week for which they hold or seek employment. If fractional values were permitted, it might also be appropriate to use them for unemployment. A person working four days during a particular week could be classified as 20 percent unemployed for that week. The introduction of fractional values would stress the concept of utilization of existing labor potential. This would be fine for a problem that emphasized the use of resources, and almost as good for assessing the impact of economic depression. Such an approach has several practical difficulties, but at the moment we are not concerned with them.

There is one major question that we must answer in connection with the universe: Are we interested in persons working or living in the Philadelphia Standard Metropolitan Statistical Area? The concept of unemployment becomes quite difficult *unless residency is the basis.* An unemployed person is unemployed in many different geographic areas, each of which might be a potential source of employment. An unemployed resident of Wilmington, Delaware, is unemployed in Philadelphia as well as in Wilmington. Indeed, he is also unemployed in San Francisco! These statements are correct, regardless of whether the person was ever employed in those areas. When residence is the criterion, no such complication arises.

Let us summarize the definition we have given to the problem: "Is Philadelphia an economically depressed area?" Philadelphia has been assumed to mean the eight-county area defined by the Bureau of the Census as the Philadelphia SMSA, and June 30, 1973 has been taken as the appropriate date. The degree of unemployment among the labor force is assumed to be a proper measure of economic depression, and residents of the area who are willing and able to work constitute the labor force. Each person is classified both with respect to his membership in the labor force and his degree of unemployment in fractional values, ranging from 0 to 1. The total size of the labor force will be given by

$$\sum_{i=1}^{N} P_i$$

where P_i is the portion of a full work week for which each resident of the area held or sought employment, and N is the total number of residents. The amount of unemployment in the area will be given by

$$\sum_{i=1}^{N} U_i P_i$$

where U_i is the portion of P_i for which each resident of the area was unemployed. For example, a person seeking two days of work per week and employed for only one-half day would be identified with $P_i = 0.4$ and $U_i = 0.75$. The resulting multiplication ($U_i P_i = 0.3$) would show the portion of a full work week for which he was unemployed. The degree of unemployment, L, in the area is then given as

$$L = \frac{\sum_{i=1}^{N} U_i P_i}{\sum_{i=1}^{N} P_i}$$

a fraction that indicates the portion of labor that is idle. Notice that both membership in the labor force and unemployment have been defined so that a person cannot be in the labor force more than once, nor can he be "overemployed." This is admittedly arbitrary and could be changed.

In our restricted problem (which has not included actions), there are two alternative answers: yes and no. What degree of unemployment characterizes an economically depressed area? The ordered pairs will take the following form: if $L \leq X_1$—representing a specific level—the answer is no; if $L > X_1$, the answer is yes.[3] The equality sign could be affixed to either inequality but not to both. We include it with the first, stating the area is economically depressed only if X_1 is exceeded. The selection of X_1 is dependent upon personal judgment and on one's philosophy of the role and responsibility of government. One person might pick 0.07 while another selects 0.03. Let us arbitrarily choose 0.05.

We do not have perfect information concerning L. How do we get a satisfactory basis upon which to reach a decision? We shall not pursue this problem, but the definition of the universe and the pertinent characteristics permit the identification of potential difficulties. Although the time and geographic limits of this problem cause difficulty, the definitions are reasonably clear. The P_i and U_i values are a different matter; here the individuals themselves may have difficulty in determining their own willingness, capabilities, and appropriate fractional values. The identification of residents may pose some practical problems, but the major problem would be in the P_i and U_i values, principally in P_i, since U_i is automatically determined if the respondent can indicate the extent of his present employment.

With two admissible answers, the research study, short of perfect information, is subject to two possible errors: (1) calling the area depressed when it is not, and (2) calling it not depressed when it is. We saw in an earlier example that another problem with two alternatives gave rise to two possible errors. This is quite general. In fact, it is so general that the two errors have been given names: Type I and Type II errors. The state of nature corresponding to one alternative is established as the hypothesis to be tested, and the other is identified as the alternative hypothesis. In our illustration let us test the hypothesis that the area is not depressed, that is, $L \leq X_1$, and identify it as H_0. H_1, the alternative hypothesis, will be $L > X_1$, or the area is depressed. There are four possible results as shown by the paradigm below:

		True State of Nature	
		H_0	H_1
Conclusion	H_0:	No error	Type II error
	H_1:	Type I error	No error

[3] If we had included the selection of actions, the sets of ordered pairs would have taken the following form: $L \leq X_1$, no action; $X_1 < L \leq X_2$, action A; $X_2 < L \leq X_3$, action B; $X_3 < L \leq X_4$, action C, etc., with each successive action, A, B, C, $\cdots$, more drastic.

No error occurs if we conclude H_0 and H_0 is true, or if we conclude H_1 and H_1 is true. However, suppose we conclude H_1 and H_0 is true; that is, we conclude the area is depressed and it is not. We identify this as a Type I error; the hypothesis being tested is true, but has been rejected. If H_1 is true but rejected, a Type II error is committed; the hypothesis being tested is accepted, although it is not true. Which is the more serious error? Different individuals may give different answers, but the experiment would be designed in a manner that reflected the individual's point of view. We shall consider such designs in Chapter 10.[4]

2.2 DUMMY TABLES

The two illustrations of the purchasing agent and the relief of depressed areas did not require much analysis of the pertinent data. The first required the calculation of two averages, and the second the calculation of a single ratio. A device that is quite useful at the planning stage, when analysis is more involved, is the dummy table. Such a table contains column and row descriptions, but not data. It indicates the type of data needed, and the investigator should be able to determine whether these will permit the selection of one of the admissible alternatives.

Table 2.1   Frequency Distribution of Department Store Clerks by Hourly Wage Rate, Memphis, Tenn., May 1973

Hourly Wage Rate ($)	Number of Clerks
1.75–1.79	
1.80–1.84	
1.85–1.89	
1.90–1.94	
etc.	

Table 2.1 is a dummy table to be used in the study of the wage rates of department store clerks in Memphis, Tenn. This table, when filled, would show the extent of similarities and differences among the wage rates received by these clerks; various calculations could be made to summarize the properties of the data.

The table focuses attention on several problems that might otherwise have been ignored. Care must be taken to assure that the data correspond to the

[4] Type I and Type II errors are frequently discussed with the assumption that there is no systematic error present. In such a case, their probabilities can be calculated.

problem and are properly interpreted. The attention here is on similarities and differences among clerks, not among stores. Wage rates must be expressed for some time period. The dummy table indicates hourly rates, but they could have been weekly or annual. Different time periods will produce the same distributions only if the clerks all work the same number of hours and no complicating factors are introduced by diverse overtime policies. The specific wage rates of the table are merely illustrative of the classes that might be employed. If they are established before the collection process, one of two situations is implied: either the problem has been defined so that the classes specified are the appropriate ones, or the investigator is familiar enough with the subject to know that they will yield a satisfactory frequency distribution. Regardless of the time at which the class limits are specified, it is necessary to determine the degree of precision demanded; for example, should the rate be specified to the nearest cent, the nearest mill, or is it permissible to round out to multiples of five cents? Once again, the problem and its alternative answers indicate the necessary precision; it cannot be determined in a vacuum.

The choice of the class intervals in such a table requires a careful statement. The classes should be mutually exclusive and exhaustive. "Mutually exclusive" means that there are no overlaps; it is impossible for an element to fall into two classes. The intervals "$1.75–1.80" and "$1.80–1.85" are not mutually exclusive since it is unclear where a clerk earning $1.80 should be placed. "Exhaustive" means that there are no gaps; each element must be in some class. If there are fractional rates, the classes suggested by Table 2.1 are not exhaustive, since a clerk earning $1.795 would be in neither the first nor the second class.

A quite different approach to the study of wage rates of department store clerks in Memphis is shown in Table 2.2. The investigator, in this case, has selected a certain wage rate as critical ($1.90), and is seeking to determine whether large and small stores differ with respect to average hourly wage rates. In this illustration, two subdivisions have been selected for each characteristic, but more could be employed. The critical values, unless dictated by the problem, might be selected after the collection process in order to divide the respondents in predetermined proportions among the classes: for example, 50 percent in each class.

Note that Table 2.2, contrary to Table 2.1, will show data for stores. Hourly rates for individual clerks must come first, but each store will contribute only one observation. In Table 2.1 the elements that compose the universe are clerks; in Table 2.2 the elements are stores. If Table 2.2 were constructed with clerks as elements, each store would contribute as many observations as it had clerks. Consequently, a few very large stores could dominate the analysis. If one argues that such a procedure is proper, one is arguing in favor of a universe composed of clerks. The problem posed for

Table 2.2   Distribution of Department Stores by Average Wage Rate of Clerks and Number of Clerks, Memphis, Tenn., May 1973

Number of Clerks in Store	Average Hourly Wage Rate		Total
	Less than $1.90	$1.90 or More	
Less than 10			
Ten or more			
Total			

Table 2.2, however, asks whether there are differences in wage rates by size[5] of *store*. One might want more classes, but the principle would be the same.

How would Table 2.2, when filled, enable us to answer the question? A comparison is implicit in the table: compare the percentage of small stores whose average wage rate is below $1.90 with the percentage for large stores. If we have accurate information from a complete census, this comparison will give a clear answer to the question, and will also indicate how much of a difference exists.

2.3   ATTRIBUTES AND VARIABLES

It is useful in many cases to make a distinction between two types of data: one involving a measurement and the other a classification. It is tempting to think that characteristics such as age are examples of the first and that others such as color are examples of the second. This is not the case! The characteristic is not the determining factor; the handling of the data is the key.

The term "variable" will be used when a measurement is involved, and the term "attribute" when it is a matter of classification.[6] In order for the characteristic to be treated as a variable, one must construct a scale, assign values on that scale to the relevant elements, and employ those values in the analysis. When the quantification is dropped at any of these stages in favor of a yes-no or qualitative distinction, an attribute has been introduced.

Consider income as a characteristic. A market research agency wished to advise a client on merchandising policies in a new store. Total income for 1965 was ascertained from prospective customers. Each respondent reported his income to the nearest $100. The agency determined the average income by

[5] Number of clerks is only one possible measure of size. Others might be total sales, square feet of selling space, or total number of employees.

[6] Attributes can be viewed as a special case of variables for which only two values are possible: 0 if the element does not possess the characteristic, and 1 if it does.

summing the incomes of all respondents and dividing by their number. The result of $5125.18[7] was presented as a summary statistic. Income, in this case, was a variable. With this same collection process, income would have been an attribute if each respondent were classified as "under $5000" or "$5000 and over." The summary statistic, in this case, could be: 56 percent, the percentage of elements who had incomes of $5000 or more. In a supplementary study of various areas this 56 percent might be a variable. The elements in this study would be areas, and in each the percentage of potential customers having incomes of $5000 or more would be calculated.

If a summary statistic indicates the number or percentage of elements that are members of a certain subset, the characteristic is an attribute. If, however, a particular value of the characteristic is presented as descriptive for a set of elements, the characteristic is a variable. Table 2.1 is instructive. It contains a scale for wages consisting of positive real numbers. Each element will be assigned a value on this scale, but the next step introduces some confusion. A series of categories is to be established with each clerk to be placed in one of them. If the summary statistics indicate the number or percentage of clerks who are in wage group 1 (identified by upper and lower limits if desired), group 2, etc., then wage rate is an attribute. On the other hand, if the analyst assumes that $1.77 is a reasonable estimate of the rate received by all persons in the $1.75–1.79 group and employs that figure ($1.77) in his calculations, wage rate is a variable. It is a variable in the latter case even if the original information is collected by asking which class is appropriate for each clerk.

Although the distinction between an attribute and a variable is not dependent on the characteristic being considered, the establishment of a scale and the assignment of values on the scale are crucial for variables. As a consequence, one might view progress in knowledge as proceeding from attributes to variables and within variables, proceeding to more and more precise scales. If this be true, the development of better measuring instruments is an indication of progress. More elaborate equipment for the medical profession supplies the physician with more complete information concerning the patient, and thus, if the right characteristics are measured, permits more intelligent treatment. In the same way, more detailed information on business, human behavior, aptitudes, finance, engineering, and even baseball are collected in the hope that more intelligent decisions can be made in these fields.

[7] The figure $5125.18 should be rounded to $5100, since the original data were rounded to the nearest $100. Furthermore, the store would certainly not require any more precision than that in establishing a merchandising policy. If $5125.18 were presented, it would be based on the assumption that the rounding process did not introduce any bias; that is, the sum of the deviations above the stated income was equal to the sum of the deviations below that income.

A resort hotel reviewed its advertising program and decided that it should purchase spot radio announcements. It then had to select the time and the station in order to do the best possible job of reaching its potential guests. The problem confronting the staff was accepted as: "At what time and over what station should we place a series of spot announcements in order to reach potential guests in the most efficient manner?" The universe of "potential guests" is rather vague; but the hotel was satisfied to define the universe in terms of age, income, and geographical location. Note also that the purchase of some announcements has been presupposed. This was based on the assumption that the long-run effects would be beneficial in terms of contacts and institutional advertising even if the short-run effects were not. The problem could have been posed as: "What, if any, spot announcements should be purchased?" Also the problem has presupposed that efficiency, not number of listeners, should be the determining factor. After discussion, efficiency was defined as profit realized, divided by cost of the announcement. The staff recognized that this kind of information could not be obtained, although the discussion was useful because it forced the decision maker to choose his goals and recognize later compromises. With perfect information, what sort of dummy table would be required?

Table 2.3   Efficiency of Alternative Spot Announcements by Station and by Time, July–September 1969 (Profit per Dollar of Cost)

Time	Radio Station			
	WNBC-AM	WOR-AM $\cdots$	WNBC-FM	$\cdots$
6:00–6:14:59 A.M.				
6:15–6:29:59 A.M.				
etc.				

The staff prepared Table 2.3. The table indicates that AM and FM listening should be separated; this is a very important distinction in terms of cost.

The fact that a spot announcement is placed at a specific point in time has considerable bearing on the time intervals accepted as relevant. The table suggests that an interval of 15 minutes is satisfactory. What information is required to complete the table, given the definition of the universe? Each cell represents a certain station and a certain time. First, it must be ascertained for each element (that is, person) in the study which of these cells represents a time and station in his listening behavior. For those that are a part of his listening behavior, the profit realized by the hotel as a result of the listening must be determined. The sum of the profit realized from all elements divided by the cost is the entry within that cell. Those cells with the highest entries are the most efficient. If the profit is operating profit, gross with respect to advertising, only the cells with an entry of 1.0 or more earn enough to cover the cost of the commercial.

Will Table 2.3 present attributes or variables? To the extent that each element is classified as listening or not listening, it seems to present attributes. Each element is measured, however, in terms of a variable—profit produced. The whole problem is seen in terms of variables when it is realized that each element is assigned a number: zero if a nonlistener or noncontributor to profit, and a positive real number if a contributor to profit.

The number of spot announcements has been unspecified, except that the minimum is one. For this problem the following decision rules were tentatively accepted, although later revised. The order of selection was to be based on rank in efficiency. The maximum number selected was restricted by whichever of three limiting conditions was encountered first: no more than ten, a total expenditure not to exceed a stipulated figure, and no cell for which the entry was less than 1.0. In the event that no cell had an entry of 1.0 or above, the cell with the highest value was to be chosen.[8]

2.4   HOMOGENEITY

Before proceeding to imperfect information, let us consider one final point in the formulation of a research project. We may be misguided in our conclusions because we inspect the data from an incorrect perspective. This is always possible, and only a careful consideration based on knowledge of the substantive area can minimize the danger. A recent study indicated that the average dividend yield for mutual funds in 1958 was 2.5 percent. Such a finding is not very informative because mutual funds are dissimilar in many respects. Some funds hold common stocks almost exclusively; others hold only bonds; still others hold only preferred stocks; and other funds hold a mixture of different types of securities. If the funds are divided into groups based on the type of securities held, and dividend yields are calculated for each group, it is found that the yields are quite dissimilar.

The basic question is whether the result for the whole group conceals differences among subgroups. Can the universe be subdivided on the basis of a characteristic other than the one under investigation so as to reveal such differences? If it is impossible to find subdivisions which differ with respect to the characteristic under study, the universe is classified as "homogeneous"

---

[8] This project was not completed. Efficiency, as defined, was obviously unobtainable, and the staff was not satisfied with any of the compromises proposed.

with respect to that characteristic. If, however, one discovers a basis of subdivision which reveals differences among the subgroups, the universe is considered "heterogeneous" with respect to the characteristic.[9] It is meaningless to refer to a universe as homogeneous or heterogeneous without specifying a particular characteristic. Almost all universes are homogeneous with respect to some characteristics but heterogeneous with respect to others.

The process can be extended to several subdivisions. In the example of dividend yields for mutual funds, the various funds announce different investment objectives. These could serve as a second basis of subdivision.

Table 2.4   Dividend Yields for Groups of Mutual Funds, 1958

Principal Type of Securities	*Percent*
Common stock	3.1
Preferred stock	5.9
Bonds	5.1
Balanced, that is, a combination	3.8
Net Assets[a] (*Common Stock Funds Only*)	
Small	3.1
Small-medium	3.1
Medium-large	3.1
Large	3.1
Investment Objective (*Common Stock Funds Only*)	
Income	4.5
Growth	2.3
Mixed	3.4

[a] Special reclassification for this table.

Other bases could be introduced, with some showing significant differences among subgroups in dividend yield and others not demonstrating such differences. Table 2.4 gives results obtained from other bases of division.

The net-assets subgroups do not reveal any differences in dividend yields, but there are marked differences among the subgroups based on investment objective. State of incorporation, number of issues in portfolio, number of

[9] When the analysis is inductive rather than descriptive, the sample differences are termed "statistically significant" in the case of heterogeneity and "not statistically significant" in the case of homogeneity.

letters in last name of chief executive, and color of eyes of secretary are all possibilities, but not all equally likely. The conclusion drawn from Table 2.4 is that mutual funds are not homogeneous with respect to dividend yield. If common stock funds with an income objective could not be subdivided on some basis other than dividend yield into subgroups that differ with respect to dividend yield, these funds would be homogeneous in that characteristic.

A related question is whether groups are homogeneous with respect to a characteristic. For example, are common stock funds and bond funds homogeneous with respect to dividend yield? The answer is obviously no, since the two groups differ considerably. When the question of homogeneity is raised with respect to a particular characteristic, a complication may develop. It is possible that a difference between two groups is more apparent than real.

A few years ago, one of us was impressed by the difference between men and women in mathematical aptitude test scores. The average for men was 560 points, and that for women was 521. A difference of this magnitude had strong implications for the teaching of quantitatively oriented courses.

Table 2.5   Average Mathematical Aptitude Scores of Men and Women by School Within a Certain University

School	Average Score	
	Men	Women
Engineering	610	608
Liberal arts	514	517
Nursing	467	473
Others	526	522
All university	560	521

Radically different performances by men and women had not been observed in these courses, and the data were inspected further. Examination of the scores within various schools supplied the explanation. Scores in the engineering schools were high for both sexes, but there were few women in the schools. The school of nursing, on the other hand, was almost exclusively composed of women, and most students in this school recorded low scores in the examination. Table 2.5 indicates that males and females within a given school had similar averages. What superficially appeared to be a difference associated with sex, became, on closer examination, a difference associated with school. Within schools, men and women were homogeneous with respect to mathematical aptitude.

2.5 PROBLEMS IN THE COLLECTION OF DATA

As we move from complete to incomplete information, the question becomes: How do we get the best possible data in the most efficient manner? In defining the problem, the elements of the universe are identified and the relevant characteristics are specified, including the precision required.

The practical research man must decide whether to study the universe identified in the problem or some approximation that he believes is a satisfactory compromise. If the latter approach is employed, he must evaluate subjectively any bias involved. One might be willing to study registered voters with children in the public school system rather than all registered voters for some elections, but it would seem a dangerous compromise if a bond issue for school construction were on the ballot.

After the universe has been selected, the researcher must establish a procedure for obtaining the required data. Various lists of techniques for collecting data have been prepared, but in the final analysis all collection takes the same form: the researcher asks the observer to record his observations concerning an element or elements of the universe. There need not be three distinct parties, but there are three roles: researcher, observer, and observed.

There may be instances in which the researcher is also the observed. This is not usually the case, and the objectivity of observations may be suspect where it occurs. The researcher is, however, frequently free to decide whether the other roles should be played by separate persons. The difficulties that arise when researcher and observer are different individuals usually involve communication and cooperation: Does the observer understand the question posed, and is he willing to supply the information? These two points tend to make it desirable for the researcher to act as observer. However, one must also consider whether the individual is capable of so acting. Capability involves both technical competence and the availability of time. In most large studies it would be impossible for the researcher to act as observer for even a substantial part of the observations.[10]

The possibility of the observed acting as observer depends on the three points raised in the preceding paragraph.

1. Will he understand the questions and the instructions?

2. Will he be cooperative and attempt to supply the information?

3. Does he possess the information, or is he capable of obtaining it?

The answers to these questions depend on the elements of the universe and

---

[10] Differentials in the monetary costs of the research might also lead the researcher to spend his time otherwise.

the characteristics under study. The student should note that the definitions adopted in the problem may not be appropriate for presentation to the observer. He may not possess the objectivity of the researcher. This may be particularly true when the observer is also the observed. Consider a study of racial prejudice. If the respondent suspects the object of the research, he might attempt to hide such tendencies. Questions would be disguised so that the respondent would not guess the characteristics being measured. Some cigarette companies have been notorious for the opposite procedure. They have been known to distribute samples of their own brand immediately prior to the collection of data. As one would expect, the results of such studies generally favor the sponsor. Technical definitions must also be avoided. A respondent should not be asked for his "personal disposable income"; instead a series of questions should enable the researcher to determine the figure indirectly.

A problem that is even more troublesome concerns the use of data on one characteristic as an approximation to data for another. For example, let us return to the determination of spot announcements for the hotel. It would be useless to ask a respondent whether he would visit the hotel if he heard the commercial, or how much he would spend if he visited the hotel. He cannot supply such information. What data could be collected? Probably that he did or did not listen to certain stations at certain times. How much of a leap is it from listening to spending? The hotel staff thought it reasonable to assume that the rankings of the cells, which represent specific times for specific stations, would be approximately the same for both spending and listening. However, they were unwilling to make any assumption concerning the number of listeners or the number of listeners per dollar of cost that would make an announcement profitable. As a result, the project was abandoned.

The problems considered thus far concern systematic error and accuracy. The second source of difficulty—experimental error—relates to two principal questions. How large a sample is required? How should the sample be selected? Much of modern statistics and a large portion of this text are devoted to these questions, which we shall pursue in only a general way in the next section. We shall then complete this chapter with a detailed discussion of systematic error.

2.6   SAMPLING PROCEDURES

The task of collecting and analyzing data is huge and extremely expensive. Sampling is frequently introduced in order to reduce the enormity of the task and to cut expenses. This is an intelligent course of action as long as the sample yields reasonably good estimates of the universe characteristics. But how does one select a sample so that such estimates can be obtained? The size of the sample is of some import, but let us temporarily assume that size is predetermined. Our problem, then, is to choose elements that in the aggregate will be fairly representative of the universe. In slightly different language, we are attempting to select a sample of n elements from a population of N elements in such a way that the characteristics of that sample will not differ by very much from the corresponding characteristics of the population. We shall use the term "statistics" for the characteristics of the sample, and "parameters" for those of the population. In sampling, we are never sure that we have a representative sample, but we choose so that we have a high "probability" that it will not mislead us by very much.

The foundation of all probability sampling is the simple random sample. A sample of this kind is defined as a subset of size n selected from a universe of size N $(n \leq N)$ so that every possible subset of size n is equally likely to be chosen. As a consequence of this condition, every element of the universe has an equal chance of becoming a part of the sample. One attractive feature of a simple random sample is that several of the more frequently used statistics— for example, the arithmetic mean—are *unbiased estimates* of the corresponding universe parameters when computed from such a sample. Let us hasten to add that they are unbiased estimates of what the results of a complete census using the same procedure would have been. There may be bias in the overall procedure, but none is introduced by the sampling method.

Suppose we wished to select a simple random sample of three students from a class of 20. There would be 1140 different samples of size three that could be selected; if we select a simple random sample, no one of these 1140 is more or less likely than the other. Also, each of the 20 students is equally likely to be a member of the sample chosen; each has a probability of 0.15 of being in the sample. Notice that no mention has been made of the characteristic to be studied. The selection of a simple random sample is in no way related to the relevant characteristics. The actual selection of the three elements could be made in any manner that satisfied the basic condition. In practice, a table of random numbers, such as Table E.4 of Appendix E, is frequently used. For this particular problem, we number the students from 1 to 20 and enter the table at an arbitrary point, determined without inspecting the table. Suppose we select as our starting point the third column of single digits and sixth row. Our sample of three is found by reading two-digit numbers from the third and fourth columns beginning with 89. The first three two-digit numbers less than 21 are 18, 08, and 05; the three persons who have been assigned these numbers constitute our sample.

A simple random sample is unbiased (in the sense just defined), but it may not be very reliable. A sample of one person chosen by simple random sampling might provide an unbiased estimate of a characteristic in the universe from which he was chosen,[11] but such a result could be quite misleading. Consider the man from Mars who came to Earth and returned with the report that the inhabitants were 5 ft 3 in. high, weighed 125 lb, had red hair, were female, and were anxious to enter something called "wedlock." A sample of size two might have changed his ideas considerably. Our objective in sampling is a reliable and unbiased estimate. Given the universe, reliability increases with sample size. This increase in reliability can be expressed mathematically, but we shall leave that until Chapter 8.

Simple random sampling is the basis of all probability sampling, but other forms are often used. We depart from simple random sampling in two ways and for two reasons. Stratified random sampling divides the universe into homogeneous subsets in order to take advantage of the similarity among the elements in these subsets. Cluster sampling divides the universe into sets of adjacent elements that can be studied simultaneously at relatively low costs.

We have stated that a simple random sample is selected without regard to the characteristic under study. In stratification, this is not the case. Suppose we wish to study expenditures by persons living within a small geographical area. If we wished to determine the allocation of these expenditures among four or five broad categories, it would be important to consider what factors are related to this allocation. Then, instead of selecting a simple random sample from the entire population, we would divide the population into subsets (strata) based on the factors specified, and sample from each stratum. In this way we can avoid selecting the most unusual samples (unusual, that is, with respect to the characteristics that are of interest to us). In our example, we might think that marital status and number of children are important. Appropriate strata could consist of single persons, married persons without children, and several classes of married persons with children. In this way we would avoid simple random samples in which any of these subsets would be overly represented. Technically, the gain comes about because the parameter is estimated quite reliably in each stratum, and then these estimates are combined. The elements within each stratum should be more similar with respect to the characteristics under study than are the elements of the entire population. If this is not the case, stratification is not an improvement over simple random sampling.

A simple or a stratified random sample of the same size may be very costly. This is particularly true if personal interviews are spread over a large geographical area. Travel costs can be reduced by interviewing elements located near one another, and a much larger sample can be studied for the same

---

[11] A sample consists of any subset of a population ranging in size from 1 to N. The null set is thus excluded.

total cost. When properly employed, clustering will result in greater reliability for the same total cost. In cluster sampling, one uses the principles of simple random sampling, but applies them to clusters of elements (and clusters within clusters) rather than to the individual elements at only one stage.

There are numerous ways of combining stratification and clustering, but the principle is the same in any well-conceived sampling design. The population is subdivided, and elements or groups are selected by simple random sampling methods with the objective of securing an optimum allocation of resources in making reliable estimates of universe parameters. As long as a probability sample is employed, the reliability of estimates can be ascertained. A nonprobability sample does not permit an objective appraisal of reliability.

2.7   EXAMPLES OF SYSTEMATIC ERROR

The movement from the ideal to the real is accompanied by a movement from perfect to imperfect information. Sampling introduces experimental error and less than perfect reliability. Procedures for collecting and processing data introduce systematic error and inaccuracies, potentially present whether a census or sample be employed.

Assuming the problem, universe, and appropriate characteristics have been clearly defined, systematic errors are introduced by failure to make the data collected conform to the accepted definitions or by failure to follow proper procedures in tabulation and analysis.[12] At the moment we are concerned with examples of difficulties at the collection stage.

We have cited the dangers involved in studying a population that is not quite the same as the one specified by the problem. Consider the department store manager who wishes to ascertain various characteristics of the store's customers (defined in a certain way). Suppose a list of these customers is not available. How can the manager identify them? A frequently followed procedure is to restrict the study to those customers who have charge accounts, since the store has a list of those individuals. Depending on the store, charge customers may represent almost 100 percent of all customers or a very small percentage. The possible magnitude of the error introduced is larger with the small percentage, but the nature of the problem is the same in either case. How do the charge and other customers compare in the characteristics studied? If the results of the study are accepted as valid for the population of "customers," one is assuming that the two types of customers (charge and noncharge) are homogeneous with respect to the characteristics studied. Since we know that they are not homogeneous with respect to "charge-account status," it might be tenuous to assume that they are homogeneous with

---

[12] Certain estimating procedures also introduce a bias. A discussion of such procedures is beyond the scope of this text.

respect to other characteristics, particularly if there is any reason to suspect that these are associated with charge-account status.

At the next stage of the study, a sample of charge customers would be selected. Let us assume that the store has a competent statistician who selects a probability sample. Mail questionnaires with clear, relevant questions are sent to a sample of 4000 charge customers, and 1600 responses are received. This is an excellent response rate, and the statistician is pleased.

Upon examination, it is found that 80 percent of the respondents have at least a high-school education. Do you think this statistic is an unbiased estimate of the corresponding parameter? Not unless you think the respondents and nonrespondents are similar with respect to educational background. Frequently one can compare the two groups with respect to one or more characteristics. Here, it may be possible to compare them with respect to dollar value of charge-account purchases. Regardless of the outcome of such a check, there is no assurance that the respondents are representative of the original sample in the characteristics studied. One can have some degree of confidence, but no way of appraising that confidence objectively.

Final follow-up requests and personal visits are frequently employed to cut down the size of the nonresponse group and minimize the magnitude of the possible error, but short of a 100 percent response the problem remains. An alternative that reduces the cost of follow-ups is subsampling. By selecting probability samples of nonrespondents, the number of follow-ups is reduced without introducing additional systematic error, although this procedure is less reliable than if the entire sample had been covered.

Note from both of the preceding illustrations that the data collected may be correct and the universe properly defined, but the elements supplying the data may not be representative of that universe. If significant compromises are made in selecting the elements to study or if those responding represent a particular segment of the universe, the study will not permit valid inferences.

It is all too easy to collect data without realizing the extent to which they are biased. Different results concerning income might be obtained from a membership study conducted by a country club and a similar study of the same population conducted by a tax agency. The respondents might overstate to the country club for prestige reasons and understate to the tax agency to reduce tax liability. A similar difficulty arose in a house-to-house survey of magazine readership. The results showed a high readership for prestige magazines. A drive to collect magazines in the same neighborhood a few weeks later produced quite different results. Admittedly the characteristics were different ("What do you read?" versus "What are you willing to give away?"), but the great disparity was suspicious. Both examples illustrate situations in which the respondent was capable of giving the desired information but perhaps unwilling to be truthful.

The specific wording of a question can bias the results in a certain direction. "Don't you think · · · ?" will cause a greater degree of agreement, regardless of the rest of the question, than a more neutrally worded question. "What is your opinion of the ultrareactionary (or radical liberal) · · · ?" will usually produce a much less favorable rating than a simple identification of a congressman. Many other examples of question phrasing and the introduction of "leading" words are possible. The student must consider each problem and ask how alternative forms would lead to different results. The form chosen should be the one that has the least danger of introducing a systematic error.

A rather subtle form of systematic error appears in the list question:

Which of the following is your favorite supermarket?

A & P
Market Basket
Safeway
Thriftimart

Even in a list as short as this, an element of bias is introduced in favor of the first store. The bias increases with the number on the list, and the upward bias extends beyond the first item. There is also an additional sort of bias associated with the list question:

Which of the following have you read (or visited, etc.)?

When the list includes nonexistent books, places, etc., there are always respondents who check them. This number, too, is higher when the nonexistent books and places appear near the beginning of the list. It is obvious that items excluded from the list, but admissible as a write-in, have the question heavily biased against them.

Questions requiring only a check ($\sqrt{}$) have the advantage of facilitating completion by the respondent and yielding generally higher response rates, but they have accompanying disadvantages. One is that cited above, biasing the results away from the choices not listed. Another is that of forcing the respondent into categories that are not appropriate. This is particularly true in motivation research. "Why did you choose a particular product?" The open-end question, which provides no clues but just a line or two, is being used more than formerly in order to avoid stereotyped groupings. It, however, has the disadvantage of possibly yielding 45 different reasons from 56 respondents. A pretest of such questions has been helpful in many studies. Through the pretest, the researcher can acquire an idea of the types of answers that will be forthcoming. He can then set up provisional categories for his analysis, even though the respondents are unaware of that grouping. Too much diversity in responses may indicate a poor question or simply an area in which the results will not provide useful conclusions. In either case, the researcher is warned that the question will probably not be satisfactory.

Another common error in collecting data is to ask for information that the respondent never knew or cannot recall. How many students were in your mathematics class last term? How many tubes of toothpaste did you use in 1968? It is conceivable that some students could supply such information, but they are the exceptions. If, on the other hand, the data need not be very precise, it might be convenient to establish classes from which the respondent is to select the one that is appropriate. He may be able to supply the information in that form. If not, or if more precision is required, the researcher should attempt a different approach. A preferable source for the first question would be the mathematics department rather than the students. The second query, typical of many questions regarding the frequency of an activity, can be changed in either of two ways: (1) to cover a shorter interval, or (2) to secure data concerning the data of most recent purchase. The respondent may be able to provide such data, but that is no advantage unless they are pertinent. Each project must be reviewed before one can decide if either approach would be fruitful. The two most common reasons why the alternative approaches may be unsatisfactory are the presence of seasonal variations in the activity and the need for crossclassification of respondents simultaneously on several characteristics.

Suppose we wish to ascertain the average number of tubes of toothpaste purchased during the most recent 12-month period. We doubt if persons will recall this number, but they may recall the figure for the most recent month—August. Can we use the result for August in calculating an annual figure? Only if we know how August compares with the rest of the year. It may be appropriate to multiply the August figure by 12, but it may not. The problem would be more difficult if we were studying suntan lotion. In order to make an annual estimate from data for one month, the investigator must have a thorough knowledge of the subject, or the shorter interval will not suffice.

When it is necessary to classify respondents simultaneously with respect to two or more characteristics, one of which is frequency of participation in a specific activity, it is dangerous to cover a short interval or secure data concerning the date of most recent participation. For example: Is there any relation between a person's education and the frequency with which he attends athletic events? If the frequency classification is based on the time interval since the respondent last attended an athletic event, some of the classifications might be misleading. The individual who went to a baseball game the day before the survey but had not attended any other athletic events in years would be misclassified. The rabid fan who has been hospitalized for several months would be another example of a misclassification. Over the entire study there would be a tendency for such errors to cancel one another, but the data would have some inaccuracies.

A final comment is that each question should provide information that is required for the study. It is tempting to include related questions that are interesting, but each additional question increases the probability of a refusal as well as tabulation time and cost.

2.8 METHODS OF COLLECTING AND TABULATING DATA

Mail questionnaires and personal interviews have been mentioned as methods of collecting data. Telephone interviews have been used in situations requiring only a few simple questions but are not well suited for extensive questioning. Personal observation has been used for years in the physical sciences and is not uncommon in the social sciences when the accuracy of questionnaires is suspect. Unfortunately, observation is usually more expensive than other methods. Telephone interviews are usually employed over fairly narrow geographic regions, although the coverage can be extended to several areas if the interviewers are strategically located.[13] There is also the possibility of collecting data by instruments. A. C. Nielsen installs recording devices in TV sets to determine viewing habits. Another instrument, familiar to most of us, is the traffic counter used on roads. These and similar devices provide economical and quite accurate substitutes for the human observer.

On the surface the personal interview is the most expensive method, but this is not always true in the long run. The final evaluation should be in terms of cost per completed questionnaire with proper weight given to reliability and accuracy. Long and involved questionnaires require personal interviews unless both cooperation and understanding on the part of the respondents can be presumed. There are no easy rules for deciding on the proper method of collection. Each problem is separate, and the best method depends on the interaction among costs, required reliability, and potential sources of bias.

Although the personal interview often permits the gathering of more data than the mail questionnaire, the respondent can choose the most convenient time for completion in the latter. The respondent may refuse a personal interview because the timing is inconvenient. Confidential information can be anonymous in a mail questionnaire, but as far as the respondent is concerned it is never anonymous in a personal interview.

The interviewer himself is a potential source of bias in the personal interview. Depending on the nature of the material, this bias may be small or great, but studies have shown that some interviewer effect is normally introduced. This effect is reduced by thorough training of the interviewers but may be present with open-end questions. It is most pronounced in depth interviews where the interviewer directs questions in a general way and may

---

[13] Recent work in telephone interviewing suggests that it can be used successfully for fairly involved studies with long distance calls via WATS lines.

vary the specific questions as he deems appropriate. In cases where the interviewer is known to have an interest in the results of the study, the respondents will probably be influenced by his presence. A political preference survey by a Democratic ward leader and church-attendance figures gathered by church groups are illustrations of this difficulty. Despite these drawbacks the personal interview usually produces a much higher response rate and permits the gathering of more detailed and, frequently, more confidential data. The presence of the interviewer is an encouragement to the respondent in a variety of ways, but the student should recognize the importance of cost and not turn blindly to the personal interview. At the same time, he should not limit his attention to a comparison of mailing and interviewing costs. Accuracy and response rate should not be ignored. As mentioned earlier, the possibility of using the mail questionnaire initially and later introducing the personal interview for all or a sample of nonrespondents is frequently an efficient procedure.

Once the data have been collected, they must be processed. This processing involves editing of the data into proper form followed by the necessary calculations. The amount of editing is dependent on the way in which the data are to be tabulated. If electronic computers are to be employed, the editing may be rather involved before the data are translated into a form suitable for machine tabulation. If simple hand tabulation is involved, the editing may be less demanding, with the possibility that most of it may accompany the tabulation. The method of tabulation is determined by the number of elements in the study, the number of characteristics investigated, and the complexity of the analysis—modified, of course, by the equipment, money, and personnel available. Generally speaking, the greater the number and complexity of the computations, the more one should consider using computational aids.

Editing comprises two basic elements: correcting obvious errors and preparing the data for convenient tabulation. In the first group, we include filling in missing information; for example, sex where names are given. It is not the editor's job to guess at information, but frequently he can ascertain the answer to one question from the answers to others. A hotel that has dining facilities for 300 persons and receives 25 percent of its revenue from meals would seem properly classified as a "hotel serving meals" rather than "hotel not serving meals," as was indicated in one study. An answer that is clearly wrong but not as easily corrected is that of an adult in a recent survey who listed his date of birth as April 3, 1967. The editor must indicate the proper classification of each answer. This is a problem with open-end questions where the various responses must be categorized. Each answer must be translated into the form required in the next stage before tabulation can proceed.

The tabulation consists of counting the number of elements supplying various types of answers, summing the answers for some questions, and performing various calculations on groups of questions, frequently with the results manipulated in some fashion. We shall have more to say about these operations in subsequent chapters, but the main advantages of an electronic computer lie in the speed with which it can perform complex computations and the way in which it can store bits of information until they are required.

IMPORTANT TERMS AND CONCEPTS

Accuracy
Bias
Census
Characteristic
  Attribute
  Variable
Collection
  Role of researcher
  Role of observer
  Role of observed
Data
  Exhaustive classes
  Mutually exclusive classes
  Editing of
  Tabulating of

Homogeneity
Parameter
Population
Sample
  Judgment
  Nonprobability
  Probability
    Cluster
    Simple random
    Stratified
    Representative
Statistic
Statistics
Universe

EXERCISES

1. Would you classify the following characteristics as attributes or variables? Give a classificatory scheme to justify your answer in each case.
   a. Horse power of an auto.
   b. Sex of a child.
   c. Color of a typewriter.
   d. Religious preference.
   e. Age of a building.
   f. Marketing budget of a firm.
2. Define each of the following terms and illustrate each definition with an original example or case.
   a. Bias.
   b. Nonsampling error and sampling error.
   c. Sampled population and theoretical population.
   d. Homogeneous data.
   e. Statistical universe.
   f. Type I and Type II errors.

3. a. Why is the concept of homogeneity important? Give an original example, indicating how your conclusions would differ if you did or did not classify the data into homogeneous subgroups.

  b. Would you agree that data are homogeneous if all of the elements are influenced by the same set of factors? Discuss.

4. How does the nature of the problem being studied affect what is done in the tabulation phase of a statistical investigation?

5. "Bias can occur with or without prejudice and prejudice can occur with or without bias." Criticize or explain this statement using an original example.

6. Give an original example of a situation where a stratified random sample would be no better than a simple random sample.

7. Is a random sample chosen unsystematically? Explain.

8. Criticize or explain the following statements.

  a. When using mail questionnaires, one should keep in mind that more responses tend to be achieved from persons with a special interest in the outcome of the survey than from others.

  b. Data collected from a sample of firms manufacturing sporting goods would probably be quite homogeneous.

  c. Students are classified as undergraduates because they are homogeneous.

  d. If the responses to a telephone survey are all truthful and accurate, then they are unbiased.

  e. Data on chemical pollution in a river furnished by a company suspected of being a pollution source is so biased that it is unusable.

9. Discuss and criticize:
One should always choose a probability sample rather than a judgment sample because the former is always more representative.

10. In an article in the June 1959 issue of *Fortune*, it was noted that the members of the class of 1949 of a highly reputed graduate school of business were earning in 1959 an average salary of $14,000. The average 1959 salary for members of the class of 1949 of a leading Eastern undergraduate school was under $10,000. The author of the article concluded that the difference between these figures was ". . . an indication at least that the two extra years of study and some $10,000 in tuition, expenses, and lost salary were a good investment." Data on which the salary figures were based were obtained by use of mail questionnaires.

  a. Discuss several possible sources of bias in the average figures quoted above. In your discussion include a definition of bias and indicate how the instances that you cite fulfill the qualifications of this definition.

b. In addition to the statements above, the author noted a problem of nonhomogeneity that limited his conclusion about the value of graduate business education. Discuss at least two factors that may have been responsible for his problem, indicating how they might cause the data to lead one to an invalid conclusion, even though the averages were correct and representative of the universes for which they were determined. Suggest ways by which this problem of non-homogeneity might be overcome.

11. The Ace TV Rating Service offers to program sponsors its estimates of the total number of viewers and of key characteristics of the total viewing audience based on sample surveys. The following statements deal with key aspects of the method used by the Ace TV Rating Service. Discuss each statement critically.
   a. Since only 1000 persons were contacted per night (out of roughly 30 million viewers), one critic claimed the results were worthless.
   b. In order to have results available for the sponsors of an evening program early the next morning, the estimates of the national audience are based upon data obtained in the eastern half of the United States, where the program is shown at an earlier hour.
   c. The respondents are contacted by telephone and asked the following questions:
      (1) Is there a television set turned on in your home? If the answer is "yes," then:
      (2) Which program is being watched? If the answer is that it is the sponsor's program, then:
      (3) How many persons are there in your family?
      The answers to these questions are used to estimate the total number of viewers.

12. Analyze, criticize, and explain:
   a. The average college entrance examination score at Culture College for Northern High graduates was higher than for other high school graduates on the same examination. Therefore, Northern has a better course of instruction than other high schools.
   b. Tom received a higher grade in Economics 1 than Jim did. This shows that Tom would make a better tutor than Jim, since Tom knows more about economics.
   c. A vice-president of the Standard Electric Company stated that the favorable comparison between the death rate under the company's group life insurance plan and the national death rate points up the effectiveness of the company's medical program.
   d. Only 20 percent of the persons who took cod-liver oil at breakfast

last winter caught colds. This is a clear indication that cod-liver oil is effective in preventing winter colds.

e. A department of motor vehicles in a certain state wanted to assess public opinion on the question: "Should liability insurance be compulsory for automobile owners in this state?" Therefore, it included this question on the operator's license application forms that were sent out during the next calendar year.

13. Assume that you had been asked to supervise a study of trust accounts held by banks in the northeast United States.
   a. State a more precise problem that has economic significance.
   b. Define the universe that is appropriate for the problem stated in *a*.
   c. Would it be feasible to study the universe defined in *b*? Discuss.

14. A study of the expenditures of welfare recipients is to be undertaken by the city of Hartford, Connecticut in order to influence welfare planning being done for the state legislature. State the universe that you think should be studied and defend your choice.

15. A political organization wanted to obtain the opinion of residents of an eastern city on having a woman as vice-president of the United States. On a week day in 1969 a survey of households, made by telephone between the hours of 9 A.M. and 4 P.M., showed that 80 percent of the persons reached favored having a woman as vice-president. Discuss the validity of this finding.

16. The data below resulted from a survey of unemployment in the United States labor force in January 1961. The survey defined "labor force" as those who have jobs plus those who are looking for work, and "unemployed" as those looking for work.

	Race	
	White (%)	Nonwhite (%)
Employed	93	86
Unemployed	7	14
	100	100

Would you be willing to accept the above information as evidence of racial discrimination? Explain why or why not?

17. Criticize the following questions designed to obtain information from respondents. Rephrase each question so it could be used in a particular situation, spelling out just what situation you have in mind.

a. Is your car in better condition than most other cars of the same make and year of production?

b. Please complete the blanks for the following question:

Born _____ Age _____

c. How many boxes of frozen peas did you purchase during the last year?

d. When the word automobile is mentioned, does the name Cadillac or some other brand first come to your mind?

e. Do you like Burpo or all other cigarettes better? Answer yes or no.

f. How many bottles of soft drink did you purchase last week?

g. Do you favor issuing drivers' licenses to teenagers, even though some teenagers may cause serious accidents from driving too fast?

h. Do you agree with others that the Dyhard Company is a reputable firm?

i. Please indicate your opinion of the campus newspaper by checking the appropriate box below:

☐ Excellent   ☐ Enlarge sports coverage
☐ Good for the community ☐ Expand editorials
☐ Interesting to students

j. How many shoestrings have you purchased in the last two weeks?

k. Do you favor freedom?

l. What three things are most wrong with our schools today?

m. Are you unemployed?

n. How much was your income for the last six months?

18. Is there any advantage in setting up statistical tables during the planning stage of a project? Explain.

19. a. Construct a set of dummy tables to show how you might classify data from a mail questionnaire sent to business executives. The purpose of the survey is to ascertain the opinions of business executives on desirable national unemployment and inflation policies.

b. Compose the questions needed to generate the data required for these tables.

20. A survey was conducted to estimate the average monthly salary received in 1970 by persons receiving bachelor's degrees from accredited colleges and universities in the Boston area in June 1969. Lists of such persons were obtained and arranged in alphabetical order. A questionnaire was then sent to every tenth name appearing on this list.

a. Do you believe that the method followed would give an accurate estimate of the average monthly salary of June 1969 graduates? Why or why not?

b. Define the population that the survey covered.

    c. Is the characteristic studied an attribute or a variable? Explain your answer, and distinguish clearly between the two terms.

21. A research organization wished to study the viewing habits of television-set owners. It selected a sample of 500 names from the San Francisco telephone book. Among the questions asked was the following: "What is your favorite television program?"

    a. What is the statistical universe of this survey?

    b. An advertiser, on seeing the results of the survey, noted that a respected organization published quite different national rankings. He concluded that one of the organizations was definitely in error. Should he have so concluded? Discuss.

22. Many companies send their senior executives to a diagnostic clinic periodically for complete health examinations. They feel that the cost of these examinations to the company is more than offset by savings in many forms. The clinic decides to undertake a study to evaluate periodic health examinations from several points of view:

    A. The company.

    B. The executive.

    C. The clinic.

    D. The family doctor of the examinee.

    E. Society in general.

    a. List two advantages and two disadvantages afforded each of the above by the examination.

    b. Formulate six hypotheses which you think should be tested in this study.

    c. List six parameters which you think should be estimated.

    d. One of the hypotheses you might have formulated in *b* is: the test used to detect high blood pressure should be discontinued. Describe how you would go about designing a study to test this hypothesis.

    e. In part *d* above:

      (1) Define the statistical universe.

      (2) Discuss the representativeness of the sample taken from that universe.

      (3) Describe the Type I and Type II errors that might occur and their consequences.

23. The Sun 'n' Fun is a beach-front hotel in New Jersey. It remains open for the entire year, but 75 percent of its patronage is concentrated in the period between July 4 and Labor Day. The Sun 'n' Fun relies on the surrounding community as little as possible and is now considering an expansion of its facilities to build up its off-season business. The Sun 'n' Fun maintains a complete file of its guests. A separate card is prepared for each person or group of persons on the first visit to the hotel. All subsequent visits with dates and number of days stayed are recorded on

the same card. The management is considering three capital expenditures: an indoor swimming pool, air conditioning of all rooms, and an indoor theatre. Funds can be secured for only one such expenditure at present, but the president insists that none of these three should be undertaken unless it will stimulate patronage.

a. What universe is implicit in the president's view of the problem?

b. If practical considerations dictate that a different universe be studied, indicate that universe and justify your choice.

c. What problems would be involved in selecting a sample from the universe that you suggest? Discuss each.

d. Assume that you have selected a sample for study. Compose a set of questions that would yield the information required by management.

e. Construct two sets of tables based on hypothetical answers to your questions. One set should indicate that one conclusion is proper, and the other set should indicate that another conclusion is proper. Specify the risks associated with each conclusion.

24. In Exercise 23, assume that a theatre was constructed and has been in use for one complete year. The hotel wishes to ascertain its guests' opinion of the theatre.

a. Define precisely the statistical universe that should be studied. Defend your choice.

b. Phrase a specific question that would be appropriate for a questionnaire, and defend its form.

c. Indicate how management could use the results as a guide to future policy.

25. The school board of Lower Fenwick wished to ascertain voter opinion concerning a special assessment to permit the expansion of school services. Lower Fenwick has a population of 25,000. There are 5000 pupils enrolled in the public schools of the community. The board selected a random sample of 500 of these children and sent questionnaires to their parents.

a. Identify the universe from which the above sample was drawn.

b. Is the sample chosen a random sample of parents? Why or why not?

c. If you had been asked to assist the board, would you have approved the universe they studied? Defend your position.

d. Assume that the sample was taken from the proper universe. All 500 questionnaires were completed. There were 75 percent who favored the special assessment and 25 percent who opposed it. The board concluded that the assessment would be approved if submitted to a vote. Evaluate this conclusion, indicating the possibilities of both sampling and nonsampling errors.

26. A labor economist was interested in a possible relationship between the size of firm and the extent to which the work force was unionized in 256 firms in the southwestern region of the United States. He obtained the following data:

Size of Firm	Percent of Firms with		Total	
	Union Work Force	Nonunion Work Force	Percent	Number of Firms
Small or medium	58	42	100	141
Large	46	54	100	115

Source. Hypothetical.

a. Is there any evidence in the above table of a statistical relationship between size of firm and extent of unionization? Explain

b. Could the second table be based on the same data as the first table? Why or why not?

Type of Industry	Size of Firm					
	Small or Medium			Large		
	Percent with Union Work Force	Percent with Nonunion Work Force	Number of Firms	Percent with Union Work Force	Percent with Nonunion Work Force	Number of Firms
Tobacco	80	20	74	80	20	30
Textile	23	77	40	24	76	47
Furniture	48	52	27	47	53	38
	—	—	—	—	—	—
Total	58	42	141	46	54	115

Source. Hypothetical.

c. Assuming that the data in the above two tables are consistent and for the same firms, would you modify the answer you gave to part *a* after observing this additional information? Discuss.

d. What are the implications of the situation in parts *a*, *b*, and *c*, for the general problem of making causal inferences, that is, inferences about the effect of independent variables upon a dependent variable?

e. In the table in part *b* the number 80 appears in the upper left cell. What is the meaning of this number?

3 Probability

3.1 RELATION OF PROBABILITY TO STATISTICS

The theory of probability is a well-established branch of mathematics. Although some statistical methods are not probabilistic, many of them fall in this category. In statistical studies, no other mathematical topic is as useful as probability. The reason for this is not hard to discover. Statistical studies attempt to shed light on unknown phenomena. But the phenomena with which modern research studies are concerned almost never involve only one or two variables. If we refer to the five problems mentioned at the beginning of Chapter 1, we will note that missile thrust, cancer causes, economic growth, retail buying, and executive behavior are highly complex. Some of them involve dozens of interacting factors. In general, it is possible to include only a limited number of the most important factors in any research study, and hence a complete solution, valid for all sets of circumstances, cannot be obtained. What will evolve is a statement that result A may be expected 30 percent of the time, result B 40 percent of the time, etc. These are probabilistic statements. The reasons for couching statistical studies in probabilistic terms will be pointed out in more detail during this chapter.

Probability is generally presented as a deductive system. Axioms are assumed from which theorems are derived. Probability can be studied in various ways, ranging in difficulty from the elementary approach adopted here to highly abstract material suitable for advanced graduate work.

The student is warned that problems in probability often have a deceptively simple appearance. Consider the following game. The player takes a well-shuffled deck and starts turning over the cards one at a time. He stops when he has found two aces or when he has turned over 24 cards, whichever occurs first. If the player finds two aces among these 24 cards, he wins. Otherwise he loses. Would you bet with him or against him—at even money?

Keep this problem in mind as you read the ensuing sections in which we shall develop the concepts and techniques needed to attack such situations.

3.2   RANDOM EXPERIMENTS

The starting point of an empirical approach to probability is the random experiment. We shall describe several such experiments and analyze one in some detail.

A man's coat pocket contains eight dimes and nothing else. Three are Mercury dimes dated 1928, 1930, and 1936. The other five are Roosevelt dimes dated 1962, 1963, 1967, 1967, and 1970. This man, entering a phone booth, reaches into his pocket and selects a dime at random to drop into the slot. We are interested in his selection process.

His choice interests us because it constitutes what statisticians call a random experiment. For our purpose, we shall construe the term random experiment as meaning an observed phenomenon which has three properties: (1) it can be repeated physically or conceptually; (2) the set consisting of all of its possible outcomes can be specified in advance; and (3) its various repetitions will not always yield the same outcome. Simple examples of random experiments are such dissimilar activities as rolling a die, determining the boiling point of a 2 percent saline solution, playing a bridge game for six spades with a particular holding after a particular bidding sequence, taking a driver's examination in the state of California, and buying a Patagonian National Defense bond redeemable in 10 years at par.

But a question might be raised: it is evident that the outcomes of these experiments will differ from trial to trial. What about the first stipulation? Can these experiments be repeated? Does not something always change from trial to trial so that we are running a different experiment each time, not a repetition of the same one?

Consider the random experiment of selecting a dime. Can this experiment be repeated? The answer is both yes and no. If by "repeated" we mean repeated exactly, this would imply the identical position of fingers, the identical arrangement of coins in the pocket, the identical thrust of the arm, etc., etc. It would be difficult, if not impossible, to control factors such as these in order to repeat the experiment exactly, and it is not desirable to do so. Indeed, it is the operation of these uncontrolled variables that imparts uncertainty to the outcome of the experiment. Consider all factors which have any bearing on the outcome of an experiment. The experimenter divides these into two classes—one which is duplicated exactly and one which is left free to vary. When the experiment is repeated, all variables in the first class are kept constant (same eight coins in the pocket, no other objects in the pocket, selection with the hand, not with a pair of tweezers). However, variables in the second class (thrust of arm, position of coins) are not controlled, and consequently the same dime will not be selected on all repetitions.

Notice that the random experiment called "taking a driver's examination in the state of California" will not be performed very often using the same individual. However, it may be thought of as the first in a series of repetitions using persons who are similar in certain respects—perhaps in age, sex, county of residence, and driving experience. Similar reasoning applies to the purchase of the Patagonian bond.

The second condition for a random experiment is that it must be possible to list all outcomes in advance. In the coin-selection experiment, there are eight outcomes. Any one of the coins might be picked. Rolling a die has six possible outcomes: the integers 1, 2, 3, 4, 5, and 6. Determining the boiling point of a saline solution will result in some real number on the centigrade scale. True, the experimenter will probably be able to guess the outcome within much narrower limits, but in order that the experiment may be called random he only needs to specify the reals as the set of possible outcomes. Possible outcomes in the bridge-game experiment are making an overtrick, making the contract exactly, or going down some number of tricks from 1 to 12. The outcomes resulting from the bond purchase might be amounts received in interest and in proceeds from sale or redemption. This could be done by a simple accumulation which would yield some dollar and cents figure, that is, $C/100$ where C is an integer in dollars. The third condition, that the outcome of the experiment be not always the same, is clear in each instance.

What relation do random experiments have to the activities of a business executive? Perhaps we feel that random experimentation denotes the surest road to insolvency and disaster. The close relation between executive decisions and random experiments becomes clear, however, when we consider the activities of an executive. Of what does his job consist?

Basically, the chief skill required of a business executive lies in the area of decision making. Other abilities include skill in selecting key personnel, skill in working effectively with his associates, and the ability to implement decisions. But these latter are subsidiary; the choice of a key man is, in itself, a business decision. It is important to find the right man for the right job because the wrong man will make the wrong decision and hence harm the whole enterprise. Again, ability to work effectively with one's associates and skill in implementing decisions are the results of long sequences of small decisions, many of which fall in the area of personal relations. To say that these decisions are small must not of course convey any idea of unimportance.

Now the making of business decisions is a difficult matter because in all practical situations it takes place in a state of uncertainty. If the executive knew the exact outcomes of the alternative courses of action confronting him, he would have no problem. He would relate actions and outcomes and adopt that action leading to the outcome he considered most desirable. He could then give his full attention to problems of implementation. However, sure things almost never arise in the conduct of business operations. The merchant wondering whether to replace his line of "Old Reliable" household appliances with the new "Satellite Special" line has to reckon with the known durability of the Old Reliable models, the higher price of the Satellites, the differences in the two warranty contracts, etc. These factors are known to some extent, but their impact and interrelationships with the consumer are extremely uncertain.

Consider also the plant manager who will decide whether to produce on the next run only the 10,000 air-conditioner compressor bases needed to fill present orders or to manufacture an additional 20,000 for inventory. He must compare costs of the different procedures in the light of market predictions; costs of storage, materials, and labor; competitors' actions, etc.—factors replete with uncertainty. He tries to evaluate all manner of contingencies, as does the president of the company faced with a different problem. This executive must give the final OK to a plan to buy out a nuisance competitor at the high price demanded. If there is one characteristic of business decisions, it is uncertainty—as to outcomes of possible courses of action and as to associated costs.

Business executives spend their lives attempting to evaluate the outcomes of complex random experiments. They must decide which possible outcomes are likely, what they can do to influence these likelihoods, and what actions seem optimal in the face of this uncertainty. Then they must make decisions to try to arrive at favorable results. The random experiments that we study here will be simple compared to the difficult problems of the corporation executive. However, by examining the simple cases, great light can be shed on complex practical situations.

Of course, not all or even most business decision problems can be solved by the methods discussed in this book. However, the executive who is familiar with probability and statistics will be able to meet his responsibilities more successfully than his competitor who is ignorant of them. Furthermore, the use of these methods will increase and become more profitable as information on the various phases of business operation accumulates, and as more attention is given to its systematic study.

3.3 SAMPLE SPACE

For convenience, let us represent each outcome of a random experiment in some way. In the case of a single roll of one die, the natural representation of the outcome in which the face with three spots appears uppermost is the number 3. However, if the experimenter chose to represent this outcome by any other symbol, for instance "*a*" or "Δ," he could do so. The set of symbols chosen to represent all the outcomes of a random experiment is called the *sample space* of the experiment, and is denoted by *S*. In the die roll, if the natural representation is used, the sample space is $S = \{1, 2, 3, 4, 5, 6\}$. In the driving-test experiment the sample space contains only two elements, for example $S = \{P, F\}$, where *P* indicates pass and *F* failure. In the boiling-point experiment the sample space might be the set of real numbers. Thus, we see that a sample space may contain a finite or an infinite number of elements.

If $S = \{a_1, a_2, \cdots\}$ is the sample space of a random experiment, then the elements or points $a_1, a_2, \cdots$ are representations of the only possible outcomes of the experiment. The listing $a_1, a_2, \cdots$ is then said to be exhaustive. The use of the term *space* is related to this idea. Since only one of $a_1, a_2, \cdots$ may occur as the outcome, *S* is called a space—indicating that no other outcomes can enter into the discussion of this experiment.

Another term is in need of introduction—*event*. An event is simply a subset of sample space. In the coin-selection experiment, three possible events are: "selection of a Roosevelt dime," "selection of a 1967 dime," and "selection of a dime dated before 1964." The term exhaustive is used in connection with events as well as with points; thus the two events "selection of a Roosevelt dime" and "selection of a Mercury dime" form an exhaustive set. In other words, a set of events is exhaustive if its union is the whole of the sample space.

In addition, the events "Roosevelt dime" and "Mercury dime" cannot both occur as outcomes of the same repetition of the experiment. These two outcomes are mutually exclusive. A set of events is said to be mutually exclusive if the intersection of each pair of its events is the null set. That is, events are said to be mutually exclusive when none of them can happen simultaneously as outcomes of a random experiment. The three events, "1967 dime," "1930 dime," and "1970 dime" are mutually exclusive but not exhaustive, whereas the two events "dime dated before 1964" and "dime dated after 1931" are exhaustive but not mutually exclusive.

Let us consider a different experiment. From a position 6 feet away a circular disc, 6 inches in diameter, is tossed upon a circular table 2 feet in diameter. The minimum distance from the edge of the disc to the edge of the table is measured and recorded. If the disc falls to the floor or projects beyond the table's edge, the experiment is rerun. We are interested in the experiment's sample space, that is, in the set of all possible minimum distances.

There are two ways to look at this sample space even if we represent its elements by the real numbers measured. On the one hand, we may regard it as dependent upon the measuring device. If a ruler is employed and distance recorded to the nearest sixteenth of an inch, then the sample space is

$$S = \{9, 8\tfrac{15}{16}, 8\tfrac{7}{8}, \cdots, \tfrac{1}{16}, 0\}.$$

From this point of view the sample space consists of 145 rational numbers. If a more sensitive instrument is used, it would be possible to measure the distance to the nearest hundredth or thousandth of an inch so that the number of points in sample space would be multiplied enormously.

On the other hand, it seems evident that the minimum distance from the disc to the table's edge might well be any real number not smaller than 0 and not exceeding 9. At least there is no value in that range that a reasonable man would rule out. Statements such as "the minimum distance could not be 4.2380196 inches" are nonsensical—assuming a sufficiently precise measuring device. From this point of view, one would regard the sample space as consisting of the interval from zero to 9 with the end points included.

Although we have said that the choice of the symbols representing the outcomes of an experiment is up to the experimenter, it is convenient to proceed in a systematic fashion. Any set of all possible outcomes will be either finite, countably infinite, or uncountably infinite. Hence, any sample space used will be in one-to-one correspondence either with the real numbers or with a proper subset of the real numbers. It follows that the points in sample space can always be shown in terms of real numbers. Consider the disc-tossing experiment. According to the second approach suggested, the sample space was

$$S = \{x \mid 0 \le x \le 9\}$$

where x is a real number. Consider the dime-selection experiment where, now, two phone calls are to be made. First, one dime is selected, a call is made, and then a second dime is chosen. Let the eight dimes be represented as follows:

1928:0	1963	:4
1930:1	first 1967	:5
1936:2	second 1967:	6
1962:3	1970	:7

To distinguish "first 1967" from "second 1967" imagine a nick cut in the edge of "first 1967." Then we have

$$\begin{aligned}
S = \{&(0, 1), (0, 2), (0, 3), (0, 4), (0, 5), (0, 6), (0, 7),\\
&(1, 0), (1, 2), (1, 3), (1, 4), (1, 5), (1, 6), (1, 7),\\
&(2, 0), (2, 1), (2, 3), (2, 4), (2, 5), (2, 6), (2, 7),\\
&(3, 0), (3, 1), (3, 2), (3, 4), (3, 5), (3, 6), (3, 7),\\
&(4, 0), (4, 1), (4, 2), (4, 3), (4, 5), (4, 6), (4, 7),\\
&(5, 0), (5, 1), (5, 2), (5, 3), (5, 4), (5, 6), (5, 7),\\
&(6, 0), (6, 1), (6, 2), (6, 3), (6, 4), (6, 5), (6, 7),\\
&(7, 0), (7, 1), (7, 2), (7, 3), (7, 4), (7, 5), (7, 6)\}
\end{aligned}$$

where x, the first number in each pair, refers to the first dime drawn, and y, the second number, to the result of the second selection. Notice that points with the same first and second member are omitted; once a dime goes in the slot, it is not available for the second call. If we wished, we could exhibit this sample space in more concise form as

$$S = \{(x, y) \mid x, y = 0, 1, \cdots, 7; x \neq y\}$$

Geometrically, it is the set of points in the plane whose coordinates are integers from zero to 7, with no equal coordinates allowed. Clearly the sample space of an experiment need not consist of a unique set of elements. We could have denoted the 56 points in S by the integers 1001 to 1056 if we had so desired.

3.4   RELATIVE FREQUENCY OF OUTCOMES

The decision maker tries to weigh the merits of the various courses of action open to him. In order to do this he must determine, as well as he can, the real likelihood of each of the possible outcomes of his experiment. He will certainly not decide to put many eggs into a basket which, he feels, will actually occur only one time in a thousand unless the reward is extremely high. Let us consider a simple case.

Each Friday the Dyno-Therm Corporation, a government contractor, must send a representative from its Chugville, N.J., office to a conference in Washington. The representative may travel either by rail or by plane. The train trip takes roughly four hours one way and the plane trip two hours—on a portal to portal basis. But the plane trip is more expensive, and in bad weather flights are canceled. Dyno-Therm's business manager needs to know the proportion of the time that Friday morning jet flights from Chugville to Washington are canceled. How can he determine this?

He first obtains the information given in Table 3.1. In 1968 there were

Table 3.1   Number and Proportion of Canceled Friday Morning Flights, Chugville, N.J. to Washington, D.C., Shown Cumulatively

	1968		1968–1969		1968–1970	
	Total Number	Proportion	Total Number	Proportion	Total Number	Proportion
Flights operating	47	0.904	93	0.886	141	0.898
Flights canceled	5	0.096	12	0.114	16	0.102
Total	52	1.000	105	1.000	157	1.000

five Friday mornings when flights were canceled, seven in 1969, and four in 1970. If we assume that types of airplanes and their operating characteristics remain roughly the same over the next several years, we would expect the cumulated proportions shown in Table 3.1 to settle down toward some fixed value; indeed, they already show signs of doing this. This limiting proportion is the figure which the business manager needs. Note that the relative frequency of cancellations may depend upon the season of the year. If the data are nonhomogeneous when divided on the basis of season, the manager would have to obtain his information from relevant periods.

Let us look at a simpler case—simpler because it involves no assumption about changes in the characteristics of aircraft. Suppose an incipient gambler is completely ignorant of the facts of life involved in the simultaneous rolling of two dice. He is in an unenviable position. He intends to make decisions about the number of spots showing after a roll and to back up his decision with cash. He decides to conduct an experiment to obtain estimates of the relative frequencies involved. Notice that what he intends to do is to obtain a relative frequency for a total of, for instance, 7; that is, to assign a number to the point labeled 7 in sample space. Suppose he experiments for 12 hours and arrives at the data shown in Table 3.2—excluding the last column.

Many persons, over the years, have conducted similar experiments with unloaded dice. This mass of accumulated evidence all points to one conclusion: as the number of throws increases, the relative frequencies of the outcomes tend to approach limiting values—the numbers $\frac{1}{36}, \frac{2}{36}, \frac{3}{36}, \frac{4}{36}, \frac{5}{36}, \frac{6}{36}, \frac{5}{36}, \frac{4}{36}, \frac{3}{36}, \frac{2}{36}, \frac{1}{36}$ appearing in decimal form in the last column of Table 3.2. We shall discuss the heading of this column shortly. Notice that whenever

Table 3.2   Relative Frequencies of the Various Outcomes After 36, 360, and 3600 Rolls of Two Dice

	36 Rolls		360 Rolls		3600 Rolls		
Outcome	Frequency	Relative Frequency	Frequency	Relative Frequency	Frequency	Relative Frequency	Probability
2	0	0.000	7	0.019	96	0.027	0.028
3	2	0.056	18	0.050	212	0.059	0.056
4	1	0.028	35	0.097	292	0.081	0.083
5	2	0.056	36	0.100	399	0.111	0.111
6	8	0.222	55	0.153	510	0.142	0.139
7	10	0.278	74	0.206	635	0.177	0.167
8	4	0.111	32	0.089	484	0.135	0.139
9	7	0.194	46	0.128	410	0.114	0.111
10	1	0.028	29	0.081	285	0.079	0.083
11	0	0.000	16	0.044	183	0.051	0.056
12	1	0.028	12	0.033	94	0.026	0.028
	36	1.001	360	1.000	3600	1.002	1.001

one throws two unbiased dice 3600 times, he obtains a different set of relative frequencies for the various totals. These differ at 36,000 rolls and also at 36,000,000 rolls, if one cares to persevere that long. The feature common to all possible sequences of rolls of this sort is that the relative frequencies of the various outcomes all seem to be settling down toward a single set of values as the number of rolls increases. We repeat that the relative frequencies can be expected to approach a limit only if the *same* experiment is repeated. In the aircraft illustration, over a 20-year period, the experiment would not be the same.

3.5   PROPERTIES OF PROBABILITY MODELS

The concept of a model arises when the scientist is trying to describe the real world. Whether the various aspects of the real world are studied by the physicist, the biologist, the economist, or the businessman, the data almost always show variation from experiment to experiment. Yet these data must be used if new problems are to be solved. What is to be done? Generally the investigator decides to employ a model—that is, a conceptual structure for the problem which simplifies the complexities of reality and seems to approximate his data in a reasonable fashion. The model is often chosen for theoretical reasons, but it cannot be overemphasized that comparison with data is the acid test of its worth. Many of the models that have been used are mathematical. This is inevitable when one considers the sorts of problems in which our civilization is interested.

All of the experiments that we have been considering differ, but our interest is centered in one of their common features. They are all random experiments. We are concerned with the relative frequencies of their uncertain outcomes. Several of them employ tractable material such as cards and dice, but later we shall be discussing more pertinent and complex experiments involving machines, markets, finances, and above all, people. Now we ask the question, "What models are appropriate when dealing with problems involving sets of relative frequencies?"

We recall that an event is a subset of sample space. If a model is to be useful, it must be capable of approximating the relative frequency with which the experiment will lead to the event in which the experimenter is interested. Thus, the model must assign a real number to each event in the sample space under consideration.

To formalize the idea of probability, we need the notion of a *function*. A function is a relation between two sets, D and R, and is expressed as a set of ordered pairs $f = \{(x, f(x))\}$, where x is an element of D and $f(x)$ is an element of R. The set D is called the *domain* and the set R is called the *range* of the function. Each element of D is paired with one and only one element of R, but an element of R may be paired with more than one element of D. For example, if $D = \{1, 2, 3, 4\}$ and $R = \{5, 6, 7, 8\}$, the set of ordered pairs

$$U_1 = \{(1, 5), (2, 6), (3, 6), (4, 8)\}$$

is a function even though the element 6 in R is paired with two elements, 2 and 3, in D. The set of ordered pairs

$$U_2 = \{(1, 5), (2, 6), (2, 7), (3, 6), (4, 8)\}$$

is not a function because the element 2 in D is paired with two elements, 6 and 7, in R. A more familiar way of expressing U_1 is

$$f(1) = 5, \qquad f(2) = 6, \qquad f(3) = 6, \qquad f(4) = 8$$

In general, the elements of D and R need not be real numbers. However, in the definition of probability D is the sample space, S, and R must be a subset of the real numbers. We will consider functions in more detail in Chapter 4, but we can now understand a more formal definition of probability.

Definition. Let S be the sample space of a random experiment. Let $A_1, A_2, \cdots, A_n, \cdots$ be any finite or countably infinite sequence of events in S. A function that assigns a real number $P(A_i)$ to each event $A_i \subseteq S$ is called a *probability distribution* on the sample space S if

1. $P(A_i) \geq 0$ for all A_i

2. $P(S) = 1$ $\hspace{4cm}$ (3.1)

3. $P(\bigcup_i A_i) = \sum_i P(A_i)$ whenever $A_i \cap A_j = \emptyset$ for all A_i and A_j in the union with $i \neq j$.

We note that in the above definition the union in part (3) and hence the sum in (3) must hold for infinite sequences of events as well as finite sequences of events.

Parts 1, 2, and 3 of (3.1) may easily be seen to be properties of relative frequencies. For example, suppose the telephoner repeats the coin-selection experiment 100 times. The relative frequencies associated with a particular set of events are shown in Table 3.3.

We note that the relative frequencies are all real numbers greater than (or equal to) zero. Also the relative frequency corresponding to the set of all possible outcomes is unity. And for mutually exclusive events such as A and B, the relative frequencies add. Let D be the event "dime dated earlier than 1967," $D = A \cup B$, $A \cap B = \emptyset$ and the relative frequency of D is, indeed $0.28 + 0.40 = 0.68$.

Table 3.3 Relative Frequencies on 100 Repetitions of the Coin-Selection Experiment

Event	Relative Frequency
A (dime dated earlier than 1932)	0.28
B (dime dated from 1932 thru 1966)	0.40
C (dime dated later than 1966)	0.32
Total	1.00

From the definition it is possible to derive many properties of probability distributions. We shall obtain several of the most important. The notation $\bar{A}$ will be used to represent the complement of A in S, the sample space.

THEOREM. $\qquad\qquad$ $P(\bar{A}) = 1 - P(A)$ $\qquad\qquad\qquad$ (3.2)

Proof. $\qquad\qquad$ $A \cup \bar{A} = S,$ $\quad$ and $\quad$ $A \cap \bar{A} = \varnothing.$

Using part 3 and then part 2 of (3.1) we have

$$P(S) = P(A \cup \bar{A}) = P(A) + P(\bar{A})$$
$$1 = P(A) + P(\bar{A})$$
$$P(\bar{A}) = 1 - P(A)$$

To illustrate this theorem, consider again the problem of the eight dimes. They are dated 1928, 1930, 1936, 1962, 1963, 1967, 1967, and 1970, the first three being Mercury dimes. Let D represent the event that a 1928 dime is selected on one thrust into the pocket. Then $\bar{D}$ is the event that the dime selected bears some other date than 1928. You will agree that $P(D)$ is $\frac{1}{8}$. From the above result, then,

$$P(\bar{D}) = 1 - P(D) = 1 - \frac{1}{8} = \frac{7}{8}$$

THEOREM. $\qquad\qquad$ $P(\varnothing) = 0$ $\qquad\qquad\qquad$ (3.3)

Proof. This follows immediately from the previous theorem when S itself is used as the set A.

This theorem states that, if a dime is chosen at random from the pocket containing the eight dimes, the probability is zero that it will bear a date other than 1928, 1930, 1936, 1962, 1963, 1967, or 1970.

"either or"   *"and intersection"*

THEOREM. $P(A \cup B) = P(A) + P(B) - P(A \cap B)$.

Proof.   We need to write $A \cup B$ as the union of two mutually exclusive events;

$$A \cup B = A \cup (B \cap \bar{A})$$

so that

$$P(A \cup B) = P(A) + P(B \cap \bar{A}) \tag{3.4}$$

However, we may also rewrite B as

$$B = (A \cap B) \cup (B \cap \bar{A})$$

where the two sets in the right-hand member are mutually exclusive. Hence

$$P(B) = P(A \cap B) + P(B \cap \bar{A})$$

and

$$P(B \cap \bar{A}) = P(B) - P(A \cap B) \tag{3.5}$$

Substituting (3.5) in (3.4),

$$P(A \cup B) = P(A) + P(B) - P(A \cap B) \tag{3.6}$$

This theorem is often called the *addition rule.*

Let B be the event that the dime selected is dated an even year. Let A be the event that a Mercury dime is selected. We wish to find $P(A \cup B)$, the probability that the chosen dime is either a Mercury dime or dated an even year.

We know that $P(A) = \frac{3}{8}$ and that $P(B) = \frac{5}{8}$. Also $A \cap B$ is the selection of a coin dated 1928, 1930, or 1936. Hence, by (3.6)

$$P(A \cup B) = P(A) + P(B) - P(A \cap B) = \frac{3}{8} + \frac{5}{8} - \frac{3}{8} = \frac{5}{8}$$

If A and B are mutually exclusive (that is, if $A \cap B = \varnothing$), (3.6) becomes

$$P(A \cup B) = P(A) + P(B) \tag{3.7}$$

Thus, if A_1 is the event that the coin is dated before 1940 and B_1 is the event that the coin is dated after 1965, using (3.7)

$$P(A \cup B) = P(A) + P(B) = \frac{3}{8} + \frac{3}{8} = \frac{3}{4}$$

The following two theorems are handy in establishing limits on the magnitude of probabilities.

THEOREM.   If $B \subseteq A$, then $P(B) \leq P(A)$.

Proof.   For any events A and B,

$$A = (A \cap B) \cup (A \cap \bar{B}) \qquad \text{where} \qquad (A \cap B) \cap (A \cap \bar{B}) = \varnothing$$

Thus

$$P(A) = P(A \cap B) + P(A \cap \bar{B})$$

But since

$$B \subseteq A, \qquad A \cap B = B$$

$$P(A) = P(B) + P(A \cap \bar{B})$$

$$P(A) - P(B) = P(A \cap \bar{B})$$

Now

$$P(A \cap \bar{B}) \geq 0$$

Thus

$$P(B) \leq P(A)$$

THEOREM.   For any event A, $0 \leq P(A) \leq 1$.

Proof.   By part 1 of (3.1), $P(A) \geq 0$. Using the previous theorem in the case where $A \subseteq S$, we have $P(A) \leq P(S) = 1$. This theorem sets the limits of probability as 1 for certainty and zero for impossibility.

Let us now introduce the idea of conditional probability, an important concept used to describe how additional information can change our concept of which probability function will be appropriate as a model. To return to the coin-selection experiment, the telephone caller knows that he has the eight dimes in his pocket. As he chooses a dime at random, he would say that the probability of a 1930 dime is 1/8. However, suppose that a casual glance shows that the coin is a Mercury dime. Then the model is due for a radical revision. The appropriate probability now appears to be 1/3. We say that the (unconditional) probability of a 1930 dime was 1/8, but the probability of a 1930 dime conditional upon a Mercury dime is 1/3. The Roosevelt dimes are thus excluded from the sample space.

Definition.   Let S be the sample space of a random experiment, and let A and B be two events in S. The conditional probability of the event A, given the event B, is denoted by $P(A \mid B)$, and defined to be

$$P(A \mid B) = \frac{P(A \cap B)}{P(B)} \tag{3.8}$$

when $P(B) \neq 0$. When $P(B) = 0$, $P(A \mid B)$ is arbitrary.

"$P(A)$ given B"

We see that the effect of the additional information that B has occurred is to exclude a portion of sample space from the computation of the probability that A has occurred. The unconditional probability $P(A)$ may be written

$$P(A) = \frac{P(A \cap S)}{P(S)}$$

since $P(S) = 1$ and $P(A \cap S) = P(A)$. Thus the unconditional probability $P(A)$ is, in fact, a special case of the conditional probability $P(A \mid B)$ in which B is taken to be S; that is, when there is no additional information.

The coin problem just discussed may be solved directly from (3.8). Let A = selection of a 1930 dime. Let B = selection of a Mercury dime. Then $A \cap B$ is selection of a 1930 Mercury dime.

$$P(A \mid B) = \frac{\frac{1}{8}}{\frac{3}{8}} = \frac{1}{3}$$

As a direct consequence of the definition of conditional probability we find, on multiplying (3.8) by $P(B)$:

$$P(A \cap B) = P(B)P(A \mid B) \tag{3.9}$$

This reasonable result is sometimes called the *multiplication rule*. If two events A and B are to occur, then the event B must occur, and the event A must also occur, given the occurrence of B. The fact that the probabilities multiply is a consequence of the definition of conditional probability, and does not follow from (3.1), the definition of a probability function. Of course, the letters A and B may be interchanged giving the valid symmetrical result:

$$P(A \cap B) = P(A)P(B \mid A)$$

Definition.   Let S be the sample space of a random experiment, and let A and B be two events in S. If $P(A \mid B) = P(A)$, the events A and B are said to be *statistically independent*.

Under what conditions will $P(A \mid B) = P(A)$? We have shown that

$$P(A \mid B) = \frac{P(A \cap B)}{P(B)} \quad \text{and that } P(A) = \frac{P(A \cap S)}{P(S)}$$

Equating these two expressions, we see that $P(A \mid B) = P(A)$ whenever

$$\frac{P(A \cap B)}{P(B)} = \frac{P(A \cap S)}{P(S)}$$

that is, whenever the ratio of probabilities for the occurrence of A is the same in B as for the whole sample space. In such a case, the additional information "B has occurred" is useless as far as giving any help in the computation of $P(A)$ is concerned. In this special case where $P(A \mid B) = P(A)$, we may also equate

$$P(A) = \frac{P(A \cap B)}{P(B)}$$

and it follows at once that for independent events A and B:

$$P(A \cap B) = P(A)P(B) \tag{3.10}$$

as a special case of the multiplication rule.

As an illustration of statistical independence, consider the following question. What is the probability of selecting a queen on a single draw from a well-shuffled deck of cards?

$$P(Q) = \frac{4}{52} = \frac{1}{13}$$

What is the probability of selecting a queen on one draw from a well-shuffled deck of cards from which all spades and hearts have been removed?

$$P(Q \mid C \cup D) = \frac{2}{26} = \frac{1}{13}$$

Thus, we see that the probability of drawing a queen is independent of the number of thirteen-card suits present.

Let us examine some problems using the theorems that we have developed—particularly the addition and multiplication laws.

3.6   ILLUSTRATIVE EXAMPLE

The personnel office of the J. B. Whickers Company has files for 18,000 employees. Their breakdown by age and sex is as follows:

	Sex		
Age	Female (F)	Male (M)	Total
Under 25 (A)	2700	900	3600
25–35 (B)	4320	2880	7200
Over 35 (C)	2160	5040	7200
Total	9180	8820	18,000

1. If one file is selected at random from the personnel office, what is the probability that it represents:

(a) An employee 35 years old or under?

(b) A female employee 35 or under?

(c) Either a male employee or an employee over 35?

(d) A male employee over 35?

(e) A female employee or an employee 25 or older?

(f) A female employee over 35, given that the file represents a female employee?

(g) A female employee over 35, given that the file represents an employee over 35?

We shall denote the various events involved by

A, under 25;   B, 25–35;   C, over 35;   M, male; and F, female

and give the solutions.

(a) P(35 or under) = $P(A \cup B)$ where $A \cap B = \varnothing$; so, by (3.7),

$$P(A \cup B) = P(A) + P(B) = \frac{3600}{18,000} + \frac{7200}{18,000} = \frac{3}{5}$$

(b) P(female 35 or under) = $P[(A \cap F) \cup (B \cap F)]$

where

$$(A \cap F) \cap (B \cap F) = \varnothing$$

so, by (3.7),

$$P[(A \cap F) \cup (B \cap F)] = P(A \cap F) + P(B \cap F)$$

$$= \frac{2700}{18,000} + \frac{4320}{18,000} = \frac{39}{100}$$

(c) P(male or over 35) = $P(M \cup C)$ where $M \cap C \neq \varnothing$; thus, by (3.6),

$$P(M \cup C) = P(M) + P(C) - P(M \cap C)$$

$$= \frac{8820}{18,000} + \frac{7200}{18,000} - \frac{5040}{18,000} = \frac{61}{100}$$

Note that this result may be obtained directly from that of *b* above. Since an employee is either a female 35 or under *or* male or over 35, and since these two sets are mutually exclusive, we may write:

$$P[(A \cap F) \cup (B \cap F)] + P(M \cup C) = P(S) = 1$$

Thus

$$P(M \cup C) = 1 - \frac{39}{100} = \frac{61}{100}$$

(d)   P(male and over 35) $= P(M \cap C) = \frac{5040}{18,000} = \frac{7}{25}$

(e) $P[F \cup (B \cup C)] = P(F) + P(B \cup C) - P[F \cap (B \cup C)]$

$$= \frac{9180}{18,000} + \frac{14,400}{18,000} - \frac{6480}{18,000} = \frac{19}{20}$$

(f) $P(C \cap F \mid F) = \dfrac{P[(C \cap F) \cap F]}{P(F)}$

$$= \frac{P(C \cap F)}{P(F)} = \frac{2160}{18,000} \cdot \frac{18,000}{9180} = \frac{12}{51} = \frac{4}{17}$$

(g) $P(C \cap F \mid C) = \dfrac{P[(C \cap F) \cap C]}{P(C)} = \dfrac{2160}{18,000} \cdot \dfrac{18,000}{7200} = \dfrac{3}{10}$

2. Suppose, now, that one file is selected at random from the 18,000 examined, and returned to its place. Then a second file is chosen at random. A sample of size two has been selected by the procedure called "sampling with replacement." Find the probability that:
(a) Both files chosen are those of female employees.
(b) Neither file is that of a female under 25.
(c) The first file is that of an employee over 35, and the second of a male employee under 25.
(d) One file is that of an employee over 35, and the other of a male employee under 25.
The solutions for *a*, *b*, and *c* are obtained by (3.10), the multiplication rule for independent events.

(a)   P(both female) $= P(F) \cdot P(F) = \left[\dfrac{9180}{18,000}\right]^2 = \dfrac{2601}{10,000}$

(b)   P(neither female under 25) $= [1 - P(F \cap A)][1 - P(F \cap A)]$

$$= \left[1 - \frac{2700}{18,000}\right]^2 = \frac{289}{400}$$

(c) $P(C) \cdot P(A \cap M) = \dfrac{7200}{18,000} \cdot \dfrac{900}{18,000} = \dfrac{1}{50}$

(d)   We may find $P(C) \cdot P(A \cap M) + P(A \cap M) \cdot P(C)$

$$= \frac{1}{50} + \frac{1}{50} = \frac{1}{25}$$

using (3.7), since the event of interest can occur only in two mutually exclusive ways, or we may reason that $P(C) \cdot P(A \cap M)$ and $P(A \cap M) \cdot P(C)$ are equal and simply double the result of c.

3. Answer question (2) if the first file selected is not returned before the second is drawn. This procedure is called sampling without replacement. In this problem, the probabilities obtained will be very close to those found in (2). However, if the total number of files was small, the results would differ considerably.

(a) $P(\text{both female}) = \dfrac{9180}{18,000} \cdot \dfrac{9179}{17,999}$

(b) $P(\text{neither female under 25}) = \left[1 - \dfrac{2700}{18,000} \right]\left[1 - \dfrac{2700}{17,999} \right]$

(c) $P(C)P(A \cap M) = \dfrac{7200}{18,000} \cdot \dfrac{900}{17,999}$

(d) $P(C)P(A \cap M) + P(A \cap M)P(C) =$

$$\frac{7200}{18,000} \cdot \frac{900}{17,999} + \frac{900}{18,000} \cdot \frac{7200}{17,999} = \frac{7200 \cdot 1800}{18,000 \cdot 17,999}$$

4. Suppose the J. B. Whickers Company keeps all male files in filing area X and all female files in filing area Y. If an area is selected at random from X and Y and then two files are picked at random from that area, what is the probability that both represent employees under 25 if the drawing is done without replacement?

Since area X is as likely to be chosen as area Y, we have

$$P(X) = P(Y) = \frac{1}{2}$$

Then, using (3.9),

$$P(\text{both under 25}) = P(X)P(A_1 \mid X)P(A_2 \mid X \cap A_1)$$
$$+ P(Y)P(A_1 \mid Y)P(A_2 \mid Y \cap A_1)$$

that is, one must either pick X, pick A on draw 1, and follow by A on draw 2 (no replacement); or he must pick Y and obtain the two A's there. The possibilities are mutually exclusive.

$$P(\text{both under 25}) = \frac{1}{2} \cdot \frac{900}{8820} \cdot \frac{899}{8819} + \frac{1}{2} \cdot \frac{2700}{9180} \cdot \frac{2699}{9179} = 0.048$$

3.7 COMBINATIONS AND PERMUTATIONS

There are various methods for simplifying probability computations. The most useful involve permutations and combinations. Consider S, a finite set with distinct elements. Let

$$S = \{a_1, a_2, \cdots, a_n\}.$$

Definition. The number of distinct arrangements that can be made from the n elements of S, using r of them at a time, is denoted by $(n)_r$ and called the number of *permutations* of n things taken r at a time. Note that $r \leq n$.

Definition. The number of distinct subsets of size r that can be formed from the n elements of S is denoted by $\binom{n}{r}$, and is called the number of *combinations* of n things taken r at a time. Note that $r \leq n$.

Definition.

$$n! = n(n-1) \cdots 3 \cdot 2 \cdot 1 \qquad \text{when } n \text{ is an integer and } n > 0.$$
$$0! = 1$$

That is,

$$3! = 3 \cdot 2 \cdot 1 = 6; \qquad 8! = 8 \cdot 7 \cdot 6 \cdot 5 \cdot 4 \cdot 3 \cdot 2 \cdot 1 = 40,320, \text{ etc.}$$

In this text the symbol $n!$ is defined *only* when n is a nonnegative integer.

To develop convenient ways of counting $(n)_r$ and $\binom{n}{r}$, we shall first work with a set of four items, $s_4 = \{a_1, a_2, a_3, a_4\}$. Suppose we wish to see how many arrangements can be made from these four elements, using three at a time. Consider three positions to be filled: We may place any one of a_1, a_2, a_3, a_4 in the first position; there are four possibilities here. Then any of the remaining three may be put in the second position. Finally, one has a choice of two for the third spot. Thus, $(4)_3 = 4 \cdot 3 \cdot 2 = 24$ permutations of four things taken three at a time.

Similar reasoning holds for the set $S = \{a_1, a_2, \cdots, a_n\}$ when we wish to count the number of permutations of these n elements taken r at a time. There are now r positions to be filled. Any of the n elements may be placed in the first, any of the remaining $n - 1$ in the second, any of the residual $n - 2$ in the third, etc. Finally, there remain only $n - (r - 1) = n - r + 1$ possibilities for the rth position. Thus,

$$(n)_r = n(n-1) \cdots (n-r+1)$$

which in turn is equal to $n!/(n-r)!$ since the factors from 1 to $n-r$ cancel. It follows that

permutation $(n)_r = \dfrac{n!}{(n-r)!}$ (3.11)

From (3.11) it is clear that $(n)_n = n!$

How many combinations may be formed from four items, using three at a time? How many subsets consisting of three elements does the set $S_4 = \{a_1, a_2, a_3, a_4\}$ have? These questions are entirely equivalent. We may answer by enumerating them: $a_1\, a_2\, a_3$, $a_1\, a_2\, a_4$, $a_1\, a_3\, a_4$, and $a_2\, a_3\, a_4$—four subsets in all. But enumeration would be time consuming if S had, for example, 96 elements. An easy way to count combinations is to relate them to the permutation formula (3.11).

Given $S = \{a_1, a_2, \cdots, a_n\}$, we wish to evaluate $\binom{n}{r}$. We need only notice that each subset consisting of r elements can be arranged in $r!$ ways. Hence, there are $r!$ times as many permutations of n elements, r at a time, as there are combinations.

$$r!\binom{n}{r} = (n)_r = \frac{n!}{(n-r)!}$$

combination $\binom{n}{r} = \dfrac{n!}{r!\,(n-r)!}$ (3.12)

Using this formula we may check our previous enumeration.

$$\binom{4}{3} = \frac{4!}{3!\,1!} = \frac{4 \cdot 3 \cdot 2 \cdot 1}{3 \cdot 2 \cdot 1 \cdot 1} = 4$$

There is one further matter to be investigated in this section. Suppose we have a set containing four elements, two of which cannot be told apart; $S = \{a, a, b, c\}$. Then the number of distinguishable permutations of four elements, taken four at a time, is reduced from the 24 obtained when all four items differ. We enumerate:

aabc, abac, abca, baac, baca, bcaa,

aacb, acab, acba, caab, caba, cbaa.

There are now 12 distinct permutations instead of $4! = 24$. What is the general relation?

Let S be a set consisting of n_1 elements a_1, n_2 elements a_2, $\cdots$, n_j elements a_j, where $\sum_{1}^{j} n_i = n$. We wish to find the number of distinguishable permutations of n elements, taken n at a time. The customary symbol is $\binom{n}{n_1 \cdots n_j}$.

If all the elements of S differed, then there would be $(n)_n = n!$ permutations which could be identified. But here, of the $n!$, $n_1!$ differ only in the ordering given to the elements a_1 and are indistinguishable, $n_2!$ differ only in the ordering given to the elements $a_2, \cdots, n_j!$ differ only in the ordering given to the elements a_j. This means that there are $n_1!\, n_2! \cdots n_j!$ times as many identifiable permutations in the case with all items distinguishable as in the present case. Symbolically,

$$n_1!\, n_2! \cdots n_j! \binom{n}{n_1 n_2 \cdots n_j} = n!$$

$$\binom{n}{n_1 n_2 \cdots n_j} = \frac{n!}{n_1!\, n_2! \cdots n_j!}$$

(3.13)

Thus the number of distinct permutations, four at a time, which may be made from $S = \{a, a, b, c\}$ is

$$\binom{4}{2\ 1\ 1} = \frac{4!}{2!\,1!\,1!} = \frac{4 \cdot 3 \cdot 2 \cdot 1}{2 \cdot 1 \cdot 1 \cdot 1} = 12$$

When S consists of n objects, r of one kind and $n - r$ of another, the distinguishable permutations are counted by

$$\binom{n}{r\ n-r} = \frac{n!}{r!\,(n - r)!} = \binom{n}{r}$$

the number of combinations of n things taken r at a time. This is to be expected. We are going to arrange the objects by placing one in each of n positions. We do so by choosing r positions for objects of the first kind; those of the second kind will be placed in the remaining $n - r$ positions. There are $\binom{n}{r}$ ways to choose the r positions for objects of the first kind. Once these r positions have been selected, the arrangements of objects of the first kind in these positions and objects of the second kind elsewhere will be indistinguishable. For our purposes, these $r!\,(n - r)!$ arrangements all count as one. For example, consider the possible arrangements of the symbols $AABB$. If we number the positions 1, 2, 3, 4, there are $\binom{4}{2}$ positions for the A's, namely: 1 and 2, 1 and 3, 1 and 4, 2 and 3, 2 and 4, and 3 and 4. The B's go in the remaining positions, and we get the six arrangements:

$$AABB \quad ABAB \quad ABBA \quad BAAB \quad BABA \quad BBAA$$

How may these ideas be applied? Dacy's department store sells eight complete lines of kitchen equipment. During the week of November 15, three show windows are available for kitchen displays—the displays will be on exhibit during the whole week.

1. If three lines are to be displayed and no line is to appear in more than one window, how many different sets of three lines are possible?

2. How many different allocations of the eight lines to three windows are possible if no line appears in more than one window?

The solutions follow from (3.12) and (3.11), respectively.

(1)   *comb* $$\binom{8}{3} = \frac{8!}{3!\,5!} = \frac{8 \cdot 7 \cdot 6}{3 \cdot 2 \cdot 1} = 56$$

(2)   *perm* $$(8)_3 = \frac{8!}{5!} = 8 \cdot 7 \cdot 6 = 336$$

Dacy's furniture department also has 17 sofas, all of the same design, to be placed along one aisle for immediate clearance. Five are upholstered in green nylon, two in brown checked nylon, seven in red checked wool, and three in grey plush. How many distinct arrangements are possible? By (3.13)

permut

$$\binom{17}{5\,2\,7\,3} = \frac{17!}{5!\,2!\,7!\,3!} = \frac{17 \cdot 16 \cdot 15 \cdot 14 \cdot 13 \cdot 12 \cdot 11 \cdot 10 \cdot 9 \cdot 8}{5 \cdot 4 \cdot 3 \cdot 2 \cdot 1 \cdot 2 \cdot 1 \cdot 3 \cdot 2 \cdot 1}$$

$$= 49{,}008{,}960$$

In the next section we shall employ combinations and permutations in the solution of probability problems.

3.8   ILLUSTRATIVE PROBLEMS

Ten percent of the J. B. Whickers Company's personnel files are known to contain errors. If eight files are selected at random with replacement what is the probability that: $m = 18{,}000$

1. None of those selected contains an error?

2. Exactly three of those selected contain errors?

3. At most, three of those selected contain errors?

4. At least, three of those selected contain errors?

Solutions.   (1) P(no errors) $= \left(\dfrac{9}{10}\right)^8 = 0.431$

(2) We consider first the probability that the first three files chosen contain errors and the remaining five do not. This is given by

$$\frac{1}{10} \cdot \frac{1}{10} \cdot \frac{1}{10} \cdot \frac{9}{10} \cdot \frac{9}{10} \cdot \frac{9}{10} \cdot \frac{9}{10} \cdot \frac{9}{10} = \left(\frac{1}{10}\right)^3 \left(\frac{9}{10}\right)^5$$

But these are $\begin{pmatrix} 8 \\ 3\,5 \end{pmatrix} = \begin{pmatrix} 8 \\ 3 \end{pmatrix}$ distinct permutations of the three files with errors and the five without. Each of these arrangements occurs with probability:

$$\left(\frac{1}{10}\right)^3 \left(\frac{9}{10}\right)^5$$

Thus,

$$P(\text{exactly three errors}) = \begin{pmatrix} 8 \\ 3 \end{pmatrix} \left(\frac{1}{10}\right)^3 \left(\frac{9}{10}\right)^5 = 56 \cdot 9^5 \cdot 10^{-8} = 0.033$$

(3) $P(\text{at most 3}) = P(\text{exactly 3}) + P(\text{exactly 2}) + P(\text{exactly 1}) + P(\text{exactly 0})$

$$= \begin{pmatrix} 8 \\ 3 \end{pmatrix} \left(\frac{1}{10}\right)^3 \left(\frac{9}{10}\right)^5 = \begin{pmatrix} 8 \\ 2 \end{pmatrix} \left(\frac{1}{10}\right)^2 \left(\frac{9}{10}\right)^6$$

$$+ \begin{pmatrix} 8 \\ 1 \end{pmatrix} \left(\frac{1}{10}\right)^1 \left(\frac{9}{10}\right)^7 + \begin{pmatrix} 8 \\ 0 \end{pmatrix} \left(\frac{1}{10}\right)^0 \left(\frac{9}{10}\right)^8$$

$$= 0.033 + 0.149 + 0.383 + 0.430 = 0.995$$

(4) $\qquad P(\text{at least 3}) = P(\text{exactly 3}) + P(\text{more than 3})$

$$= 0.033 + 1 - P(\text{at most 3})$$

$$= 0.033 + 1.000 - 0.995 = 0.038$$

Of course, this problem may also be solved by direct computation similar to that used in (3).

On a blind date, six male freshmen from Ironclad University meet six coeds from Honeydew Junior College. Among the freshmen, three are handsome (H), two of the others are very studious (S), and the remaining one is a star athlete (A). Among the girls, three are musical (M), two of the others are drama majors (D), and the sixth is a beauty contest winner (B). Assuming that the couples pair up at random, what is the probability that:

1. The athletic freshman dates the beautiful coed?

2. The two studious freshmen date the two drama majors?

3. Not more than two handsome frosh date musical coeds?

4. At least two handsome frosh do not date musical coeds?

5. Either no studious freshman dates a drama major, or no handsome freshman dates the beautiful coed?

It is interesting to examine the sample space of this most random of random experiments. We determine the number of points in sample space by counting permutations, noting that a point represents a complete set of six pairs. Suppose that the athlete chooses a date first. He has six girls to choose from. Suppose the first studious freshman chooses second; he has five possibilities, etc. Thus the number of possible pairs is

$$(6)_6 = 6 \cdot 5 \cdot 4 \cdot 3 \cdot 2 \cdot 1 = 720$$

and there are 720 points in the experiment's sample space.

(1) The probability that the athlete dates the beautiful coed is given by the number of these 720 points at which they do date, divided by 720. If these two date each other, there are 5! ways in which the other couples may pair off. Thus,

$$P(A; B) = \frac{5!}{6!} = \frac{1}{6}$$

It could also be argued that, with six equally likely girls, the probability that the athlete would date any one particular girl is one out of six.

(2) As in the previous problem, we may reason that there are 4! ways that the others may pair off, and two ways that this may be done between the studious and dramatic subsets.

$$P(S, S; D, D) = \frac{2 \cdot 4!}{6!} = \frac{1}{15}$$

Or we could argue that there are exactly two mutually exclusive ways that this arrangement could come about. Either S_1 dates D_1 and S_2 dates D_2 or S_1 dates D_2 and S_2 dates D_1. Here, by (3.7) and (3.9),

$$P(S, S; D, D) = \frac{1}{6} \cdot \frac{1}{5} + \frac{1}{6} \cdot \frac{1}{5} = \frac{1}{15}$$

(3) There are three mutually exclusive ways in which not more than two handsome freshmen can date musical coeds: none can; exactly one can; or exactly two can. We can again use (3.7) and (3.9) directly.

$$P(0) = \frac{3}{6} \cdot \frac{2}{5} \cdot \frac{1}{4} = \frac{1}{20}$$

$$P(1) = \frac{3}{6} \cdot \frac{3}{5} \cdot \frac{2}{4} + \frac{3}{6} \cdot \frac{3}{5} \cdot \frac{2}{4} + \frac{3}{6} \cdot \frac{2}{5} \cdot \frac{3}{4} = \frac{9}{20}$$

$$P(2) = \frac{3}{6} \cdot \frac{2}{5} \cdot \frac{3}{4} + \frac{3}{6} \cdot \frac{3}{5} \cdot \frac{2}{4} + \frac{3}{6} \cdot \frac{3}{5} \cdot \frac{2}{4} = \frac{9}{20}$$

$$P = P(0) + P(1) + P(2) = \frac{19}{20}$$

We note that the reasoning shown in computing P(1) may be given a short cut. Instead of saying "first does, second doesn't, third doesn't"; or "first doesn't, second does, third doesn't"; or "first doesn't, second doesn't, third does"; we may say that the first term is one of three equally likely possibilities so that

$$P(1) = 3 \cdot \frac{3}{6} \cdot \frac{3}{5} \cdot \frac{2}{4} = \frac{9}{20}$$

As an alternative procedure, note that the three events whose probabilities have been found do not form an exhaustive set. There is one other possibility and only one: that all three handsome freshmen date musical coeds.

$$P(3) = \frac{3}{6} \cdot \frac{2}{5} \cdot \frac{1}{4} = \frac{1}{20}$$

Hence, using (3.2), $P = 1 - P(3) = 1 - \frac{1}{20} = \frac{19}{20}$ as previously found.

(4) "At least two do not" is equivalent to "either two do not or three do not," which is the same as "either one does or none do."

$$P = P(0) + P(1) = \frac{1}{20} + \frac{9}{20} = \frac{1}{2}$$

(5) Perhaps it is simplest to translate this problem into positive terms. Either: (I) both studious freshmen date beautiful or musical coeds, *or* (II) all handsome freshmen date musical or dramatic girls. Events I and II are not mutually exclusive; for instance, the studious freshmen could date two musical coeds, while the handsome freshmen could date the remaining musical girl and the two drama majors. Thus,

$$P(I) = \frac{4}{6} \cdot \frac{3}{5} = \frac{12}{30} = \frac{8}{20}$$

$$P(II) = \frac{5}{6} \cdot \frac{4}{5} \cdot \frac{3}{4} = \frac{60}{120} = \frac{10}{20}$$

It remains to count the number of points in I ∩ II. Suppose the two studious lads date musical coeds. This can be done in $(3)_2 = 3 \cdot 2 = 6$ ways. In each case, one musical girl is not chosen. Thus the three handsome boys may choose from one musical girl and two drama majors. This may be done in $(3)_3 = 3 \cdot 2 \cdot 1 = 6$ ways. So there are $6 \cdot 6 = 36$ points in sample space in I ∩ II at which both studious boys date musical girls. The only other possibility is for one studious freshman to date the beautiful girl and the other to date a musical coed. Again, this can be done in six ways. But now there are four possibilities for the handsome freshman leading to $(4)_3 = 4 \cdot 3 \cdot 2 = 24$ arrangements and $6 \cdot 24 = 144$ points in I ∩ II. Hence I ∩ II contains

$36 + 144 = 180$ points, each having probability $1/720$. Finally,

$$\frac{180}{720} = \frac{5}{20}$$

and we use (3.6).

$$P(I \cup II) = P(I) + P(II) - P(I \cap II)$$

$$= \frac{8}{20} + \frac{10}{20} - \frac{5}{20} = \frac{13}{20}$$

The game of bridge leads to many probability problems. What is the probability of holding three one-point bridge hands in succession if distribution points are not considered?

In the point-count system of evaluating hands, an ace counts 4 points, a king 3, a queen 2, and a jack one. Eliminating distribution points, the question asks for the probability of holding three hands in succession, each containing one jack and no aces, kings, or queens.

We first find the probability for a single hand. There are $\binom{52}{13}$ possible subsets of the deck that a player may hold. We wish to enumerate those that contain exactly one jack and no higher honors.

First, choose the jack. This may be done in $\binom{4}{1}$ ways. Then choose the other 12 cards, remembering that four aces, four kings, four queens, and four jacks are not available. This can be done in $\binom{36}{12}$ ways. The required probability for one hand is then:

$$P = \frac{\binom{4}{1}\binom{36}{12}}{\binom{52}{13}} = \frac{4!}{1!\,3!} \cdot \frac{36!}{12!\,24!} \cdot \frac{13!\,39!}{52!} = 0.00788$$

For three hands,

$$P^3 = (0.00788)^3 = 4.89 \times 10^{-7}$$

It is often desirable to write the expression for P as

$$P = \frac{\binom{4}{1}\binom{36}{12}\binom{12}{0}}{\binom{52}{13}}$$

where the upper and lower figures in the numerator add respectively to the upper and lower figures in the denominator. The factor $\binom{12}{0}$ indicates that no ace, king, or queen may be chosen. The value of P is unchanged, since

$$\binom{12}{0} = \frac{12!}{0!\,12!} = \frac{12!}{1\cdot 12!} = 1$$

For accurate approximations to large factorials, reference should be made either to a table of logarithms of factorials, such as Table E.5, or to Stirling's formula, which states

$$N! \approx \sqrt{2\pi N}\, N^N e^{-N} \tag{3.14}$$

As N becomes large, the relative error in this approximation becomes smaller and smaller.

We assume that the reader has been keeping the problem of the two aces (posed in Section 3.1) in mind. If he hasn't already solved it, the suspense must be unbearable by now. We keep an implied promise by using it to close the chapter. We are really asked to find the probability that 24 cards, selected from a standard deck of 52, will contain two or more aces. If we let P_j be the probability that 24 cards contain j aces, we can reason as follows: We are selecting 24 cards from 52. This can be done in $\binom{52}{24}$ ways. In order to get j aces from the 4 available, we must select these j and then $24 - j$ other cards from the 48 available. This can be done in $\binom{4}{j}\binom{48}{24-j}$ ways. Then

$$P_j = \frac{\binom{4}{j}\binom{48}{24-j}}{\binom{52}{24}}$$

Letting $j = 0, 1, 2, 3, 4$, we can compute

$$P_0 = 2925/38{,}675 = 0.0756 \qquad P_3 = 8096/38{,}675 = 0.2093$$

$$P_1 = 11{,}232/38{,}675 = 0.2904 \qquad P_4 = 1518/38{,}675 = 0.0393$$

$$P_2 = 14{,}904/38{,}675 = 0.3854$$

These probabilities add to unity. The probability of two or more aces is thus

$$P_2 + P_3 + P_4 = 0.6340$$

At even money, it looks like a good game to play.

IMPORTANT TERMS AND CONCEPTS

Domain
Elements
  Combinations of
  Permutations of
Events
  Exhaustive set of
  Independent
  Mutually exclusive set of
Experiment, random
Function

Probability
  Addition of
  Conditional
  Multiplication of
  Unconditional
Range
Relative frequency
Sample space
Sets
  Disjoint
  Intersection of
  Union of

SYMBOLS AND ABBREVIATIONS

$A \cap B$ and - intersect

$A \cup B$ or - either or

$P(A)$ - prob of A

$P(A \mid B)$ - " ", given B

$\bar{A}$ -

$n!$

$(n)_r$

$\dbinom{n}{r}$

$\dbinom{n}{n_1 \, n_2 \cdots n_m}$

$\varnothing$

$A \subseteq B$

$A \supseteq B$

OFTEN-USED FORMULAS

$$(n)_r = n(n-1)(n-2)\ldots(n-r+1) = \frac{n!}{(n-r)!}$$

$$\binom{n}{r} = \frac{n!}{r!\,(n-r)!}\,; \qquad \binom{n}{n_1 \, n_2 \cdots n_m} = \frac{n!}{n_1!\,n_2! \cdots n_m!}$$

$$P(\bar{B}) = 1 - P(B)$$

$$P(A \mid B) = \frac{P(AB)}{P(B)} = \frac{P(A \cap B)}{P(B)}$$

$$P(A \cap B) = P(AB) = P(A)P(B \mid A) = P(B)P(A \mid B)$$

$$P(A \cup B) = P(A) + P(B) - P(A \cap B)$$

EXERCISES

1. Given two sets:

$$V = \{7, 3\} \qquad W = \{4, 5, 6\}$$

   a. Construct a function with V as domain and a subset of W as range.
   b. Construct a function with W as domain and V as range.
   c. Construct a set of ordered pairs whose first elements are taken from V and whose second elements are taken from W that is not a function.

2. Given the following sets:

$$A = \{7, 8, 9\} \qquad B = \{4, 5, 6\}$$

   and the following sets of pairs constructed from them:

$$T = \{(7, 4), (8, 5), (9, 6)\}$$
$$U = \{(7, 4), (8, 4), (9, 4)\}$$
$$V = \{(4, 7), (4, 8), (4, 9)\}$$
$$W = \{(4, 9), (5, 8), (6, 9)\}$$
$$X = \{(7, 6), (8, 4), (9, 5)\}$$
$$Y = \{(4, 9), (5, 8), (6, 7)\}$$
$$Z = \{(4, 9), (5, 8), (4, 7)\}$$

   a. Which of the sets of pairs are functions?
   b. What is the domain of W?
   c. What is the range of U?

3. a. To what extent does taking a Statistics 1 examination at the University of Colorado qualify as a random experiment? Justify your answer.
   b. Assume that taking a Statistics 1 examination does meet the qualifications of a random experiment. Define precisely a statistical problem and universe in which this experiment would be useful.

4. Define sample space in each of the following random experiments:
   a. Taking a Statistics 1 examination.
   b. Tossing two dice once.
   c. Counting the number of packages in a shipment.
   d. Taking a course in economics.
   e. Crossing a street on foot.
   f. Taking an automobile trip on Labor Day.
   g. Seeking a job after graduation.
   h. Rendering a verdict in a criminal court of law.
   i. Studying during an evening.

5. Evaluate each of the following:

   a. 7!   b. 15!   c. 0!   d. 40!

6. Evaluate:

   a. $(5)_3$ e. $(10)_2$

   b. $(6)_1$ f. $\begin{pmatrix} 9 \\ 5\,2\,2 \end{pmatrix}$

   c. $\begin{pmatrix} 9 \\ 4 \end{pmatrix}$ g. $\begin{pmatrix} 4 \\ 1\,1\,2 \end{pmatrix}$

   d. $\begin{pmatrix} 8 \\ 6 \end{pmatrix}$ h. $\begin{pmatrix} 10 \\ 7\,2\,1 \end{pmatrix}$

7. How many permutations are there of two of the last four letters in the alphabet?

8. Stirling's formula states that $N! \approx \sqrt{2\pi N}\, N^N e^{-N}$. Evaluate the following by the use of Stirling's formula:

   a. $(9)_9$ b. $\begin{pmatrix} 50 \\ 25 \end{pmatrix}$

9. A university has planned to build five buildings on one city block. Assume that there are only five spaces available and that any of the planned buildings would fit into any of the available spaces.

   a. How many arrangements are possible?

   b. One of the five planned buildings is for the English Department. Suppose that the English Department prefers a particular space. What is the probability that its building will be assigned to the space the English Department prefers? State any assumptions you make.

   c. Describe the probability model that you used in part *b*.

   d. Criticize and evaluate the reasonableness of the assumptions of your model if this problem were in an actual situation.

10. On a reviewing stand at a local Army Reserve parade, there stood two colonels, three lieutenant colonels, and four captains.

   a. How many possible arrangements are there for these 9 officers if each person is distinguishable?

   b. If persons of the same rank are not distinguishable from each other, how many different arrangements are possible?

   c. If persons of the same rank are not distinguishable from each other, and if the two colonels must stand in the two end positions, how many arrangements are possible?

   d. How many arrangements are possible, if each officer is assigned a position by name, with a condition that the two colonels must be assigned the two middle positions?

11. A student wishes to arrange one statistics book, one accounting book, two economics texts, and four paperback novels on a shelf. How many arrangements are possible if:

    a. The books may be arranged in any order?

    b. The books on each subject must all stand together, and the novels are regarded as one subject class?

    c. Only the novels must stand together?

    If the books are drawn out of a box at random and placed on the shelf, what is the probability that:

    d. The novels are all adjacent?

    e. The books in each subject are standing together?

12. There are seven unfilled positions along a fountain pen assembly line for the Penco Corporation. One of the seven positions is that of a foreman. The Penco Corporation personnel office has 13 applicants for jobs, of which three are for the position of foreman on the line, and the other 10 are for the position of laborer. How many different combinations may be chosen from the applicants to fill the seven unfilled positions of six laborers and one foreman if all positions as laborer are regarded as identical?

13. John J. Stokes is coach of a Little League baseball team. Each boy will play any position, and 11 boys show up for practice. How many "fielding teams" can be assigned to the nine positions by coach Stokes? (*Note.* A switching of players among the nine positions represents a new "fielding team.")

14. Both John B. and Paul S. (class of 1969) upon graduation accepted trainee positions in the marketing department of a local company. There were a total of six trainees hired by the company (including John and Paul). Each was assigned one of the six desks on the back row of the large room housing the marketing staff. Suppose that the six desks were assigned at random by the person in charge. What is the probability that John and Paul were assigned to adjacent desks?

15. There are 51 seats in a particular classroom at Ironclad University, 12 seats in the first row, and 13 seats in each of the three other rows. Suppose that 48 students enter this room and choose seats in a truly random fashion.

    a. How many different combinations of seats may be chosen?

    b. What is the probability that no one will sit in the last seat in the last row?

    c. What is the probability that no one will sit in the fifth seat of the first row?

d. What is the probability that the first two seats at the left in the front row will not be chosen?

e. Define the sample space and briefly describe the probability model that you used for parts *b*, *c*, and *d*.

f. Criticize the probability model of part *e* in a real situation, indicating what modifications might be desirable.

16. Given that $A \cup B \subset S$, show that:

a. $A \cup S = S$

b. $A \cup A = A$

c. $A \cup (A \cap B) = A$

d. $A \cap (A \cup B) = A$

e. $(A \cap B) \cup (A \cap \bar{B}) = A$

17. Prove that if $A \subseteq S$ and $B \subseteq S$,

$$P(A \cap B) \leq P(A) \leq P(A \cup B) \leq P(A) + P(B)$$

18. Given the events $A_1, A_2, \cdots, A_n$, such that $A_i \cap A_j = \varnothing$, $i \neq j$, prove that

$$P\left(\bigcup_{i=1}^{n} A_i\right) = \sum_{i=1}^{n} P(A_i)$$

(*Hint.* Use mathematical induction.)

19. Parts *a* through *e* of this question refer to the following table.

U.S. Institutions of Higher Education—Number of Degrees Conferred (All Data Rounded to the Nearest Thousand and Adjusted for Consistency of Totals)

	School Year Ending	B_1 Bachelor's or First Prof.	B_2 Master's or Second Prof.	B_3 Doctor's or Equivalent	All Degrees
A_7	1957	337	62	9	408
A_6	1956	309	59	9	377
A_5	1955	285	58	9	352
A_4	1954	291	57	9	357
A_3	1953	303	61	8	372
A_2	1952	330	63	8	401
A_1	1951	383	65	7	455
	Total	2238	425	59	2722

Source. Historical Statistics of the United States, U.S. Census, 1960.

a. Explain in words the meaning of the following symbols, given that the sample space consists of all degrees of institutions of higher learning in the United States conferred during the school years from 1951 to 1957.

(1) $P(A_1)$

(6) $P(B_2 \cup B_3)$

(2) $P(B_2)$

(7) $P(A_7 \cap A_6)$

(3) $P(A_4 \mid B_1)$

(8) $P[(B_2 \cup B_3) \cap (A_7 \cup A_6)]$

(4) $P(B_1 \cap A_2)$

(9) $P(B_1 \mid A_7 \cup A_6)$

(5) $P[(B_2 \cup B_3) \cap A_7]$

b. Calculate the numerical ratio representing each of the probabilities in part *a*.

c. Give the symbolic notation and compute the probability that a conferred degree from an institution of higher education in the United States during the school years from 1951 to 1957, selected at random, was:

(1) A master's degree in 1957.

(2) A bachelor's degree or a master's degree.

(3) A doctor's degree prior to 1955.

(4) Conferred between 1953 and 1956 inclusive as a master's or a doctor's degree.

(5) A bachelor's degree, given that it was conferred before 1954.

d. Suppose that one selected a name at random from the names on the 2,722,000 conferred degrees issued by institutions of higher learning in the United States during 1951 to 1957. Would the probability that a particular name was chosen equal 1/2,722,000 and be equal for all names? Explain.

20. Derive formulas that express the following probabilities in terms of the probabilities of their component events.

a. $P(A \cap B \cap C)$

c. $P(A \cap B \mid C)$

b. $P(A \cup B \cup C)$

d. $P(A \mid B \cup C)$

21. The following information pertains to all sophomore undergraduate students at Blibo college during the 1965 fall term.

(1) There were 20 percent who received a grade of A in Accounting 1.

(2) Of those receiving a grade other than A in Accounting 1, 10 percent received a grade of A in Statistics 1.

(3) Of those receiving a grade of A in Statistics 1, 20 percent received a grade of A in Accounting 1.

(4) All sophomore students were required to take both Statistics 1 and Accounting 1.

If a sophomore student is selected at random, what is the probability that he received:
a. A grade of A in Statistics 1?
b. An A in both Statistics 1 and Accounting 1?
c. A grade of A in Accounting 1 but some other grade in Statistics 1?
d. A grade other than A in both Accounting 1 and Statistics 1?
e. A grade of A in Statistics 1 given that he got an A in Accounting 1?
f. A grade of A in either Statistics 1 or Accounting 1?
g. A grade of A in some other subject?

22. The information given in the preceding problem indicates a special kind of relationship between the event "received a grade of A in Statistics 1" and the event "received a grade of A in Accounting 1." Is this relationship likely to be true in your school? Spell out the implications of this relationship, relating it specifically to the subject matter of Exercise 21.

23. At Ironclad University the president's office is being picketed by a group consisting of 20 students, 6 of whom identify with the extreme right and 8 of whom identify with the extreme left. If 2 students are selected at random from the pickets to interview the President, what is the probability that 1 extreme leftist and 1 extreme rightist are selected?

24. What is the probability that a bridge hand contains
    a. No clubs?
    b. Six spades?
    c. No clubs and six spades?
    d. A void in at least one suit?

25. If a die is thrown twice, what is the probability that the highest throw is exactly twice the lowest?

26. In a selected list of 10 rail stocks, 4 rose in 1970 and 6 fell. In a selected list of 10 utility stocks, 7 rose in 1970 and 3 fell. If a speculator purchased 2 rails and 2 utilities at the beginning of 1970, what is the probability that more than half of his stocks rose during that year if he selected stocks at random from the two lists?

4 Probability Distributions

4.1 RANDOM VARIABLES

The events in the sample space of an experiment often have complicated descriptions such as "three tosses of a 1962 Roosevelt dime resulted in two heads and one tail," or "the skinny sophomore with the Beatle haircut got a 93 in the sociology mid-term," or "Throstle, the new salesman in the men's wear department, sold $1367.42 worth of merchandise last week, which included $503.64 in neckties alone." We are seldom interested in such detail, and we would like a concise way of describing the important aspects of the event. When these aspects can be quantified, a numerical description of the event is convenient. We call such a numerical description a *random variable*.

Definition. A *random variable* X is a numerical-valued or vector-valued function defined on the elements of a sample space, S.

Recall from Section 3.5 that a function is a pairing of elements in the set D, the domain of the function, with elements in the set R, the function's range, in such a way that every element of D is paired with one and only one element of R. The probability distribution defined on S pairs the elements of S with the real numbers lying between zero and unity. The random variable X accomplishes a more general kind of pairing. The elements of S often are paired with a subset of the reals, but there are times when we may want to pair them with points in a space of more than one dimension. An example is in order.

In tossing the 1962 Roosevelt dime, we are interested in neither the date nor the denomination of the coin; we are interested only in the outcomes of the three tosses. We can represent these outcomes by triples consisting of the elements H and T where the first, second, and third elements are respectively the outcomes of the first, second, and third tosses. The set S will consist of eight events.

$$S = \{\text{HHH, HHT, HTH, THH, TTH, THT, HTT, TTT}\}$$

If we are not interested in the order of occurrence but only in the number of heads and tails, we can define X so that it pairs the elements of S with a subset of the points in a two-dimensional vector space. The first coordinate represents the number of heads and the second the number of tails. This gives

$$\begin{aligned}
X(\text{HHH}) &= (3, 0) & X(\text{TTH}) &= (1, 2) \\
X(\text{HHT}) &= (2, 1) & X(\text{THT}) &= (1, 2) \\
X(\text{HTH}) &= (2, 1) & X(\text{HTT}) &= (1, 2) \\
X(\text{THH}) &= (2, 1) & X(\text{TTT}) &= (0, 3)
\end{aligned}$$

Of course, if we know that the coin was tossed three times, one of the two elements of X is superfluous. We can deduce the second element from the first. Hence, if the number of tosses is known to be three, we can define a new random variable Y, the number of heads, as

$$\begin{aligned}
Y(\text{HHH}) &= 3 \\
Y(\text{HHT}) &= Y(\text{HTH}) = Y(\text{THH}) = 2 \\
Y(\text{TTH}) &= Y(\text{THT}) = Y(\text{HTT}) = 1 \\
Y(\text{TTT}) &= 0
\end{aligned}$$

The set S consists of eight events; the random variable Y has paired each of these with one and only one of the real numbers 0, 1, 2, 3. The random variable X has transformed the set S of events to the set $X(S)$, a subset of a two-dimensional vector space, and the random variable Y has transformed S to $Y(S)$, a subset of the reals. In this chapter we will consider random variables that transform S into a subset of the real numbers; the case where $X(S)$ is a subset of a space of more than one dimension is discussed in Chapter 5.

We have now defined two functions on S, a probability distribution and a random variable. Since $X(S)$ is a set, we can define a probability distribution on it also. Because $X(S)$ is a concise way of describing S, we should derive P_X, the probability distribution on X, from P_S, the probability distribution on S. When the number of elements in S is at most countable, this is easy to do. The probability that X takes the value x is the sum of the probabilities of the events E in S which have the property that $X(E) = x$.[1] To illustrate, suppose that each of the eight events in S for the coin example is assigned probability $1/8$. We can use this probability assignment to define a probability

---

[1] Here, X denotes the *function*, and x denotes the *value* of the function.

distribution on $Y(S)$ as follows:

$$P(Y = 0) = P(TTT) = \frac{1}{8}$$

$$P(Y = 1) = P(TTH) + P(THT) + P(HTT) = \frac{3}{8}$$

$$P(Y = 2) = P(HHT) + P(HTH) + P(THH) = \frac{3}{8}$$

$$P(Y = 3) = P(HHH) = \frac{1}{8}$$

When the sample space has an at most countable number of events, the random variable can take on an at most countable number of different values, and we can calculate the probability distribution over $X(S)$ by adding as we have done in the coin example. When X takes on an at most countable number of values, we say that we have a *discrete random variable*. Sometimes, however, the number of events in S can be thought of as uncountable. If S consists of all positive weights in grams of male college sophomores, the number of events in S depends upon the precision of the scale and the patience of the observer. It is convenient in this case to think of the possible events in S as all points on a line, perhaps ranging from zero to some very large number. The number of events in S is uncountable and, if X is the weight in grams (to many decimal places), the number of elements in $X(S)$ is also uncountable. When this is so, we say that we have a continuous random variable. For brevity, we usually say, "X is continuous," or "X is discrete," when the meaning is clear. When X is continuous, it makes no sense to calculate $P(X = x)$ because the answer is always zero.

There is a function defined on $X(S)$ that does not lead to such difficulties. It is called the *cumulative probability distribution* of X. We define it here for the case when $X(S)$ is a subset of the real numbers, that is, a one-dimensional space.

Definition.   The function $F(x)$ is a *cumulative probability distribution* of the random variable X if

(1) It is defined for all real x.
(2) It is nondecreasing; that is, if $x_1 < x_2$, then $F(x_1) \leq F(x_2)$.
(3) It is right-continuous; that is, if $h > 0$, then $\lim_{h \to 0} F(x + h) = F(x)$.
(4) $0 \leq F(x) \leq 1$; $F(-\infty) = 0$; $F(+\infty) = 1$.

Any function with these properties is a cumulative probability distribution, but in order to be useful it must be possible to interpret $F(x)$ as

$$F(x) = P(X \leq x) \tag{4.1}$$

for some random variable X. This interpretation explains why $F(x)$ is called the "cumulative" probability distribution; as X increases, $F(x)$ "cumulates" the probabilities. For the coin example, $F(y)$ is tabulated as

$$F(y) = \begin{cases} 0, & y < 0 \\ \dfrac{1}{8}, & 0 \le y < 1 \\ \dfrac{1}{2}, & 1 \le y < 2 \\ \dfrac{7}{8}, & 2 \le y < 3 \\ 1, & 3 \le y \end{cases}$$

The graph of this function is shown in Figure 4.1. The heavy dots indicate the points at which $F(y)$ takes a jump.

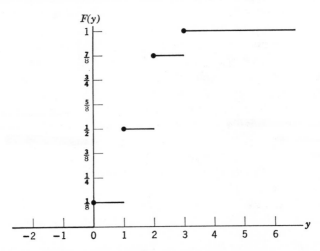

Fig. 4.1. Cumulative probability distribution for coin example.

The cumulative probability distribution can be used to make various kinds of probability statements about X; for example,

$$P(a < X \le b) = F(b) - F(a)$$

and

$$P(X > a) = 1 - F(a)$$

If X is a discrete random variable, we can also compute

$$P(X = a) = \lim_{h \to 0} [F(a) - F(a - h)], \quad h > 0$$

If X is continuous, then $F(x)$ is continuous from the left as well as from the right, and the limit just described will always be zero. When X is discrete, the limit will be positive for some values of X.

4.2 FREQUENCY FUNCTIONS FOR DISCRETE RANDOM VARIABLES

If X is a discrete, real-valued random variable and if $F(x)$ is its cumulative probability distribution, we define the frequency function of X as

$$f(x) = \lim_{h \to 0} [F(x) - F(x - h)], h > 0$$

The frequency function has the following properties:

(1) $f(x)$ is defined for all real x.
(2) $f(x) \geq 0$, but $f(x) > 0$ only over a finite or countably infinite subset of the real numbers.
(3) If we define f^+ as the set of all x for which $f(x) > 0$, then

$$\sum_{x \in f^+} f(x) = 1$$

As we have already said, $f(x)$ can be interpreted as

$$f(x) = P(X = x)$$

and the cumulative probability distribution can be computed from $f(x)$ by adding $f(x)$ for those values of X that are both in f^+ and less than or equal to x. Symbolically, if we define the set a^- as

$$a^- = \{x \mid x \leq a \text{ and } x \in f^+\}$$

then

$$F(a) = \sum_{x \in a^-} f(x)$$

In the coin illustration of the previous section, for example, $F(2) = \frac{7}{8}$, and, if $0 < h < 1$, $F(2 - h) = \frac{1}{2}$. Therefore,

how do solve this part?

$$f(2) = \lim_{h \to 0} [F(2) - F(2 - h)] = \lim_{h \to 0} \left[\frac{7}{8} - \frac{1}{2} \right] = \frac{3}{8}$$

In a similar way we can calculate

F(0)= 1/8   F(1)=1/2   F(2)=7/8   F(3)=1

$$f(0) = \frac{1}{8} \qquad f(1) = \frac{3}{8} \qquad f(2) = \frac{3}{8} \qquad f(3) = \frac{1}{8}$$

and $f(x) = 0$ for all other values. For $x = 2$, we have

$$2^- = \{0, 1, 2\}$$

and

$$F(2) = f(0) + f(1) + f(2) = \frac{1}{8} + \frac{3}{8} + \frac{3}{8} = \frac{7}{8}$$

This agrees with what is shown in Figure 4.1.

When X is discrete, $f(x)$ describes the assignment of probabilities to the points in $X(S)$. Real numbers not in $X(S)$ are assigned a probability of zero, and the probability distribution on S determines the probability distribution on $X(S)$. The frequency function, $f(x)$ describes this probability distribution, and, when confusion is unlikely, we shall call $f(x)$ the discrete probability distribution of X.

Fortunately, as we shall see in the following sections, most practical problems do not require the degree of formality we have used here. The nature of the problem dictates the definition of X, the random variable, and the sample space is simply the set of possible values for X. The underlying set of more complicated events can be ignored. It is also usually easier to derive $f(x)$ than $F(x)$. This is particularly true when X is discrete. In the next two sections we shall derive two of the more important discrete probability distributions, the binomial and the Poisson, and give examples of their use. The discussion of continuous random variables begins with Section 4.5.

4.3 BINOMIAL PROBABILITY DISTRIBUTION

The Bizzy-B Company markets honey in jars stamped "5 pounds net." Because of slight irregularities in the filling process, two-thirds of the jars marketed in a given time period contain more than five pounds of honey, while the other third contains less. If Mrs. Burchard purchases six jars during the year, what is the probability that five or more of them are overweight?

The distinguishing features of this problem are clear, once it is translated into probabilistic language. Mrs. Burchard's purchases constitute six repetitions of a random experiment having only the two possible outcomes "over 5 pounds" and "under 5 pounds." Since two-thirds of the jars placed on sale in any time period are known to be overweight, it is natural to assign a probability 2/3 to the outcome "over 5 pounds" and a probability 1/3 to the alternative.

The sample space contains two events, and we can define the random variable X as X(over 5 pounds) = 1, and X(under 5 pounds) = 0. Then Figure 4.2 shows the probability distribution commonly used as a model for a single one of Mrs. Burchard's experiments. It is called a *Bernoulli probability distribution*.

In general, a Bernoulli distribution states the probabilities in random experiments having only two possible outcomes—which we shall represent by $x = 1$ and $x = 0$. Random variables having this property were identified

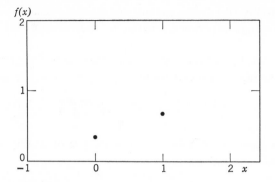

Fig. 4.2. Bernoulli probability distribution appropriate for describing one purchase of honey by Mrs. Burchard.

as attributes in Chapter 2. In a Bernoulli distribution the numbers p and q are assigned respectively to 1 and 0 where $p \geq 0, q \geq 0, p + q = 1$.

Under what conditions, then, is the Bernoulli model appropriate? It applies to those random experiments having only two possible outcomes where the probability attached to each outcome does not vary. It describes Mrs. Burchard's experiment adequately only if one does not question the statement that "two-thirds of the jars marketed in any given time period contain more than 5 pounds of honey." The statement has a suspiciously omniscient ring, and any statistician would wish to examine the grounds on which it was made. But if it is true and consequently p and q are constant, then the model is an excellent one for this instance.

Now we shall develop a model that describes Mrs. Burchard's six purchases. Since we are now dealing with a more complex experiment, the two-point sample space is no longer appropriate. Now there will be seven points in sample space corresponding to the seven outcomes "no jar is over 5 pounds," "exactly one jar is over 5 pounds," $\cdots$, "exactly 5 jars are over 5 pounds," "all jars are over 5 pounds." For these events, the random variable X assumes the values $0, 1, \cdots, 6$ corresponding to the number of jars purchased that are over 5 pounds in weight.

Consider a compound experiment consisting of n trials of a simple experiment. The simple experiment can be represented by a Bernoulli probability distribution, that is, it has two possible outcomes occurring with constant probability. Furthermore, the trials are independent; the outcome of any trial is not influenced by the outcome of any previous one. It is easy to derive a good model for such a compound experiment.

Let us represent the two possible outcomes of the simple experiment by 1, occurring with probability p, and 0, occurring with probability q. We wish to find the probability $f(x)$ associated with the outcome "exactly x ones" in one trial of the compound experiment, that is, in n independent trials of the simple experiment.

Let the event A_1 be that the first x trials yield ones and the remaining trials zeros. Since the trials are independent,

$$P(A_1) = \underbrace{p \cdots p}_{x} \cdot \underbrace{q \cdots q}_{n-x} = p^x q^{n-x}$$

Let A_2 be the event that the first $x - 1$ trials give ones, the xth a zero, the $(x + 1)$st a one, and the rest zeros.

$$P(A_2) = \underbrace{p \cdots p}_{x-1} \cdot q \cdot p \cdot \underbrace{q \cdots q}_{n-x-1} = p^x q^{n-x}$$

Thus the probability $p^x q^{n-x}$ evidently obtains whenever we have x ones and $n - x$ zeros, regardless of the order in which these appear. Since the events $A_1, A_2, \cdots$ are mutually exclusive, their probabilities add. We only need to count them to find $f(x)$. But counting them is easy; the question is how many distinct permutations can be made from x ones and $n - x$ zeros. In Section 3.7 the answer was shown to be

$$\binom{n}{x \quad n - x} = \binom{n}{x}$$

Consequently the probability of exactly x ones in n independent trials of a simple experiment with two outcomes occurring with constant probabilities p and q where $p + q = 1$ is given by

$$f(x) = \binom{n}{x} p^x q^{n-x} \qquad x = 0, 1, \cdots, n$$
$$= 0 \qquad \text{other values}$$

This expression is called the *binomial probability distribution.* If we write it as

$$f(x) = \binom{n}{x} p^x (1 - p)^{n-x} \qquad x = 0, 1, \cdots, n \qquad (4.2)$$
$$= 0 \qquad \text{other values}$$

it is seen to contain two variables in addition to x. Hence, it represents a whole family of functions. A particular one may be specified by assigning values to p and n.

How do we prove that the binomial is really a probability distribution? First, $f(x)$ is defined for all real numbers and nonzero on a finite set. Second, since x, n, and p cannot be negative, $f(x)$ is never negative. Finally, we add all the function's values:

$$\sum_{x=0}^{n} \binom{n}{x} p^x q^{n-x} = \binom{n}{0} p^0 q^n + \binom{n}{1} p^1 q^{n-1} + \cdots + \binom{n}{n-1} p^{n-1} q^1 + \binom{n}{n} p^n q^0$$

$$= (q + p)^n = (1 - p + p)^n = 1$$

The sum is exactly the expansion of $(q + p)^n$, using the binomial theorem. The expression $q + p$ is unity, since $q = 1 - p$.

Figures 4.3, 4.4, and 4.5 exhibit several binomial probability distributions.

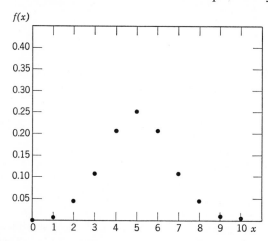

Fig. 4.3. Binomial probability distribution, $p = 1/2$, $n = 10$.

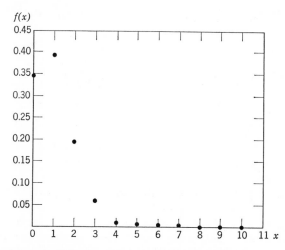

Fig. 4.4. Binomial probability distribution, $p = 1/10$, $n = 10$.

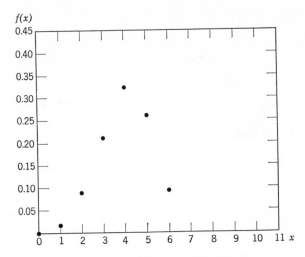

Fig. 4.5. Binomial probability distribution, $p = 2/3$, $n = 6$.

The computed functional values of the binomial of Figure 4.3 are

x	0	1	2	3	4	5	6	7	8	9	10
$f(x)$	0.0010	0.0097	0.0440	0.1172	0.2051	0.2460	0.2051	0.1172	0.0440	0.0097	0.0010

The function is symmetric with respect to a vertical line drawn through its maximum value. Binomial probability distributions have this property if and only if $p = 1/2$. We know that

$$\binom{n}{x} = \frac{n!}{x!\,(n-x)!} = \frac{n!}{(n-x)!\,x!} = \binom{n}{n-x}.$$

Hence, when $p = 1/2$,

$$f(x) = \binom{n}{x}\left(\frac{1}{2}\right)^{x}\left(\frac{1}{2}\right)^{n-x} = \frac{\binom{n}{x}}{2^{n}}$$

while

$$f(n-x) = \binom{n}{n-x}\left(\frac{1}{2}\right)^{n-x}\left(\frac{1}{2}\right)^{x} = \frac{\binom{n}{x}}{2^{n}}$$

When rounded to four decimals, the function of Figure 4.4 yields

x	0	1	2	3	4	5	6	7	8	9	10
$f(x)$	0.3487	0.3874	0.1937	0.0574	0.0112	0.0015	0.0001	0.0000	0.0000	0.0000	0.0000

Thus the effect of decreasing *p* below 1/2 while holding *n* fixed is seen to be a concentration of the probabilities on the left side of the function's domain. Such a function is said to be positively skewed, or skewed toward the right. If *p* were now changed to 9/10 while *n* were kept at 10, the resulting function would have a form similar to that shown in Figure 4.4 but skewed to the left.

In Figure 4.5 we show the binomial used as a model in Mrs. Burchard's honey problem. There $p = 2/3$ and $n = 6$, so from (4.2),

$$f(x) = \binom{6}{x}\left(\frac{2}{3}\right)^{x}\left(\frac{1}{3}\right)^{6-x}, \qquad x = 0, \cdots, 6.$$

The values of $f(x)$ corresponding to the points $x = 0, \cdots, 6$ are 0.0014, 0.0164, 0.0823, 0.2195, 0.3292, 0.2634, 0.0878. We shall frequently omit the statement that $f(x) = 0$ for other values of x when this is obvious—as it is here.

By drawing additional sketches, the student can easily show that the larger *n* is for a fixed $p \neq 1/2$, the smaller the skewness of the binomial in question.

Originally we asked for the probability that five or more of the six jars purchased were overweight. If our model is appropriate, we can use

$$f(5) + f(6) = \binom{6}{5}\left(\frac{2}{3}\right)^{5}\left(\frac{1}{3}\right)^{1} + \binom{6}{6}\left(\frac{2}{3}\right)^{6}\left(\frac{1}{3}\right)^{0}$$

$$= 0.2634 + 0.0878 = 0.35$$

Too much emphasis cannot be placed upon the fact that the number 0.35 is valuable only to the degree that the binomial model really pictures the true situation. Let us reconsider the problem.

There are two places where trouble is likely to arise—the assumption of constant probabilities already mentioned and the assumption of independent trials. Has an investigation been made to show that the overweight jars do not occur in long sequences so that shipments to retailers are likely to be mostly overweight or underweight? Is it known whether Mrs. Burchard's purchases took place several months apart? Did she buy all six jars at once? Points such as these have to be thoroughly investigated before one can say that "two-thirds of the jars marketed in a given time period are overweight," and before independence of trials can safely be assumed. One frequently sees examples of binomial models for dice throwing, coin tossing, and card selecting. Where the physical form of the experimental materials is permanent and tractable, the assumptions of independence of trials and stability of probability may be approximately true. However, in most practical situations that the businessman faces, he must worry about both points.

Consider the following problem. A stamping machine cuts bicycle fenders from steel strips. During the first six months of 1970 it turned out 20,000 fenders of which 1000 required smoothing before they could be used. If five fenders are selected at random from the machine's output, what is the probability that exactly one of them requires smoothing?

One may approach this problem by selecting as a model the binomial probability distribution with $n = 5$ and $p = 1/20$. Then, using (4.2) with the random variable X representing the number of defective fenders,

$$f(x) = \binom{5}{x} \left(\frac{1}{20}\right)^x \left(\frac{19}{20}\right)^{5-x}, \qquad x = 0, 1, \cdots, 5$$

and

$$f(1) = \binom{5}{1} \left(\frac{1}{20}\right)^1 \left(\frac{19}{20}\right)^4 = 0.20$$

Clear, simple—and almost certainly in serious error. In all likelihood a poorly stamped fender results when the machine is out of adjustment or when some moving part becomes worn. But such conditions do not develop for a single fender and then vanish. One badly cut fender would be followed by another and another until the machine was shut down and repaired. In the terms that we have been using the probability of a bad fender is almost certainly not constant. It will vary with time.

One should also be concerned with the way in which the five fenders are selected. Unless a randomizing scheme is used, the independence of the trials is questionable. If the fenders are taken one after another as they come off the machine, there is trouble, and if they are selected from the inventory on hand on a given day, there is more trouble.

Given a class of 20 students, what is the probability that no more than 3 will be women if only 5 percent of the student body are women? Again we must ask if the binomial model is appropriate. If so, the cumulative probability distribution (4.1) is required. The answer is found simply by summing the functional values of $f(x)$.

$$F(3) = \sum_{x=0}^{3} \binom{20}{x} \left(\frac{1}{20}\right)^x \left(\frac{19}{20}\right)^{20-x} = \binom{20}{0} \left(\frac{1}{20}\right)^0 \left(\frac{19}{20}\right)^{20} + \binom{20}{1} \left(\frac{1}{20}\right)^1 \left(\frac{19}{20}\right)^{19}$$
$$+ \binom{20}{2} \left(\frac{1}{20}\right)^2 \left(\frac{19}{20}\right)^{18} + \binom{20}{3} \left(\frac{1}{20}\right)^3 \left(\frac{19}{20}\right)^{17}$$

Both the binomial probability and cumulative probability distributions have been tabulated extensively. A good tabular source is *Tables of the Binomial Probability Distribution*, published by the National Bureau of Standards. The problem is left for the student to finish.

4.4   POISSON PROBABILITY DISTRIBUTION

Another important probability distribution is the Poisson distribution—named after a French mathematician. The discussion in this section will make use of real number "*e*" and of the MacLaurin series expansion. These topics are discussed in Appendices A and B, and the student should study them carefully. We shall approach the Poisson distribution by considering a problem.

A total of 15,600 trucks unloaded merchandise at the main warehouse of the J. B. Whickers Company during the last year. The warehouse is open 5 days a week, 52 weeks per year, from 7:00 A.M. to 7:00 P.M. There has been no noticeable pattern of truck arrivals, either seasonal, weekly, daily, or hourly. What is the probability that 8 trucks will arrive to unload cargo at the warehouse between 10 and 11 A.M. tomorrow morning?

This problem is typical of a class of situations in which we are concerned not with n independent trials of a single simple experiment (as in the binomial model), but with a predetermined time or space interval and an observation of the number of times a specified event occurs within that interval. We do not determine the number of truck arrivals in advance; the factor that is predetermined is the number of hours over which a count of unloadings is kept. Also the experiment does not have the feature of having two and only two possible outcomes on a single trial. Trucks arrive and are counted. Zero truck arrivals is only one of many possibilities.

Let us consider a more general situation. Let ϵ represent a short interval of time. It is chosen in such a way that, if some event is recurring in time, for some real number r the following statements are true:

(a) The probability that exactly one of the events being counted occurs in an interval of length ϵ is approximately $r\epsilon$.

(b) The probability that none of the events being counted occurs in an interval of length ϵ is approximately $1 - r\epsilon$. $\hspace{2em}$ (4.3)

(c) The probability that two or more of the events being counted occur in an interval of length ϵ is approximately zero.

The number r may be thought of as the average occurrence rate for the events being counted. For example, if the average arrival rate of trucks at the Whickers warehouse was one per 100 minutes, that is, $r = 1/50$ for $\epsilon = 2$ minutes, then it would seem reasonable that the probability of two arrivals in two minutes was tiny enough to be overlooked—assuming that the arrivals were occurring at random. Then the probability of exactly one arrival in a two-minute interval would be $r\epsilon = 1/50 \cdot 1 = 1/50$ and the probability of no arrivals in two minutes would be $1 - r\epsilon = 1 - 1/50 \cdot 1 = 49/50$. Notice that in these computations 2 minutes = 1 unit of time.

Now let T be a longer time interval during which an event occurs repeatedly. Divide this interval into n equal parts; each subinterval will then be of length T/n. Let $T/n = \epsilon$, and assume that ϵ satisfies (4.3). Assume that the number of occurrences of the event in question in any subinterval is independent of the number of occurrences in any previous subinterval. The probability that exactly x events will take place during the interval T may be approximated by the probability that a single event has taken place in exactly x of the n subintervals. The approximation could be expected to improve as n becomes larger and the subintervals become shorter. But by (a), (b), and (c) of (4.3), and the assumed independence, this probability is identical with the probability that we obtain exactly x ones on n independent trials of an experiment for which the binomial model is suitable. The quantity p, the probability of a one, is given by $p = r\epsilon = rT/n$. The probability of exactly x ones is, by (4.2),

$$g(x) = \binom{n}{x}\left(\frac{rT}{n}\right)^x\left(1 - \frac{rT}{n}\right)^{n-x} \qquad x = 0, 1, \cdots, n$$

We wish to find the probability that exactly x events will take place in the time interval, that is, we want to know the form of the function approached by $f(x)$ as n becomes large. Thus, we wish to find

$$f(x) = \lim_{n \to \infty} g(x) = \lim_{n \to \infty} \binom{n}{x}\left(\frac{rT}{n}\right)^x\left(1 - \frac{rT}{n}\right)^{n-x}$$

Let us first set $rT = \lambda$, the average number of subintervals in which an event occurs and rewrite the expression, rearranging and using the fact that the limit of a product is the product of the limits of the respective factors.

$$\begin{aligned}
f(x) &= \lim_{n \to \infty} \frac{n!}{x!\,(n-x)!\,n^x}\,\lambda^x\left(1 - \frac{\lambda}{n}\right)^n\left(1 - \frac{\lambda}{n}\right)^{-x} \\
&= \frac{\lambda^x}{x!}\lim_{n \to \infty}\frac{n!}{(n-x)!\,n^x}\,\lim_{n \to \infty}\left(1 - \frac{\lambda}{n}\right)^n\lim_{n \to \infty}\left(1 - \frac{\lambda}{n}\right)^{-x}
\end{aligned}$$

We evaluate these limits separately.

To evaluate the first limit, first cancel $(n-x)!$, then pair the x factors of the numerator with the x factors of the denominator and evaluate the resulting limits separately.

$$\begin{aligned}
\lim_{n \to \infty}\frac{n!}{(n-x)!\,n^x} &= \lim_{n \to \infty}\frac{n(n-1)\cdots(n-x+1)}{n \cdot n \cdots n} \\
&= \lim_{n \to \infty}\frac{n}{n}\lim_{n \to \infty}\left(1 - \frac{1}{n}\right)\cdots\lim_{n \to \infty}\left(1 - \frac{x-1}{n}\right) \\
&= 1 \cdot 1 \cdots 1 = 1
\end{aligned}$$

The second limit is more complicated. To find it we recall that λ is a constant and then set $y = -\lambda/n$. This implies that $n = -\lambda/y$ and that when $n \to \infty$, $y \to 0$. Thus

$$\lim_{n \to \infty} \left(1 - \frac{\lambda}{n}\right)^n = \lim_{y \to 0} (1 + y)^{-\lambda/y} = \left[\lim_{y \to 0} (1 + y)^{1/y}\right]^{-\lambda}$$

But, by Appendix A, the quantity within the square bracket is exactly the limit defining e, and

$$\lim_{n \to \infty} \left(1 - \frac{\lambda}{n}\right)^n = e^{-\lambda}$$

The third and last limit is simple. Since x is a nonnegative integer,

$$\lim_{n \to \infty} \left(1 - \frac{\lambda}{n}\right)^{-x} = 1$$

Assembling the various factors, we see that it has been shown that

$$f(x) = \frac{\lambda^x e^{-\lambda}}{x!} \qquad x = 0, 1, 2, \cdots \qquad (4.4)$$

This function is called the *Poisson probability distribution.*

We should next show that this function is a true probability distribution. First, we ask if it is always nonnegative and defined for all real numbers. The answer is affirmative as long as λ is a positive number, since x cannot be negative. It will be shown in Chapter 6 that λ can never be negative, here we shall simply restrict λ to positive values.

The remaining point is crucial: Do the probabilities sum to one?

$$\sum_{x=0}^{\infty} \frac{\lambda^x e^{-\lambda}}{x!} = e^{-\lambda} \sum_{x=0}^{\infty} \frac{\lambda^x}{x!}$$

But this last sum is exactly the MacLaurin series expansion of e^λ, which is discussed in Appendix B, x being used in place of n as the index of summation. Hence

$$\sum_{x=0}^{\infty} \frac{\lambda^x e^{-\lambda}}{x!} = e^{-\lambda} e^{\lambda} = 1$$

This completes the proof that (4.4) is a probability distribution.

Next we show graphs for two Poisson probability distributions (Figures 4.6 and 4.7), the first with $\lambda = 1$. For $\lambda = 1$, remembering that e is approximately 2.718, we obtain $e^{-1} = 0.368$. Therefore, from (4.4),

$$f(x) = \frac{\lambda^x e^{-\lambda}}{x!} = \frac{1^x (0.368)}{x!} = \frac{0.368}{x!} \qquad x = 0, 1, 2, \cdots$$

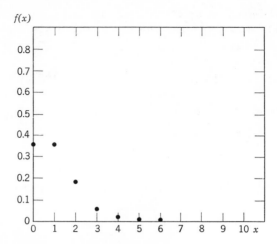

Fig. 4.6. Poisson probability distribution, $\lambda = 1$.

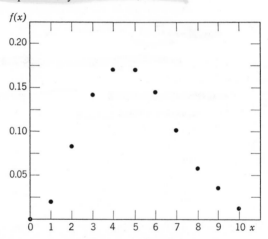

Fig. 4.7. Poisson probability distribution, $\lambda = 5$.

It follows that $f(0) = 0.368$, $f(1) = 0.368$, $f(2) = 0.184$, $f(3) = 0.061$, $f(4) = 0.015$, $f(5) = 0.003$, etc. These computations are facilitated by Table E. 2 of Appendix E. Although the function is nonzero for all positive integers, it is close to zero for large positive integers. The function is strongly skewed to the right.

For $\lambda = 5$, the shape of the function is quite different. Since $e^{-5} = 0.00674$, the Poisson distribution for $\lambda = 5$ is

$$f(x) = \frac{5^x(0.00674)}{x!} \qquad x = 0, 1, 2, \cdots$$

Easy computations yield:

x	0	1	2	3	4	5	6	7	8	9	10
$f(x)$	0.00674	0.03370	0.08425	0.14042	0.17552	0.17552	0.14625	0.10445	0.06528	0.03627	0.01813

Notice that this function is much less skewed than when $\lambda = 1$. If the student takes time to sketch Poisson functions for a number of values of λ, he will find that, as λ becomes larger, the functions become less skewed but continue to be centered near the value of λ used. A contrast between the binomial and the Poisson should also be noticed. The former contains two other variables, n and p, in addition to x. The Poisson, however, contains only a single additional variable, λ. Thus the Poisson probability distribution is a one-parameter family of functions, while the binomial probability distribution is a two-parameter family of functions.

Returning to the problem which touched off our investigation of the Poisson distribution, we recall that the Whickers warehouse was open five days per week, 12 hours per day during all 52 weeks of the year, or 3120 hours per year. Thus the 15,600 truck arrivals took place at the average rate of five per hour. Setting $\lambda = 5$ and using the Poisson model

$$f(x) = \frac{5^x e^{-5}}{x!} \qquad x = 0, 1, 2, \cdots$$

we obtain the required probability that eight trucks arrive in a single hour

$$f(8) = \frac{5^8 e^{-5}}{8!} = 0.065$$

This is a simple enough result; however, let us examine the problem more carefully than we have done thus far. The key question, of course, concerns the assumptions. Are all these met at least approximately so that the Poisson model may be expected to produce probabilities which lie close to the actual relative frequencies of truck arrivals?

First, it appears that assumptions (a), (b), and (c) of (4.3) are reasonable. Consider truck arrivals in a given minute. There should be a probability connected with one arrival in one minute. The probability of no arrivals should be approximately one minus this, since the probability of two or more arrivals during the same minute would be tiny by comparison. Then shift the time scale to one second; everything checked for one minute would be true to an even greater degree here. Finally the assumption of independence of number of arrivals in the various hours should be examined. The flat statement was made that "there had been no noticeable pattern of truck arrivals." Of course, if a regular pattern was evident, independence would be a poor assumption; for instance, if the morning arrival rate was always roughly twice the afternoon arrival rate, or if very few trucks arrived during the 7 to 8:00 A.M. and the 6 to 7:00 P.M. hours. But, if no regular pattern appeared, would independence necessarily be a good assumption?

Hardly, although we do not have enough information to make a decision. Suppose, however, that the store has a restocking policy based on total inventory. When total inventory falls below a certain dollar figure, restocking orders go out to all departments. (It is recognized that this is not a reasonable policy; the idea is introduced only as an illustration of the effect which inventory policy could have on truck arrivals.) Then, as those orders are filled, truck arrivals could be expected to rise; high arrival rate in one hour would be tied to high arrival rate in the neighboring hours.

As another example of failure of the independence assumption, consider a different problem concerning a busy warehouse where only one truck at a time could unload. Suppose we were counting unloadings per hour, not arrivals, and suppose the time at which the first case touched the platform was arbitrarily defined as the unloading time. Obviously an independence assumption is poor. When an hour appears in which several trucks have unloaded, the chances are good that a waiting line has formed so that there will be numerous unloadings in the following hour. But, as the problem is concerned with arrival time, not unloading time, we are likely to decide to use the model and maintain a reservation regarding independence.

As a final example of the Poisson distribution, we introduce the following problem. The Silver Dollar Supermarket sold giant-sized boxes of Bleecho detergent during a five-week period as shown in Table 4.1. What is the probability of selling no giant-sized boxes of Bleecho during the week of April 10?

The weekly sales rate of giant Bleecho averages as $\frac{100}{5} = 20$ boxes per week. Again the assumption of independence would have to be carefully checked, but all of the assumptions appear satisfactory. Using (4.4), one then computes

$$f(0) = \frac{20^0 e^{-20}}{0!} = 0.000$$

Table 4.1   Supermarket Sales of Bleecho

Week	Number of Sales
March 6	18
March 13	21
March 20	19
March 27	24
April 3	18
Total	100

No sales of giant Bleecho would be most unlikely. Note that more meaningful questions would be: "What is the probability of more than 21 sales?" or "What is the probability of between 16 and 24 sales?" We could answer these questions by computing a number of Poisson ordinates and adding them. (A useful Poisson table may be found in *Tables for Statisticians* by Arkin and Colton published by Barnes and Noble, Inc.)

4.5   CONTINUOUS RANDOM VARIABLES

A pilot making a 200-mile flight between two cities is told to land at the nearer of the two cities if mechanical difficulties arise on the flight. If he does have mechanical difficulty, what is the probability that he will have to fly less than 30 miles in order to land? Before answering the question, we will make a simplifying (and false) assumption: if there is mechanical difficulty, it is as likely to occur at one point in the flight as at any other. The pilot is within 30 miles of one of the cities during the first 30 miles of his flight and within 30 miles of the other during the last 30 miles—a total of 60 miles out of 200. Under our simplifying assumption, the probability of having to fly less than 30 miles in order to land is 60/200 or 0.3. If we define the random variable X to be the distance to the nearer city, X is *continuous*, and its cumulative probability distribution is

$$F(x) = P(X \leq x) = \frac{2x}{200} = 0.01x \qquad 0 \leq x < 100$$

$$= 0 \qquad x < 0$$

$$= 1 \qquad x > 100$$

We pointed out in Section 4.1 that, when X is continuous, $F(x)$ is continuous from both the left and the right. In this case, the probability that X takes on a particular value is always zero. For example, if $h > 0$,

$$P(X = 30) = \lim_{h \to 0} [0.01(30) - 0.01(30 - h)] = \lim_{h \to 0} [0.01h] = 0$$

We cannot calculate a meaningful frequency function for a continuous random variable. When the discrete random variable X changes in increments of one unit (one jar of honey, one truck, one giant-sized box of Bleecho), then $f(x)$ gives the change in $F(x)$ as X moves from $x - 1$ to x. It is a limit of differences:

$$f(x) = \lim_{h \to 0} [F(x) - F(x - h)] \qquad h > 0$$

This suggests an analogous function for continuous random variables. In the continuous case, X can change by any arbitrarily small increment, and we obtain the function by *differentiating* $F(x)$ instead of *differencing* it as we do in the discrete case. We call the derivative the *density function* and, as with the frequency function, we denote it by a lower case symbol such as $f(x)$. Although $F(x)$ is both left and right continuous when X is continuous, this need not be true of $f(x)$.[2] We have the following definition of a density function.

Definition.   If X is a continuous random variable and $F(x)$ is its cumulative probability distribution, then its *density function* is defined by

$$f(x) = \frac{dF(x)}{dx}$$

at points where $F(x)$ is differentiable.[3] The density function has the following properties:

1. $f(x)$ is defined for all real x.

2. $f(x) > 0$ over an at most countable set of intervals, and $f(x) = 0$ otherwise.

3. $\int_{-\infty}^{\infty} f(x)\, dx = 1.$

We will often call both frequency and density functions "probability distributions."

For the emergency landing problem we have

$$f(x) = \begin{cases} 0 & x \le 0 \\ 0.01 & 0 < x \le 100 \\ 0 & x > 100 \end{cases}$$

It is easy to see that properties (1) and (2) hold for this function. For property (3) we see that

$$\int_{-\infty}^{\infty} f(x)\, dx = \int_{-\infty}^{0} 0\, dx + \int_{0}^{100} 0.01\, dx + \int_{100}^{\infty} 0\, dx = 0 + [0.01x]_{0}^{100} + 0 = 1$$

From the definition of the density function as a derivative, it is clear that we can obtain the cumulative probability distribution and make other probability statements about X by integrating the density function over

---

[2] For the situations discussed in this book, the question of left and right continuity will not cause any problems. The student might note that in the emergency landing problem there are questions of this sort that arise when one takes the derivative of $F(x)$ at the two points $x = 0$ and $x = 100$.

[3] At points where $F(x)$ is not differentiable, and for $h > 0$, we would define the density function to be

$$f(x) = \lim_{h \to 0} \frac{[F(x + h) - F(x)]}{h}$$

if we were presenting this topic in a mathematically rigorous way.

appropriate intervals:

$$F(a) = \int_{-\infty}^{a} f(x)\,dx = P(X \le a)$$

$$P(a < X \le b) = \int_{a}^{b} f(x)\,dx = F(b) - F(a)$$

$$P(X > a) = \int_{a}^{\infty} f(x)\,dx = 1 - F(a)$$

Any function with properties (1), (2), and (3) of the definition of density function can serve as a density function, although we might be hard pressed to find a realistic example of a random variable that has the probabilistic behavior described by the density. Consider.

$$f(x) = x^{-2} \qquad 1 \le x < \infty$$
$$= 0 \qquad \text{other values}$$

This function is defined for all real x and is positive only over the interval $1 \le x < \infty$. We can check property (3) by integrating over this interval:

$$\int_{1}^{\infty} x^{-2}\,dx = [-x^{-1}]_{1}^{\infty} = 0 - (-1) = 1$$

Hence $f(x)$ is a density function. It is a special case of the Pareto density function used in the theory of income distribution. The cumulative probability distribution of X is

$$F(x) = \int_{1}^{x} t^{-2}\,dt = 1 - \frac{1}{x} \qquad 1 \le x < \infty$$
$$= 0 \qquad\qquad -\infty < x < 1$$

When X is continuous, the set $X(S)$ is uncountable, and the assignment of probabilities in S determines $F(x)$. This cumulative probability distribution has as elements of its domain subsets of the form

$$x^{-} = \{x' \mid -\infty < x' \le x\}$$

in $X(S)$. The density function describes the way in which $F(x)$ changes as x changes; in this sense $f(x)$ describes the probability distribution over points of $X(S)$. As was the case of the frequency function, when confusion is unlikely, we shall call $f(x)$ the (continuous) probability distribution of X. We now have the background to consider some important continuous probability distributions.

4.6 THE EXPONENTIAL PROBABILITY DISTRIBUTION

The SUMAC electronic computer has been found to break down at an average rate of two failures during one of its usual 18-hour operating days.

If the SUMAC has performed perfectly during the last three days, what is the probability that it will break down during the next workday?

There are many situations of this sort; basically they may be grouped under the heading of "time to first failure" problems. How long will a light bulb last? How long will it be before the first of a jeweler's diamond pendants is sold? In certain cases these problems can be easily approached.

These are cases in which it is appropriate to represent the probability of exactly x occurrences of the event in question during a particular interval by a Poisson probability distribution. Notice that the Poisson assumptions are met in the SUMAC problem, providing that breakdowns are caused by various unrelated occurrences in the machine's operation and maintenance. (This may not always be true, of course. Breakdowns might occur when Operator C pushes the wrong button.)

It is easy to obtain the cumulative distribution of the time to first failure if the number of failures in any time period follows the Poisson probability distribution. Suppose that the average number of failures per unit time period (the failure rate) is c. Then the average number of failures in a time period of t units is ct, and the actual number of failures in a time period of t units has the Poisson probability distribution with parameter ct. The probability that the time to first failure is less than or equal to t is the same as the probability of one or more failures in a time period of t units. If T is time to first failure and $X(t)$ is the number of failures in t time units, then

$$F(t) = P(T \leq t) = P[X(t) > 0] = 1 - P[X(t) = 0]$$
$$= 1 - e^{-ct} \qquad 0 \leq t < \infty \tag{4.5}$$

because $X(t)$ follows the Poisson distribution with parameter ct. The probability density of T can be obtained from the definition in the preceding section:

$$f(t) = \frac{d}{dt}(1 - e^{-ct}) = ce^{-ct} \qquad 0 < t < \infty \tag{4.6}$$
$$= 0 \qquad \qquad \text{other values}$$

This density function is called the *exponential probability distribution* with parameter c. When $c > 0$, $f(t)$ is positive for all nonnegative values of t and zero otherwise, and

$$c \int_0^\infty e^{-ct} \, dt = [-e^{-ct}]_0^\infty = 0 + 1 = 1$$

Hence the exponential is a probability distribution.

For the SUMAC problem, $c = 2$, and T is measured in working days of 18 hours each. We want to know the probability that T is less than or equal to 4 given that it is greater than 3. We can compute such a conditional probability from the definition.

$$P(T \leq 4 \mid T > 3) = \frac{P[(T \leq 4) \cap (T > 3)]}{P(T > 3)}$$

For the numerator we have

$$P[(T \leq 4) \cap (T > 3)] = P(3 < T \leq 4) = \int_3^4 2e^{-2t}\, dt$$

$$= [-e^{-2t}]_3^4 = e^{-6} - e^{-8}$$

and for the denominator

$$P(T > 3) = 1 - P(T \leq 3) = 1 - (1 - e^{-6}) = e^{-6}$$

directly from (4.5). Hence,

$$P(T \leq 4 \mid T > 3) = \frac{e^{-6} - e^{-8}}{e^{-6}} = 1 - e^{-2}$$

$$= 1 - 0.135 = 0.865$$

Notice that the probability of failure on the first day is, by (4.5), also

$$P(T \leq 1) = 1 - e^{-2} = 0.865$$

The probability of a failure on the fourth day, given that none occurred within the first three days, is the same as the probability that the first failure will occur during the first day. This should not be unexpected, since the Poisson distribution assumes that the number of failures in any day is independent of the number of failures on any other day. In fact, we can show that P (first failure on nth day $\mid$ no failure until then) = P (first failure on first day). This is not to say that the unconditional probabilities for first failure on specific days are all equal; a glance at Figure 4.8 will quickly reveal that $f(x)$ differs considerably for different days.

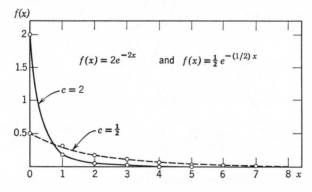

Fig. 4.8. Exponential probability distributions with parameters 2, 1/2.

In the trucking problem at the J. B. Whickers warehouse,[4] we pose an additional question. What is the probability that on July 18 the first truck arrives between 7:15 and 7:30 A.M.? To solve this problem, we need only employ the exponential distribution, using a new time interval of 15 minutes for which $\lambda = 1.25$. Thus

$$f(t) = 1.25\, e^{-1.25t}$$

so that

$$\int_1^2 e^{-1.25t}(1.25\, dt) = [-e^{-1.25t}]_1^2 = -e^{-2.5} + e^{-1.25} = 0.20$$

4.7   THE NORMAL PROBABILITY DISTRIBUTION

One of the most useful distributions in statistics is the *normal probability distribution*, which is a family of continuous functions of the form:

$$f(x) = \frac{1}{\sigma\sqrt{2\pi}}\, e^{-(x-\mu)^2/2\sigma^2}, \qquad -\infty < x < \infty \tag{4.7}$$

The function is defined for all x, and so long as σ is a positive real number the function is nonnegative. It can be shown that the function integrates to one, but we shall defer presentation of the proof to Section 4.8.

Figure 4.9 shows three normal functions with the same σ and different μ. Figure 4.10 exhibits three normal functions with the same μ and varying σ. Notice that the location of the curve is determined by μ; the curves are

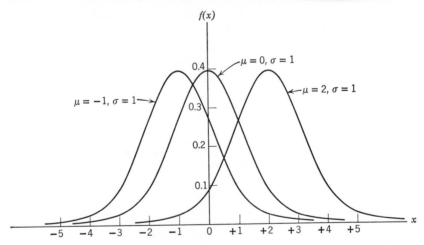

Fig. 4.9. Normal probability distributions for fixed σ and 3 values of μ.

[4] See Section 4.4

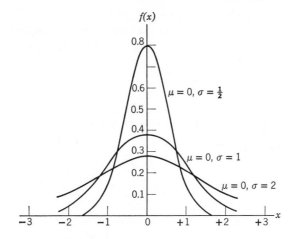

Fig. 4.10. Normal probability distributions for fixed μ and 3 values of σ.

centered at μ. And the parameter σ is related to the spread or dispersion of the function around its central point; the larger the value of σ, the greater the spread of the function. Suppose we are considering the particular normal probability distribution for which $\mu = 1$, $\sigma = 2$. From (4.7)

$$f(x) = \frac{1}{2\sqrt{2\pi}} e^{-(x-1)^2/2 \cdot 2^2} \qquad -\infty < x < \infty \qquad (4.8)$$

We wish to find the probability that $X \geq 2$. This would be obtained by integrating (4.8). It is equivalent to the area below the curve, to the right of the line $x = 2$, and above the x axis.

$$P(X \geq 2) = \frac{1}{2\sqrt{2\pi}} \int_{x=2}^{\infty} e^{-(x-1)^2/2 \cdot 2^2} \, dx$$

Let $z = (x - 1)/2$. Then $dz = dx/2$; when $x = 2$, $z = 1/2$, and when $x = \infty$, $z = \infty$. As a result,

$$P(X \geq 2) = \frac{1}{2\sqrt{2\pi}} \int_{z=\frac{1}{2}}^{\infty} e^{-z^2/2} 2 \, dz = \frac{1}{\sqrt{2\pi}} \int_{z=\frac{1}{2}}^{\infty} e^{-z^2/2} \, dz = P(Z \geq \tfrac{1}{2}) \quad (4.9)$$

which shows that $P(X \geq 2)$, with reference to the normal distribution with $\mu = 1$, $\sigma = 2$, is equal to $P(Z \geq \tfrac{1}{2})$, with reference to the normal distribution with $\mu = 0$, $\sigma = 1$, namely:

$$f(z) = \frac{1}{\sqrt{2\pi}} e^{-z^2/2} \qquad -\infty < z < \infty \qquad (4.10)$$

This function is called the unit normal probability distribution.

This property is perfectly general; probabilities for any normal probability distribution may be calculated from the unit normal probability distribution by means of a change of variable. Consider the function (4.7):

$$f(x) = \frac{1}{\sigma\sqrt{2\pi}} e^{-(x-\mu)^2/2\sigma^2} \qquad -\infty < x < \infty$$

We wish to determine the probability that a single value of X, selected at random from a population described by $f(x)$, lies in the interval $c < x < d$. This is found by integrating (4.7). Figure 4.11 shows the required probability

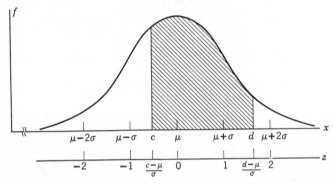

Fig. 4.11. Probability that X lies between c and d for the normal distribution.

(area) with reference to the scales in x and in z. The numerical values of c and d will determine the location of these points. They may be on opposite sides of μ or on the same side.

$$P(c < X < d) = \frac{1}{\sigma\sqrt{2\pi}} \int_{x=c}^{d} e^{-(x-\mu)^2/2\sigma^2}\, dx$$

Let $z = (x - \mu)/\sigma$, $dz = dx/\sigma$; when $x = c$, $z = (c - \mu)/\sigma$, and when $x = d$, $z = (d - \mu)/\sigma$. This is the general transformation corresponding to that of the preceding example.

$$P(c < X < d) = \frac{1}{\sigma\sqrt{2\pi}} \int_{z=(c-\mu)/\sigma}^{(d-\mu)/\sigma} e^{-z^2/2}\sigma\, dz = \frac{1}{\sqrt{2\pi}} \int_{z=(c-\mu)/\sigma}^{(d-\mu)/\sigma} e^{-z^2/2}\, dz$$

Unfortunately, the expression $\int e^{-y^2}\, dy$ cannot be expressed in terms of the elementary functions. Hence an integral such as the previously obtained

$$P(X \geq 2) = \frac{1}{\sqrt{2\pi}} \int_{z=\frac{1}{2}}^{\infty} e^{-z^2/2}\, dz$$

must be evaluated by some process of approximation. It has been found convenient to construct tables of areas under the unit normal distribution in order to facilitate such computation. Table E.3 of Appendix E is a typical table of areas.

This table gives the area above the x axis and under the unit normal probability distribution lying between the fixed ordinate at μ and the ordinate at x, when σ is used as the unit of measurement along the x axis. Such a table permits one to find probabilities of the type occurring in (4.9). There, we found for $\mu = 1$ and $\sigma = 2$ that $P(X \geq 2)$ is given by

$$P\left(Z \geq \frac{1}{2}\right) = \frac{1}{\sqrt{2\pi}} \int_{z=\frac{1}{2}}^{\infty} e^{-z^2/2} \, dz$$

$$= P(Z \geq 0) - P\left(0 < Z < \frac{1}{2}\right)$$

$$= 0.50000 - 0.19146 = 0.30854$$

If we wished to find $P(X < 2)$, we could use the fact that the total area under the curve is unity, and write

$$P(X < 2) = 1 - P(X > 2) = 1 - P\left(Z > \frac{1}{2}\right) = 1 - 0.30854 = 0.69146$$

Given the same μ and σ, what is the probability that X falls between -3 and $+2$? To find the probability, simply transform to Z, break the area into two parts, and evaluate these separately, that is, given $\mu = 1$, $\sigma = 2$,

$$P(-3 < X < 2) = P\left(\frac{-3-1}{2} < Z < \frac{2-1}{2}\right) = P\left(-2 < Z < \frac{1}{2}\right)$$

$$= P(-2 < Z < 0) + P\left(0 < Z < \frac{1}{2}\right)$$

$$= 0.47725 + 0.19146 = 0.66871$$

Let us turn to the production of cylindrical spindles. An automatic lathe receives rough steel rods and grinds them into circular cylinders $\frac{1}{2}$ in. in diameter. However, precise measurements show minute variation in the spindle diameter around the $\frac{1}{2}$ in. figure. If we assume that these deviations are brought about by the interplay of a large number of independent factors, each factor leading to a small error in the fixed value, that the errors produced by all factors are of the same size, and that positive and negative errors are equally likely, the normal probability distribution is appropriate. Note that these conditions really specify a binomial distribution. Section 7.4 shows that the normal is a good approximation of the binomial when n is large. Even if we are willing to make these rather strong assumptions, we still are unable to calculate probabilities of the various possible events. One must have either the exact values of the parameters μ and σ or, what is more likely, workable estimates of both quantities. Suppose, however, that we knew that the population of spindle diameters was not only normal, but also had $\mu = 0.500$ in. and $\sigma = 0.001$ in. Then, letting X be spindle diameter, we could compute, for example, the probability that one spindle selected at random would have a diameter not differing from 0.500 in. by more than 0.001 in.

$$P(0.499 < X < 0.501)$$

$$= P\left(\frac{0.499 - 0.500}{0.001} < Z < \frac{0.501 - 0.500}{0.001}\right)$$

$$= P(-1 < Z < 1) = 2P(0 < Z < 1) = 2(0.34134) = 0.68268$$

Or one could find

$$P(0.498 < X < 0.502)$$

$$= P\left(\frac{0.498 - 0.500}{0.001} < Z < \frac{0.502 - 0.500}{0.001}\right)$$

$$= P(-2 < Z < 2) = 2P(0 < Z < 2) = 2(0.47725) = 0.95450$$

Or finally

$$P(0.497 < X < 0.503)$$

$$= P\left(\frac{0.497 - 0.500}{0.001} < Z < \frac{0.503 - 0.500}{0.001}\right)$$

$$= P(-3 < Z < 3) = 2P(0 < Z < 3) = 2(0.49865) = 0.99730$$

Thus it is extremely unlikely—less than three times in a thousand—that one spindle selected at random from a population described by a normal probability distribution with $\mu = 0.500$ in., $\sigma = 0.001$ in. would have a diameter deviating more than 0.003 in. from the central value 0.500 in. This type of result is perfectly general. Given a normal probability distribution with parameters μ and σ, less than three times in a thousand will a single item selected at random from a population described by that function lie further than 3σ units from μ. More information concerning μ and σ will be given in Chapter 6.

*4.8   PROOF THAT THE NORMAL FUNCTION IS A PROBABILITY DISTRIBUTION

The usual proof that the normal is a probability distribution requires a knowledge of the polar transformation and uses double integration. Since this section may be omitted without causing repercussions later, we have starred it. However, double integration will be used frequently in succeeding chapters, and the conscientious student should read Appendix C at this point.

In (4.7) we defined the normal probability distribution to be the family of continuous functions:

$$f(x) = \frac{1}{\sigma\sqrt{2\pi}} e^{-(x-\mu)^2/2\sigma^2} \qquad -\infty < x < \infty, \qquad \sigma > 0$$

The function $f(x)$ is defined for all x and is nonnegative, since σ is a positive real number. It remains to be shown that the function integrates to one. Unfortunately, this cannot be done directly, since the integral

$$\int_{y=-\infty}^{\infty} e^{-y^2} dy$$

does not exist in terms of the elementary functions. However, an interesting special method has been found whereby the expression

$$\left[\int_{y=-\infty}^{\infty} e^{-y^2} dy\right]^2$$

can be evaluated.

We wish to show that the integral of (4.7) is unity. We first transform

$$\int_{-\infty}^{\infty} f(x) \, dx = \frac{1}{\sigma\sqrt{2\pi}} \int_{x=-\infty}^{\infty} e^{-(x-\mu)^2/2\sigma^2} dx$$

by letting $z = (x - \mu)/\sigma$. Then, when $x = \infty$, $z = \infty$, and when $x = -\infty$, $z = -\infty$. Also $dx = \sigma \, dz$. Hence

$$\int_{x=-\infty}^{\infty} f(x) \, dx = \frac{1}{\sqrt{2\pi}} \int_{z=-\infty}^{\infty} e^{-z^2/2} dz$$

Representing

$$\left[\int_{-\infty}^{\infty} f(x) \, dx\right]^2 \qquad \text{by} \quad A^2$$

since the particular variable of integration used is of no import,

$$A^2 = \left[\int_{x=-\infty}^{\infty} f(x) \, dx\right]^2 = \int_{z=-\infty}^{\infty} f(z) \, dz \int_{w=-\infty}^{\infty} f(w) \, dw$$

$$= \frac{1}{\sqrt{2\pi}} \int_{z=-\infty}^{\infty} e^{-z^2/2} \, dz \, \frac{1}{\sqrt{2\pi}} \int_{w=-\infty}^{\infty} e^{-w^2/2} \, dw$$

$$= \frac{1}{2\pi} \int_{z=-\infty}^{\infty} \int_{w=-\infty}^{\infty} e^{-(z^2+w^2)/2} \, dw \, dz$$

Functions of z are constants with respect to w, and can be moved back and forth across the w integral at will.

By changing w and z to polar coordinates, the element of area $dz\,dw$ for rectangular coordinates is replaced by the element $r\,dr\,d\theta$ in polar coordinates (see any calculus text). Then

$$w = r\cos\theta, \qquad z = r\sin\theta$$

$$z^2 + w^2 = r^2\sin^2\theta + r^2\cos^2\theta = r^2$$

Also, since the limits $z = -\infty$ to $+\infty$, $w = -\infty$ to $+\infty$ cover the whole wz-plane, we must also cover the plane in terms of r and θ, for example, by using $\theta = 0$ to 2π while $r = 0$ to ∞. Note that the limits $r = -\infty$ to ∞, $\theta = 0$ to 2π cover the plane twice and hence should not be used. Thus

$$A^2 = \frac{1}{2\pi}\int_{\theta=0}^{2\pi}\int_{r=0}^{\infty} e^{-r^2/2}r\,dr\,d\theta = \frac{1}{2\pi}\int_{\theta=0}^{2\pi} d\theta \cdot \int_{r=0}^{\infty} e^{-r^2/2}r\,dr$$

$$= \frac{1}{2\pi}\Big[\theta\Big]_0^{2\pi} \cdot \Big[-e^{-r^2/2}\Big]_0^{\infty} = \frac{1}{2\pi}\cdot 2\pi \cdot [0+1] = 1$$

Since the square of our integral

$$A = \frac{1}{\sigma\sqrt{2\pi}}\int_{x=-\infty}^{\infty} e^{-(x-\mu)^2/2\sigma^2}\,dx$$

is unity, A must be either plus 1 or minus 1. However, $\sigma > 0$, and the integrand is always positive. The direction of the limits is from left to right. Hence A can never be negative. By exclusion, $A = +1$, so that the normal is a true probability distribution.

IMPORTANT TERMS AND CONCEPTS

Distribution
  Cumulative probability
  Probability
  Bernoulli
  Binomial
  Exponential
  Normal
  Poisson
Function
  Frequency
  Density

MacLaurin series
Model
  Probability
  Statistical
Parameter
Polar coordinates
Random variable
  Discrete
  Continuous
Sample space

SYMBOLS AND ABBREVIATIONS

X $\ln x$

x $\int f(x)\,dx$

f^+ $F(x)$

a^- λ

$f(x)$ μ

e σ

OFTEN-USED FORMULAS

Binomial distribution:

$$f(x) = \binom{n}{x} p^x (1-p)^{n-x} \qquad x = 0, 1, \cdots, n$$

Poisson distribution:

$$f(x) = \frac{\lambda^x e^{-\lambda}}{x!}\,; \qquad x = 0, 1, 2, \cdots$$

Exponential distribution:

$$f(x) = \lambda e^{-\lambda x}; \qquad x \geq 0$$

Normal distribution:

$$f(x) = \frac{1}{\sigma\sqrt{2\pi}} e^{-(x-\mu)^2/2\sigma^2}; \qquad -\infty < x < \infty$$

EXERCISES

1. a. Graph the following functions:

     (1) $f(x) = \dfrac{1}{3}x$; $x = 1, 2$

     (2) $f(x) = -x$; $x = -0.75, -0.50, +0.25$

     (3) $f(x) = x - 1$; $x = 1, 2, 3, 4, 5, 6$

     (4) $f(x) = \dfrac{1}{8}$; $1 \leq x \leq 9$

     (5) $f(x) = 3x^2$; $0 \leq x \leq 1$

    b. What is the range of each of the functions listed in part *a*?

    c. Are any of the functions in part *a* frequency or density functions? Justify your answer for each function.

2. a. Are any of the following frequency or density functions? Prove your answer in each case.

      (1) $f(x) = 1$; $x = 1$

      (2) $f(x) = \dfrac{x}{6}$; $x = 1, 2, 3$

      (3) $f(x) = 2x$; $0 \le x \le 1$

      (4) $f(x) = x$; $x = \dfrac{1}{16}, \dfrac{3}{16}, \dfrac{1}{4}, \dfrac{1}{2}$

      (5) $f(x) = \dfrac{3}{10}(2 - x^2)$; $-1 \le x \le 1$

    b. What is the range of each of the functions in part *a*?

3. For each of the functions in Exercise 2 which are probability distributions, give the corresponding cumulative probability distribution.

4. Six unbiased coins are tossed in an unbiased manner.

    a. Is this a random experiment? Why?

    b. Define the sample space for the experiment.

    c. What is the probability that precisely one coin will be "heads?"

    d. What is the meaning of the probability calculated in part *c*?

    e. What is the probability, if the experiment is run three times, that precisely one head will result at least once?

5. The game of Russian roulette is played using a six shooter with a loaded shell in one chamber but no shells in the other chambers. The cylinder is spun; the pistol is aimed at the player's head; the trigger is pulled. The process is repeated indefinitely until the lone shell is hit with the hammer.

    a. Define the sample space for this problem.

    b. Would the following probability model be appropriate for this problem?

$$f(x) = \frac{1}{6}\left(\frac{5}{6}\right)^{x-1}; \qquad x = 1, 2, 3, \cdots$$

    where $f(x)$ denotes the probability of "losing" on the xth try.

    c. Prove that the function given in part *b* is a probability distribution. What does this imply about the eventual fate of the player?

6. Assume that the probability of a male birth is 0.5 and that the binomial distribution is applicable. What is the probability that a couple with 2 children will have 1 boy and 1 girl?

7. Assume that in a very large lot of similar articles produced by a manu-facturer, nine-tenths are known to be perfect and one-tenth are known to be defective. If 9 of these articles are selected at random and tested, what is the probability of getting exactly 3 defectives? At most, 3 defectives? At least, 3 defectives?

8. Suppose that 10 dice are thrown simultaneously. Each 5 or 6 spot appearing is considered to be a success. What is the probability that no more than 2 successes will occur?

9. If the probability is 0.25 that a male graduate student will be married, what is the probability that a random sample of 12 male graduate students will contain:
   a. Exactly 2 married men?
   b. No more than 3 married men?

10. What is the probability of throwing 9 heads exactly twice in 4 throws of 10 true coins?

11. In a very large shipment of washing machines, it is known that 2 percent of the machines are nonautomatic. What is the smallest sized random sample necessary to yield a probability of 0.95 of getting at least 1 non-automatic washing machine?

12. Two dice are rolled. What is the probability of obtaining a sum greater than 8?

13. Assume that it is known that 20 percent of the books in a lot of 100,000 volumes are rare editions. In a random sample of 4 items, what is the probability of finding:
   a. Exactly zero rare editions?
   b. At least one rare edition?

14. Suppose that 5 percent of the items in a shipment are defective. For samples of 10 items from this shipment, the binomial probability distribution for the number of defectives in the sample is as follows:

Number of Defectives	Probability
0	0.599
1	0.315
2	0.075
3	0.010
4 or more	0.001
	1.000

    a. Note that P(2) = 0.075. Show how this value would be calculated.

    b. Discuss in a sentence or two the meaning of P(2) = 0.075.

    c. An acceptance sampling plan specifies: accept a shipment if no more than 1 item in a sample of 10 items is defective. If the binomial distribution is applicable, what is the probability that this sampling plan will lead to the acceptance of a shipment in which 5 percent of the items are defective?

15. The Rush Trucking Company has found that 5 percent of the time some truck paint is marred when a truck backs into a loading stall at the warehouse.

    a. Would a binomial probability model be appropriate for this situation? Justify your answer by discussing some factors that should be investigated.

    b. One person investigating this situation suggested that there is a non-homogeneity problem here because of length of driver experience. What would this mean?

    For the remaining parts of this problem assume that a binomial probability model is appropriate.

    c. If 5 trucks back into stalls, what is the probability that some paint is marred on no more than 4 of the trucks?

    d. If 5 trucks back into stalls, what is the probability that some paint is marred on all of the trucks?

    e. What is the probability that no more than 2 trucks have marred paint when 5 trucks back into stalls?

    f. Define the probability model used in part c.

    g. Define the cumulative distribution function for part c.

    h. How many trucks would have to back into stalls to make the probability of marring paint on at least one truck equal to 0.99?

16. The Drew-Jacobs Accounting Agency employs a clerk who is responsible for entering items into the ledgers of various clients. Mr. Drew made a spot check of this clerk's work by examining 20 entries selected at random, and about one-fourth of the entries were in error. Mr. Drew concluded that the clerk was doing unsatisfactory work and reported this to Mr. Jacobs. Mr. Jacobs was hesitant. He maintained that an error rate of 5 percent was not uncommon for this grade of clerk and that it was highly probable that the error rate of this clerk was 5 percent, since this sample could have been nonrepresentative.

    a. How likely is it that one would get an error rate of 25 percent in a random sample of size 20 if the true error rate were really only 5 percent?

    b. Suppose the clerk's true error rate is 50 percent. What is the probability of getting a 25 percent error rate from a random sample of 20?

c. What is the meaning of the numerical probabilities that you calculated in parts *a* and *b*?

d. Suppose that the true error rate was 50 percent. Which is more likely, (1) 5 errors in a random sample of size 10 or (2) 10 errors in a random sample of size 20? Explain.

17. An automobile insurance company knows that 0.002 of all compact cars are involved in accidents each year. It has insured 20,000 compact cars. What is the probability that not more than 2 of the compacts it has insured are involved in accidents this year? (Omit computation.)

18. If the village of Peaceful Valley averages 6 unsolved murders per year, what is the probability that next year it will have no unsolved murders? Comment on the reasonableness of the model you have used.

19. A newspaper proofreader states that he misses only one misprint in a thousand. If his statement is true, what is the probability of his missing more than one misprint in 5000? Comment upon the reasonableness of the assumptions underlying your model.

20. The lost and found department of the Jonas Department Store receives an average of three calls during its first five minutes of operation (from 9:00 to 9:05 A.M.) Monday through Friday.

a. Would a Poisson probability model be appropriate for this situation? Justify your answer.

In the remaining parts of this exercise, assume that a Poisson probability model is appropriate.

b. What is the probability of no calls next Monday between 9:00 and 9:05 A.M.?

c. What is the probability of one call during the first five minutes of operation tomorrow?

d. What is the probability that a total of exactly two calls will be received in the next three working days during the 9:00 to 9:05 A.M. time periods?

21. For the Styleking Clothing Store, it has been determined that the number of times a customer repurchases in the store during a 5-year period is well approximated by a Poisson distribution with $\lambda = 3$.

a. Calculate:

1. $P(X < 1)$ 3. $P(X < 3)$

2. $P(X = 1)$ 4. $P(X > 4)$

b. Describe in words each of the probabilities you calculated in part *a*.

22. The number of thunderstorms occurring in a certain area each year can be approximated by a Poisson distribution with $\lambda = 22$.

a. Calculate the probability that in one year 18 thunderstorms will occur in this area.
b. Find $P(20 \leq X \leq 22)$, and state the meaning of this probability in words.

23. One instructor said that his students' IQ's were distributed as follows:

$$f(x) = \frac{1}{b - a} \qquad a \leq x \leq b$$

with $a = 50$ and $b = 150$.
a. Criticize the use of the above probability model in a "typical" college class.
b. What distribution might be more appropriate? Justify.
c. Assume that the model given above is a correct one. Calculate the following:

1. $P(X < 100)$ 4. $P(75 \leq X \leq 125)$

2. $P(X \geq 100)$ 5. $P(X > 150)$

3. $P(75 < X < 125)$ 6. $P[(X > 145) \cup (X < 70)]$

24. Given the following probability distribution:

$$f(x) = \frac{3}{125} x^2 \qquad 0 < x < 5$$

a. What is the corresponding cumulative distribution?
b. Calculate the following probabilities:

1. $P(X = 0)$ 3. $P(2 < X < 3)$

2. $P(X = 2)$ 4. $P(X > 2)$

25. Given the following probability distribution:

$$f(x) = \frac{1}{18}(3 + 2x) \qquad 2 < x < 4$$

a. Find the probability that $2 < X < 2.5$.
b. Sketch the above distribution and shade the area denoting the probability you calculated in part *a*.
c. What is the cumulative probability distribution which corresponds to the above probability distribution?

26. The distribution of length of life in months of one type of small retail

store is adequately approximated by an exponential function of the form:

$$f(x) = \frac{1}{70} e^{-x/70} \qquad 0 \le x < \infty$$

a. What is the cumulative distribution corresponding to the above probability distribution?
b. What is the probability that a small retail store selected randomly will have a length of life of:
  1. Less than 2 years?
  2. More than 4 years?

27. A child who is learning to walk falls and bumps his head at the average rate of twice per hour. What is the probability that he does not fall and bump his head during the first half-hour of walking tomorrow? Comment upon the appropriateness of the exponential model in this problem.

28. A financier receives confidential reports on his investments at the average rate of three reports per day. What is the probability that two days will elapse without his receiving such a report?

29. a. Find the maximum ordinate of the normal probability distribution.
   b. Can the maximum ordinate of the Poisson function be found by differentiating and equating the derivative to zero? Explain.

30. a. Graph the probability distribution of a random variable X which is normally distributed with $\mu = 80$ and $\sigma = 5$.
   b. What is the probability that an item drawn at random from this distribution will have a value greater than 76?
   c. Shade the area of your graph in part *a* which corresponds to the probability in part *b*.

31. Assume that the distribution of heights of adult males is normal with $\mu = 5$ ft 9 in., $\sigma = 2.5$ in.
   a. What percentage of adult males are between 5 ft 8 in. and 6 ft 0 in. in height?
   b. What percentage of adult males are shorter than 5 ft 5 in.?
   c. What percentage are shorter than 6 ft?

32. The ABC Company uses a machine to fill boxes with soap powder. In a state of statistical quality control, the net weights of the boxes of soap are normally distributed with $\mu = 15$ oz and $\sigma = 0.8$ oz.
   a. What proportion of the boxes will have net weights of more than 14 oz? More than 15 oz?
   b. Twenty-five percent of the boxes will be heavier than a certain net weight and 75 percent of the boxes will be lighter than this net weight. What is the value of the net weight that divides the heavier 25 percent and the lighter 75 percent of the boxes?

33. The Dain Company produces widgets. It is known that the process used produces widgets whose lengths are normally distributed with $\mu = 6.00$ in. and $\sigma = 0.30$ in. Suppose specifications for the length are 5.60 to 6.50 in.
    a. What proportion of widgets are too short?
    b. What proportion of widgets are too long?
    c. Widgets that are too short must be thrown out (salvage). Widgets that are too long can be reworked for a slight additional cost. If salvage cost is much more than rework cost per item, what suggestions do you have about possible changes in the process?

34. If the exact times at which the 20,000 office employees of the Rodann Corporation report for work in the morning are approximately normally distributed with mean 8:55 A.M. and standard deviation 5 minutes, what is the probability that
    a. One office employee picked at random will report for work later than 9:00 A.M. next Thursday?
    b. Two out of three office employees picked at random will report for work later than 9:00 A.M. next Thursday?
    c. Comment on your answer to part b since the sample of three employees would probably be selected without replacement.

35. If the duration of student sit-ins in the United States is an approximately normally distributed random variable with mean 6 days and standard deviation 2 days, what is the probability that a sit-in, chosen at random, lasts at least 5 days?

5 Probability Distributions of Two or More Random Variables

5.1 MULTIVARIATE RANDOM VARIABLES

Our definition of random variable in Section 4.1 included the possibility that X, the random variable defined on S, the sample space, could be a vector. In this chapter we will consider situations where it is useful to think of a random variable as a vector of more than one element. Such random variables are called "multivariate" random variables, and their study is an important branch of our subject.

Suppose, for example, that the owner of a small machine shop has received an order for 10,000 steel spindles and must now order the stock from which they are to be turned. The spindles are to be 12 inches long and to taper from a diameter of one-half inch at one end to an inch at the other. To be acceptable to the buyer, the spindles must come within 0.001 inches of the specified diameters and 0.01 inches of the specified length. These tolerances are given because both parties to the order know that cutting tools vary during the production process so that the spindles will not all be precisely of the same dimensions. In ordering the stock, the shop owner must allow for the fact that, because of this variation, some of the spindles will have to be either scrapped or reworked. He is interested, therefore, in the variation in the length and in the end diameters of spindles produced to the given specifications. Conceptually, the sample space consists of all such spindles, and the random variable is a vector with three components: length, diameter at the wide end, and diameter at the narrow end. Thus the random variable is a vector-valued function whose domain is the set of all spindles produced by this machine shop to these specifications and whose range is a three-dimensional vector space.

As an easy, but more specific, illustration of a multivariate random variable, suppose that S, the sample space, consists of the sides of a die. The event E_j in S denotes the side of the die with j spots so that we can write

$$S = \{E_1, E_2, E_3, E_4, E_5, E_6\}$$

Suppose also that we are interested in two aspects of E_j: first, whether or not j is even; and second, whether or not j is divisible by three. Our random variable will consist of two components, X_1 and X_2, which are defined by

$$X_1(E_j) = \begin{cases} 1, & \text{if } j \text{ is even} \\ 0, & \text{otherwise} \end{cases}$$

$$X_2(E_j) = \begin{cases} 1, & \text{if } j \text{ is divisible by three} \\ 0, & \text{otherwise} \end{cases}$$

The random variable $X = (X_1, X_2)$ can take four possible values: $(0, 0)$, $(0, 1)$, $(1, 0)$, and $(1, 1)$. Our function from S to X is

$$X(E_1) = (0, 0), \qquad X(E_2) = (1, 0), \qquad X(E_3) = (0, 1),$$

$$X(E_4) = (1, 0), \qquad X(E_5) = (0, 0), \qquad X(E_6) = (1, 1)$$

If we have defined a probability distribution on S, we can use it to define a probability distribution on X just as we did in the case of a one-dimensional random variable.

$$P_X[(0, 0)] = P_S(E_1) + P_S(E_5)$$

$$P_X[(0, 1)] = P_S(E_3)$$

$$P_X[(1, 0)] = P_S(E_2) + P_S(E_4)$$

$$P_X[(1, 1)] = P_S(E_6)$$

The probability distribution we have just constructed describes the simultaneous or "joint" probabilistic behavior of 2 one-dimensional random variables, X_1 and X_2; for this reason P_X is sometimes called the joint probability distribution of X_1 and X_2. We may be interested in the probabilistic behavior of X_1 alone and of X_2 alone. The probability distributions of X_1 and X_2, each regarded as one-dimensional random variables, can be deduced from their joint distribution. Suppose, for example, we want the probability distribution of X_1. It is easily computed.

$$P_{X_1}(0) = P\{X_1 = 0\} = P_X[(0, 0)] + P_X[(0, 1)]$$

$$P_{X_1}(1) = P\{X_1 = 1\} = P_X[(1, 0)] + P_X[(1, 1)]$$

Similarly

$$P_{X_2}(0) = P\{X_2 = 0\} = P_X[(0, 0)] + P_X[(1, 0)]$$

$$P_{X_2}(1) = P\{X_2 = 1\} = P_X[(0, 1)] + P_X[(1, 1)]$$

These probability distributions are called the "marginal probability distributions" of X_1 and X_2. In order to see the reason for the word "marginal," it is convenient to assign numbers to P_S. Let's make things easy for ourselves by assigning

$$P_S(E_j) = \frac{1}{6} \qquad E_j \subset S$$

The joint probability distribution of X_1 and X_2 can now be presented in the form of a two-way table (Table 5.1).

Table 5.1 Joint Probability Distribution for Die Example

X_2 \ X_1	0	1	$P_{X_2}(x)$
0	1/3	1/3	2/3
1	1/6	1/6	1/3
$P_{X_1}(x)$	1/2	1/2	1

The body of Table 5.1 gives $P_X[(x_1, x_2)]$. The row sums are called the row "marginal" totals. They are formed by holding X_2 constant and summing over X_1, and it is easy to check that they give the probability distribution of X_2. Similarly, the column sums are called the column "marginal" totals, and they give the probability distribution of X_1. Hence the marginal probability distributions are the marginal totals obtained when the joint probability distribution is presented in the form of a two-way table and summed over the rows and columns.

We see that, when X is a two-element vector, we can construct three probability distributions: the joint distribution of the two elements and the marginal distributions of each—considered as a one-dimensional random variable. As the number of elements of X increases, the number of probability distributions that can be constructed proliferates at an alarming rate. When X has three elements, a total of seven distributions can be constructed. These are: the joint distribution of the three elements of X, three joint distributions of the elements considered in pairs, and three distributions of the elements considered as single random variables. In general, if X has r elements, a total of $2^r - 1$ distributions can be constructed. (Why is this so?) In order to keep the length of this chapter within reasonable bounds, we shall consider only two-dimensional examples.

In Chapter 4 we called a one-dimensional random variable discrete if its range was a countable set and continuous if its range was an interval or countable set of intervals. This is true for each of the elements of a vector-valued random variable. Thus there are four kinds of two-dimensional random variables: X_1 and X_2 both discrete, X_1 discrete and X_2 continuous, X_1 continuous and X_2 discrete, and X_1 and X_2 both continuous. There are 2^r possibilities for an r-dimensional random variable. The fact that some elements of the vector can be discrete while others are continuous means that we must be careful in defining frequency and density functions when the random variable is a vector-valued function.

5.2 CUMULATIVE PROBABILITY DISTRIBUTIONS

The definition of a cumulative probability distribution for an r-dimensional random variable is analogous to that for a one-dimensional random variable.

Definition. The function $F(x_1, x_2, \cdots, x_r)$ is a cumulative probability distribution for the r-dimensional random variable $X = (X_1, X_2, \cdots, X_r)$ if

(1) It is defined for all real $x_1, x_2, \cdots, x_r$.

(2) It is nondecreasing in each of its arguments; that is, if $x_j' > x_j$, then for some $j = 1, \cdots, r$,

$$F(x_1, \cdots, x_j', \cdots, x_r) \geq F(x_1, \cdots, x_j, \cdots, x_r)$$

(3) It is right continuous in each of its arguments; that is, if $h_j > 0$, then

$$\lim_{h_j \to 0} F(x_1, \cdots, x_j + h_j, \cdots, x_r) = F(x_1, \cdots, x_j, \cdots, x_r) \quad j = 1, \cdots, r$$

(4) $0 \leq F(x_1, x_2, \cdots, x_r) \leq 1$, for all real $x_1, x_2, \cdots, x_r$.

(5) $F(-\infty, -\infty, \cdots, -\infty) = 0$, and $F(+\infty, +\infty, \cdots, +\infty) = 1$.

Any function with these properties is a cumulative probability distribution for an r-dimensional random variable, but, as in the case of a one-dimensional random variable, it must be possible to interpret $F(x_1, x_2, \cdots, x_r)$ as

$$F(x_1, x_2, \cdots, x_r) = P\{(X_1 \leq x_1) \cap (X_2 \leq x_2) \cap \cdots \cap (X_r \leq x_r)\} \quad (5.1)$$

where X_j denotes the name of the element and x_j its value. For our example of Section 5.1, the cumulative probability distribution is

$$F(x_1, x_2) = \begin{cases} 0, & (x_1 < 0) \cup (x_2 < 0) \\ \frac{1}{3}, & (0 \leq x_1 < 1) \cap (0 \leq x_2 < 1) \\ \frac{1}{2}, & (0 \leq x_1 < 1) \cap (1 \leq x_2 < \infty) \\ \frac{2}{3}, & (1 \leq x_1 < \infty) \cap (0 \leq x_2 < 1) \\ 1, & (1 \leq x_1 < \infty) \cap (1 \leq x_2 < \infty) \end{cases}$$

The graph of this function is shown in Figure 5.1. The heavy edges indicate the points at which $F(x_1, x_2)$ takes a jump.

Given $F(x_1, x_2, \cdots, x_r)$, we can in principle compute the probability that the point $(X_1, X_2, \cdots, X_r)$ lies in any region of the r-dimensional space over which it is defined. However, even when X is two-dimensional and the region is a rectangle, one must be careful. Suppose, for example, we wish to compute $P\{(a_1 < X_1 \leq b_1) \cap (a_2 < X_2 \leq b_2)\}$. We can do this with the help of Figure 5.2. The function $F(x_1, x_2)$ evaluated at the point we have marked (1) gives $P\{(X_1 \leq b_1) \cap (X_2 \leq b_2)\}$. If we subtract from this probability the

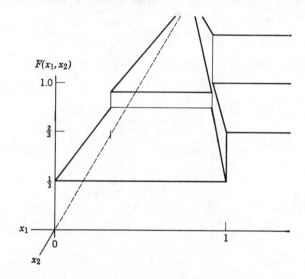

Fig. 5.1. Cumulative probability distribution for die example.

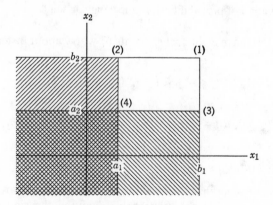

Fig. 5.2. Evaluation of probability over a rectangle.

values of the function evaluated at the points we have marked (2) and (3), we will have subtracted twice the probability over the doubly cross-hatched area, so that we must add back this probability once. It is given by the value of the function at the point (4). Now we have computed

$$P\{(a_1 < X_1 \leq b_1) \cap (a_2 < X_2 \leq b_2)\} = F_{(1)} - F_{(2)} - F_{(3)} + F_{(4)}$$

$$= F(b_1, b_2) - F(a_1, b_2) - F(b_1, a_2) + F(a_1, a_2) \quad (5.2)$$

Figure 5.3 will help us to make a similar calculation for a three-dimensional random variable. Reasoning similar to that used in the case of two-dimensions

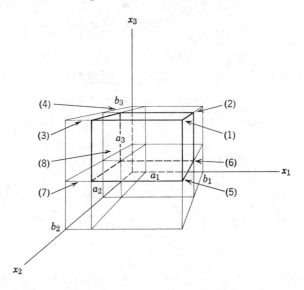

Fig. 5.3. Evaluation of probability over a rectangular solid.

will show that we have eight corner points to worry about instead of four and that

$$P\{(a_1 < X_1 \leq b_1) \cap (a_2 < X_2 \leq b_2) \cap (a_3 < X_3 \leq b_3)\}$$
$$= F_{(1)} - F_{(2)} - F_{(3)} - F_{(5)} + F_{(4)} + F_{(6)} + F_{(7)} - F_{(8)}$$
$$= F(b_1, b_2, b_3) - F(b_1, a_2, b_3) - F(a_1, b_2, b_3) - F(b_1, b_2, a_3)$$
$$+ F(a_1, a_2, b_3) + F(b_1, a_2, a_3)$$
$$+ F(a_1, b_2, a_3) - F(a_1, a_2, a_3) \quad (5.3)$$

It is possible to generalize this result to a similar region in an r-dimensional space by noting in (5.3) the relationship between the sign attached to a particular value of F and the number of its arguments which are at their lower levels, but the generalization is difficult to express succinctly and will not be needed in this text. For the balance of this chapter we shall confine ourselves to two dimensions.

5.3 JOINT FREQUENCY FUNCTIONS

When X_1 and X_2 are both discrete-valued random variables, we can write

$$P\{(X_1 = x_1) \cap (X_2 = x_2)\}$$
$$= \lim_{\substack{h_1 \to 0 \\ h_2 \to 0}} P\{(x_1 - h_1 < X_1 \leq x_1) \cap (x_2 - h_2 < X_2 \leq x_2)\}$$

assuming h_1 and h_2 are both positive. For example, in our die illustration,

$$P\{(X_1 = 1) \cap (X_2 = 1)\}$$
$$= \lim_{\substack{h_1 \to 0 \\ h_2 \to 0}} \{F(1, 1) - F(1, 1 - h_2) - F(1 - h_1, 1) + F(1 - h_1, 1 - h_2)\}$$
$$= \lim_{\substack{h_1 \to 0 \\ h_2 \to 0}} \left\{1 - \frac{2}{3} - \frac{1}{2} + \frac{1}{3}\right\} = \frac{1}{6}$$

which agrees with the value computed earlier. When X_1 and X_2 are both discrete, we define their *frequency function* as

$$f(x_1, x_2) = P\{(X_1 = x_1) \cap (X_2 = x_2)\}$$
$$= \lim_{\substack{h_1 \to 0 \\ h_2 \to 0}} \{F(x_1, x_2) - F(x_1, x_2 - h_2)$$
$$- F(x_1 - h_1, x_2) + F(x_1 - h_1, x_2 - h_2)\} \qquad (5.4)$$

where h_1 and h_2 pass through positive values only on the way toward their limits. The frequency function for two discrete random variables has properties similar to the frequency function for one discrete random variable.

(1) $f(x_1, x_2)$ is defined for all real (x_1, x_2).

(2) $f(x_1, x_2) \geq 0$, but $f(x_1, x_2) > 0$ only for a countable subset of points in the real (x_1, x_2) plane.

(3) If we define f^+ as the set of points in the real (x_1, x_2) plane for which $f(x_1, x_2)$ is positive, then

$$\sum_{(x_1, x_2) \in f^+} f(x_1, x_2) = 1$$

In applications, it is frequently convenient to derive the frequency function from the statement of the problem, and then, if needed, to compute the cumulative probability distribution from the frequency function by addition.

We define the set a^- as

$$a^- = \{(x_1, x_2) \mid (x_1 \leq a_1) \cap (x_2 \leq a_2) \cap (x_1, x_2) \in f^+\}$$

then

$$F(a_1, a_2) = \sum_{(x_1, x_2) \in a^-} f(x_1, x_2)$$

For an example with a little more realism then our die illustration, let us return to Mrs. Burchard and the Bizzy-B Company. Recall that one-third of the five pound jars of honey sold by the Bizzy-B Company were under-weight and that two-thirds were overweight. Suppose that in an overweight jar of honey the air-seal is tight so that the honey cannot possibly turn to sugar. In an underweight jar, however, the air-seal need not be tight, and prolonged exposure to air may turn some of the honey near the mouth of the jar to sugar by the time that the honey reaches the grocer's shelf. Suppose that in one-fifth of the underweight jars the honey has begun to turn to sugar by the time the jars are put on the shelf. Mrs. Burchard buys six jars of honey. We will let X_1 be the number of underweight jars and X_2 the number of jars in which the honey has begun to turn to sugar.

Now, given X_1, the number of underweight jars, X_2, has the binomial distribution. We can write

$$P\{(X_2 = x_2) \mid (X_1 = x_1)\} = \binom{x_1}{x_2}\left(\frac{1}{5}\right)^{x_2}\left(\frac{4}{5}\right)^{x_1-x_2} \qquad x_2 = 0, 1, \cdots, x_1$$

In Chapter 3 we learned that

$$P(A \cap B) = P(A)P(B \mid A)$$

and we can apply this to the problem at hand. First let's assume that Mrs. Burchard buys n jars of honey instead of 6. This will give a general result that can be specialized to $n = 6$. The event "A" in our problem is "X_1 jars are underweight," and the event "B" is "in X_2 jars the honey has begun to turn to sugar." We have

$$P(A) = P\{X_1 = x_1\} = \binom{n}{x_1}\left(\frac{1}{3}\right)^{x_1}\left(\frac{2}{3}\right)^{n-x_1} \qquad x_1 = 0, 1, \cdots, n$$

and

$$P(B \mid A) = P\{X_2 = x_2 \mid X_1 = x_1\} = \binom{x_1}{x_2}\left(\frac{1}{5}\right)^{x_2}\left(\frac{4}{5}\right)^{x_1-x_2} \qquad x_2 = 0, 1, \cdots, x_1$$

Then

$$P(A)P(B \mid A) = P\{X_1 = x_1\}P\{X_2 = x_2 \mid X_1 = x_1\}$$

$$= \binom{n}{x_1}\left(\frac{1}{3}\right)^{x_1}\left(\frac{2}{3}\right)^{n-x_1}\binom{x_1}{x_2}\left(\frac{1}{5}\right)^{x_2}\left(\frac{4}{5}\right)^{x_1-x_2}$$

$$x_1 = 0, 1, \cdots, n \qquad x_2 = 0, 1, \cdots, x_1$$

This is our frequency function, and with a little manipulation we can write it as

$$f(x_1, x_2) = \frac{n!}{(n - x_1)! \, (x_1 - x_2)! \, x_2!} \left(\frac{10}{15}\right)^{n-x_1} \left(\frac{4}{15}\right)^{x_1-x_2} \left(\frac{1}{15}\right)^{x_2}$$

$$x_1 = 0, 1, \cdots, n \qquad x_2 = 0, 1, \cdots, x_1.$$

Notice that the jars fall into three sets:

Set 1. Overweight. Two-thirds of the jars marked have this property, and there are $n - x_1$ of them.

Set 2. Underweight but not turning to sugar. Four-fifths of one-third, or four-fifteenths, of the jars marked have this property, and there are $x_1 - x_2$ of them.

Set 3. Underweight and turning to sugar. One-fifth of one-third, or one-fifteenth, of the jars have this property, and there are x_2 of them.

Notice further that we have n objects (jars) to be divided into three sets, the first set containing $n - x_1$ objects, the second $x_1 - x_2$, and the third x_2. We have learned in Chapter 3 that this can be done in

$$\binom{n}{n - x_1 \quad x_1 - x_2 \quad x_2} = \frac{n!}{(n - x_1)!(x - x_2)!x_2!}$$

ways. In solving our problem we have arrived at a generalization of the binomial frequency function, and we shall now summarize our discovery.

Suppose that a single trial of an experiment can result in any one of r mutually exclusive outcomes, and that the probability of an outcome in category j is p_j where

$$\sum_{j=1}^{r} p_j = 1$$

Then, if n independent trials of the experiment are made, the probability of x_1 outcomes in category 1, x_2 outcomes in category 2, $\cdots$, x_r outcomes in category r is

$$P\{(X_1 = x_1) \cap (X_2 = x_2) \cap \cdots \cap (X_r = x_r)\}$$

$$= f(x_1, x_2, \cdots, x_r)$$

$$= \frac{n!}{x_1! x_2! \cdots x_r!} p_1^{x_1} p_2^{x_2} \cdots p_r^{x_r} \quad (5.5)$$

where $x_1 + x_2 + \cdots + x_r = n$, and $p_1 + p_2 + \cdots + p_r = 1$. When $r = 2$, we have the binomial frequency function. Our result, (5.5) is called the multinomial frequency function.

Now back to Mrs. Burchard for whom $n = 6$ and

$$f(x_1, x_2) = \frac{6!}{(6 - x_1)!(x_1 - x_2)!x_2!} \left(\frac{10}{15}\right)^{6-x_1} \left(\frac{4}{15}\right)^{x_1-x_2} \left(\frac{1}{15}\right)^{x_2}$$

$$x_1 = 0, 1, \cdots, 6 \qquad x_2 = 0, 1, \cdots, x_1$$

This joint frequency function is tabulated in Table 5.2; its joint cumulative probability distribution is given in Table 5.3. We now illustrate the use of these tables by answering two questions about Mrs. Burchard's purchase.

First, what is the probability that two of Mrs. Burchard's jars will be underweight and that in none of the jars has the honey begun to turn to

Table 5.2   Joint Frequency Function for Mrs. Burchard's Problem

X_2	X_1 0	1	2	3	4	5	6
0	0.0878	0.2107	0.2107	0.1124	0.0337	0.0054	0.0004
1		0.0527	0.1054	0.0843	0.0337	0.0067	0.0005
2			0.0132	0.0211	0.0126	0.0034	0.0003
3				0.0018	0.0021	0.0003	0.0001
4					0.0001	0.0001	0.0000[a]
5						0.0001	0.0000
6							0.0000

[a] 0.0000 means less than 0.00005.

Table 5.3   Cumulative Distribution for Mrs. Burchard's Problem

X_2	X_1 0	1	2	3	4	5	6
0	0.0878	0.2985	0.5092	0.6216	0.6553	0.6607	0.6611
1	0.0878	0.3512	0.6673	0.8640	0.9314	0.9435	0.9444
2	0.0878	0.3512	0.6805	0.8983	0.9783	0.9938	0.9950
3	0.0878	0.3512	0.6805	0.9001	0.9822	0.9935	0.9998
4	0.0878	0.3512	0.6805	0.9001	0.9823	0.9987	1.0000[a]
5	0.0878	0.3512	0.6805	0.9001	0.9823	0.9988	1.0000
6	0.0878	0.3512	0.6805	0.9001	0.9823	0.9988	1.0000

[a] 1.0000 means greater than 0.99995.

sugar? Here $X_1 = 2$ and $X_2 = 0$; Table 5.2 shows that

$$P\{(X_1 = 2) \cap (X_2 = 0)\} = 0.2107$$

Mrs. Burchard stands slightly better than one chance in five of getting two underweight jars and no sugar.

Second, what is the probability that no more than two of Mrs. Burchard's jars will be underweight and that the contents of no more than one jar will have begun to turn to sugar? To answer this question we enter Table 5.3 with $X_1 = 2$ and $X_2 = 1$, and we see that

$$P\{(X_1 \leq 2) \cap (X_2 \leq 1)\} = 0.6673$$

The chances are slightly better than two out of three that Mrs. Burchard will purchase no more than two underweight jars and that no more than one of them will contain sugar.

5.4   JOINT DENSITY FUNCTIONS

When X_1 and X_2 are both continuous, the limit we computed to obtain the frequency function in the discrete case will be identically zero. Therefore, when both variables are continuous, we compute the probability density in a way similar to that used in the case of one continuous random variable. In Chapter 4 we defined the probability density of the continuous random variable X as

$$f(x) = \lim_{h \to 0} \frac{1}{h} P\{x - h < X \leq x\} \qquad h > 0$$

In that case we were concerned with the probability that X lay in an interval of length h whose right end was the point $X = x$. The ratio was the probability per unit length of this interval, and the limit of this ratio was the probability density. In the case of two random variables, we calculate the limit of the probability per unit area in the (x_1, x_2) plane and call the limit of this ratio the probability density. We designate this density by lower case f.

$$f(x_1, x_2) = \lim_{\substack{h_1 \to 0 \\ h_2 \to 0}} \frac{1}{h_1 h_2} P\{(x_1 - h_1 < X_1 \leq x_1) \cap (x_2 - h_2 < X_2 \leq x_2)\}$$
$$h_1, h_2 > 0$$

We can write this out as

$$f(x_1, x_2) = \lim_{\substack{h_1 \to 0 \\ h_2 \to 0}} \frac{1}{h_1 h_2} \{[F(x_1, x_2) - F(x_1 - h_1, x_2)]$$

$$- [F(x_1, x_2 - h_2) - F(x_1 - h_1, x_2 - h_2)]\}$$

and, when we take the limit and recall what we know about partial derivatives, we see that

$$f(x_1, x_2) = \frac{\partial^2 F(x_1, x_2)}{\partial x_1 \, \partial x_2} \qquad (5.6)$$

This idea extends to r continuous random variables. If $x_1, x_2, \cdots, x_r$ are r continuous random variables whose cumulative probability distribution is $F(x_1, x_2, \cdots, x_r)$, then the probability density of $x_1, x_2, \cdots, x_r$ at the point $X_1 = x_1, X_2 = x_2, \cdots, X_r = x_r$ is

$$f(x_1, x_2, \cdots, x_r) = \frac{\partial^r F(x_1, x_2, \cdots, x_r)}{\partial x_1 \, \partial x_2 \cdots \partial x_r} \qquad (5.7)$$

The density function (5.7) has the following properties:

(1) $f(x_1, x_2, \cdots, x_r)$ is defined for all real points $(x_1, x_2, \cdots, x_r)$.

(2) $f(x_1, x_2, \cdots, x_r) \geq 0$.

(3) $\displaystyle\int_{x_r=-\infty}^{\infty} \cdots \int_{x_2=-\infty}^{\infty} \int_{x_1=-\infty}^{\infty} f(x_1, x_2, \cdots, x_r) \, dx_1 \, dx_2 \cdots dx_r = 1$

In applications it is frequently convenient to begin with the density function and to derive the cumulative distribution by integration. If $f(x, y)$ is the density, we have

$$F(x, y) = \int_{v=-\infty}^{y} \int_{u=-\infty}^{x} f(u, v) \, du \, dv \qquad (5.8)$$

and the probability content of a rectangle can be computed by

$$P\{(a_1 < X_1 \leq b_1) \cap (a_2 < X_2 \leq b_2)\} = \int_{v=a_2}^{b_2} \int_{u=a_1}^{b_1} f(u, v) \, du \, dv \qquad (5.9)$$

It is a simple exercise in double integration to show that (5.9) will produce the same answer as (5.2).

In a study of costs for a certain type of transistor, A. P. Foote Electronics has learned that the density function for size of order, X, and total cost for the order, Y, is reasonably well approximated by

$$f(x, y) = \frac{1}{2.4}, \quad 1 \leq x \leq 5, \quad 0.1 + 0.9x \leq y < 0.1 + 1.1x$$

where x is in thousands of transistors and y is in thousands of dollars. If the company sets a price of \$1.10 per transistor, on what proportion of orders for this transistor will it either break even or make a profit? The region over which $f(x, y)$ is positive is sketched in Figure 5.4, where we have also drawn the total revenue curve assuming a selling price of \$1.10 per unit and shaded the region in which A. P. Foote either breaks even or makes a profit. In

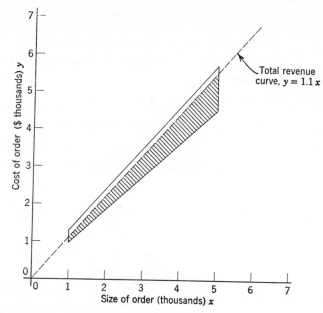

Fig. 5.4. Sketch for A. P. Foote's problem.

order to answer our question, we must integrate the density $f(x, y)$ over the shaded region.

$$P\{\text{break even or profit}\} = \frac{1}{2.4} \int_{x=1}^{5} \int_{y=0.1+0.9x}^{1.1x} dy \, dx$$

$$= \frac{1}{2.4} \int_{x=1}^{5} (0.2x - 0.1) \, dx = \frac{2.0}{2.4} = \frac{5}{6}$$

A. P. Foote Electronics will either break even or make a profit on 5/6 of the orders received for this transistor.

Consider another problem that can be solved by using the joint distribution of two random variables. The Collins Metals Company has a waste disposal problem. It must deactivate before disposal a useless slurry consisting chemically of three ingredients that we shall simply call ingredients A, B, and C.

Let X be the proportion of a day's slurry formed by ingredients A and B. Let Y be the proportion formed by A alone. A study of past data indicates that the composition of the slurry on one day does not seem to be related to its composition on succeeding days. Also the proportions X and Y appearing from day to day appear to have approximately the probability distribution

$$f(x, y) = 8xy \qquad 0 \le x \le 1 \qquad 0 \le y \le x \qquad (5.10)$$

The upper limit for x indicates days when the slurry is composed of a mixture of A and B only. The limits shown for y simply say that the proportion of A in the slurry cannot exceed the proportion of A and B combined.

We pose two questions. What is the probability that on a day selected at random the slurry contains:

(1) More than 20 percent ingredient A?

(2) Less than 40 percent ingredients A and B combined?

To solve (1) we must find the probability $P(Y > 0.2)$. Figure 5.5 illustrates the area over which we must integrate. Notice that a point such as $(0.1, 0.1)$

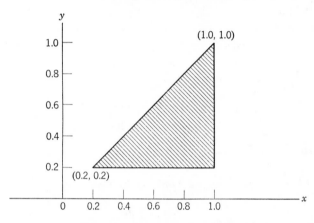

Fig. 5.5. Region of integration for part 1 of the waste disposal problem using (5.10).

corresponds to a slurry composed mostly of C, while the point $(0.9, 0.9)$ corresponds to one composed mostly of A, and the point $(0.9, 0.1)$ corresponds to one composed mostly of B. Finding the integral of the function over this area, we obtain

$$P(Y > 0.2) = \int_{x=0.2}^{1} \int_{y=0.2}^{x} 8xy \, dy \, dx = \int_{x=0.2}^{1} 8x \left[\frac{y^2}{2} \right]_{0.2}^{x} dx$$

$$= \int_{x=0.2}^{1} 4x^3 \, dx - \int_{x=0.2}^{1} 4(0.04)x \, dx$$

$$= 4 \left[\frac{x^4}{4} \right]_{0.2}^{1} - 0.16 \left[\frac{x^2}{2} \right]_{0.2}^{1}$$

$$= 1 - 0.0016 - 0.08 + 0.0032 = 0.9216$$

The probability is slightly more than 0.92 that a single day's slurry will contain more than 20 percent ingredient A.

For the answer to question 2 we require the probability that X, the proportion of ingredients A and B, should be less than 0.4. We ask the student to locate the region of integration on Figure 5.5 and then check that it gives the following calculation.

$$P(X < 0.4) = \int_{x=0}^{0.4} \int_{y=0}^{x} 8xy \, dy \, dx = \int_{x=0}^{0.4} 8x \left[\frac{y^2}{2} \right]_0^x dx$$

$$= 4 \int_{x=0}^{0.4} x^3 \, dx = 4 \left[\frac{x^4}{4} \right]_0^{0.4} = (0.4)^4 = 0.0256$$

The probability is about 0.026 that a single day's slurry will contain less than 40 percent of ingredients A and B combined.

Thus far in two dimensions we have considered cases where either both variables are discrete or both variables are continuous. We shall omit the mixed case where one variable is discrete and the other continuous. It is important to professional statisticians but not to the elementary student.

5.5 MARGINAL DISTRIBUTIONS

Suppose that our friend, Mrs. Burchard, regards the extent to which a jar of honey may be overweight or underweight as negligible and is primarily concerned with the number of jars whose contents may have begun to turn to sugar. She is interested in the distribution of X_2 alone and, as we learned in Section 5.1, this distribution is called the "marginal" distribution of X_2. Since X_1 and X_2 are both discrete, we can obtain $f(x_2)$, the marginal distribution of X_2, by summing across the rows of Table 5.2, and we can obtain $F(x_2)$, the marginal cumulative distribution of X_2, by looking at the column of Table 5.3 under $X_1 = 6$. This is easily checked by cumulating the row sums of Table 5.2 and comparing the result with the rightmost column of Table 5.3. Regardless of whether the variables are discrete or continuous, we can always obtain marginal cumulative distributions from joint cumulative distributions as follows:

If $F(x_1, x_2)$ is the joint cumulative distribution of X_1 and X_2, the marginal cumulative distribution of X_1 is given by

$$G(x_1) = F(x_1, \infty) \tag{5.11}$$

and the marginal cumulative distribution of X_2 by

$$H(x_2) = F(\infty, x_2) \tag{5.12}$$

While the general expressions, (5.11) and (5.12), appear simple, they are often difficult to compute because $F(x_1, x_2)$ must first be computed from the appropriate joint frequency or density function. It is simpler to go directly from $f(x_1, x_2)$, to $g(x_1)$ and $h(x_2)$, the marginal frequency or density functions, by summing or integrating out the unwanted variable.

If X_1 and X_2 are discrete, we can begin by defining two sets:

$$a(x_1) = \{(x_1, x_2) \mid X_1 = x_1, (x_1, x_2) \in f^+\}$$
$$a(x_2) = \{(x_1, x_2) \mid X_2 = x_2, (x_1, x_2) \in f^+\}$$

Then the marginal frequency function of X_1 is given by

$$P\{X_1 = x_1\} = g(x_1) = \sum_{(x_1, x_2)\epsilon a(x_1)} f(x_1, x_2)$$

and the marginal frequency function of X_2 by

$$P\{X_2 = x_2\} = h(x_2) = \sum_{(x_1, x_2)\epsilon a(x_2)} f(x_1, x_2)$$

The tricky part is in the definition of the sets $a(x_1)$ and $a(x_2)$, as we can see by computing marginal distributions for Mrs. Burchard's problem. The joint frequency function for this problem has the general form

$$f(x_1, x_2) = \frac{n!}{(n - x_1)!\,(x_1 - x_2)!\,x_2!}\, p_1^{n-x_1} p_2^{x_1-x_2}(1 - p_1 - p_2)^{x_2},$$

$$x_1 = 0, \cdots, n \qquad x_2 = 0, \cdots, x_1$$

A sketch of the set f^+ is given by the heavy dots in Figure 5.6 for the case

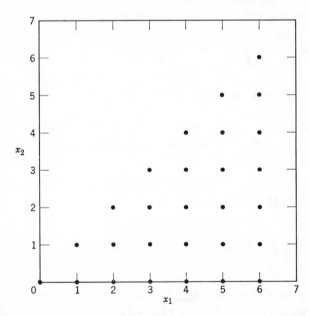

Fig. 5.6. The set f^+ for Mrs. Burchard's problem.

where $n = 6$. We have described this set by saying that X_1 takes values between $x_1 = 0$ and n and X_2 takes values between $x_2 = 0$ and x_1, but f^+ can also be described by saying that X_2 takes values between $x_2 = 0$ and n and X_1 takes values between x_2 and n or, more succinctly, by writing $x_2 = 0, \cdots, n; \; x_1 = x_2, \cdots, n$. These two ways of describing f^+ mean that we can write

$$a(x_1) = \{(x_1, 0), (x_1, 1), (x_1, 2), \cdots, (x_1, x_1)\}$$

and

$$a(x_2) = \{(x_2, x_2), (x_2 + 1, x_2), (x_2 + 2, x_2), \cdots, (n, x_2)\}$$

Now it is easy to obtain the marginals for Mrs. Burchard's problem.

$$g(x_1) = \sum_{x_2=0}^{x_1} \frac{n!}{(n - x_1)! \, (x_1 - x_2)! \, x_2!} \, p_1^{n-x_1} p_2^{x_1-x_2} (1 - p_1 - p_2)^{x_2}$$

$$= \frac{n!}{(n - x_1)! \, x_1!} \, p_1^{n-x_1} \sum_{x_2=0}^{x_1} \frac{x_1!}{(x_1 - x_2)! \, x_2!} \, p_2^{x_1-x_2} (1 - p_1 - p_2)^{x_2}$$

$$= \frac{n!}{(n - x_1)! \, x_1!} \, p_1^{n-x_1} (1 - p_1)^{x_1} \qquad x_1 = 0, \cdots, n$$

$$h(x_2) = \sum_{x_1=x_2}^{n} \frac{n!}{(n - x_1)! \, (x_1 - x_2)! \, x_2!} \, p_1^{n-x_1} p_2^{x_1-x_2} (1 - p_1 - p_2)^{x_2}$$

$$= \frac{n!}{x_2! \, (n - x_2)!} \, (1 - p_1 - p_2)^{x_2} \sum_{x_1=x_2}^{n} \frac{(n - x_2)!}{(n - x_1)! \, (x_1 - x_2)!} \, p_1^{n-x_1} p_2^{x_1-x_2}$$

In the sum, it is convenient to let $j = x_1 - x_2$. Then $x_1 = j + x_2$, and

$$h(x_2) = \frac{n!}{x_2! \, (n - x_2)!} \, (1 - p_1 - p_2)^{x_2} \sum_{j=0}^{n-x_2} \frac{(n - x_2)!}{j! \, (n - x_2 - j)!} \, p_1^{j} p_2^{n-x_2-j}$$

$$= \frac{n!}{x_2! \, (n - x_2)!} \, (1 - p_1 - p_2)^{x_2} (p_1 + p_2)^{n-x_2} \qquad x_2 = 0, \cdots, n$$

For Mrs. Burchard's problem, $n = 6$, $p_1 = 2/3$, $p_2 = 4/15$, and we have

$$g(x_1) = \frac{6!}{x_1! \, (6 - x_1)!} \left(\frac{2}{3}\right)^{x_1} \left(\frac{1}{3}\right)^{6-x_1} \qquad x_1 = 0, \cdots, 6$$

and

$$h(x_2) = \frac{6!}{x_2! \, (6 - x_2)!} \left(\frac{1}{15}\right)^{x_2} \left(\frac{14}{15}\right)^{6-x_2} \qquad x_2 = 0, \cdots, 6$$

The probability that none of her honey has begun to turn to sugar is

$$h(0) = \left(\frac{14}{15}\right)^{6} = 0.6611$$

or, roughly, two chances out of three.

In the continuous case, sums are replaced by integrals in obtaining the marginal density functions, and the integrals are taken over sets like the sets $a(x_1)$ and $a(x_2)$ in the discrete case. In the A. P. Foote Electronics example of the previous section, when X, the size of order, is fixed, Y, the total cost, can vary in the interval

$$0.1 + 0.9x \leq y < 0.1 + 1.1x$$

and

$$g(x) = \frac{1}{2.4} \int_{0.1+0.9x}^{0.1+1.1x} dy = \frac{0.2x}{2.4} = \frac{x}{12} \qquad 1 \leq x < 5$$

When total cost is held fixed, the region over which size of order can vary is most easily determined with the help of Figure 5.4. There are three cases. First, when $1.0 \leq y < 1.2$, then $1.0 \leq x < (y - 0.1)/0.9$, and

$$h(y) = \frac{1}{2.4} \int_{1.0}^{(y-0.1)/0.9} dx = \frac{y - 1}{2.4(0.9)} \qquad 1.0 \leq y < 1.2$$

Next, when $1.2 \leq y < 4.6$, then

$$\frac{y - 0.1}{1.1} \leq x < \frac{y - 0.1}{0.9}$$

and

$$h(y) = \frac{1}{2.4} \int_{(y-0.1)/1.1}^{(y-0.1)/0.9} dx = \frac{0.2(y - 0.1)}{2.4(0.99)} \qquad 1.2 \leq y < 4.6$$

Finally, when $4.6 \leq y < 5.6$, then

$$\frac{y - 0.1}{1.1} \leq x < 5$$

and

$$h(y) = \frac{1}{2.4} \int_{(y-0.1)/1.1}^{5} dx = \frac{5.6 - y}{2.4(1.1)} \qquad 4.6 \leq y < 5.6$$

Summarizing, we have

$$h(y) = \begin{cases} \dfrac{y - 1}{2.16} & 1.0 \leq y < 1.2 \\[2mm] \dfrac{y - 0.1}{11.88} & 1.2 \leq y < 4.6 \\[2mm] \dfrac{5.6 - y}{2.64} & 4.6 \leq y < 5.6 \\[2mm] 0 & \text{otherwise} \end{cases}$$

The reader should check that $h(y)$ as given above is a density function.

The Collins Metals Company provides a somewhat more straightforward illustration of the calculation of marginal density functions. Recall that the joint density function was

$$f(x, y) = 8xy \qquad 0 \le x \le 1 \qquad 0 \le y \le x$$

The limits over which $f(x, y)$ is positive could just as easily have been written as $0 \le y < 1$ and $y \le x < 1$. We can define the sets

$$a(x) = \{(x, y) \mid 0 \le y \le x\}$$

and

$$a(y) = \{(x, y) \mid y \le x \le 1\}$$

Then the marginal densities are given by

$$g(x) = 8 \int_0^x xy \, dy = 4x^3 \qquad 0 \le x \le 1$$

$$h(y) = 8 \int_y^1 xy \, dx = 4y(1 - y^2) \qquad 0 \le y \le 1$$

Here, X is the proportion of the slurry formed by ingredients A and B together, and Y is the proportion formed by A alone.

Marginal densities and distributions permit us to answer questions about one of the variables when the value of the other is either unknown or of no interest. Suppose, for example, that the management of A. P. Foote Electronics wishes to know the proportion of orders with a total cost of \$3000 or less. This can be readily computed from $h(y)$ as follows.

$$P\{Y \le 3\} = \int_{-\infty}^3 h(y) \, dy = \frac{1}{2.16} \int_{1.0}^{1.2} (y - 1) \, dy + \frac{1}{11.88} \int_{1.2}^3 (y - 0.1) \, dy$$

$$= \frac{0.02}{2.16} + \frac{3.6}{11.88} = 0.0093 + 0.3030 = 0.3123$$

Almost one-third of the orders will have a total cost of \$3000 or less.

For purposes of pollution control, it is important to the Collins Metals Company that no more than 50 percent of a given day's slurry be made up of ingredient A. When the slurry exceeds this limitation, it must be recycled. The probability that no more than 50 percent of the slurry is made up of ingredient A is

$$P\{Y \le 0.5\} = \int_{-\infty}^{0.5} h(y) \, dy = \int_0^{0.5} 4y(1 - y^2) \, dy$$

$$= [2y^2 - y^4]_0^{0.5} = 0.4375$$

Only about 44 percent of the slurrys meet pollution control specifications.

5.6   CONDITIONAL DISTRIBUTIONS

Mrs. Burchard can make a better informed guess as to the number of jars in which the honey has begun to turn to sugar if she knows how many jars are underweight. For example, if she knows that three jars are underweight, she also knows that no more than three jars can contain sugar. She can compute the probability that 0, 1, 2, or 3 jars contain sugar given that only three jars are underweight. So can we, for we learned about conditional probability in Chapter 3. We are given a condition, namely that three jars are underweight. Define the event, B, by

$$B: X_1 = 3$$

and suppose we want the probability that no jars contain sugar. Then we define the event, A, by

$$A: X_2 = 0$$

In Chapter 3 we learned

$$P(A \mid B) = \frac{P(A \cap B)}{P(B)}$$

Applying this gives

$$P\{X_2 = 0 \mid X_1 = 3\} = \frac{P\{(X_2 = 0) \cap (X_1 = 3)\}}{P\{X_1 = 3\}}$$

We can compute the necessary probabilities from Table 5.2 and the definition of marginal probability.

$$P\{(X_2 = 0) \cap (X_1 = 3)\} = 0.1124$$

$$P\{X_1 = 3\} = 0.1124 + 0.0843 + 0.0211 + 0.0018$$

$$= 0.2196$$

Hence

$$P\{X_2 = 0 \mid X_1 = 3\} = \frac{0.1124}{0.2196} = 0.5118.$$

There is a slightly better than even chance that none of Mrs. Burchard's jars contain sugar.

We could make a similar calculation for the remaining values of X_2, but it is more satisfying to produce a result that is generally useful. We define the conditional frequency function of X_2 given X_1 by

$$g_1(x_2 \mid x_1) = P\{X_2 = x_2 \mid X_1 = x_1\} = \frac{f(x_1, x_2)}{g(x_1)}$$

We must be careful in applying this, however, especially when X_1 gives information about the range of possible values for X_2. In Mrs. Burchard's case, for example, we know that X_2 cannot exceed X_1. We also know that X_2 cannot be negative. Applying the results of the previous sections to the problem in hand gives

$$g_1(x_2 \mid x_1) = \left[\frac{n!}{(n - x_1)!\,(x_1 - x_2)!\,x_2!} \, p_1^{n-x_1} p_2^{x_1-x_2}[1 - p_1 - p_2]^{x_2} \right]$$

$$\div \left[\frac{n!}{x_1!\,(n - x_1)!} \, p_1^{n-x_1}(1 - p_1)^{x_1} \right]$$

$$= \frac{x_1!}{x_2!\,(x_1 - x_2)!} \left(\frac{p_2}{1 - p_1} \right)^{x_1-x_2} \left(\frac{1 - p_1 - p_2}{1 - p_1} \right)^{x_2}$$

and we must remember that $x_2 = 0, 1, 2, \cdots, x_1$. It is clear that $g(x_2 \mid x_1)$ is a binomial frequency function, and a little manipulation will show that

$$\sum_{x_2=0}^{x_1} g_1(x_2 \mid x_1) = 1$$

Conditional frequency functions have all of the properties of ordinary frequency functions when they are properly treated. To check on our calculation when $X_2 = 0$ and $X_1 = 3$, we note that $p_1 = 2/3$ and $p_2 = 4/15$. Then

$$g_1(0 \mid 3) = \frac{3!}{0!\,3!} \left(\frac{4/15}{1/3} \right)^3 \left(\frac{1/15}{1/3} \right)^0 = \left(\frac{4}{5} \right)^3 = \frac{64}{125} = 0.5120$$

There is rounding error in Table 5.2.

If Mrs. Burchard knows the number of jars containing sugar, X_2, then she knows that the number of underweight jars, X_1, cannot be less than X_2 or greater than n, the number of jars she has bought. If she were interested, she could compute

$$h_1(x_1 \mid x_2) = \frac{f(x_1, x_2)}{h(x_2)}$$

$$= \frac{(n - x_2)!}{(n - x_1)!\,(x_1 - x_2)!} \left(\frac{p_1}{p_1 + p_2} \right)^{n-x_1} \left(\frac{p_2}{p_1 + p_2} \right)^{x_1-x_2}$$

$$x_1 = x_2, x_2 + 1, \cdots, n$$

Conditional density functions can also be calculated in the continuous case. Suppose, for example, that A. P. Foote Electronics, has an order for 4000 transistors. From the joint density of order cost and size, we know that the cost of the order must lie between \$3700 and \$4500. At a price of \$1.10 per transistor, what is the probability that A. P. Foote will break even or make a profit on this order? We want the probability that Y is less than or equal to 4.4 given that X is 4. We can calculate the conditional density of

Y given X by the same principles we used in Mrs. Burchard's problem:

$$g_1(y \mid x) = \frac{f(x, y)}{g(x)} = \frac{1}{2.4} \div \frac{x}{12} = \frac{5}{x}$$

where we must have $0.1 + 0.9x \leq y < 0.1 + 1.1x$. For us, $X = 4$, and we want

$$P\{3.7 \leq Y \leq 4.4 \mid X = 4\} = \frac{5}{4} \int_{3.7}^{4.4} dy = \frac{3.5}{4} = 0.875$$

The chief accountant at A. P. Foote is looking at a record of an order which had a total cost of \$3300 and a selling price of \$1.10 per transistor. The size of the order is not shown, and the accountant wonders if the company made a profit on the order. He knows that, provided $1 \leq x < 5$, then $0.1 + 0.9x \leq y < 0.1 + 1.1x$. Rearranging the inequality on y tells him that $3.2/1.1 < x \leq 3.2/0.9$. It is also clear that the company either broke even or made a profit if the order was for 3000 units or more. Hence, we can help the accountant by computing the probability that X was greater than or equal to 3 given that $Y = 3.3$. From the preceding section, we know that, when $1.2 \leq y < 4.6$, then

$$h(y) = \frac{y - 0.1}{11.88}$$

Here,

$$h(y) = \frac{3.2}{11.88}$$

and

$$h_1(x \mid Y = 3.3) = \frac{1}{2.4} \div \frac{3.2}{11.88} = \frac{99}{64}, \qquad \frac{32}{11} < x \leq \frac{32}{9}$$

Then

$$P\{3 < X \leq 32/9 \mid Y = 3.3\} = \frac{99}{64} \int_{3}^{32/9} dx = \left(\frac{99}{64}\right)\left(\frac{5}{9}\right)$$

$$= \frac{55}{64} = 0.859$$

There is a better than 85 percent chance that A. P. Foote made a profit on this order.

5.7 INDEPENDENCE

In the examples of the previous section, the conditional distribution of one variable depended on the other. For Mrs. Burchard, the conditional distribution of the number of jars of honey whose contents have begun to turn to sugar depends on the number of jars that were underweight; for A. P. Foote, the distribution of the cost of an order depends on the size of the order. This dependence of the conditional distribution of a variable on the conditioning variable means that we can make predictions from the conditional distribution which are in some sense "better" than predictions made from the marginal distribution. Thus, if the cost accountant at A. P. Foote doesn't know the size of the order, then all he can say about its total cost is that it will lie somewhere between $1000 and $5600. If he knows that the order is for 3000 transistors, however, he can say that the total cost will lie between $2800 and $3400, which is a considerable reduction in the range of his uncertainty. Thus, information about the size of the order is useful in making probability statements about its total cost because total cost and size of order are dependent random variables. When X and Y are dependent random variables, the conditional distribution of Y given X depends on X and is not the same as the marginal distribution of Y.

When the conditional distribution of Y given X does not depend on X, it will be the same for all values of X and, in fact, will be the same as the marginal distribution of Y. Suppose, for example, that John agrees to meet Jane at the Student Union at 2 o'clock on a Friday afternoon. Let X be the time in minutes after 2 o'clock at which John arrives, and let Y be the time in minutes after 2 o'clock at which Jane arrives, and assume that the joint density of these two random variables is

$$f(x, y) = 0.02e^{-0.2x-0.1y} \qquad 0 \le x < \infty \qquad 0 \le y < \infty$$

A little calculation will show that the marginal densities are

$$g(x) = 0.2e^{-0.2x} \qquad 0 \le x < \infty$$

and

$$h(y) = 0.1e^{-0.1y} \qquad 0 \le y < \infty$$

Further, the conditional densities are

$$g_1(y \mid x) = \frac{f(x, y)}{g(x)} = 0.1e^{-0.1y} \qquad 0 \le y < \infty$$

$$h_1(x \mid y) = \frac{f(x, y)}{h(y)} = 0.2e^{-0.2x} \qquad 0 \le x < \infty$$

The marginal densities are the same as the conditional densities, so that information about one of the variables tells us nothing about the density of the other. The two variables are independent.

Recall that, in obtaining the joint frequency function for Mrs. Burchard's problem in Section 5.2, we used the fact that

$$P\{A \cap B\} = P\{A\}P\{B \mid A\} = P\{B\}P\{A \mid B\}$$

This rule applies also to frequency and density functions, so that we can write

$$f(x, y) = g(x)g_1(y \mid x) = h(y)h_1(x \mid y)$$

If X and Y are independent, then

$$g_1(y \mid x) = h(y) \qquad \text{and} \qquad h_1(x \mid y) = g(x)$$

This gives

$$f(x, y) = g(x)h(y)$$

when X and Y are independent, their joint frequency or density function is the product of the marginals.

We now have two tests for independence: (1) the conditional frequency or density function is the same as the marginal, and (2) the joint frequency or density function is the product of the marginals. The second test is usually easier to apply than the first, and we will apply it to the example in Table 5.4 below. It is clear that the cell entries are the products of the marginal totals; hence, X and Y are independent.

Table 5.4 Joint and Marginal Frequency Functions of Two Discrete Random Variables

		x		
y	0	1	2	$g(x)$
0	1/32	1/16	1/32	1/8
1	3/32	3/16	3/32	3/8
2	3/32	3/16	3/32	3/8
3	1/32	1/16	1/32	1/8
$h(y)$	1/4	1/2	1/4	1

*5.8 THE BIVARIATE NORMAL PROBABILITY DISTRIBUTION

Much of the theory in successive chapters will be built on the assumption that the random variables on which observations are made either follow the normal probability distribution or can be transformed into variables which follow that distribution. If we are dealing with only one normally distributed random variable, then the normal distribution of Chapter 4 can be used to describe its behavior. However, if we are concerned with more than one normally distributed random variable, we modify the probability distribution of Chapter 4 to take account of the additional variables. Here, we shall consider the joint distribution of two normally distributed random variables. It is given by

$$f(x, y) = \frac{1}{2\pi\sigma_1\sigma_2\sqrt{1 - \rho^2}} \exp\left\{- \frac{1}{2(1 - \rho^2)}\left[\left(\frac{x - \mu_1}{\sigma_1}\right)^2 - 2\rho\left(\frac{x - \mu_1}{\sigma_1}\right)\right.\right.$$

$$\left.\left. \times \left(\frac{y - \mu_2}{\sigma_2}\right) + \left(\frac{y - \mu_2}{\sigma_2}\right)^2\right]\right\} \quad (5.13)$$

$$-\infty < x < \infty \qquad -\infty < y < \infty$$

The symbol "exp" stands for "exponential" and means "e raised to the power in braces." If $\sigma_1 > 0$, $\sigma_2 > 0$, and $-1 < \rho < 1$, we can show that

$$\int_{-\infty}^{\infty}\int_{-\infty}^{\infty} f(x, y)\, dy\, dx = 1$$

Since f is defined and positive for each point in R_2, it follows that $f(x, y)$ is a probability distribution.

(5.13) can be simplified considerably by making changes of the sort used to simplify the normal distribution in Chapter 4. Instead of X and Y, let us deal with

$$U = \frac{X - \mu_1}{\sigma_1} \qquad V = \frac{Y - \mu_2}{\sigma_2}$$

These new variables can be considered as special cases of X and Y, with μ_1 and μ_2 both equal to zero and σ_1 and σ_2 both equal to unity. Now, instead of (5.13), we can write

$$f(u, v) = \frac{1}{2\pi\sqrt{1 - \rho^2}} \exp\left\{- \frac{1}{2(1 - \rho^2)}(u^2 - 2\rho uv + v^2)\right\} \quad (5.14)$$

$$-\infty < u < \infty \qquad -\infty < v < \infty$$

If we look at (5.14) carefully, we can see that it is symmetric in u and v. That is, if we interchanged these two symbols, the function would not be changed. Therefore, the marginal distribution of V must be of the same form as the marginal distribution of U, and the conditional distribution of V given u must be of the same form as the conditional distribution of U given v. Hence we can get two marginal and two conditional distributions by deriving a marginal and a conditional distribution for one of the variables and then interchanging variables.

In order to derive the marginal distribution of U, we must integrate $f(u, v)$ as v goes from $-\infty$ to $+\infty$. To accomplish this, we must express the exponent in (5.14) as the product of a constant and the sum of two square terms. One of these terms should involve only u, so that we can factor out a term in u alone before we integrate. First, we "complete the square" in that part of the exponent involving u and v so as to get a term involving u alone and a term involving both u and v.

$$u^2 - 2\rho uv + v^2 = u^2 + v^2 - 2\rho uv + \rho^2 u^2 - \rho^2 u^2$$

$$= u^2(1 - \rho^2) + v^2 - 2\rho uv + \rho^2 u^2$$

$$= u^2(1 - \rho^2) + (v - \rho u)^2$$

We can write the exponent of (5.14) as

$$-\frac{1}{2(1 - \rho^2)}(u^2 - 2\rho uv + v^2) = -\frac{1}{2}u^2 - \frac{1}{2}\left(\frac{v - \rho u}{\sqrt{1 - \rho^2}}\right)^2$$

With this form of the exponent, $f(u, v)$ can be expressed as the product of two functions, one involving u alone and the other involving u and v.

$$f(u, v) = \frac{1}{\sqrt{2\pi}}e^{-u^2/2}\frac{1}{\sqrt{1 - \rho^2}\sqrt{2\pi}}e^{-[(v-\rho u)/\sqrt{1-\rho^2}]^2/2} \qquad (5.15)$$

We are now ready to obtain the marginal distribution of U by integrating out v.

$$g(u) = \int_{-\infty}^{\infty} f(u, v)\, dv$$

$$= \frac{1}{\sqrt{2\pi}}e^{-u^2/2} \cdot \frac{1}{\sqrt{2\pi}\sqrt{1 - \rho^2}}\int_{-\infty}^{\infty} e^{-[(v-\rho u)/\sqrt{1-\rho^2}]^2/2}\, dv$$

The second factor looks like the integral of the normal probability distribution with a μ of ρu and a σ of $\sqrt{1 - \rho^2}$. Since the integral is over the whole domain of such a function, it is equal to unity. Therefore

$$g(u) = \frac{1}{\sqrt{2\pi}}e^{-u^2/2} \qquad (5.16)$$

The marginal distribution of U is normal, and because of symmetry, the marginal distribution of V is also normal.

$$h(v) = \frac{1}{\sqrt{2\pi}}e^{-v^2/2} \qquad (5.17)$$

The function (5.15) is written in such a way that it is easy to divide it by $g(u)$ as given by (5.16) to obtain the conditional distribution of V given u.

$$g(v \mid u) = \frac{f(u, v)}{g(u)} = \frac{1}{\sqrt{1 - \rho^2}\sqrt{2\pi}}e^{-[(v-\rho u)/\sqrt{1-\rho^2}]^2/2} \qquad (5.18)$$

(5.18) says, given a particular value for u, V is normally distributed with a μ of ρu and a σ of $\sqrt{1 - \rho^2}$. The conditional distribution of U given v can be obtained from (5.18) simply by interchanging u and v.

$$h(u \mid v) = \frac{1}{\sqrt{1 - \rho^2}\,\sqrt{2\pi}}\, e^{-[(u-\rho v)/\sqrt{1-\rho^2}]^2/2} \tag{5.19}$$

Hence, given a particular value for v, U is normally distributed with a μ of ρv and a σ of $\sqrt{1 - \rho^2}$.

In the bivariate normal distribution the marginal and conditional distribution of both variables are normal. This means that Table E. 3 of Appendix E can be used to make marginal and conditional probability statements about random variables which have the bivariate normal distribution. We shall consider the interpretation of the constants in these distributions in Chapter 6, but it is possible to draw some general conclusions now. Equation (5.16) says that, if we know nothing about v, then U is normally distributed with a μ of zero and a σ of unity. In Chapter 4 we learned that the normal distribution reaches its maximum at μ, and that σ is a measure of its "spread." Hence, knowing nothing about V, we should say that values of U close to zero are more "likely"—that is, have a greater probability density—than values of U that are not close to zero. Suppose we consider two nonoverlapping intervals of equal width along the u axis in a sketch of $g(u)$, one interval centered on zero, the other centered on a value other than zero. The probability that U will lie in the first interval is greater than the probability that U will lie in the second. Now, suppose we are told that V is equal to some value other than zero. Since we know v, we can use (5.19), the conditional distribution of U, instead of the marginal distribution of U. The value of μ in the conditional distribution of U is ρv, $h(u \mid v)$ reaches its maximum at ρv, and values of U that are close to ρv have a higher probability density than values of U that are not. Given v, we know that a shift has occurred in the peak of the probability distribution, but we also know that the distribution has become more concentrated about its peak. In the marginal distribution of U, the value of σ is unity; in the conditional distribution, it is $\sqrt{1 - \rho^2}$. As we said, when we gave the joint distribution of X and Y, ρ must lie between -1 and $+1$ in order for $f(x, y)$ to be a probability distribution. If $-1 < \rho < 1$, then $\sqrt{1 - \rho^2} < 1$, and the dispersion of the conditional distribution of U given v is less than that of the marginal distribution of U. In the case of $\rho = 0$, $\sqrt{1 - \rho^2} = 1$, and the two dispersions will be equal.

Suppose we want to make a probability statement about the weight of a male college freshman. From a study of the health records of several thousand male college freshmen we conclude that the joint probability distribution of the height in inches, X, and the weight in pounds, Y, of a male college freshman can be approximated by (5.13) with:

$$\mu_1 = 68 \qquad \mu_2 = 150 \qquad \rho = 0.6$$

$$\sigma_1 = 2 \qquad \sigma_2 = 5$$

Now we can transform X and Y into U and V, respectively, and use the conditional and marginal distributions that we have derived. We shall let $V = (Y - 150)/5$ and $U = (X - 68)/2$. Suppose we want to determine the probability that the weight, Y, of our male freshman will be between 145 and 155 pounds. With a little arithmetic, we see that we want $P(-1 < V < 1)$. We have been told nothing about the height of this freshman, so we have to use the marginal distribution of V. This distribution has a μ of zero and a σ of 1, so we can use Table E.3 without further calculation. From this table we compute

$$P(-1 < V < 1) = 2P(0 < V < 1) = 0.68268.$$

The chances are about 68 out of 100 that a freshman of unknown height will weigh between 145 and 155 pounds.

Now, suppose that someone tells us that this particular freshman is 69 inches tall. Then

$$u = \frac{69 - 68}{2} = 0.5$$

Since we are given u, we use the distribution of V given u. This is a normal distribution with:

$$\mu = \rho u = 0.6(0.5) = 0.3$$

$$\sigma = \sqrt{1 - \rho^2} = \sqrt{1 - 0.36} = \sqrt{0.64} = 0.8$$

We can again use Table E.3 to find:

$$P(-1 < V < 1 \mid v = 0.5) = P\left(\frac{-1 - 0.3}{0.8} < Z < \frac{1 - 0.3}{0.8}\right)$$

$$= P(-1.625 < Z < 0.875)$$

$$= P(0 < Z < 1.625) + P(0 < Z < 0.875)$$

$$= 0.44738 + 0.31057 = 0.75795$$

The chances are about 76 out of 100 that a freshman who is 69 inches tall will weigh between 145 and 155 pounds. The distribution of weight of a freshman 69 inches tall reaches its maximum at a weight which makes V equal to 0.3 (0.3, remember, is the μ in $h_1(v \mid u)$). This weight is 151.5 pounds. Furthermore, about 76 percent of the conditional distribution is concentrated between 145 and 155 pounds whereas only 68 percent of the marginal distribution is concentrated within these limits. If the 10-pound interval were centered at 151.5 pounds, the proportion would be even higher (79 percent). Information about the height of our freshman has been used to increase our information about his weight. Figure 5.7 gives a sketch of the bivariate normal distribution with $\mu_1 = 68$, $\sigma_1 = 2$, $\mu_2 = 150$, $\sigma_2 = 5$, and $\rho = 0.6$ used to calculate these probabilities.

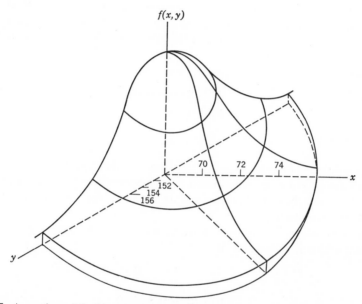

Fig. 5.7. A portion of the bivariate normal distribution used for heights and weights of college freshmen.

In the bivariate normal density, when $\rho \neq 0$ the marginal distributions of U and V are different from their conditional distributions. In a certain sense, however, a knowledge of U narrows the limits of V and a knowledge of V narrows the limits of U. In Chapter 4 we learned that the normal density function reaches its maximum value at μ. In discussing (5.18) and (5.19), we pointed out that the point at which $h_1(u \mid v)$ reaches its maximum depends on v, and the point at which $g_1(v \mid u)$ reaches its maximum depends on u. We also learned in Chapter 4 that the constant σ measures the "spread" of the normal density. When σ is small, there is a higher probability that the random variable will lie in any fixed interval centered on μ than when σ is large. When $\rho \neq 0$, the measure of spread of the conditional distribution is less than that of the marginal distribution, and it is in this sense that a knowledge of U narrows the limits of V and a knowledge of V narrows the limits of U. It is obvious that $\sqrt{1 - \rho^2}$ decreases as ρ^2 increases. Hence, we see by (5.18) and (5.19) that as ρ^2 increases, both the probability that U will lie in any fixed interval centered on ρv and the probability that V will lie in any fixed interval centered on ρu increase. Further, if ρ is positive, ρv increases as v increases and ρu increases as u increases, while, if ρ is negative, the reverse is true.

Hence, increasing the value of ρ^2 narrows the spread of $h_1(u \mid v)$ and $g_1(v \mid u)$ and, at the same time, increases the "sensitivity" of ρv to changes in v and ρu to changes in u. If we are going to use information about U to make probability statements about V or vice versa, we would like ρ^2 to be as close to unity as possible.

Suppose now that ρ is equal to zero. When we compare (5.18) with (5.17) and (5.19) with (5.16), setting $\rho = 0$, we see that

$$g_1(v \mid u) = h(v)$$

and $\qquad\qquad\qquad\qquad\qquad\qquad\qquad\qquad\qquad\qquad$ (5.20)

$$h_1(u \mid v) = g(u)$$

The conditional distributions are the same as the marginal distributions. Knowledge of V is of no help in making statements about U, and knowledge of U is of no help in making statements about V. The random variables U and V are independent.

The expressions (5.20) are consistent with what we learned about independent events in Chapter 3. If

$$P(A \mid B) = P(A) \qquad \text{and} \qquad P(B \mid A) = P(B)$$

then

$$P(A \cap B) = P(A)P(B),$$

and the events A and B are independent. Similarly, if (5.20) holds, then

$$f(u, v) = g(u)h(v)$$

and the variables U and V are independent. This equation says that, if U and V are independent, their joint distribution is equal to the product of their marginal distributions.

If ρ is equal to zero in (5.14),

$$f(u, v) = \frac{1}{2\pi} e^{-(u^2+v^2)/2} = \frac{1}{\sqrt{2\pi}} e^{-u^2/2} \cdot \frac{1}{\sqrt{2\pi}} e^{-v^2/2}$$

We have factored $f(u, v)$ into a product of two normal distributions, one involving only u and the other involving only v. Hence, when ρ is equal to zero in (5.14), U and V are independent. We have already seen that this means that knowledge about one variable is of no help in making probability statements about the other.

IMPORTANT TERMS AND CONCEPTS

Function
  Joint
  Multivariate
  Cumulative
  Density
  Frequency
Probability distribution
  Conditional
  Of two random variables
    Normal random variables
  Joint
  Marginal
  Multivariate

Variables
  Dependent
  Independent
  Interdependent

SYMBOLS AND ABBREVIATIONS

$F(x_1, \cdots, x_r)$

$f(x_1, \cdots, x_r)$

$f(x, y)$

$g_1(y \mid x)$

$h_1(x \mid y)$

ρ

ρ^2

OFTEN-USED FORMULAS

$$g(x) = \sum_y f(x, y) \quad \text{or} \quad g(x) = \int_y f(x, y)\, dy$$

$$h(y) = \sum_x f(x, y) \quad \text{or} \quad h(y) = \int_x f(x, y)\, dx$$

$$g_1(y \mid x) = \frac{f(x, y)}{g(x)} \; ; \quad h_1(x \mid y) = \frac{f(x, y)}{h(y)}$$

$$f(x, y) = g(x)g_1(y \mid x) = h(y)h_1(x \mid y)$$

For independence, $f(x, y) = g(x)h(y)$

$$f(x, y) = \frac{1}{2\pi\sigma_1\sigma_2\sqrt{1 - \rho^2}} \exp\left\{-\frac{1}{2(1 - \rho^2)} \left[\left(\frac{x - \mu_1}{\sigma_1}\right)^2 - 2\rho\left(\frac{x - \mu_1}{\sigma_1}\right)\right.\right.$$

$$\left.\left. \times \left(\frac{y - \mu_2}{\sigma_2}\right) + \left(\frac{y - \mu_2}{\sigma_2}\right)^2\right]\right\}$$

$$-\infty < x < \infty, \qquad -\infty < y < \infty$$

EXERCISES

1. In the general case, what conditions are necessary for any function to qualify as a probability distribution?

2. Given the probability distribution

$$f(x, y) = 1 \qquad 0 < x < 1 \qquad 0 < y < 1$$

find the following probabilities:

a. $P(X \leq 1/2)$ d. $P(X - Y > 0)$

b. $P(Y = 3/4)$ e. $P[(X < Y) \cup (Y > 1/2)]$

c. $P(X = Y)$

3. Consider the function

$$f(x, y) = ke^{-(2x+2y)} \qquad 0 \leq x < \infty \qquad 0 \leq y < \infty$$

a. Determine k so that the function really is a probability distribution. [*Hint.* Integrate $f(x, y)$ and then set k equal to the reciprocal of your result.]

b. Find $P(Y = 1)$.

c. Find $P(Y \leq 2)$.

d. Find $P(X > Y)$.

4. Two dice are rolled twice. Let X be the number of times that no ones occur, and let Y be the number of times that no twos occur. What is the probability that both X and Y are less than two?

5. Six cards are drawn at random from a standard deck. What is the probability that the number of black cards equals the number of red cards drawn? What is the probability that the number of diamonds exceeds the number of clubs?

6. Given the probability distribution

$$f(x, y) = 3x \qquad 0 < y < x \qquad 0 < x < 1$$

   a. Find $P(Y < 1/2)$.
   b. Find $P[(X < 1/2) \cap (Y < 1/2)]$.
   c. Determine the marginal distribution of X.
   d. Determine the conditional distribution of X given Y.

7. For the conditional probability distribution

$$g_1(y \mid x) = \binom{x}{y} \left(\frac{1}{10}\right)^y \left(\frac{9}{10}\right)^{x-y} \qquad y = 0, 1, \cdots, x$$

   calculate $g_1(3 \mid 10)$.

8. Prove that if the joint distribution of X_1 and X_2 is a bivariate normal probability distribution with parameters μ_1, μ_2, σ_1, σ_2, and ρ, then

$$Y_1 = \frac{X_1 - \mu_1}{\sigma_1} \qquad \text{and} \qquad Y_2 = \frac{X_2 - \mu_2}{\sigma_2}$$

   are also jointly distributed as a bivariate normal distribution with $\mu_1' = \mu_2' = 0$, $\sigma_1' = \sigma_2' = 1$, and the same correlation coefficient ρ.

9. A certain target area is rectangular in shape, being ten miles long in a north-south line and six miles wide in an east-west direction. Suppose that a high-speed missile is directed toward the exact center of the area. If X_1 and X_2 represent the deviation from center of point of impact, respectively in a northerly and an easterly direction, and if X_1 and X_2 are jointly independently normally distributed with $\mu_1 = \mu_2 = 0$, $\sigma_1 = 20$ miles, and $\sigma_2 = 3$ miles, calculate the probability that the missile hits the target area.

10. Given:

$$f(x, y) = \binom{5}{x} \left(\frac{1}{2}\right)^5 \binom{x}{y} \left(\frac{1}{4}\right)^y \left(\frac{3}{4}\right)^{x-y} \qquad x = 0, 1, 2, 3, 4, 5$$

$$y = 0, \cdots, x$$

   and

$$h(y) = \binom{5}{y} \left(\frac{1}{8}\right)^y \left(\frac{7}{8}\right)^{5-y} \qquad y = 0, 1, 2, 3, 4, 5$$

   a. Prove that

$$h_1(x \mid y) = \binom{5-y}{x-y} \left(\frac{3}{7}\right)^{x-y} \left(\frac{4}{7}\right)^{5-x} \qquad x = y, y + 1, \cdots, 5$$

   b. Are X and Y independent in this instance? Justify your answer.

11. Given the following joint probability distribution:

y x	0	1	2
0	0	$\dfrac{1}{12}$	$\dfrac{2}{12}$
1	$\dfrac{1}{12}$	$\dfrac{2}{12}$	0
2	$\dfrac{2}{12}$	0	$\dfrac{4}{12}$

a. Determine $g(x)$ and $h(y)$, the marginal probability distributions.
b. Determine $h_1(x \mid y)$ for each of the possible values of Y.
c. Are X and Y independent? Justify your answer.

12. Given the following joint probability distribution:

y x	2	3	4
1	$\dfrac{1}{18}$	0	$\dfrac{2}{18}$
2	$\dfrac{3}{18}$	0	$\dfrac{4}{18}$
3	$\dfrac{3}{18}$	0	$\dfrac{5}{18}$

a. Determine $g_1(y \mid x)$ for each of the possible values of X.
b. Now determine $h(y)$, the marginal distribution of Y.
c. Are X and Y independent? Justify your answer.

13. Given the function

$$f(x, y) = k(x + y) \qquad 0 < x < 4$$
$$0 < y < 6$$

a. Find the value of k for which $f(x, y)$ is a probability distribution.
b. What is the range of $f(x, y)$?
c. Derive an expression for:

    (1) $g(x)$ (3) $g_1(y \mid x)$
    (2) $h(y)$ (4) $F(x, y)$

    Be sure to specify the domains for each of these probability distributions.
d. Are X and Y independent? Justify your answer.
e. What is the probability that X and Y are both less than 3?

14. The joint probability distribution of X_1 and X_2 is:

$$f(x_1, x_2) = 20e^{-(4x_1 + 5x_2)} \qquad x_1 > 0, \quad x_2 > 0$$

Find an expression for:
a. $g(x_1)$
b. $h(x_2)$
c. $g_1(x_2 \mid x_1)$
d. $h_1(x_1 \mid x_2)$
e. $F(x_1, x_2)$
f. Are X_1 and X_2 independent? How can you tell?

15. Using your answers to Exercise 14 calculate:
a. $P(X_1 > 1)$
b. $P(X_2 < 2 \mid X_1 > 8)$
c. $P(X_1 \leq 1 \text{ and } X_2 \leq 2)$
d. $P(X_1 = 7 \text{ and } X_2 > 3)$

16. Given the following function:

$$f(x, y) = \frac{xy}{70} \qquad 2 \leq x \leq 3$$
$$5 < y < 9$$

a. Prove that this is a probability distribution.
b. What is the range of this function?
c. Derive an expression for the following, specifying the domains in each case.

    (1) $g(x)$ (3) $h_1(x \mid y)$
    (2) $h(y)$ (4) $F(x, y)$
d. Are X and Y independent? Justify your answer.

e. Calculate the following probabilities:

(1) $P(X < 2.6$ and $Y < 7)$ (5) $P(X \leq 2.7 \mid Y < 6)$

(2) $P(X < 3$ and $Y < 8)$ (6) $P(X > 2.4$ and $Y < 6)$

(3) $P(Y > 4)$ (7) $P(X > 2.4$ or $Y < 6)$

(4) $P(Y > 7)$

17. This year an auditing procedure for a certain company randomly selects 5 out of 20 junior accountants. For each person chosen, 8 of his entries are selected at random for intense scrutiny. Unknown to the auditors or the company, Mr. Spencer, one of the 20, has been embezzling funds. One percent of Mr. Spencer's entries have been used in the embezzlement and, since he is not careful in his cover-up, he is certain to be detected if any of these entries are selected for study.

    a. What is the probability that this year's audit in the accounting department will lead to a detection of embezzling by Mr. Spencer, given that he was one of the 5 chosen for study?

    b. What is the probability that this year's audit in the accounting department will fail to detect the embezzling by Mr. Spencer?

    c. Explain the probability model that you used to answer parts *a* and *b*. Be sure to spell out any assumptions you made that are not specifically stated above.

18. A perfect tetrahedron has faces numbered 1, 2, 3, and 4. Tossing a 4 occurs when the face marked 4 is facing down—in this sense, down is up! The tetrahedron is rolled, and X, the number facing down, is recorded. Then five perfect coins are tossed, and Y, the number of heads obtained, is recorded and multiplied by the X from the tetrahedron roll. This product XY is thus the outcome of the experiment. Define and determine:

    a. $g(x)$ d. $g(y \mid x)$

    b. $h(y)$ e. $h(x \mid y)$

    c. $f(x, y)$

19. Referring to Exercise 18:

    a. What is the probability of an outcome of 20 in one trial of this experiment?

    b. What is the probability of an outcome of zero?

    c. What is the probability of either a 3 or a 4 from the tetrahedron and either 3 or 4 heads?

    d. What is the probability of 5 heads?

    e. What is the probability of 5 heads given that a 3 occurred on the toss of the tetrahedron?

    f. Are X and Y independent?

    g. What is the probability of an outcome of 4?

20. The household department of the Jonas Department Store receives an average of five calls during its first five minutes of operation (from 9:00 to 9:05 A.M.), Monday through Friday. A Poisson probability model adequately approximates the random variable "number of calls" during this period. On the average, three out of every four calls received result in telephone orders being placed.
    a. What is the probability that on a particular morning exactly three orders result from seven calls?
    b. To what probability distribution did you refer in your answer above? Can you formulate a general probability distribution that will give the probability of X orders from Y incoming calls?

21. There is a severe air pollution problem in the city of Bronchus, Ohio. Recent studies have shown that the daily concentrations of both sulfur dioxide and nitrogen dioxide are very high although, strangely enough, one appears to be independent of the other. Let X and Y be, respectively, the daily concentrations of sulfur dioxide and nitrogen dioxide measured in micrograms per cubic meter. It has been found that the joint distribution of X and Y is approximately a bivariate normal distribution with parameters $\mu_X = 400$, $\mu_Y = 200$, $\sigma_X = 20$, and $\sigma_Y = 20$. What is the probability that on a day chosen at random the concentrations of both pollutants are more than ten percent above their average values?

6 Descriptive Measures of Probability Distributions

6.1 INTRODUCTION

Statistical methods are extremely useful in making decisions in the face of uncertainty. Prior experience, judgment, observation, and statistical theory are combined to predict the outcomes of alternative decisions. Then one may choose that decision whose predicted outcome is best from some point of view. This is by no means as sophisticated as it sounds. To take a classic example, consider the problem of whether or not to carry an umbrella.

The proper decision would be to carry an umbrella if it rains and not to carry one if it does not rain. Unfortunately, life is not always this simple. If it rains and we do not carry an umbrella, we shall be wet and uncomfortable, we shall spoil the crease in our trousers, and we might even catch cold. On the other hand, if it does not rain and we carry an umbrella, we might look a little silly, although this depends on our attitude toward such things. So we listen to a weather forecast, and take a look at the sky in order to form our own judgment about the probability of rain. This judgment usually will not have a number attached to it. It will take a form such as, "It definitely will rain," "It probably will rain," "It might or it might not rain," "It probably won't rain," or "It definitely won't rain," We combine the probability judgment with our feelings about being rained upon when we do not have an umbrella versus carrying an umbrella when it does not rain, and make our decision. This is exactly the procedure described in the first paragraph, and we use it in some form or other almost every day of our lives.

Consider the problem of a store manager who must decide how much inventory to carry. He must balance the costs of carrying too much inventory against the costs of carrying too little. If he carries too much, he has unnecessary funds tied up, and the items may deteriorate. If he carries too little inventory, he loses profits on the items he could have sold if he had them in stock, and he may lose customers to competitors with larger inventories.

What constitutes too much or too little inventory depends primarily on demand, which is usually uncertain.[1] The best the manager can do is to base his decision on a prediction of demand. In order to make this prediction, he must know something about the use to which it will be put and something about the probability distribution of demand. The form of the prediction depends on the use made of it. If only one inventory decision is to be made on the basis of the prediction, its form may be different from the form used if a sequence of decisions is required.

The probability distribution of demand determines the numerical magnitude of this prediction and the confidence placed in it. The predicted value should lie in that part of the domain over which the distribution takes on nonzero values. Preferably, values of the random variable which are close to the predicted value should have a higher probability than values far removed. This does not imply that the predicted value should be the most probable value of the random variable or the value at which the probability distribution reaches its maximum. As we have already pointed out, the method for choosing the predicted value depends on the use to be made of the prediction.

If the probability of a particular value of the random variable is unity and the probabilities of all other values are zero, we could then predict that demand would be equal to the first value and be certain that our prediction would come true. On the other hand, if the probability distribution has a rectangular shape over a large part of its domain and takes on zero values over all other parts, then any value of demand whose probability is not zero is as likely to occur as any other such value. Under these circumstances, we might be at a loss as to what demand to predict and would not have much confidence in the prediction. These extreme cases indicate that both the magnitude of the prediction and our confidence in it depend on the way in which the probability distribution is concentrated over parts of its domain. For this reason, we need to develop measures which describe certain properties of probability distributions.

What properties of the distribution do we wish to describe? We should indicate the order of magnitude of the random variable in that part of the domain for which the probability distribution is nonzero. We have several choices open to us. One of these, called the *mode*, is the value of the random variable which maximizes the probability distribution. If the random variable is discrete, then this value is the most probable; if the random variable is continuous, then this value has the greatest probability density. Many

---

[1] Optimum inventory may also depend on the future behavior of prices. If the manager anticipates a future rise in the price of the goods he is selling, he may increase present inventories to take advantage of the lower price at present. Similarly, an anticipated fall in future prices may lead to a reduction in present inventories. In this simple discussion, we shall ignore the complications introduced by uncertain factors other than demand.

distributions are not symmetric, however, so that values of the random variable on one side of the mode are likelier than values on the other. Hence, a sequence of predictions based on the mode may consistently tend to overestimate or underestimate the value of the random variable which actually occurs.

To avoid this difficulty, we could indicate order of magnitude by the value of the random variable which is as likely to overpredict as it is to underpredict. This value is called the *median*. The value of the random variable which actually occurs is as likely to lie above the median as below the median.[2] The median is one of the simplest and most useful measures in statistics.

Both the mode and the median are based only on probabilities. If our measure of order of magnitude is to take into account all possible values of the random variable *and* their probabilities, it becomes less easy in concept and in interpretation. One possible procedure is to multiply each possible value of the random variable by its probability and either add or integrate the result over the domain of the probability distribution. The result is called the *expected value*, the *mean*, or more familiarly, the average. The surprising thing about the arithmetic mean is its popularity, since it does not have an easy interpretation. Yet all students enter a course in statistics knowing how to compute the average of a set of numbers, and we are bombarded daily with averages—usually uninterpreted—in our newspapers.

In addition to describing the order of magnitude of the random variable— or *central tendency* of the distribution, as we shall call it—we also want to describe the variability of the random variable. This measure of variability will provide a measure of the confidence that we can put in any prediction of the random variable. These measures are of two general types, one based on the difference between two particular values of the random variable and one based on the differences between all possible values of the random variable and some measure of central tendency. Finally, we may want to describe the general shape of the distribution by describing the degree of asymmetry of the distribution and the "sharpness" of its highest peak. These properties can be described in many ways, but the commonest is by means of a set of measurements called *moments*, which describe the central tendency, variability, asymmetry, peakedness and many other aspects of a distribution. We shall consider moments in some detail later.

A knowledge of one variable is often useful in predicting another. In the A. P. Foote electronics problem of Chapter 5, for example, the management can make a better prediction of the cost of an order if the size of the order is known than otherwise. Since the range of variation of the conditional

---

[2] If the random variable is discrete, this is usually only approximately true.

distribution of Y given X is much less than that of the marginal distribution of Y, there is less uncertainty about Y when X is known than when X is unknown. In such a case, the conditional distribution should be used to predict Y.

Finally, we must recognize that in most practical situations the probability distributions of the variables with which we are dealing are unknown. Often, fortunately, our problem requires only one or two descriptive measures; at times, however, good approximations to the actual distributions may be needed. In either case, we must replace probability distributions and their descriptive measures by approximations based on observations of the random variables in question. Statisticians call such observations "data." In later chapters we shall consider methods for obtaining "good" approximations to descriptive measures. In this chapter we shall consider the computation of descriptive measures for data as well as a method for grouping data into classes so as to approximate the shape of the underlying probability distribution.

6.2 MEASURES OF CENTRAL TENDENCY

Let us now consider the three most important measures of central tendency: the mode, the median, and the arithmetic mean. Suppose that X is a random variable representing 1967 income after taxes of 18 X-ray technicians employed at the Consolidated City Clinics. The probability distribution of X in dollars is contained in the following table:

x	\$4600	4900	5000	5100	5200	5500
$f(x)$	$\dfrac{1}{18}$	$\dfrac{2}{18}$	$\dfrac{4}{18}$	$\dfrac{7}{18}$	$\dfrac{3}{18}$	$\dfrac{1}{18}$

The table was constructed from the actual incomes after taxes of the 18 girls. One earned \$4600, two \$4900, etc.

The mode of the random variable is the value at which $f(x)$ has its maximum. Here \$5100 is the mode of X, since 7/18 is the greatest of the probabilities.

The median is the halfway point, that is, the value of X which divides the total probability into two equal parts (or into two parts as nearly equal as possible). It is most conveniently found from the cumulative probability distribution, $F(x)$.

x	\$4600	4900	5000	5100	5200	5500
$F(x)$	$\dfrac{1}{18}$	$\dfrac{3}{18}$	$\dfrac{7}{18}$	$\dfrac{14}{18}$	$\dfrac{17}{18}$	$\dfrac{18}{18}$

To find the median, answer this question: For which of the possible values of X does $F(x)$ first equal or exceed $1/2$? Here, the value $5100 is the desired median.

The arithmetic mean $E(X)$—which we shall usually call the mean—is obtained by multiplying each possible value of X by its probability of occurrence and totaling these products. Here

$$E(X) = 4600 \frac{1}{18} + 4900 \frac{2}{18} + 5000 \frac{4}{18} + 5100 \frac{7}{18} + 5200 \frac{3}{18} + 5500 \frac{1}{18}$$

$$= \frac{4600 + 9800 + 20{,}000 + 35{,}700 + 15{,}600 + 5500}{18} = \$5067$$

Note that carrying this division out to dollars but not cents implies that the original salary figures were given correct to dollar accuracy only.

Now let us obtain these same basic measures in a case where the probability distribution is continuous. The only differences which arise are due to the replacement of arithmetical procedures by those of calculus.

Suppose that a study of several years duration has been made of the daily percentage of factory workers at the A. J. Romberg Manufacturing Company who are absent during the months of January, February, and March. Empirical studies have shown that the daily percentage of absentees is nicely described by the following distribution:

$$f(x) = \begin{cases} 0.1x & 0 < x \le 2 \\ 0.025(10 - x) & 2 < x \le 10 \end{cases}$$

The function is shown graphically in Figure 6.1. It is easy to check that $f(x)$ is a probability distribution by computing the area of the right triangles over the intervals $0 < x \le 2$ and $2 < x \le 10$. The area of the first is 0.2, and the area of the second is 0.8. The sum of the areas is unity. Also, $f(x)$ is defined for all x and is never negative.

We can find the mode, Mo, by inspection. Since $f(x)$ reaches its maximum at $x = 2$, $Mo = 2$ percent absentees. Ordinarily, to find the maximum or

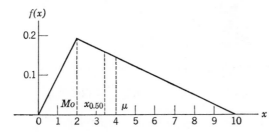

Fig. 6.1. Daily percentage of absentees x.

minimum of a continuous function, we differentiate it, set the derivative equal to zero, and solve the resulting equation for x. This procedure will find only relative maxima and minima, however. The equation $f'(x) = 0$ may have several roots, some at maxima, others at minima, and still others in neighborhoods over which $f(x)$ is "flat." Furthermore, to be successful the procedure requires that $f'(x)$ be continuous at the point at which $f(x)$ reaches its maximum. For our function, $f'(x)$ is not continuous at $x = 2$. We can see, however, that $f(2) \geq f(x)$ for all x.

The median in the continuous case divides the area under the curve into two equal parts. Because the area of the right triangle over the interval $0 < x \leq 2$ is only 0.2, we can conclude that the median of this particular distribution must lie in the interval $2 < x \leq 10$. The area to the right of any point in this interval is the area of a right triangle. Suppose that the point $x_{0.50}$ in Figure 6.1 is the median of the distribution. The base of the triangle over the interval $x_{0.50} < x \leq 10$ is $10 - x_{0.50}$. The altitude is given by

$$f(x_{0.50}) = 0.025(10 - x_{0.50})$$

The area of this triangle must be 0.50, hence

$$\tfrac{1}{2} 0.025(10 - x_{0.50})(10 - x_{0.50}) = 0.50$$

or

$$(10 - x_{0.50})^2 = 40$$

$$(10 - x_{0.50}) = \pm\sqrt{40} = \pm 6.32$$

This last equation has two roots, $x_{0.50} = 3.48$ and $x_{0.50} = 16.32$. Since 16.32 lies outside that part of the domain over which $f(x)$ takes on positive values, we conclude that $x_{0.50} = 3.48$ percent absentees. We also could have found the median by solving the equation:

$$0.5 = \int_{-\infty}^{x_{0.50}} f(x)\, dx = \int_{0}^{2} 0.1x\, dx + \int_{2}^{x_{0.50}} 0.025(10 - x)\, dx$$

$$= 0.2 + 0.025 \left(10x - \frac{x^2}{2} \right)_{2}^{x_{0.50}}$$

$$0.5 = 0.25x_{0.50} - 0.0125x_{0.50}^2 - 0.25$$

When we rearrange this equation, we reduce the problem to that of solving

$$0.0125[x_{0.50}^2 - 20x_{0.50} + 60] = 0.$$

The roots of this equation are those found previously.

$$x_{0.50} = 10 \pm \sqrt{40}$$

Finally, the mean, $E(X)$, is found by

$$E(X) = \int_{-\infty}^{\infty} xf(x)\, dx$$

Here

$$E(X) = \int_{0}^{2} x \cdot 0.1x\, dx + \int_{2}^{10} x \cdot 0.025(10 - x)\, dx$$

$$= 0.1 \int_{0}^{2} x^2 dx + 0.025 \int_{2}^{10} (10x - x^2)\, dx$$

$$= 0.025\left[\left(4\frac{x^3}{3}\right)_{0}^{2} + \left(10\frac{x^2}{2} - \frac{x^3}{3}\right)_{2}^{10} \right]$$

$$= 0.025\left[\frac{32}{3} + \frac{500}{3} - \frac{52}{3} \right] = 4$$

The average daily absentee rate is 4 percent. The mode, the median, and the mean of the distribution lie within two percentage points of each other. The fact that the three measures of central tendency lie fairly near one another indicates that the distribution does have a meaningful "central tendency."

6.3 FURTHER DISCUSSION OF CENTRAL TENDENCY

A study made by a statistical consultant to the manager of a supermarket has shown that the number of customers X entering the market between 9 and 10 A.M. on Thursday morning has approximately the Poisson distribution with $\lambda = 10$. This implies that

$$g(x) = \frac{e^{-10}10^x}{x!} \qquad x = 0, 1, 2, \cdots$$

The same study showed that ten percent of the customers bought Ice Crop frozen foods. If we assume that decisions by customers to buy Ice Crop frozen foods are made independently and with a constant probability of purchase, then, conditional on X customers entering the store on Thursday morning, the number Y buying Ice Crop has the binomial distribution

$$g_1(y \mid x) = P(Y = y \mid X = x) = \binom{x}{y}(0.1)^y(0.9)^{x-y} \qquad y = 0, 1, \cdots, x$$

Combining these two distributions gives

$$f(x, y) = e^{-10}\frac{10^x}{x!}\binom{x}{y}(0.1)^y(0.9)^{x-y}$$

$$x = 0, 1, 2, \cdots \qquad y = 0, 1, \cdots, x \quad (6.1)$$

We leave it to the reader to satisfy himself that the marginal distribution of Y and the conditional distribution of X given Y are respectively

$$h(y) = \frac{e^{-1}}{y!} \qquad y = 0, 1, \cdots \tag{6.2}$$

$$h_1(x \mid y) = e^{-9} \frac{9^{x-y}}{(x-y)!} \qquad x = y, y+1, y+2, \cdots \tag{6.3}$$

Suppose that the manager wants to predict Y, the sales of Ice Crop frozen foods. Making this prediction well ahead of time, he has no knowledge of X, the number of customers entering the store. Therefore, he must base his prediction on (6.2), the marginal distribution of Y.

Let us assume, first, that he has made a bet with the district manager that he can predict the sales of Ice Crop frozen foods "on the nose" during the time period in question. No matter what the stakes, the manager wants to maximize the probability that he will win the bet. Therefore, he should predict the mode: that value of Y which maximizes (6.2). To avoid ambiguity, we shall assume that if more than one value of Y maximizes (6.2) the manager will predict the smallest. Since (6.2) is a special case of the Poisson probability distribution, the most efficient thing for us to do is to solve the problem for any Poisson distribution and apply the solution to (6.2) or any similar problem.

The general form of the Poisson distribution is

$$f(y) = e^{-\lambda} \frac{\lambda^y}{y!} \qquad y = 0, 1, 2, \cdots \tag{6.4}$$

If y_p, ("p" for "predicted"), is the smallest value of y which maximizes (6.4), then

$$f(y_p) > f(y_p - 1) \tag{6.5}$$

and

$$f(y_p) \geq f(y_p + 1) \tag{6.6}$$

Substituting (6.4) into (6.5),

$$e^{-\lambda} \frac{\lambda^{y_p}}{y_p!} > e^{-\lambda} \frac{\lambda^{y_p-1}}{(y_p - 1)!}$$

Since all quantities are positive, we can divide the inequality by $e^{-\lambda}\lambda^{y_p-1}$ and then multiply it by $y_p!$ Since $y_p! = y_p(y_p - 1)!$, we get

$$y_p < \lambda \tag{6.7}$$

By substituting (6.4) into (6.6) and performing the same kind of manipulations,

$$y_p \geq \lambda - 1 \tag{6.8}$$

Combining (6.7) and (6.8) gives

$$\lambda - 1 \leq y_p < \lambda$$

This combined inequality says that, if λ is an integer, then the best prediction (in the sense of the mode) is $\lambda - 1$. If λ is not an integer, then the best prediction is the largest integer which is less than λ. In our problem, $\lambda = 1$ so that the best prediction is $y_p = 0$. In Table 6.1 we have computed the first few values of $h(y)$ as given by (6.2). This table shows that $y = 0$ is the *smallest* value of y that maximizes (6.2), although $y = 1$ gives the same ordinate. Thus, in this case, $h(y)$ has two modes, 0 and 1. Since they are adjacent, we do not make much of the fact that $h(y)$ has two modes. If they were separated by intervening values of Y for which $h(y)$ was not zero, we would say that $h(y)$ was bimodal and seek the reasons for this.

Table 6.1 Values of $h(y) = e^{-1}(1/y!)$, for $y = 0, 1, 2, \cdots, 7$

y	$f(y)$	y	$f(y)$
0	0.3679	4	0.0153
1	0.3679	5	0.0031
2	0.1839	6	0.0005
3	0.0613	7	0.0001

To summarize with regard to the mode, we give the following definition.

Definition I. If X is a random variable and $f(x)$ is its probability distribution, the values of X which maximize $f(x)$ are called the *modes* of $f(x)$.

Before considering other measures of central tendency, let us consider the stakes in the bet between the store manager and the district manager. What stakes would make the bet "fair?" The first question is: What do we mean by "fair?" Suppose that the two managers have a standing bet; that is, they make the same bet every time (6.2) describes the probabilistic behavior of the sales of Ice Crop frozen foods. Table 6.1 shows that, in the long run, if the store manager persistently bet on zero, he would win about 37 per cent of the time and the district manager would win about 63 percent. A "fair" bet is one that equalizes the long-run winnings of each bettor. Suppose the store manager wins $\$W$ if he predicts correctly and loses $\$L$ if he predicts incorrectly. Then, over a large number of bets, he can expect to win $\$(0.3679W - 0.6321L)$ per bet on the average. The only quantity which is its own negative is zero. Hence, to make the bet "fair":

$$0.3679W - 0.6321L = 0$$

or

$$W = 1.718L$$

That is, if the store manager pays the district manager $1 when he loses, then the district manager should pay the store manager $1.72 when the store manager wins. The bet is slightly favorable to the store manager because of rounding.

In the language of statistics, a "fair" bet equalizes the "expected" winnings of each bettor. The store manager's winnings are a random variable; hence, they have a probability distribution. If the bets are as described, and we designate the value of the random variable by W,

$$f(W) = \begin{cases} 0.3679, & W = +\$1.72 \\ 0.6321, & W = -\$1.00 \end{cases} \tag{6.9}$$

The expected value of a random variable is defined as follows.

Definition II. If X is a random variable and $f(x)$ is its probability distribution, then the *expected value* of X is denoted by $E(X)$ and given by

$$E(X) = \sum_{x=-\infty}^{\infty} xf(x) \tag{6.10}$$

if X is discrete, and by

$$E(X) = \int_{-\infty}^{\infty} xf(x)\,dx \tag{6.11}$$

if X is continuous.

The expected value of X need not exist, but such cases will hardly ever occur in this book. The expected value of X is also called the *arithmetic mean* of the distribution, popularly known as the *average*. We have simply been calling it the *mean* and will continue to do so.

When we apply (6.10) to (6.9) and note that $f(W)$ is zero for all values of W except $1.72 and $-$1.00, we have

$$E(W) = \sum_{W=-\infty}^{\infty} Wf(W) = (\$1.72)(0.3679) + (-\$1.00)(0.6321) = +\$0.000688$$

Over 100 bets, the store manager can expect to win about seven cents. This is about as close to "fair" as we can get without making the bets considerably larger. We shall consider the expected values of other random variables throughout this chapter.

Next, suppose the manager wants to decide how many avocados to put on his produce shelves. Avocados are delivered daily from the warehouse, and any avocados that are left over at the end of the day are sold at a loss. (To keep matters simple, we shall assume that all left-over avocados can be sold.) Suppose that a profit of P is made on each avocado sold during the day and that a loss of L is incurred on each left over. Each day the manager must place an order for the next day's supply. He wants to find an ordering policy that maximizes his expected daily profit. If he orders A avocados and the demand is X, his profit, $Pr(A)$, is

and
$$Pr(A) = \begin{cases} Px - L(A - x) & \text{if} \quad x < A \\ \\ PA & \text{if} \quad x \geq A \end{cases} \tag{6.12}$$

The profit is a function of x, and X is a random variable. Any function of a random variable is itself a random variable. It has a probability distribution and, usually, an expected value. The manager wants to choose A, the number of avocados that he orders, so as to maximize the expected value of a function of a random variable. This is defined as follows.

Definition III.   If X is a random variable with probability distribution $f(x)$, and $g(X)$ is any function of X, then the expected value of $g(X)$ is denoted by $E[g(X)]$ and given by

$$E[g(X)] = \sum_{x=-\infty}^{\infty} g(x)f(x) \tag{6.13}$$

if X is discrete, and by

$$E[g(X)] = \int_{-\infty}^{\infty} g(x)f(x)\,dx \tag{6.14}$$

if X is continuous. $E[g(X)]$ need not exist.

There are three properties of expected values that will prove useful later. These are

$$E[c] = c$$
$$E[cg(X)] = cE[g(X)] \tag{6.15}$$
$$E[g_1(X) + g_2(X)] = E[g_1(X)] + E[g_2(X)]$$

In words, the expected value of a constant is that constant; the expected value of a constant times a function of X is the constant times the expected value of the function; and the expected value of the sum of two functions is the sum of the two expected values. We shall prove these three properties for discrete random variables; proofs are similar in the continuous case.

$$E[c] = \sum_x cf(x) = c \sum_x f(x) = c$$
$$E[cg(X)] = \sum_x cg(x)f(x) = c \sum_x g(x)f(x) = cE[g(X)]$$
$$E[g_1(X) + g_2(X)] = \sum_x [g_1(x) + g_2(x)]f(x)$$
$$= \sum_x g_1(x)f(x) + \sum_x g_2(x)f(x) = E[g_1(X)] + E[g_2(X)]$$

Now let $f(x)$ be the probability distribution of X, the daily demand for avocados. We can find the expected profit from (6.11). The manager wishes to maximize $E[Pr(A)]$

$$E[Pr(A)] = \sum_{x=0}^{A-1} [Px - L(A - x)]f(x) + \sum_{x=A}^{\infty} PAf(x)$$

$$= (P + L) \sum_{x=0}^{A-1} xf(x) - LA \sum_{x=0}^{A-1} f(x) + PA\left[1 - \sum_{x=0}^{A-1} f(x)\right]$$

$$= (P + L) \sum_{x=0}^{A-1} xf(x) - (P + L) \sum_{x=0}^{A-1} Af(x) + PA$$

$$= (P + L) \sum_{x=0}^{A-1} (x - A)f(x) + PA \tag{6.16}$$

Because he does not want to carry more stock than is necessary, he wishes to find the *smallest* value of A that maximizes (6.16). This means that he wants to find A such that

$$E[Pr(A)] > E[Pr(A - 1)]$$

and $\tag{6.17}$

$$E[Pr(A)] \geq E[Pr(A + 1)]$$

Now since the difference $E[Pr(A)] - E[Pr(A - 1)]$ is given by

$$E[Pr(A)] - E[Pr(A - 1)] = (P + L) \sum_{x=0}^{A-1} (x - A)f(x) + PA$$

$$- (P + L) \sum_{x=0}^{A-2} (x - A + 1)f(x) - P(A - 1)$$

$$= (P + L) \sum_{x=0}^{A-2} (x - A - x + A - 1)f(x)$$

$$+ (P + L)(-1)f(A - 1) + P$$

$$= P - (P + L) \sum_{x=0}^{A-1} f(x)$$

$$= P - (P + L)F(A - 1)$$

where $F(x)$ is the cumulative probability distribution of the random variable X, we may write

$$E[Pr(A - 1)] = E[Pr(A)] + (P + L)F(A - 1) - P \tag{6.18}$$

When we substitute $A + 1$ for A in (6.18) and rearrange terms,

$$E[Pr(A + 1)] = E[Pr(A)] - (P + L)F(A) + P \tag{6.19}$$

The conditions on A are given by (6.17). Substituting (6.18) into the first inequality of (6.17)

$$E[Pr(A)] > E[Pr(A)] + (P + L)F(A - 1) - P$$

which implies

$$F(A - 1) < \frac{P}{P + L}$$

Similarly, when we substitute (6.19) into the second inequality of (6.17),

$$\frac{P}{P + L} \leq F(A)$$

We can combine these results to get the condition that must hold if A is the smallest number that maximizes $E[Pr(A)]$.

$$F(A - 1) < \frac{P}{P + L} \leq F(A) \tag{6.20}$$

This condition, (6.20), is not as complicated as it appears. We must compute the ratio, $P/(P + L)$, and cumulate $f(x)$ until $F(x)$ either equals or exceeds the computed ratio. When this occurs, we stop cumulating. The value of X at which we have stopped is the required value of A. To illustrate: suppose that P is 20¢, $L = 10$¢, and that demand has the Poisson distribution with $\lambda = 5$. First, we compute the ratio

$$\frac{P}{P + L} = \frac{20}{30} = 0.6667$$

Then we write down $f(x)$ and begin cumulating. We stop as soon as the cumulated sum either equals or exceeds 0.6667. The value of X at which we stop is the required value of A. The calculations are carried out in Table 6.2. In this table, we continue to cumulate beyond the point at which we should stop so that we can calculate the expected daily profits shown in the last column. These are calculated by computing $E[Pr(0)]$ from (6.16) and then using (6.19). From the table, we see that the manager should order six avocados daily in order to maximize expected daily profits.

The solution is illustrated graphically in Figure 6.2. We have made the probability of meeting the demand roughly proportional to the profit per item sold and the probability of not meeting the demand roughly proportional to the loss per unsold item. As the profit per item sold increases relative to the loss per item left unsold, the optimum number of items to order increases, while, as the loss per item left unsold increases relative to the profit per item sold, the optimum number of items to order decreases. Our manipulations

Table 6.2 Probability Distribution and Cumulative Probability Distribution of Daily Demand for Avocados and Expected Daily Profit for Various Quantities Ordered

Daily Demand x	Probability Distribution $f(x)$	Cumulative Distribution $F(x)$	Expected Daily Profit if X Avocados Are Ordered $E[Pr(X)]$
0	0.0067	0.0067	0.000 ¢
1	0.0337	0.0404	19.799
2	0.0842	0.1246	38.587
3	0.1404	0.2650	54.849
4	0.1755	0.4405	66.899
5	0.1755	0.6160	73.368
6	0.1462	0.7622 (Stop!)	75.204 (Maximum)
7	0.1044	0.8666	72.338
8	0.0653	0.9319	66.340
9	0.0363	0.9682	58.383
10	0.0181	0.9863	49.337
11	0.0082	0.9945	39.748
12	0.0034	0.9979	29.913
13	0.0013	0.9992	19.976
14	0.0005	0.9997	10.000
15	0.0002	0.9999	−29.991

have led to an ordering policy which seems to make sense; if they had not, we should have to check our assumptions.

If we were to determine the optimum order quantity for fuel oil, gasoline, or some other divisible commodity, X would be a continuous random variable, and $F(x)$ would be a smooth curve instead of a step function. In this case, we could make the right hand inequality in (6.20) hold as an equality. The probability of meeting demand would be precisely equal to the ratio $P/(P + L)$. The optimum order quantity would divide the area under the probability distribution into two parts, $100 P/(P + L)$ percent of the area lying to the left of the optimum order quantity and $100 L/(P + L)$ percent lying to its right.

Values of the random variable that divide the area under the probability distribution in such a way that a given proportion of the area lies to the left of the dividing line are called *quantiles*. These quantities are given descriptive names. Thus, 60 percent of the area under the probability distribution lies to the left of the third quintile (or sixtieth percentile), and 25 percent of the area lies to the left of the first quartile (or twenty-fifth percentile). Quantiles are often used as descriptive measures of probability distributions. In particular, the median, or fiftieth percentile, is often used as a measure of central tendency.

If the random variable is continuous, any quantile can be computed at least in principle. When the variable is discrete, however, as it is in the case of the demand for avocados, we must be careful. A glance at the cumulated distribution given in Table 6.2 is enough to show that there is no value of X such that 50 percent of the time the demand will be less than or equal to x and 50 percent of the time the demand will be greater than x. The best we can say is that about 62 percent of the time the demand will be less than or equal to five avocados and about 44 percent of the time the demand will be

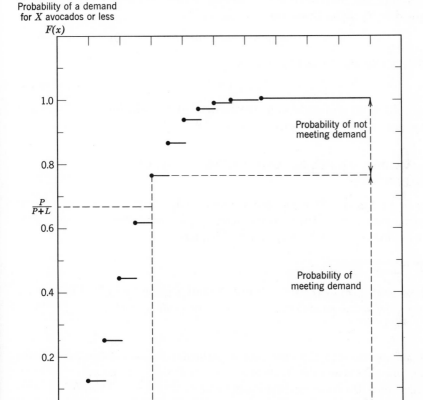

Fig. 6.2. Graphic solution of inventory problem.

less than or equal to four. It is tempting to interpolate linearly, as we do in a table of logarithms, and say that 50 percent of the time the demand will be less than or equal to 4.339 avocados. This is meaningless and misleading. The cumulative probability distribution is a step function and is equal to 0.4405 for any value of X equal to or greater than four and less than five. Hence, the probability that demand will be less than or equal to 4.339 avocados is the same as the probability that demand will be less than or equal to four. Most probability distributions of discrete random variables do not have medians in the strict sense. If we allow for this, we can define the median as follows.

Definition IV. If X is a random variable and $F(x)$ is its cumulative probability distribution, then the median of the probability distribution is denoted by $x_{0.50}$ and defined by

$$x_{0.50} = \text{minimum}(x \text{ such that } F(x) \geq 0.50) \tag{6.21}$$

If X is continuous, it will be true that

$$F(x_{0.50}) = 0.50 \tag{6.22}$$

According to this definition, the median of the distribution of demand for avocados is five avocados.

6.4 MODES, MEDIANS, AND MEANS OF SPECIAL DISTRIBUTIONS

Sections 6.2 and 6.3 introduced the most important measures of central tendency. We now review these measures by computing them for a number of distributions that will be used in later chapters.

The Poisson Distribution

The general form of the Poisson distribution is given by (6.4), and we have already derived a general rule for finding the *mode*, namely,

$$\lambda - 1 \leq Mo < \lambda$$

All we need to find the mode for a particular Poisson distribution is the value of λ. If λ is an integer, there are two modes, $\lambda - 1$ and λ; if λ is not an integer, then Mo is the smallest integer greater than $\lambda - 1$. Table 6.3 presents $f(x)$, $F(x)$, and $xf(x)$ for a Poisson distribution for which $\lambda = 7.3$. According to the rule, Mo should be 7 because that is the smallest integer greater than $7.3 - 1 = 6.3$. Table 6.3 shows that the mode is indeed 7.

Unless a simple formula is available for $F(x)$, the *median* must be found by cumulating $f(x)$ and applying Definition IV. If X is a continuous random

Table 6.3 Calculation of the Mode, Median, and Mean of a Poisson Distribution with $\lambda = 7.3$

x	$f(x)$	$F(x)$	$xf(x)$	x	$f(x)$	$F(x)$	$xf(x)$
0	0.0007	0.0007	0.0000	11	0.0531	0.9319	0.5841
1	0.0049	0.0056	0.0049	12	0.0323	0.9642	0.3876
2	0.0180	0.0236	0.0360	13	0.0181	0.9823	0.2353
3	0.0438	0.0674	0.1314	14	0.0095	0.9918	0.1330
4	0.0799	0.1473	0.3196	15	0.0046	0.9964	0.0690
5	0.1167	0.2640	0.5835	16	0.0021	0.9985	0.0336
6	0.1420	0.4060	0.8520	17	0.0009	0.9994	0.0153
7	0.1481	0.5541	1.0367	18	0.0004	0.9998	0.0072
8	0.1351	0.6892	1.0808	19	0.0001	0.9999	0.0019
9	0.1096	0.7988	0.9864	20	0.0001	1.0000	0.0020
10	0.0800	0.8788	0.8000				
					Total		7.3003

variable, the median may be approximated graphically by drawing $F(x)$ and reading off the value of X for which $F(x) = 1/2$. The calculation of the median for a Poisson distribution which has $\lambda = 7.3$ is illustrated in Table 6.3. Applying Definition IV, we see that $F(6) < 0.50 < F(7)$. Hence, the median is 7.

We can, however, derive a formula for the *expected value* (mean). Applying Definition II to the Poisson probability distribution,

$$E(X) = \sum_{x=0}^{\infty} xe^{-\lambda} \frac{\lambda^x}{x!}$$

$$= 0 \cdot e^{-\lambda} + 1 \cdot e^{-\lambda} \frac{\lambda^1}{1!} + 2 \cdot e^{-\lambda} \frac{\lambda^2}{2!} + 3 \cdot e^{-\lambda} \frac{\lambda^3}{3!} + \cdots$$

$$= e^{-\lambda} \left[\lambda + \frac{\lambda^2}{1!} + \frac{\lambda^3}{2!} + \frac{\lambda^4}{3!} + \cdots \right]$$

$$= e^{-\lambda} \lambda \left[1 + \frac{\lambda^1}{1!} + \frac{\lambda^2}{2!} + \frac{\lambda^3}{3!} + \cdots \right]$$

Now, we have previously used the McLaurin series expansion of e^x.

$$1 + \frac{x^1}{1!} + \frac{x^2}{2!} + \frac{x^3}{3!} + \cdots = e^x$$

Therefore

$$1 + \frac{\lambda^1}{1!} + \frac{\lambda^2}{2!} + \frac{\lambda^3}{3!} + \cdots = e^\lambda$$

and

$$E(X) = e^{-\lambda}\lambda e^\lambda = \lambda$$

The constant, λ, of the Poisson distribution is the expected value of X. For the Poisson distribution used for illustration in Table 6.3, $E(x) = 7.3 = \lambda$. This is calculated from the definition of expected value by computing $xf(x)$ and adding. The difference between the value 7.3 and the calculated value of $E(X)$ is due to rounding.

The Binomial Distribution

Suppose that the manager of our supermarket wants to predict the number of customers buying Ice Crop frozen foods when he knows that 20 customers have entered the store. Since he knows x, he can use the conditional distribution of Y. This is the binomial distribution given at the beginning of Section 6.3. Our results will be more useful if we consider the general binomial distribution

$$f(x) = \binom{n}{x} p^x (1-p)^{n-x} \qquad x = 0, \cdots, n \tag{6.23}$$

We can then use the results in any special case once we know the values of n and p.

According to Definition I, the mode maximizes $f(x)$. Since X is discrete, we must deal in inequalities, namely,

$$f(Mo) \geq f(Mo + 1)$$
$$f(Mo) > f(Mo - 1) \tag{6.24}$$

When we substitute (6.23) into the first inequality of (6.24), we obtain

$$\frac{n!}{(Mo)!\,(n - Mo)!} p^{Mo}(1 - p)^{n-Mo}$$
$$\geq \frac{n!}{(Mo + 1)!\,(n - Mo - 1)!} p^{Mo+1}(1 - p)^{n-Mo-1}$$

Many things cancel; we can then reduce the inequality to

$$\frac{1-p}{n-Mo} \geq \frac{p}{Mo+1}$$

We now solve the inequality for Mo. Since all quantities are nonnegative, we can cross multiply to clear fractions. The rest of the algebra is left to the reader. When completed,

$$Mo \geq (n + 1)p - 1$$

By substituting (6.23) into the second inequality in (6.24), we obtain, through a similar process,

$$Mo < (n + 1)p$$

We can combine these to locate Mo in an interval.

$$(n + 1)p - 1 \leq Mo < (n + 1)p \tag{6.25}$$

Once we know n and p we can find the mode—or modes—of any binomial distribution. If $(n + 1)p$ is not an integer, then Mo is the integer which lies between $(n + 1)p - 1$ and $(n + 1)p$. If $(n + 1)p$ is an integer, then the distribution has two adjacent modes, $(n + 1)p - 1$ and $(n + 1)p$. In the supermarket problem, see Section 6.3, p is 0.1 and x plays the role of n. Since x is 20, $(n + 1)p = (20 + 1)(0.1) = 2.1$. The inequality (6.25) says, in this case,

$$1.1 \leq Mo < 2.1$$

The only integer lying in this interval is 2. Thus, when 20 customers have entered the store, the most probable number buying Ice Crop frozen foods is 2. This may be seen in Table 6.4, in which we also show the calculations required to obtain the median and the expected value. The work in this table has been carried to five decimal places, and a value of 0.00000 for $f(x)$ indicates that $f(x)$ is very small, but not zero.

Table 6.4 Calculation of the Mode, Median, and Mean of a Binomial Distribution with $n = 20$ and $p = 0.10$

x	$f(x)$	$F(x)$	$xf(x)$	x	$f(x)$	$F(x)$	$xf(x)$
0	0.12158	0.12158	0.00000	11	0.00000	1.00000	0.00000
1	0.27017	0.39175	0.27017	12	0.00000	1.00000	0.00000
2	0.28518	0.67693	0.57036	13	0.00000	1.00000	0.00000
3	0.19011	0.86704	0.57033	14	0.00000	1.00000	0.00000
4	0.08978	0.95682	0.35912	15	0.00000	1.00000	0.00000
5	0.03192	0.98874	0.15960	16	0.00000	1.00000	0.00000
6	0.00887	0.99761	0.05322	17	0.00000	1.00000	0.00000
7	0.00197	0.99958	0.01379	18	0.00000	1.00000	0.00000
8	0.00036	0.99994	0.00288	19	0.00000	1.00000	0.00000
9	0.00005	0.99999	0.00045	20	0.00000	1.00000	0.00000
10	0.00001	1.00000	0.00010				
					Total		2.00002

As in the case of the Poisson distribution, there is no simple formula for the median. It must be calculated by cumulating $f(x)$ until $F(x)$ equals or exceeds 0.50000. When we apply Definition IV to the binomial distribution in Table 6.4, we see that the median is 2. A strict interpretation of the result would be: when 20 customers enter the store, 68 percent of the time, two or fewer buy Ice Crop frozen foods and 32 percent of the time three or more buy Ice Crop frozen foods.

By applying Definition II to the binomial distribution in (6.23),

$$E(X) = \sum_{x=0}^{n} xf(x) = \sum_{x=0}^{n} x \frac{n!}{x!\,(n-x)!} p^x (1-p)^{n-x}$$

$$= np \sum_{x=1}^{n} \frac{(n-1)!}{(x-1)!\,(n-x)!} p^{x-1} (1-p)^{n-x}$$

The last summation is from one to n because the first term in the preceding summation is zero. Now, as x advances from 1 to n, $x-1$ goes from zero to $n-1$. This suggests the following substitutions

$$z = x - 1 \qquad m = n - 1$$

giving

$$E(X) = np \sum_{z=0}^{m} \frac{m!}{z!\,(m-z)!} p^z (1-p)^{m-z} = np \qquad (6.26)$$

The summation in (6.26) adds up all the terms of a binomial distribution with m instead of n and z instead of x. Hence the sum is unity. $E(X)$, remember, is called the expected value of X. In (6.26) we see why this name makes sense in the case of the binomial distribution. This distribution applies when we perform n identical independent experiments and, in each experiment, the probability of one of the two outcomes is p. In such a situation, the statement, "I expect the particular outcome to occur np times in n independent trials" has some meaning. Thus, if we toss a "true" coin ten times, we might say, "I expect five heads." This does not mean that we expect exactly five heads. It means that, if we tossed the coin a very large number of times, recording H when heads occurred and T when tails occurred, and broke our record down into groups of 10 tosses each, the average number of heads per group of ten tosses would be very close to five. For the binomial distribution of Table 6.4, $np = 20(0.1) = 2.0$. The difference between $np = 2.0$ and $\sum xf(x) = 2.00002$ is due to the rounding error.

The Exponential Distribution

Under fairly plausible assumptions about the behavior of clerks at super-market check-out counters, it is possible to show that the time, T (in minutes), that a customer spends at a check-out counter is a random variable with the probability distribution:

$$f(t) = ce^{-ct} \qquad 0 \le t < \infty, \qquad c > 0$$

It turns out that the parameter c is equal to the average number of customers a clerk can serve in a minute. We shall see that the average time that a customer spends at a check-out counter is $1/c$. This is called the average service time. The function $f(t)$ is called a "service time" distribution.

Since the parameter, c, is positive, when $t > 0, f(t)$ decreases as t increases. Hence, $f(t)$ reaches its maximum at $t = 0$. According to Definition I, then, the mode of $f(t)$ is zero.

The formula for the cumulative exponential distribution, $F(t)$, is quite simple. It is

$$F(t) = c \int_0^t e^{-cx} \, dx = 1 - e^{-ct}$$

We find the median service time by setting $F(t_{0.50})$ equal to 0.5 and solving for $t_{0.50}$. Thus

$$1 - e^{-ct_{0.50}} = 0.5$$

or

$$e^{-ct_{0.50}} = 1 - 0.5 = 0.5$$

Taking logarithms (to the base 10) of both sides yields

$$-ct_{0.50} \log_{10} e = \log_{10} 0.5 = 9.69897 - 10 = -0.30103$$

$t_{0.50}$ is then found by dividing both sides of the above expression by $-c \log_{10} e$

$$t_{0.50} = \frac{-0.30103}{-c \log_{10} e} = \frac{0.30103}{c(0.43429)} = (0.69315) \cdot \frac{1}{c}$$

Finally, to find the mean of the distribution, we compute

$$E(T) = \int_{-\infty}^{\infty} tf(t) \, dt = c \int_0^{\infty} te^{-ct} \, dt$$

The integral can be evaluated by parts.[3] Let $u = t$ and $dv = e^{-ct} \, dt$. Then $du = dt$ and $v = -e^{-ct}/c$. Then

$$E(T) = c \left[\left(-te^{-ct}/c \right)_0^{\infty} + \frac{1}{c} \int_0^{\infty} e^{-ct} \, dt \right]$$

$$= c \left[(-0 + 0) + \frac{1}{c^2}(-0 + 1) \right] = \frac{1}{c}$$

---

[3] See any standard calculus text.

Before interpreting our results, let us assume that for the supermarket, $c = 1/3$. In this case,

$$Mo = 0$$

$$t_{0.50} = (0.69315)\frac{1}{1/3} = (0.69315) \cdot 3 = 2.07945 \text{ minutes}$$

$$E(T) = \frac{1}{c} = \frac{1}{1/3} = 3 \text{ minutes}$$

The mode is zero. This does not mean that more customers will have zero service time than any other; it means that zero is the service time with the greatest probability density. If $h > 0$ and $t_0 > 0$, then, in this case, $Mo = 0$ implies that

$$P\{0 < T < h\} > P\{t_0 < T < t_0 + h\}$$

The median is about 2.1 minutes. Therefore we conclude that one-half of the customers will have a service time of 2.1 minutes or less and that one-half of the customers will have a service time of more than 2.1 minutes. The average service time is 3 minutes. In our earlier discussion we showed that during a certain time period the average number of customers entering the store was 10 per hour. If there is one check-out counter open, it will take the clerk an average of 3 minutes per customer to pass customers through the check-out counter. Hence, during this time period, the clerk must spend 30 minutes per hour on the average in checking. On the average, then, he can spend 30 minutes in performing other duties.

The Normal Distribution

Strictly speaking, situations in which the normal distribution applies are rare. The domain of the function stretches from $-\infty$ to $+\infty$, and it is difficult to conceive of many random variables that vary over such a wide range. There are numerous situations, however, where the normal distribution gives an excellent approximation to the distribution of a random variable with a more limited range. Because the normal distribution has been extensively tabulated and is fairly easy to handle mathematically, it is often used as an approximation to more complicated probability distributions. Loosely speaking, we require that the distribution be roughly symmetrical about its mode and approach zero rather rapidly as the random variable departs in either direction from the mode. The normal distribution is an excellent approximation to the binomial distribution, for example, when p is one-half and n is large—as will be shown in Chapter 7.

The normal distribution is

$$f(x) = \frac{1}{\sigma\sqrt{2\pi}} e^{-(x-\mu)^2/2\sigma^2} \qquad -\infty < x < \infty$$

It is continuous over its entire domain. When we differentiate $f(x)$ with respect to x, we obtain

$$f'(x) = -\frac{1}{\sigma}\left(\frac{x-\mu}{\sigma}\right)f(x)$$

Thus $f'(x)$ is continuous over the entire domain of the function. Since $f(x)$ is always positive, $f'(x)$ is positive when x is less than μ and negative when x is greater than μ. Hence, $f(x)$ increases as x approaches μ from either the right or the left, and we can conclude that

$$f(\mu) > f(x)$$

for all x in the domain of $f(x)$. The mode of the normal distribution, therefore, is μ. Notice that $x = \mu$ is the only root of $f'(x) = 0$.

That the median of the normal probability distribution is also μ is most easily seen by noting that $f(x)$ is symmetrical about $x = \mu$. Suppose $x_1 = \mu + y$ and $x_2 = \mu - y$. Then

$$|x_1 - \mu| = |x_2 - \mu| = |y|$$

that is, x_1 and x_2 are equidistant from μ and on opposite sides of μ. Then

$$f(x_1) = f(x_2) = \frac{1}{\sigma\sqrt{2\pi}} e^{-y^2/2\sigma^2}$$

This is true for any two points, x_1 and x_2 that are equidistant from μ but on opposite sides of μ. If we were to draw a sketch of $f(x)$, one-half of the area under the curve would lie to the left of μ. We can write

$$F(\mu) = \int_{-\infty}^{\mu} f(x)\,dx = 0.5$$

According to Definition IV, the median of the normal probability distribution must be μ.

Having discovered that the mode and the median of the normal probability distribution are both equal to μ, we are not going to be too surprised to learn that the mean of the distribution is also μ.

$$E(X) = \frac{1}{\sigma\sqrt{2\pi}} \int_{-\infty}^{\infty} x e^{-(x-\mu)^2/2\sigma^2}\,dx$$

Let $z = (x - \mu)/\sigma$. Then $x = \sigma z + \mu$ and $dx = \sigma\,dz$. Substituting

$$E(X) = \frac{1}{\sqrt{2\pi}} \int_{-\infty}^{\infty} (\sigma z + \mu) e^{-z^2/2}\,dz$$

$$= \frac{\sigma}{\sqrt{2\pi}} \int_{-\infty}^{\infty} z e^{-z^2/2}\,dz + \frac{\mu}{\sqrt{2\pi}} \int_{-\infty}^{\infty} e^{-z^2/2}\,dz$$

Write the first integral as

$$\int_{-\infty}^{\infty} ze^{-z^2/2}\, dz = \int_{-\infty}^{0} ze^{-z^2/2}\, dz + \int_{0}^{\infty} ze^{-z^2/2}\, dz$$

Since $e^{-z^2/2}$ is positive, the expressions under the integral signs will be positive when z is positive and negative when z is negative. For every positive value of z in the second integral on the right, there will be a corresponding negative value of z in the first integral. Hence

$$\int_{-\infty}^{0} ze^{-z^2/2}\, dz = -\int_{0}^{\infty} ze^{-z^2/2}\, dz$$

and

$$\int_{-\infty}^{\infty} ze^{-z^2/2}\, dz = 0$$

The expression for $E(X)$ now becomes

$$E(X) = \mu \cdot \frac{1}{\sqrt{2\pi}} \int_{-\infty}^{\infty} e^{-z^2/2}\, dz = \mu(1) = \mu$$

To summarize: *for the normal probability distribution, the mode, the median, and the mean are numerically the same.* Conceptually, of course, they are much different.

6.5   MEASURES OF DISPERSION

As has been pointed out in the introduction to this chapter, there are two general methods of measuring dispersion. One method is based on the difference between two quantiles, while the other is based on the expected value of some function of the difference between the random variable and a measure of central tendency. The method used depends on the purpose of the measurement.

Any prediction of a random variable should take account of the probabilistic nature of the prediction. One way of doing this is to predict that the random variable may take any one of several values and to state the probability that it will do so. This most usually implies finding the difference between two quantiles and stating the associated probability. As an example, we shall compute the interquartile range of an exponential distribution. This statistic is the measure of dispersion found by subtracting the first quartile of a probability distribution from the third quartile. The probability that a value of the random variable will lie in this interval is 0.5. Any two quantiles can be used to form a measure of dispersion in this way, however, the interquartile range is the most common of these statistics.

Consider the supermarket service time distribution discussed in Section 6.4. For $c = 1/3$ this distribution is

$$f(t) = \frac{1}{3} e^{-t/3} \qquad 0 \leq t < \infty$$

From our earlier work with this distribution, we know that

$$F(t) = 0 \qquad\qquad -\infty < t < 0$$
$$F(t) = 1 - e^{-t/3} \qquad 0 \leq t < \infty$$

In finding t_p, the pth percentile, we use the same method that we used to find the median

$$1 - e^{-(1/3)t_p} = p$$
$$1 - p = e^{-(1/3)t_p}$$

$$\log_{10}(1 - p) = -\frac{1}{3} t_p \log_{10} e$$

$$t_p = \frac{-3 \log_{10}(1 - p)}{\log_{10} e} = \frac{-3 \log_{10}(1 - p)}{0.43429}$$

For $100p_1 = 25$ percent and $100p_2 = 75$ percent, we have

$$t_{0.25} = \frac{-3 \log_{10} 0.75}{0.43429} = \frac{-3(-0.12494)}{0.43429} = 0.86 \text{ minutes}$$

$$t_{0.75} = \frac{-3 \log_{10} 0.25}{0.43429} = \frac{-3(-0.60206)}{0.43429} = 4.16 \text{ minutes}$$

Thus the interquartile range of the service time distribution is $4.16 - 0.86 = 3.30$ minutes, and the probability is 0.5 that a value of the random variable will lie there. Interquartile ranges for discrete random variables can be found approximately by the same methods.

A prediction that states the probability that the random variable will lie in an interval provides both a measure of the variability of the variable and the degree of confidence that can be placed in the prediction. As a measure of dispersion, however, the width of the interval has its shortcomings. First the probability content of the interval can be chosen arbitrarily so that, by judicious choice of interval, conflicting impressions of dispersion can sometimes be conveyed. Second, the measure is based on the difference between two values of the random variable, and the contribution of other values to dispersion is ignored. Two distributions which differ markedly in their "tails" can have the same interquartile range, for example. What is needed is a measure of dispersion which considers every possible value of the random variable and assigns to each its proper probability "weight." Such a measure might be based on the average difference between the random variable and some measure of central tendency.

Suppose that we decide to use as a measure of dispersion the expected value of the difference between the random variable and its expected value. Let us call this measure δ.

$$\delta = E[X - E(X)]$$

For simplicity, let us assume that X is discrete and has probability distribution $f(x)$. Then

$$\delta = \sum_{x=-\infty}^{\infty} [x - E(X)]f(x)$$

$$= \sum_{x=-\infty}^{\infty} xf(x) - E(X) \sum_{x=-\infty}^{\infty} f(x)$$

$E(X)$ is a constant and can be factored out of the summation. According to Definition II, the first summation on the right is precisely $E(X)$. The second summation is unity by the definition of $f(x)$ as a probability distribution. This gives

$$\delta = E(X) - E(X) = 0$$

A measure of dispersion that is always equal to zero is not very informative, so we had better revise it. When x is less than $E(X)$, the quantity $x - E(X)$ will be negative, and when x is greater than $E(X)$, it will be positive. These positive and negative values cancel in the averaging process. We can avoid this difficulty by seeing to it that we average only nonnegative quantities. There are two easy ways to do this. One way is to ignore the sign of $x - E(X)$, calling all differences positive. That is, we average the absolute values of $x - E(X)$. We denote absolute value by vertical lines, thus

$$|x| = \begin{cases} x & x \geq 0 \\ -x & x < 0 \end{cases}$$

Hence, the absolute value is always nonnegative. The other way of being sure that we average only nonnegative quantities is to square $x - E(X)$ before averaging. We shall consider each of these devices in turn.

In a preceding section, we arrived at three measures of central tendency by considering three problems in prediction. Each measure can be shown to minimize the expected cost of error in prediction where the cost of error is measured in a certain way. If the cost of error is zero if we predict correctly and a fixed amount if we are wrong, no matter what the magnitude of the error is, we minimize the expected cost of error by predicting the mode. If the cost of error is proportional to the absolute value of the error, we minimize the expected cost of error by predicting the median. Finally, if the cost of error is proportional to the square of the error, we minimize the expected cost of error by predicting the mean. Hence, the expected value of $|X - x_{0.50}|$ is a measure of the cost of error if the median is the best prediction, and the expected value of $[X - E(X)]^2$ is a measure of the cost of error if the mean is the best prediction. If we measure dispersion by absolute differences, we should take them from the median; if we measure dispersion by squared differences, we should take them from the mean.

In an inventory problem, if the penalty for a shortage of a given amount is the same as the penalty for an overage of the same amount and is proportional to the amount over or short, then the optimum size of inventory is the median of the probability distribution of demand. The expected cost of stocking this amount will be proportional to the expected value of the absolute deviation from the median. This expected value is called the *mean deviation from the median.*

Definition V.   If X is a random variable with probability distribution $f(x)$, the mean deviation from the median is denoted by the symbol M.D. and given by

$$\text{M.D.} = \sum_{x=-\infty}^{\infty} |x - x_{0.50}| \, f(x) \qquad \text{if } X \text{ is discrete}$$

$$\text{M.D.} = \int_{x=-\infty}^{\infty} |x - x_{0.50}| \, f(x) \, dx \quad \text{if } X \text{ is continuous}$$

(6.27)

The mean deviations of probability distributions of continuous random variables are often difficult to compute, but for discrete random variables the computation follows directly from the definition. Table 6.5 illustrates the calculation of the mean deviation of the probability distribution of demand for avocados. The median of this distribution, remember, is five avocados. The mean deviation from the median is 1.75 avocados. For the distribution of number of customers buying Ice Crop foods the mean deviation is approximately 0.74. Should we conclude that the distribution of demand for avocados has a greater dispersion than the number of customers buying Ice Crop frozen foods? Not unless in some sense we are willing to equate one avocado with one customer. If we divide each mean deviation by its median and multiply by 100, we find that the mean deviation of the demand for avocados is 35 percent of the median while the mean deviation of the number of customers buying Ice Crop is 74 percent of the median. The distribution of the number of customers buying Ice Crop has relatively greater dispersion.

As we have suggested, another way of making sure that we average only nonnegative quantities when measuring dispersion is to square the deviations before averaging them. A measure of dispersion based on squared deviations

Table 6.5 Calculation of Mean Deviation from the Median of the Probability Distribution of Table 6.2

Daily Demand x	Absolute Deviation from Median $\lvert x - 5 \rvert$	Probability Distribution $f(x)$	$\lvert x - 5 \rvert f(x)$
0	5	0.0067	0.0335
1	4	0.0337	0.1348
2	3	0.0842	0.2526
3	2	0.1404	0.2808
4	1	0.1755	0.1755
5	0	0.1755	0.0000
6	1	0.1462	0.1462
7	2	0.1044	0.2088
8	3	0.0653	0.1959
9	4	0.0363	0.1452
10	5	0.0181	0.0905
11	6	0.0082	0.0492
12	7	0.0034	0.0238
13	8	0.0013	0.0104
14	9	0.0005	0.0045
15	10	0.0002	0.0020
16	11	0.0001	0.0011
17	12	0.0000	0.0000
Total		1.0000	1.7548

from the expected value is appropriate when the expected value of the distribution is the best measure of central tendency to use. The expected value of the squared deviation from the mean of the probability distribution is called the *variance* of the distribution.

Definition VI. If X is a random variable with probability distribution $f(x)$, the variance of $f(x)$ is denoted by the symbol σ^2 and given by

$$\sigma^2 = \sum_{x=-\infty}^{\infty} [x - E(X)]^2 f(x)$$

if X is discrete, and by

$$\sigma^2 = \int_{-\infty}^{\infty} [x - E(X)]^2 f(x)\, dx$$

If X is continuous.

To avoid ambiguity, we shall sometimes use the notation $\sigma^2(X)$ or $\sigma_X{}^2$ to indicate the variance of $f(x)$ and $\sigma^2(Y \mid x)$ to indicate the variance of $f(y \mid x)$.

Computable formulas for the variance can be derived for the most important distributions in statistics such as the binomial, Poisson, exponential, and normal distributions. Because of the extensive use of the mean as a measure of central tendency—and for other reasons—the variance is the most commonly used measure of dispersion.

Statistics has been called the study of variation. If measurable quantities did not vary unpredictably because of error in measurement and variations in environmental conditions, there would be no need for either a theory of probability or a science of statistics. Hence, the variance is one of the most important measures in statistics.

Before we proceed to the next section, let us compute the variances of the two simple distributions given in Section 6.2. For the X-ray technicians we found a mean of $5067 based on the following distribution:

x	$4600	4900	5000	5100	5200	5500
$f(x)$	$\dfrac{1}{18}$	$\dfrac{2}{18}$	$\dfrac{4}{18}$	$\dfrac{7}{18}$	$\dfrac{3}{18}$	$\dfrac{1}{18}$

For the variance of 1967 income after taxes we compute:

$$\sigma^2 = (4600 - 5067)^2 \frac{1}{18} + (4900 - 5067)^2 \frac{2}{18} + (5000 - 5067)^2 \frac{4}{18}$$

$$+ (5100 - 5067)^2 \frac{7}{18} + (5200 - 5067)^2 \frac{3}{18} + (5500 - 5067)^2 \frac{1}{18}$$

$$= \frac{218{,}089 \cdot 1 + 27{,}889 \cdot 2 + 4489 \cdot 4 + 1089 \cdot 7 + 17{,}689 \cdot 3 + 187{,}489 \cdot 1}{18}$$

$$= \frac{540{,}002}{18} = 30{,}000$$

Two points should be made. First, since the dollar differences were squared, the variance is not expressed in dollars. Second, the computations are somewhat lengthy, even in so tiny a problem as this one. A better method of computation will be forthcoming in the next section.

For the distribution of daily absentee rates at the A. J. Romberg Manufacturing Company, recall that

$$f(x) = \begin{cases} 0.1x & 0 < x \le 2 \\ 0.025(10 - x) & 2 < x \le 10 \\ 0 & \text{other values} \end{cases}$$

and that $E(X) = 4$. We want to compute:

$$\sigma^2 = E\{(X - 4)^2\} = E\{(X^2 - 8X + 16)\}$$

$$= \int_{-\infty}^{\infty} (x^2 - 8x + 16)f(x)\, dx$$

$$= \int_{-\infty}^{\infty} x^2 f(x)\, dx - 8\int_{-\infty}^{\infty} xf(x)\, dx + 16\int_{-\infty}^{\infty} f(x)\, dx$$

$$= \int_{-\infty}^{\infty} x^2 f(x)\, dx - 8E(X) + 16 \cdot 1$$

$$= \int_{-\infty}^{\infty} x^2 f(x)\, dx - 8 \cdot 4 + 16 = \int_{-\infty}^{\infty} x^2 f(x)\, dx - 16$$

Because $f(x)$ is zero except in the interval $0 < x \leq 10$,

$$\int_{-\infty}^{\infty} x^2 f(x)\, dx = \int_{0}^{2} x^2(0.1x)\, dx + \int_{2}^{10} x^2[0.025(10 - x)]\, dx$$

$$= \left[0.1\frac{x^4}{4}\right]_0^2 + 0.025\left[10\frac{x^3}{3} - \frac{x^4}{4}\right]_2^{10}$$

$$= 0.4 + 20.2667 = 20.6667$$

Hence

$$\sigma^2 = 20.6667 - 16 = 4.6667$$

6.6   VARIANCES OF SPECIAL DISTRIBUTIONS

Before obtaining the variances of some special distributions, we shall obtain a useful shortcut for their calculation. From the definition,

$$\sigma^2 = E\{[X - E(X)]^2\}$$

$$= E\{X^2 - 2E(X)X + [E(X)]^2\}$$

Now $E(X)$ is a constant as is $[E(X)]^2$. Using each of the three properties of (6.15), we find

$$\sigma^2 = E(X^2) - 2E(X)E(X) + [E(X)]^2 = E(X^2) - [E(X)]^2 \qquad (6.29)$$

The variance is the expected value of the square minus the square of the expected value. We have already obtained the expected values of several probability distributions. To obtain the variances of these distributions, all we need is the expected value of the square of the random variable.

We begin by finding the variance of the Poisson distribution. All we need is $E(X^2)$.

$$E(X^2) = \sum_{x=0}^{\infty} x^2 e^{-\lambda} \frac{\lambda^x}{x!}$$

$$= e^{-\lambda} \sum_{x=0}^{\infty} x \frac{\lambda^x}{(x-1)!}$$

The first term is zero, so we can sum as x moves from 1 to infinity. Next, we can factor out a λ and let $y = x - 1$. As x moves from 1 to infinity, y moves from zero to infinity, and

$$E(X^2) = e^{-\lambda} \lambda \sum_{y=0}^{\infty} (y+1) \frac{\lambda^y}{y!}$$

$$= e^{-\lambda} \lambda \sum_{y=0}^{\infty} y \frac{\lambda^y}{y!} + e^{-\lambda} \lambda \sum_{y=0}^{\infty} \frac{\lambda^y}{y!}$$

$$= \lambda^2 + \lambda$$

(The algebra is similar to that used in the derivation of $E(X)$ for the Poisson distribution.) When we apply (6.29),

$$\sigma^2 = \lambda^2 + \lambda - \lambda^2 = \lambda$$

The expected value and the variance of the Poisson distribution are both λ.

Since the units of the variance are the square of the units of the underlying random variable, the relative measure of dispersion based on the variance is the ratio of the variance to the *square* of the expected value. This ratio is called the "*rel-variance*." If we want a measure of dispersion in the same units as the underlying random variable, we take the square root of the variance. This quantity is called the *standard deviation*.

Definition VII. If X is a random variable with probability distribution $f(x)$, expected value $E(X)$, and variance σ^2, the *standard deviation* of $f(x)$ is denoted by σ and is equal to the positive square root of σ^2.

$$\sigma = +\sqrt{\sigma^2}.$$

The *coefficient of variation* of $f(x)$ is denoted by V and given by

$$V = |\sigma/E(X)|$$

Notice that V^2 is the rel-variance of $f(x)$. Both V and V^2 are often expressed as percentages.

For the Poisson distribution:

$$\sigma = \sqrt{\lambda}$$

$$V = |\sqrt{\lambda}/\lambda| = 1/\sqrt{\lambda} \qquad V^2 = 1/\lambda$$

The coefficient of variation of the probability distribution of the number of customers buying Ice Crop frozen foods is $1/\sqrt{1}$ or 100 percent, while the coefficient of variation of the probability distribution of demand for avocados is $1/\sqrt{5}$ or, roughly, 45 percent.

If X has the binomial probability distribution,

$$E(X^2) = \sum_{x=0}^{n} x^2 \frac{n!}{x!\,(n-x)!}\, p^x(1-p)^{n-x}$$

$$= \sum_{x=1}^{n} x \frac{n!}{(x-1)!\,(n-x)!}\, p^x(1-p)^{n-x}$$

Again, we substitute $y = x - 1$.

$$E(X^2) = np \sum_{y=0}^{n-1} (y+1) \frac{(n-1)!}{y!\,(n-1-y)!}\, p^y(1-p)^{n-1-y}$$

Breaking this sum into two parts,

$$E(X^2) = np[(n-1)p + 1] = n^2p^2 - np^2 + np$$

and

$$\sigma^2 = n^2p^2 - np^2 + np - n^2p^2$$

$$= np(1-p)$$

Now that the variances of both the binomial and the Poisson have been found, we can compare the variance of the marginal distribution of the number of customers buying Ice Crop frozen foods with the variance of the conditional distribution of the number of customers buying Ice Crop frozen foods given that 20 customers have entered the store. Thus

$$\sigma^2(Y) = 1$$

$$\sigma^2(Y \mid x = 20) = 20(0.1)(0.9) = 1.8$$

Next, consider the exponential distribution.

$$f(t) = ce^{-ct} \qquad 0 \le t < \infty$$

We have previously shown that the mean of this distribution is $1/c$. Let us find the expected value of T^2.

$$E(T^2) = \int_{t=0}^{\infty} t^2 ce^{-ct}\, dt = c \int_{0}^{\infty} t^2 e^{-ct}\, dt$$

Integrating by parts, we let $u = t^2$, $du = 2t\, dt$, $dv = e^{-ct}\, dt$, $v = -e^{-ct}/c$:

$$E(T^2) = c\left\{ \left[\frac{-t^2 e^{-ct}}{c}\right]_{0}^{\infty} + \frac{2}{c} \int_{0}^{\infty} te^{-ct}\, dt \right\}$$

The first term evaluates to zero. The integral in the second term has been shown in Section 6.4 to be $1/c^2$. Therefore

$$E(T^2) = c \left(\frac{2}{c}\right)\left(\frac{1}{c^2}\right) = \frac{2}{c^2}$$

From (6.29) it follows that for the exponential distribution

$$\sigma^2 = E(T^2) - E^2(T) = \frac{2}{c^2} - \left(\frac{1}{c}\right)^2 = \frac{1}{c^2}$$

Thus in the service time distribution the variance of service times is 9.

Finally, we shall consider the variance of the normal distribution. We wish to evaluate:

$$E(X - \mu)^2 = \frac{1}{\sigma\sqrt{2\pi}} \int_{-\infty}^{\infty} (x - \mu)^2 e^{-(x-\mu)^2/2\sigma^2} \, dx$$

First, we shall make the usual simplifying transformation:

$$z = \frac{x - \mu}{\sigma} \qquad dz = \frac{dx}{\sigma}$$

so that

$$E(X - \mu)^2 = \frac{\sigma^2}{\sqrt{2\pi}} \int_{-\infty}^{\infty} z^2 e^{-z^2/2} \, dz$$

We perform this integration by parts using

$$u = z \qquad du = dz \qquad dv = e^{-z^2/2} z \, dz \qquad v = -e^{-z^2/2}$$

This gives

$$E(X - \mu)^2 = \frac{\sigma^2}{\sqrt{2\pi}} \left[-ze^{-z^2/2} \right]_{-\infty}^{\infty} + \frac{\sigma^2}{\sqrt{2\pi}} \int_{-\infty}^{\infty} e^{-z^2/2} \, dz = \sigma^2$$

since the bracket evaluates to zero at each limit and the multiplier of σ^2 in the second term is the integral of a normal distribution over its whole domain.

The constants, μ and σ, in the normal probability distribution now have a specific meaning. The constant μ is the mean of the distribution and, because of symmetry, also the median and mode, while σ is the standard deviation of the distribution.

6.7 MOMENTS

Thus far we have discussed various methods of describing the central tendency and dispersion of a probability distribution. There are other properties that we may want to describe. Consider, for example, the exponential service time distribution discussed earlier. There

$$f(t) = ce^{-ct} \qquad 0 \leq t < \infty$$

This function is a maximum when $t = 0$ and decreases steadily as t increases. The point we wish to make is that $f(t)$ is not symmetric about its mode—far from it, since none of that part of the function's domain over which it is nonzero lies to the left of the mode. We say that such a distribution is "skewed" to the right, the direction of the skewness being indicated by the "long tail" of the distribution. If a unimodal probability distribution is not skewed, it is symmetrical about the mode, and the mean, median, and mode have the same value. If the distribution is skewed, the mean, median, and mode differ, and the direction and degree of skewness influence the way in which the three measures differ. A knowledge of skewness also tells something about the probabilistic behavior of the random variable. In the case of service times no service time can be below the mode, and extremely long service times are possible. If we want to make statements of this general type, our measures of central tendency and dispersion are not sufficient; we need a measure of skewness. In this section we shall develop a system of descriptive measures for probability distributions. These quantities are called *moments*, and they measure central tendency, dispersion, skewness, and other properties of probability distributions. We begin with a formal definition as follows.

Definition VIII. If X is a random variable with probability distribution $f(x)$, the kth *moment about the origin* of $f(x)$ is denoted by the symbol μ_k' and defined by

$$\mu_k' = \sum_{x=-\infty}^{\infty} x^k f(x)$$

if X is discrete, and by

$$\mu_k' = \int_{-\infty}^{\infty} x^k f(x)\, dx$$

if X is continuous. μ_k' need not exist. We shall sometimes us such notation as $\mu_k'(Y \mid x)$ to avoid ambiguity.

From this definition, we see that the kth moment about the origin of $f(x)$ is the expected value of the kth power of x. In particular, the first moment about the origin is the mean of the probability distribution; hence, a measure of central tendency, and its computation and interpretation have already been illustrated. In this text, we shall use the symbol μ instead of μ_1' to denote the mean of a probability distribution.

The second and third moments about the origin are related to dispersion and skewness, but they are also influenced by the first moment. The effect of the latter is eliminated if we take moments of higher order than the first about the mean. Therefore, we introduce another definition.

Definition IX. If X is a random variable with probability distribution $f(x)$ and mean μ, the kth *moment about the mean* of $f(x)$ is denoted by the symbol μ_k and defined by

$$\mu_k = \sum_{x=-\infty}^{\infty} (x - \mu)^k f(x)$$

if X is discrete, and by

$$\mu_k = \int_{-\infty}^{\infty} (x - \mu)^k f(x) \, dx$$

if X is continuous. Of course, μ_k need not exist. We shall sometimes use notations like $\mu_k(X)$ and $\mu_k(Y \mid x)$ to avoid ambiguity.

It is plain from the definition that the first moment about the mean is identically zero and that the second moment about the mean is $E[(X - \mu)^2]$, the variance. Hence, the second moment about the mean is the measure of dispersion already discussed and illustrated in Sections 6.5 and 6.6.

The third moment about the mean is a measure of skewness. It is positive if the probability distribution is skewed to the right, zero if the distribution is symmetrical, and negative if the distribution is skewed to the left. The proof of these assertions is tedious. We shall not give it. Instead we shall provide two examples of skewness.

Before computing measures of skewness for particular distributions, we shall need a formula for computing the third moment about the mean from the first, second, and third moments about the origin. In general, we can write the third moment about the mean as

$$\mu_3 = E[(X - \mu)^3]$$

We expand the expression inside the square brackets and take the expected value, remembering that the expected value of an algebraic sum is the algebraic sum of the expected values.

$$\mu_3 = E[(X - \mu)^3] = E[X^3 - 3X^2\mu + 3X\mu^2 - \mu^3]$$

$$= E(X^3) - 3\mu E(X^2) + 3\mu^2 E(X) - \mu^3$$

$$= \mu_3' - 3\mu\mu_2' + 2\mu^3 \tag{6.30}$$

We can use (6.30) to compute the third moment about the mean from the first three moments about the origin.

We have already noted that the distribution of service time is skewed to the right, so a logical illustration would be a measure of skewness for that distribution. In Sections 6.4 and 6.6 we found that the first and second moments about the origin were given by

$$E(T) = \frac{1}{c}$$

$$E(T^2) = \frac{2}{c^2}$$

(6.31)

We now compute the third moment about the origin directly from Definition VIII.

$$E(T^3) = \int_{t=0}^{\infty} t^3 c e^{-ct}\, dt$$

Let

$$u = t^3 \qquad du = 3t^2\, dt \qquad dv = e^{-ct} c\, dt \qquad v = -e^{-ct}$$

$$E(T^3) = \left[-t^3 e^{-ct}\right]_0^{\infty} + 3\int_0^{\infty} t^2 e^{-ct}\, dt = 0 + \frac{3}{c} E(T^2)$$

since the integral would be $E(T^2)$ if multiplied by c. Hence

$$E(T^3) = \frac{6}{c^3}$$

(6.32)

To find the third moment about the mean, we substitute (6.31) and (6.32) in (6.30):

$$\mu_3 = E\{[T - E(T)]^3\} = E(T^3) - 3E(T)E(T^2) + 2[E(T)]^3$$

$$= \frac{6}{c^3} - 3\frac{1}{c}\frac{2}{c^2} + 2\frac{1}{c^3} = \frac{2}{c^3}$$

Since $c > 0$, the distribution of T is always skewed to the right—as initially reasoned. This measure of skewness is an absolute measure whose unit is the cube of the unit in which the random variable is measured. However, skewness is usually measured relative to dispersion by the quantity:

$$\alpha_3 = \frac{\mu_3}{\sigma^3}$$

where μ_3 is the third moment about the mean and σ the standard deviation. For the exponential, since $\sigma^2 = 1/c^2$

$$\alpha_3 = \frac{2}{c^3} \div \left(\frac{1}{c}\right)^3 = 2$$

Relative to its dispersion, the skewness of the exponential is constant—in fact, double the dispersion when the latter is measured by σ^3.

The direction of skewness of the binomial distribution depends on the relationship between p and q. The calculation of μ_3 for the binomial distribution is lengthy and not very instructive. It may be shown to be

$$\mu_3 = npq(q - p)$$

so that

$$\alpha_3 = \frac{q - p}{\sqrt{npq}} \tag{6.33}$$

For fixed values of q and p, the absolute value of μ_3 increases with n, but the absolute value of α_3 decreases. Hence, as n increases, the skewness of the binomial distribution decreases relative to the dispersion. Later we shall show that, as n increases, a form of the binomial distribution approaches the normal distribution. From (6.33) we see that, if q is greater than p, the binomial distribution is skewed to the right; if q is equal to p, it is symmetric; and, if q is less than p, it is skewed to the left. This makes sense. The binomial distribution applies if we perform n identical and independent random experiments, and the probability of a particular outcome in a single trial of the experiment is p. If p is less than q, we expect more failures than successes so that the distribution of the number of successes in n trials should reach its peak at less than $n/2$. If p is equal to q, we expect about as many successes as failures so that the distribution should be symmetrical about $n/2$. Finally, if p is greater than q, we expect more successes than failures and a peaking of the distribution at a number of successes greater than $n/2$. In Figure 6.3 we show three binomial distributions with n equal to 10 and three different values of p.

At this point, we should discuss notation. Thus far, we have been discussing descriptive measures for theoretical probability distributions. These distributions have either been "pulled out of the air" or derived from a consideration of the problem at hand. We can also construct probability distributions from observations, and these distributions have descriptive measures. It is important to distinguish the moments of a probability distribution based on observations from those describing the behavior of a random variable in a universe. To do this, we use different notations, employing *Greek* letters to denote the moments of a probability distribution which describes a *universe* and *Roman* letters to denote the moments of a probability distribution which describes a *sample*. Thus, μ and σ denote the mean and standard deviation of a universe distribution, and $\bar{x}$ and s the corresponding measures of a sample. As mentioned in Chapter 2, descriptive measures of universe distributions are called *parameters*, while those of sample distributions are called *statistics*. What constitutes a universe and what constitutes a sample depend on the problem; one man's sample may be another man's universe.

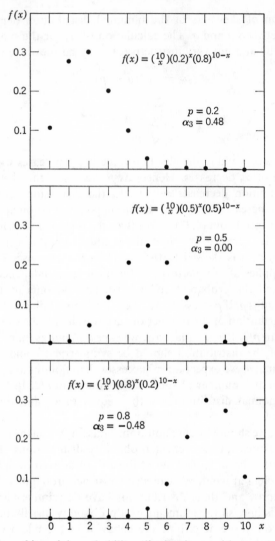

Fig. 6.3. Three binomial probability distributions with $n = 10$ and different values of p and α_3.

6.8   EMPIRICAL PROBABILITY DISTRIBUTIONS

The practicing statistician does not decide arbitrarily what probability distribution is appropriate in a given situation. Instead he must either construct a mathematical model of the process that generates the random variables of his problem or make observations on the random variable and choose a mathematical model that "fits" the observations fairly well. In many situations he will do both. First, he will construct a mathematical model. Then he will estimate the parameters of the model and check its appropriateness using actual observations. In later chapters we shall consider the problems of estimating the parameters of a probability model. Here, we describe methods for constructing approximations to probability distributions from data and the computation of some of their more important descriptive measures.

The Heterodyne Corporation makes electronic equipment for military aircraft. Because the use of the equipment is secret, it is called the Black Box. (Actually, in accordance with military specifications, it is painted grey.) Before the Black Box can be accepted for military use, Heterodyne must provide the Department of Defense with a reliability analysis of the equipment. This analysis must give an estimate of the average number of hours that the equipment will operate before failing, as well as an approximation to the probability distribution of the operating time until failure. In developing this reliability analysis, Heterodyne has operated 100 Black Boxes until they failed, and has recorded their operating times until failure. The Black Boxes were operated in an environment that simulated actual military operating conditions as closely as possible. The operating times until failure appear in Table 6.6, where they have been arranged in increasing order of magnitude.[4]

Descriptive measurements for observations can be computed by thinking of the probability distribution of N observations as

$$f(x) = \begin{cases} \dfrac{1}{N} & \text{if } x \text{ is the value of an observation.} \\ 0 & \text{otherwise.} \end{cases} \tag{6.34}$$

For hand computation, 100 observations are too many to treat in this way, so to illustrate suppose that the operating times until failure of ten additional

[4] In actual reliability tests, fewer than 100 observations are usually taken. Since one Black Box in the test operated for over 3000 hours, the test described here would require more than four months of full-time operation to complete. In practice, therefore, life tests are either "accelerated" by making the test-operating environment much more severe than the "real-life" environment or "truncated" by terminating the test before all test items have failed. Such test procedures are much too complicated for discussion here.

Table 6.6   Operating Time (in Hours) Until Failure of 100 Black Boxes

382	946	1315	1577	1886
571	949	1316	1592	1891
575	977	1323	1666	1909
625	1003	1342	1669	1972
645	1044	1344	1674	1976
677	1053	1399	1679	1986
686	1063	1404	1683	1996
699	1084	1440	1687	2008
700	1126	1462	1700	2094
716	1143	1469	1710	2125
794	1188	1477	1721	2131
795	1195	1483	1725	2287
800	1209	1486	1729	2448
822	1214	1510	1744	2489
842	1225	1514	1753	2511
843	1261	1520	1765	2639
884	1266	1554	1776	2679
906	1274	1557	1785	2738
916	1287	1560	1841	2775
917	1307	1574	1875	3008

Mean time to failure: 1465.57 hours

$$s^2 = 303,289.4451 \qquad s = 550.717 \text{ hours}$$

Black Boxes are those given in column 2 of Table 6.7. Descriptive measures of these observations can be computed by applying the definitions of the preceding section to $f(x)$ in (6.34) and to Table 6.7.

Since each observation has probability $1/N$, or $1/10$ in our example, there are ten modes. Since this is meaningless, the mode is not generally computed for a set of observations. Later, however, we shall group the data in Table 6.6 into a more compact form, and it will then be meaningful to compute a measure analogous to the mode. For the mean,

$$E(X) = \sum_{i=1}^{N} x_i f(x_i) = \sum_{i=1}^{10} x_i \frac{1}{10} = \frac{1}{10} \sum_{i=1}^{10} x_i$$

$$= \frac{1}{10} (14,189) = 1418.9 \text{ hours}$$

Since the data are observations which we regard as a sample from an infinitely large universe of operating times, we use $\bar{x}$ instead of $E(X)$ or μ and write

$$\bar{x} = 1418.9 \text{ hours}$$

The definition of the variance is given by Definition VI, but it is most easily computed from

$$s^2 = E(X^2) - [E(X)]^2$$

where we use the symbol s^2 instead of σ^2 because we regard the data as a sample. Continuing with the calculation,

$$E(X^2) = \sum_{i=1}^{N} x_i^2 f(x_i) = \sum_{i=1}^{10} x_i^2 \frac{1}{10} = \frac{1}{10} \sum_{i=1}^{10} x_i^2$$

$$= \frac{1}{10}(22,633,299) = 2,263,329.9$$

Hence

$$s^2 = 2,263,329.9 - (1418.9)^2 = 250,052.69$$

No units are assigned to the variance, but units are assigned to the standard deviation, which is

$$s = \sqrt{250,052.69} = 500.05 \text{ hours}$$

Since one-half of the observations are equal to or less than 1446 hours, this is the value of the median. There are shortcut methods for computing the mean and the variance when the observations are as unwieldy as those in Table 6.7, but we shall not illustrate them because we do not want to emphasize methods of calculation.

What do we conclude from our calculations? They were made from a sample, and in later chapters we shall consider in detail the problem of drawing inferences from samples. The sample seems to indicate that the

Table 6.7 Operating Times (in Hours) Until Failure of 10 Black Boxes

Item i	Operating Time x_i	x_i^2
1	517	267,289
2	868	753,424
3	1,035	1,071,225
4	1,096	1,201,216
5	1,446	2,090,916
6	1,533	2,350,089
7	1,667	2,778,889
8	1,951	3,806,401
9	1,979	3,916,441
10	2,097	4,397,409
Total	14,189	22,633,299

average operating time until failure is about 1420 hours and that one-half of the Black Boxes will fail in less than 1450 hours. Since the mean and the median are fairly close together relative to the total range of variation of the data, we have some evidence of central tendency in the underlying probability distribution. We must remember, however, that these conclusions are based on a sample and that another sample would probably lead to slightly different ones. The sample-to-sample variability of sample means and medians depends on the variability of the underlying universe as measured by the variance of the universe. Since we ordinarily do not know this variance, we must estimate it from the sample, and it is for this reason that we compute the variance and the standard deviation of the sample. By themselves, they tell us very little, but we need them to draw inferences about the magnitude of universe means and medians from similar measures for samples.

We could make similar calculations for the data given in Table 6.6; an electronic computer could do the work in a few seconds, but a desk calculator would take longer. Since the data are given in increasing order of magnitude, we can see that the median is 1469 hours. The mean, variance, and standard deviation are indicated at the bottom of the table. The observations in Tables 6.6 and 6.7 were both drawn from the same universe. The differences between their various descriptive measures are due to sampling variation.

We can make the calculation of descriptive measures for the data in Table 6.6 somewhat easier and, at the same time, get some idea of the shape of the underlying (universe) probability distribution if we group the data into classes. The data range roughly from 300 to 3100 hours. We can break this range into subintervals and record the number of observations in each. We must decide, however, on the width of the subintervals or, equivalently, on their number. Since the range 300 to 3100 is 2800 hours in width, subintervals of widths 200 hours, 400 hours, and 700 hours would be convenient. The width of the subinterval is called the class interval. In Table 6.8 we show groupings by each of the convenient class intervals. The groupings are called frequency distributions.

Which frequency distribution is best? The answer, of course, depends on what we hope to accomplish by grouping the data. As we have already suggested, we hope to do two things. First, we want to make the calculation of descriptive measures easier than with the ungrouped data. Second, we want to get some idea of the shape of the underlying distribution of the observations. These two objectives are, in a sense, conflicting. Although we would like to simplify the calculatinn of the descriptive measures, we would also like them to be reasonably close to those of the ungrouped data. After grouping the data, we no longer know the value of any observation. With a 200-hour class interval, for example, we know only that there was one observation between 300 and 499 hours, seven observations between 500

Table 6.8 Grouping of the Data in Table 6.6 by Three Different Class Intervals

200-Hour Class Interval		400-Hour Class Interval		700-Hour Class Interval	
Operating Time (Hours)	Number of Black Boxes	Operating Time (Hours)	Number of Black Boxes	Operating Time (Hours)	Number of Black Boxes
300–499	1	300–699	8	300–999	23
500–699	7	700–1099	20	1000–1699	45
700–899	9	1100–1499	25	1700–2399	24
900–1099	11	1500–1899	29	2400–3099	8
1100–1299	11	1900–2299	10	Total[1]	100
1300–1499	14	2300–2699	5		
1500–1699	15	2700–3099	3	$\bar{x} = 1468.5$ hours	
1700–1899	14				
1900–2099	7	Total	100		
2100–2299	3				
2300–2499	2	$\bar{x} = 1459.5$ hours			
2500–2699	3				
2700–2899	2				
2900–3099	1				
Total	100				

$\bar{x} = 1465.5$ hours

and 699 hours, and so on. In general, the smaller the class interval, the more we know about the individual observations, so that descriptive measures for frequency distributions with relatively small class intervals will *tend* to be closer to the corresponding descriptive measures for the ungrouped data than measures for frequency distributions with relatively large class intervals. We say "tend" because the agreement between descriptive measures also depends on the location of the end points of the classes. If possible, these should be chosen so that the average of the observations in a class is near the middle of the class. A comparison of the means for the three groupings in Table 6.8 with the mean of the ungrouped data in Table 6.6 shows that the means obtained using a 200-hour interval and a 700-hour interval are both closer to the mean of the ungrouped data than the mean obtained using a 400-hour interval.[5] In general, however, the desire for agreement between descriptive measures of the frequency distribution and those of the ungrouped data implies a relatively small class interval.

Our other objective in grouping is to get some idea of the shape of the underlying distribution of observations. Many common probability distributions are "smooth." The frequency or density function rises smoothly from the left-hand tail to a peak at the mode, then falls away again in the right-hand tail. There are no irregularities or "bumps" in the graph. We usually would like the number of observations in the classes of the frequency distribution to rise smoothly to a peak and fall away again without bumps, irregularities, or long flat sections. This desire for "smoothness" leads to the choice of a large class interval. Of course, if we put all of our observations into one class with a class interval equal to the range of the ungrouped data, we would have a smooth frequency distribution but no idea about the way in which the data were concentrated. Hence, the class interval cannot be too large, or we will lose most of the information contained in the ungrouped data.

There are no hard and fast rules about the choice of class interval, but less than six classes or more than 18 are rarely used. The 700-hour class interval in our problem leads to too few classes. Either of the others would be satisfactory, however, we shall use the 400-hour interval. The lower end points are multiples of 100, which is convenient; and the "error" in the mean of the frequency distribution is well within 1 percent of the mean of the ungrouped data. This is an acceptable error for most purposes. We show this grouping in Table 6.9 as it might be presented in Heterodyne's bid to supply Black Boxes to the Department of Defense. Table 6.9 is illustrated in Figure 6.4. A graph that illustrates a frequency distribution by means of adjacent vertical bars is called a histogram.

---

[5] Methods for computing means for frequency distributions will be described in the next section. For the present, the reader should take them as given.

Table 6.9 Operating Times Until Failure of 100 Black Boxes in Simulated Operational Reliability Test

Operating Time to Failure (Hours)	Number of Black Boxes
300–699	8
700–1099	20
1100–1499	25
1500–1899	29
1900–2299	10
2300–2699	5
2700–3099	3
Total black boxes tested:	100

Source. Heterodyne Test Laboratories, Incorporated; Test Run No. DOD-65-3.

Table 6.9 and Figure 6.4 tell us quite a bit about the data in Table 6.6 which cannot be discerned from an examination of either the basic data or the descriptive measures. More than half the Black Boxes tested failed after operating between 1100 and 1899 hours, and more than 80 percent failed in less than 1900 hours. The underlying distribution appears to have a peak in the neighborhood of 1500 hours and to be slightly skewed.

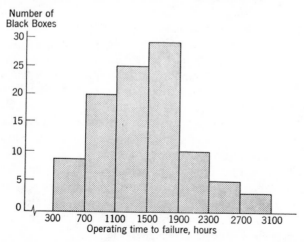

Fig. 6.4. Operating times until failure of 100 Black Boxes in simulated operational reliability test. (*Source* Table 6.9.)

It will help to introduce some terms at this point. We have broken the range of the operating times into classes. The number of observations in a class is called the class frequency, and the ratio of the frequency of a given class to the total number of observations is called the relative frequency. If we think of our observations as a statistical universe instead of as a sample and assign to each observation the probability $1/N$, where N is the total number of observations, then the relative frequency of a class is the probability that an observation will fall in that class. In computing descriptive measures, we shall treat the relative frequencies as probabilities. The classes are arranged so that there is no ambiguity as to the class into which a particular observation is put. The boundaries of the classes are called class limits. The underlying variable of our example, time, is continuous, and Heterodyne's test engineers have apparently decided to measure it to the nearest hour. The "true" values of the operating times are known only to within one-half of an hour. Therefore, all that we know about the eight observations in the first class in Table 6.9 is that their true values were somewhere between 299.5 and 699.5 hours. The numbers 299.5 and 699.5 are called the true limits of the first class, and the numbers 300 and 699 are called its written limits. Written limits are usually given to the same degree of precision as observations. The observations in Table 6.6 are to the nearest hour; hence the written limits in Table 6.9 are in hours. The mean of either the upper and lower true limits or the upper and lower written limits of a class is called the class midpoint. The class midpoints in Table 6.9 are 499.5, 899.5, 1299.5, 1699.5, 2099.5, 2499.5, and 2899.5 hours. These class midpoints and limits will play an important part in the calculation of descriptive measures for frequency distributions.

As already indicated, the difference between the upper and lower true limits of a class is called the class interval. In Table 6.9, we have made all class intervals the same length. This is usually the most convenient arrangement, but it is not essential. Suppose, for example, that we had a list of the 1963 incomes of a random sample of 1000 American families. These incomes might range from $1000 to $100,000. We would need about ten classes in our frequency distribution, and, if we insist on equal intervals, our interval would be about $10,000. The incomes of most of the families would be clustered in the $5000 to $10,000 range, and the variation within this range would be hidden because all incomes in this range are in the first class. We really want the class intervals at the lower end of the income scale to be smaller than those at the higher end of the scale. In this situation, a geometric progression of class limits is sometimes useful. In presenting income distributions in published reports the highest income class is often left open because people with high incomes are easily identified, and income information is usually regarded as confidential. In Table 6.10 we show a hypothetical distribution of the incomes of 1000 American families. The class intervals are in approximate geometric progression, and we have left the last class, "60,000 and over," open.

Table 6.10   1963 Incomes (Before Taxes) of 1000 American Families

Income	Number of Families
1,000–1,499	5
1,500–2,499	41
2,500–3,999	135
4,000–5,999	240
6,000–9,999	297
10,000–14,999	173
15,000–24,999	80
25,000–39,999	23
40,000–59,999	5
60,000 and over	1
	1000

Source. Hypothetical (very).

6.9 DESCRIPTIVE MEASURES FOR FREQUENCY DISTRIBUTIONS

In grouping, individual observations lose their identity. We know their magnitudes only to within one-half of a class interval. This means that we must make an assumption about the way in which they are distributed within the classes before we can compute any descriptive measures. In fact, the standard methods for computing the mean, median, mode, and variance of a frequency distribution imply different, and, in the case of the median, inconsistent assumptions about the way in which the observations are distributed within the classes.

The mode, mean, and variance of a frequency distribution are usually computed under the somewhat unrealistic procedure of assigning to every item in a class the value of the class midpoint. Suppose there are k classes in the frequency distribution. Let N be the total number of observations, f_i be the frequency of the ith class, and m_i be the midpoint of the ith class. We convert the frequency distribution into a discrete probability distribution:

$$f(x) = \frac{1}{N} f_i \quad \text{if} \quad x = m_i, i = 1, \cdots, k \qquad (6.35)$$

x has nonzero probability only if it is the value of a class midpoint. Applying this technique to the Black Box data in Table 6.9 gives as a probability distribution:

$$f(499.5) = 0.08 \qquad f(2099.5) = 0.10$$
$$f(899.5) = 0.20 \qquad f(2499.5) = 0.05 \qquad\qquad (6.36)$$
$$f(1299.5) = 0.25 \qquad f(2899.5) = 0.03$$
$$f(1699.5) = 0.29 \qquad f(x) = 0 \qquad \text{all other values of } x$$

We can now apply the definitions of the preceding sections to this probability distribution. The class with the greatest frequency is called the modal class, and its midpoint is defined to be *Mo*, the mode. Hence, for the Black Box data, the mode is 1699.5 hours. For the probability distribution, defined by (6.35), the median is found by cumulating the probabilities, beginning with the smallest class midpoint, and stopping as soon as the cumulated probability equals or exceeds 0.5. For the Black Box data, using the probability distribution given by (6.36),

$$F(899.5) = 0.28$$

$$F(1299.5) = 0.53$$

By Definition IV, the median of the frequency distribution is 1299.5 hours. Many statisticians, however, find this method unsatisfactory and insist on finding the median and other quantiles by interpolation. Interpolation involves the assumption that the individual observations are uniformly distributed within the classes. As this assumption conflicts with the one underlying (6.35), we shall return to the median and the other quantiles after finding the mean and variance of the probability distribution given by (6.35) and of the data in Tables 6.9 and 6.10.

From (6.35) and Definition II, we have for the mean of a frequency distribution

$$E(X) = \sum_{i=1}^{k} m_i \cdot \frac{1}{N} f_i = \frac{1}{N} \sum_{i=1}^{k} f_i m_i = \bar{x} \qquad (6.37)$$

We use the symbol $\bar{x}$ because we are describing a sample. We shall apply (6.37) to the Black Box data after writing a formula for the variance of a frequency distribution. Combining Definition VI, (6.29), and (6.37) and applying them to (6.35) gives

$$s^2 = \sum_{i=1}^{k} m_i^2 \frac{1}{N} f_i - \bar{x}^2 = \frac{1}{N} \sum_{i=1}^{k} f_i m_i^2 - \bar{x}^2 \qquad (6.38)$$

In Table 6.11, we show the calculation of the mean and variance of the Black Box frequency distribution using (6.37) and (6.38). The mean and variance are reasonably close to those of the ungrouped data in Table 6.6. The mean is within 0.5 percent, the variance within 5 percent, and the standard deviation within 3 percent of the corresponding measures for the ungrouped data.

Table 6.11 Computation of Mean and Variance of Operating Time Until Failure Using Table 6.9 and Equations (6.37) and (6.38)

i	Operating Time (Hours)	Midpoint m_i	Frequency f_i	$f_i m_i$	$f_i m_i^2$
1	300–699	499.5	8	3,996.0	1,996,002.00
2	700–1099	899.5	20	17,990.0	16,182,005.00
3	1100–1499	1299.5	25	32,487.5	42,217,506.25
4	1500–1899	1699.5	29	49,285.5	83,760,707.25
5	1900–2299	2099.5	10	20,995.0	44,079,002.50
6	2300–2699	2499.5	5	12,497.5	31,237,501.25
7	2700–3099	2899.5	3	8,698.5	25,221,300.75
	Totals		100	145,950.0	244,694,025.00

$$\bar{x} = \frac{1}{100}(145,950.0) = 1459.5 \text{ hours}$$

$$s^2 = \frac{1}{100}(244,694,025.00) - (1459.5)^2$$

$$= 2,446,940.25 - 2,130,140.25 = 316,800$$

$$s = \sqrt{316,800} = 562.8 \text{ hours}$$

A glance at the calculations in Table 6.11 is enough to discourage anyone who has only pencil, paper, and average ability in arithmetic. Fortunately, shortcuts are possible, especially when the class interval is constant. Then we can perform the calculations in class interval units by first "coding" the class midpoints by a transformation. This transformation shifts the origin to an arbitrary class midpoint and divides the unit scale by the size of the class interval. The procedure is much less complicated than it sounds. Let c be the class interval. Pick a class midpoint (any one will do) and call it m_0. For each class midpoint, compute:

$$d_i' = \frac{1}{c}(m_i - m_0) \qquad i = 1, 2, \cdots, k$$

The result of this calculation will be a sequence of integers such as $\cdots -2$, $-1, 0, 1, 2, 3, \cdots$. In the Black Box data, if we pick $m_0 = 1699.5$, we obtain $d_1' = -3$, $d_2' = -2$, $d_3' = -1$, $d_4' = 0$, $d_5' = 1$, $d_6' = 2$, $d_7' = 3$. The quantity d_i' simply measures how many class intervals the ith class is from the class whose midpoint is m_0. Now,

$$m_i = cd_i' + m_0 \qquad i = 1, 2, \cdots, k$$

Hence

$$\bar{x} = \frac{1}{N}\sum_{i=1}^{k} f_i m_i = \frac{1}{N}\sum_{i=1}^{k} f_i(cd_i' + m_0)$$

$$= \frac{c}{N}\sum_{i=1}^{k} f_i d_i' + m_0 \tag{6.39}$$

The same kind of a calculation applied to (6.38) will yield

$$s^2 = \frac{c^2}{N}\sum_{i=1}^{k} f_i(d_i')^2 - \frac{c^2}{N^2}\left(\sum_{i=1}^{k} f_i d_i'\right)^2 \tag{6.40}$$

These formulas (6.39) and (6.40) are applied in Table 6.12 to our example.

Table 6.12 Computation of Mean and Variance of Operating Time Until Failure, Using Table 6.9 and Equations (6.39) and (6.40)

Interval i	Operating Time (Hours)	Midpoint m_i	Frequency f_i	d_i'	$f_i d_i'$	$f_i(d_i')^2$
1	300–699	499.5	8	−3	−24	72
2	700–1099	899.5	20	−2	−40	80
3	1100–1499	1299.5	25	−1	−25	25
4	1500–1899	1699.5	29	0	0	0
5	1900–2299	2099.5	10	1	10	10
6	2300–2699	2499.5	5	2	10	20
7	2700–3099	2899.5	3	3	9	27
	Totals		100		−60	234

$$m_0 = 1699.5 \qquad c = 400$$

$$\bar{x} = \frac{400}{100}(-60) + 1699.5 = -240 + 1699.5 = 1459.5 \text{ hours}$$

$$s^2 = \frac{(400)^2}{100}(234) - \frac{(400)^2}{(100)^2}(-60)^2 = 1600(234) - 16(3600) = 316,800$$

$$s = \sqrt{316,800} = 562.8 \text{ hours}$$

Table 6.13 Computation of Mean and Variance of Family Incomes Using Table 6.10 and Equations for Variable Class Intervals

Interval i	Income	Midpoint m_i	Number of Families f_i	d_i	$f_i d_i$	$f_i d_i^2$
1	1,000–1,499	1,249.5	5	−3,750	−18,750	70.3125 × 10⁶
2	1,500–2,499	1,999.5	41	−3,000	−123,000	369.0000 × 10⁶
3	2,500–3,999	3,249.5	135	−1,750	−236,250	413.4375 × 10⁶
4	4,000–5,999	4,999.5	240	0	0	0
5	6,000–9,999	7,999.5	297	3,000	891,000	2,673.0000 × 10⁶
6	10,000–14,999	12,499.5	173	7,500	1,297,500	9,731.2500 × 10⁶
7	15,000–24,999	19,999.5	80	15,000	1,200,000	18,000.0000 × 10⁶
8	25,000–39,999	32,499.5	23	27,500	632,500	17,393.7500 × 10⁶
9	40,000–59,999	49,999.5	5	45,000	225,000	10,125.0000 × 10⁶
10	60,000–99,999	79,999.5	1	75,000	75,000	5,625.0000 × 10⁶
			1000		3,943,000	64,400.7500 × 10⁶

$$m_0 = 4999.5$$

$$\bar{x} = \frac{1}{1000}(3{,}943{,}000) + 4999.5 = \$8942.50$$

$$s^2 = \frac{1}{1000}(64{,}400.75 \times 10^6) - \frac{1}{(1000)^2}(3{,}943{,}000)^2$$

$$64{,}400{,}750 - 15{,}547{,}249 = 48{,}853{,}501$$

$$s = \$6990$$

The computations are much easier than those in Table 6.11. They can be done in a few minutes, using only the pencil, paper, and average ability in arithmetic with which most of us are equipped.

Even when the class interval is not constant, some saving in computation can be achieved if the class intervals are convenient numbers. In this case, we can define, after picking an arbitrary midpoint, m_0.

$$d_i = m_i - m_0 \qquad i = 1, 2, \cdots, k$$

A little algebra will show that

$$\bar{x} = \frac{1}{N}\sum_{i=1}^{k} f_i d_i + m_0$$

$$s^2 = \frac{1}{N}\sum_{i=1}^{k} f_i(d_i)^2 - \frac{1}{N^2}\left(\sum_{i=1}^{k} f_i d_i\right)^2$$

We illustrate the use of these formulas in Table 6.13 by applying them to the family income data in Table 6.10 after closing the last class at \$99,999. A desk calculator is required, but the numbers are much more convenient than if the class midpoints were used.

Time, as we remarked earlier, is a continuous variable. Underlying the observations in Table 6.6 is a continuous probability distribution. In constructing Table 6.9, we have superimposed on this underlying distribution a set of classes whose width and beginning point are random variables because they depend on the magnitudes of the largest and smallest observations. If we were to take 100 new observations and group them, we might use a different class interval and a different beginning point, and we would come to a slightly different conclusion about the shape of the underlying distribution. In Figure 6.5 we show a sketch of a continuous distribution on which

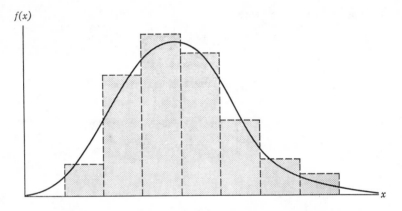

Fig. 6.5. Histogram superimposed on a continuous probability distribution.

we have superimposed arbitrary classes and a hypothetical histogram which might have resulted when 100 observations were drawn at random from the underlying distribution. Our method of computing the mode, mean, and variance assigns all the relative frequency to the class midpoint and ignores both the shape of the underlying distribution (which is unknown in any case) and the distribution of the individual observations within the classes. Because the underlying distribution is a smooth curve which rises to a peak at the mode and falls away in the tails, the midpoints of classes below the mode tend to understate the averages of the observations in their classes, while the class midpoints of classes above the mode tend to overstate them. If the underlying distribution is symmetric, the understatement will tend to cancel the overstatement in the calculation of the mean. The biases do not cancel in the calculation of the variance, however. In spite of the fact that, in calculating the variance, we have concentrated all of the probability in a class at its midpoint and thereby ignored the variation of the individual items within classes, the variance of a frequency distribution tends to overstate the variance of the individual observations.[6] Most statisticians, however, ignore this bias.

In the calculation of the median and other quantiles, however, the concentration of the probability at the class midpoints is too gross an approximation for many statisticians. They prefer, instead, to assume that the individual items are uniformly distributed within classes. Under this assumption, the quantiles can be calculated by linear interpolation within classes. No specific formulas are necessary, but we shall illustrate the procedure. In Table 6.14 we give the frequency distribution, the relative frequencies, and the cumulated relative frequencies of the family income data in Table 6.10. We have left the last class open. In computing quantiles by interpolation, we must pay attention to true class limits. We see from Table 6.14 that 42.1 percent of the

Table 6.14 Basic Computations for the Calculation of Quantiles for Family Income Data in Table 6.10

i	Income	Number of Families f_i	Relative Frequency $p_i = f_i/1000$	Cumulated Relative Frequency $P_i = \sum_{j=1}^{i} p_j$
1	1,000–1,499	5	0.005	0.005
2	1,500–2,499	41	0.041	0.046
3	2,500–3,999	135	0.135	0.181
4	4,000–5,999	240	0.240	0.421
5	6,000–9,999	297	0.297	0.718
6	10,000–14,999	173	0.173	0.891
7	15,000–24,999	80	0.080	0.971
8	25,000–39,999	23	0.023	0.994
9	40,000–59,999	5	0.005	0.999
10	60,000–and over	1	0.001	1.000
	Totals	1000	1.000	6.226

[6] There is an approximate correction for this overstatement of the variance. Subtract $c^2/12$ from the variance of the frequency distribution. When we subtract

$$\frac{c^2}{12} = \frac{(400)^2}{12} = 13,333$$

from the variance in Tables 6.11 and 6.12, we get $s^2 = 303,467$, which is very close to the variance of the data in Table 6.6. This refinement will not be used in the sequel.

incomes were equal to or less than 5999.50, the true upper limit of the fourth class. Therefore, the median income lies in the fifth class. Because of the uniformity assumption, we can interpolate linearly into the fifth class to obtain the median. We set up a proportionality equation,

$$\frac{x_{0.50} - 5999.5}{9999.5 - 5999.5} = \frac{0.500 - 0.421}{0.718 - 0.421}$$

and solve for $x_{0.50}$. We obtain

$$x_{0.50} = 5999.5 + \frac{(4000)(0.079)}{0.297} = \$7063.97$$

or \$7064 when rounded to the nearest dollar. To provide other illustrations, let us find the lower limit of the upper 5 percent of the incomes, $x_{0.95}$, and the upper limit of the lower 10 percent of the incomes, $x_{0.10}$. In Table 6.14 we see that $x_{0.95}$ lies in the seventh class

$$\frac{x_{0.95} - 14,999.5}{24,999.5 - 14,999.5} = \frac{0.950 - 0.891}{0.971 - 0.891}$$

$$x_{0.95} = 14,999.5 + \frac{(10,000)(0.059)}{0.080} = \$22,374$$

Ninety-five percent of the families had income equal to or less than that amount. Finally, for the tenth percentile,

$$\frac{x_{0.10} - 2499.5}{3999.5 - 2499.5} = \frac{0.100 - 0.046}{0.181 - 0.046}$$

$$x_{0.10} = 2499.5 + \frac{(1500)(0.054)}{0.135} = \$3100$$

Ten percent of the families had incomes of this amount or less. The assumption that individual items are uniformly distributed within classes is no more reasonable than the assumption that the items are concentrated at the class midpoints. Hence, although the quantiles just computed are in accordance with standard statistical practice, they are no more accurate than similar quantiles computed under our earlier assumption.

The student will notice that the material covered in Sections 6.8 and 6.9 is mathematically simple. This should not create the impression that it is unimportant. In fact, it is basic to all applied statistics.

IMPORTANT TERMS AND CONCEPTS

Arithmetic mean
Bimodal probability distribution
Central tendency
Class interval
Coefficient of variation
Expected value of a random variable
Frequency distribution
Histogram
Interpolation
Interquartile Range
Mean deviation

Median
Mode
Moments about the mean
Moments about the origin
Percentile
Quantile
Quartile
Range
Skewness
Standard deviation
Variance

SYMBOLS AND ABBREVIATIONS

$\mu_k' = E(X^k)$

$\mu_k = E[(X - \mu)^k]$

$E[g(X)]$

$\mu = E(X)$

$\sigma^2 = \mu_2 = E[(X - \mu)^2]$

M.D.

V

$\bar{x}$

$x_{0.50}$

$x_{0.25}$

$x_{0.75}$

s

s^2

x_i

d_i

d_i'

OFTEN-USED FORMULAS

$$\mu = E(X) = \begin{cases} \sum_x xf(x) & \text{discrete random variables} \\ \int_{-\infty}^{\infty} xf(x)\,dx & \text{continuous random variables} \end{cases}$$

$$\mu_2 = \sigma^2 = E[(X - \mu)^2] = \begin{cases} \sum_x (x - \mu)^2 f(x) & \text{discrete} \\ \int_{-\infty}^{\infty} (x - \mu)^2 f(x)\,dx & \text{continuous} \end{cases}$$

$$E(X^k) = \begin{cases} \sum_x x^k f(x) & \text{discrete} \\ \int_{-\infty}^{\infty} x^k f(x)\, dx & \text{continuous} \end{cases}$$

$$E[(X - \mu)^k] = \begin{cases} \sum_x (x - \mu)^k f(x) & \text{discrete} \\ \int_{-\infty}^{\infty} (x - \mu)^k f(x)\, dx & \text{continuous} \end{cases}$$

For the binomial distribution: $\mu = np;$ $\sigma^2 = npq$

For the Poisson distribution: $\mu = \lambda;$ $\sigma^2 = \lambda$

For the normal distribution: $\mu = \mu;$ $\sigma^2 = \sigma^2$

$$\text{M.D.} = \begin{cases} \sum_x |x - x_{0.50}|\, f(x) & \text{discrete} \\ \int_{-\infty}^{\infty} |x - x_{0.50}|\, f(x)\, dx & \text{continuous} \end{cases}$$

$$\sigma^2 = \mu_2 = \mu_2' - \mu^2 = E(X^2) - [E(X)]^2$$

$$V = |\sigma/E(X)|$$

Mean, ungrouped data:

$$\bar{x} = \frac{1}{N} \sum_{i=1}^{N} x_i$$

Mean, grouped data:

$$\bar{x} = \frac{1}{N} \sum_{i=1}^{k} f_i m_i \qquad \bar{x} = \frac{c}{N} \sum_{i=1}^{k} f_i d_i' + m_0$$

Standard deviation, ungrouped data:

$$s = \sqrt{\sum_{i=1}^{N} (x_i - \bar{x})^2 / N} = \frac{1}{N} \sqrt{N \sum_{i=1}^{N} x_i^2 - \left(\sum_{i=1}^{N} x_i \right)^2}$$

Standard deviation, grouped data:

$$s = \frac{c}{N} \sqrt{N \sum_{i=1}^{k} f_i (d_i')^2 - \left(\sum_{i=1}^{k} f_i d_i' \right)^2}$$

EXERCISES

1. Prove the following.
    a. For discrete distributions, $\sum_x (x - t)^2 f(x)$ is a minimum when $t = \mu$.

    b. For continuous distributions, $\int_{-\infty}^{\infty} (x - t)^2 f(x)\, dx$ is a minimum when $t = \mu$.

2. a. Why is $\mu_2 (= \sigma^2)$ a better measure of dispersion than μ_2'?
    b. Let μ_1 be defined by

$$\mu_1 = \sum_x (x - \mu) f(x)$$

    for discrete distributions. Would μ_1 be a good measure of dispersion? Why or why not?

3. Prove that, in general:
    a. $\mu_2 = \mu_2' - \mu^2$
    b. $\mu_3 = \mu_3' - 3\mu_2'\mu + 2\mu^3$

4. Prove that for the binomial distribution:
    a. $\mu = np$
    b. $\sigma^2 = np(1 - p)$

5. Explain the meaning of the following terms.
    (a) Expected value
    (b) Skewness
    (c) Symmetry
    (d) Variance
    (e) Standard deviation
    (f) Median
    (g) Mode
    (h) Mean

6. Mr. Norton, proprietor of the Dineeze Restaurant, stated that the average (mean) number of persons ordering chicken dinners at his establishment during one day is 53. Mr. Thor, a statistician, remarked that if the number of persons ordering chicken is distributed binomially, the expected number of persons ordering chicken tomorrow is 53; however, if the number of persons ordering chicken has a Poisson distribution, this statement is false. Do you agree with Mr. Thor? State clearly any assumptions you make; explain why you agree or disagree.

7. The number of calls received by the lost and found department of the Jonas Department Store during the first five minutes of operation each working day is approximated by a Poisson distribution with $\lambda = 2$.
    a. What is the expected number of calls during that period tomorrow (assuming that tomorrow is a regular working day)?

b. What are the mean and variance of the above distribution? How would you interpret these two parameters?

8. If the distribution of heights of adult American males is normal with parameters: $\mu = 5$ ft 8 in. $\sigma^2 = 6.25$ square in.

   a. Find the mean and standard deviation of this distribution.

   b. What is the probability that if a person is selected at random from this population his height will be exactly 6 ft?

   c. What is the probability that his height will be 6 ft when measured to the nearest inch?

9. For each of the following distributions, calculate $\mu_1, \mu_2, \mu_3, \mu_1', \mu_2', \mu_3'$.

   a. $f(x) = \dfrac{1}{7}$ $1 \leq x \leq 8$

   b. $f(x) = 3x^2$ $0 \leq x \leq 1$

   c. $f(x) = \dfrac{3}{10}(2 - x^2)$ $-1 \leq x \leq 1$

   d. $f(x) = \dfrac{x}{4}$ $1 \leq x \leq 3$

10. A random variable X is normally distributed with $\mu = 80$, $\sigma = 5$.

    a. What is the value of μ_3 for this distribution?

    b. What does this fact imply about this distribution?

    c. What is the value of the median of this distribution? The mode?

    d. Do your answers above imply that

    $$P(70 < X < 75) = P(85 \leq X \leq 90)?$$

    Justify your answer.

11. Calculate the mean and standard deviation for each of the following functions which are probably distributions.

    a. $f(x) = \dfrac{x}{3}$ $x = 1, 2$

    b. $f(x) = \dfrac{x - 1}{15}$ $x = 1, 2, 3, 4, 5, 6$

    c. $f(x) = -x$ $x = -0.75, -0.50, +0.25$

    d. $f(x) = x$ $x = \dfrac{1}{16}, \dfrac{3}{16}, \dfrac{1}{4}, \dfrac{1}{2}$

12. Calculate the mean, variance, and a measure of skewness for each of the following distributions.

   a. $f(x) = \dfrac{1}{b-a}$ $a \leq x \leq b$

   b. $f(x) = \dfrac{3x^2}{125}$ $0 < x < 5$

   c. $f(x) = \dfrac{1+x}{6}$ $1 < x < 3$

   d. $f(x) = 1$ $x = \dfrac{1}{2}$

   e. $f(x) = \dfrac{2}{3x}$ $x = 1, 2$

13. A random experiment is conducted in which four unbiased coins are tossed.
   a. What is the expected value of the number of heads obtained?
   b. What is the meaning of the value computed in part *a*?
   c. What is the variance of the outcome in part *a*? Of what use is this number?
   d. Are the numerical values calculated in parts *a* and *c* statistics or parameters? Explain.
   e. Suppose the experiment was repeated three times. What is the expected value of the sum of the three outcomes?

14. The probability function used to describe the game of Russian roulette in Exercise 5 of Chapter 4 was

$$f(x) = \frac{1}{6}\left(\frac{5}{6}\right)^{x-1} \qquad x = 1, 2, 3, \cdots$$

   where $f(x)$ denotes the probability of "losing" on the xth try.
   a. What is the expected value of this function? Do not evaluate.
   b. Give an interpretation of this expected value in terms of this specific situation.

15. Given the following probability distribution:

$$f(x) = e^{-x} \qquad 0 \leq x < \infty$$

   a. Calculate the mean and variance of this distribution.
   b. Plot this distribution on graph paper.
   c. For this distribution would μ_3 be greater or less than zero? Explain.

16. A random sample of 25 articles is taken from a stream of production which is 20 percent of type A.
    a. What percentage of the sample would you expect to be of type A? Explain.
    b. What is the probability that you would get exactly the percentage that you derived in part *a*?
    c. What is the expected number in the sample which are not of type A? How did you derive this number? What is its meaning?
    d. Is the distribution of the number of type A articles in a sample of size 25 skewed or symmetrical? If skewed, is it skewed to the left or right? Justify your answer, using any logic or computations necessary.

17. Given that the distribution of births in Polynesia is binomially distributed with the probability of a male birth $= 0.5$.
    a. What is the expected value of this distribution when $n = 1$? When $n = 2$?
    b. Interpret the answers that you gave in part *a*.

18. a. Prove that the following are probability distributions.

    1. $f(x) = \dfrac{3}{4} x(2 - x) \qquad 0 < x < 2$

    2. $f(x) = \dfrac{1}{\pi(1 + x^2)} \qquad -\infty < x < \infty$

    b. Find μ, μ_2', and μ_2 for the function in subpart 1 of part *a*.
    c. Find the mean of the function in subpart 2 of part *a*.
    d. Is the function in subpart 2 symmetric or skewed? Justify your answer.
    e. For the function in subpart 1, what is the value of $f(x)$ when $x = \mu$?
    f. For the function in subpart 2, what is the value of $f(x)$ when $x = \mu$?

19. The function

$$f(x) = \frac{\alpha 2^\alpha}{x^{\alpha+1}} \qquad x \geq 2 \qquad \alpha > 0$$

is called a Pareto probability distribution.
    a. Prove that it is a probability distribution.
    b. What is the corresponding cumulative distribution function?
    c. What are the mean and variance of the above distribution?
    d. If $\alpha = 3$ what are the numerical values of:
       1. The mean?
       2. The variance?
       3. The standard deviation?
    e. Is this distribution symmetric?

f. If $\alpha = 3$, what is the probability that an item drawn at random from the above distribution would have a value:

1. Of two?
2. Of less than two?
3. Of more than two?
4. Greater than eight?
5. Less than nine?
6. Between eight and nine?
7. More than the mean?

20. The beta probability distribution is

$$f(x) = \frac{(\alpha + \beta + 1)!}{\alpha! \beta!} x^{\alpha}(1 - x)^{\beta} \qquad 0 \le x \le 1$$

a. Find the mean of this distribution when $\alpha = 0$ and $\beta = 0$. Sketch this distribution. It is called a uniform distribution.
b. Derive the mean of this distribution if $\alpha = 1$, $\beta = 0$. Sketch this distribution.
c. Prove that the function in part *b* is a probability distribution.
d. Derive the cumulative distribution for the distribution in part *b*.

21. The normal probability distribution is

$$f(x) = \frac{1}{\sigma\sqrt{2\pi}} e^{-(x-\mu)^2/2\sigma^2} \qquad -\infty < x < \infty$$

a. What is the mode of this distribution?
b. What is the median of this distribution?
c. If X, the height of male undergraduates at the University of Connecticut during 1964, is distributed normally with $\mu = 5$ ft 10 in., $\sigma = 2$ in., what percent of the male undergraduates are over 6 ft tall? Under 6 ft 3 in. tall?
d. Referring to part *c*, 67 percent of the male undergraduates exceed what height?

22. A wholesale bakery, which caters exclusively to restaurants, must bake bread each evening for delivery the next day. The number of loaves that a restaurant will take is not known until the truck arrives at the delivery entrance of the restaurant. The total demand for loaves of bread on a particular day is approximated by a Poisson probability distribution with a mean of 4 dozen loaves. The bakery makes a profit of three cents on each loaf of bread sold to restaurants. Loaves not sold to restaurants are sold at a loss of two cents per loaf to a discount shop.

a. If the bakery wants to maximize short-run profits from the sale of bread, how many loaves of bread should be baked each day?
b. If the bakery maximizes short-run profits by baking the number of loaves indicated in part *a*, what effect is this likely to have on the expected value of long-run profits? How would this alter the actual number of loaves of bread baked each day?

23. The beta probability distribution is given in Exercise 20.
    a. Deriving the first-order condition only, show that the mode of the beta distribution is

$$x = \frac{\alpha}{\alpha + \beta} \qquad \text{if} \qquad \alpha > 0, \qquad \beta > 0$$

    b. Is $x = \alpha/(\alpha + \beta)$ the mode if $\alpha \leq 0$ or $\beta \leq 0$? Explain.

24. Given that the 1965 personal income tax paid by seven members of the Brandingham Family was, respectively, $6500; 12,200; 8000; 7500; 18,500; 9000; and 5500:
    a. Find the arithmetic mean tax.
    b. Find the median tax.
    c. Which of these two measures of central tendency would you consider the more representative?

25. The ages of nine girls in a beauty·contest are 16, 17, 17, 17, 18, 21, 21, 22, and 22. Suppose that you were trying to guess the age of the winner before this was announced, and all of the girls were so beautiful that, as far as you could estimate, all had an equal probability of winning. What measure of central tendency would you use in the following instances?
    a. If you win a prize only by guessing the exact age of the winner?
    b. If you win a prize if your total error in ten such beauty contests with the same age distribution is the smallest?
    c. Find the arithmetic mean of the girls' ages.

26. Ten production workers in the assembly department of the Northcote Gyroscopic Stabilizer Company completed, in one week's time, 12, 16, 21, 11, 10, 15, 14, 11, 14, and 14 stabilizer units, respectively.
    a. Find the arithmetic mean number of units completed by the ten in that week.
    b. Find the median number.
    c. Find the modal number.
    d. Which of these measures of central tendency do you consider to be the most representative? Why?

27. It has been stated that the presence of two modes in a frequency distribution suggests that the objects represented in the frequency distribution may not be homogeneous. Why is this true? Your answer should include a definition and illustration of the concept of homogeneity.

28. Define each of the following concepts.
    a. Frequency distribution   d. Percentile
    b. Median   e. Skewness
    c. Histogram   f. Interpolation

29. Table 6.15 gives the relative frequency distribution of annual payrolls for 500 small retail establishments in a Pennsylvania city for 1970.

Table 6.15

Annual Payroll (Thousands of Dollars)	Percent of Establishments
less than 10	12
10 and less than 20	12
20 and less than 30	18
30 and less than 40	30
40 and less than 50	20
50 and less than 60	8
	100

a. Calculate the arithmetic mean annual payroll of the above distribution.
b. Calculate the median annual payroll of the above distribution.
c. What is your best estimate of the total payroll of these 500 establishments? Comment briefly on the accuracy of this estimate.
d. Would you agree that your answer to the median value (part *b*) can be given the following interpretation: "Fifty percent of the total payroll of these 500 establishments was paid by firms with an annual payroll above (*your answer* to part *b*)?" Why or why not?
30. Table 6.16 shows the cost of manufacturing flour for selected companies.
a. Calculate the median net cost of manufacturing a barrel of flour from column 1.
b. Explain the meaning of your answer in terms of this problem.
c. The median net cost of manufacturing a barrel of flour calculated from column 2 is $5.10. Why does this answer differ from your answer in part *a*?
31. A frequency distribution showing men classified by weight has a mode of 160 lb and a mean at 175 lb.
a. What can you say about the value of the median of this distribution?
b. What can you say about the skewness of this distribution?
32. Table 6.17 gives the hourly wage rates of the 200 truck drivers employed by the Springtime Company for the week ending April 1, 1968.
a. Calculate the mean hourly wage rate per driver for this company for the week ending April 1, 1968.

Table 6.16

Net Cost of Manufacturing Flour per Barrel	Column 1	Column 2
	Number of Companies Operating at Given Cost	Barrels Produced (Millions)
$4.40–4.79	14	20
4.80–5.19	15	40
5.20–5.59	35	25
5.60–5.99	19	7
6.00–6.39	10	4
6.40–6.79	4	2
6.80–7.19	2	1
7.20–7.59	1	1
	100	100

Source. Hypothetical

b. Explain precisely the meaning of the number you computed in part *a*.

c. Would the average that you computed in part *a* be the same as the ratio of total wages paid to truck drivers of the Springtime Company during the week ending April 1, 1968 to the total man hours worked by truck drivers during that week? Why or why not?

33. Criticize or explain the following statements.

a. If statistical calculations are to be made from a frequency distribution instead of from the ungrouped data, it is essential that all class intervals be of the same size.

Table 6.17

Hourly Wage Rate	Number of Drivers
$2.250–2.3749	6
2.375–2.4999	14
2.500–2.6249	30
2.625–2.7499	110
2.750–2.8749	24
2.875–2.9999	16
	200

b. When concentrations of items appear around certain numerical values in an array, the class limits in a frequency table should be adjusted insofar as possible to make these concentrations fall at the class limits.

c. Sixty-five percent of college graduates in the first quartile of their graduating class smoke more than the average number of cigarettes per day. This suggests that the higher the IQ the more cigarettes consumed.

d. A statistician once said that the same percentage of frequencies occur between the first and third quartile of a symmetrical distribution as occur between the first and third quartile of a skewed distribution.

34. The distribution given in Table 6.18 refers to hourly workers of a certain company.

Table 6.18

Hourly Wage	Number of Workers
$2.25–2.29	10
2.30–2.34	17
—	—
—	—
—	—
Total	175

a. The arithmetic mean or the above distribution was $2.47 and the arithmetic mean number of hours worked by these 175 men was 38 during a certain week. Would $2.47 × 38 × 175 equal total wages paid by the company to these men for that week? Explain.

b. The median of the above distribution was $2.43. Interpret this value specifically in terms of this problem.

35. Criticize or explain the following statements.

a. Sixty percent of the graduates of Ironclad University Medical School received higher than the average score on the National Board Examinations. Our graduates should be congratulated on their fine showing.

b. A student at College A transferred to College B, thus raising the average IQ in both schools.

c. Men and women are homogeneous with respect to IQ but not with respect to height.

d. The average college entrance examination score at Culture College for Northern High graduates was higher than for other high school graduates on the same examination. Therefore, Northern has a better course of instruction than other high schools.

36. Give an example of a frequency distribution, constructed from actual data, in which it would be impossible to close the end classes. Give a second example of a frequency distribution with open end classes in which it would be relatively simple to close the end classes.

37. Listed in Table 6.19 are total dollar sales for each day of the month of April 1968 at Joe Blott's newsstand in Chicago. Total sales for the entire month of April 1968 were $3767.87.

   a. Construct a frequency distribution representing daily sales at Blott's newsstand for April 1968.

Table 6.19

Day of Month	Total Sales (Dollars)	Day of Month	Total Sales (Dollars)
1	107.60	16	122.67
2	92.65	17	155.68
3	151.02	18	165.92
4	164.68	19	116.34
5	102.06	20	115.27
6	162.21	21	137.72
7	93.77	22	127.66
8	94.01	23	93.66
9	112.44	24	106.70
10	146.42	25	146.79
11	159.59	26	119.99
12	126.97	27	135.41
13	134.31	28	114.17
14	113.23	29	101.70
15	128.94	30	118.29

   b. Draw a histogram showing the distribution of part *a*.
   c. Construct a cumulative frequency distribution of sales at Blott's newsstand for April 1968.
   d. Calculate the arithmetic mean of the frequency distribution that you constructed in part *a*.

e. Calculate the median of the frequency distribution constructed in part *a*.

f. Calculate the standard deviation of the frequency distribution that you constructed in part *a*.

g. Now, find the mean daily sales at Blott's newsstand direct from the original 30 items.

h. Why do the results of parts *d* and *g* differ? Under what conditions would they be the same?

i. Find the median of daily sales at Blott's newsstand direct from the original 30 items.

j. Why do the results of parts *e* and *i* not differ? Under what conditions would they differ?

k. If you were to find the standard deviation of the original 30 items directly, would it agree with the result obtained in part *f*? Explain.

l. Do any of your results in this problem suggest that the data may not be homogeneous? Explain after examining the original data carefully.

38. Listed in Table 6.20 are the amounts shown on the 423 sales slips issued at Counter H of the Monahan Brothers Department Store during October 1969.

a. Construct a frequency distribution of these amounts.

b. Draw a histogram for this distribution.

c. Find the mean amount of sales at Counter H during October 1969.

d. Find the median amount of sales.

e. In which class would the mode of the distribution be located?

f. Compute the standard deviation for this distribution.

39. For the data of Exercise 24, calculate the following.

a. The range.

b. The standard deviation.

c. The coefficient of variation.

40. For the data of Exercise 25, calculate the following.

a. The range.

b. The standard deviation.

c. The coefficient of variation.

41. Table 6.21 gives the frequency distribution for all salaried employees of the Jones Plastic Co.

a. Compute the arithmetic mean of this distribution.

b. Is the arithmetic mean a good measure of central tendency for this distribution? Discuss.

c. Compute the standard deviation of the above distribution.

d. Would you say that there is a great deal of dispersion in this distribution? Why or why not?

Table 6.20

Sales Slip Number	Amount of Sale	Sales Slip Number	Amount of Sale	Sales Slip Number	Amount of Sale	Sales Slip Number	Amount of Sale	Sales Slip Number	Amount of Sale
1	3.73	57	14.27	113	6.76	169	4.84	225	1.89
2	6.28	58	13.09	114	3.06	170	20.03	226	5.29
3	8.52	59	1.06	115	23.09	171	7.96	227	13.48
4	8.32	60	7.76	116	6.83	172	8.43	228	2.52
5	1.57	61	6.76	117	18.64	173	8.41	229	6.43
6	16.15	62	2.16	118	17.68	174	2.23	230	20.14
7	7.56	63	1.31	119	1.52	175	2.29	231	7.77
8	4.03	64	1.78	120	1.66	176	5.29	232	13.38
9	20.31	65	15.27	121	9.88	177	7.07	233	9.01
10	25.78	66	5.47	122	4.51	178	21.18	234	5.24
11	19.05	67	6.76	123	2.07	179	9.52	235	2.68
12	19.94	68	1.19	124	4.53	180	9.94	236	20.44
13	4.82	69	1.77	125	21.16	181	21.60	237	7.00
14	1.37	70	5.99	126	9.67	182	1.87	238	2.52
15	1.37	71	3.44	127	2.49	183	3.30	239	6.07
16	6.84	72	19.63	128	13.48	184	18.89	240	6.91
17	9.66	73	1.70	129	2.74	185	26.67	241	2.16
18	4.59	74	9.06	130	6.81	186	1.57	242	4.19
19	13.71	75	9.34	131	26.45	187	8.10	243	5.04
20	6.57	76	19.53	132	4.93	188	5.76	244	13.48
21	6.87	77	5.85	133	8.24	189	15.63	245	6.00
22	9.38	78	3.33	134	1.78	190	4.57	246	8.42
23	11.33	79	1.93	135	13.58	191	16.31	247	9.02
24	2.24	80	1.67	136	8.18	192	13.39	248	14.26
25	1.89	81	24.09	137	9.77	193	9.81	249	12.33
26	26.94	82	2.76	138	1.23	194	18.32	250	11.20
27	7.18	83	1.20	139	7.79	195	23.79	251	28.06
28	4.37	84	6.87	140	23.72	196	23.79	252	29.36
29	6.59	85	1.67	141	5.68	197	26.67	253	5.64
30	10.60	86	3.87	142	7.99	198	1.27	254	7.51
31	5.79	87	2.66	143	8.81	199	22.31	255	14.00
32	8.61	88	13.75	144	14.65	200	10.28	256	8.69
33	10.50	89	2.99	145	1.71	201	4.78	257	5.91
34	14.15	90	8.41	146	1.51	202	11.35	258	4.65
35	2.68	91	1.84	147	4.65	203	10.95	259	5.68
36	12.11	92	4.62	148	3.36	204	1.18	260	1.91
37	7.05	93	6.63	149	15.76	205	1.32	261	1.76
38	9.36	94	2.31	150	1.17	206	9.20	262	9.09
39	1.94	95	7.13	151	5.18	207	3.44	263	4.76
40	8.13	96	7.66	152	20.57	208	7.28	264	1.81
41	10.02	97	17.39	153	2.05	209	1.99	265	2.58
42	5.26	98	1.92	154	4.41	210	26.28	266	6.11
43	7.73	99	7.26	155	4.24	211	4.30	267	11.29
44	22.87	100	3.10	156	25.06	212	2.01	268	2.82
45	6.36	101	28.77	157	4.64	213	1.65	269	3.51
46	4.77	102	7.86	158	9.22	214	4.86	270	2.98
47	8.54	103	20.92	159	1.01	215	1.91	271	7.13
48	5.60	104	3.75	160	20.47	216	24.37	272	29.48
49	11.39	105	6.67	161	3.59	217	25.49	273	21.29
50	7.21	106	1.62	162	12.76	218	15.42	274	3.72
51	22.51	107	1.62	163	26.90	219	1.95	275	2.53
52	12.64	108	10.29	164	1.65	220	14.26	276	9.65
53	7.67	109	5.49	165	19.23	221	1.47	277	14.34
54	4.14	110	11.87	166	4.24	222	7.99	278	2.73
55	8.76	111	8.38	167	9.87	223	9.62	279	4.59
56	6.79	112	2.46	168	7.00	224	2.62	280	2.21

(continued)

226

Table **6.20** (*continued*)

Sales Slip Number	Amount of Sale	Sales Slip Number	Amount of Sale	Sales Slip Number	Amount of Sale	Sales Slip Number	Amount of Sale	Sales Slip Number	Amount of Sale
281	4.86	310	2.82	339	7.23	368	4.35	397	8.86
282	7.86	311	14.59	340	10.42	369	6.97	398	18.90
283	25.72	312	1.28	341	15.81	370	2.48	399	12.37
284	17.78	313	9.82	342	12.97	371	9.47	400	14.71
285	7.49	314	11.00	343	1.00	372	7.17	401	2.61
286	5.97	315	17.59	344	1.81	373	1.25	402	3.53
287	21.35	316	8.48	345	1.90	374	2.53	403	18.31
288	5.86	317	2.24	346	2.23	375	13.70	404	16.96
289	27.09	318	28.48	347	6.42	376	5.84	405	5.49
290	1.71	319	1.52	348	1.11	377	21.39	406	8.73
291	6.92	320	18.61	349	5.07	378	3.39	407	4.73
292	10.56	321	7.81	350	7.99	379	1.02	408	1.50
293	5.08	322	7.64	351	2.92	380	4.66	409	4.57
294	9.27	323	8.69	352	21.69	381	1.22	410	15.48
295	20.25	324	2.87	353	7.99	382	17.00	411	2.20
296	2.06	325	20.04	354	10.56	383	5.40	412	9.69
297	3.04	326	13.20	355	14.36	384	3.49	413	2.57
298	22.30	327	4.15	356	9.64	385	5.58	414	19.92
299	3.51	328	13.03	357	3.17	386	16.29	415	6.82
300	7.19	329	2.68	358	9.91	387	7.77	416	1.19
301	14.15	330	1.16	359	5.95	388	2.10	417	5.26
302	22.28	331	8.92	360	13.22	389	1.17	418	2.42
303	3.75	332	1.43	361	3.28	390	1.71	419	11.49
304	8.14	333	9.28	362	6.32	391	11.60	420	2.73
305	21.85	334	4.22	363	25.18	392	18.47	421	8.26
306	8.84	335	29.01	364	6.03	393	9.54	422	5.83
307	7.58	336	5.95	365	1.62	394	21.99	423	13.76
308	18.33	337	1.62	366	9.58	395	1.34		
309	1.88	338	8.45	367	22.47	396	6.38		

Table **6.21**

Weekly Wage ($)	Number of Employees
60 and less than 70	7
70 and less than 80	20
80 and less than 90	62
90 and less than 100	50
100 and less than 110	20
110 and less than 120	15
120 and less than 130	6
	180

e. The age distribution for these employees has the following characteristics: first quartile = 26, arithmetic mean = 42, third quartile = 54,
median = 38, standard deviation = 18, range = 49. Do these
employees exhibit more dispersion in weekly wages or in age?

42. Table 6.22 gives the frequency distribution of the life of Brand A tires
in a road test.

Table 6.22

Life of Tire (Thousands of Miles)	Percentage of Tires Tested
10 and under 15	7
15 and under 20	15
20 and under 25	40
25 and under 30	30
30 and under 35	8
	100

a. Compute the standard deviation and the arithmetic mean of the above
distribution.
b. A laboratory test of Brand B tires showed a mean life of 500 hours
and a standard deviation of 165 hours. On the basis of the data given,
would you conclude that there is greater variability in the life of
Brand B tires than in Brand A tires? Justify statistically.
c. Given that 25 percent of the Brand A tires tested had a life of less
than 20,375 miles, compute the range (in miles) that would include
the middle 50 percent of the tires tested.

43. The distribution in Table 6.23 refers to total costs per dollar of sales,
that is, sales of services, for the 80 firms in the Shoe Repair Trade
Association of West Falls, Pa.
a. Compute the standard deviation and the arithmetic mean of this
distribution.
b. Is the arithmetic mean computed in part *a* the same value as the ratio
of total costs to total sales for these 80 companies? Why or why not?
c. A similar distribution for tailors in West Falls yielded a mean of
$0.61 and a standard deviation $0.098. Are costs per dollar of sales
more uniform for tailors than for shoe repairmen?

Table 6.23 Number of Shoe Repair Establishments Classified by Cost per Dollar of Sales, West Falls, Pa.

Cost per Dollar of Sales	Number of Establishments
0.50 and under 0.60	4
0.60 and under 0.70	8
0.70 and under 0.80	14
0.80 and under 0.90	30
0.90 and under 1.00	16
1.00 and under 1.10	8
Total	80

d. Assume that the data in Table 6.23 were collected by means of mail questionnaires. Under what conditions would you be willing to say that the data are representative of all shoe repair establishments in West Falls? Discuss fully.

e. If the 80 ratios referred to above had been presented to you in the form of an array, list each operation that you would have to perform in order to compute the standard deviation from these individual values.

f. In what sense, if any, is the standard deviation an "average?" Discuss.

44. A leading labor journal published the figures shown in Table 6.24 on the average number of hours worked per week by production employees of 100 selected industries in the United States in September, 1964.

a. Compute the coefficient of variation of hours worked from the distribution shown in Table 6.24.

Table 6.24

Hours Worked per Week	Number of Industries
30.0–32.99	2
33.0–35.99	4
36.0–38.99	25
39.0–41.99	48
42.0–44.99	15
45.0–47.99	6
	100

    b. Explain what each element of the coefficient of variation measures as well as what the coefficient itself measures.

    c. Compute the median for the distribution and explain its meaning.

    d. If this value, which you computed in part *c*, differs from the measure of central tendency you computed as part of *a*, explain the difference. If they do not differ, explain why they are equal.

45. The arithmetic mean sales volume of drug stores in County A is $20,000 per month, and the standard deviation is $4000. The arithmetic mean sales volume of food stores in County A is $100,000 per month and the standard deviation is $15,000. Using sales as a measure of size, is there greater variability in size among drug stores in County A or among food stores in County A? Support your conclusion with calculations.

46. a. Sketch two frequency distributions having the same median value and the same total frequency, but differing considerably in dispersion. Explain what criteria you used to fit your sketch to the above restrictions.

    b. Sketch two frequency distributions with equal total frequency and the same standard deviation, but with definitely different medians.

    c. Is it true that a skewed frequency distribution has greater dispersion than one which is symmetric? Explain.

7 Moment-Generating Functions

7.1 INTRODUCTION AND DEFINITION

The statistician often works with random variables that are functions of other random variables. He is interested in determining the probability distribution of the function from the distributions of the variables in its domain. If he cannot find it, he would at least like to know its mean and variance and perhaps find a simple probability distribution that approximates it.

For example, suppose we want to find out how long it takes to walk from the dormitory to our statistics class. The ordinary person might time himself once, trying to walk at a "normal" pace. This would give a time from which he could compute how late he could sleep and still get to class on schedule. One observation might be "good enough" in this case. A little thought, however, will show that the time to walk from the dormitory to statistics class is a random variable. It depends on the weather (we tend to hurry when it rains, for example), on whom we meet on the way, on the traffic on any streets that we have to cross, on how crowded the hallways are, and on other factors that may increase or decrease walking time and that may operate in different directions at different times.

An estimate based on only one observation might not be very good. Perhaps a better procedure would be to time oneself under a variety of conditions—say on ten days picked at random from the next 20 days on which one has to take this walk. Having done this, we might use the average of these times as our estimate. This average is the sum of ten random variables divided by ten. It is a random variable, and its probability distribution depends on the distributions of the ten random variables. It turns out that, under fairly reasonable assumptions about the distribution of the individual walking times, the distribution of the average is easy to obtain. Also, if we are interested only in the mean and variance of the distribution, they are easy to compute—provided one knows a few "tricks." Problems like this one will be discussed in Chapter 8, but in the present chapter we shall introduce one of the tricks: the use of the *moment-generating function.*

Since we cannot easily create a situation in which a moment-generating function is the logical thing to use, we begin with a definition and then proceed by discussion and example.

Definition. If X is a random variable with probability distribution $f(x)$, the moment-generating function of $f(x)$ is denoted by the symbol $m_X(\theta)$ and defined by

$$m_X(\theta) = \sum_{x=-\infty}^{\infty} e^{\theta x} f(x) \tag{7.1}$$

if X is discrete, and by

$$m_X(\theta) = \int_{x=-\infty}^{\infty} e^{\theta x} f(x)\, dx \tag{7.2}$$

if X is continuous. In this text θ is always a real number. When this is true, there are functions $f(x)$ for which $m_X(\theta)$ does not exist. However, they are unusual; for any probability distribution discussed in this text, $m_X(\theta)$ will exist.

Now, $e^{\theta X}$ is a function of a random variable X, and is therefore a random variable. $m_X(\theta)$ is the expected value of the random variable $e^{\theta X}$, according to Definition III of Section 6.3. Sometimes $m_X(\theta)$ is either difficult or impossible to compute. When we can obtain it in simple form, however, it is often extremely useful. To illustrate the calculation of the moment-generating function, we shall obtain it for the binomial and the uniform distributions. For the binomial distribution,

$$f(x) = \binom{n}{x} p^x (1 - p)^{n-x} \qquad x = 0, 1, \cdots, n$$

Thus we have

$$m_X(\theta) = \sum_{x=0}^{n} e^{\theta x} \binom{n}{x} p^x (1 - p)^{n-x}$$

$$= \sum_{x=0}^{n} \binom{n}{x} (pe^\theta)^x (1 - p)^{n-x} = [pe^\theta + (1 - p)]^n \tag{7.3}$$

For the uniform distribution, with $a = 0$, $b = 1$,

$$f(x) = 1 \qquad 0 \le x \le 1$$

and

$$m_X(\theta) = \int_0^1 e^{\theta x}\, dx = \frac{1}{\theta}\left[e^{\theta x} \right]_0^1 = \frac{1}{\theta}(e^\theta - 1) \tag{7.4}$$

A partial check of the correctness of the calculation of $m_X(\theta)$ is to take its limit as θ approaches zero. This limit should be equal to unity because when θ is zero, $e^{\theta X}$ is equal to unity, and the definition of $m_X(\theta)$ reduces to the sum or integral of a probability distribution over its entire domain. The moment-generating functions of both the binomial and the uniform distributions satisfy this condition, although it is slightly more difficult to show it in the case of the uniform distribution.[1]

There is a simple property of moment-generating functions which we will introduce at this point although it will not be needed until Chapter 8. It is stated as

$$m_{cX}(\theta) = m_X(c\theta) \qquad (7.5)$$

If we form a new variable by multiplying X by the constant c, then we can obtain the moment-generating function of the new variable by replacing θ by $c\theta$ in the moment-generating function of X. We show the simple proof in the continuous case; the discrete case follows if sums replace integrals.

On the one hand

$$m_{cX}(\theta) = \int e^{\theta c x} f(x)\, dx$$

On the other hand

$$m_X(c\theta) = \int e^{c\theta x} f(x)\, dx$$

The two expressions are identical.

7.2   MOMENT-GENERATING PROPERTIES OF MOMENT-GENERATING FUNCTIONS

Why is $m_X(\theta)$ called a *moment-generating* function? Properly manipulated, it can be made to "generate" the moments of $f(x)$. To see this, we first write $e^{\theta x}$ in a power series. From Appendix B we know that

$$e^{\theta x} = 1 + \theta x + \frac{\theta^2 x^2}{2!} + \frac{\theta^3 x^3}{3!} + \cdots \qquad (7.6)$$

---

[1] To show that the limit as θ approaches zero of $m_X(\theta)$ is unity in the case of the uniform distribution, we may use one of two methods. One procedure is to use L'Hospital's rule for evaluating limits of the form $0/0$. This may be found in any standard calculus text. Another method is to expand $e^{\theta X}$ in its MacLaurin series obtaining the form shown in (7.8). As θ approaches zero, it is at once evident that

$$1 + \frac{1}{2}\theta + \frac{1}{3}\frac{\theta^2}{2!} + \frac{1}{4}\frac{\theta^3}{3!} + \cdots$$

approaches 1 as a limit.

Now we substitute (7.6) in (7.1). We get

$$m_X(\theta) = \sum_{x=-\infty}^{\infty} \left(1 + \theta x + \frac{\theta^2 x^2}{2!} + \frac{\theta^3 x^3}{3!} + \cdots\right) f(x)$$

$$= \sum_{x=-\infty}^{\infty} f(x) + \theta \sum_{x=-\infty}^{\infty} x f(x) + \frac{\theta^2}{2!} \sum_{x=-\infty}^{\infty} x^2 f(x) + \cdots$$

$$= 1 + \theta E(X) + \frac{\theta^2}{2!} E(X^2) + \frac{\theta^3}{3!} E(X^3) + \cdots \qquad (7.7)$$

We would get the same result by substituting (7.6) in (7.2) and integrating. This result, (7.7), means, that if we can write $m_X(\theta)$ as a power series in θ, we can read off the moments about the origin immediately. In particular, $E(X^k)$ is the coefficient of $\theta^k/k!$. Consider, for example, the moment-generating function for the uniform distribution given in (7.4). We can write this as

$$\frac{1}{\theta}(e^\theta - 1) = \frac{1}{\theta}\left(1 + \theta + \frac{\theta^2}{2!} + \frac{\theta^3}{3!} + \frac{\theta^4}{4!} + \cdots -1\right)$$

$$= \frac{1}{\theta}\left(\theta + \frac{\theta^2}{2!} + \frac{\theta^3}{3!} + \frac{\theta^4}{4!} + \cdots\right)$$

$$= \left(1 + \frac{1}{2}\theta + \frac{1}{3}\frac{\theta^2}{2!} + \frac{1}{4}\frac{\theta^3}{3!} + \cdots\right) \qquad (7.8)$$

The first moment about the origin of $f(x)$ is the coefficient of θ, namely 1/2. The second moment, $E(X^2)$, is the coefficient of $\theta^2/2!$, that is, 1/3. In general $E(X^k)$ is given by $1/(k + 1)$. All we need to do to determine any moment about the origin of this uniform distribution is to read (7.8) in the context of (7.7).

If we expand $e^{\theta x}$ as a power series in the moment-generating function for the binomial distribution and collect coefficients of like powers of θ, we run into a bookkeeping problem. Fortunately, there is a way around this difficulty. Suppose we differentiate a few times with respect to θ the expression for $m_X(\theta)$ given by (7.7). We get

$$m_X'(\theta) = E(X) + \theta E(X^2) + \frac{\theta^2}{2!} E(X^3) + \frac{\theta^3}{3!} E(X^4) + \cdots$$

$$m_X''(\theta) = E(X^2) + \theta E(X^3) + \frac{\theta^2}{2!} E(X^4) + \frac{\theta^3}{3!} E(X^5) + \cdots$$

$$\cdots \qquad \cdots \qquad \cdots \qquad \cdots \qquad \cdots \qquad (7.9)$$

$$m_X^{(k)}(\theta) = E(X^k) + \theta E(X^{k+1}) + \frac{\theta^2}{2!} E(X^{k+2}) + \frac{\theta^3}{3!} E(X^{k+3}) + \cdots$$

$$\cdots \qquad \cdots \qquad \cdots \qquad \cdots \qquad \cdots$$

Now, if we set θ equal to zero, we shall have the moments.

$$m_X'(0) = E(X)$$
$$m_X''(0) = E(X^2)$$
$$\cdots \qquad \cdots \qquad (7.10)$$
$$m_X^{(k)}(0) = E(X^k)$$
$$\cdots \qquad \cdots$$

Hence, in one way or another, we can make the moment-generating function "generate" the moments of $f(x)$.

To illustrate the method of (7.9) and (7.10), we shall obtain the first three moments about the origin of the binomial distribution by differentiating $m_X(\theta)$ three times with respect to θ and setting θ equal to zero. We have, differentiating (7.3),

$$m_X'(\theta) = n[pe^\theta + (1 - p)]^{n-1}pe^\theta$$
$$m_X''(\theta) = n(n - 1)[pe^\theta + (1 - p)]^{n-2}p^2e^{2\theta} + n[pe^\theta + (1 - p)]^{n-1}pe^\theta$$
$$m_X'''(\theta) = n(n - 1)(n - 2)[pe^\theta + (1 - p)]^{n-3}p^3e^{3\theta} + 3n(n - 1)$$
$$\times [pe^\theta + (1 - p)]^{n-2}p^2e^{2\theta} + n[pe^\theta + (1 - p)]^{n-1}pe^\theta$$

Now, we set θ equal to zero and use (7.10) to get the first three moments about the origin.

$$E(X) = np$$
$$E(X^2) = n(n - 1)p^2 + np$$
$$E(X^3) = n(n - 1)(n - 2)p^3 + 3n(n - 1)p^2 + np$$

With a little manipulation, this can be shown to agree with our earlier results.

7.3   THE MOMENT-GENERATING FUNCTION FOR THE NORMAL DISTRIBUTION

In Chapter 8 we shall need the moment-generating function for the normal distribution. It is not difficult to compute this function directly. Since the normal distribution is given by

$$f(x) = \frac{1}{\sigma\sqrt{2\pi}} e^{-(x-\mu)^2/2\sigma^2} \qquad -\infty < x < \infty$$

the moment-generating function is

$$m_X(\theta) = \frac{1}{\sigma\sqrt{2\pi}} \int_{z=-\infty}^{\infty} e^{\theta x} e^{-(x-\mu)^2/2\sigma^2} \, dx$$

Now let $z = (x - \mu)/\sigma$, $x = \mu + \sigma z$, $dx = \sigma\, dz$.

$$m_X(\theta) = \frac{1}{\sigma\sqrt{2\pi}} \int_{z=-\infty}^{\infty} e^{\theta(\mu+\sigma z)} e^{-z^2/2} \sigma\, dz$$

$$= \frac{e^{\mu\theta}}{\sqrt{2\pi}} \int_{z=-\infty}^{\infty} e^{-(z^2 - 2\sigma\theta z)/2}\, dz$$

Next we complete the square in the exponent.

$$-\frac{1}{2}(z^2 - 2\sigma\theta z) = -\frac{1}{2}(z^2 - 2\sigma\theta z + \sigma^2\theta^2) + \frac{\sigma^2\theta^2}{2}$$

$$= -\frac{1}{2}(z - \sigma\theta)^2 + \frac{\sigma^2\theta^2}{2}$$

So, substituting,

$$m_X(\theta) = e^{\mu\theta} e^{\sigma^2\theta^2/2} \cdot \frac{1}{\sqrt{2\pi}} \int_{z=-\infty}^{\infty} e^{-(z-\sigma\theta)^2/2}\, dz$$

$$m_X(\theta) = e^{\mu\theta + \sigma^2\theta^2/2} \tag{7.11}$$

Since the last factor is the integral of a normal distribution with mean $\sigma\theta$ and standard deviation unity over its whole domain, it is equal to one. We repeat that several references will be made to (7.11) in Chapter 8. The student may easily verify, by differentiating and setting $\theta = 0$, that the mean and variance of a normal distribution are respectively μ and σ^2.

7.4   OTHER USES OF THE MOMENT-GENERATING FUNCTION

The moment-generating function is unique in the sense that to every moment-generating function there corresponds one and only one probability distribution.[2] This means that if two probability distributions have the same moment generating function they are really the same. This property of uniqueness is useful in finding approximate distributions. For example, binomial probabilities are difficult to compute when n is large. By looking at the limit of the moment-generating function of the binomial probability distribution as n increases, perhaps we can identify it. If so, we can use the probability distribution corresponding to this moment-generating function as an approximation to the binomial distribution.

If instead of X, the *number* of successes in n trials of an experiment to which the binomial distribution applies, we consider X/n, the *proportion* of successes, we get a good approximation for the binomial distribution when

---

[2] This is true only if $m_X(\theta)$ exists when θ lies in an interval containing zero. In this text this restriction will not trouble us.

n is large. Let $P = X/n$. Then we can find the moment-generating function of P from the moment-generating function of X.

$$m_P(\theta) = m_{X/n}(\theta) = E(e^{\theta X/n}) = m_X\left(\frac{\theta}{n}\right)$$

$$= [pe^{\theta/n} + (1 - p)]^n \qquad \text{using (7.3).}$$

We first expand $e^{\theta/n}$ in a power series in θ.

$$m_P(\theta) = \left[1 - p + p\left(1 + \frac{\theta}{n} + \frac{\theta^2}{n^2 2!} + \frac{\theta^3}{n^3 3!} + \cdots\right)\right]^n$$

Now, if n is large and θ is close to zero, θ^k/n^k will approach zero very rapidly so that we can ignore the terms involving high powers of θ. Let us ignore all powers of θ higher than the second. Thus

$$m_P(\theta) \approx \left[1 + p\frac{\theta}{n} + p\frac{\theta^2}{2n^2}\right]^n$$

Consider the logarithm to the base e of $m_P(\theta)$ as n grows large. If we expand $\ln(1 + x)$ in MacLaurin series, we obtain (see Appendix B):

$$\ln(1 + x) = x - \frac{x^2}{2} + \frac{x^3}{3} - \frac{x^4}{4} + \cdots$$

Hence

$$\ln m_P(\theta) = n \ln\left[1 + p\frac{\theta}{n} + p\frac{\theta^2}{2n^2}\right]$$

$$\approx n\left[p\frac{\theta}{n} + p\frac{\theta^2}{2n^2} - \frac{1}{2}\left(\frac{p^2\theta^2}{n^2} + \frac{p^2\theta^3}{n^3} + \frac{p^2\theta^4}{4n^4}\right) + \cdots\right]$$

$$\approx p\theta + \frac{1}{2}\frac{p(1 - p)}{n}\theta^2$$

Since this is, approximately, $\ln m_P(\theta)$ when n is large, then, when n is large,

$$m_P(\theta) \approx e^{p\theta + [p(1-p)/n]\theta^2/2} \qquad (7.12)$$

When we compare (7.12) with (7.11), we see that they look alike. Instead of μ we have p, and instead of σ^2 we have $p(1 - p)/n$. Hence, when n is large, we can approximate the probability distribution of X/n, where X has the binomial distribution, with a normal distribution with a mean of p and a variance of $p(1 - p)/n$. In practice, this approximation is good if np is equal to or greater than five. It can be improved if we work with the cumulated normal distribution of

$$u = \frac{x + \frac{1}{2} - np}{\sqrt{npq}} \qquad q = 1 - p$$

Table 7.1   Illustration of the Normal Approximation to the Cumulated Binomial Distribution with $n = 10$ and $p = 0.5$

x	u	$F(u)$ (Normal)	$F(x)$ (Binomial)
0	−2.85	0.0022	0.0010
1	−2.22	0.0132	0.0108
2	−1.58	0.0571	0.0547
3	−0.95	0.1711	0.1719
4	−0.32	0.3745	0.3770
5	0.32	0.6255	0.6231
6	0.95	0.8289	0.8282
7	1.58	0.9430	0.9454
8	2.22	0.9868	0.9893
9	2.85	0.9978	0.9991
10	3.48	0.9997	1.0000

The approximation is illustrated and compared with the binomial in Table 7.1 using an n of 10 and a p of 0.5.

Suppose, next, that we want an approximation to the binomial probability distribution when n is large but p so small that the condition that np must be equal to or greater than five does not hold. Specifically, let us make the assumption that p goes to zero and n goes to infinity in such a way that

$$np = \lambda$$

We can write $m_X(\theta)$ for the binomial as

$$m_X(\theta) = \left[1 + \frac{\lambda}{n}(e^\theta - 1) \right]^n$$

Now, let

$$v = \frac{n}{\lambda(e^\theta - 1)}$$

Then

$$m_X(\theta) = \left[\left(1 + \frac{1}{v} \right)^v \right]^{\lambda(e^\theta - 1)}$$

It is easy to show that (see Appendix A)

$$\lim_{v \to \infty} \left(1 + \frac{1}{v} \right)^v = e$$

Hence

$$\lim_{n \to \infty} m_X(\theta) = \lim_{v \to \infty} \left[\left(1 + \frac{1}{v} \right)^v \right]^{\lambda(e^\theta - 1)} = e^{\lambda(e^\theta - 1)}$$

Table 7.2   Some Common Probability Distributions and Their Moment-Generating Functions

Name of Distribution	$f(x)$ and values of X at which $f(x) \neq 0$	$m_X(\theta)$
1. Uniform (discrete)	$1/n, \; x = 0, 1, \cdots, n - 1$	$(1 - e^{n\theta})/n(1 - e^{\theta})$
2. Binomial	$\binom{n}{x} p^x (1 - p)^{n-x}, \; x = 0, 1, \cdots, n$	$(1 - p + pe^{\theta})^n$
3. Poisson	$e^{-\lambda} \lambda^x / x!, \; x = 0, 1, \cdots$	$e^{\lambda(e^{\theta}-1)}$
4. Uniform (continuous)	$1/(b - a), \; a \leq x \leq b$	$(e^{b\theta} - e^{a\theta})/(b - a)\theta$
5. Exponential	$ce^{-cx}, \; 0 \leq x < \infty$	$c/(c - \theta)$
6. Normal	$\dfrac{1}{\sigma\sqrt{2\pi}} e^{-[(x-\mu)/\sigma]^2/2}, \; -\infty < x < \infty$	$e^{\mu\theta + \sigma^2\theta^2/2}$

In Table 7.2 we list some common probability distributions and their moment-generating functions. If we look in this table, we see that the function given above is the moment-generating function for the Poisson probability distribution. Hence, when n is large and p is small, we can approximate the binomial probability distribution with a Poisson probability distribution using a λ of np. In Table 7.3 we show such an approximation for a binomial distribution having an n of 20 and a p of 0.1.

Table 7.3   Poisson Approximation to the Binomial when $n = 20$ and $p = 0.1$

x	Poisson Approximation $\lambda = 20\,(0.1) = 2$	Binomial Distribution
0	0.1353	0.1216
1	0.2707	0.2702
2	0.2707	0.2852
3	0.1804	0.1901
4	0.0902	0.0898
5	0.0361	0.0319
6	0.0120	0.0089
7	0.0034	0.0020
8	0.0009	0.0004
9	0.0002	0.0001
10	0.0001	0.0000
11	0.0000	0.0000

7.5 MOMENTS AND MOMENT-GENERATING FUNCTIONS
FOR SEVERAL RANDOM VARIABLES

In Section 5.4 we defined a continuous probability distribution of the n random variables $X_1, \cdots, X_n$ to be a function $f(x_1, \cdots, x_n)$ defined for all points $(x_1, \cdots, x_n)$ in an n-dimensional space for which

$$f(x_1, \cdots, x_n) \geq 0$$

and

$$\int_{x_1} \cdots \int_{x_n} f(x_1, \cdots, x_n) \, dx_1 \cdots dx_n = 1$$

$$-\infty < x_1 < \infty \qquad -\infty < x_2 < \infty \qquad \cdots \qquad -\infty < x_n < \infty$$

For discrete distributions, sums replace integrals. In this text we shall have no use for probability distributions of several discrete random variables. As an example of a probability distribution of several random variables, the reader is referred to Appendix C where, in showing that the integral of the function

$$\frac{8}{9}(x_1 + x_2 + x_3)$$

was unity over a particular domain, we also showed that it is a probability distribution.

Each of the random variables $X_1, \cdots, X_n$ has a mean $E(X_i)$, $i = 1, \cdots, n$, which is its first moment about the origin. Each has a variance $\sigma_i^2 = E[X_i - E(X_i)]^2$ which is its second moment about the mean. And each pair of variables has a joint first moment about the mean called a *covariance*. In the case of two continuous variables X_1 and X_2 whose joint distribution is $f(x_1, x_2)$

$$E(X_1) = \int_{x_1=-\infty}^{\infty} \int_{x_2=-\infty}^{\infty} x_1 f(x_1, x_2) \, dx_1 \, dx_2$$

$$E(X_2) = \int_{x_1=-\infty}^{\infty} \int_{x_2=-\infty}^{\infty} x_2 f(x_1, x_2) \, dx_1 \, dx_2$$

$$E(X_1^2) = \int_{x_1=-\infty}^{\infty} \int_{x_2=-\infty}^{\infty} x_1^2 f(x_1, x_2) \, dx_1 \, dx_2$$

$$E(X_2^2) = \int_{x_1=-\infty}^{\infty} \int_{x_2=-\infty}^{\infty} x_2^2 f(x_1, x_2) \, dx_1 \, dx_2$$

$$\sigma_1^2 = E(X_1^2) - [E(X_1)]^2 \qquad \sigma_2^2 = E(X_2^2) - [E(X_2)]^2$$

For the covariance of X_1 and X_2, the definition is

$$\text{cov}\,(X_1,\,X_2) = E\{[X_1 - E(X_1)][X_2 - E(X_2)]\}$$

$$= \int_{x_1=-\infty}^{\infty} \int_{x_2=-\infty}^{\infty} [x_1 - E(X_1)][x_2 - E(X_2)]$$

$$\times f(x_1,\,x_2)\,dx_1\,dx_2 \qquad (7.13)$$

For many calculations we use a simplified formula obtained by expanding (7.13).

$$\text{cov}\,(X_1,\,X_2) = \int_{x_1=-\infty}^{\infty} \int_{x_2=-\infty}^{\infty} x_1 x_2 f(x_1,\,x_2)\,dx_1\,dx_2$$

$$- E(X_1) \int_{x_1=-\infty}^{\infty} \int_{x_2=-\infty}^{\infty} x_2 f(x_1,\,x_2)\,dx_1\,dx_2$$

$$- E(X_2) \int_{x_1=-\infty}^{\infty} \int_{x_2=-\infty}^{\infty} x_1 f(x_1,\,x_2)\,dx_1\,dx_2$$

$$- E(X_1)E(X_2) \int_{x_1=-\infty}^{\infty} \int_{x_2=-\infty}^{\infty} f(x_1,\,x_2)\,dx_1\,dx_2$$

Denoting the first term on the right by $E(X_1 X_2)$ and simplifying the last three terms, we have

$$\text{cov}\,(X_1,\,X_2) = E(X_1 X_2) - E(X_1)E(X_2) - E(X_1)E(X_2)$$

$$+ E(X_1)E(X_2)$$

$$\text{cov}\,(X_1,\,X_2) = E(X_1 X_2) - E(X_1)E(X_2) \qquad (7.14)$$

The covariance of two random variables is a basic measure of the association between them. It will be used extensively in later chapters in the discussions of regression and correlation.

Let us now illustrate by computing some moments for a particular distribution. Consider

$$f(x_1, x_2) = e^{-(x_1+x_2)} \qquad 0 \le x_1 < \infty \qquad 0 \le x_2 < \infty \qquad (7.15)$$

We have, using "integration by parts"—a standard technique discussed in all calculus books,

$$E(X_1) = \int_{x_1=0}^{\infty} \int_{x_2=0}^{\infty} x_1 e^{-x_1-x_2}\,dx_1\,dx_2 = \int_{x_1=0}^{\infty} x_1 e^{-x_1}\,dx_1 \int_{x_2=0}^{\infty} e^{-x_2}\,dx_2$$

$$= \left[-x_1 e^{-x_1} \right]_0^{\infty} + \int_{x_1=0}^{\infty} e^{-x_1}\,dx_1 = 0 + 1 = 1$$

Similarly, $E(X_2) = 1$. Again

$$E(X_1{}^2) = \int_{x_1=0}^{\infty} \int_{x_2=0}^{\infty} x_1{}^2 e^{-x_1-x_2} dx_1\, dx_2 = \int_{x_1=0}^{\infty} x_1{}^2 e^{-x_1}\, dx_1 \int_{x_2=0}^{\infty} e^{-x_2}\, dx_2$$

$$= [x_1{}^2 e^{-x_1}]_0^{\infty} + 2\int_{x_1=0}^{\infty} x_1 e^{-x_1}\, dx_1 = 0 + 2(1) = 2$$

Hence

$$\sigma_1{}^2 = E(X_1{}^2) - [E(X_1)]^2 = 2 - 1^2 = 1$$

By symmetry, $\sigma_2{}^2 = 1$. Finally,

$$E(X_1 X_2) = \int_{x_1=0}^{\infty} \int_{x_2=0}^{\infty} x_1 x_2 e^{-x_1-x_2}\, dx_1\, dx_2$$

$$= \int_{x_1=0}^{\infty} x_1 e^{-x_1}\, dx_1 \int_{x_2=0}^{\infty} x_2 e^{-x_2}\, dx_2 = 1 \cdot 1 = 1$$

so that from (7.14),

$$\mathrm{cov}\,(X_1, X_2) = E(X_1 X_2) - E(X_1)E(X_2) = 1 - 1 = 0$$

This result is to be expected. Whenever X_1 and X_2 are independent random variables, their covariance will be zero. To see that X_1 and X_2 are independent here, one need only show that the joint distribution is the product of the marginals.

Given that $X_1, \cdots, X_n$ have the continuous joint probability distribution $f(x_1, \cdots, x_n)$, then we define their moment-generating function to be

$$m(\theta_1, \cdots, \theta_n) = E(e^{\theta_1 X_1 + \cdots + \theta_n X_n})$$

$$= \int_{x_1=-\infty}^{\infty} \int_{x_2=-\infty}^{\infty} e^{\theta_1 x_1 + \cdots + \theta_n x_n} f(x_1, \cdots, x_n)\, dx_1 \cdots dx_n \quad (7.16)$$

Just as in the case of a single random variable, if a probability distribution of several random variables has a moment-generating function, it is unique, and we can use it to identify the probability distribution. Moment-generating functions for several random variables will be useful in developing some of the sampling theory in Chapter 8. If we wish to obtain the moment-generating function corresponding to the joint distribution of several discrete random variables, we may do so by replacing the integrals in (7.16) by sums.

The moment-generating function of several random variables can be made to generate moments in a way analogous to the case of a single random variable. We first calculate $m(\theta_1, \cdots, \theta_n)$, then differentiate it an appropriate number of times with respect to some of the θ_i, and finally set all $\theta_i = 0$. We conclude this chapter by recomputing the moments of the distribution (7.15) by this method.

$$m(\theta_1, \theta_2) = E(e^{\theta_1 X_1 + \theta_2 X_2}) = \int_{x_1=0}^{\infty} \int_{x_2=0}^{\infty} e^{\theta_1 x_1 + \theta_2 x_2} e^{-(x_1+x_2)} dx_1 \, dx_2$$

$$= \int_{x_1=0}^{\infty} \int_{x_2=0}^{\infty} e^{-(1-\theta_1)x_1} e^{-(1-\theta_2)x_2} dx_1 \, dx_2$$

$$= \int_{x_1=0}^{\infty} e^{-(1-\theta_1)x_1} dx_1 \int_{x_2=0}^{\infty} e^{-(1-\theta_2)x_2} dx_2 \qquad (7.17)$$

To evaluate the first integral, let

$$v = (1 - \theta_1)x_1 \qquad x_1 = \frac{v}{1 - \theta_1} \qquad dx_1 = \frac{dv}{1 - \theta_1}$$

Then

$$\int_{x_1=0}^{\infty} e^{-(1-\theta_1)x_1} dx_1 = \int_{v=0}^{\infty} e^{-v} \frac{dv}{1 - \theta_1} = (1 - \theta_1)^{-1} \int_{v=0}^{\infty} e^{-v} dv = (1 - \theta_1)^{-1}$$

By symmetry, the second integral of (7.17) is equal to $(1 - \theta_2)^{-1}$. Thus we have

$$m(\theta_1, \theta_2) = (1 - \theta_1)^{-1}(1 - \theta_2)^{-1}$$

Now that we have obtained the moment-generating function, we can use it to find moments of the distribution. To obtain $E(X_1)$, differentiate $m(\theta_1, \theta_2)$ once with respect to θ_1.

$$\frac{\partial}{\partial \theta_1} m(\theta_1, \theta_2) = -1(1 - \theta_1)^{-2}(-1)(1 - \theta_2)^{-1} = (1 - \theta_1)^{-2}(1 - \theta_2)^{-1}$$

Then set both θ_1 and θ_2 equal to zero.

$$E(X_1) = (1 - 0)^{-2}(1 - 0)^{-1} = 1$$

To obtain the variance of X_1, we first find $E(X_1^2)$. Differentiate $m(\theta_1, \theta_2)$ twice with respect to θ_1.

$$\frac{\partial^2}{\partial \theta_1^2} m(\theta_1, \theta_2) = -2(1 - \theta_1)^{-3}(-1)(1 - \theta_2)^{-1} = 2(1 - \theta_1)^{-3}(1 - \theta_2)^{-1}$$

Set both θ_1 and θ_2 equal to zero.

$$E(X_1^2) = 2(1 - 0)^{-3}(1 - 0)^{-1} = 2$$

Then

$$\sigma_1^2 = E(X_1^2) - [E(X_1)]^2 = 2 - 1^2 = 1$$

To obtain the covariance of X_1 and X_2, we commence by finding $E(X_1X_2)$. Differentiate once with respect to θ_1 and once with respect to θ_2.

$$\frac{\partial^2}{\partial\theta_1\,\partial\theta_2}\,m(\theta_1,\theta_2) = (1-\theta_1)^{-2}(-1)(1-\theta_2)^{-2}(-1) = (1-\theta_1)^{-2}(1-\theta_2)^{-2}$$

Again set θ_1 and θ_2 equal to zero.

$$E(X_1X_2) = (1-0)^{-2}(1-0)^{-2} = 1$$

Then from (7.14)

$$\text{cov}\,(X_1X_2) = E(X_1X_2) - E(X_1)E(X_2) = 1 - 1\cdot 1 = 0$$

These results agree with those obtained earlier in this section. The values of the mean and variance of X_2 can be checked in the same way.

The moment-generating function furnishes a powerful weapon. On the one hand, such functions are useful in statistical theory, often leading to great simplification of otherwise difficult proofs. On the other hand, they are useful in computing moments and in determining approximate distributions in ways similar to those illustrated in this chapter.

The moment-generating function was invented by the French mathematician Pierre Simon Laplace (1749–1827) and was first described by him in a paper on probability theory published in 1812. It fell into disuse for many years and has, only recently, been restored to its present prominent place in statistics. A history of mathematics written in 1908 said of the method of moment-generating functions, "The method is cumbersome, and in consequence of the increased power of analysis is now rarely used."[3] Perhaps some of the black arts known in mathematics in 1908 have since been lost in antiquity.

IMPORTANT TERMS AND CONCEPTS

Covariance

MacLaurin series

Mean

Moment

Moment-generating function

Uniform distribution

Variance

SYMBOLS AND ABBREVIATIONS

$m_X(\theta)$

$E(e^{\theta X})$

$m(\theta_1,\cdots,\theta_n)$

$\text{cov}(X_1,X_2)$

$\dfrac{\partial m}{\partial\theta}$

[3] W. W. Rouse Ball, *A Short Account of the History of Mathematics*, New York: Dover Publications, Inc., 1960, p. 418.

OFTEN-USED FORMULAS

$$m_X(\theta) = E(e^{\theta X}) = \sum_{x=-\infty}^{\infty} e^{\theta x} f(x) \qquad \text{(discrete)}$$

$$= \int_{x=-\infty}^{\infty} e^{\theta x} f(x)\, dx \qquad \text{(continuous)}$$

$$m(\theta_1, \cdots, \theta_n) = E(e^{\theta_1 X_1 + \cdots + \theta_n X_n})$$

$$= \int_{x_1=-\infty}^{\infty} \cdots \int_{x_n=-\infty}^{\infty} e^{\theta_1 x_1 + \cdots + \theta_n x_n} f(x_1, \cdots, x_n)\, dx_1 \cdots dx_n$$

EXERCISES

1. Find the moment-generating function of the probability distribution:

$$f(x) = \frac{1}{70} e^{-x/70} \qquad 0 \le x < \infty$$

2. Calculate the mean and variance of the probability distribution in Problem 1. Use the moment-generating function that you have derived.

3. Find the moment-generating function of the probability distribution

$$f(x) = \frac{3 e^{3x}}{e^3 - 1} \qquad 0 < x < 1$$

4. Find the moment-generating function of the probability distribution

$$f(x) = \begin{cases} 0.25, & x = 0 \\ 0.50, & x = 1 \\ 0.25, & x = 2 \end{cases}$$

5. Calculate the mean and variance of the probability distribution in problem 4 from the moment-generating function.

6. A fair coin is tossed n times. Let X be the number of heads obtained. We know that

$$f(x) = \binom{n}{x} \frac{1}{2^n} \qquad x = 0, 1, \cdots, n$$

Derive the moment-generating function of this probability distribution.

7. Obtain the mean and variance of the probability distribution in Problem 6 from this moment-generating function.

8. Without a derivation, write down the moment-generating function of a normal distribution whose mean is 10 and whose standard deviation is 5.

9. Give a complete description of the probability distribution specified by each of the following moment-generating functions.

a. $m_X(\theta) = \dfrac{e^{2\theta} - 1}{2\theta}$

b. $m_X(\theta) = e^{(\theta + \theta^2)/4}$

c. $m_X(\theta) = e^{2(e^\theta - 1)}$

d. $m_X(\theta) = \dfrac{1}{1 - 5\theta}$

e. $m_X(\theta) = \left(\dfrac{1}{3} + \dfrac{2}{3} e^\theta\right)^n$

f. $m_X(\theta) = e^{5\theta + \theta^2}$

10. Find the mean and variance of the probability distribution whose moment-generating function is that of:
    a. 9c
    b. 9e
    c. 9f
    In each case, use the given moment-generating function.

11. If Z is a random variable whose moment-generating function is

$$m_Z(\theta) = e^{ae^\theta - a}$$

and if Y is a second random variable with moment-generating function

$$m_Y(\theta) = e^{a(e^\theta - 1)}$$

what can you conclude about Z and Y?

12. If Q is a statistic whose moment-generating function is

$$m_Q(\theta) = e^{(a+b)\theta + (c^2 + d^2)\theta^2}$$

identify the distribution of Q, and find its mean and variance.

13. If the random variable Y has moment-generating function

$$m_Y(\theta) = e^{c(\theta^2 + \theta) - d(\theta^2 - \theta)}$$

identify the probability distribution of Y, and find its mean and variance.

14. Compute $E(X_1)$, $E(X_2)$, $\sigma_1{}^2$, $\sigma_2{}^2$, and cov (X_1, X_2) for the distribution

$$f(x_1, x_2) = 1 \qquad 0 \leq x_1 \leq 1 \qquad 0 \leq x_2 \leq 1$$

Do not use moment-generating functions.

15. For the probability distribution

$$f(x, y) = \frac{2^x 3^y}{x!\, y!\, e^5} \qquad x = 0, 1, 2, \cdots \qquad y = 0, 1, 2, \cdots$$

compute means, variances, and covariance without using moment-generating functions.

16. In Exercise 15, compute the required moments by the use of moment-generating functions.

17. Consider the probability distribution

$$f(x, y) = 8xy \qquad 0 \leq x \leq 1 \qquad 0 \leq y \leq x$$

a. Are X and Y independent random variables?
b. Compute the covariance of X and Y.

18. For the probability distribution (7.15), find $E(X_2)$ and $\sigma_2{}^2$ using moment-generating functions.

19. Consider the probability distribution

$$f(x, y) = \frac{e^{-(x^2+y^2)/2}}{2\pi} \qquad -\infty < x < \infty \qquad -\infty < y < \infty$$

a. Are X and Y independent?
b. Compute the covariance of X and Y.

8 Sampling

8.1 BASIC CONSIDERATIONS

Society is making a continuing attack upon its problems with methods that can be characterized as scientific. These methods are systematic and rational. In them theory is checked against fact—which implies that facts must be sought out and accumulated. This process of acquiring and recording facts is carried out by organizations ranging from individuals to the Federal government. The data are collected by means of laboratory studies, street-corner interviews, searches of already published materials, large-scale field tests, and many other approaches. This passion for piling up data may well be one of the distinguishing attributes of our civilization.

Business enterprises are particularly active in this respect. Data on sales, taxes, personnel, production, and facilities are periodically collected and studied. Similar figures for competitors are eagerly sought out for comparison. The movements of important economic time series are watched. And we are not noting a pointless artifact; the conduct of the modern enterprise's operations requires a basis of detailed fact for its managerial decisions.

The task of collecting, recording, and analyzing data is of vast proportions even within a single large corporation. The advent of electronic computers has made it less tedious than before; however, any procedure that can simplify the process is of value. Probably the most important of these procedures are those summarized under the title "Sampling."

In any investigation, there is some set of objects about which information is required. As stated in Chapter 2, this fundamental set is called a population or universe. It may consist of such diverse items as all persons over the age of 21 living in the state of New Hampshire, all television sets manufactured by the National Transistor Company during the year 1970, or those words used in the works of Shakespeare which do not appear in Webster's Collegiate

Dictionary—latest edition. Populations may be small; for example, the 16 members of last term's Statistics 12 course. They may be huge. Consider the populations consisting of all living things on our planet, or the loaves of bread baked in the United States during the past 20 years. We cannot emphasize too strongly that the population in a statistical problem is determined by the problem itself. If we are concerned with the median cost of a ton of bituminous coal in the city of Cincinnati during the year 1966, we have a definite population. The populations appropriate to other questions would usually be different; for example, if the question concerned average cost to all United States purchasers of a ton of bituminous coal during 1966, or cost at the mine, or cost during July 1966, or cost of anthracite, and so on.

A complete tabulation of the figure of interest for all elements of the population is called a *census*. These are often tedious and expensive, particularly when the population is large. Often it is possible to obtain most of the information that a census would reveal and to avoid a great deal of the work. This is done by examining, instead of the whole population, a sample selected from it.

A sample is defined as a subset of a population; however, a sample must have at least one element. We thus exclude the null set and allow sample size to run from unity to census size. Most sample sizes lie between these extremes. One does not obtain much information by examining one or two items. On the other hand, one does not save much time or money by examining 90 per cent of a large population. Later we shall discuss the problem of selecting an appropriate sample size.

To take a simple example, imagine that we are interested in finding the arithmetic mean dollar sale of the H. H. Varnway Shoe Store on August 20, 1968. There were 25 customers to whom sales were made on that day with dollar amounts per customer shown in Table 8.1.

For the sake of illustration, suppose that we decide to obtain information about the arithmetic mean of this small population by sampling, and that a sample size of four has been agreed upon. We see that whether we obtain helpful information or misleading twaddle depends on the particular sample chosen. Actually, from Table 8.1, the population's mean is

$$\mu = \frac{384.02}{25} = \$15.36$$

However, if our sample should happen to consist of the four items marked \$8.50, the sample mean would be $\bar{x} = \$8.50$, far too low a figure. Or, if the four largest sales were employed, we would have $\bar{x} = 122.03/4 = \$30.51$, roughly double the correct amount. On the other hand, if we used a sample consisting of \$8.50, \$10.00, \$18.00, and \$31.00, the result would be $\bar{x} = 67.50/4 = \$16.88$, a figure that would appear to be more useful.

Table 8.1 Dollar Sales per Customer, H. H. Varnway Shoe Store, August 20, 1968

Dollar Sale x_i	Frequency f_i	$f_i x_i$
7.75	1	7.75
8.50	4	34.00
9.75	1	9.75
10.00	7	70.00
12.12	1	12.12
15.87	1	15.87
18.00	4	72.00
20.25	2	40.50
23.75	1	23.75
25.00	1	25.00
31.00	1	31.00
42.28	1	42.28
	25	384.02

Ideally, we would like our sample to be a small-scale image of the population from which it was selected. In practical situations, however, one does not attempt to obtain samples that are completely representative of the population. When one ignores a large number of population items in the interest of speed and economy, one must pay the piper in some way. One pays by getting less exact information than from a census. In practice, then, we can say that sample A does not seem to be representative of the population or that sample B appears more representative than sample A. At best we can remark that sample B appears to be reasonably representative in terms of the population characteristics in which we are interested. For the problem under consideration, the sample consisting of the four items $8.50 and the sample consisting of the items $23.75, $25.00, $31.00, $42.28 seem to be unrepresentative of the population, whereas the sample $8.50, $10.00, $18.00, $31.00 would be much more representative. More or less representative samples, then, yield more or less correct information about the population.

Statisticians have given much thought to the problem of choosing samples that would always be highly representative of their populations without solving it. However, they have discovered methods whose use insures that the probability of obtaining a reasonably representative sample is very great. Central to these methods is the idea of a simple random sample.

We can define a simple random sample easily. Let S be a population of size N from which a sample of size n is to be selected. We shall call the sample

T_n to emphasize that it contains n elements. Thus $T_n \subseteq S$. If

$$P(T_n) = \frac{1}{\dbinom{N}{n}} \qquad \text{all } T_n$$

then T_n is called a simple random sample.

It is instructive to consider the following example. Ten slips of paper are numbered 1 to 10 in sequence on one side and on the reverse side appear 11 to 20. The integers 11 and 1 appear on the same slip, as do 12 and 2, etc. The ten slips are tossed into a hat and mixed thoroughly. One slip will be picked by a blindfolded class member. It will be tossed on a flat surface so that one of the two sides falls uppermost. It will not be replaced. Then another slip will be selected and processed identically. A sample of two items has thus been selected from the population of 20 integers. The point we wish to make is that this is *not* a simple random sample.

Suppose we examine the probability that the sample consists of the pair $\{5, 13\}$. Let A_1 be the event that 5 is obtained on the first draw, and A_2 that 5 is obtained on the second draw. Let B_1 and B_2 be, respectively, the events that a 13 is obtained on the first and second draws. Then

$$P(5, 13) = P(A_1)P(B_2 \mid A_1) + P(B_1)P(A_2 \mid B_1)$$

Now $P(A_1) = 1/20$ and $P(B_2 \mid A_1) = 1/18$, since there are only 18 possible outcomes for the second draw once the 5 has occurred on the first—thus also eliminating the possibility of a 15. The probabilities in the second term can be found by the same reasoning. Thus

$$P(5, 13) = \frac{1}{20} \cdot \frac{1}{18} + \frac{1}{20} \cdot \frac{1}{18} = \frac{1}{180}$$

Now consider the probability of selecting the sample $\{5, 15\}$. Let C_1 and C_2 be, respectively, the events that a 15 is obtained on the first and second draws. Then we have $P(A_1) = 1/20$, $P(C_2 \mid A_1) = 0$. Hence

$$P(5, 15) = \frac{1}{20} \cdot 0 + \frac{1}{20} \cdot 0 = 0$$

The conditions for a simple random sample are not fulfilled. All possible pairs are not equally likely.

Consider S, a population, and T_n, a subset of S consisting of n elements. We now select a sample of n items from S. If it is possible to calculate the probability that T_n is the sample chosen (for each subset T_n), then the sample is called a probability sample. In other words, for a sample to be a probability sample, the probability that the sample consists of any set of n elements from the population must be calculable. The problem of the 10 slips of paper involves a probability sample.

A simple random sample is now seen to be one kind of probability sample, namely, one in which the probabilities for all subsets of a given size are not merely calculable but equal. How does one actually go about obtaining a simple random sample? Various means are available in the usual case when the population is finite. The simple device of drawing numbered tickets from a hat is theoretically sound. However, in practice, it is usually difficult to insure a thorough mixing. Tickets have a tendency to stick together in bunches, to become wedged in corners, or to behave in other recalcitrant ways. The best practical way of choosing a simple random sample involves the use of tables of random numbers such as Table E.4. Suppose we have a population consisting of 512 oil wells, and we wish to select 30 wells at random to study their 1971 yields. First we number the wells from 001 to 512. Next we enter Table E.4 at random, for instance, by closing the eyes and stabbing the page with a pencil point. Since the wells are distinguished by three digit numbers, we read groups of threes starting at the one struck by the pencil point (the three at the intersection of row 34 and column 23). We may read horizontally, vertically, or in any other systematic manner. Suppose we read horizontally and obtain 335. Well 335 is included in the sample. Next we reach 905. No well corresponds to this number, so we skip it. The next triple is 282, so well number 282 is included. We proceed in this fashion until 30 triples have been found which are actually numbers originally given to certain wells. These 30 wells form the required sample.

8.2   OTHER SAMPLING METHODS

The theory of sampling is based on the concept of a simple random sample. From it evolve all the more complex sampling plans. For example, the problem with the ten slips of paper, numbered on each side, consists of two simple random samples. First, a slip of paper was drawn from a universe of ten slips by simple random sampling. Second, one side of a particular slip was selected in the same manner from the two sides available. In addition to serving as the basis of all probability samples, there are many instances in which the simple random sample itself will prove satisfactory. However, it is frequently advisable to employ a more complex sampling plan, particularly in a large-scale investigation. Following a brief discussion of two of these without any consideration of mathematics, we shall return in the next section to the simple random sample and a discussion of the reliability associated with it.

A device that frequently increases the probability of getting a representative sample is stratification. The stratified random sample is most useful when the population is composite in nature; that is, when it can be divided into subpopulations that are distinct in the characteristic(s) of interest. For example, suppose that we were about to choose a sample of 300 employees from the 6000 now working at the Rayton Aviation Corporation's Los Angeles plant. Questionnaires will be distributed to the 300 asking for opinions on company labor policy. If a simple random sample is chosen from the population of 6000, it may be highly unrepresentative. It may consist entirely of persons over 50 years of age, or of men. If these compositions seem unlikely, the sample may at least represent some groups disproportionately. Stratification is a procedure that allows us to eliminate all possibility of obtaining certain obviously unrepresentative samples.

To obtain a representative sample in the Rayton case, an obvious variable on which to stratify is type of employee. A meaningful subdivision involves the three classes: "managerial employees," "clerical employees," and "factory employees." If the 6000 employees are broken down into these three groups, if a simple random sample is selected from each, and if the results are combined in some way, the benefits are clear. It is impossible to come up with a sample consisting entirely of managers, or of factory hands. Thus, a highly undesirable type of unrepresentativeness has been eliminated.

However, stratification can be useless or even harmful if the variable used to form the subpopulations is not germane to the investigation. If, in the Rayton example, we were to stratify on color of hair, we would be eliminating the possibility of obtaining 300 blond employees or 300 redheads, but what this accomplishes is far from clear. We have removed any possibility of obtaining a set of samples, some of which may be quite representative of employee's opinions but others of which may be quite unrepresentative. It is difficult to know whether such stratification would increase or decrease the probability of obtaining a representative sample, but it would certainly seem that a more intelligent basis of stratification could be chosen.

Stratification can be used on more than a single variable. In the Rayton illustration we subdivided only on type of employee. It seems reasonable that other variables such as sex, years of employment by Rayton, and union membership might also be meaningful. One could envision a study using three types of employee strata, two sex strata, two years of employment strata, and two strata representing "union" and "nonunion." In this study $3 \times 2 \times 2 \times 2 = 24$ subpopulations would be isolated, and 24 simple random samples would be obtained and their results combined.

But such subdivision can be carried to ridiculous extremes if a large number of possibly pertinent variables are selected so that thousands of subpopulations are delineated. How far should stratification be carried? A few general rules of thumb may be pointed out. For one thing, it is theoretically desirable to stratify until the items within each subpopulation are very much alike, that is, until they are homogeneous with respect to the variable under consideration. And, concomitantly, it is desirable to stratify until the items within each stratum differ to a decided degree from those in other strata— again with respect to the variable of concern. But these principles indicate the fragmentation that we have termed undesirable. They must be balanced against the practical notion that for sampling to make sense there must be a fair number of items in each of the subpopulations. Thus, one tries to include several relevant variables in one's study without reducing the groups to be sampled to too small a size.

Another important question in stratified sampling is how large a sample should be picked from each subpopulation. One method is to pick each sample with size proportional to the size of the subpopulation from which it is drawn. The method is called proportional stratified sampling. If one wished to use it for the Rayton sample of 300 and if there were 500 managers, 1500 clerks, and 4000 factory workers employed, then one would draw random samples of 25, 75, and 200 from the three groups, respectively, since

$$\frac{25}{500} = \frac{75}{1500} = \frac{200}{4000} = \frac{300}{6000} = \frac{1}{20}$$

It is not true that all stratified sampling should be done proportionally. A solution to the problem of sample size for each stratum is a generalization of the problem of proper sample size for a simple random sample discussed in Chapter 9.

A second type of probability sample that is useful is the cluster sample. In some contexts it is referred to as an area sample. Suppose that a study was to be made of undertakers in the United States. If interviews were to be obtained from each man in a simple random sample of 200, a rather expensive situation would develop. Interviewers would have to be sent to all parts of the country. On the other hand, considerable savings might be realized by "clustering" the interviews. In this procedure, a simple random sample of ten counties could be selected and the interviews restricted to those counties. Within each county chosen, a simple random sample of undertakers would be selected.

Notice that the illustration with the slips of paper was a cluster sample. There, each cluster consisted of two numbers, and one number was selected from the cluster initially chosen. Each element had an equal probability of inclusion in the sample. This need not be true. In the study of undertakers one might choose the same number of establishments from each county. This would mean that the probability associated with each element would vary from county to county. The distinctive feature of the cluster sample is the grouping of elements together and the application of simple random sampling to these groups.

An important feature of cluster sampling is that a listing of all elements is not required. Lists are needed, as is always the case in probability sampling, but lists of population elements at only the final stage. In a typical problem one might need a list of all counties in the universe and a list of all census tracts within those counties selected at the first stage, but require a list of the ultimate elements for only those tracts selected at the second stage.

All of the sampling methods discussed thus far have been probability methods. As examples of nonprobability sampling, we mention studying the "four largest companies in the petroleum industry" or interviewing the owner of every fifth house on the east side of Fifty-seventh Street in West Philadelphia commencing with the southeast corner of Market and Fifty-seventh Streets and moving south to Baltimore Avenue. There is no randomness here. An oil company or a home owner is either in the sample or out. Both of these examples are of a type called judgment samples. Selection of the items depends on someone's judgment as to what constitutes representativeness for the problem at hand.

Now if one change is made in Fifty-seventh Street interviewings, the concept of probability can be brought into the picture. Pick the starting house at random from the first five on the east side of Fifty-seventh below Market. Then each owner has a chance of being interviewed—depending upon which house is picked as a starting point. Such a sample—random initial choice and every nth item thereafter—constitutes systematic sampling. Be sure to understand that a systematic sample is a probability sample only because of the initial randomness.[1] If the initial point is fixed, the result is a judgment sample.

8.3 EMPIRICAL SAMPLING FUNCTIONS

A sample settles for incomplete information. More than that, probability samples leave to chance the determination of the particular sample that will serve as the basis for conclusions concerning the universe. For this reason we shall now pursue the general question; "But if chance had given us another sample, how similar would our results have been?"

First, a review of some terminology. In statistical work a population characteristic is called a parameter. If we are concerned with the annual incomes earned by United States citizens, the median income, the modal income, the standard deviation of incomes, and the percentage of incomes

---

[1] A systematic sample is a rather unusual example of a cluster sample. Observe that the universe is divided into n clusters and one of those clusters is selected at random. For example, if there are 200 elements and every tenth element is chosen with a random start between 1 and 10, the universe is divided into 10 clusters of 20 elements each: 1, 11, $\cdots$, 191; 2, 12, $\cdots$, 192; etc. One of these clusters is selected as the sample.

above \$10,000 are each parameters of this population. In a given year, for example 1969, each of these parameters has a value, and its determination might be the object of a statistical study. Suppose that it was decided to conduct the study by use of sampling. When the sample has been selected, one may compute corresponding numbers—the median and modal income of the sample, the standard deviation, and the percentage above \$10,000. These figures are called statistics, and one of the major problems of statistics (the subject) is that of estimating parameters from statistics (the sample characteristics). In the Varnway Shoe Store problem (Section 8.1), we were really concerned with estimating the population's arithmetic mean, given the sample's arithmetic mean. Our conclusion was that sometimes the sample statistic was a "reasonably good" estimate and that occasionally it was a poor one. Now let us study the relation between sample statistic and population parameter with more care.

In the case of the Varnway Shoe Store, the population was small, consisting of 25 elements. Consider all possible samples of size four that could be selected from the population. There are

$$\binom{25}{4} = \frac{25 \cdot 24 \cdot 23 \cdot 22}{4 \cdot 3 \cdot 2 \cdot 1} = 12,650$$

distinct subsets of a set with 25 elements, any one of which might be obtained when a random sample of size four is chosen. In fact the probability of selecting any particular subset of four elements is exactly $1/12,650$. Three of these subsets are the samples \$8.50, \$8.50, \$8.50, \$8.50; \$23.75, \$25.00, \$31.00, \$42.28; and \$8.50, \$10.00, \$18.00, \$31.00, previously discussed. Their arithmetic means were found to be \$8.50, \$30.51, and \$16.88, respectively. Imagine now that we wrote down each one of the other 12,647 samples and computed each of the 12,647 sample arithmetic means. Tabulating these would yield the probability distribution of $\bar{X}$ in samples of size four from the Varnway population.

Now the prospect of computing and tabulating 12,650 arithmetic means is not enticing. However, the student will gain by seeing this process actually carried through. Let us introduce a tiny population for demonstration purposes only. No one would sample from a population as small as the one about to be discussed.

Consider a population consisting of six executives (A to F) of the Lohrman Corporation on November 23, 1970. The characteristic of interest, X, the number of hours worked on that day, is respectively 2, 5, 6, 6, 8, and 10 hours for executives A to F. Suppose we are interested in samples of size two. There are

$$\binom{6}{2} = \frac{6 \cdot 5}{2 \cdot 1} = 15$$

such samples. We compute their arithmetic means in Table 8.2. The population would be represented by the probability distribution $f(x)$, which has ordinate $\frac{1}{6}$ at each of the points 2, 5, 8, 10 and ordinate $\frac{2}{6}$ at $x = 6$. Now the sample mean, $\overline{X}$, is also a random variable. Its probability distribution is

Table 8.2   Samples of Size Two and Sample Arithmetic Mean Hours Worked on November 23, 1970; Lohrman Corporation Executives

Sample	$\bar{x}$	Sample	$\bar{x}$
AB	3.5	BF	7.5
AC	4	CD	6
AD	4	CE	7
AE	5	CF	8
AF	6	DE	7
BC	5.5	DF	8
BD	5.5	EF	9
BE	6.5		

given by Table 8.3 for samples of size two. A probability distribution of a sample statistic will be called a *sampling distribution*. We distinguish the sampling distribution $f_2(\cdot)$ from the population distribution $f(\cdot)$ by the use of the subscript representing sample size. Notice that in the discrete case the sampling distribution of $\overline{X}$ leads to the same general types of statements as does the population distribution: the probability is 2/15 that the arithmetic mean of a sample of size two drawn at random from the Lohrman population

Table 8.3   Sampling Distribution of $\overline{X}$ in Samples of Size Two from the Lohrman Population

$\bar{x}$	Frequency	$f_2(\bar{x})$
3.5	1	1/15
4.0	2	2/15
5.0	1	1/15
5.5	2	2/15
6.0	2	2/15
6.5	1	1/15
7.0	2	2/15
7.5	1	1/15
8.0	2	2/15
9.0	1	1/15

is 7.0 hours; the probability is 3/15 that such an arithmetic mean is less than 5 hours. The place to obtain probability information regarding the location of $\bar{x}$ is the sampling distribution of $\bar{X}$.

Care should be used to distinguish an additional type of distribution. This third type is the distribution of the items in a particular sample of size n. It would be expected to resemble $f(\cdot)$ in many ways if the sample were selected at random. Keep firmly in mind that there are three different functions associated with any sampling problem: the population distribution, the sampling distribution, and the distribution within a particular sample.

The sampling distribution of a statistic depends strongly on sample size. To point up this fact we shall now determine the sampling distribution of $\bar{X}$ in samples of size three from the Lohrman population. At this point, attempt to visualize this function's appearance before proceeding.

There are $\binom{6}{3} = \dfrac{6 \cdot 5 \cdot 4}{3 \cdot 2 \cdot 1} = 20$ possible samples of size three, as is shown in Table 8.4. Table 8.5 summarizes the sampling distribution of $\bar{X}$ in this case. The two probability questions previously posed have different answers when referred to $f_2(\bar{x})$ than when referred to $f_3(\bar{x})$. In the latter case, the probability that the sample mean should turn out to be 7.0 is 2/20 while the probability that it should be less than 5 hours has shrunk to 3/20. For comparative purposes we graph $f_2(\bar{x})$ and $f_3(\bar{x})$ in Figure 8.1.

There are two features that should be emphasized. The arithmetic mean of the population is

$$\mu = \frac{2 + 5 + 6 + 6 + 8 + 10}{6} = \frac{37}{6}$$

Table 8.4 Samples of Size Three and Sample Arithmetic Mean Hours Worked on November 23, 1970; Lohrman Corporation Executives

Sample	$\bar{x}$	Sample	$\bar{x}$
ABC	4.3	BCD	5.7
ABD	4.3	BCE	6.3
ABE	5.0	BCF	7.0
ABF	5.7	BDE	6.3
ACD	4.7	BDF	7.0
ACE	5.3	BEF	7.7
ACF	6.0	CDE	6.7
ADE	5.3	CDF	7.3
ADF	6.0	CEF	8.0
AEF	6.7	DEF	8.0

Table 8.5   Sampling Distribution of $\bar{X}$ in Samples of Size Three from the Lohrman Population

$\bar{x}$	Frequency	$f_3(\bar{x})$
4.3	2	2/20
4.7	1	1/20
5.0	1	1/20
5.3	2	2/20
5.7	2	2/20
6.0	2	2/20
6.3	2	2/20
6.7	2	2/20
7.0	2	2/20
7.3	1	1/20
7.7	1	1/20
8.0	2	2/20

This value appears to be roughly central to both $f_2(\bar{x})$ and $f_3(\bar{x})$. Later we shall show that the mean of the sampling distribution of $\bar{X}$ is always μ, regardless of sample size. The other feature of interest is that the standard deviation of $f_3(\bar{x})$ appears to be somewhat smaller than that of $f_2(\bar{x})$. This is a reflection of a theorem which states that the variance of $f_n(\bar{x})$ is inversely proportional to sample size, although not uniquely determined by it. Let us check these two statements before leaving the Lohrman problem.

We shall find $f_5(\bar{x})$, the sampling distribution of $\bar{X}$ for sample size five. This is formed from the six means:

$$\frac{2+5+6+6+8}{5} = 5.4; \qquad \frac{2+5+6+6+10}{5} = 5.8$$

$$\frac{2+5+6+8+10}{5} = 6.2; \qquad \frac{2+5+6+8+10}{5} = 6.2$$

$$\frac{2+6+6+8+10}{5} = 6.4; \qquad \frac{5+6+6+8+10}{5} = 7.0$$

each occurring with equal probability. The function $f_5(\bar{x})$ defined by

$\bar{x}$	5.4	5.8	6.2	6.4	7.0
$f_5(\bar{x})$	$\dfrac{1}{6}$	$\dfrac{1}{6}$	$\dfrac{1}{3}$	$\dfrac{1}{6}$	$\dfrac{1}{6}$

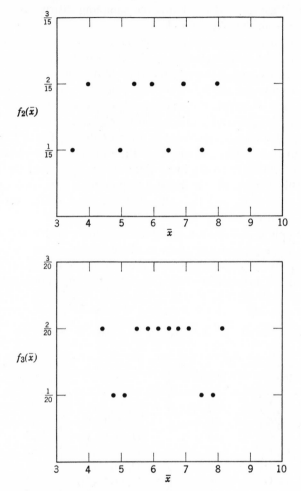

Fig. 8.1. $f_2(\bar{x})$ and $f_3(\bar{x})$; Lohrman population.

again seems centered close to the population mean. The standard deviation of $f_5(\bar{x})$ is greatly reduced over $f_2(\bar{x})$ and $f_3(\bar{x})$.

We have illustrated the construction of a sampling distribution for one particular statistic, the arithmetic mean. The procedure is valid for any statistic. Suppose that ζ (zeta) is some parameter of a finite population and that Z is the corresponding statistic. We wish to find the sampling distribution of Z in samples of size n from the given population. Conceptually, one lists all the possible samples of size n, computes the statistic z from each of these, and tabulates the frequency with which each z occurs. Dividing by the number of samples, one obtains the sampling distribution of Z in samples of size n from the given population.

Let us take one further classroom example of the construction of a sampling distribution. Seven prototype models of the Bronco heavy-duty truck are submitted for intensive field testing. Actually two of these have serious defects, which will show up in the testing, while the other five will pass with flying colors. Because of a shortage of trained personnel, only four of the trucks can be tested. If a random sample of size four is chosen from the seven trucks, what are the possible results, and what is the probability of each?

The answer to this question is given by the sampling distribution of P, the percentage of defective trucks in samples of size four from the Bronco population. Table 8.6 shows the basic computations. The two defective trucks are denoted by D_1 and D_2, while the five good trucks are labeled G_1, G_2, G_3, G_4, and G_5.

Here, the sampling distribution is extremely simple. Table 8.7 supplies the answer to the initial question. As was obvious, the sample can contain 0, 1, or 2 trucks with serious defects. The probabilities associated with them are 1/7, 4/7, and 2/7, respectively. We notice that the population percentage

Table 8.6 Sample Percentage Defective in Samples of Size Four; Bronco Population

Sample	$p(\%)$	Sample	$p(\%)$
$D_1\,D_2\,G_1\,G_2$	50	$D_1\,G_2\,G_4\,G_5$	25
$D_1\,D_2\,G_1\,G_3$	50	$D_1\,G_3\,G_4\,G_5$	25
$D_1\,D_2\,G_1\,G_4$	50	$D_2\,G_1\,G_2\,G_3$	25
$D_1\,D_2\,G_1\,G_5$	50	$D_2\,G_1\,G_2\,G_4$	25
$D_1\,D_2\,G_2\,G_3$	50	$D_2\,G_1\,G_2\,G_5$	25
$D_1\,D_2\,G_2\,G_4$	50	$D_2\,G_1\,G_3\,G_4$	25
$D_1\,D_2\,G_2\,G_5$	50	$D_2\,G_1\,G_3\,G_5$	25
$D_1\,D_2\,G_3\,G_4$	50	$D_2\,G_1\,G_4\,G_5$	25
$D_1\,D_2\,G_3\,G_5$	50	$D_2\,G_2\,G_3\,G_4$	25
$D_1\,D_2\,G_4\,G_5$	50	$D_2\,G_2\,G_3\,G_5$	25
$D_1\,G_1\,G_2\,G_3$	25	$D_2\,G_2\,G_4\,G_5$	25
$D_1\,G_1\,G_2\,G_4$	25	$D_2\,G_3\,G_4\,G_5$	25
$D_1\,G_1\,G_2\,G_5$	25	$G_1\,G_2\,G_3\,G_4$	0
$D_1\,G_1\,G_3\,G_4$	25	$G_1\,G_2\,G_3\,G_5$	0
$D_1\,G_1\,G_3\,G_5$	25	$G_1\,G_2\,G_4\,G_5$	0
$D_1\,G_1\,G_4\,G_5$	25	$G_1\,G_3\,G_4\,G_5$	0
$D_1\,G_2\,G_3\,G_4$	25	$G_2\,G_3\,G_4\,G_5$	0
$D_1\,G_2\,G_3\,G_5$	25		

Table 8.7 Sampling Distribution of P in Samples of Size Four from the Bronco Population

$p(\%)$	Frequency	$f_4(p)$
0	5	1/7
25	20	4/7
50	10	2/7

defective, 28.6 percent, seems central to the sampling distribution. If samples of various sizes were chosen we would again see the standard deviation of the sampling distribution decrease as sample size increases.

8.4 INDEPENDENT RANDOM VARIABLES

The discussion in Section 8.3 should provide a good understanding of the basic concept of a sampling distribution. We shall wish to apply the concept, however, to populations that are very large—perhaps infinite. Before we can do this, we shall have to investigate the way in which random sampling affects the process. The important point is that simple random sampling makes each item selected an independent random variable if the population is continuous. Since only simple random samples will be used in the rest of this book, we shall hereafter use the term "random sampling" to mean "simple random sampling."

We first extend the idea of independence. Let $X_1, X_2, \cdots, X_n$ be n random variables. Let the probability distribution of X_1 be $g_1(x_1)$, the distribution of X_2 be $g_2(x_2)$, $\cdots$, and the distribution of X_n be $g_n(x_n)$. Let the joint probability distribution of $X_1, X_2, \cdots, X_n$ be $f(x_1, x_2, \cdots, x_n)$. If

$$f(x_1, x_2, \cdots, x_n) = g_1(x_1) \cdot g_2(x_2) \cdots g_n(x_n)$$

$$-\infty < x_i < \infty \qquad i = 1, \cdots, n$$

the random variables $X_1, X_2, \cdots, X_n$ are said to be independent. In other words, for n random variables to be independent their joint probability distribution must factor into the product of their marginal probability distributions and the domain of each variable must not be stated in terms of any of the other variables.

As an example of independence, let X_1, X_2, X_3, and X_4 be four random variables, each having a Poisson distribution with mean μ. That is

$$f(x_i) = \frac{\mu^{x_i} e^{-\mu}}{x_i!} \qquad x_i = 0, 1, 2, \cdots \qquad i = 1, 2, 3, 4$$

Suppose we know that the joint distribution of X_1, X_2, X_3, and X_4 has the form

$$f(x_1, x_2, x_3, x_4) = \frac{\mu^{x_1+x_2+x_3+x_4}e^{-4\mu}}{x_1!\,x_2!\,x_3!\,x_4!} \qquad x_i = 0, 1, 2, \cdots \qquad i = 1, 2, 3, 4$$

What can be said about the independence or interdependence of these four random variables? Since the function can be factored as

$$f(x_1, x_2, x_3, x_4) = \frac{\mu^{x_1}e^{-\mu}}{x_1!} \cdot \frac{\mu^{x_2}e^{-\mu}}{x_2!} \cdot \frac{\mu^{x_3}e^{-\mu}}{x_3!} \cdot \frac{\mu^{x_4}e^{-\mu}}{x_4!} \qquad x_i = 0, 1, 2, \cdots$$

$$i = 1, 2, 3, 4$$

the four variables are independent. This implies, of course, that probability statements made about one of them are not affected by values taken on by the others.

Suppose now that we have a population represented by the random variable X and its distribution $f(x)$. We are about to select one item from this population. Without specifying the method of selection, we can say that its result is a random variable, X_1, having a probability distribution. Note that if we pick one item at random from the population, the probabilities that it will lie in different intervals will be the same as for X in the original population. We can then select X_1, X_2, $\cdots$, X_n and consider the result of each draw as the value of a random variable with some distribution. Let the probability distribution of X_i be $g_i(x_i)$, $i = 1, \cdots, n$. Then if the random variables are independent, that is, if

$$f_n(x_1, x_2, \cdots, x_n) = g_1(x_1)g_2(x_2) \cdots g_n(x_n)$$

we say that the sampling method is independent. Note that one great advantage of random sampling is that it assures independence of sampling method in certain cases, as is shown in the following example.

Consider the exponential population:

$$f(x) = 2e^{-2x} \qquad 0 \le x < \infty \tag{8.1}$$

In selecting an item, X_1, at random,

$$f_1(x_1) = 2e^{-2x_1} \qquad 0 \le x_1 < \infty$$

After this selection is made, the model is unchanged, so that when a second item X_2, is picked at random, its distribution is not dependent on x_1:

$$f_2(x_2 \mid x_1) = f_2(x_2) = 2e^{-2x_2} \qquad 0 \le x_2 < \infty$$

Thus

$$f_2(x_1, x_2) = f_1(x_1)f_2(x_2 \mid x_1) = f_1(x_1)f_2(x_2)$$

$$= (2e^{-2x_1})(2e^{-2x_2}) \qquad 0 \le x_1 < \infty \qquad 0 \le x_2 < \infty$$

Similarly, for a sample of size n,

$$f_n(x_1, x_2, \cdots, x_n) = f_1(x_1)f_2(x_2) \cdots f_n(x_n)$$
$$= (2e^{-2x_1})(2e^{-2x_2}) \cdots (2e^{-2x_n}) \qquad 0 \le x_i < \infty$$
$$i = 1, 2, \cdots, n$$

Thus the random sample is an independent sample—as we knew would be the case when we saw the form of the marginals $f_i(x_i)$.

To give a final illustration of the connection between independent sampling and random sampling, consider the use of a table of random numbers to select 10 names from a list of 10,000 names. The method is surely random sampling. If we do not rule out the possibility that a name be chosen on more than one draw, then the sampling method is independent, that is

$$f(x_1, x_2, \cdots, x_n) = g_1(x_1)g_2(x_2) \cdots g_n(x_n)$$

This is sampling with replacement. If we do not allow repetitions (sampling without replacement), then the probability of obtaining a particular name on the fourth draw depends upon the names obtained on the first three draws, and the sampling method is not independent. In short, random sampling is independent sampling only when the population's form is not changed by the act of selection—as in the case with continuous populations.

Random sampling and independence have interesting effects upon the moment-generating functions of the variables involved. These effects are summed up in the two theorems with which we conclude this section.

THEOREM.   The moment-generating function of a sum of n independent random variables is equal to the product of the moment-generating functions of the variables themselves.

Proof. Let $X_1, \cdots, X_n$ be independent random variables. Let $V = X_1 + \cdots + X_n$. Let $m_V(\theta)$ be the moment-generating function of V. Let $m_i(\theta_i)$ be the moment-generating function of X_i, $i = 1, \cdots, n$. Then,

$$m_V(\theta) = E(e^{V\theta}) = E(e^{(X_1 + \cdots + X_n)\theta})$$
$$= E(e^{X_1\theta} \cdots e^{X_n\theta}) = E(e^{X_1\theta}) \cdots E(e^{X_n\theta})$$

because of independence. Finally,

$$m_V(\theta) = m_1(\theta) \cdots m_n(\theta) \tag{8.2}$$

From this theorem we easily obtain another.

THEOREM.   Let $X_1, \cdots, X_n$ be a random sample selected from a continuous population. The moment-generating function of $V = X_1 + \cdots + X_n$ is the nth power of the population's moment-generating function.

Proof. Since in this case random sampling implies independence, we may use the preceding result (8.2),

$$m_V(\theta) = m_1(\theta) \cdots m_n(\theta)$$

But random sampling from a continuous population also implies that

$$m_1(\theta) = \cdots = m_n(\theta) = m_X(\theta)$$

where $m_X(\theta)$ is the population's moment-generating function. Hence

$$m_V(\theta) = m_X(\theta) \cdots m_X(\theta) = [m_X(\theta)]^n \qquad (8.3)$$

The proofs of these two theorems assume that the random variables are continuous; if they are discrete, integrals must be replaced by sums.

We illustrate the last theorem by finding the moment-generating function of the sum of n random variables selected from the distribution (8.1). Let $V = X_1 + \cdots + X_n$. Since $f(x)$ is continuous

$$m_V(\theta) = [m_X(\theta)]^n$$

From Table 7.2, the moment-generating function of this exponential distribution is $m_X(\theta) = 2/(2 - \theta)$, so

$$m_V(\theta) = 2^n(2 - \theta)^{-n}$$

8.5 MEAN AND VARIANCE OF THE SAMPLING DISTRIBUTION OF THE SAMPLE ARITHMETIC MEAN

It has, no doubt, become obvious that the arithmetic mean is often germane to the solution of practical problems. Furthermore, since decisions are frequently based on sample evidence, we should be interested in knowing something about the accuracy and reliability of the sample mean. These properties are shown by the expected value of the pertinent sampling distribution and the amount of dispersion in it. In this section we shall find the mean and variance of the sampling distribution of the sample mean.

Consider a random sample of size n, $X_1, \cdots, X_n$, chosen from some population of unknown form. Based on our work in Section 8.3, we would expect that the mean of the sampling distribution of $\bar{X}$ would be the population mean μ. It is easy to prove this formally.

$$E(\bar{X}) = E\left(\frac{X_1 + \cdots + X_n}{n}\right) = \frac{E(X_1) + \cdots + E(X_n)}{n}$$

$$= \frac{\mu + \cdots + \mu}{n} = \frac{n\mu}{n} = \mu \qquad (8.4)$$

According to the terminology introduced in Chapter 2, the sample mean of a simple random sample is an unbiased estimate of the population mean.[2]

We next obtain a similar result for the standard deviation of the sampling distribution of $\bar{X}$. Our empirical work in Section 8.3 suggests strongly that this quantity decreases as n increases, but it gives no hint as to the exact form of $\sigma_{\bar{X}}^2$. However, we are now in a position to find this variance directly in the case where the population is infinite. For other populations the form of $\sigma_{\bar{X}}^2$ is discussed briefly in Section 8.10. We commence with the variance of $\bar{X}$.

$$\sigma_{\bar{X}}^2 = E[(\bar{X} - \mu)^2] = E\left[\left(\frac{X_1 + \cdots + X_n}{n} - \mu\right)^2\right]$$

$$E\left[\left(\frac{X_1 + \cdots + X_n - n\mu}{n}\right)^2\right] = \frac{1}{n^2} E\{[(X_1 - \mu) + \cdots + (X_n - \mu)]^2\}$$

$$= \frac{1}{n^2}\left\{E\left[\sum_{i=1}^{n}(X_i - \mu)^2 + 2\sum_{i=1}^{n}\sum_{j=1}^{i-1}(X_i - \mu)(X_j - \mu)\right]\right\}$$

that is, when we square a sum of n terms, we obtain n squared terms and $\binom{n}{2}$ cross products. By (6.15) we now can write

$$\sigma_{\bar{X}}^2 = \frac{1}{n^2}\sum_{i=1}^{n}E(X_i - \mu)^2 + \frac{2}{n^2}\sum_{i=1}^{n}\sum_{j=1}^{i-1}E(X_i - \mu)(X_j - \mu)$$

$$= \frac{1}{n^2}\sum_{i=1}^{n}\sigma^2 + \frac{2}{n^2}\sum_{i=1}^{n}\sum_{j=1}^{i-1}\text{cov}\,(X_i X_j)$$

Since X_i and X_j are independent random variables, their covariance is zero, and we have

$$\sigma_{\bar{X}}^2 = \frac{n\sigma^2}{n^2} = \frac{\sigma^2}{n} \tag{8.5}$$

Thus the variance of $\bar{X}$ does not depend upon the form of the population, and $\sigma_{\bar{X}}$, the standard error of the sample mean, is given by

$$\sigma_{\bar{X}} = \frac{\sigma}{\sqrt{n}} \tag{8.6}$$

Note that, as sample size increases, $\sigma_{\bar{X}}$ decreases. We have used mathematics to uncover the underlying structure which explains the empirical results about $\sigma_{\bar{X}}$ obtained in Section 8.3.

---

[2] Of course, any systematic error in the collection process would carry over to the estimate. This is unbiased only when one considers errors introduced by sampling as opposed to taking a census.

It is important for the student to keep in mind that (8.4) holds exactly for all populations, but that we have proved (8.5) only for continuous populations. It will be shown in Section 8.10 that (8.5) holds approximately for many other populations and can be used in most sampling problems.

8.6 SAMPLING DISTRIBUTION OF THE SAMPLE ARITHMETIC MEAN; NORMAL POPULATION

The normal probability distribution holds a very important place in statistics from the point of view of both theory and of applications. The value of the normal distribution is particularly apparent in the study of sampling. This section will study the following question, "What is the sampling distribution of the random variable $\bar{X}$ in random samples of size n from a normal population?"[3] Later we shall indicate how the normal distribution can be useful in many cases where the population is not normal.

In Chapter 7 it was shown that the moment-generating function of a normal distribution with random variable X, mean μ, and variance σ^2 is

$$m_X(\theta) = e^{\mu\theta + \sigma^2\theta^2/2} \tag{8.7}$$

It can also be shown (see Section 8.9) that the moment-generating function of the sampling distribution of the arithmetic mean in samples of size n drawn from the same normal population is

$$m_{\bar{X}}(\theta) = e^{\mu\theta + (\sigma^2/n)(\theta^2/2)} \tag{8.8}$$

A comparison of (8.7) and (8.8) reveals that both have the same functional form with μ as the coefficient of θ and that the coefficients of $\theta^2/2$ are, respectively, σ^2 and σ^2/n. According to Chapter 7, this establishes the important conclusion that the sampling distribution of $\bar{X}$ is normal whenever the population is normal. Also the results for the mean and variance agree with those of the previous section, that is, the sampling distribution of $\bar{X}$ must have mean μ and variance σ^2/n regardless of the form of the population from which it is drawn.

Let us now use these results. Experience over 15 years has shown that type B copper rods purchased from the Ajax Corporation have a mean breaking strength of 200 pounds and a standard deviation of breaking strength of 12 pounds. Furthermore, the breaking strengths have been observed to have a normal distribution. What is the probability that a sample of 16 rods selected at random from the next shipment will have an arithmetic mean breaking strength of more than 208 pounds? Between 198 and 202 pounds?

---

[3] We shall use the expression "normal population" as meaning a "population that has a normally distributed characteristic" in cases where there is no possibility of confusion. Similarly, other adjectives may be applied as descriptive of the population.

Since the population is normal with $\mu = 200$ and $\sigma = 12$, we are sure that the sampling distribution of $\bar{X}$ in samples of size 16 is again normal with mean 200 and standard deviation $\sigma_{\bar{x}} = 12/\sqrt{16} = 3$. This sampling distribution is shown in Figure 8.2.

We first find $P(\bar{X} > 208)$. The problem is now simply one of reading probabilities from a normal distribution such as was discussed in Chapter 4.

$$P(\bar{X} > 208) = P\left(\frac{\bar{X} - 200}{3} > \frac{208 - 200}{3}\right) = P(Z > 2.67)$$

From Table E.3 we obtain

$$P(\bar{X} > 208) = 0.50000 - 0.49621 = 0.00379$$

It was also required to find $P(198 < \bar{X} < 202)$. By the same reasoning,

$$P(198 < \bar{X} < 202) = P\left(\frac{198 - 200}{3} < \frac{\bar{X} - 200}{3} < \frac{202 - 200}{3}\right)$$
$$= P(-0.67 < Z < 0.67) = 2P(0 < Z < 0.67)$$
$$= 2(0.24857) = 0.49714$$

We shall give one further example. Yearly wages paid to the 30,000 unskilled laborers employed by the Blascomb Steel Company are known to be approximately normally distributed each year. In the unskilled group for 1948, the mean wage was \$2800 and the standard deviation was \$240.

1. If a random sample of 36 unskilled laborers is selected from this population, what is the probability that its arithmetic mean differs from the population mean by more than \$50?

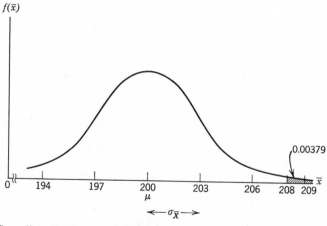

Fig. 8.2. Sampling distribution of $\bar{X}$ in the Ajax problem.

2. Within what range would the sample mean fall 95 percent of the time in random sampling from this population for samples of size 36?

3. How large a random sample has to be taken before the probability that the sample mean lies within $20 of the population mean reaches 0.90?

Solution of 1.

$$\sigma_{\bar{X}} = \frac{240}{6} = \$40$$

$$P(2750 < \bar{X} < 2850) = P\left(\frac{-50}{40} < \frac{\bar{X} - 2800}{40} < \frac{50}{40}\right)$$

$$= P(-1.25 < Z < 1.25) = 2P(0 < Z < 1.25)$$

$$= 2(0.39435) = 0.78870$$

The probability that the difference is greater than $50 is

$$1 - 0.7887 = 0.2113$$

Solution of 2. Assuming that the required interval is centered on μ and has length $2c$,

$$P(-c + 2800 < \bar{X} < c + 2800) = 0.95$$

which is to be solved for c. In terms of Z this reduces to

$$P\left(\frac{-c}{40} < \frac{\bar{X} - 2800}{40} < \frac{c}{40}\right) = 0.95$$

$$2P\left(0 < Z < \frac{c}{40}\right) = 0.95; \qquad P\left(0 < Z < \frac{c}{40}\right) = 0.475$$

Reading from the normal table, we find that $c/40 = 1.96$ and $c = 78.4$. We would then expect the sample mean to lie within $78.40 of the population mean 95 percent of the time in random samples of size 36.

Solution of 3. Since n is to be determined, we can only write

$$\sigma_{\bar{X}} = 240/\sqrt{n}$$

$$P(2780 < \bar{X} < 2820) = P\left(\frac{-20}{\frac{240}{\sqrt{n}}} < \frac{\bar{X} - 2800}{\frac{240}{\sqrt{n}}} < \frac{20}{\frac{240}{\sqrt{n}}}\right) = 0.90$$

$$P\left(-\frac{\sqrt{n}}{12} < Z < \frac{\sqrt{n}}{12}\right) = 2P\left(0 < Z < \frac{\sqrt{n}}{12}\right) = 0.90$$

$$P\left(0 < Z < \frac{\sqrt{n}}{12}\right) = 0.45$$

From the table of normal areas,

$$\frac{\sqrt{n}}{12} = 1.64 \qquad \sqrt{n} = 19.68 \qquad n = 387.30 = 388$$

We would need a sample of at least 388 in order to have that high a probability that the sample mean is not off by more than \$20 from the population
mean.

8.7 SAMPLING DISTRIBUTION OF THE SAMPLE MEAN: NONNORMAL POPULATION

Derivation of the mean and variance of the sampling distribution of sample
means in Section 8.5 did not depend upon the functional form of the parent
population. Suppose that it is known that the mean 1970 annual income for
all practicing United States psychiatrists was \$29,000 and that the standard
deviation of this population was \$6000. Find the mean and standard deviation
of the sampling distribution of $\bar{X}$ when random samples of size 9 are selected
from this population.

By the previous discussion, $E(\bar{X}) = \mu = \$29,000$, and

$$\sigma_{\bar{X}} = \frac{\sigma}{\sqrt{n}} = \frac{6000}{\sqrt{9}} = \$2000$$

But, as yet, no probability statements are possible. Almost certainly the
parent population is not normal. There is one further important fact about
the sampling distribution of $\bar{X}$ that holds no matter what the form of the
population. This fact is known as the "Central Limit Theorem." Its proof
will not be given; we shall, however, state and use it.

> **THEOREM.** Given any population whose variance exists. Let $X_1, \cdots, X_n$
> be a random sample of size n selected from this population. Then the
> sampling distribution of $Z = (\bar{X} - \mu)/(\sigma/\sqrt{n})$ approaches a normal dis-
> tribution with mean zero and variance one as n becomes large.

The conditions under which the central limit theorem is true are not
restrictive. There are relatively few populations that do not have a finite
variance.[4] If we take larger and larger random samples from almost any
population, the sampling distribution of $\bar{X}$ will tend to assume a form closer

---

[4] Perhaps the simplest such renegade is one that follows the Cauchy distribution:

$$f(x) = \frac{1}{\pi(x^2 + 1)} \qquad -\infty < x < \infty$$

and closer to a normal distribution. Its mean and variance will, of course, always be given by $\mu_{\bar{X}} = \mu$ and $\sigma_{\bar{X}}^2 = \sigma^2/n$ as has been proved. It then can be shown that the random variable

$$Z = \frac{\bar{X} - \mu}{\sigma/\sqrt{n}}$$

has an approximately normal sampling distribution when n is large and that this function has mean zero and variance 1.

When should a sample be called large? The answer is really a matter of opinion. In the uses of the central limit theorem the size of the sample that should be drawn depends on the degree of reliability needed. The larger the sample the more reliable the results. If a rule of thumb is required, we might say that many statisticians have found approximations based on samples as small as size 30 to be satisfactory for their purposes. The student may thus, if he wishes, think of samples of 30 or over as being "large" and of samples of 29 and under as "small." But he must always keep in mind, as sample size is decreased, that there is no cut-off point at which the approximation suddenly ceases to be satisfactory. Rather, there is a steady falling-off in reliability; no statistician would use the central limit theorem on an unknown population in samples of size 4, but in samples of sizes 15 to 40 he might apply it in some situations but not in others.

Let us use the central limit theorem in a problem. Loads of scrap paper are weighed as they enter the R. K. Hildek Company's warehouse. Then the paper is compressed into standard bales and stored for sale. On October 31, 1968, the warehouse contained 2,768,500 lb of paper packed in 13,000 bales. From past experience the standard deviation of bale weights is known to be 27 lb.

1. In a random sample of 324 bales, what is the probability that the sample mean will not differ from the population mean by more than 2 lb?

2. Within what range will the sample mean fall 99 percent of the time in random samples of size 81?

Solution of 1.

$$\sigma_{\bar{X}} = \frac{\sigma}{\sqrt{n}} = \frac{27}{18} = 1.5$$

$$P\{|\bar{X} - \mu| \leq 2\} = P\left\{\left|\frac{\bar{X} - \mu}{\sigma_{\bar{X}}}\right| \leq \frac{2}{\sigma_{\bar{X}}}\right\} = P\left\{|Z| \leq \frac{2}{1.5}\right\} = 2P\{0 \leq Z \leq 1.33\}$$

$$= 2\{0.4082\} = 0.8164$$

The odds are roughly 4 to 1 that the sample mean will not be more than 2 lb away from the population mean.

Solution   of   2.   Here $\mu = 2,768,500/13,000 = 212.96$ lb   (why?),   and $\sigma_{\bar{X}} = 27/\sqrt{81} = 3.00$ lb.

$$P\{-c + 212.96 < \bar{X} < c + 212.96\} = P\left\{-\frac{c}{3} < \frac{\bar{X} - 212.96}{3} < \frac{c}{3}\right\} = 0.99$$

$$2P\left\{0 < Z < \frac{c}{3}\right\} = 0.99, \qquad P\left\{0 < Z < \frac{c}{3}\right\} = 0.495$$

$$\frac{c}{3} = 2.57, c = 7.71;$$

therefore

$$P\{205.25 < \bar{X} < 220.67\} = 0.99$$

The probability is 0.99 that a random sample of 81 bales, drawn from the contents of the warehouse, will have a mean lying between 205.25 and 220.67 lb.

8.8   OTHER SAMPLING DISTRIBUTIONS

There are a large number of sampling distributions that are of interest in the business applications of statistics. In theory, any sample statistic gives rise to a sampling distribution when it is computed and tabulated in all possible samples of a fixed size from the population of interest. We shall limit the discussion to various sampling distributions involving means and pro-portions—perhaps the simplest and most useful of all statistics.

Consider the following problem—which cannot be solved by referring to the sampling distribution of $\bar{X}$ already derived. In order to select personnel suited for work on an intricate small-parts assembly job, the Buchanan Calculator Company decides to give certain of its employees the Hansco Manual Skills Test, a standard timed test using pegs and blocks. The Hansco firm has announced that men's scores on this test are normally distributed with mean 200 and variance 2500, while women's scores are normal with mean 210 and variance 3025. If 30 men and 20 women from the Buchanan Company take the test, what is the probability that the sample mean score for men is more than 5 points higher than the sample mean score for women?

When one starts out to solve this problem, one first has to worry about the representativeness of the samples. Can the 30 men and 20 women be considered to form groups similar to those that would have been obtained by drawing random samples from the two populations consisting of all men and all women who have taken the Hansco tests? Assume that this point has been checked and the samples found reasonably satisfactory, what then? In order to proceed we need to know the form of a new sampling distribution. Since the probability question concerns the difference between the means of two independent samples taken from normal populations, we need to find the sampling distribution of such a difference. We note that if the samples were not independent, the sampling distribution of the difference would have an entirely different form. Under what conditions might these samples be dependent?

Conceptually, just what is the sampling distribution of the difference between the means of two independent samples? Consider all samples of size n from the first population. Compute the mean of each of these. Then consider all samples of size m from the second population and compute their means. Then form all possible pairs of samples one from the first population and one from the second. Subtract and tabulate the difference of these sample means to obtain the required sampling distribution.

The moment-generating function for this sampling distribution is derived in Section 8.9, and is given by

$$m_{\bar{X}-\bar{Y}}(\theta) = e^{(\mu_X - \mu_Y)\theta + [(\sigma_X^2/n) + (\sigma_Y^2/m)]\theta^2/2} \tag{8.9}$$

By comparison with the moment-generating function of (8.7), we see that the sampling distribution of $\bar{X} - \bar{Y}$ in independent samples of size n and m from populations that are normal with means μ_X and μ_Y and variances σ_X^2 and σ_Y^2 is again normal with mean $\mu_X - \mu_Y$ and variance $\sigma_X^2/n + \sigma_Y^2/m$.

To solve the Buchanan Calculator Company's problem, we note that $\mu_X = 200$, $\sigma_X^2 = 2500$, $n = 30$; $\mu_Y = 210$, $\sigma_Y^2 = 3025$, $m = 20$. Then the sampling distribution of $\bar{X} - \bar{Y}$ is approximately normal, as is shown in Figure 8.3, with mean $\mu_X - \mu_Y = -10$ and standard deviation.

$$\sigma_{\bar{X}-\bar{Y}} = \sqrt{\frac{2500}{30} + \frac{3025}{20}} = \sqrt{\frac{14{,}075}{60}} = 15.3$$

We require

$$P\{\bar{X} - \bar{Y} > 5\} = P\left\{\frac{(\bar{X} - \bar{Y}) + 10}{15.3} > \frac{5 + 10}{15.3}\right\}$$

$$= P\{Z > 0.98\} = 0.5 - 0.3365 = 0.1635$$

The probability is roughly 16 in a 100 that the 30 men would "on the average" outscore the 20 women by at least 5 points on the Hansco Manual Skills Test.

To enlarge the scope of the applications of this sampling distribution, consider this additional problem. Each year the Murphy and Helmer mail order house takes a random sample of 2000 from its sales invoices in order to estimate certain of its operating parameters. One of these is the quantity "average dollar amount per order." In 1970, however, a complete census of all that year's invoices was made from which the values $\mu = \$18.75$ and $\sigma = \$4.31$ were laboriously computed. If the mean and standard deviation of the

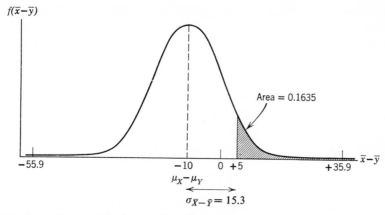

$f(\bar{x}-\bar{y})$

Area = 0.1635

-55.9

-10 0 $+5$

$\mu_X-\mu_Y$

$+35.9$ $\bar{x}-\bar{y}$

$\sigma_{\bar{X}-\bar{Y}} = 15.3$

Fig. 8.3. Sampling distribution of $\bar{X} - \bar{Y}$ in the Buchanan problem.

population of dollar amounts per order remain the same after 1970, and if the 1971 sample mean was $19.00:

1. What is the probability that the 1972 sample mean will exceed the 1971 sample mean?

2. What is the probability that the 1973 sample mean will exceed the 1972 sample mean by $0.15 or more?

Solution of 1. In 1971 and 1972,

$$m = n = 2000, \qquad \mu_X = \mu_Y = 18.75, \qquad \sigma_X = \sigma_Y = 4.31$$

However, here we need only the sampling distribution of $\bar{Y}$, since the question really asks for the probability that the 1972 sample mean will exceed $19. By the central limit theorem, this sampling distribution is approximately normal with

$$\mu_Y = 18.75 \qquad \text{and} \qquad \sigma_{\bar{Y}} = \frac{4.31}{\sqrt{2000}} = 0.096$$

$$P\{\bar{Y} > 19.00\} = P\left\{\frac{\bar{Y} - 18.75}{0.096} > \frac{19 - 18.75}{0.096}\right\}$$

$$= P\left\{Z > \frac{0.25}{0.096}\right\} = P\{Z > 2.60\}$$

$$= 0.5000 - 0.4953 = 0.0047$$

It is unlikely that the 1972 sample mean will exceed the 1971 figure of $19.00—given that the population is as assumed.

Solution of 2. Here we do require the sampling distribution of the difference of sample means. By the central limit theorem, this function is approximately normal with

$$\mu_{\bar{X}-\bar{Y}} = \mu_X - \mu_Y = 0$$

and

$$\sigma_{\bar{X}-\bar{Y}} = \sqrt{\frac{(4.31)^2}{2000} + \frac{(4.31)^2}{2000}} = \frac{4.31}{10\sqrt{10}} = \frac{4.31}{31.62} = 0.136$$

$$P\{\bar{Y} \geq \bar{X} + 0.15\} = P\{\bar{X} - \bar{Y} \leq -0.15\} = P\left\{\frac{(\bar{X} - \bar{Y}) - 0}{0.136} \leq \frac{-0.15 - 0}{0.136}\right\}$$

$$= P\{Z \leq -1.10\} = 0.5 - 0.3643 = 0.1357$$

Roughly 14 times in 100 we would expect to find the 1973 mean exceeding the 1972 mean by at least $0.15. The student should consider the validity of the independence assumption used here.

We now shift our attention away from problems involving means. Many of the basic questions asked by businessmen are phrased in terms of proportions or percentages. The remainder of this section discusses sampling distributions for percentages.

It is known that, in a certain large midwestern city, 40 percent of all dwelling units are occupied by five or more persons. What is the probability that, in a random sample of 2000 homes taken in this city, less than 38 percent of the dwelling units would be occupied by five or more persons?

To answer probability questions concerning a percentage based on a single random sample requires a knowledge of the form of the sampling distribution of P, the percentage of sample elements possessing some characteristic of interest. Here P is the sample percentage of homes occupied by more than four people. But we have already studied a problem closely related to this. Here is a Bernoulli population—each home either is or is not occupied by five or more people. The sample is formed by repeating independently 2000 times the experiment of picking a home from a list of all homes in the city. Therefore the sampling distribution of X, the number of homes in the sample occupied by five or more people, must be binomial if we sample with replacement according to the argument of Chapter 4.

$$f(x) = \binom{n}{x}\left(\frac{\pi}{100}\right)^x \left(\frac{\phi}{100}\right)^{n-x} \qquad x = 0, 1, 2, \cdots, n$$

where π is the population percentage having the characteristic in question and $\phi = 100 - \pi$. (If the sampling is done without replacement, the sampling distribution is approximately binomial whenever the sample is small relative to the population.) In terms of p, the sample percentage, and on a percentage scale for p, the function becomes the binomial

$$f(p) = \binom{n}{\frac{np}{100}} \left(\frac{\pi}{100}\right)^{np/100} \left(\frac{\phi}{100}\right)^{n-(np/100)} \qquad p = 0, \frac{100}{n}, \frac{200}{n}, \cdots, 100$$

since the sample number with a given characteristic is placed in percentage form by multiplying by $100/n$, that is,

$$p = \frac{100x}{n} \tag{8.10}$$

The mean and variance of $f(x)$ are known from Chapter 6 to be

$$E(X) = n\frac{\pi}{100} \qquad \sigma_X{}^2 = n\frac{\pi}{100}\frac{\phi}{100} \tag{8.11}$$

Again multiplying by $100/n$ to arrive at a percentage scale for P and focusing our attention on $f(p)$, we change (8.11) into

$$E(P) = \pi \qquad \sigma_P{}^2 = \frac{\pi\phi}{n} \tag{8.12}$$

If one has a set of tables of the binomial distribution, one can solve many problems in sampling by reading off probability figures corresponding to different intervals. This is particularly simple when the tables are given in cumulative form. However, as is shown in Section 7.4, for large n the normal distribution furnishes a good approximation to the binomial when the parameter representing the probability of success is close neither to zero nor to one. We solve the present problem using the approximation.

For the home occupancy problem $n = 2000$; $\pi = 40\% = \mu_P$; $\phi = 60\%$

$$\sigma_P{}^2 = \frac{40 \cdot 60}{2000} = 1.2 \qquad \sigma_P = \sqrt{1.2} = 1.095\%$$

We shall approximate the sum of the ordinates of the binomial $p < 38$ percent by taking the normal area less than 38 percent. Since the binomial is a discrete distribution, we really should not include 38 percent but should cumulate up to the first figure less than 38 percent (759/2000 or 37.95 percent in this case). This distinction is of little practical significance whenever n is large enough for the normal to be a satisfactory approximation. Using 38 percent, we say that

$$P_{\text{binominal}}\{P < 38\%\} \approx P_{\text{normal}}\{P < 38\%\}$$

$$P_{\text{normal}}\{P < 38\%\} = P\left\{\frac{P - 40\%}{1.095\%} < \frac{38\% - 40\%}{1.095\%}\right\}$$

$$= P\{Z < -1.83\} = 0.5000 - 0.4664 = 0.0336$$

We have used capital P here to represent both a probability statement and a random variable. This notation will cause no problem to the reader as P used as a random variable is always italicized and P used in the sense of probability is always roman.

In addition to single-sample percentages one frequently encounters two-sample situations. The Central Electricity Company and Radix Industries are manufacturers of household appliances. Central produces a refrigerator model called "The Aristofreeze." Radix puts out a model called "The Chillerator," which is comparable to the Aristofreeze in construction and price. If 1971 sales of both models were "large" with 70 percent of sales of both models in pastel colors, and if independent random samples of 500 and 400 are taken from the 1971 sales of Aristofreeze and Chillerator, respectively, what is the probability that the sample percentage of pastel Aristofreezes exceeds the sample percentage of pastel Chillerators by less than 2 percent?

Here the question concerns a difference in percentages in two samples which fall within the "large" category. One reasonable approach to such a problem can be made using normal approximations. We replace each of the binomials by an approximating distribution and then proceed as in the case of the difference of two independent sample means.

In general, let us consider two independent Bernoulli populations, the first with parameter π_1 and the second with parameter π_2. Earlier in this section we have shown that the sampling distribution of the sample percentages P_1 and P_2 are each binomial with means and variances

$$E(P_1) = \pi_1 \qquad E(P_2) = \pi_2 \qquad \sigma_{P_1}^2 = \frac{\pi_1 \phi_1}{n} \qquad \sigma_{P_2}^2 = \frac{\pi_2 \phi_2}{m}$$

where n and m are the respective sample sizes, $\phi_1 = 100 - \pi_1$, and $\phi_2 = 100 - \pi_2$. The sampling distribution of differences between sample proportions has mean $\pi_1 - \pi_2$ and variance $\pi_1 \phi_1 / n + \pi_2 \phi_2 / m$. For reasonably large samples the normal is again a satisfactory approximation (see Section 8.9).

As in the preceding problem we should recognize that we have a discrete situation and might wish to modify our procedure to take this into account.[5]

---

[5] If we wish to modify our procedure to take account of the discrete nature of the distribution, we must recognize that all differences will be divisible by $(1/m - 1/n)100\%$. In this case $(1/400 - 1/500)100\% = 0.05\%$. Thus the only possible values for which Aristofreezes exceed Chillerators by less than 2 percent must lie between 0.05 percent and 1.95 percent. Since the normal is a continuous function, we should split the difference between 0.00 and 0.05 and between 1.95 and 2.00. We would then solve

$$\mathrm{P}_{normal}\{0.025\% < P_1 - P_2 < 1.975\%\} = \mathrm{P}\left\{\frac{0.025}{3.07} < \frac{P_1 - P_2}{3.07} < \frac{1.975}{3.07}\right\}$$

$$= \mathrm{P}\{0.008 < Z < 0.643\} = 0.240 - 0.003 = 0.237$$

However, in the refrigerator problem we shall simply let

$$P_{\text{binomial}}\{0 < P_1 - P_2 < 2\%\} \approx P_{\text{normal}}\{0 < P_1 - P_2 < 2\%\}$$

$$\pi_1 = \pi_2 = 70\% \qquad \mu_{P_1-P_2} = \pi_1 - \pi_2 = 0\%$$

$$\sigma_{P_1-P_2} = \sqrt{\frac{\pi_1\phi_1}{n} + \frac{\pi_2\phi_2}{m}} = \sqrt{\frac{70 \cdot 30}{500} + \frac{70 \cdot 30}{400}} = 3.07\%$$

Therefore

$$P_{\text{normal}}\{0 < P_1 - P_2 < 2\%\} = P\left\{\frac{0-0}{3.07} < \frac{(P_1 - P_2) - \mu_{P_1-P_2}}{\sigma_{P_1-P_2}} < \frac{2-0}{3.07}\right\}$$

$$= P\{0 < Z < 0.651\} = 0.242$$

If the 1971 Aristofreeze and Chillerator populations do, in fact, each contain 70 percent pastel refrigerators, then the probability is roughly 0.242 that sample percentages in samples of size 500 and 400, respectively, would show pastel Aristofreezes outnumbering pastel Chillerators by less than 2 percent.

We have now seen how a certain sort of probability statement about a mean or a proportion can be made. The statement has been of the type, "If a population has form A, what is the probability that a random sample of size n chosen from it will have characteristic B?" Notice that the population was assumed known and the reasoning was from population to sample. In the next chapter we shall use these ideas to attack a set of much more important problems in which this process is reversed. They will appear as, "If a random sample of size n is chosen from a population and if the sample has form C, should one conclude that the *population* has characteristic D?" Problems in which one reasons from sample to population are called problems of inference.

In any problem involving a probability statement about a statistic and the corresponding parameter, attention is focused on the sampling distribution of the statistic. If its form is known, exactly or approximately, probability statements about the statistic can be made and checked; if the form is unknown and no approximation is available, there are still ways of dealing with some probability statements. However, these are, in general, either more difficult or less satisfactory than those that could have been made if the sampling distribution was available. In the next chapter we shall see how the sampling distribution concept is central to statistical inference.

All sampling distributions discussed here have been either exactly normal or approximately so. Often, in first statistics courses, students receive the impression that all sampling distributions are normal. Nothing could be more false. It happens that many of the simplest and most useful sampling distributions are normal—or nearly so—but by far the majority have other forms.

In the next chapter an important statistic will be used which has a sampling distribution called the *t* distribution.

*8.9   MOMENT-GENERATING FUNCTIONS OF SAMPLING DISTRIBUTIONS

In this section we shall derive the sampling distributions of three statistics already used in this chapter. The first is the distribution of $\overline{X}$ used in Section 8.6, the second is the distribution of $\overline{X} - \overline{Y}$ that appeared in Section 8.8, and the third is the distribution of $P_1 - P_2$ also from Section 8.8. We shall state these three theorems and prove them in order.

THEOREM.   Let $X_1, \cdots, X_n$ be a random sample selected from a population which is normal with mean μ and variance σ^2. Let

$$\overline{X} = \sum_{i=1}^{n} \frac{X_i}{n}$$

be the mean of the sample. Then the sampling distribution of $\overline{X}$ is normal with mean μ and variance σ^2/n.

Proof.   From (7.11) we recall that the moment-generating function of a normal distribution with mean μ and variance σ^2 is

$$m_X(\theta) = e^{\mu\theta + \sigma^2\theta^2/2}$$

We now find the moment-generating function of $\overline{X}$. Since the sample is random, $\overline{X} = X_1/n + \cdots + X_n/n$ is a sum of independent random variables, and we may use (8.3)

$$m_{\overline{X}}(\theta) = [m_{X/n}(\theta)]^n$$

Now by (7.5)

$$m_{X/n}(\theta) = m_X(\theta/n)$$

$$m_{X/n}(\theta) = \int_{x=-\infty}^{\infty} e^{\theta x/n} \frac{1}{\sqrt{2\pi}\,\sigma} e^{-(x-\mu)^2/2\sigma^2} dx$$

$$= \frac{1}{\sqrt{2\pi}\,\sigma} \int_{x=-\infty}^{\infty} e^{-(1/2\sigma^2)[(x-\mu)^2 - (2\sigma^2\theta/n)x]} dx$$

We complete the square in the exponent.

$$(x-\mu)^2 - \frac{2\sigma^2\theta}{n}x = x^2 - 2\left(\mu + \frac{\sigma^2\theta}{n}\right)x + \left(\mu + \frac{\sigma^2\theta}{n}\right)^2 + \mu^2 - \left(\mu + \frac{\sigma^2\theta}{n}\right)^2$$

$$= \left(x - \mu - \frac{\sigma^2\theta}{n}\right)^2 - \left(2\frac{\mu\sigma^2\theta}{n} + \frac{\sigma^4\theta^2}{n^2}\right)$$

Hence

$$m_{X/n}(\theta) = e^{(\mu\theta/n)+(\sigma^2\theta^2/2n^2)}\frac{1}{\sqrt{2\pi}\,\sigma}\int_{x=-\infty}^{\infty}e^{-[x-\mu-\sigma^2\theta/n]^2/2\sigma^2}\,dx$$

The second factor is the integral from $-\infty$ to ∞ of a normal distribution with mean $\mu + \sigma^2\theta/n$ and variance σ^2. Hence it equals unity, and

$$m_{X/n}(\theta) = e^{(\mu\theta/n)+(\sigma^2\theta^2/2n^2)}$$

But then

$$m_{\bar{X}}(\theta) = [m_{X/n}(\theta)]^n = e^{\mu\theta+(\sigma^2/n)\theta^2/2}$$

By comparing this with the moment-generating function of a normal distribution given initially, we see that $m_{\bar{X}}(\theta)$ is the moment-generating function of a normal distribution with mean μ and variance $\sigma_{\bar{X}}^2 = \sigma^2/n$, which establishes the theorem. Remember that this result has already been employed in Section 8.6.

THEOREM. Let $X_1, \cdots, X_n$ be a random sample selected from a population which is normal with mean μ_X and variance $\sigma_X{}^2$. Let $Y_1, \cdots, Y_m$ be an independent random sample selected independently from a second normal population—this one having mean μ_Y and variance $\sigma_Y{}^2$. Let $\bar{X}$ and $\bar{Y}$ be respectively the means of these samples. Then the sampling distribution of $\bar{X} - \bar{Y}$ is normal with mean $\mu_X - \mu_Y$ and variance $\sigma_X{}^2/n + \sigma_Y{}^2/m$.

Proof.   Since the first population is normal, from (7.11)

$$m_{\bar{X}}(\theta) = e^{\mu_X\theta+(\sigma_X{}^2/n)\theta^2/2}$$

And by (7.5) with $c = -1$,

$$m_{-\bar{Y}}(\theta) = m_{\bar{Y}}(-\theta) = e^{\mu_Y(-\theta)+(\sigma_Y{}^2/m)(-\theta)^2/2}$$
$$= e^{-\mu_Y\theta+(\sigma_Y{}^2/m)(\theta^2/2)}$$

But since the sampling is random, $\bar{X}$ and $\bar{Y}$ are independent and, hence,

$$m_{\bar{X}-\bar{Y}}(\theta) = m_{\bar{X}}(\theta) \cdot m_{-\bar{Y}}(\theta)$$
$$m_{X-Y}(\theta) = e^{\mu_X\theta+(\sigma_X{}^2/n)\theta^2/2} \cdot e^{-\mu_Y\theta+(\sigma_Y{}^2/m)\theta^2/2}$$
$$= e^{(\mu_X-\mu_Y)\theta+[(\sigma_X{}^2/n)+(\sigma_Y{}^2/m)]\theta^2/2}$$

Thus the sampling distribution of the difference between means of independent samples selected from normal populations is normal with mean $\mu_X - \mu_Y$ and variance $(\sigma_X{}^2/n) + (\sigma_Y{}^2/m)$.

THEOREM. **Let P_1 be the percentage of a random sample of size n possessing a certain characteristic, the sample being chosen from a population in which the percentage having that characteristic is π_1. Let P_2 and π_2 be a similar statistic and parameter arising from a second population and an independent random sample of size m. When n and m are large, the sampling distribution of $P_1 - P_2$ is approximately normal with mean $\pi_1 - \pi_2$ and variance $\pi_1\phi_1/n + \pi_2\phi_2/m$.**

Proof. Since both samples are large, we may use Section 7.4 to approximate each binomial sampling distribution by a normal distribution obtaining
for P_1:

$$f(p_1) = \sqrt{\frac{n}{2\pi\pi_1\phi_1}}\, e^{-n(p_1-\pi_1)^2/2\pi_1\phi_1}$$

and, for P_2:

$$f(p_2) = \sqrt{\frac{m}{2\pi\pi_2\phi_2}}\, e^{-m(p_2-\pi_2)^2/2\pi_2\phi_2}$$

The corresponding moment-generating functions are

$$m_{P_1}(\theta) = e^{\pi_1\theta+(\pi_1\phi_1/n)(\theta^2/2)} \qquad m_{P_2}(\theta) = e^{\pi_2\theta+(\pi_2\phi_2/m)(\theta_2/2)}$$

and furthermore, by (7.5) with $c = -1$,

$$m_{-P_2}(\theta) = e^{-\pi_2\theta+(\pi_2\phi_2/m)(-\theta)^2/2}$$

But P_1 and P_2 are independent random variables; hence by (8.2)

$$m_{P_1-P_2}(\theta) = m_{P_1}(\theta)m_{-P_2}(\theta)$$

$$m_{P_1-P_2}(\theta) = e^{\pi_1\theta+(\pi_1\phi_1/n)\theta^2/2}e^{-\pi_2\theta+(\pi_2\phi_2/m)\theta^2/2}$$

$$= e^{(\pi_1-\pi_2)\theta+\,[(\pi_1\phi_1/n)+(\pi_2\phi_2/m)]\theta^2/2}$$

By (8.7) this is the moment-generating function of a normal distribution with mean $\pi_1 - \pi_2$ and variance

$$\sigma^2_{P_1-P_2} = \frac{\pi_1\phi_1}{n} + \frac{\pi_2\phi_2}{m}$$

This establishes that in large samples the sampling distribution of $P_1 - P_2$ may be approximated by such a normal distribution.

8.10   CORRECTION FACTORS FOR THE STANDARD ERROR

In Section 8.5 we have stated that the mean of the sampling distribution of $\bar{X}$ is always equal to the mean of the population. But we suggested circumstances under which the standard error of $\bar{X}$ took on different forms. As long as the population is infinite or even when it is finite and we sample with replacement, $\sigma_{\bar{x}}$ is given by $\sigma/\sqrt{n}$. But when the population is finite and we sample without replacement it can be shown that

$$\sigma_{\bar{x}} = \sqrt{\frac{N-n}{N-1}} \cdot \frac{\sigma}{\sqrt{n}}$$

where N is the population size and n is the sample size.

Does this mean that many of our problems in this chapter have been shown with erroneous solutions? Not so! Whenever n is small relative to N,

$$\sqrt{\frac{N-n}{N-1}}$$

is close to unity and can be ignored. This was the case in all problems discussed in this chapter.

Only when sample size becomes large relative to a finite population size must the correction factor be employed. A rule of thumb, which lacks very convincing supporting evidence but is often used, states that the correction factor can be ignored as long as the sample is less than one-tenth of the population. Under these conditions, the correction factor will be between 0.95 and 1.00 unless the population is unusually small. It is not usual to sample from tiny populations. The limits on the size of the correction factor in the case mentioned are easy to obtain, for example,

$$\sqrt{\frac{N-n}{N-1}} > \sqrt{\frac{N-0.1N}{N-1}} = \sqrt{\frac{0.9N}{N-1}} \approx \sqrt{0.9} = 0.95$$

Other correction factors should be used for cases of statistics other than $\bar{X}$ when sample size is large relative to population size. An investigation of these is not a desirable part of a first course in statistics.

IMPORTANT TERMS AND CONCEPTS

Binomial probability distribution
  Normal approximation to
Correction factor
Moment-generating function
Population
  Parameter
  Subset of
Random variable

Sampling
  Independent
Sampling distribution
  Empirical
  Theoretical
  Differences in means
  Differences in proportions
  Means
  Proportions

Sample
  Nonprobability (judgment)
  Probability
    Area
    Cluster
    Proportional stratified
    Simple random
    Stratified
    Systematic
  Statistic

Standard error
Table of random numbers

SYMBOLS AND ABBREVIATIONS

$f(\cdot)$	P	$\mu_{\bar{X}-\bar{Y}}$
$f_i(\cdot)$	p	$\sigma_{\bar{X}}$
$m(\theta_1, \cdots, \theta_n)$	$\mu_{\bar{X}}$	σ_P
π	μ_P	$\sigma_{P_1-P_2}$
ϕ	$\mu_{P_1-P_2}$	$\sigma_{\bar{X}-\bar{Y}}$

OFTEN-USED FORMULAS

$$m(\theta_1, \cdots, \theta_n) = \int_{x_1=-\infty}^{\infty} \cdots \int_{x_n=-\infty}^{\infty} e^{\theta_1 x_1 + \cdots + \theta_n x_n} f(x_1, \cdots, x_n)\, dx_1 \cdots dx_n$$

$$m_V(\theta) = m_1(\theta) \cdots m_n(\theta)$$

$$m_V(\theta) = [m_X(\theta)]^n$$

$$E(\bar{X}) = \mu_X; \quad \sigma_{\bar{X}}^2 = \frac{\sigma_X^2}{n}; \qquad E(P) = \pi; \quad \sigma_P^2 = \frac{\pi\phi}{n}$$

$$\mu_{\bar{X}-\bar{Y}} = \mu_X - \mu_Y; \qquad \sigma_{\bar{X}-\bar{Y}}^2 = \frac{\sigma_X^2}{n} + \frac{\sigma_Y^2}{m} \qquad \mu_{P_1-P_2} = \pi_1 - \pi_2;$$

$$\sigma_{P_1-P_2}^2 = \frac{\pi_1\phi_1}{n} + \frac{\pi_2\phi_2}{m}$$

$$\sigma_{\bar{X}} = \sqrt{\frac{N-n}{N-1}} \cdot \frac{\sigma_X}{\sqrt{n}};$$

EXERCISES

1. Define or explain each of the following:
   a. Sampling distribution.
   b. Standard error of the mean.
   c. Statistical independence.
   d. Standard error of the difference of two percentages.
   e. Simple random sample.
   f. Probability sample.
   g. Independent sampling.
   h. Proportional stratified random sample.
   i. Sampling distribution of differences in means.

2. Consider the following three distributions:
   a. Frequency distribution of the income of all lawyers in the United States for 1970.
   b. Frequency distribution of the incomes of a random sample of 300 lawyers in the United States for 1970.
   c. Probability distribution of the sample mean income of lawyers in the United States for 1970. (Also called the sampling distribution of the mean.)
   Compare these three distributions with respect to:
   Elements in the distributions.　　Standard deviations.
   Arithmetic means.　　Skewness.

3. A research group has been commissioned to conduct a survey in a certain state. The first objective is to estimate the percentage of unemployment among males in the labor force. Assume that a complete list of names and addresses of all males in the labor force is available and that a random sample is desired. Would sending out mail questionnaires to be answered on a voluntary basis by every tenth name on the list produce a simple random sample? Why or why not? Would this constitute a probability sample? Explain.

4. In Section 8.8 there was discussion of the Hansco Manual Skills Test. Answer the following questions relating to that problem.
   a. How might one go about checking to see if the employees were similar to those persons whose scores were used by the Hansco firm to establish the standard scores for men and women?
   b. Under what conditions or situations would the two samples taken from the Buchanan Calculator Company's employees be *dependent*?

5. a. Is a larger sample always a better sample? Explain.
   b. Would you agree that sometimes a judgment sample is better than a probability sample? Explain your position using concrete examples.
   c. What are the advantages of random sampling?

6. Prove that the moment-generating function of a sum of n independent random variables is equal to the product of the moment-generating functions of the variables themselves for probability distributions which are discrete. (*Hint.* This is proved in the text for continuous distributions.)

7. If four random variables are independent and each has a binomial distribution with parameters n and p,
   a. Find the moment-generating function of their sum.
   b. Use this moment-generating function to find the mean of the sum.
   c. Check your computation by finding the mean of the sum directly.

8. If X_1, X_2 represents a random sample of size two selected from a Poisson distribution with mean λ,
   a. Find the moment-generating function of $V = X_1 + X_2$ and thus identify the probability distribution of V.
   b. What is the variance of V?
   c. What is the covariance of X_1 and X_2?

9. If X is a random variable that is normally distributed with mean zero and variance unity, and if $Y = a + bX$, use moment-generating functions to identify the distribution of Y and its parameters.

10. In a manufacturing process, it was observed over a long period of time, that the mean weight of the articles produced was 30 lb with a standard deviation of 2 lb. The distribution of the weights of these articles was approximately normal.
    a. What is the probability that an article selected at random from the output of this process will have a weight of less than 25 lb?
    b. If a random sample of 49 articles was selected from this process, what is the probability that it would have a mean weight between 30.5 and 30.9 lb?
    c. Explain precisely the meaning of the probabilities that you calculated in parts a and b.

11. A certain type of truck tire is known to have a mean weight of 50 lb with a standard deviation of 2 lb for all tires produced. If random samples of size 25 are drawn from a warehouse containing thousands of these tires, what is the probability of a single sample having a mean weight per tire of between 50.4 and 50.8 lb?

12. Assume that it is desired to estimate the arithmetic mean income per family in a large city. On the basis of past information, we are willing to assume that the standard deviation of family incomes is $2000. How large a simple random sample would be required to make the probability 0.954 that the error in estimating average income would not exceed $100?

13. Find the moment-generating function of the following probability distribution.

$$f(x) = xe^{-x} \qquad x \geq 0$$

Use your result to find the mean of the distribution. (*Hint.* Integration by parts will be useful here.)

14. There are 12 first-year junior executives of the Wilson Corporation. Their housing expenditures are as follows:

Individual	Housing Expenditure Per Month
A	$425.00
B	475.00
C	500.00
D	425.00
E	450.00
F	525.00
G	475.00
H	450.00
I	500.00
J	475.00
K	475.00
L	525.00

a. Calculate the mean and standard deviation of housing expenditure per month for these 12 first-year junior executives.

b. What is the mean of the sampling distribution of means from random samples of size ten from this population?

c. Of size five?

d. What is the standard deviation of the sampling distribution of means from random samples of size ten from this population?

e. Of size five?

f. Were your measures in parts *b* and *c* the same or different? Explain the reason for your results.

g. Were your answers in parts *d* and *e* the same or different? Explain the reason for your results.

h. Why were the standard deviations that you calculated in parts *d* and *e* smaller than the standard deviation you computed in part *a*?

    i. Draw four simple random samples of size five from the above distribution, using a table of random numbers.

       (1) Calculate the mean and standard deviation for each sample.

       (2) Compare the sample means and standard deviations with the corresponding population characteristics calculated in part *a*.

       (3) Using means from the four samples you have chosen, estimate empirically the mean of the sampling distribution of sample means from simple random samples of size five.

       (4) Is your result in part *i(3)* the same or different from that obtained in part *c*? Explain the reason for any discrepancy.

   j. In part *i* you drew four simple random samples of size five from the population. If you drew all possible simple random samples of five from the above population, how many would you obtain?

15. Mr. McMichael's television set is not operating properly. He looks in the yellow pages of the telephone directory and his eyes fall on a list of fifteen television repair establishments. Since he has just moved to this locality he is ignorant of the fact that certain of these establishments give unsatisfactory service. Below is a list of the establishments and their performance as rated by the local better business bureau. Mr. McMichael does not have the information shown in the second column (S means satisfactory; U unsatisfactory).

Repair Establishment	Performance
1	S
2	U
3	S
4	U
5	S
6	S
7	S
8	U
9	U
10	S
11	S
12	U
13	U
14	S
15	S

   a. Mr. McMichael selects a firm at random. What is the probability that the establishment picked is rated satisfactory?

   b. If Mr. McMichael narrows his choice by selecting a simple random sample of four from the list, what is the probability that it will consist of firms all of which are rated unsatisfactory? That it will contain three firms rated satisfactory?

c. Select five random samples of size four from the above population, and calculate p, the sample proportion rated satisfactory, for each.

d. Estimate empirically $E(P)$ and σ_P using the results obtained in part c.

e. How would you go about calculating the frequency distribution of all p's from all possible random samples of size four from the population? Is there an alternative way of doing this when π is known as is true in this problem? Explain.

f. Suppose that Mr. McMichael selected a firm at random, dialed that firm, and found that there was no answer. He then picked a second firm at random from those remaining and dialed that firm only to find that again there was no answer. A third firm was selected, again at random, and this time there was an answer. What is the probability that the third firm called was rated satisfactory?

g. In actual practice, is it likely that firms listed in the yellow pages of the telephone book under Television Repair would be chosen by a random procedure? Discuss.

16. Refer to Exercise 37 of Chapter 6.

$\mu = \$125.595$ and $\sigma = \$22.4236$ for this set of sales data for the month of April 1968.

a. Calculate $E(\overline{X})$ and $\sigma_{\overline{X}}$ for simple random samples of size nine from these data.

b. Draw five simple random samples of size nine from the population of total sales for the 30 days of April, 1968, using a table of random numbers.

c. Compute $\overline{x}$ and s for each sample and compare these results with values of μ and σ given above.

d. Using the results you obtained in part c, estimate empirically the first and second moments about the origin and the first and second moments about the mean in the distribution of means from all possible simple random samples of size nine taken from the set of sales data.

e. Can you attach a name to any of these moments? Do so.

f. Compare your results in part d with those in part a. Should they be identical? If so, why? If not, what accounts for any difference?

17. Refer to Exercise 38 of Chapter 6.

The mean and standard deviation of this distribution are $\mu = \$8.86$ and $\sigma = \$7.035$.

a. What are the mean and standard deviation of the sampling distribution of the sample mean from samples of size 25?

b. What assumption regarding the nature of the samples did you make in your calculation of part *a*?

c. If the samples taken in part *a* were not probability samples, would your answer to part *a* be altered? If not, explain. If so, how would you revise your calculations?

d. Assume that the sampling distribution of means from sample size 25 is approximated by a normal distribution. What is the probability of drawing a sample of size 25 and finding:
   1. $\$8.00 < \bar{X} < \$9.00$?   3. $\bar{X} \leq \$8.86$?
   2. $\bar{X} > \$9.00$?

   Using symmetrical limits around the population mean, within what range will the sample mean fall:
   4. 95 percent of the time?
   5. 99 percent of the time?
   6. 100 percent of the time?

e. Interpret each of the probabilities that you calculated in part *d*.

f. Draw three simple random samples of size 25 from this population of sales amounts on 423 sales slips. (The amounts are listed in Exercise 38 of Chapter 6.)

g. Make an empirical estimate of $E(\bar{X})$ and $\sigma_{\bar{X}}$ by direct calculation from the means of the three samples that you drew in part *f*.

h. Compare the results in part *g* to the results from part *a*. What accounts for the difference?

i. If you had drawn 20 samples of size 25, instead of 3, would your answer to part *g* have been closer to the $E(\bar{X})$ and $\sigma_{\bar{X}}$ calculated in part *a*? Discuss.

j. What proportion of sales slips in the population had amounts under $\$2.00$?

k. Let π equal the population proportion of sales slips with amounts under $\$2.00$. Calculate $E(P)$ and σ_P where P is the proportion of sales slips with amounts under $\$2.00$ in random samples of size 25.

l. Within what range will the sample proportion lie 95.4 percent of the time? (Use symmetrical limits around π.)

m. For each of the samples that you drew in part *f* calculate *p*.

n. Estimate empirically $E(P)$ and σ_P from the results in part *m*.

18. Yearly wages (excluding very substantial commissions) paid to the 3000 salesmen employed by the Frockter and Scramble Corp. are known to be approximately normally distributed each year. For 1969 the mean wage was $\$8100$ and the standard deviation of wages was $\$630$.

a. What percentage of the salesmen were paid more than $\$7000$ in wages during 1969?

b. What percentage of the salesmen were paid between $6000 and $7000 in wages during 1969?

c. If a simple random sample of 81 salesmen is selected from this population, what is the probability that the arithmetic mean in this sample differs from the population mean by more than $20? By more than $10?

d. Within what range would the sample mean fall 99 percent of the time in simple random sampling from this population for samples of size 81?

e. How large a simple random sample has to be taken before the probability that the sample mean lies within $5 of the population mean reaches 0.9545?

19. The Washum Corporation owns a machine that fills boxes of laundry flakes. The machine is set for 15 oz net weight, and the net weights of boxes filled from the machine have a mean of 15 oz, a standard deviation of 0.5 oz, and are normally distributed.

a. What proportion of the boxes will have net weights of more than 14 oz?

b. More than 16 oz?

c. Differing from the mean weight for all boxes by more than 1 oz?

d. If a sample of 16 boxes is drawn, what is the probability that its mean net weight will be greater than 15.6 oz? Less than 14 oz?

20. The Crackup Special, an express commuter train, makes one run each weekday morning from the suburb of Oldlyn to the city of Newlyn. The train is scheduled to arrive at the downtown station at 8:43 A.M. CST. A railroad executive explained that while the mean arrival time was 8:45 A.M. the company had determined that the standard deviation of arrival times was 0.8 minutes and that the arrival times were approximately normally distributed.

a. The executive further stated that while there was some variation in arrival time, the probability was small that the train would be as much as four minutes late and that the arrival of the train five minutes behind schedule was an extremely rare event. Do you agree or not? Support your answer with numerical calculations.

b. Suppose one picks four incoming runs of the Crackup Special at random from the runs of the past year. What is the probability that the average arrival time in the sample will be later than 8:44 A.M.?

21. Salesman A and Salesman B both work for the Joynsville Company. Recently a contest was announced. The first prize was a week's vacation at a mountain resort. Salesmen A and B tied for first place, but the company was unwilling to award two first prizes. It was decided that A and B would be assigned five regular "small order" clients each. From

sales made to these clients, a random sample of two was selected for each salesman. The salesman having the highest total sales *in the sample* was the winner of the contest. The amounts of sales made to the regular "small order" clients by the two salesmen are shown below.

Salesman A Sale No.	Amount of Sale	Salesman B Sale No.	Amount of Sale
1	$30	1	$40
2	45	2	50
3	40	3	40
4	40	4	55
5	35	5	45
Total	$190	Total	$230

a. Which salesman would you expect to win?

b. What is the probability that Salesman A won?

c. What is the expected value of total sales for A in samples of size two from his universe of five small order clients?

d. What is the analogous expected value of total sales for B?

e. B's expected total sales found in d are higher than A's expected total sales found in c. Does it follow that B must have a greater probability of winning than does A? Discuss.

22. If 45 percent of all customers of a dairy company prefer large curd cottage cheese to small curd cottage cheese:

   a. What is the probability that a simple random sample of 100 of these customers would contain at least 57 persons who preferred small curd cottage cheese?

   b. Define the universe to which the parameter 45 percent applies.

   c. How would you undertake a census of this universe? What problems can you anticipate?

   d. In actual practice, which is more feasible: (1) taking a census of opinions of all customers buying cottage cheese, or (2) taking a census of the opinions from the purchaser of each box of cottage cheese sold? What is the difference?

23. Two brands of desk calculator are being considered by the Ace Accounting Firm. Brand A and Brand B are judged equal in convenience, so a decision to purchase a large number of machines is to be made by comparing the average time before first breakdown in a sample of sixteen from each brand. The brand whose sample shows the longer average time

before first breakdown is to be selected. Sixteen machines of each brand are rented, and the time before first breakdown is recorded for each machine. (Note that time in this context refers to time in use—not calendar time.) Operators of the machines are assigned at random each day in order to minimize the possible effect of other factors.

The manufacturer of brand A has determined that the average time before first breakdown is 1200 hours with a standard deviation of 100 hours. The manufacturer of Brand B has determined that the average time before first breakdown is 1250 hours with a standard deviation of 60 hours. Both variables are approximately normally distributed.

Assume that the above are true statements of universe parameters and that the Ace operators are comparable to the group used by the manufacturers in their calculations.

a. Which machine would you expect Ace to purchase? Why?

b. What percentage of Brand A machines last more than 1325 operating hours before the first breakdown?

c. What percentage of Brand B machines last more than 1325 operating hours before the first breakdown?

d. Do the results in parts *b* and *c* suggest that different decisions would be made if the criteria were altered slightly?

e. What is the probability that the results of the experiment will lead to the selection of Brand B?

f. Of Brand A?

g. What is the probability that Brand B will show a mean life before breakdown between 53 and 56 hours more than the mean life for Brand A?

h. What probability distribution was used in computing the probabilities in parts *b*, *c*, *e*, *f*, and *g*?

24. The MacDonald Corporation has received two very large shipments of blank punch cards for use in electronic computers. The manufacturer of the punch cards, unknown to the MacDonald Corporation, has determined that in the first shipment 8 percent of the cards are defective, while in the second shipment only 4 percent of the cards are defective. Defective cards do not tend to occur in any definite sequence. If one box of 400 cards is chosen from each of the shipments:

a. What is the probability that the number of defective cards in the sample from the second shipment is greater than the number of defective cards in the sample from the first shipment?

b. What is the probability that the percentage defective in the sample from the first shipment exceeds the percentage defective in the sample from the second shipment by more than eight percentage points?

25. If 25 percent of United States university faculty members favor abolition of all grading systems, if 35 percent of all United States university students have similar opinions, and if 400 faculty and 400 students are selected independently and at random from these populations, what is the probability that the percentages in the two samples favoring abolition of all grading systems differ by more than 3 percent?

26. The H. K. Stein Company, a retail mail-order firm, sells many thousands of individual products both through its dry-goods facility and through its hardware facility. As part of a large-scale operations research study, it has been found that Stein makes an average profit of 16 cents per item sold through dry goods and one of 19 cents per item sold through hardware. The standard deviations are 3 cents for dry goods and 2 cents for hardware. The profits per item sold are approximately normally distributed in each case. What is the probability that a random sample of 10 items selected at random from those sold by the hardware facility shows a smaller mean profit than random sample of 20 items taken independently from the dry goods facility?

9 Inference—Estimation

9.1 INTRODUCTION

Statisticians use the term "inference" to denote the process of generalizing sample evidence to the population from which the sample is selected. This type of inductive reasoning is valuable in many kinds of scientific investigation. It is thought by many to take a central place in the field of statistics. We repeat that inferential procedures generally cannot prove results concerning the population of interest; they only establish results subject to a probability qualification. Whether these statements are reasonable depends on the degree of the sample's representativeness. If the sample reflects the population fairly well, then the inferential process will impute an approximately true characteristic to the population. If the sample is unrepresentative, erroneous statements about the population may be labeled as probably correct. Methods incorporating randomness are the best procedures for selecting representative samples.

Statistical inference is generally discussed under three headings: point estimation, interval estimation, and hypothesis testing. In a point-estimation problem we use the evidence provided by a sample as a basis for guessing the exact value of some population characteristic. Interval estimation deals with a closely associated problem. Here we use the sample evidence to determine some interval within which the population characteristic is likely to lie. Tests of hypotheses are methods of using sample evidence to discover whether statements made about populations are likely to be true or false. We shall follow this three-way breakdown—covering point estimation and interval estimation in this chapter and discussing hypothesis testing in the next.

The material in Chapters 9 and 10, as we have just outlined it, is commonly called classical statistical inference. The ultimate purpose of inference is to aid in the making of decisions, and in recent years new techniques have been developed which build upon traditional inference in an attempt to bring all relevant information to bear in reaching the right decision. These modern developments are discussed in Chapters 11 and 12.

The next four chapters are thus closely related because, in one way or another, they all address the general problem of *decision making*. Hence, before we commence our discussion of estimation, we shall, in this section and the next, give a brief discussion of how statisticians view the process of decision making. We will then, as the later materials are developed, tie them into Section 9.2 and thus relate them to each other.

A decision is a choice between competing courses of action. A decision maker, if he is behaving in a rational fashion, will first try to identify each of the possible actions. Then he will choose the one that seems most likely to yield the results he wants and act upon his choice. The decision maker may be an individual as when Jimmy removes the phone from its cradle and debates whether to call Joan, Gloria, Carol, or Yvonne. Or the decision maker may be a group of persons as when the board of directors of the Central National Bank discusses the merger offer made by the First National Bank. In either case the decision is not said to be made until the action is taken—Joan was dialed in the first case, and a letter was written rejecting the merger offer in the second.

Upon what is the choice based in a decision problem? Simply upon all available evidence. This may be of two sorts. One is the accumulated experience of the decision maker including other sources upon which he can draw. The other is sample evidence, accumulated specifically as an aid in making the decision in question. It is only in the case of important decisions that the decision maker will collect directly relevant sample evidence as this is usually a matter of planning and conducting several experiments. One of the important problems of decision making is how the two kinds of evidence should be combined in the decision process so as to give a reasonably accurate picture of the *state of nature* that actually holds.

An additional important consideration is the gain or loss to be expected from each action. Consider a physician testing a desperately ill patient who has just been diagnosed as probably having disease A but possibly disease B. Drug 1 is known to bring excellent results in 90 percent of cases of disease A but to be nearly always fatal in cases of disease B. Drug 2 is known to bring excellent results in 50 percent of cases of disease A and to have no effect at all

	Disease A	Disease B
Drug 1		
Drug 2		

upon disease B. In order to reach a rational decision, the physician must consider the gains and losses in each of the four situations and weigh them against each other. A method of doing this will be presented in Chapter 11.

When students first encounter the concepts of decision theory and statistical inference, they tend to think of them as something brand new—something quite foreign to their experience. Quite the contrary is true; every thinking person has been using this mode of reasoning all his life. All that these chapters will do is to use the concepts of probability to treat this generalizing process numerically—which is to say, more exactly, more rationally than the student has done in the past.

When the bases were loaded and the count was three and two, the batter, remembering that the opposing pitcher did not have control of his curve, dug in and swung from the heels, guessing it would be a fast ball. Actually he was using the sample evidence that the percentage of tight situations in which this hurler would come in with his blazer was very high. The batter was performing statistical inference.

Did Joan, in turning down three bids to the high school prom on the chance that Jimmy would call, estimate the probabilities carefully? Did Jim, after the dance when driving down Mosby Road at 65 and running the blind red light at Ackert Drive, realize he was rather stupidly testing the hypothesis that there is never any traffic on Ackert Drive at 2:45 A.M. on Sunday?

Every decision that one makes suggests a certain opinion concerning the state of a particular universe. Almost without exception, this opinion is based on an inference. One has a limited amount of evidence from the population of interest or some closely related population and, from this evidence, one infers the state of the universe. Let us discuss this process in a more systematic and explicit manner.

9.2 DECISION THEORY

A large shipment of cheap ballpoint pens has arrived at the main warehouse of the R. J. Flagler Five and Dime Stores. Because of the poor quality of recent shipments from this manufacturer, Flagler will not automatically accept this shipment. The store has set standards for blotting, skipping, mechanical failure, etc., and it intends to accept the shipment only if 95 percent of the pens it contains are acceptable by these standards. We note then that Flagler's decision to accept or reject the shipment depends upon a population parameter—in this case the percentage of defective pens in the shipment.

We are discussing a particular case of a very general decision problem. Suppose a decision maker must choose one from a set of possible actions.

But which action is best depends upon an unknown parameter θ of a probability distribution $f(x; \theta)$. If θ were known, then f would be known and the best action would be obvious. Since θ is not known, the decision maker should draw a sample from the population, use this sample to estimate θ, and choose the appropriate action on the basis of this estimate.

Let $\{A\}$ be the set of all possible actions. In the Flagler problem, there are only two although in general infinitely many are possible.

$$A_0: \text{accept shipment}$$

$$A_1: \text{reject shipment}$$

Next we list all values of the parameter in question. Of course there are infinitely many values possible, but from a practical view we may decide that many of these are not distinguishable in their effect upon the decision. Suppose in the Flagler problem we use values differing by 5 percent:

$$0, 5, 10, 15, 20, 25, 30, 35, 40, 45, 50, 55,$$

$$60, 65, 70, 75, 80, 85, 90, 95, 100$$

If π is percentage defective in the population, we would wish to accept the sample only if $\pi = 0\%$ or $\pi = 5\%$.

Now Flagler's warehouse inspector picks from the shipment a random sample of six pens. He will accept the shipment if his sample results lead him to think that $\pi = 0\%$ or $\pi = 5\%$ for the whole shipment. For example, if there are no defectives in the sample ($p = 0\%$), he will suspect that π is very small and thus decide to accept the shipment. A *strategy* in a decision problem is a function whose domain is the set of all possible random samples of the given size from the population and whose range is the set of actions. A possible strategy for Flagler's inspector is shown below. Notice that the order of defective and acceptable pens is of no importance, the sample percentage defective P contains all the relevant information.

p	action
0%	accept
17	reject
33	reject
50	reject
67	reject
83	reject
100	reject

A different strategy, which does not appear as desirable, would call for accepting the shipment when $p = 0\%$ or 17%. A ridiculous strategy would suggest accepting the shipment only when $p = 50\%$ or 67%. Symbolically if $X_1, \cdots, X_n$ is a random sample from the population of interest, and if $\{A\}$ is the set of all possible actions, a strategy s is a function such that

$$s(X_1, \cdots, X_n) = A$$

for all samples. A strategy simply states what action the decision maker will take when he obtains each possible sample result.

In any real situation, the decision maker usually has a choice among many strategies. In the last paragraph it became clear that some are much better than others. We need to have a formal procedure for comparing strategies so that one may be chosen which is in some sense best. To develop such a procedure we need to be able to compare the consequences of the various actions for various values of the unknown parameter θ. This can be done by introducing the *opportunity loss* function $l(A, \theta)$. The range of this function is a set of nonnegative real numbers. One of these numbers, say $l(A_i, \theta_j)$, represents the opportunity loss occurring when action A_i is taken and the value of the parameter θ is really θ_j. For instance, in the Five and Dime example, if action A_1 (accept the shipment) were taken when the true percentage of defective pens was $\pi = 70\%$, a large opportunity loss would be incurred. As is always the case with opportunity losses, $l(A, \theta) = 0$ when the most favorable combination of action and parameter value has occurred. In the future we shall abbreviate and call $l(A, \theta)$ simply the *loss function*, but the reader should remember that opportunity losses are always implied by this term.

Now the action A to be selected in a particular decision problem is a random variable since it depends upon the sample obtained. Hence the corresponding loss $l(A, \theta)$ is also a random variable. We can now define what is meant by a "best" strategy.

Definition. A strategy is said to be "best" if it minimizes the expected loss for all possible values of θ.

In practice, it is often difficult to set up a realistic loss function and hence to decide upon a best strategy. Some of the problems involved are discussed in Chapters 11 and 12 where the ideas of this section are explained in detail.

9.3 POINT ESTIMATION

The Radox Corporation, manufacturer of the Transport portable transistor radio, is considering equipping its product with the type 38-Y-21 battery. Radox needs to obtain an estimate of the mean life of such batteries. Thus the population of concern is the set of all 38-Y-21 batteries that would be supplied to Radox. Since it is futile to think of obtaining a random sample from such a time-oriented population, an assumption is made that future 38-Y-21 product will have the same mean life as available past product. This assumption may be warranted as long as the company producing the 38-Y-21 maintains its production standards. Suppose Radox selects a random sample of size 81 from available past product, tests these batteries, and finds that the sample mean life is given by $\bar{x} = 600$ hours. What is the best estimate that can be given for the mean of the population? Note that this refers to the mean life of available past product; however, Radox is assuming this figure to be the same as that for all batteries supplied to it in the future.

Most of us would state that the best estimate of the population mean, μ, was given by the sample mean $\bar{x} = 600$. Indeed, this is a correct statement. However, we wish to raise the often embarrassing question, "Why?" What allows us to say that 600 is a better estimate than 590 or 603? If we are reaching such a conclusion on the basis of the presupposition that the best estimator of any population characteristic is the corresponding sample characteristic, this idea must be nipped in the bud. In fact, we shall show later that the best estimate of the population variance is *not* the sample variance. In the battery problem we are asked to estimate μ, a parameter, given that a random sample has been taken giving the statistic $\bar{x} = 600$ hours. We now use Section 9.2 in an attempt to develop a criterion for judging the goodness of an estimator.

If a decision maker is in a situation where he will incur a loss unless he guesses the population parameter exactly, he is said to have a *point estimation* problem. Furthermore, his strategies are usually called estimators. His loss function is zero only when the estimator (strategy) $\hat{\theta} = \theta$. It is also reasonable, though not essential, to assume that the farther away the estimator is from the parameter, the greater the loss incurred.[1] More succinctly, the worse the decision maker's guess, the more it costs him. Two of the most common loss functions used by statisticians are the quadratic

$$l(\hat{\theta}, \theta) = C(\hat{\theta} - \theta)^2 \qquad C > 0$$

and the linear

$$l(\hat{\theta}, \theta) = C|\hat{\theta} - \theta| \qquad C > 0.$$

Unfortunately neither type of loss function leads to a unique solution of the problem of selecting a best estimator—that is, one with the minimum expected loss.

---

[1] It is not necessary either to assume that overestimation by a fixed amount leads to the same loss as underestimation by that amount.

Since decision theory does not lead to a unique criterion for judging the goodness of estimators, statisticians are forced to adopt arbitrary criteria. Many have been suggested; in this book we shall use only the simplest.

Definition. Let θ be a population parameter and $\hat{\theta}$ a statistic computed from a random sample of size n selected from the population. $\hat{\theta}$ is said to be an *unbiased estimator* of θ provided that $E(\hat{\theta}) = \theta$.

Is the sample mean an unbiased estimate of the population mean? Does the relation

$$E(\overline{X}) = \mu \tag{9.1}$$

always hold? The answer is yes, and the proof of (8.4) should be consulted. Notice that to say $\hat{\theta}$ is unbiased merely means that the mean of $\hat{\theta}$'s sampling distribution is θ.

There are a number of other criteria whereby statisticians customarily evaluate the goodness of a point estimate. The interested student can find these discussed in more advanced statistics texts under the headings of consistency, sufficiency, efficiency, invariance, etc., but these concepts will not be examined here. The method of maximum likelihood estimation, which will be discussed later yields estimates that often satisfy many of these other criteria.

Since only the criterion of unbiasedness will be considered, we shall not claim that our estimators are "best." Indeed, the term "best estimator" will not occur again in this text; instead, we shall merely speak of unbiased estimators. We note that unbiased estimators are not unique; there may be many of them for one parameter. For example, the arithmetic mean, the median, and the midrange of a random sample are all unbiased estimators of the mean of a normal population. We shall find a single unbiased estimator for each of several important parameters. For the Radox example, we have already shown that $\overline{x} = 600$ is an unbiased estimate of the population mean μ. Note that the random variable $\overline{X}$ is called an estimator. A particular value of an estimator, that is, 600, is called an estimate.

Now, averages are not very valuable unless accompanied by measures of variation. The Radox Corporation was interested in the dispersion of actual battery lives as well as in their average length. From the same sample of 81 batteries the variance was found to be

$$s^2 = \frac{\sum_{i=1}^{n} (x_i - \overline{x})^2}{n} = 1600 \text{ hr}^2$$

Let us determine an unbiased estimator of σ^2, the population variance, based on this sample variance. An algebraic identity is helpful.

$$\sum_{i=1}^{n}(X_i - \mu)^2 = \sum [(X_i - \bar{X}) + (\bar{X} - \mu)]^2$$

$$= \sum (X_i - \bar{X})^2 + 2 \sum (X_i - \bar{X})(\bar{X} - \mu) + \sum (\bar{X} - \mu)^2$$

$$= \sum (X_i - \bar{X})^2 + 2(\bar{X} - \mu) \sum (X_i - \bar{X}) + n(\bar{X} - \mu)^2$$

$$= \sum_{i=1}^{n}(X_i - \bar{X})^2 + n(\bar{X} - \mu)^2$$

since

$$\sum (X_i - \bar{X}) = \sum X_i - n\bar{X} = n\bar{X} - n\bar{X} = 0.$$

We may then write the identity as

$$\sum_{i=1}^{n}(X_i - \bar{X})^2 = \sum_{i=1}^{n}(X_i - \mu)^2 - n(\bar{X} - \mu)^2 \tag{9.2}$$

We are now ready to find out whether S^2 is an unbiased estimator for σ^2. Using (9.2),

$$E(S^2) = E\left[\frac{\sum_{i=1}^{n}(X_i - \bar{X})^2}{n} \right] = \frac{1}{n} E[\sum (X_i - \mu)^2 - n(\bar{X} - \mu)^2]$$

$$E(S^2) = \frac{1}{n} [\sum E(X_i - \mu)^2 - nE(\bar{X} - \mu)^2]$$

The quantity $E(X_i - \mu)^2$, which occurs in the first term within the bracket, is by definition σ^2, the variance of X. Furthermore, since in (8.4) we have established that the mean of the sampling distribution of $\bar{X}$ is μ, it follows that the quantity $E(\bar{X} - \mu)^2$ from the second term is simply the second moment of $\bar{X}$ about its mean or the variance of $\bar{X}$. But by (8.5) we may substitute $\sigma_{\bar{X}}^2 = \sigma^2/n$. We then obtain

$$E(S^2) = \frac{1}{n}\left[\sum_{i=1}^{n} \sigma^2 - n\frac{\sigma^2}{n} \right] = \frac{1}{n} [n\sigma^2 - \sigma^2] = \frac{n-1}{n} \sigma^2 \tag{9.3}$$

establishing the interesting fact that S^2 is a *biased* estimator of σ^2. But all is not lost! See how simple it is to find a new statistic, closely related to S^2, which is indeed an unbiased estimator of σ^2. Merely examine the statistic:

$$\hat{\sigma}^2 = \frac{n}{n-1} S^2 = \frac{n}{n-1} \frac{\sum (X_i - \bar{X})^2}{n} = \frac{\sum (X_i - \bar{X})^2}{n-1} \tag{9.4}$$

It follows that

$$E(\hat{\sigma}^2) = E\left[\frac{n}{n-1}\, S^2\right] = \frac{n}{n-1}\, E(S^2)$$

$$= \frac{n}{n-1} \cdot \frac{n-1}{n}\, \sigma^2 = \sigma^2 \tag{9.5}$$

so that $\hat{\sigma}^2$ is an unbiased estimator of the population variance σ^2.

To estimate the population variance in the battery problem, we find

$$\hat{\sigma}^2 = \frac{n}{n-1}\, s^2 = \frac{81}{80}\, 1600 = 1620 \text{ hr}^2$$

The reader may question whether the difference of 20 between s^2 and $\hat{\sigma}^2$ is important enough to warrant the extra bother. We call attention to the statement that a correct answer is preferable to an incorrect one, but more decisively we suggest a pause for computation of the same discrepancy for a sample size of ten or four. The large divergences observable should make it clear that the correction factor $n/(n-1)$ is an important quantity.

Note that the square root of an unbiased estimate of a population variance is *not* an unbiased estimate of a population standard deviation. $\hat{\sigma} = \sqrt{1620} = 40.25$ hr is an estimate of σ, but a biased one.

Next, let us consider point estimation of a population percentage. The city council of Hiawatha, Minnesota, was faced with a political problem. A study group had recommended the purchase and installation of fluoridation equipment for the city's water supply. Several conservative groups had expressed opposition. The council favored the recommendation but hesitated to take steps until it made sure that its support was widespread. A polling service was consulted and asked to determine public opinion on the proposal.

A representative of the service met with the council and agreed to carry out a series of brief interviews. It was established that the council was really not interested in the opinions of all the populace of Hiawatha, as had originally been stated, but in the opinions of those eligible to vote in the elections the next November. Hence the pollster did not set up a sampling procedure based on the whole city. Rather, the lists of registered voters available in city hall formed his point of departure. He selected 1000 names from these lists with the help of a table of random numbers and conducted a three-minute interview with each person whose name had been drawn. The results of his poll showed that 600 of those interviewed favored fluoridation, 100 opposed it, and 300 ventured no opinion. What unbiased estimate of the population percentage favoring fluoridation can be obtained? Does the corresponding sample percentage furnish such an estimator?

Referring to (8.12) of Section 8.8, we find that indeed the mean of the sampling distribution of P, the sample percentage, is π, the population percentage. This shows that P is an unbiased estimator of π. We shall always use the sample percentage as an estimate of the corresponding population percentage. In the case of the Hiawatha city council, the unbiased estimates of the percentage of eligible voters favoring fluoridation, opposing it, and neutral were respectively 60 percent, 10 percent , and 30 percent.

We conclude this section with one further investigation. (8.12) also shows that the variance of the sampling distribution of P is given by

$$\sigma_P^2 = \frac{\pi(100 - \pi)}{n}$$

Suppose that we do not know π and estimate it by p; is the quantity

$$s_p^2 = \frac{p(100 - p)}{n}$$

an unbiased estimate of σ_P^2? Let us see.

Remember that $P = 100X/n$ where X, the number of items in the sample having the characteristic in question, has a binomial distribution.

$$E(S_P^2) = E\left[\frac{P(100 - P)}{n}\right] = \frac{1}{n} E\left[\frac{100X}{n}\left(100 - \frac{100X}{n}\right)\right]$$

$$= \frac{100^2}{n^2} E(X) - \frac{100^2}{n^3} E(X^2)$$

Now in the discussion of Section 6.6 it is shown that for the binomial, with π now representing the parameter,

$$E(X^2) = \frac{n^2\pi^2}{100^2} - \frac{n\pi^2}{100^2} + \frac{n\pi}{100}$$

Then since $E(X) = n\pi/100$ we have

$$E(S_P^2) = \frac{100^2}{n^2}\frac{n\pi}{100} - \frac{100^2}{n^3}\left(\frac{n^2\pi^2}{100^2} - \frac{n\pi^2}{100^2} + \frac{n\pi}{100}\right)$$

$$= \frac{1}{n^2}[100n\pi - n\pi^2 + \pi^2 - 100\pi]$$

$$= \frac{1}{n^2}[(n - 1)100\pi - (n - 1)\pi^2]$$

$$= \frac{n - 1}{n}\left[\frac{100\pi - \pi^2}{n}\right]$$

$$= \frac{n - 1}{n}\frac{\pi(100 - \pi)}{n} \tag{9.6}$$

In other words the situation holds as when we estimate the variance. Define the new estimator

$$\hat{\sigma}_P^2 = \frac{n}{n-1} S_P^2 \tag{9.7}$$

and it follows at once that

$$E(\hat{\sigma}_P^2) = \sigma_P^2 \tag{9.8}$$

Suppose, as is unlikely, that we knew that exactly 58 percent of the voters of Hiawatha favored fluoridation. Then

$$\sigma_P = \sqrt{\frac{58 \cdot 42}{1000}} = 1.56\% \text{ for samples of size } 1000$$

In the more usual case where π is not known, we could still estimate σ_P by estimating π from p, that is, for the sample of 1000.

$$\sigma_P \approx s_p = \sqrt{\frac{60 \cdot 40}{1000}} = 1.55\%$$

The multiplier can safely be ignored in such a large sample.

*9.4 MAXIMUM LIKELIHOOD ESTIMATION

The maximum likelihood method is a general approach to the problem of point estimation. Results obtained by its use generally satisfy several of the criteria by which statisticians judge the goodness of a point estimator. Consequently, it is frequently employed. We remark, however, that maximum likelihood estimators may be biased.

Suppose that we are interested in X, a random variable which has a Poisson probability distribution with parameter λ. Then

$$f(x; \lambda) = \frac{\lambda^x e^{-\lambda}}{x!} \qquad x = 0, 1, \cdots$$

Suppose we draw a random sample of four items from this population. Think of the drawings as being one at a time. We are concerned with the probability that various population elements are chosen to be in the sample; for example, the probability that the first item selected has a value of unity is given by

$$f(1; \lambda) = \frac{\lambda^1 e^{-\lambda}}{1!} = \lambda e^{-\lambda}$$

Since random sampling insures independence of the individual events, the probability that the sample consists of the four elements 1, 4, 8, 0 in that order is obtained by multiplying the individual probabilities. Thus

$$f(1; \lambda)f(4; \lambda)f(8; \lambda)f(0; \lambda) = \lambda e^{-\lambda} \cdot \frac{\lambda^4 e^{-\lambda}}{4!} \cdot \frac{\lambda^8 e^{-\lambda}}{8!} \cdot e^{-\lambda} = \frac{\lambda^{13} e^{-4\lambda}}{4! \, 8!}$$

This function of the sample items and λ is called a likelihood function. In the case where X has a discrete probability distribution, the likelihood function represents the probability of securing the random sample obtained. We now express the same idea in more general form.

Let X be a random variable having a discrete probability distribution $f(x; \theta)$ with one parameter θ. Then the likelihood function of the random sample $X_1, X_2, \cdots, X_n$ is given by

$$L(\theta) = f(x_1; \theta)f(x_2; \theta) \cdots f(x_n; \theta) \tag{9.9}$$

and represents the probability of obtaining the random sample $x_1, x_2, \cdots, x_n$ from the population $f(x; \theta)$.

Returning now to the likelihood function $L(\lambda)$ of our sample from the Poisson population, we see that this probability varies when λ changes. That is, for different Poisson populations, the probabilities of obtaining our particular sample are different. Since we know that λ is the mean of the population, we would be surprised to obtain a random sample made up of such small numbers as 1, 4, 8, and 0 if λ were equal to 100. Substituting 100 for λ in $L(\lambda)$ would yield a tiny number. However, the substitution of $\lambda = 3$ in the same expression would yield a probability which, although small, would be much larger than for $\lambda = 100$. This backs up the belief that the random sample 1, 4, 8, 0 is much more likely to arise from a population with mean 3 than from one with mean 100.

How can we use these notions to help us estimate λ? If λ is unknown, its maximum likelihood estimate is that value of λ which makes the likelihood function as large as possible, that is, it is the value of λ which maximizes the probability of obtaining our particular sample.

But the problem then is reduced to a standard situation of elementary calculus. We differentiate the likelihood function with respect to the parameter, set the resulting function equal to zero and solve, obtaining all candidates for maxima. Of these candidates all that satisfy the further condition that the second derivatives of the function with respect to λ should be negative are the relative maximum points.

One further idea may be introduced to simplify the algebra involved. Consider a function $f(x; \lambda)$, which is differentiable in λ, and its derivative $(d/d\lambda)f(x; \lambda)$. Now examine the function $\ln f(x; \lambda)$ and its derivative

$$\frac{d}{d\lambda} \ln f(x; \lambda) = \frac{1}{f(x; \lambda)} \frac{d}{d\lambda} f(x; \lambda)$$

When we set this last expression equal to zero, we may, in general multiply each side by the expression $f(x; \lambda)$, thus obtaining the same equation

$$\frac{d}{d\lambda} f(x; \lambda) = 0$$

as we would get by setting $df/d\lambda$ equal to zero. This argument shows that, for functions which can be differentiated with respect to a parameter, maximizing the natural logarithm of a function yields the same results as maximizing the function itself. We now proceed to find the maximum likelihood estimate of λ based on our sample.

$$L(\lambda) = \frac{\lambda^{13} e^{-4\lambda}}{4! 8!}$$

$$\ln L(\lambda) = 13 \ln \lambda - 4\lambda - \ln 4! - \ln 8!$$

$$\frac{d}{d\lambda} \ln L(\lambda) = \frac{13}{\lambda} - 4$$

$$\frac{13}{\lambda} - 4 = 0$$

$$\hat{\lambda} = \frac{13}{4}$$

The caret appears as soon as the derivative is set equal to zero and indicates the required estimator. It only remains to check $\hat{\lambda}$ in the second derivative.

$$\frac{d^2}{d\lambda^2} \ln L(\lambda) = \frac{-13}{\lambda^2}$$

which for $\lambda = 13/4$ yields a negative number. This proves that 13/4 is indeed a relative maximum.

We next solve a more general problem. We shall find the maximum likelihood estimator of p in a particular binomial probability distribution

$$f(x; p) = \binom{50}{x} p^x (1 - p)^{50-x} \qquad x = 0, 1, \cdots, 50$$

based on the random sample $x_1, \cdots, x_n$. Note that p here is a probability as in Chapter 4, not a percentage. We have a population whose probability distribution is $f(x; p)$, and we select the above sample of n items at random obtaining the likelihood function. (Note that each x_i is based upon 50 observations.)

$$L(x_1, \cdots, x_n; p) = \binom{50}{x_1} p^{x_1}(1-p)^{50-x_1} \cdots \binom{50}{x_n} p^{x_n}(1-p)^{50-x_n}$$

$$= \binom{50}{x_1} \cdots \binom{50}{x_n} p^{\sum_1^n x_i} (1-p)^{\sum_1^n (50-x_i)}$$

Next we take the natural logarithm.

$$\ln L = \ln \left[\binom{50}{x_1} \cdots \binom{50}{x_n} \right] + \sum_1^n x_i \cdot \ln p + \sum_1^n (50 - x_i) \cdot \ln (1-p)$$

Differentiating with respect to p, we obtain

$$\frac{d(\ln L)}{dp} = \frac{\sum x_i}{p} - \frac{\sum (50 - x_i)}{1 - p}$$

Setting the derivative equal to zero gives

$$\frac{\sum x_i}{\hat{p}} - \frac{\sum (50 - x_i)}{1 - \hat{p}} = 0$$

And solving for $\hat{p}$ yields

$$(1 - \hat{p}) \sum x_i - \hat{p} \sum (50 - x_i) = 0$$

$$\sum x_i - \hat{p} \sum x_i - 50n\hat{p} + \hat{p} \sum x_i = 0$$

$$\sum_1^n x_i - 50n\hat{p} = 0$$

$$\hat{p} = \frac{\sum_1^n x_i}{50n} = \frac{\bar{x}}{50}$$

Checking for a maximum, we take the second derivative

$$\frac{d^2(\ln L)}{dp^2} = \frac{-\sum x_i}{p^2} - \frac{\sum (50 - x_i)}{(1 - p)^2}$$

Both terms are negative, since the sums in the numerators are both positive and since the denominators are squared. Hence $\hat{p}$ is a true maximum.

As an example, suppose five samples of 50 items each are chosen at random from this year's output of Chillerator refrigerators. The respective numbers of "frost-free" refrigerators observed in these samples are 28, 35, 22,

39, and 26. The maximum likelihood estimator of p, the proportion of frost-free Chillerators produced this year is

$$\hat{p} = \frac{\sum x_i}{50n} = \frac{28 + 35 + 22 + 39 + 26}{50 \cdot 5} = \frac{150}{250} = 0.6$$

If only one sample had been selected, we would have had simply $\hat{p} = x_1/50$, the sample proportion.

We conclude this section by considering one problem of maximum likelihood estimation in the case where the population is continuous. The student should notice that we cannot give a probabilistic interpretation of the likelihood function in the continuous case. The probability of obtaining any sample of n items by selection from a continuous population is zero. However, abandoning the probability notion as it affects the likelihood function, we keep the algebraic definition and find the estimators by the same procedures.

If a population contains two parameters as does a normal one, we may use maximum likelihood procedures to estimate them jointly. One differentiates once with respect to each parameter, sets the resulting two equations both equal to zero, and solves the resulting system simultaneously. Solutions will be candidates for maxima, and will indeed be true relative maxima if a certain condition involving second partial derivatives is satisfied. In this book we shall not discuss that condition; however, it is found in most texts on elementary calculus. Thus, given the population,

$$f(x; \mu, \sigma) = \frac{1}{\sqrt{2\pi}\,\sigma} e^{-(x-\mu)^2/2\sigma^2} \qquad -\infty < x < \infty$$

we find maximum likelihood estimators for μ and σ.

First, we write down the likelihood function.

$$L(x_1, \cdots, x_n; \mu, \sigma) = \frac{1}{\sqrt{2\pi}\,\sigma} e^{-(x_1-\mu)^2/2\sigma^2} \cdots \frac{1}{\sqrt{2\pi}\,\sigma} e^{-(x_n-\mu)^2/2\sigma^2}$$

$$= \frac{1}{(2\pi)^{n/2}\sigma^n} e^{-\sum\limits_1^n (x_i-\mu)^2/2\sigma^2}$$

Next, take the natural log.

$$\ln L = -\frac{n}{2}\ln(2\pi) - n \ln \sigma - \frac{1}{2\sigma^2} \sum_1^n (x_i - \mu)^2$$

Now, take the partial derivatives (see Section 13.6) with respect to μ and σ.

$$\frac{\partial \ln L}{\partial \mu} = -\frac{1}{2\sigma^2} \sum_1^n 2(x_i - \mu)(-1) = \frac{1}{\sigma^2} \sum_1^n (x_i - \mu)$$

$$\frac{\partial \ln L}{\partial \sigma} = -\frac{n}{\sigma} + \frac{1}{\sigma^3} \sum_1^n (x_i - \mu)^2$$

Setting these both equal to zero, we see that we can solve the first for μ without reference to the second:

$$\frac{1}{\hat{\sigma}^2} \sum_1^n (x_i - \hat{\mu}) = 0$$

$$\sum_1^n (x_i - \hat{\mu}) = 0 \qquad \sum_1^n x_i - n\hat{\mu} = 0$$

$$\hat{\mu} = \frac{\sum x_i}{n} = \bar{x}$$

Then, for the estimator of σ:

$$-\frac{n}{\hat{\sigma}} + \frac{1}{\hat{\sigma}^3} \sum_1^n (x_i - \hat{\mu})^2 = 0$$

$$-n\hat{\sigma}^2 + \sum_1^n (x_i - \bar{x})^2 = 0$$

$$\hat{\sigma}^2 = \frac{\sum_{i=1}^n (x_i - \bar{x})^2}{n}$$

$$\hat{\sigma} = \sqrt{\frac{\sum_{i=1}^n (x_i - \bar{x})^2}{n}} = s$$

The student will have to take on faith the statement that the second degree condition for a maximum is satisfied.

It is pleasant to find that the maximum likelihood estimators of the population mean and standard deviation in the normal case are the sample mean and standard deviation. From our previous work we know that $\bar{X}$ is unbiased while S is biased.

One further fact: the procedures of calculus suffice to find relative maxima of continuous functions. However, when the likelihood function is not differentiable in its parameters or when absolute, not relative, maxima exist, the problem of estimation by maximum likelihood methods becomes more difficult than is indicated by the examples given here.

9.5   INTERVAL ESTIMATION—ARITHMETIC MEANS—SINGLE SAMPLE

For this second type of inference we shall use the problem situations of Section 9.3 and obtain *interval estimates* for population means and percentages. Although interval estimation for standard deviations will not be discussed, it will be necessary to refer to the point estimator of σ on several occasions.

Suppose the Radox Corporation, before equipping its Transport radio with 38-Y-21 batteries, had asked for an interval estimate of the mean life of these batteries. It would then be required to find the smallest interval which included the mean life of the population some specified percentage of the time, for instance, 95 percent. In statistical terminology the problem would read, "Set a 95 percent confidence interval for the population mean life based on a random sample of size 81 yielding a sample mean of 600 hours and a sample standard deviation of 40 hours." A more abbreviated wording would be, "Find 95 percent confidence limits for μ when $n = 81$, $\bar{x} = 600$, and $s = 40$." Later in this section we shall point out a sense in which statements about confidence intervals may be given a probability interpretation.

As a preliminary we shall discuss a simpler type of confidence interval problem. Suppose our population of battery lives had a normal probability distribution with unknown mean μ and known standard deviation $\sigma = 36$ hours. A random sample of $n = 81$ items is drawn, and $\bar{x}$ is found to be 600 hours. Here s need not be computed, since the exact value of σ is known. Remember that in Chapter 8 it was shown that under these conditions $\bar{X}$ has a normal distribution with mean μ and standard deviation:

$$\sigma_{\bar{x}} = \frac{\sigma}{\sqrt{n}} = \frac{36}{\sqrt{81}} = 4 \text{ hours}$$

The probability is 0.95 that a single random sample of size 81 from this population will have a mean $\bar{x}$ lying in the interval from $\mu - 1.96\sigma_{\bar{x}}$ to $\mu + 1.96\sigma_{\bar{x}}$. Letting $\sigma_{\bar{x}} = 4$ hours, the probability is 0.95 that such a sample would have a mean $\bar{x}$ lying between $\mu - 7.84$ hours and $\mu + 7.84$ hours. The figure 1.96 is taken from Table E.3 and indicates the number of standard deviations from the mean required to leave an area of 0.025 in one tail of a normal distribution and hence a total area of 0.05 in both tails.

The interval just constructed is of little value, since it is centered on the unknown population mean and hence cannot be located. Emphatically, we state that the interval just found is not a confidence interval. The latter should be concerned with bounding the population mean while the interval in the preceding paragraph sets bounds for the sample mean.

Suppose, however, that we reverse the process and center an interval of the same length on $\bar{x}$ rather than on μ. This will be the actual confidence limit procedure, as will be shown shortly. This interval would be given by $\bar{x} \pm 1.96\sigma_{\bar{x}} = 600 \pm 7.84$, that is, its limits would be 592.16 hours and 607.84 hours. Let us now relate the two intervals that we have found, referring to Figure 9.1 for a clear picture of the relationship.

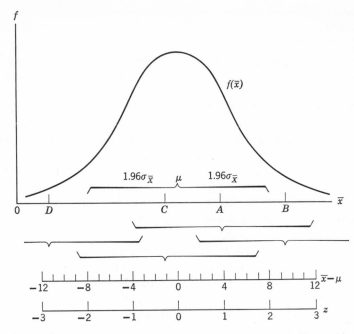

Fig. 9.1. Relationship between the sampling distribution of $\bar{X}$ and confidence limits for μ.

In Figure 9.1 the normal curve shown represents the sampling distribution of $\bar{X}$ in samples of size 81 from the given population. The standard error, $\sigma_{\bar{X}}$, has been shown to equal 4 hours. However, we do not know its mean μ, a fact that forces us to omit any origin on this axis. We do show, at the bottom of the figure, two scales for measuring from μ; the first indicating measurements in units of 1 hour and the second in units of one standard error, that is, 4 hours.

Now, when a random sample of size 81 is selected from the population, $\bar{X}$ can take on any value along the horizontal axis in Figure 9.1. Suppose $\bar{X}$ fell at point A. Lay off $1.96\sigma_{\bar{X}} = 7.84$ hours on either side of Point A, and examine the resulting interval as shown in the figure. Notice that μ is included within this interval. Now fix on point B. Again, construct a lower limit 7.84 hours below B and an upper limit 7.84 hours above. Note that μ is not included within this second interval. Moving to the left we find that an interval $3.92\sigma_{\bar{X}} = 15.68$ hours in length includes μ when centered on C but fails to do so when centered on D. The main point is now clear. Whenever a particular random sample leads to an $\bar{x}$ which lies within $1.96\sigma_{\bar{X}} = 7.84$ hours of the unknown population mean, the unspecified parameter μ will lie within

$1.96\sigma_{\bar{X}} = 7.84$ hours of $\bar{x}$. But this last interval $\bar{x} \pm 1.96\sigma_{\bar{X}}$ is the same as the interval 600 ± 7.84 (which we discussed in the preliminary problem) whenever $\bar{x} = 600$.

We have, therefore, shown that μ will be included in the interval $\bar{X} \pm 1.96\sigma_{\bar{X}}$ whenever $\bar{x}$ lies within $1.96\sigma_{\bar{X}}$ hours of μ. But from the preliminary problem we know that the probability that $\bar{x}$ lies within $1.96\sigma_{\bar{X}}$ of μ is 0.95 in the case where the population is normal with known variance. This implies that, in the long run, on repeated independent trials of this experiment, approximately 95 out of 100 trials will see the population mean included in the interval $\bar{X} \pm 1.96\sigma_{\bar{X}}$. More succinctly, we call the interval $\bar{X} \pm 1.96\sigma_{\bar{X}}$ a 95 percent confidence interval for μ because, before we construct one such interval, the probability that it will include μ is 0.95. Students often reason as follows. Suppose that the sample of size 81 gives rise to an $\bar{x}$ of 600 hours. Then substitution gives an interval bounded below by $\bar{x} - 1.96\sigma_{\bar{X}} = 592.16$ hours and above by $\bar{x} + 1.96\sigma_{\bar{X}} = 607.84$ hours. Thus, they conclude, in approximately 95 trials out of 100, μ will be included in the interval from 592.16 to 607.84. The fallacy is that $\bar{X}$ is a random variable, but μ is not. Since $\bar{X}$ is a random variable, the interval $\bar{X} \pm 1.96\sigma_{\bar{X}}$ is also a random variable. The interval 592.16 to 607.84 is but one of an infinite number of possible intervals. The quantity μ either lies within this particular interval or it does not—μ, although unknown, is one fixed real number!

What, then, should we conclude? Given the sample with mean $\bar{x}$, we shall find the interval 592.16 to 607.84 hours just as was done in the preceding paragraph. We shall call it a 95 percent confidence interval for μ. But we shall be very careful to interpret it not in terms of μ falling within this specific interval 95 times in 100 but in terms of μ falling within intervals established by this procedure for various sample means in 95 cases out of 100. We shall say that our "degree of confidence" in the interval estimate is 95 percent. Other commonly used confidence coefficients are 99, 98, and 90 percent.

Notice that the confidence interval just constructed is centered at $\bar{x}$. This procedure is customary but arbitrary; we shall use it because it is the simplest way to construct unique confidence intervals for means and percentages. However, there is nothing wrong with using off-center confidence intervals; in fact, the usual procedure for constructing confidence limits for σ in the case of a normal population leads to off-center intervals.

Returning to our original discussion, we were asked to set 95 percent confidence limits for μ in the case where $n = 81$, $\bar{x} = 600$ hours, and $s = 40$ hours. This original problem differs from the one just discussed in two ways: σ is not known, and the functional form of the population is not specified. Problems in which the form of the population is unknown occur much more frequently in practice than the sort where the population is conveniently normal and its standard deviation magically available. These latter problems occur most often between the covers of statistics texts. However, they are useful in introducing the more usual cases.

We have ample ammunition to demolish the two obstacles that have arisen. The key to the situation is the sample size, n. This quantity is quite large so we expect the estimator $\hat{\sigma} = S\sqrt{n/(n-1)}$ to be a fine approximation for σ. Even S, itself, would be an adequate estimator, although not unbiased. We have

$$\hat{\sigma} = s\sqrt{\frac{n}{n-1}} = 40\sqrt{\frac{81}{80}}$$

$$\hat{\sigma}_{\bar{X}} = \frac{\hat{\sigma}}{\sqrt{n}} = \frac{1}{\sqrt{81}}\sqrt{\frac{81}{80}} \cdot 40 = \frac{40}{\sqrt{80}} = 4.47 \text{ hours}$$

Because the sample size is large, we can use the central limit theorem to find the approximate sampling distribution of $\bar{X}$. Recall that this very important theorem tells us what probability distribution the sampling distribution of $\bar{X}$ approaches as n becomes large. This limiting function is normal with mean equal to μ, the population mean, and $\sigma_{\bar{X}} \approx 4.47$ hours. The arguments about confidence intervals containing μ whenever $\bar{X}$ falls within $1.96\sigma_{\bar{X}}$ hours of μ are again valid, and the 95 percent confidence limits for μ in this more practical problem are given approximately by

$$\bar{x} \pm 1.96\sigma_{\bar{X}} = 600 \pm 1.96(4.47)$$

$$= 600 \pm 8.76 \text{ hours}$$

In the long run, confidence intervals established in this manner will contain μ in roughly 95 percent of the repetitions of this experiment.

The problem of interval estimation, like point estimation, can be viewed as a special case of the general decision problem. In this case a strategy relates each possible sample to the interval that will be used as the estimate of θ when that particular sample is obtained. The action involved is the choice of a particular interval I. Suppose that the loss function is the following particularly simple one:

$$l(I, \theta) = \begin{cases} 0 & \theta \in I \\ 1 & \theta \notin I \end{cases}$$

That is, the decision maker will receive the maximum payoff if indeed, his choice of interval does include θ. For any other choice he will lose a fixed amount. For such a loss function, the expected loss is

$$E(l) = \sum_{l} lf(l) = 0f(0) + 1f(1) = f(1)$$

But $f(1)$ is the probability that l will take on the value 1—that is, the probability that the interval I will not include θ. If we construct confidence intervals in the way indicated earlier in this section, and if the confidence level (that is, the a priori probability that the interval will include the parameter) is set at $(1 - \alpha)$ percent, then the expected loss associated with the choice of an interval is α.

9.6 *t* DISTRIBUTION

There is one further set of circumstances under which an interval estimate of μ can be easily obtained. We shall discuss this briefly without developing any of the requisite theory.

Suppose that the population of battery lives was known to have a normal density function, but that the standard deviation of this population was not known. If sample size was large, the central limit theorem would give us the approximate probability distribution of $(\bar{X} - \mu)/\hat{\sigma}_{\bar{X}}$ and allow us to set confidence limits for μ. But if sample size was small, the central limit theorem would be of no help. Furthermore, the fact that σ was not known would make it impossible to use the normal distribution.

If we could find the form of the sampling distribution of $(\bar{X} - \mu)/\hat{\sigma}/\sqrt{n}$, we could set confidence limits for μ by means of the reasoning already brought out. Through various procedures that are beyond the scope of this text, it may be shown that, when the population is normal and σ is estimated by $\hat{\sigma} = S\sqrt{n/(n - 1)}$, then $(\bar{X} - \mu)/\hat{\sigma}/\sqrt{n}$ has a sampling distribution that follows a form called the *t* distribution.

This form is

$$f(x) = K\left(1 + \frac{x^2}{m}\right)^{-(m+1)/2}, \qquad -\infty < x < \infty$$

where K is chosen so that the area under the curve and above the x axis is equal to unity. We referred to $f(x)$ as representing a distribution; actually, it is a family of functions, particular curves being obtained by substituting particular values for m. K is not a parameter; it can be expressed entirely in terms of m so that assigning a value to m completely determines $f(x)$. The parameter m is called the "degrees of freedom" of the *t* function and, in this text, will always be a positive integer. Graphs of several *t* curves are shown in Figure 9.2.

All of these curves are symmetric with mean zero; that curve for which $m = 1$ is lower in the center than the curves for other degrees of freedom and higher in the tails. As the number of degrees of freedom increases, successive curves become higher at the mean and lower in the tails approaching the curve marked $m = \infty$ as a limit. It is important for us to know that this limiting curve is exactly normal in form, and that no other *t* function is

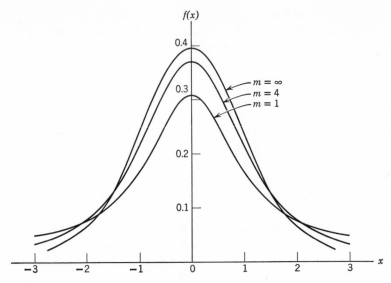

Fig. 9.2. *t* distributions corresponding to 1, 4, and infinitely many degrees of freedom.

normal. We shall not attempt the proof of this statement; however, it allows us to approximate *t* functions with large *m* by normal functions.

It has already been stated that, when the population is normal $f[(\bar{x} - \mu)\sqrt{n}/\hat{\sigma}]$ is a *t* density function. Furthermore, the number of degrees of freedom appropriate depends only on sample size and, in fact, is given by $m = n - 1$. To set 95 percent confidence limits for μ in the battery problem, given that the population is normal, σ is unknown, $n = 81$, $\bar{x} = 600$ hours, and $s = 40$ hours, we approximate the *t* distribution by the normal distribution, finding

$$\sigma_{\bar{x}} = \frac{\sigma}{\sqrt{n}} \approx \frac{\hat{\sigma}}{\sqrt{n}} = \frac{s}{\sqrt{n-1}} = \frac{40}{\sqrt{80}} = 4.47 \text{ hours}$$

and then writing $\bar{x} \pm 1.96\,(4.47)$. The approximate confidence limits obtained are 591.24 hours and 608.76 hours. As we shall show in the next problem, the appropriate coefficient for $\sigma_{\bar{x}}$ is determined by m and the confidence required. With $m = 80$ and a specification of 95 percent confidence, the coefficient would be 1.99 if we did not approximate.

Now let us examine the same problem in the case where the sample size is small; the problem now reads population normal, σ unknown, $n = 5$, $\bar{x} = 600$ hours, and $s = 40$ hours. What changes in procedure does the reduction in sample size necessitate? $\bar{x}$ is still 600 hours. Our proofs that $\hat{\sigma}^2$ is an unbiased estimate of σ^2 do not depend on population form, hence they are valid when the population is represented by a *t* function or by any other probability distribution. We shall still use $\hat{\sigma}$ to estimate σ. But $\sigma_{\bar{x}}$ is greatly affected by the diminution of the sample size.

$$\sigma_{\bar{x}} = \frac{\sigma}{\sqrt{n}} \approx \frac{\hat{\sigma}}{\sqrt{n}} = \frac{s}{\sqrt{n-1}} = \frac{40}{\sqrt{4}} = 20 \text{ hours}$$

The other adjustment comes when we replace the multiplier 1.96. What did this figure represent? It was the number of standard deviations from the mean which left an area equal to 0.025 in a single tail of the normal distribution. We must now discover the corresponding number of standard deviations which leave 0.025 in one tail of the appropriate *t* function. Which one is appropriate? The one for which $m = n - 1$, that is, the one whose number of degrees of freedom is one less than sample size. Referring to Table E.6, which shows percentage points for the various *t* functions, we see that 2.77 standard deviations from the mean leave 0.025 in one tail of the *t* function with four degrees of freedom. The confidence interval is thus bounded by

$$\bar{x} \pm 2.77\sigma_{\bar{x}} = 600 \pm 2.77(20)$$

The 95 percent confidence limits are 544.6 and 655.4. It is evident that a serious error would be made if 1.96 were carelessly used instead of 2.77.

Intuition should have told us that this small sample would yield a much broader, less useful confidence interval than would a sample of size 81. For one thing, we know that sample size occurs in the denominator of the standard error of the mean so that $\sigma_{\bar{x}}$ diminishes as *n* increases. But even without algebra, it should have been apparent that much less information can be obtained from a sample of four items than from a sample of 81 items. The former stands a good chance of being quite unrepresentative of the population. Consequently, any inferential statement based on the small sample will be less incisive than its large sample counterpart. For a given $\hat{\sigma}$ the smaller sample will always lead to the wider confidence interval, as long as the population and confidence coefficient are unchanged and a particular parameter is being estimated.

9.7   INTERVAL ESTIMATION—PERCENTAGES—
SINGLE LARGE SAMPLES

This text will not consider the problem of fixing confidence intervals for population percentages in small samples, although the procedures are analogous to those discussed for population means. Finding the percentage points of the sampling distribution of P is tedious, since $f(p)$ is binomial and the percentage points are found by summing in a binomial table. We shall deal only with the large sample case in which $f(p)$ can be easily approximated.

We shall find 90 percent confidence limits for the percentage of voters of Hiawatha, Minnesota, favoring fluoridation of the water supply. The population is Bernoulli in form—each voter falls either into Class I favoring fluoridation or into Class II consisting of those who oppose the move or give no opinion.

π is the unknown population percentage favoring fluoridation for which we are to obtain an estimate; $p = 60$ is the percentage favoring fluoridation in the random sample of size $n = 1000$. The sampling distribution of P has been shown in Section 8.8 to be binomial with mean and standard deviation

$$E(P) = \pi \qquad \sigma_P = \sqrt{\frac{\pi\phi}{n}}$$

We can approximate it by a normal distribution with the same mean and standard deviation since n is large. Also we have shown in Section 9.3 that for large samples we may approximate σ_P by

$$\sigma_P \approx \sqrt{\frac{p(100 - p)}{n}} = \sqrt{\frac{60 \cdot 40}{1000}} = 1.55 \%$$

Hence, the 90 percent confidence limits for π are

$$p \pm z_{0.05}\sigma_P = p \pm z_{0.05}\sqrt{\frac{p(100 - p)}{n}} = 60 \pm 1.64(1.55)$$

yielding 57.46 percent to 62.54 percent for the approximate interval. Note that $z_{0.05} = 1.64$ is the figure that leaves 0.05 in one tail of the unit normal probability distribution and hence 0.10 (the complement of 0.90) as the total from both.

The reasoning validating this confidence interval is exactly that which we exhibited in the case of the mean. Whenever a random sample of size 1000 leads to a value of P lying in the interval $\pi \pm z_{0.05}\sigma_P$, it follows that the population percentage π lies within the related interval $p \pm z_{0.05}\sigma_P$. Probability statements must be interpreted as before in terms of long-run relative frequencies.

To emphasize how generally this rationale applies, consider a population having a parameter $\flat$ which we shall call "flat." Suppose that a statistic $\sharp$, "sharp," can be computed for random samples from the population and that sharp is an unbiased estimator of flat, that is, $E(\sharp) = \flat$. To set a $100(1 - \alpha)$ percent confidence interval for $\flat$, we need to know the sampling distribution of $\sharp$ for random samples of size n. The identification of this sampling distribution is a mathematical problem. Suppose it has been solved and sharp is found to have a Parthian probability distribution, which is symmetric. $\sigma_\sharp$, the standard error of $\sharp$, can then be found. Also, perhaps after considerable computation, $\sharp_{\alpha/2}$, that value of $\sharp$ that leaves $\alpha/2$ in a single tail of Parthian distribution, can be identified. Then the $100(1 - \alpha)$ percent confidence limits for $\flat$ are given exactly by $\sharp \pm \sharp_{\alpha/2}\sigma_{\sharp}$. Whenever a random sample of size n leads to a value of $\sharp$ lying in the interval $\flat \pm \sharp_{\alpha/2}\sigma_{\sharp}$, the parameter $\flat$ will be within the $100(1 - \alpha)$ percent confidence limits $\sharp \pm \sharp_{\alpha/2}\sigma_{\sharp}$.

9.8 PROBLEMS OF SAMPLE SIZE—PERCENTAGES

When information is needed about a population, the first question that should be raised is whether the value of the information is likely to exceed the cost of obtaining it. If this is not true, the logical procedure is to act without acquiring the information. Now it is possible to consider obtaining the information either by means of a census or by sampling. In most practical cases censuses are so time consuming and awkward to control that sampling is much to be preferred. We begin a discussion here of the cost of sampling. This will be extended in Chapters 11 and 12.

One of the most critical variables determining the cost of sampling is n, the sample size. The more items that have to be selected, the costlier the process. In instances where secondary material is being scanned or where questionnaires are being mailed, sample size is important, but perhaps not overriding. If interviewers are being maintained in the field, sample size may well be the dominant cost factor. The problem is simply to determine how large a sample should be taken. Clearly, as sample size increases, information obtained tends to increase, but so do costs. How shall we balance one of these variables against the other so as to obtain the smallest sample that will provide sufficient information?

Let us take up a more specific instance. Suppose the purpose of drawing a sample is to obtain an estimate of a certain parameter, for example, a population percentage. The larger the sample, the better the estimate. It will be necessary to determine how reliable an estimate is required before an adequate sample size can be found.

The Commercial Haulers Combine is a trade association whose members engage in long-distance hauling. In general, the individual loads hauled can be characterized either as perishable or non-perishable, and are so designated on the standard bills of lading. Any load containing even a small shipment of perishable items is labeled "perishable" and must be given special scheduling and handling. The transportation of perishables has become an important portion of the business of several of Commercial Haulers' members. The association, as part of a study to determine trends in the distance hauling business, wishes to know what percentage of all hauls made by the members of the Combine in 1968 involved perishable loads.

A statistician was consulted by J. F. Donnelly, a vice-president of the Combine. It developed that the population to be studied consisted of 282,810 carbons of the 1968 bills of lading kept in the files of the member companies. Each bill was presumably marked "perishable" or "nonperishable." Taking a census seemed undesirable to Mr. Donnelly; the statistician agreed and explained the benefits of a well-designed sampling procedure. It was decided to draw a simple random sample from the carbons in the following manner. First, order the member companies alphabetically: Aardvark Truckers, Ace-High Express, etc. Then, consider a conceptual listing of the 282,810 bills of lading, arranged with Aardvark's 25,812 carbons occurring first in the order in which they were filed, then Ace-High's 4004 carbons in their filing order, etc. Select n numbers between 1 and 282,810 from a table of random digits. Pull the corresponding n carbons (rather laboriously) from the files and check for perishables. Compute p, the sample percentage of perishable loads. Before reading further, reread this paragraph concentrating on sampling procedures. Does any alternative procedure suggest itself? We hope so.

The statistician next inquired how accurate an estimate was needed. After considerable hemming and hawing, Mr. Donnelly agreed that the Combine would be satisfied with an estimate of π, the percentage of perishable hauls in the 1968 population, which lay within four percentage points of the true value. The statistician further indicated that he could not assert with certainty that this could be achieved, and Mr. Donnelly finally settled for a 98 percent confidence interval.

It was clear to the statistician that no small sample would provide the accuracy desired. So he assumed that a large sample would be needed, and carried out the estimation process in terms of the normal approximation to the actual binomial distribution. From a table of normal areas he found that the abscissa 2.33 leaves 0.01 in one tail of the standardized normal distribution. Thus, in random sampling, the sample percentage P will lie within $2.33\sigma_P$ of π, the population percentage, approximately 98 times in 100. Since

$$\sigma_P = \sqrt{\frac{\pi(100 - \pi)}{n}}$$

the problem can be handled by setting

$$2.33\sqrt{\frac{\pi(100 - \pi)}{n}} = 4$$

and solving for n. But wait a minute! What about π? Its value is not known; in fact, it is the very parameter that the statistician is attempting to estimate. Is this a dead end? Fortunately not; even if π is not known, limits can be placed on it, and thus a sample size can be found that will be sufficiently large to cause the estimate to lie in the desired range with the given probability. We need to study the behavior of σ_P as a function of π.

For what value of π is σ_P the greatest? It is easier to discuss $\sigma_P{}^2$ than σ_P, and surely $\sigma_P{}^2$ increases when σ_P increases and diminishes when σ_P diminishes. Thus σ_P has its maximum at the same value of π for which $\sigma_P{}^2$ is maximized. Let us examine $\sigma_P{}^2$.

$$\sigma_P{}^2 = \frac{\pi(100 - \pi)}{n} = \frac{1}{n}(100\pi - \pi^2)$$

To discover the maximum value of $\sigma_P{}^2$, we differentiate

$$\frac{d(\sigma_P{}^2)}{d\pi} = \frac{d}{d\pi}\left[\frac{1}{n}(100\pi - \pi^2)\right] = \frac{1}{n}(100 - 2\pi)$$

Setting $d(\sigma_P{}^2)/d\pi = 0$ and solving; $2\pi = 100$, $\pi = 50\%$. This is a maximum point, since

$$\frac{d^2(\sigma_P{}^2)}{d\pi^2} = \frac{1}{n}(-2) = \frac{-2}{n}$$

Thus we see that, when n is fixed, σ_P is largest when $\pi = 50\%$ and decreases gradually as π decreases toward 0% or increases toward 100%. The function is shown in Figure 9.3 for $n = 100$. It is a portion of a parabola.

After some judicious prodding, Mr. Donnelly said he was sure that π, the population percentage of perishable loads, was less than 20 percent. So the

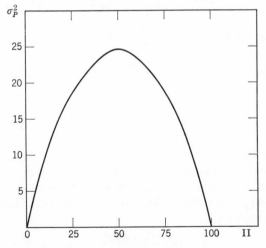

Fig. 9.3. Graph of the function $\sigma_P{}^2$ when $n = 100$.

statistician used 20 percent in place of π in the standard error and computed sample size in that way. Let us see why he did this. Let $\pi^* \leq 50\%$ be an upper limit on the desired population percentage. Then $\pi^* \geq \pi$. But, from our previous discussion, this means that

$$\sigma_P = \sqrt{\frac{\pi(100 - \pi)}{n}} \leq \sqrt{\frac{\pi^*(100 - \pi^*)}{n}} = \sigma_P{}^*$$

Squaring and multiplying by n gives

$$\pi(100 - \pi) \leq \pi^*(100 - \pi^*)$$

Now, if we set $2.33\sigma_P = 4$ and solve for n,

$$2.33\sqrt{\frac{\pi(100 - \pi)}{n}} = 4$$

$$\frac{(2.33)^2\pi(100 - \pi)}{n} = 16$$

$$n = \frac{(2.33)^2\pi(100 - \pi)}{16}$$

This is the value of n which insures a sample value lying within 4 percentage points of π on 98 percent of all repeated trials. But it is useless, since π is not known. Consider now

$$2.33\sqrt{\frac{\pi^*(1 - \pi^*)}{n}} = 4$$

Solving this equation yields a different sample size n^*.

$$\frac{(2.33)^2\pi^*(100 - \pi^*)}{n^*} = 16$$

$$n^* = \frac{(2.33)^2\pi^*(100 - \pi^*)}{16}$$

We have shown that $\pi(100 - \pi) \leq \pi^*(100 - \pi^*)$, so a comparison of the formulas for n and n^* shows at once that $n \leq n^*$. Thus the use of an upper bound $\leq 50\%$ for π will always give a sample size sufficiently large to insure the desired accuracy. The sample taken for the Commercial Haulers study of 1968 loads was then of size

$$n^* = \frac{(2.33)^2(20)(80)}{16} = 543$$

Suppose that Mr. Donnelly had been unable to place a bound on π. The situation is still not impossible. In cases where there is no evidence about π, we use $\pi^* = 50\%$. No matter what the true value of π, it can in no wise yield a larger sample size than the n^* corresponding to 50 percent. In many cases, this procedure leads to taking a larger sample than is necessary; however, it is helpful if a sample must be taken in a state of nearly complete ignorance about π. In the Commercial Haulers study, without Mr. Donnelly's upper bound, the statistician would have suggested a sample size of

$$n^* = \frac{(2.33)^2(50)(50)}{16} = 848$$

Thus, 300 extra bills of lading would have had to have been checked in the "no upper bound" case. There would have been a gain in reliability, but such great reliability was not needed.

A general formula for n^*, derived by these procedures, is

$$n^* = \frac{z_{\alpha/2}^2 \pi^*(100 - \pi^*)}{D^2} \tag{9.10}$$

where D is the tolerated deviation in percentage points, $1 - \alpha$ is the required confidence that p lies within D of π, and $z_{\alpha/2}$ is the abscissa of the point leaving $\alpha/2$ in one tail of the standardized normal probability distribution.

Before leaving this section we ask the student to return to the beginning of the Commercial Haulers problem and investigate the question of whether the percentage of perishable loads is a meaningful statistic for the industry. What are some more important quantities?

9.9   PROBLEMS OF SAMPLE SIZE—MEANS

Suppose that we are asked what sample size is necessary to estimate a population mean. Our discussion of the similar problem in the percentage case shows how to proceed. The problem requires a knowledge of the sampling distribution of the statistic involved and specification of both the deviation that will be tolerated and the confidence that is demanded. Designating the tolerated deviation by D and the required confidence by $1 - \alpha$, we must determine from the sampling distribution a number $z_{\alpha/2}$ which leaves $\alpha/2$ in one tail of the distribution. We equate

$$z_{\alpha/2}\sigma_{\bar{X}} = D$$

Replacing $\sigma_{\bar{X}}$ by $\sigma/\sqrt{n}$ and solving for n, we obtain

$$n = \frac{z_{\alpha/2}^2 \sigma^2}{D^2} \tag{9.11}$$

whose form resembles (9.10) quite closely.

If the population variance is known, well and good. But if we are estimating the population mean it is likely that we do not know σ^2 either. When this point is reached in a class discussion there is usually one man in the back row who says, "Estimate it by $\hat{\sigma}^2$." But in order to follow his advice the sample must already have been taken. Our problem is how to delimit its size initially.

For many populations an interval of 3σ on either side of the mean includes practically all elements of the population. Hence 6σ is a rough approximation to the range of the population. If we have some idea as to the size of its largest and smallest elements, we can base an estimate of σ upon the range, substitute, and compute n. This gives a rough estimate for σ and not an upper bound, so the resulting value of n is not guaranteed to be large enough to estimate μ with the desired accuracy. Such a value of n is only an approximation and, if the estimate of σ is very bad, the value of n may be too small or much larger than necessary. However, an alternative procedure may be used. We may deliberately overestimate σ, in which case the resulting sample size will always be adequate since the variance occurs in the numerator of n in (9.11). If the research is important and expensive so that sample size is critical, a good procedure is to draw a preliminary sample for the express purpose of estimating σ.

The fashion editor of the magazine *Young Style* wishes to conduct a survey to determine the average waist measurement of coeds in American colleges. How large a simple random sample would she need in order to estimate this parameter, correct to the nearest tenth of an inch with 99 percent confidence? It is important to consider the theoretical problem of defining this population as well as the practical problem of how the sample data should be collected. Also, does the desired tenth of an inch allowable deviation appear reasonable?

Now coeds with waist measurements under, for instance 18 in., are rare, as are those whose waists exceed 48 in. Thus a range of 30 in. should lead to a considerable overestimation of σ; $6\sigma^* = 30$ in., $\sigma < \sigma^* = 5$. The quantity σ^* will represent an overestimate of σ. By the central limit theorem the large sample sampling distribution of $\bar{X}$ is approximately normal with mean μ and variance of σ^2/n, regardless of the form of the population (which may be normal anyway). For the normal distribution, we recall that $z_{0.005} = 2.58$. The value of D is 0.1 in. Thus

$$n^* = \frac{(2.58)^2 25}{0.01} = 16{,}641$$

This is a large sample, and we would expect that a large value of n would be needed to yield so high a probability of so reliable an estimate.

A more reasonable estimate of the population standard deviation might be 4 in., in which case n would be reduced to 10,650—or cut by one-third. This demonstrates the sensitivity of sample size to a rough estimate of σ.

9.10   INTERVAL ESTIMATION—ARITHMETIC MEANS— TWO INDEPENDENT SAMPLES

We shall examine one further type of problem involving confidence intervals— interval estimation of the difference of two population means.

For several years the Achilles Tire and Rubber Company has put out a standard tire called the "Dependable" which is suitable for use on compact cars. At the completion of the manufacturing process, these tires have been sight inspected and classified as Dependable A or Dependable B according to whether they displayed no flaws or minor flaws. Any tire with a serious defect was rejected. Dependable B's had been sold at roughly 75 percent of the price of Dependable A's.

Annual figures compiled by the sales department revealed an interesting trend. Total number of Dependable A tires sold showed a slight gain each year for the past four years. But sales of Dependable B's, which were in- significant in the first year, had more than doubled each succeeding year until they now stood at about one-half of the A sales. An investigation revealed that the rapid gains for B were occurring in the replacement segment. Many persons were buying B's instead of A's when their old tires wore out. The company's executives began to wonder if the average lives of Dependable A's and B's were the same—which would occur if the minor flaws in the latter were superficial. An experiment was initiated to see if the price reduction was simply money lost to the company.

Independent random samples of sizes $n = 100$ and $m = 60$ were selected from the large stock of Dependable A's and B's on hand. The tires were mounted on testing machines and their miles to wearout determined. For the A's the mean mileage was $\bar{x} = 24{,}204$ miles with standard deviation $s_x = 400$ miles. For the B's the mean mileage was $\bar{y} = 23{,}850$ with standard deviation $s_y = 900$ miles. The presence of minor flaws tended to produce a less regular performance.

It was decided to set 90 percent confidence limits for the difference $\mu_X - \mu_Y$. Such inference was based on the sampling distribution of $\bar{X} - \bar{Y}$. Since the two samples were large and chosen independently, $f(\bar{x} - \bar{y})$ is sure to be approximately normal by the central limit theorem applied to the population of differences. The inferential reasoning is the same as in other confidence interval problems; $\mu_X - \mu_Y$ must lie within $1.64\sigma_{\bar{X}-\bar{Y}}$ of $\bar{x} - \bar{y}$ whenever $\bar{x} - \bar{y}$ falls within $1.64\sigma_{\bar{X}-\bar{Y}}$ of $\mu_X - \mu_Y$. This occurs in random sampling with probability 0.90.

We know from Section 8.9 that

$$\hat{\sigma}^2_{\bar{X}-\bar{Y}} = \frac{\sigma_X{}^2}{n} + \frac{\sigma_Y{}^2}{m}$$

To estimate $\sigma_X{}^2$ and $\sigma_Y{}^2$, we might use

$$\hat{\sigma}_X{}^2 = \frac{n}{n-1}\, s_x{}^2 = \frac{100}{99}\,(400)^2 \qquad \hat{\sigma}_Y{}^2 = \frac{m}{m-1}\, s_y{}^2 = \frac{60}{59}\,(900)^2$$

If we did employ $\hat{\sigma}_X{}^2$ and $\hat{\sigma}_Y{}^2$, however, the results would be so close to $s_x{}^2$ and $s_y{}^2$ as to make the added arithmetic useless. When sample sizes are large, we can get good approximations by using the biased estimates s_x and s_y.

$$s_{\bar{x}-\bar{y}} = \sqrt{\frac{(400)^2}{100} + \frac{(900)^2}{60}} = 122.9 \text{ miles}$$

Thus

$$(\bar{x} - \bar{y}) \pm 1.64 s_{\bar{x}-\bar{y}} = (24{,}204 - 23{,}850) \pm 1.64(122.9)$$

$$= 354 \pm 202$$

Ninety percent confidence limits for $\mu_X - \mu_Y$ are 152 miles and 556 miles. The reader should now write down the confidence statement corresponding to this result. If he thinks it means that one A tire picked at random has a probability equal to 0.90 of lasting between 152 and 556 miles longer than a single B tire picked at random, he should commence a reappraisal of fundamental concepts.

IMPORTANT TERMS AND CONCEPTS

Confidence coefficient

Confidence interval

Decision maker

Degrees of freedom

Estimate

Estimator

Inference

Interval estimation

Likelihood function

Loss function

Maximum likelihood estimator

Opportunity loss

Parameter

Partial derivative

Sampling distribution

Standard error

  of difference

  of X

  of P

Statistic

Strategy

t distribution

Unbiased estimator

SYMBOLS AND ABBREVIATIONS

n	p
$\overline{X}$	P
$\overline{x}$	π
S	ϕ
s	$\sigma_{\overline{X}}$
μ	σ_P
σ	$\sigma_{\overline{X}-\overline{Y}}$
$\hat{\sigma}$	

OFTEN-USED FORMULAS

$$\overline{X} = \frac{\sum X_i}{n}, \qquad S = \sqrt{\frac{\sum (X_i - \overline{X})^2}{n}}$$

$$E(\overline{X}) = \mu \qquad \sigma_{\overline{X}} = \frac{\sigma}{\sqrt{n}}$$

$$\hat{\sigma} = \sqrt{\frac{\sum (X - \overline{X})^2}{n - 1}}, \qquad E(\hat{\sigma}^2) = \sigma^2$$

$$E(P) = \pi \qquad \sigma_P = \sqrt{\frac{\pi\phi}{n}}$$

$$\sigma_{\overline{X}-\overline{Y}} = \sqrt{\frac{\sigma_X{}^2}{n} + \frac{\sigma_Y{}^2}{m}}$$

EXERCISES

1. Define the following terms: statistic, parameter, sampling distribution of sample means, sampling distribution of sample percentages, random sample.
2. a. Distinguish between a point estimate and an interval estimate.
   b. Which of these must be based on a random sample?

3. If X, Y, and Z are three independent random variables each of whose probability distributions is Poisson with parameter μ, show that

$$\hat\mu = \frac{2X + 5Y + 3Z}{10}$$

is an unbiased estimator of μ.

4. Let ψ be a parameter in a probability distribution. Let g_1 and g_2 be independent and unbiased estimators for ψ. Let w_1 and w_2 be weights such that $w_1 + w_2 = 1$. Show that $w_1 g_1 + w_2 g_2$ is an unbiased estimator of ψ.

5. A random sample of 50 delinquent charge accounts at a certain department store shows a mean of $66 and a standard deviation of $20.
   a. Estimate the mean size of the store's delinquent charge accounts.
   b. Construct a 99 percent confidence interval for the mean size of all delinquent charge accounts at this store.
   c. If the range that you obtained in part *b* is larger than you are willing to tolerate, how can you narrow it?

6. A random sample of 1000 names selected from a state's male labor force showed 900 employed and the rest unemployed.
   a. What is your estimate of the percentage of unemployed persons in the population?
   b. Is your estimate unbiased or biased?
   c. Set up limits that you are reasonably certain (90 percent confidence) include the true percentage unemployed for the entire state's male labor force.
   d. Interpret your answer to part *c* specifically in terms of this problem.

7. A market research firm wished to study characteristics of the guests of a certain hotel. The following results were obtained from a random sample of 400 of these guests:

Arithmetic mean income = $9800
Standard deviation (income) = $2000

100 were residents of the state of New York
15 of the residents of New York were single

   a. Estimate the mean income of the population from which the sample was taken.
   b. Is your estimate biased or unbiased?
   c. Estimate the standard deviation of incomes in the population from which the sample was taken.
   d. Is this estimate biased or unbiased?

   e. Estimate the proportion of single residents of New York in the population from which the sample was taken.

   f. Is this estimate biased or unbiased?

   g. To what population do your various estimates apply?

8. Explain why the maximum likelihood criterion is a logical device to use in point estimation problems.

9. Find the maximum likelihood estimator of the parameter π in the binomial population

$$f(x) = \binom{500}{x} \pi^x (1 - \pi)^{500-x} \qquad x = 0, 1, \cdots, 500$$

based on a random sample of size two.

10. Find the maximum likelihood estimator in samples of size n of the parameter μ in a normal population in which $\sigma = 4$.

11. Find the maximum likelihood estimator in samples of size n of the parameter σ in a normal population in which $\mu = 41$.

12. Suppose that you wish to estimate average family income in the city of Philadelphia for the calendar year 1966 with 95.4 percent confidence.

   a. If a random sample of 100 families yielded an arithmetic mean income of \$4500, a modal income of \$5000, and a standard deviation of \$1200, what would your interval estimate of average family income be?

   b. Interpret specifically in terms of the problem your answer to part *a*.

   c. Discuss how you would obtain the sample discussed. Are you really sampling from the population of interest?

13. In a survey of the coffee-drinking habits of the American people, 225 adults were randomly sampled in each region. The following means and standard deviations were obtained:

     New England: 20.0 pounds of coffee per adult
       per annum with $s_x = 9$.
     West North Central Region: 24.0 pounds of coffee
       per adult per annum with $s_y = 12$.

   a. Set 90 percent confidence limits for the difference $\mu_X - \mu_Y$.

   b. State the exact meaning of the limits that you have found in part *a*.

14. If a statistician wished to be 95.4 percent confident in estimating the percentage of defective products in a shipment within 2 percentage points, what size sample should he take if:

   a. He knew that no more than 50 percent of the products would be defective?

   b. He knew that no more than 20 percent would be defective?

   c. He had no idea what percentage would be defective?

15. a. A random sample of 100 units drawn from a manufacturing process showed 15 units to be defective. Construct the 90 percent confidence interval for the percentage of all units that are defective.
    b. Is the interval constructed in part *a* too large? Briefly explain your answer.

16. a. A large shipment of barrels is to be sampled in order to estimate mean barrel weight. In the past the standard deviation of the weights of the barrels has been found to be between 15 and 20 pounds. How large a random sample is necessary in order to estimate the universe mean so that the estimate will deviate from the true parameter by no more than 3 pounds, with 99.7 percent confidence?
    b. What effect on required sample size would each of the following have:
       (1) Decreasing confidence level?
       (2) Decreasing allowable error?
       (3) Decreasing the estimate of the standard deviation of the universe?

17. A statistician wishes to forecast what is expected to be a very close election by taking a random sample of the voting population on election eve. He wants to be practically certain that his error in estimating the percentage of votes to be received by the winner will not exceed 3 per cent. He has $850.00 available for interviews at $1.00 per interview. Are his financial resources compatible with his aim concerning reliability? (*Note.* You may assume that a simple majority will win the election; there are only two candidates; there are no undecided votes; and no "overnight" shifts in opinion.)

18. Set 95 percent confidence limits for the mean increase in the selling price of unrenovated row houses in Baltimore, Md. during a quarter in which a random sample of 10 such houses showed a mean increase of $400 and a standard deviation of $100 if the selling price increase may be assumed normally distributed. Do you think selling price increase would be normally distributed? Discuss. If selling price increase was not normally distributed, what effect would this have on your original confidence limits?

19. Scores on a standardized college entrance examination are known to be normally distributed. Set 99 percent confidence limits for the mean score
    a. If a random sample of 17 applicants has a mean score of 85 and a standard deviation of scores of 15.
    b. If, in addition to the information given in *a*, it is known that the standard deviation of all scores on the examination is 18.

20. A random sample of 225 undergraduates in the United States yielded mean age of 20.25 years and standard deviation 1.65 years.

   a. Construct the 92 percent confidence interval for the mean age of all undergraduates in the United States.

   b. What is the meaning of the "92 percent" figure in part *a*?

   c. How would you go about drawing the sample mentioned?

21. From past experience it is known that the diameters of shafts produced by a manufacturing process are normally distributed with a mean of 3.330 in. and a standard deviation of 0.020 in. Samples of 16 shafts are to be examined regularly in order to determine whether any change in the process mean has taken place.

   a. Calculate the appropriate three standard deviation control limits $(\mu \pm 3\sigma_{\bar{x}})$ for the above inspection plan.

   d. Discuss the action, if any, that would be taken by plant personnel after a sample mean of 3.313 in. had been observed.

   c. What is the probability that this inspection plan will detect a change in the process mean from 3.330 to 3.310 in.?

   d. What proportion of the shafts that are produced by this process have diameters that exceed 3.345 in.?

22. If 68 out of a random sample of 340 households had a television set turned on between 8:05 and 8:15 P.M. on October 20, what is the 90 percent confidence interval for the percentage of the population of households with sets turned on during this period?

23. a. Assume that in a random sample of 1000 of its subscribers a magazine finds that 700 would like to see a change in the type of cover. What are the 99 percent confidence limits for the proportion of all subscribers who favor a change in the cover?

   b. Is this sample likely to be a biased one? Discuss.

24. How large a random sample is needed to estimate the average number of days that books loaned by a public library are kept before return to within two days with 90 percent confidence? It has been observed that in recent years all books have been returned within 70 days.

10 Inference—Tests of Hypotheses

10.1 INTRODUCTION

The term "hypothesis" appears in most high school geometry courses. There, and in most other mathematical contexts, it indicates a set of known truths or assumed propositions—the "given" of a particular proof. In statistics the word is used in a very different sense.

A statistical hypothesis is a statement about a population. The statement may be true or it may be false. In a study limited to automobiles produced in the United States during 1970, the following statements were considered.

1. Only 15 companies manufactured automobiles.

2. Seventy-five percent of the autos produced had some type of automatic gear shift.

3. More of the autos produced were painted blue and white than any other color combination.

4. The arithmetic mean weight of autos produced exceeded two tons.

5. The highest list price of any automobile was $10,699.

The above five statements concern a population. They are five hypotheses. What is the best way to check their validity?

In statement 4, for example, the best procedure is to obtain from each manufacturer the weight of each model that he produced in 1970 plus the total number produced. Perform the requisite multiplication, addition, and division, thus finding the population's mean weight exactly. Then compare it to the stated figure of two tons. Or, for statement 5, obtain from each manufacturer the list price for each model made in 1970 and compare prices. Similar census procedures should be used to check each of the five statements. Thus, many hypotheses can be shown to be true or false without employing sampling procedures. Furthermore, if a hypothesis is checked by means of a census, a definite conclusion will be reached that the statement is either true or false. The conclusion will be correct as long as no errors have occurred in the census; that is, as long as there is no nonsampling error.

Now, consider the same five statements with one small modification. Let the statements refer to all automobiles manufactured in the United States during 1970 and driven more than 5000 miles during 1970! This is quite another matter. No manufacturer or dealer has records of the 1970 mileage on cars sold by him. In fact, no one has such information on any group of cars; it must be obtained from the individual owners very shortly after the close of 1970 or it will not be available at all. Few owners would have retained their exact mileage figure after several months had passed. By the end of the next year, many would be unable to state whether the figure was above 5000 miles or below it. A census is, then, next to impossible. The information would have to be obtained from the owners themselves early in 1971—a difficult and costly undertaking if we really intend to locate all American automobiles manufactured and driven more than 5000 miles in 1970.

A test of a hypothesis is simply a procedure for checking the validity of the statement made. We have already mentioned that, when the procedure is based upon a census, we will decide that the hypothesis is either true or false. In the case where sample evidence is used, the result is different; there, we conclude only that the statement is probably true or probably false. The reason for qualification is that no sample can sum up all the information of interest. The larger the sample, the more information it contains, but for complete information the sample must become a census.

10.2   ALTERNATIVE HYPOTHESES AND ERRORS

The hypothesis to be tested is customarily called the null hypothesis. We shall also speak of the alternative hypothesis; this is simply the negation of the null hypothesis. If we were testing statement 2 of the previous section in the population of automobiles manufactured in the United States during 1970 and driven more than 5000 miles in that year, we might write our hypotheses in any of three forms.

1. H_0 (null hypothesis): 75 percent of these autos had some type of automatic gear shift. H_1 (alternative hypothesis): Not 75 percent of these autos had some type of automatic gear shift.

2. H_0 (null hypothesis): 75 percent or more of these autos had some type of automatic gear shift. H_1 (alternative hypothesis): Less than 75 percent of these autos had some type of automatic gear shift.

3. H_0 (null hypothesis): 75 percent or less of these autos had some type of automatic gear shift. H_1 (alternative hypothesis): More than 75 percent of these autos had some type of automatic gear shift.

For obvious reasons, formulation 1 is often called "two-sided" or "two-tailed," while formulations 2 and 3 are spoken of as "one-sided" or "one-tailed."

The choice of form depends upon the problem under consideration and the alternative actions available.[1] Each hypothesis should be uniquely associated with an action; that is, if we really knew which of the hypotheses was true, we would also know the proper action to adopt.

Returning to the statements in Section 10.1, let us consider statement 4. Here we might construct our hypotheses according to formulation 3 of this section.

H_0: The mean weight of these autos was two tons or less.

H_1: The mean weight of these autos exceeded two tons.

The null and alternative hypotheses are thus woven closely together. If one decides that the null hypothesis is probably true, one automatically decides that the alternative is probably false and vice versa.[2]

When we decide that the null hypothesis is probably true, we shall say that we accept the null hypothesis (and reject the alternative). In cases where we decide that the null hypothesis is probably false, we shall use the nomenclature: "reject H_0" and "accept H_1." This wording emphasizes that any test of a hypothesis reaches a tentative conclusion. It tells us to act as though H_0 were true (or false). Consider the following situation.

The manager of the testing division of the Roquart Company has the final responsibility for clearing all parts before shipment. In the case of 12AT7 transistors, specifications call for no more than 10 percent defective under a severe test. Since the test is a destructive one, sampling must be employed. The transistors are produced in runs of 100,000 and shipped in various quantities. The manager decides to test the null hypothesis

H_0: 10 percent or less of the 12AT7 transistors in the January 1969 run are defective.

The alternative hypothesis is

H_1: More than 10 percent of the transistors in the January 1969 run are defective.

---

[1] We shall later see that formulation 1 is frequently a set of three hypotheses:

1. H_0 (null hypothesis): 75 percent of these autos had some type of automatic gear shift.

2. H_1 (first alternative hypothesis): Less that 75 percent of these autos had some type of automatic gear shift.

3. H_2 (second alternative hypothesis): More than 75 percent of these autos had some type of automatic gear shift.

[2] With two or more alternative hypotheses the procedure is only slightly more involved.

The manager decides to test 200 transistors selected at random from this production run of 100,000 and to accept or reject the null hypothesis based on the test results.

A moment's reflection shows that there are four possible outcomes for his test. The statement H_0 may be true or false; the manager may decide to accept it or reject it. Schematically,

		H_0 is really	
		True	False
Manager	Accept H_0	III	II
decides to	Reject H_0	I	IV

In two of the situations, those marked III and IV in the diagram, he makes a correct decision. In III he decides that 10 percent or less of the 100,000 transistors would probably fail this test, and he is right. In IV he decides that more than 10 percent would probably fail, and again he is right.

In the other two cases, the manager errs. We speak of these as errors of the first and second kinds. Specifically, an error of the first kind consists of the rejection of a true null hypothesis. An error of the second kind consists of the acceptance of a false null hypothesis. We have shown earlier that in a sampling situation, as distinct from a census, the decision will be a qualified one—a probability will be attached. The statistician must devise techniques to insure that the probability of a correct decision will be high—that is, that low probabilities attach to both errors of the first and second kind.

Suppose that none of the 200 transistors failed the test. The manager cannot claim that H_0 is definitely true. In order to validate H_0 he would have to test (and destroy) 89,800 more transistors. The statistician "accepts" or "rejects" hypotheses; except in very unusual conditions the word "prove" is inappropriate.

The null hypothesis, like the sitting duck in the shooting gallery, is placed before the customers to be filled with buckshot if possible. It is carefully chosen, and then all the sample evidence is brought forward in an attempt to discredit it. In fact, when a statistician "accepts" a null hypothesis, he means that he has been unable to reject it. It has resisted his efforts, but he still has one eye on it.

We now return to Roquart's testing division and ask how the consequences of errors of the first and second kind affect the manager's decision. This is an interesting question. Its answer depends upon the attitude of the company toward the stipulated tolerances. This, in turn, depends upon the consequences of the two types of error. Here the cost of a Type II error (sending out transistors from a run with more than 10 percent failing the test) would stem from too high a rate of unsatisfactory performance by TV sets in which the transistors were used. Assuming that this means nothing more catastrophic than missing a TV program, the cost to Roquart would be in ill will from wholesalers, retailers, and customers, transformed into fewer sales. If the true parameter for the run is 10.1 percent, H_1 is true, and if the manager concludes H_0, a Type II error will be made. This is also the case when the true value of the parameter is 20.0 percent. In each case H_1 is true, but the cost to Roquart differs greatly.

A similar situation obtains for Type I errors. If the complete run of 100,000 is classified as "outgoing trash," the company suffers losses equal to raw material and production costs plus the markup which could have been realized. But it is not that simple! The cost is really dependent upon the universe parameter and thus how much the run betters specifications. If the parameter is 2.0 percent, this may be a horrible error in terms of costs. On the other hand, at 10.0 percent, it may not be such a disaster, given the ill will that would accompany such a shipment even though specifications call it "satisfactory." The guiding principle is simple. The manager must decide which of the two types of error is likely to be costlier to Roquart. Then he should construct a test in such a way that the probability of the more serious type of error is the less likely. This reasoning will be extended in Chapter 12 where an explicit comparison of costs is brought into the picture.

What does an actual test look like? We shall find out shortly; however, it is necessary to discuss the principles controlling such tests before their mechanics can be explained. Remember that a hypothesis is simply a statement about a population, and that a test of a hypothesis is a procedure for deciding whether the statement is likely to be true or untrue.

10.3   CONSTRUCTION OF A TEST

Let us examine another problem. Sam Sage, the poultry buyer for the Food-Lux supermarket chain specifies that Thanksgiving turkeys supplied by Alfonso Farms should have mean weight 13 lb. Mr. Sage wishes to find out if Alfonso Farms is meeting this specification. Since Alfonso ships about 60,000 turkeys to Food-Lux each November, a sampling procedure is indicated—followed by a statistical test. Mr. Sage selects a random sample of 65 birds from this year's November shipments from Alfonso and weighs each one. He finds the sample mean to be 13.6 lb and the sample standard deviation 4 lb. Is it likely that Alfonso Farms is meeting the weight specification?

In the customary notation we have $\mu =$?, $\sigma =$?, $n = 65$, $\bar{x} = 13.6$, $s = 4$. A two-sided test is needed, since Mr. Sage wishes to detect deviations in weight in either direction. The appropriate hypotheses are

$$H_0: \mu = 13 \text{ lb} \qquad H_1: \mu \neq 13 \text{ lb}$$

We are now ready to attack the details of test construction. What is the test supposed to do? For each sample mean weight that Sam might obtain from his 65 turkeys, the test must tell him whether to accept H_0 or reject it. To do this, the test must associate with each possible $\bar{x}$ one of the two statements "accept H_0" or "reject H_0." Speaking more generally, a statistical test is a function whose domain is the statistic of interest and whose range consists of two elements: acceptance of the null hypothesis and its rejection.

It is helpful to picture such a test geometrically. Here, an axis labeled $\bar{x}$ is partitioned into two mutually exclusive exhaustive subsets, one labeled "reject H_0" and the other "accept H_0." The first is called the critical region or the region of rejection; the second the region of acceptance. One possible test of Mr. Sage's null hypothesis is that shown in Figure 10.1. In other

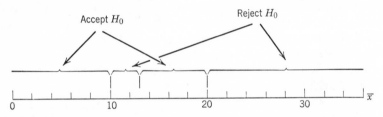

Fig. 10.1. Acceptance and rejection regions for test T_1 of the turkey problem.

language, we could divide the domain of all real numbers into two sets, R_1 and A_1, such that

$$R_1 = \{\bar{x} \mid (10 \leq \bar{x} < 13) \cup (\bar{x} \geq 20)\}$$

and

$$A_1 = \{\bar{x} \mid (\bar{x} < 10) \cup (13 \leq \bar{x} < 20)\}$$

(that is, R_1 consists of all real numbers $\bar{x}$ lying either in $10 \leq \bar{x} < 13$ or in $\bar{x} \geq 20$, and A_1 is the rest of the $\bar{x}$ axis). The test, say T_1, is then the function given by

$$T_1(\bar{x}) = \begin{cases} \text{reject } H_0 \mid \bar{x} \in R_1 \\ \text{accept } H_0 \mid \bar{x} \in A_1 \end{cases}$$

Now in calling this partitioning a statistical test we refrained from saying that it was a good test. As a matter of fact, it is a thoroughly miserable test for two reasons. It tells Mr. Sage to decide that the mean turkey weight in the population is not 13 when the sample mean is $\bar{x} = 12$, 12.5, or even 12.9 lb.

Since it is unusual for the mean of a random sample selected from a population to fall very far from the mean of the population, this test tells Sam Sage to reject his null hypothesis when an event occurs that is quite usual when H_0 is true. And from the opposite point of view the test accepts H_0 when $\bar{x} =$ 4 lb although this is a much less likely outcome than 12 lb for the sample mean when H_0 is true. Let us abandon T_1 and consider a more reasonable test, T_2, of the same null hypothesis.

Given $a < 13 < b$, let

$$A = \{\bar{x} \mid a < \bar{x} < b\}$$
$$R = \{\bar{x} \mid (\bar{x} \leq a) \cup (\bar{x} \geq b)\}$$
$$T_2(\bar{x}) = \begin{cases} \text{reject } H_0 \mid \bar{x} \in R \\ \text{accept } H_0 \mid \bar{x} \in A \end{cases}$$

In other words, we shall lay off an interval surrounding the hypothesized value of μ, in this case 13, and reject H_0 when $\bar{x}$ falls outside this interval. Although it is possible to center this interval elsewhere than at the hypothesized value μ_0, on two-sided tests in this text we shall set a and b so that $\mu_0 - a = b - \mu_0$. A diagram illustrating the acceptance and rejection regions for T_2 is given in Figure 10.2.

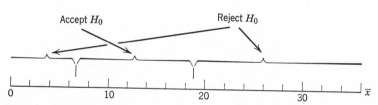

Fig. 10.2. Acceptance and rejection regions for a more reasonable test T_2 in the turkey problem.

Note that we are not rehashing a confidence interval problem. In confidence intervals the limits are set on either side of the sample statistic. Here, a and b are placed on either side of the hypothesized population parameter. Hence, although the same sampling distribution is involved in the two types of inference, the reasoning is very different. We now consider the problem of determining a and b.

They depend upon α, the probability of a Type I error, or β, the probability of a Type II error. Let us simplify our reasoning as a preliminary tactic. Imagine that additional information was available to Mr. Sage, which enabled him to know in advance that the mean weight of turkeys shipped by Alfonso to Food-Lux was either 13 or 15 lb. No other weights were possible. What test could the buyer use in this simpler case? First, he should use a different alternative hypothesis:

$$H_0; \mu = 13 \text{ lb} \qquad H_1': \mu = 15 \text{ lb}$$

Next, the central limit theorem guarantees that the distribution of $\bar{X}$, the statistic of interest, is approximately normal with mean μ and $\sigma_{\bar{X}}^2 = \sigma^2/n$. We estimate $\sigma_{\bar{X}}^2$, using the unbiased $\hat{\sigma}^2$, although no damage would be done if s^2 were used with this large a sample size.

$$\hat{\sigma}^2 = \frac{n}{n-1} s^2 = \frac{65}{64} \cdot 16$$

$$\sigma_{\bar{X}}^2 = \frac{\hat{\sigma}^2}{n} = \frac{65}{64} \cdot \frac{16}{65} = \frac{1}{4} \qquad \sigma_{\bar{X}} = 0.5 \text{ lb}$$

Figure 10.3 shows both $f_0(\bar{x})$, the sampling distribution of $\bar{X}$ when H_0 is true, and $f_1(\bar{x})$, the sampling distribution of $\bar{X}$ when H_1' is true. What is a good test of H_0 against H_1'?

Let us examine several possible tests. Any reasonable test here is one-sided. All $\bar{x}$ below 13 suggest H_0 rather than H_1', and all values above 15 indicate H_1' rather than H_0.[3] We only need to find a demarcation point somewhere between 13 and 15 lb. Suppose we choose the following critical region.

$$R_1^* = \{\bar{x} \mid \bar{x} \geq 13.8\}$$

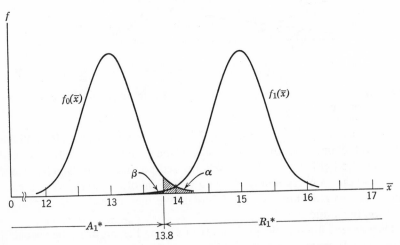

Fig. 10.3. Sampling distributions of $\bar{X}$ under the null and alternative hypotheses with errors of the first and second kind—simplified turkey problem.

[3] If either a Type I or a Type II error were considered serious enough, this might not be true.

Note that A_1^* is then the complement of R_1^* in the real line. The test is:

$$T(\bar{x}) = \begin{cases} \text{reject } H_0 \mid \bar{x} \in R_1^* \\ \text{accept } H_0 \mid \bar{x} \in A_1^* \end{cases}$$

We want to examine the probability of a Type I error (α) and the probability of a Type II error (β) for this test. Each can be uniquely determined here, since there are only two possible "states of nature."

Since α is the probability of rejecting a true H_0, it is the area under $f_0(\bar{x})$, the sampling distribution that holds when H_0 is true, corresponding to $\bar{x}$ in the region of rejection R_1^*. It is shaded and labeled in Figure 10.3. But such areas can be represented as definite integrals: hence

$$\alpha = \int_{\bar{x}=13.8}^{\infty} f_0(\bar{x})\, d\bar{x} = \frac{1}{\sqrt{2\pi}\,(0.5)} \int_{\bar{x}=13.8}^{\infty} e^{-(\bar{x}-13)^2/2(0.25)}\, d\bar{x}$$

By letting $z = (\bar{x} - 13)/0.5$ and referring to Table E.3 we find that

$$\alpha = \frac{1}{\sqrt{2\pi}} \int_{z=1.6}^{\infty} e^{-z^2/2}\, dz = 0.0548$$

As for β, it is the probability of accepting a false H_0, and hence is the integral of $f_1(\bar{x})$ over the region of acceptance A_1^*. Mathematically, letting

$$z' = \frac{\bar{x} - 15}{0.5}$$

$$\beta = \int_{\bar{x}=-\infty}^{13.8} f_1(\bar{x})\, d\bar{x} = \frac{1}{\sqrt{2\pi}\,(0.5)} \int_{\bar{x}=-\infty}^{13.8} e^{-(\bar{x}-15)^2/2(0.25)}\, d\bar{x}$$

$$= \frac{1}{\sqrt{2\pi}} \int_{z'=-\infty}^{-2.4} e^{z'^2/2}\, dz' = 0.0082$$

At this point a dilemma arises. Refer now to Figure 10.3, and consider the reasonable one-sided tests that might be used to check the hypothesis H_0. Each of these is determined by specifying a point of demarcation separating a region of rejection from a region of acceptance. Suppose we choose $\bar{x} = 13.7$ instead of 13.8. From the figure, it is clear that the resulting test will have a larger α and a smaller β than the original one based on 13.8. The reader can verify that for this test:

$$\alpha = \frac{1}{\sqrt{2\pi}\,(0.5)} \int_{13.7}^{\infty} e^{-(\bar{x}-13)^2/2(0.25)}\, d\bar{x} = 0.08076$$

$$\beta = \frac{1}{\sqrt{2\pi}\,(0.5)} \int_{-\infty}^{13.7} e^{-(\bar{x}-15)^2/2(0.25)}\, d\bar{x} = 0.00464$$

And, if we move the point of demarcation to the right, we shall diminish α but increase β. If the value $\bar{x} = 14$ lb is employed, the resulting test has

$$\beta = \alpha = \int_{\bar{x}=14}^{\infty} f_0(\bar{x}) \, d\bar{x} = 0.02275$$

In other words any action that we take to reduce α by changing our choice of tests will result in an increase in β, and vice versa. Unfortunately, this is true of all statistical tests. If a Type I error were very serious, we would reduce α and hence move the rejection region to the right.

To return to Mr. Sage, before he can run his test, he must decide how to balance the two errors. This is usually done by specifying α, which determines the region of rejection and thus the test—once it has been decided that a one-tailed (or two-tailed) test is appropriate. Suppose that he is satisfied with an α of 0.05. Then

$$\alpha = 0.05 = \frac{1}{\sqrt{2\pi}\,(0.5)} \int_{\bar{x}=c}^{\infty} e^{-(\bar{x}-13)^2/2(0.25)} \, d\bar{x} = \frac{1}{\sqrt{2\pi}} \int_{z=(c-13)/0.5}^{\infty} e^{-z^2/2} \, dz$$

From Table 3 of Appendix E, $(c - 13)/0.5 = 1.64$. Thus, $c - 13 = 0.82$; $c = 13.82$. The test is then to accept H_0 whenever $\bar{x} < 13.82$ and to reject H_0 whenever $\bar{x} \geq 13.82$. Since Mr. Sage's sample gave an $\bar{x} = 13.6$, he accepts H_0 and concludes that Alfonso is probably maintaining the required average weight in this year's deliveries to Food-Lux. We note that the Type II error for this test is

$$\beta = \frac{1}{\sqrt{2\pi}\,(0.5)} \int_{\bar{x}=-\infty}^{13.82} e^{-(\bar{x}-15)^2/2(0.25)} \, d\bar{x} = 0.00914$$

$T(\bar{x})$ is a good test to use if it is important that Food-Lux should not decide that the mean turkey weight was 13 lb when, in fact, it was 15 lb.

10.4   THE POWER OF A TEST

We return now to Mr. Sage's original hypothesis and a more practical situation. Food-Lux has had difficulty in the past in disposing both of small and king-sized turkeys. Therefore, the buyer decides to construct the "two-tailed" test:

$$H_0: \mu = 13 \qquad H_1: \mu \neq 13$$

using an α of 0.05. The term "level of significance of the statistical test" is also often used for α.

This test differs from the foregoing one in that its alternative hypothesis subsumes not just a single value of μ, but an infinity of values. In fact, the set for which H_1 is true is the union of all single values of μ other than 13.0. Each element in this union should be thought of as giving rise to a test similar to the one just developed using $H_0: \mu = 13$ versus $H_1': \mu = 15$. That is, while we still shall deal with one sampling distribution, $f_0(\bar{x})$, when H_0 is true, we have to consider an infinity of sampling distributions each of which corresponds to a point alternative under H_1. This implies that α will be found from $f_0(\bar{x})$ exactly as before, but that β will change as the sampling distribution changes with the possible values of μ in H_1. Figure 10.4 illustrates this change for the

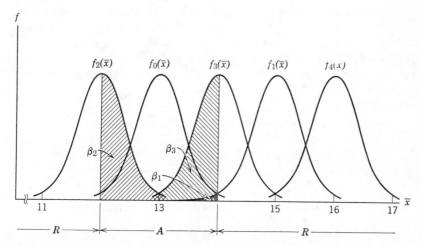

Fig. 10.4. Variation of β with several point alternatives—turkey problem.

version of the turkey problem now being examined. Although only a few functions can be shown, the reader should visualize a set of normal distributions with mean at each value of μ.

Let us set up an appropriate test at the 0.05 level of significance. Since the alternative hypothesis is two-sided, we shall arbitrarily divide α equally between the two tails of $f_0(\bar{x})$. That is, we shall determine that value of $\bar{x}$ which leaves an area equal to 0.025 in a single tail of $f_0(\bar{x})$.

$$\frac{\alpha}{2} = 0.025 = \frac{1}{\sqrt{2\pi}\,(0.5)} \int_c^\infty e^{-(\bar{x}-13)^2/2(0.25)}\,d\bar{x} = \frac{1}{\sqrt{2\pi}} \int_{z=(c-13)/0.5}^\infty e^{-z^2/2}\,dz$$

From Table E.3 $(c - 13)/0.5 = 1.96$; $c = 13.98$. The test is thus specified by

$$A = \{12.02 < \bar{x} < 13.98\} \qquad R = \{(\bar{x} \leq 12.02) \cup (\bar{x} \geq 13.98)\}$$

Mr. Sage's sample value is $\bar{x} = 13.6$ lb. H_0 is accepted, and the Alfonso shipments are considered as meeting specifications.

The principal point to be noted is the variation in β shown in Figure 10.4. Since β is the integral of the particular alternative sampling distribution over the region of acceptance, it is seen to be nearly 0.5 for both $f_2(\bar{x})$ and $f_3(\bar{x})$. On the other hand, it is small for $f_1(\bar{x})$ and so tiny for $f_4(\bar{x})$ that it cannot be shown.

We note that the closer a particular value of μ under the alternative hypothesis is to the value μ_0 under the null hypothesis, the larger is the value of β. These concepts are discussed by introducing the power of a test.

The power of a test against a particular value under the alternative hypothesis is defined to be $1 - \beta$ where β is computed from the particular alternative in question. Thus, for the test $T_2(\bar{x})$, the power is a constant since there is only one value of μ possible under H_1'. For the test $T(\bar{x})$, we proved that $\beta = 0.0082$; therefore the power is $Pw = 0.9918$. Since β is the probability of accepting a false null hypothesis, Pw is the probability of rejecting a false null hypothesis.

In the test of H_0: $\mu = 13$ against the compound alternative H_1: $\mu \neq 13$, we have just discovered that β is variable. We shall write $\beta = \beta(\mu)$ to indicate that β changes as μ changes. Hence, Pw will also vary with μ, and we shall use the notation $Pw(\mu)$. Using the relation,

$$Pw(\mu) = 1 - \beta(\mu) = 1 - \int_A f_\mu(\bar{x}) \, d\bar{x} = \int_R f_\mu(\bar{x}) \, d\bar{x}$$

where $f_\mu(\bar{x})$ is the distribution of $\bar{x}$ under the particular alternative μ, we shall compute one value of $Pw(\mu)$. The student should check those given in Table 10.1.

$$Pw(14) = 1 - \frac{1}{\sqrt{2\pi}\,(0.5)} \int_{\bar{x}=12.02}^{13.98} e^{-(\bar{x}-14)^2/2(0.25)} \, d\bar{x}$$

$$= 1 - \frac{1}{\sqrt{2\pi}} \int_{z=-3.96}^{-0.04} e^{-z^2/2} \, dz$$

$$= 1 - (0.48405 - 0.00004) = 0.51599$$

Table 10.1   Values of $Pw(\mu)$ for the Turkey Problem with a Compound Alternative

μ	15.5	15	14.5	14	13.5	13[4]	12.5	12	11.5	11	10.5
$Pw(\mu)$	0.999	0.979	0.851	0.516	0.170	0.050	0.170	0.516	0.851	0.979	0.999

[4] If we define "the power of a test" as $1 - \beta$ or the power against the alternative hypothesis, the value(s) for which the null hypothesis obtain(s) is (are) not part of the "power function." We shall, however, include these figures in our presentations.

The graph of $Pw(\mu)$ is shown in Figure 10.5. It exhibits the characteristic shape of any power function for a two-sided test. The fact that the power is low when the null and alternative hypothesized values of μ are close together is a reflection of the fact that it is difficult to distinguish between means that differ only slightly. However, the large values of $Pw(\mu)$ for alternatives such as $\mu = 15$ or $\mu = 10.5$ indicate that the test distinguishes very well between cases where H_0 is true and cases where these values of μ are true. All of this discussion is, of course, in terms of Type II error with α fixed at 0.05. The value of $Pw(\mu) = 0.979$ for $\mu = 15$ says that the test used, which rejects H_0

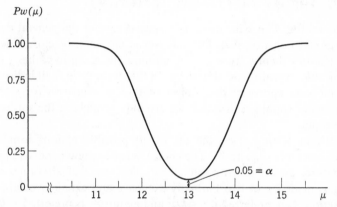

Fig. 10.5. Power function in the turkey problem with compound alternative.

when it is true only 5 times out of 100, will also reject H_0 when it is false with a mean of 15 lbs. about 98 times in 100.

The usefulness of the power function is described in just such terms as these. Since α increases whenever β is decreased and vice versa, it is necessary to commence the construction of a test by controlling one of these errors. The usual procedure is to fix α in advance, choosing a value that seems reasonable in view of the consequences of a Type I error. The next step is to determine the critical region; keep in mind that the test is entirely specified by this choice. Finally, the power function of the test is calculated. From this function the user can tell how large β is when particular values of the alternative hypothesis are, in fact, true. In general, if the power function appears as a narrow V-shaped curve, the test will discriminate well between the value stated in H_0 and most other values of the parameter. But, if the V is very broad, there will be a large interval over which the discrimination will be poor.

Also notice that the shape of the power curve is influenced by sample size. If we use the same test (that is, the same critical region), but increase the number of sample items, then we reduce $\sigma_{\bar{X}}$, since $\sigma_{\bar{X}} = \sigma/\sqrt{n}$. When the standard error of $\overline{X}$ is reduced, the area in the tails of the sampling distribution is reduced both when H_0 is true and when H_1 is true. Thus increasing sample size while maintaining the same critical region reduces α but does not uniformly reduce β. For parameters lying close to the value specified in H_0, β is increased while it is decreased for those parameters not close to this value. If, on the other hand, sample size is increased while α is maintained, β is reduced for all parameters. It is only for a fixed sample size that the statement, "anything done to diminish α increases β and vice versa" is valid.

*10.5 THE THEORY OF STATISTICAL TESTING

Hypothesis testing, like estimation, is a special case of the general decision problem stated in Section 9.2. The relation is particularly close since historically decision theory arose out of attempts to make hypothesis testing more applicable to real-world situations. In this section we shall indicate this relation and then approach the subject of goodness criteria for statistical tests. The reader should realize that we are only scratching the surface of a very large topic.

In hypothesis testing, $\{A\}$, the set of all possible actions usually has exactly two elements, A_0 and A_1. The choice between them depends upon the state of nature, an unknown parameter θ. The set Ω of all values of this parameter is made up of two mutually exclusive and exhaustive subsets Ω_0 and Ω_1. Action A_0 is preferred if $\theta \in \Omega_0$, and action A_1 is preferred if $\theta \in \Omega_1$. The loss function is quite specialized; $l(A, \theta) \geq 0$ but

$$l(A_0, \theta) = 0 \quad \text{for} \quad \theta \in \Omega_0$$

and

$$l(A_1, \theta) = 0 \quad \text{for} \quad \theta \in \Omega_1$$

Let $X_1, \cdots, X_n$ be a random sample from the population of interest. A strategy, as before, is a function

$$s(X_1, \cdots, X_n) = A$$

defined for all samples. Since A has only two elements, each strategy can be represented as a partition of sample space S into two mutually exclusive and exhaustive subsets S_0 and S_1 so that action A_0 will be taken if the sample point falls in S_0 and action A_1 will be taken if the sample point falls in S_1.

The expected loss $E[l(A, \theta)]$ is the sum of four terms corresponding to the four combinations of two actions and two subsets of Ω.

$$E[l(A, \theta)] = l(A_0, \theta \in \Omega_0)P(s \in S_0 \mid \theta) + l(A_1, \theta \in \Omega_0)P(s \in S_1 \mid \theta)$$
$$+ l(A_0, \theta \in \Omega_1)P(s \in S_0 \mid \theta) + l(A_1, \theta \in \Omega_1)P(s \in S_1 \mid \theta) \quad (10.1)$$

The first term is the loss occurring when the sample value leads to A_0, the preferred action for $\theta \in \Omega_0$. This term is zero as is the last term representing the loss when the sample indicates A_1 and this is really the preferred action. Thus, in the hypothesis-testing situation, the expected loss is seen to be composed of the losses corresponding to the Type I and Type II errors introduced in Section 10.2. For example, if we were testing the hypothesis that $\theta \in \Omega_0$ and obtained $s \in S_1$, we would opt for A_1 and thus make a Type I error if θ was in Ω_0. The second term of (10.1) would be the loss from a Type I error multiplied by its probability. In summary then, from (10.1) we have

$$E[l(A, \theta)] = l(A_1, \theta \in \Omega_0)P(s \in S_1 \mid \theta) + l(A_0, \theta \in \Omega_1)P(s \in S_0 \mid \theta) \quad (10.2)$$

Let us examine the original turkey problem (Section 10.4) in the light of these ideas. We wished to test H_0: $\mu = 13$ lb against H_1: $\mu \neq 13$ lb. Thus Ω is the real line consisting of all values of μ, Ω_0 is the set $\{13\}$ and Ω_1 consists of all other values of μ. The actions are not clearly specified, but A_1 might be "cancel Alfonso's order" while A_0 could be "let the order stand."

We set an interval for acceptance of the null hypothesis, and determined a critical region.

$$S(\bar{x}) = \begin{cases} A_0, \bar{x} \in S_0 = \{12.02 < \bar{x} < 13.98\} \\ A_1, \bar{x} \in S_1 = \{(\bar{x} \leq 12.02) \cup (\bar{x} \geq 13.98)\} \end{cases}$$

Notice that no loss function is specified in the turkey problem. The basis for acceptance or rejection is only a probability $P(\bar{x} \in S_1 \mid \theta \in \Omega_0)$ which we set equal to 0.05. One of the reasons for the development of decision theory was the failure of classical inference to consider the loss function. Where classical statistics can only ask which of the two types of error is the more costly and then set α accordingly, decision theory will demand that some formal representation of the losses be incorporated into the analysis.

We will treat one further matter in this section. In Figures 10.1 and 10.2 we showed two tests—calling one "good" and one "bad" on intuitive grounds. What do we mean by a good test or a bad test? What specific criterion is involved? And is it possible to speak of a "best" test?

Unfortunately, this problem has no general solution; neither classical statistics nor modern decision theory has been able to lay down a formal procedure for arriving at a best test under all circumstances. We shall now examine briefly one criterion that leads to best tests in a very limited class of problems.

Remember that a test is determined by a partition of the sample space of an appropriate statistic. A simple hypothesis is one corresponding to a single value of the parameter. The test of H_0: $\mu = 13$ lb versus H_1': $\mu = 15$ lb has both a simple null hypothesis and a simple alternative. The following theorem is called the Neyman-Pearson lemma. We state it without proof.

NEYMAN-PEARSON LEMMA: Consider a population $f(x, \theta)$ and all tests of the simple hypothesis $\theta = \theta_0$ against the simple alternative $\theta = \theta_1$ which have a level of significance of α or less. Let $X_1, \cdots, X_n$ be a random sample from $f(x, \theta)$. Then the test that has the greatest power is the one whose critical region is defined by

$$\frac{f(x_1, \theta_0) \ \cdots \ f(x_n, \theta_0)}{f(x_1, \theta_1) \ \cdots \ f(x_n, \theta_1)} < K$$

for some K such that the probability that the sample point will lie in the critical region is exactly equal to α.

It is reasonable to use the concept of power as a criterion of the goodness of a test, and the Neyman-Pearson lemma would give a fine solution to our problem if all tests had simple null and alternative hypotheses. Most do not. When we examine them, we find that the typical situation finds one test most powerful for certain values of the alternative hypothesis and other tests more powerful for other values. Thus we cannot go too far with the Neyman-Pearson lemma. We note, however, that the one-tailed tests of means and percentages to be discussed in Section 10.8 are best tests in the Neyman-Pearson sense. Surprisingly, their two-sided counterparts from Section 10.6 are not.

We might also mention that another criterion for best tests, called the generalized likelihood ratio criterion, can be built upon the idea of maximum likelihood estimation discussed in Section 9.4. We shall not discuss this procedure; however, all the tests discussed in this chapter are best tests when it is used as the standard.

10.6   TWO-SIDED TESTS OF MEANS AND PERCENTAGES

In this section we shall give examples illustrating two-sided tests of hypotheses in those situations already discussed relative to point and interval estimation. The student should keep before him the rationale of such problems. This does not differ from case to case. The hypotheses of interest are set down, and α is chosen. The sampling distribution of the appropriate statistic is found. The region of rejection is chosen so as to leave a total of α in both tails of the sampling distribution that obtains when H_0 is true. Then, the power function is employed to see how satisfactorily the test deals with errors of the second kind. Finally, a random sample is drawn, the statistic computed, and its location within or without the region of rejection determined. The null hypothesis is discredited or not discredited by the location of this statistic.

Mr. Caesar, president of the Reputable Insurance Company, reads an article which states that clerical employees of insurance companies do not remain for long in the employ of one company. The author estimates the mean

duration of employment at three years. The president knows that a considerable period of time is needed to "break in" new clerical personnel, and
he feels that the three-year figure, if true at Reputable, indicates a great waste
of training. To check the figure, Mr. Caesar has a clerk select 150 files at
random from the clerical employee section of the personnel office. Of these,
101 persons are found to be no longer employed at Reputable while 49 are
still working for the company. Mr. Caesar decides to discard these 49 files,
since the total time of these people with Reputable cannot be determined,
and to work with a sample of size 101—none of whom was rehired after
leaving the company. Should he have discarded the 49 files? Could he have
carried out an appropriate test based on the 150 files? Does the set of 101
files constitute a true random sample?

The 101 files yield a mean of 5.1 years and a variance of 36 (years)². Noting
that Mr. Caesar's population consists of all past clerical employees of
Reputable who were not rehired, we describe his procedures. He had decided
to test the null hypothesis that μ was three years against the alternative that
μ was not three years. (This was not a wise choice of hypothesis, as will be
noted later.) He further felt that it was important not to reject H_0 when it was
true. Thus, he chose $\alpha = 0.01$, and proceeded formally as follows:

$$H_0: \mu = 3 \qquad H_1: \mu \neq 3$$

By the central limit theorem, $f(\bar{x})$ is approximately normal with mean μ and
variance σ^2/n:

$$\sigma_{\bar{x}}^2 = \frac{\sigma^2}{n} \approx \frac{n}{n-1} s^2 \cdot \frac{1}{n} = \frac{36}{100} = 0.36 \text{ years} \qquad \sigma_{\bar{x}} = 0.6 \text{ years}$$

The acceptance region is thus $3 \pm 2.58(0.6) = 3 \pm 1.55$.

$$A = \{\bar{x} \mid 1.45 < \bar{x} < 4.55\}$$

Since 5.1 years lies in the region of rejection, the null hypothesis is rejected.
It is unlikely that the mean employment time of past unrehired clerical
employees of Reputable Insurance is three years.

Let us also find the power of this test against the alternative $\mu = 5$.

$$\beta(5) \approx \frac{1}{\sqrt{2\pi}\,(0.6)} \int_{\bar{x}=1.45}^{4.55} e^{-(\bar{x}-5)^2/2(0.36)} \, d\bar{x} = \frac{1}{\sqrt{2\pi}} \int_{z=-5.92}^{-0.75} e^{-z^2/2} \, dz = 0.227$$

$Pw(5) = 0.773$. We conclude that the test discriminates fairly well in terms
of Type II errors when the alternative is five years; however, about one-fourth
of all false null hypotheses $\mu = 3$ years are accepted by the test when μ is

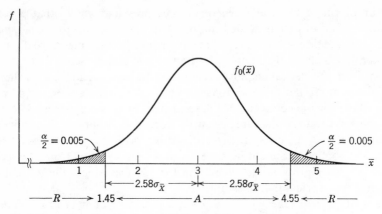

Fig. 10.6. Sampling distribution of $\overline{X}$, Reputable problem.

really five years. Figure 10.6 shows the sampling distribution when H_0 is true as well as A, R, and the Type I error.

The Eisenmann Company manufactures pencil sharpeners. In the Model T sharpener the cylindrical grinding gears should have a diameter of 0.70 in. The standard process by which the gears are produced is known to yield a normal distribution of gear diameters. A random sample of six gears is taken over a four-month interval from the many thousand produced. The mean diameter of the sample gears is 0.72 in. and the standard deviation is 0.03 in. Can the Eisenmann Company conclude at the 0.10 level of significance that the mean diameter of all gears produced during that four months was 0.70 in. ?

$$H_0: \mu = 0.70 \text{ in.} \qquad H_1: \mu \neq 0.70 \text{ in.} \qquad \alpha = 0.10$$

$$\sigma^2 \approx \frac{n}{n-1}\, s^2 = \frac{6}{5}(0.03)^2$$

$$\sigma_{\overline{x}}{}^2 = \frac{\sigma^2}{n} \approx \frac{6}{5}\frac{(0.03)^2}{6} \qquad \sigma_{\overline{x}} = \frac{0.03}{\sqrt{5}} = 0.0134$$

Here, we must use a t distribution with five degrees of freedom, since the population is normal with unknown σ (see Section 9.6). Hence the acceptance region is $0.70 \pm 2.015(0.0134) = 0.70 \pm 0.027$.

$$A = \{\overline{x} \mid 0.673 < \overline{x} < 0.727\}$$

An abscissa of ± 2.015 leaves a total of 0.10 in both tails of a t-density function with five degrees of freedom (see Table E.6). Since $\overline{x} = 0.72$ lies within the acceptance region, we accept H_0. The Eisenmann Company cannot conclude that its standards are not being met at the assumed level of significance.

We emphasize two points here. The first is the importance of the initial choice of α. It can be easily verified from the t table that if $\alpha = 0.20$ had been used, H_0 would have been rejected. Thus, every effort should be made to make sure that the α selected initially is a reasonable one. Of course, α must be chosen before the sample calculations are made; otherwise statisticians could accept or reject hypotheses according to whim—merely by picking an α that would lead to the result they favored. Such a procedure would be intolerable. The problem of which level of significance is suitable for use in a particular test is a difficult one. In Chapter 12 we shall discuss a decision-theory approach to such questions. This will provide a more sensitive means of relating decisions to costs.

The second point is that, if σ were known, the test could be based on the normal sampling distribution of $\overline{X}$ even though sample size was small. Power functions will not be discussed when the sampling distribution takes the form of a t distribution.

To illustrate hypothesis testing in a one-sample situation involving percentages, consider the activities of the stenographic pool at the Cogswell Radio Corporation's headquarters. Complaints were heard concerning water cooler addiction, clock watching, and malapropism. Finally, several executives, in a heated exchange with the office manager, declared that 20 percent of all letters handled by members of the pool that year had to be retyped because of stenographic errors. It was found that the stenographic pool handled in excess of 20,000 letters during that time. A random sample of 500 of these showed that 75 needed complete retyping. Does this result tend to to affirm the executives' pronouncement?

The procedure is clear; it is necessary to test

$$H_0: \pi = 20\% \text{ versus } H_1: \pi \neq 20\%\text{[5]}$$

Suppose that the 0.05 level of significance is judged to be appropriate. The sample percentage requiring retyping is given by $p = 75/500 = 15\%$. Since the sample is large, the sampling distribution of P is approximately normal with mean π and variance $[\pi(100 - \pi)]/n$. Now, under H_0,

$$\sigma_P = \sqrt{\frac{\pi(100 - \pi)}{n}} = \sqrt{\frac{(20)(80)}{500}} = 1.79\%$$

---

[5] This is a two-tailed test only if deviations from $\pi = 20$ percent have the same practical significance regardless of direction. This problem is appropriately labeled "two-sided" only if the alternative actions are, "Conclude the executives are right: $\pi = 20$ percent" versus, "Conclude they are wrong: $\pi \neq 20$ percent, but do not specify whether it is higher or lower than 20 percent." As we shall see in Section 10.8, most real problems consist of a single one-sided test or two one-sided tests. We shall postpone discussion of this feature until that section.

Compute

$$\pi \pm 1.96\sigma_P = 20 \pm 1.96(1.79) = 20 \pm 3.51$$

Then

$$A = \{p \mid 16.49\% < p < 23.51\%\}$$

Since the sample statistic $p = 15\%$ lies in R, H_0 must be rejected at the 0.05 level. The statement that 20 percent of all letters needed retyping appears to be an unjustified maligning of the stenographers.

The mechanics of running a test are sometimes done in a slightly different way. After σ_P is computed, the transformation

$$z = \frac{P - \pi}{\sigma_P}$$

is made, and the result referred to the acceptance region

$$A' = \{z \mid -1.96 < z < 1.96\}$$

That is, the sample result is transformed to the unit normal curve and the regions of rejection and acceptance are specified there. In this problem

$$z = \frac{15 - 20}{1.79} = -2.79$$

which lies outside of A' so that H_0 is rejected.

The student should ask himself other questions. Would H_0 have been rejected if α had been chosen to be 0.01? 0.10? Which of these three levels of significance is really the most appropriate? Was H_0: $\pi = 20\%$ a good null hypothesis to test? Does the fact that H_0 was rejected suggest that all is well with the pool? How would the random sample of 500 letters be chosen? Should it have included originals and retypings of the same letters? It cannot be overemphasized that the formal results obtained in the preceding paragraph are meaningful only when the proper null hypothesis has been tested at a reasonable level of significance using a correct randomizing procedure.

The power function for this test presents no new concepts. The sampling distribution under the alternatively hypothesized value, $\pi = \pi_0$, is approximately normal, and the power against that alternative is the integral of that sampling distribution over R, the region of rejection. This is no different from the situation obtaining in the test of H_0: $\mu = \mu_0$ versus H_1: $\mu \neq \mu_0$. Computationally, the student should notice that the sampling distribution of P varies with π, since $\sigma_P = \sqrt{[\pi(100 - \pi)]/n}$. Consequently, in finding the power of the test against various alternatives, a different σ_P must be computed for each value of π employed as an alternative. In this respect, tests involving percentages do differ from those involving means since the same standard error was employed for each possible μ in the case of means.

10.7 TWO-SIDED TESTS—TWO-SAMPLE CASES

Let us now move to a two-sample test. Suppose that the Internal Revenue Service wishes to check on a statement that men and women who were gainfully employed but not self-employed in the city of Chicago during 1968 had equal mean 1968 incomes. Suppose a random sample of sixty-five 1968 returns filed by Chicago males in that category had $\bar{x} = \$6180$ and $s_x = \$800$. An independent random sample of thirty-seven 1968 returns filed by Chicago females in that category yielded $\bar{y} = \$5520$ and $s_y = \$600$. Is the statement concerning equality of income reasonable in the light of the sample evidence? Use the 0.10 level of significance.

$$H_0: \mu_X - \mu_Y = 0 \qquad H_1: \mu_X - \mu_Y \neq 0 \qquad \alpha = 0.10$$

The sampling distribution of $\bar{X} - \bar{Y}$ is approximately normal[6] by the central limit theorem applied to the population of differences. (Note that populations of incomes are not usually normal but skewed to the right.) It is shown in Figure 10.7.

The mean of this sampling distribution is the difference in population means when H_0 is true, that is, $\mu_X - \mu_Y = 0$. The variance is approximated

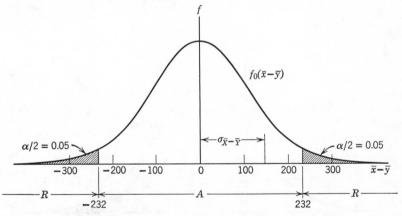

Fig. 10.7. Sampling distribution of $\bar{X} - \bar{Y}$, Internal Revenue example.

[6] The student should note that the t distribution is not appropriate here; since universe variances are unknown and assumed different, the sample sizes are large enough so that the normal is a good approximation.

from the samples:

$$\sigma_{\bar{X}-\bar{Y}} = \sqrt{\frac{\sigma_X^2}{n} + \frac{\sigma_Y^2}{m}} = \sqrt{\frac{s_x^2}{n-1} + \frac{s_y^2}{m-1}}$$

$$= \sqrt{\frac{(800)^2}{64} + \frac{(600)^2}{36}} = 100\sqrt{2} = \$141.41$$

$$0 \pm 1.64(141.41) = 0 \pm \$232$$

$$A = \{\bar{x} - \bar{y} \mid -\$232 < \bar{x} - \bar{y} < \$232\}$$

From the samples, $\bar{x} - \bar{y} = 6180 - 5520 = \$660$. The difference is large enough to discredit H_0 at the 0.10 level of significance. We conclude that it is unlikely that Chicago men and women who were gainfully employed but not self-employed had equal mean 1968 incomes. (However, the reader should challenge the population actually used.)

Let us sketch the power curve of this test. For an alternative $\mu_X - \mu_Y = 100$, the power is shown as the shaded area in Figure 10.8.

Its actual value is given by

$$Pw(\mu_X - \mu_Y) = Pw(100) = 1 - \beta(100)$$

$$= 1 - \frac{1}{\sqrt{2\pi}\,(141)} \int_{D=-232}^{232} e^{-(D-100)^2/2(141)^2}\, dD$$

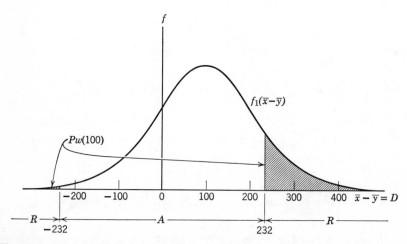

Fig. 10.8. Internal Revenue example, power of the test against the alternative hypothesis $\mu_X - \mu_Y = 100$.

where $D = \bar{x} - \bar{y}$. Letting $(D - 100)/141 = z$, as usual, we find that

$$P(100) = 1 - \frac{1}{\sqrt{2\pi}} \int_{z=-2.35}^{0.94} e^{-z^2/2} \, dz = 1 - (0.32639 + 0.49061)$$

$$= 1 - 0.81700 = 0.183$$

Such a result reinforces our intuitive idea that it will be difficult to distinguish H_0 from values under the alternate hypothesis which lie less than a standard error away. Table 10.2 gives further values of the power function for this test. The function is plotted in Figure 10.9.

Table 10.2 Power Function for Two-Sided Test, Internal Revenue Example

$\mu_X - \mu_Y$	-400	-300	-200	-100	0^7	100	200	300	400
$Pw(\mu_X - \mu_Y)$	0.883	0.684	0.414	0.183	0.100	0.183	0.414	0.684	0.883

A null hypothesis in the two-sample case is really a test for homogeneity. In the preceding problem the null hypothesis states that the particular subsets of men and women are homogeneous with respect to mean income. The results of the test led us to conclude that they were heterogeneous; that is, that the two groups should not be considered as composing a single group with respect to this characteristic.

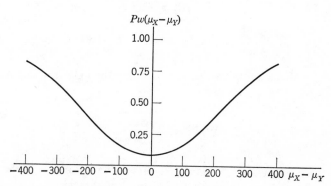

Fig. 10.9. Power function, Internal Revenue example.

---

[7] Again, the power function, as we have defined it, does not include values for which H_0 is true.

As usual, we might be wrong, and in this case we are running a 10 percent risk that we have committed a Type I error. Might we have committed a Type II error? Clearly the answer is no. Our method runs risks for both Type I and Type II errors, but once a decision is made, only one type of error is possible and this is dependent upon whether we accept or reject the null hypothesis.

As a final example of two-sample hypothesis testing, consider the dilemma of Horace T. Wilson, owner of a chain of hotels. Mr. Wilson suffered severe financial reverses necessitating the sale of several of his properties. A prospective buyer offered to purchase either of the Wilson chain's Florida hotels for a price that Mr. Wilson felt he had to accept. He ordered a quick study to see whether it made any difference which hotel he sold.

The consulting firm examined various phases of the operation of Mr. Wilson's hotels. We are concerned with only one phase. A random sample of 50 was selected from the population of persons who had spent a week or more at the Dune Sands during the past three years. Each was asked the question, "If you were to spend a week in Florida in the near future, would you come to the Dune Sands again?" Thirty-five persons replied in the affirmative, and 15 in the negative. An independent random sample was taken from the population of persons who had spent at least a week at the Galldorf Plaza during the past three years. The analogous question was asked, and 18 affirmatives versus 32 negatives were received. A test was made of the hypothesis that percentages of customers stating they would return to the same hotel, if they were to spend a week in Florida in the near future, were equal for the two populations. The 0.01 level of significance was employed.

$$H_0: \pi_1 - \pi_2 = 0 \qquad H_1: \pi_1 - \pi_2 \neq 0 \qquad \alpha = 0.01$$

$$p_1 = \left(\frac{35}{50}\right) 100 = 70 \qquad p_2 = \left(\frac{18}{50}\right) 100 = 36$$

The sampling distribution of $P_1 - P_2$ is approximately normal with mean $\pi_1 - \pi_2$ and standard deviation:

$$\sigma_{P_1-P_2} = \sqrt{\frac{\pi_1(100 - \pi_1)}{n} + \frac{\pi_2(100 - \pi_2)}{m}}$$

It was necessary to estimate this statistic from the samples, since π_1 and π_2 were not known. One might expect to use as an estimator:

$$\sqrt{\frac{p_1(100 - p_1)}{n} + \frac{p_2(100 - p_2)}{m}}$$

As a matter of fact, when the percentages p_1 and p_2 are not extreme and the samples sizes are fairly similar, the above statistic is satisfactory. But for general use in testing H_0: $\pi_1 = \pi_2$, it can be shown that another statistic provides a better estimate of $\sigma_{P_1-P_2}$. We shall not attempt a justification of this statement.

To compute this improved statistic, $\hat{\sigma}_{P_1-P_2}$, first take a weighted average of the sample percentages:

$$\bar{P} = \frac{n}{n+m}\, P_1 + \frac{m}{n+m}\, P_2 = \frac{nP_1 + mP_2}{m+n}$$

Note that the respective weights are proportional to sample size (more information is obtained from large samples than from small ones). Also $\bar{P}$ is an unbiased estimator for π in the case where both samples are drawn from populations with equal percentages of interest, $\pi_1 = \pi_2 = \pi$. The percentage $\bar{P}$ is often called a pooled estimator, since it is based jointly on the two samples. Then use $\bar{P}$ to find the desired estimator of $\sigma_{P_1-P_2}$.

$$\hat{\sigma}_{P_1-P_2} = \sqrt{\frac{\bar{P}(100 - \bar{P})}{n} + \frac{\bar{P}(100 - \bar{P})}{m}} = \sqrt{\bar{P}(100 - \bar{P})\left(\frac{1}{n} + \frac{1}{m}\right)}$$

For the Wilson hotel problem, the computations are:

$$\bar{p} = \frac{np_1 + mp_2}{n+m} = \frac{50(70) + 50(36)}{50 + 50} = 53\%\,^8$$

$$\hat{\sigma}_{P_1-P_2} = \sqrt{\bar{p}(100 - \bar{p})\left(\frac{1}{n} + \frac{1}{m}\right)} = \sqrt{(53)(47)\frac{2}{50}}$$

$$= \frac{1}{5}\sqrt{2491} = 9.98\%$$

$$0 \pm 2.58(9.98) = 0 \pm 25.75\%$$

$$A = \{p_1 - p_2 \mid -25.75\% < p_1 - p_2 < 25.75\%\}$$

Here, $p_1 - p_2 = 70 - 36 = 34\%$, a statistic that lies within R. Hence the hypothesis of equal population percentages is rejected, despite the relatively large region A accompanying the low α of 0.01. We can report that the ensuing sale of Galldorf Plaza was influenced slightly by this test which served as valuable corroboration for other parts of the study.

---

[8] Observe that the $\bar{P}$ is simply the percentage of elements in the two samples combined that possess the specified characteristic. In this problem, $\bar{p} = [(35 + 18)/100]100$.

10.8   ONE-SIDED TESTS OF MEANS AND PERCENTAGES

We shall shortly see that there is but one operational distinction between two-sided and one-sided tests which are of practical use. In two-sided tests the critical region appears as two disjoint infinite intervals, one lying under the right-hand tail of the sampling distribution and the other under the left-hand tail. This follows from the fact that in two-sided tests the null hypothesis states that a parameter has some specified value: Thus, deviations in either direction on the part of the corresponding statistic tend to discredit H_0, and it is necessary to split the critical region into two parts. In a one-sided test, although large deviations in one direction will cast doubt on H_0, we shall find that deviations in the other will only reinforce it. Hence the region of rejection for a one-tailed test will be a single infinite interval lying entirely on one side of the mean of the nully hypothesized sampling distribution. Let us see what kinds of null hypotheses will lead to one-tailed tests.

We return to Mr. Caesar and the mean duration of employment for clerical employees of the Reputable Insurance Company (Section 10.6). He tested H_0: $\mu = 3$ years versus H_1: $\mu \neq 3$ years. Did Mr. Caesar test the right hypothesis? Why did the statement cause him concern in the first place? He feared that the average period of employment in his own company was too short—resulting in too much loss of experienced personnel and too high costs of training. In terms of alternative actions, either the situation is satisfactory or corrective steps are required. Large values of μ do not indicate a need for remedial action, but small values do. Following this reasoning, he should have decided upon the smallest mean period of employment which he would have considered satisfactory and tested to see whether, in fact, that time span was or was not being exceeded. Suppose that a mean duration of employment of three years was the acceptable minimum. Then, logically, we might say that either a test of

$$H_0: \mu \leq 3 \text{ versus } H_1: \mu > 3$$

or

$$H_0': \mu \geq 3 \text{ versus } H_1': \mu < 3$$

would appear to fill the bill.

We shall adopt a convention to include the equality statements in H_0. This is convenient in the sequel. The first problem that arises concerns proper handling of the Type I error in a case such as this, in which the null hypothesis does not specify one, but infinitely many sampling distributions.

The situation resembles that which obtained under the alternative hypothesis for two-sided tests. Once a region of rejection has been chosen, the Type I error will vary from function to function among those included in

H_0, since it is an integral over the critical region of the sampling distribution and H_0 specifies many such functions.

Let us commence, arbitrarily, by selecting the most extreme value of μ under H_0 and considering a test when this value prevails. Here $\mu = 3$ years is the most extreme value. It leads to the sampling distribution $f_0(\bar{x})$, shown in Figure 10.10. This is approximately normal, with mean $\mu = 3$ and standard

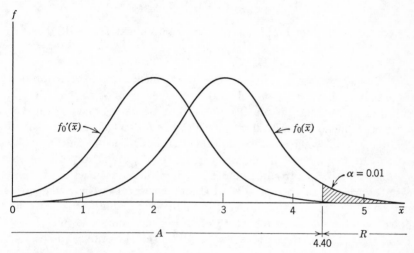

Fig. 10.10. Sampling distribution of $\bar{X}$ for two values of μ under H_0, Reputable problem, one-sided test.

deviation previously estimated as $\sigma_{\bar{x}} = 0.6$ years.

Now, H_0 is discredited by large sample means and only by these. Hence, the entire critical region must be placed in the upper tail. Since 2.33 standard errors leave 0.01 in one tail of a normal distribution, we compute

$$3 + 2.33(0.6) = 4.40 \text{ years}$$

Hence

$$R = \{\bar{x} \mid \bar{x} \geq 4.40 \text{ years}\}$$

Notice that 4.40 is smaller than the least upper bound of A in the two-sided case. This must be the case, since α is the probability of rejecting H_0 when it is true.[9] In the two-sided test with $\alpha = 0.01$, the 1 percent was distributed between the two tails leaving only 0.005 in the upper tail. In the one-sided test, the entire 1 percent is placed in the upper tail. The sampling procedure is exactly the same as for the two-sided test. The previously obtained sample

---

[9] The numerical value specified for α in the one-sided test is not the probability of rejecting H_0 when it is true, but the probability of rejecting H_0 when it is true at the equality value.

mean $\bar{x} = 5.1$ years would lead to rejection of H_0: $\mu \leq 3$ in the case where $\mu = 3$. We must now deal with the other cases.

Suppose we pick another value of μ which can obtain under H_0, for instance, $\mu = 2$. The sampling distribution corresponding to this possibility is denoted by $f_0'(\bar{x})$ in Figure 10.10. It is evident that the value of $\bar{X}$ which leaves 0.01 in the upper tail of $f_0'(\bar{x})$ is smaller than 4.40. Actually its value is

$$2 + 2.33(0.6) = 3.40 \text{ years}$$

The corresponding region of rejection for $\mu = 2$ under H_0 would then be

$$R' = \{\bar{x} \mid \bar{x} \geq 3.40 \text{ years}\}$$

Since $R \subset R'$, we see that any sample mean which leads to rejection of H_0 where R is the critical region will also lead to rejection of H_0 when R' is the critical region. In fact, broadening our vision a bit, we see that any value of μ under H_0 will lead to a critical region which has R as a subset. Consequently, a sample value $\bar{x}$ which leads to rejection of H_0 under the one-sided test based on the extreme value will lead to rejection of H_0 under any of the other possible values of μ subsumed under H_0. Since hypothesis testing is viewed by statisticians as an attempt to reject H_0, it is customary to base all one-sided tests on the extreme value under H_0. In the Reputable problem we have shown that the one-sided test based on $\mu = 3$ adequately tests H_0: $\mu \leq 3$ versus H_1: $\mu > 3$ at the 0.01 level of significance. The critical value of 4.40 means that $\alpha < 0.01$ for other portions of H_0.

What of the other possible test? We spoke of testing

$$H_0': \mu \geq 3 \text{ versus } H_1': \mu < 3$$

as a logical alternative. Which is the better null hypothesis? It depends upon the situation, the alternative actions, and which error (in terms of actions) Reputable views as the most serious. In the approach just employed, remedial action is taken if the null hypothesis is accepted. Following this reasoning, Mr. Caesar will fail to act when he should a maximum of one percent of the time. In the alternative approach using H_0': $\mu \geq 3$, remedial action, will be taken only if the null hypothesis is rejected. In order to ascertain the probability of failing to act when he should, Mr. Caesar must investigate the power function of the test.

The critical value for

$$H_0': \mu \geq 3 \qquad H_1': \mu < 3 \qquad \alpha = 0.01$$

is easily found to be 1.60. Only if the sample value is less than 1.6 years would Reputable take corrective steps. With the other approach, corrective measures would be taken unless the sample value were more than 4.4 years. In the case of the actual result, $\bar{x} = 5.1$, the same decision is reached, but any result between 1.6 and 4.4 would lead to different actions with the two approaches. Neither one is "right," but Mr. Caesar must decide which error is the more serious.

Let us consider the power of the test using H_0 and H_1. First, we recall that the power of a test is the probability of rejecting H_0 when it is false. We have shown in the case of a two-sided test that power varies with the true value of the parameter when H_0 is false. In one-sided tests the same reasoning holds, the only difference being that the null hypothesis is false only on an infinite half-line. Hence, the power function exists only on that half-line. The extreme value of the parameter under H_0 forms its bound.

Computation of points on the power curve proceeds as before. We show one computation as well as Table 10.3, which summarizes further computations, and Figure 10.11, which exhibits the form of the function. The power

Table 10.3   Power Function, Reputable Example, One-Sided Test

μ	3	4	5	6	7
$Pw(\mu)$	0.010	0.251	0.841	0.996	1.000

function of a one-sided test resembles one-half of the power function of a two-sided test.

$$P(4) = \frac{1}{\sqrt{2\pi}\,(0.6)} \int_{\bar{x}=4.40}^{\infty} e^{-(\bar{x}-4)^2/2(0.36)}\, d\bar{x}$$

$$= \frac{1}{\sqrt{2\pi}} \int_{z=0.67}^{\infty} e^{-z^2/2}\, dz = 0.25143$$

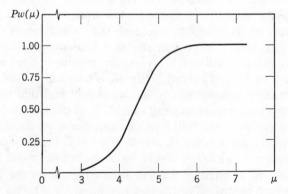

Fig. 10.11.   Power function, Reputable example, one-sided test.

The use of H_0: $\mu \leq 3$ results in Reputable running almost a 75 percent risk of instituting remedial action, even though the average be 4.0 years and about a 15 percent risk when the average reaches 5.0. The alternative of testing H_0': $\mu \geq 3$ runs high risks of failing to institute such action when needed. For example, corrective measures would be indicated by sample evidence only about 25 percent of the time if the mean were 2.0 years. The student should experiment with larger sample sizes to ascertain the effect of such a change on the conflict between the two approaches.

Next we shall reexamine several of the other tests shown in Section 10.6. In each case we shall discover a one-sided hypothesis or a set of two one-sided hypotheses which seems pertinent. The skeleton of the test will be given, a conclusion reached, and an occasional further comment made. Power curves will not be discussed as they introduce no new points.

In the Eisenmann example, suppose that the cylinders from which the gears were cut were known to have an original diameter not exceeding 0.70 in. The only question would be whether the finally machined gear diameters had been cut down too much. Suppose that the random sample of six gears had $\bar{x} = 0.67$ in. and $s^2 = 0.03$ in. Then it is pointless to test the null hypothesis that $\mu \leq 0.70$ in. Any test will accept this statement. Instead, we test:

$$H_0: \mu \geq 0.70 \qquad H_1: \mu < 0.70 \qquad \alpha = 0.10$$

(Note that this procedure effectively tests H_0: $\mu = 0.70$ versus H_1: $\mu < 0.70$, since values of μ greater than 0.70 in. are ruled out a priori.) Now $\sigma_{\bar{x}} = 0.0134$, as before, and we use a t distribution with 5 degrees of freedom. We compute

$$0.70 - 1.476(0.0134) = 0.70 - 0.0198 = 0.68$$

$$R = \{\bar{x} \mid \bar{x} \leq 0.68 \text{ in.}\}$$

Since $\bar{x} = 0.67$ in., we conclude that H_0 should be rejected and that the cutting process is reducing the diameters too much.

As a review, let us state why we reach such a conclusion. We reach it because, if H_0 is true, it is unlikely that in a random sample of size six we would obtain an $\bar{x}$ as small as 0.67. A specific meaning is given to "unlikely" by the concept of a Type I error. When H_0 is true and we examine a large number of random samples of size six, we should find that only about 10 percent of these have a mean as small as 0.68. Since our sample had a smaller mean and we are using the 0.10 level of significance, we conclude that it is rare to find such a mean when H_0 is true. If we wish to conclude that a rare event has happened, we are at liberty to do so. But we would be increasing the probability of concluding H_0 and decreasing the probability of concluding H_1—both regardless of the true parameter. What does this mean in terms of α and β?

In the Cogswell stenographic-pool example, a reasonable question would be whether the population percentage of letters needing retyping exceeded some figure, for instance, 10 percent. Given $p = 15\%$, and $\alpha = 0.05$, we would then test:

$$H_0: \pi \leq 10\% \qquad H_1: \pi > 10\%$$

Now

$$\sigma_P = \sqrt{\frac{\pi(100 - \pi)}{n}} = \sqrt{\frac{10(90)}{500}} = 1.34\%$$

under the limiting case when H_0 is true. With 0.05 on the upper tail, we write

$$10 + 1.64(1.34) = 12.20\%$$

$$R = \{p \mid p \geq 12.20\%\}$$

Since sample $p = 15\%$, we conclude that it is likely that the percentage of letters needing retyping exceeds 10 percent. It is not at all likely that a sample p of 15 percent would arise in random samples of size 500 from the population.

A problem that appears similar to the Cogswell situation is illustrated by the Kronkite Quality Product Company. Kronkite produces machine parts that are advertised as "with Kronkite, superior is the average." A potential buyer proposes the following contract to J. Oswald Kronkite, owner and president. "Industry prices will be paid if the average length of life is 1000 hours, a 10 percent bonus will be paid if the average is more than 1000 hours, but the entire shipment is to be returned if the average is less than 1000 hours." Both parties agree to use sample evidence and a speeded up test that will supply the needed means in a 24-hour period.

Here, we have a two-sided test or, more correctly, two one-sided tests. Three alternative actions are available; therefore, there are three hypotheses.

$$H_0: \mu = 1000 \qquad H_1: \mu < 1000 \qquad H_2: \mu > 1000.$$

We must now be careful in what we mean by α. It still means the probability of rejecting H_0 when it is true, but it is not uniquely associated with either H_1 or H_2. Rather, it is associated with both of them—part of the time that a Type I error is made, H_1 is concluded, and part of the time, H_2. Suppose that we set $\alpha = 0.02$. The 2 percent could be equally divided between H_1 and H_2 but need not be. If it is equally divided, we would ascertain the two critical values by employing a z value of 2.33 on either side of the hypothesized μ of 1000.

The life span of the part to be tested is known to be approximately normal with a standard deviation of 50 hours. (If the universe standard deviation were unknown or the parties were unwilling to accept it as appropriate for the shipment, that parameter would be estimated from the sample and a *t* test would be used.) Given this information and a random sample of 16 parts,

$$\sigma_{\bar{x}} = \frac{50}{\sqrt{n}} = \frac{50}{4} = 12.50$$

The critical values then become

$$1000 \pm 2.33(12.50) = 1000 \pm 29.125$$

so that

$$A = \{\bar{x} \mid 970.875 < \bar{x} < 1029.125\}$$

That is, pay a bonus if the sample of 16 parts yields a mean of 1029.125 hours or more, send the shipment back if the mean is 970.875 or less, and accept the shipment if the sample mean is between these two values.

The power of such a test would have to be evaluated against each of the alternatives. Other than the existence of two power functions and the fact that errors arise from two possible incorrect conclusions, no new concepts are involved. For example, the power of the test against H_1 depends only on the critical value 970.875, although either H_0 or H_2 might be concluded when the sample statistic was above that figure.

10.9   ONE-SIDED TESTS—TWO-SAMPLE CASES

Proceeding to the two-sample cases, we encounter (Section 10.7) the Internal Revenue case. Here, we shall check on the statement that the mean annual 1968 income of Chicago women who were gainfully employed but not self-employed during that year was less than the income of men in the analogous category.[10] For the men, $n = 65$, $\bar{x} = \$6180$, $s_x = \$800$. For the women, $m = 37$, $\bar{y} = \$5520$, $s_y = \$600$. $\hat{\sigma}_{\bar{x}-\bar{y}}$ has been found to be approximately $141. $\alpha = 0.10$.

The hypotheses should be framed as

$$H_0: \mu_X - \mu_Y \leq 0 \qquad H_1: \mu_X - \mu_Y > 0$$

We determine $0 + 1.28(141) = \$180$

$$A = \{\bar{x} - \bar{y} \mid \bar{x} - \bar{y} < \$180\}$$

---

[10] This problem might have started as two one-sided tests or, because of certain presuppositions and visualized alternative actions, it might have simply been a single one-sided test.

Here $\bar{x} - \bar{y} = 6180 - 5520 = \$660$, which leads to the rejection of H_0. We conclude that it is unlikely that the mean of the male population is equal to or less than the mean of the female population. This is equivalent to the conclusion that it is likely that the mean 1968 income of women in the category of interest is less than the mean 1968 income of men.

The alternate method of reasoning refers the test to the standardized normal distribution. Using this function,

$$A' = \{z \mid z < 1.28\}$$

We then compute

$$z = \frac{(\bar{x} - \bar{y}) - 0}{\hat{\sigma}_{\bar{X}-\bar{Y}}} = \frac{660}{141} = 4.68$$

Since $4.68 > 1.28$, we reject H_0 as before. These two methods are entirely equivalent.

Finally, in the case of Mr. Wilson and his resort hotels, we would set up two one-sided tests, since he has three actions: sell Dune Sands, sell Galldorf Plaza, or complete indifference to which one is sold. How would you proceed in the latter case if you were Mr. Wilson? Using $\alpha = 0.01$, and distributing that 1 percent equally for H_1 and H_2,

$$H_0 : \pi_1 - \pi_2 = 0 \qquad H_1 : \pi_1 - \pi_2 > 0 \qquad H_2 : \pi_1 - \pi_2 < 0$$

For Dune-Sands, $p_1 = 70\%$ and $n = 50$; for Galldorf Plaza, $p_2 = 36\%$ and $m = 50$. Thus $\hat{\sigma}_{P_1-P_2} = 9.98\%$ and

$$0 \pm 2.58(9.98) = 0 \pm 25.75$$

Hence $A = \{p_1 - p_2 \mid -25.75 < p_1 - p_2 < +25.75\}$.

$$R(\text{in favor of } H_1) = \{p_1 - p_2 \mid p_1 - p_2 \geq +25.75\}$$
$$R(\text{in favor of } H_2) = \{p_1 - p_2 \mid p_1 - p_2 \leq -25.75\}$$

But $p_1 - p_2 = 70 - 36 = 34\%$, so that H_0 is rejected in favor of H_1. Mr. Wilson concludes, as was suggested in Section 10.7, that Dune Sands has the greater percentage of returnees. It cannot be emphasized too strongly that hypotheses as well as the level of significance should be established prior to the collection of data. Even though we know at this point in time that the sample evidence will not indicate H_2, that hypothesis is still a part of our framework of analysis.

In this chapter we have introduced only a few simple tests.

1. Tests based on a normal sampling distribution.

2. Tests based on a sampling distribution that is approximately normal in large samples.

3. Tests based upon a *t*-sampling distribution.

There are many other tests in common use among statisticians. Most of these are based on sampling distributions not discussed in this text, but any test follows the pattern established here. The sampling distribution appropriate to the null hypotheses under test is designated, the critical region is determined so as to leave $\alpha/2$ in each tail of a two-tailed test (or α in the single tail of a one-tailed test), and a sample statistic is computed and checked to see whether it falls in R or in A.

IMPORTANT TERMS AND CONCEPTS

Degrees of freedom	Sampling distribution
Hypothesis	Standard error
Null	*of $\bar{x}$*
Alternate	*of P*
Inference	*of sample differences*
Level of significance	Statistic
Neyman-Pearson lemma	*t* distribution
Parameter	Tests of hypothesis
Population of differences	*One-sided*
Power of a test	*Two-sided*
Region of acceptance	Type I error
Region of rejection	Type II error

SYMBOLS AND ABBREVIATIONS

$\overline{X}$	$\hat{\sigma}$	$\sigma_{P_1-P_2}$
n	p	α
$\bar{x}$	P	β
S	π	H_0
s	$\sigma_{\bar{x}}$	H_1
μ	σ_P	$Pw(\mu)$
σ	$\sigma_{\bar{X}-\bar{Y}}$	$Pw(\pi)$

OFTEN-USED FORMULAS

$$\bar{X} = \frac{\sum X_i}{n} \qquad S = \sqrt{\frac{\sum (X_i - \bar{X})^2}{n}}$$

$$E(\bar{X}) = \mu \qquad \sigma_{\bar{X}} = \frac{\sigma}{\sqrt{n}}$$

$$\hat{\sigma} = \sqrt{\frac{\sum (X_i - \bar{X})^2}{n - 1}} \qquad E(\hat{\sigma}^2) = \sigma^2$$

$$E(P) = \pi \qquad \sigma_P = \sqrt{\frac{\pi \phi}{n}}$$

$$\sigma_{\bar{X} - \bar{Y}} = \sqrt{\frac{\sigma_X^2}{n} + \frac{\sigma_Y^2}{m}}$$

$$\bar{P} = \frac{nP_1 + mP_2}{n + m} \qquad \hat{\sigma}_{P_1 - P_2} = \sqrt{\bar{P}(100 - \bar{P})\left(\frac{1}{n} + \frac{1}{m}\right)}$$

EXERCISES

1. Explain briefly, but precisely, the meaning of each of the following.
   a. Probability sample.
   b. Standard error of the difference between two means.
   c. Power function.

2. Contrast a one-tailed test with a two-tailed test. Indicate the type of hypothesis generally associated with each.

3. Explain clearly why you agree or disagree with the following statements and defend your position.
   a. The standard error of the difference between two percentages is a standard deviation.
   b. The null hypothesis is usually set forth to be rejected, since proving it is difficult or impossible in many cases.
   c. A Type I error is more important than a Type II error.
   d. No sample statistic can ever appear in a null hypothesis.

4. a. In a random sample of 500 purchasers of white-wall tires the mean age was 30 years and the standard deviation of ages was 4 years. Is it likely at the 0.05 level of significance that the mean age of all purchasers of white-wall tires is over 28 years?

   b. Construct the power function of this test.

5. a. Is it likely at the 0.01 level of significance that the percentage of college undergraduates favoring the abolition of all grading systems is 10 percent? A random sample of 80 college undergraduates shows 12 favoring such an abolition.

   b. Construct the power function of this test.

   c. Express the Type I error of this test as a definite integral.

   d. Express the Type II error as a definite integral when the population percentage is really 15 percent.

6. It is known from past experience that the lengths of time needed to train workers to operate the 14JM2 turret lathe are approximately normally distributed. Test the hypothesis that the mean training time for all workers is 72 hours if a random sample of 10 workers shows mean training time needed to be 75 hours with standard deviation of training times 1 hour. Use the 0.05 level of significance.

7. a. In a rapid survey of monthly salaries paid by local businesses to college students holding summer jobs, Joe Sundstrum took a random sample of 115 such students and found the mean monthly salary to be $500 with standard deviation $25. Is this result compatible with a published report that the average monthly salary for such students employed in the city is $530? Use the 0.10 level of significance.

   b. Give a probabilistic statement that explains why you reached your conclusion in part *a*.

   c. If the true average monthly salary for college students holding summer jobs in that city was $540, what is the probability of concluding that the $530 figure was correct?

8. If many studies show that the number of customers entering restaurants between the hours of 11:30 A.M. and 1:30 P.M. on Fridays is approximately normally distributed, is it likely at the 0.01 level of significance that the average number of customers entering Cointreau's Restaurant between these hours on Friday does not exceed 560? A random sample of five Fridays shows an average of 600 customers entering in that time interval with standard deviation 20 customers.

9. a. A manufacturer received a shipment of 20,000 fuses from supplier A. He did not wish to accept any shipment that contained in excess of 5 percent defectives. A random sample of 200 fuses from the shipment showed 6 percent defectives. What action should he take if he is

willing to run a risk of 0.03 of rejecting a shipment containing precisely 5 percent defectives?

b. A random sample of 400 fuses from a shipment of 20,000 fuses received from supplier B showed 9 percent defectives. Would it be proper to conclude that supplier B turns out fuses of poorer quality (greater proportion of defectives) than supplier A of part *a*? Support your conclusion statistically at the 0.03 level of significance.

10. Plant A produces machine bolts in large quantities. During the past 6 months, under a state of statistical quality control, the mean length of these bolts has been 2.5000 in. and the standard deviation has been 0.0100 in. These figures coincide with specified quality standards. For a random sample of 49 bolts selected from the production line, the mean was 2.5022 in. and the standard deviation was 0.0090 in.

a. Would you conclude that standards were still being met with respect to mean length? Justify statistically. (Assume $\alpha = 0.05$.)

b. What does $\alpha = 0.05$ mean in terms of this problem?

c. Express α as a definite integral using the specific distribution employed in this problem.

11. In a random sample of 100 families in City A, a mean income of $5000 and a standard deviation of $1000 were observed. In a random sample of 500 families in City B, a mean income of $5100 and a standard deviation of $1500 were observed. There are 100,000 families in City A and 200,000 families in City B.

a. Would you conclude that there is a difference in average family income between the two cities? Assume that you are willing to tolerate a probability of 0.01 of concluding that there is a difference in average income between the two cities when there actually is no difference.

b. Did you structure this problem as a one-tailed test, a two-tailed test, or two one-tailed tests? Why?

c. There is a difference of $100 between the two sample means given above. What is the probability of observing a difference of $100 or more between the means of these two samples if the populations have equal means?

12. A random sample of 500 flash bulbs was taken from a large shipment received by a local photographic supply company. In a destructive test of these 500 bulbs, 30 turn out to be defective. The bulbs are guaranteed by the producer to contain 5 percent defectives or less. Assume that the photo supply company wishes to run a risk of not more than 0.025 of rejecting the shipment when it should be accepted.

a. Should this shipment be rejected or accepted?

b. Defend your choice of a null hypothesis.

c. Suppose that the above shipment actually contained 8 percent defective bulbs. If the above test were used, what is the probability that the shipment would be rejected?

13. A random sample of 100 parts from the production of the Morgan Metals Company showed a mean melting point for the parts of 1650°C and a standard deviation of 30°C. A random sample of 100 of the same kind of parts from the production of Albertson Alloys had a mean melting point of 1660°C and a standard deviation of 40°C.

a. Would you be willing to conclude that the mean melting point of parts from the second firm exceeded that of parts from the first firm? Justify your conclusion statistically, using a 0.01 probability of a Type I error.

b. Sketch the probability distribution for your test in part *a*. Label your sketch appropriately, showing all information that you used in making the test.

c. Would your conclusion in part *a* have been different if you had used a 0.05 level of significance? Discuss the reasoning that supports your answer, being sure to indicate the meaning of a 0.05 level of significance in terms of this problem.

14. A random sample of 100 college students at Ironclad University is taken, and the average IQ is found to be 117 with a standard deviation of 9. The average IQ for all college students in the United States is known to be 116 with a standard deviation of 10.

a. Would university officials be correct in assuming that the average IQ at Ironclad is higher than the United States college average? They only wish to take a 5 percent risk of being wrong in making this statement.

b. Explain briefly why you came to this decision.

15. Two random samples, one of alumni and one of students, of a particular university were taken to obtain opinions on a football schedule. Suppose that of the 200 alumni sampled, 120 favored playing team A, and of the 100 students, 48 favored playing team A. Should it be inferred that the alumni were more favorable than the students to including team A on the schedule? Assume that you are willing to run a risk of 0.01 of so concluding and being wrong.

16. The purchasing agent of Sloane county could buy pine seedlings from Nursery A or B for the same price and services. He examined a random sample of 100 seedlings in a lot of 50,000 being shipped from Nursery A and found 10 in poor condition. A random sample of 400 seedlings taken from a lot of 70,000 being shipped by Nursery B showed 24 in poor condition.

a. Do you think the purchasing agent could now decide which nursery was likely to ship better seedlings? If so, state which nursery, and justify your answer statistically.
b. Could the agent be wrong? Explain.
c. A standard deviation was calculated in part *a*. Of what distribution was it a measure of dispersion?

17. A labor leader wished to compare the percentage unemployed in two areas. He selected a simple random sample of 500 from the labor force in each area. There were 20 unemployed in area A and 30 in area B. The labor leader concluded that the percentage was higher in area B, since there were 50 percent more unemployed in the sample from that area. Would you agree at the 0.01 level? Support your answer with any statistical calculations that you believe are necessary.

18. Workers in two different industries were asked what they considered to be the most important labor-management problem in their industry. In industry A, which had a total of 20,000 workers, 200 out of a random sample of 400 felt that a fair adjustment of grievances was the most important problem. In industry B, which had a total of 30,000 workers, 70 out of a random sample of 100 workers felt that this was the most important problem.
a. Would you conclude that these two industries differed with respect to the proportion of workers who believed that a fair adjustment of grievances was the most important problem? Demonstrate statistically, giving a brief statement of your reasoning.
b. Draw a sketch of the probability distribution upon which your answer to part *a* depends. Show on the sketch the approximate positions of the values pertinent to the solution to the above problem.

19. The management of Bimbels Department Store wished to study aspects of the purchase patterns of customers of the New York and the San Francisco stores. In particular, it wished to know whether or not the proportion of items returned differed in these two stores. A random sample of sales slips accounting for 400 items was taken from the San Francisco store, and it was determined that 80 items had been returned. Similar data from sales slips of the New York store showed 250 of 1000 items returned.
a. Discuss briefly the manner in which the company attacked the problem, making sure to include the concepts of a statistical universe and a random sample.

(For the remainder of the question, assume that the procedure followed by the company was correct.)

   b. Using a 0.05 probability of a Type I error, would you conclude that the stores differed in the proportion of items returned?

   c. Explain precisely, in terms of this problem, what is meant by $\alpha = 0.05$.

   d. Did you compute a standard deviation in part b? If so, for what distribution is it a measure of dispersion?

20. An oil company has 100,000 active customer charge accounts. A motel owners association has proposed that the holders of these accounts be permitted to charge bills incurred at its motels on the oil company charge account.

   a. The oil company decides that unless evidence indicates that more than 20 percent of the account holders would use the privilege, charging motel bills should not be permitted. A random sample of 100 customers reveals 24 who would use the privilege. Should the company conclude that the parameter is more than 20 percent? Assume that it is willing to run a risk of 0.05 of erroneously reaching this conclusion.

   b. Suppose two persons disagreed about the level of significance that should have been used in part a. One urged a 0.05 level, the other a 0.10 level. Which person, if either, is correct? Why do they disagree?

   c. If the percentage who would use the privilege is actually 19, what is the probability that you will accept the hypothesis that you tested in part a?

   d. In the random sample of 100 charge customers, 30 percent had had a charge account with the company for five years or more. Using this information, construct an 80 percent confidence interval for the percentage of all charge customers who have had charge accounts for five years or more.

   e. Someone asserted that this sample of 100 is not large enough to estimate the mean age of all charge account customers to within one year. Explain why you agree or disagree with this assertion.

21. A prospective MBA student had narrowed his choice to two universities. He decided that the average starting salaries of the MBA graduates of the institutions were relevant to his decision. Simple random samples were selected from the recent MBA graduates of both schools, and the following statistics were obtained.

	School A	*School B*
Mean starting salary	8175	8155
Standard deviation of starting salaries	600	800
Sample size	100	100

a. Would you be willing to conclude that the mean starting salary of MBA graduates from School A is higher than that of MBA graduates from School B? Assume that you are willing to run a 1 percent risk of asserting the mean is higher at A when there is no difference in the universe means.

b. Draw a graph of the sampling distribution associated with part *a*. Label the horizontal axis; indicate the units employed; and show the location(s) of the statistic(s) observed, the hypothesized parameter, and the critical value(s) established by your decision rule.

c. Would your answer in part *a* have been different if you had been willing to accept a 5 percent probability of asserting the mean is higher at A when there is no difference in the universe means? Why?

22. In the manufacture of a space vehicle component, specifications of a mean heat resistance of at least 1650° and a standard deviation of 300°C were used. In a random sample of 100 components drawn from a particular shipment, a mean heat resistance of 1590° and a standard deviation of 300° were observed.

a. If we are willing to reject a good shipment no more than 1 time in 100, should the shipment be accepted? Justify statistically.

b. Using the same decision-making rules as in part *a*, what is the probability of making a Type II error for a shipment of components having a mean heat resistance of 1645° and a standard deviation of 300°?

c. In terms of the problem, what does this probability mean?

d. Express this probability as a definite integral.

23. a. In a simple random sample of 400 students in collegiate schools of business, 176 favored the addition of more required mathematics courses in the freshman and sophomore years. In a random sample of 600 students in colleges of liberal arts, 216 favored the addition of more required mathematics courses. Can you be reasonably sure (probability = 0.01) that the percentages of students in the two types of schools differed in their opinions on this subject?

b. Explain in terms of this problem the meaning of a Type I error.

24. A random sample of 225 families in City A revealed that 25 families had annual incomes over $8000. Another random sample of 225 families from City B contained 35 with annual incomes over $8000.

a. Would you be willing to conclude that a higher percentage of families in City B had incomes over $8000 than did families in City A? Justify your conclusion statistically, using a 0.01 level of significance.

b. Sketch the probability distribution that was relevant to your conclusion in part *a*. Label your sketch appropriately, showing all information about this distribution which you have determined in reaching your conclusion.

25. A buyer of widgets wishes to reject lots having more than 10 percent defective. He also is willing to assume a risk of 0.01 of rejecting good lots, that is, lots with 10 percent or less defective. He takes a random sample of 100 widgets from a lot of 100,000, and 11 of these 100 items are defective.
   a. Should he reject or accept the lot? Why?
   b. Suppose the lot, in reality, contained 12 percent defectives. Under the decision-making rules set up for part *a*, what is the probability of his making a Type I error? A Type II error?
   c. If this 12 percent defective lot is accepted, what is the probability that at least one of the first three widgets used will be defective?

26. In a certain year the mean interest rate on loans to all large retailers (that is, those with assets of $5,000,000 or more) was 6.0 percent and the standard deviation was 0.2 percent. Two years later, a random sample of 100 loans to large retailers yielded an arithmetic mean interest rate of 6.015 percent.
   a. Would you conclude that there has been a change in the average level of interest rates for large retailers? Assume you are willing to tolerate a 5 percent probability of concluding there has been a change when, in fact, there has been no change.
   b. Using the same decision-making rule as in part *a*, what is the probability of making a Type II error if the average interest rate for all large retailers was 6.01 percent? 5.99 percent?
   c. Explain in terms of this problem the meaning of the probabilities that you computed in part *b*.
   d. Three years after the original study, in a random sample of 81 large retailers, a mean interest rate of 6.1 percent and a standard deviation of 0.22 percent were observed. Construct a 90 percent confidence interval for the average interest rate paid by large retailers at that time.
   e. Do you think a sample of 81 is of sufficient size for part *d*? Why?
   f. Express the Type I error of this test as a definite integral.
   g. Express the power of this test as a definite integral if the mean interest rate on loans to large retailers is really 6.2 percent.

11 Statistical Decision Theory

11.1 INTRODUCTION

In Chapters 9 and 10 we introduced problems in which population characteristics were estimated and statements about them were checked. It was emphasized that inferential procedures are found not only in the textbook and the classroom. They are used daily by persons engaged in the study of practical problems in dozens of different areas. Furthermore, the reason for these studies is usually to provide a sound basis for action of some sort. This action may be taken by the researcher himself, by his employers, or by someone seeking his advice. It may be some definite step or, if the evidence appears inconclusive, it may take the form of suspending any action until more evidence is available. In other words, a major use of inference is to provide evidence useful in decision making. But we shall see later that statistics can contribute much more than this. It can, under certain circumstances, provide a structure through which a decision can be reached rationally. If this sounds like braggadocio, suspend judgment until the evidence is in—that is, until the next two chapters have been read.

If we define decision theory as that body of material that is useful in assisting a decision maker in choosing wisely among the alternatives open to him, we are speaking of a very large area. Much of the material included is not statistical nor even quantitative. For example, the selection of a wise decision may have strong psychological and/or sociological components. A decision that seems most desirable from the point of view of maximizing income may be an unhappy one because of personalities and policies involved. Witness the position of the moonlighting employee whose primary employer takes a dim view of second jobs. Nevertheless, there is a large body of statistical material that is highly relevant to decision processes. These topics are called "statistical decision theory." They have been touched upon in

Sections 9.2 and 10.5. They will be treated in some detail in this chapter and the next. As elsewhere we shall be emphasizing basic concepts.

Statistical decision theory is a relatively new area of study. Most of the important contributions have been made since 1945. As with most new subjects, additional ideas and constructs are being incorporated, and new ways of organizing the material are being tried out. A continuing controversy is in progress between decision theorists and other statisticians. The argument concerns both the validity of the concept of personalistic probability and the degree to which the decision-theory approach is useful in practice. Resolution of the second part of this dispute will take place only after a considerable period during which decision-theory methods are used extensively in the solution of actual problems. The theoretical argument is concerned with basic philosophy and may well go on indefinitely. In the meantime, the ideas seem to be provocative and revealing—particularly in the context of business activities.

Decision theory does not deny the validity of the traditional inferential procedures. Rather, it seeks to amplify them. As has already been pointed out, the selection of α is often unsatisfying. Decision theory attempts to clarify the process by bringing the costs of errors into the formal analysis. Also decision theory recognizes that valid decisions can often be made based on evidence that is not obtained from samples. Hence, it considers how this sort of information can be combined with sampling results to obtain a decision superior to the one that could have been reached by the use of either component alone. Use of the concept of utility allows the analysis to proceed in cases where it is difficult or impossible to attach dollar-and-cents cost estimates to the possible outcomes. All in all, it is fair to say that decision theory attempts to bring more refined instruments to bear on more general problems than does the traditional statistical approach.

Statistical decision theory considers situations in which the decision maker—an individual or a group—is faced with a choice among courses of action. It will be assumed in the sequel that all alternatives are known and, conceptually at least, can be listed. In some situations, such possibilities as "take no action whatever" or "hold off for two months" are legitimate entries on this list. The decision itself is the choice of an action. The action selected will be the one from the list that the decision maker feels is most likely to bring about whatever outcome he considers the most desirable.

Decisions are commonly classified according to the probabilistic environment of the possible actions.

1. If each action will inevitably lead to one particular outcome, the decision is made in an environment of *certainty*.

2. If each action will, with a known probability, lead to some element of a set of outcomes, the decision is made in an environment of *risk*.

3. If each action will lead to some element of a set of outcomes, but with unknown probability, the decision is made in an environment of *uncertainty*.

It is not difficult to see that decision making in an environment of certainty is conceptually the easiest of the three. One merely decides which possible outcome is the most desirable and opts for an action leading to it. At the other extreme, decision making is a more difficult business under uncertainty than under risk. Important information—the probabilities attaching to the outcomes—is available in the latter case but not in the former.

To point up the differences and the relative difficulty involved, let us return to the happy days of bold knights and fair ladies. We find ourselves at the castle of King Arthubad, as villainous a sovereign as was ever known. The king has three beautiful daughters. He has just announced that his daughters, each with one-third of his kingdom for a dowry, will be given away on the throw of a die! Suitors are invited to test their luck. Knights begin to arrive, and the first is Sir Lancelot. The king reads the ground rules to him. He is to throw a single die, once. If a six comes up, he receives a beautiful princess and a dowry. If a five appears, he is to be tarred, feathered, set backward on his horse, and drummed out of the castle gate. If four comes up, he will be drowned in the moat; if three, two, or one come up, he will be fed to the king's pet dragon for breakfast.

"Sir," declares Sir Lancelot, "this fateful game gladly will I play. It just happens that I have brought my dice with me."

"Hold! Forbear!" snarls Arthubad. "Thou must use my dice."

So, he places before Lancelot six large ivory cubes. (We might mention that Arthubad, second to none in evil intent, is rather on the stupid side.) The knight examines each cube carefully and notes that the first die has a one on each of its six sides, the second six twos, and so on until the sixth, each side of which bears a six. Lancelot, being no fool, selects the last die, calmly rolls a six, marries the fair lady, relieves the baffled king of one-third of his kingdom, and retires to live the good life that always awaits those fortunate ones who can make important decisions in an environment of certainty.

King Arthubad is furious. He takes the six dice and hurls them into the moat. He then goes to his large dice collection and selects six others. The first has 5 sixes and a one; the second has 4 sixes, a one, and a two; the third has 3 sixes, a one, a two, and a three; the fourth has 2 sixes, a one, a two, a three, and a four; the fifth and sixth are the usual types with one of each number showing.

Enter Sir Galahad in quest of daughter number two. After a lengthy verbal exchange, he examines the dice, selects the one that has 5 sixes and the one on its faces, rolls a six, marries the lass, divests the outraged Arthubad of another third of his kingdom, and retires to lead the good life that sometimes comes to those careful planners who often do rather well when making important decisions in an environment of risk.

King Arthubad is livid—more dice go in the moat accompanied by a few snickering men at arms. He calls in a wandering statistical consultant named Merlin who recommends the use of off-center, irregular seven-sided polyhedra with weighted faces. They are all different and there are few sixes on any of them.

Comes a knock on the portal. Enter Sir Gawain with great eagerness. The ground rules are read. The dice are produced. Gawain examines them in consternation. He seems unable to make a selection, fingering the six outrageous dice until, to make a short story shorter, he suffers a sudden apoplectic stroke and dies on the spot. Needless to say, the dragon gets him for breakfast. Arthubad keeps the last third of his kingdom, and bestows his remaining daughter on the consultant, Merlin. Thus some statisticians live happily ever after, but hard is the lot of the decision maker who must choose his actions in an environment of uncertainty.

But let us return to the 20th century and its problems. There is no need to discuss further the question of how to make decisions in an environment of either certainty or risk. The student can easily choose the action leading invariably to the outcome that he desires when certainty obtains. Or, in the second environment, he can choose the action that maximizes the probability of obtaining the desired outcome. But the remaining case, decision making under uncertainty, is trickier. It has "done in" not only Sir Gawain, but also a whole host of generals, speculators, politicians, entrepreneurs, athletes, college sophomores, and men on the street. We shall now approach this problem.

11.2   DECISION MAKING UNDER UNCERTAINTY—
TWO STATES OF NATURE

As an aid to the development of the ideas briefly stated in Section 9.2, we shall introduce a particular problem. By following the Resource Development Corporation's decision processes, we shall be able to keep our attention centered as we digress occasionally to discuss related material.

The Resource Development Corporation (RDC) is interested in the production of uranium. It holds a lease that will shortly expire on a large tract of land in the Mackenzie District of Canada. It will be unprofitable for

RDC to renew the lease unless it intends to begin large-scale mining operations. Thus, a decision will shortly be made between two alternative courses of action:

A_0: Renew the lease, and commence mining operations

A_1: Give up the lease, and abandon plans for mining

Now, if the ore is high-grade (more than one part uranium per 500 parts pitchblende) it can be extracted by a standard process. However, if the ore is low-grade (less than one part uranium per 500 parts pitchblende), a more expensive special process must be installed. The corporation executives have agreed that it is not economically feasible to install the special process so that, if the ore is really low-grade, the corporation will wish to give up the lease. Thus the correctness of the decision to be made depends on an unknown quantity, the richness of the ore deposits. Such a quantity in a decision-theory context is called a "state of nature." Here, there are two states of nature:

θ_0: Low-grade ore

θ_1: High-grade ore

In order to make a correct decision, the decision maker—that is, the executives of RDC—need information regarding which state of nature actually prevails in the Mackenzie backwoods.

When decision theory is used, gains, losses, or both, appear explicitly in the analysis. The executives of RDC can prepare rough estimates of the total profit expected to accrue from the mining operation under each decision and state of nature. Note the difficulty involved in making these estimates; at worst, they may be sheer guesses. Nevertheless, they are the best guesses available and should be used as inputs to the problem. Estimated total profits over the life of the Mackenzie mining operation are shown in Table 11.1— called a payoff table.

Table 11.1 Estimated Mining Profits (Millions of Dollars)

		State of Nature	
Action		Low-Grade θ_0	High-Grade θ_1
Renew lease	A_0	−10	15
Abandon lease	A_1	0	0

Notice that it is possible to formulate this problem in terms of more than two states of nature, since all high-grade ores will not yield the same profits nor will all low-grade ores. One could consider four states of nature:

θ_0': Ore containing less than one part uranium in 1000 parts pitchblende
θ_1': Ore containing between one part in 1000 and one part in 500
θ_2': Ore containing between one part in 500 and one part in 250
θ_3': Ore containing more than one part uranium in 250 parts pitchblende

In this case, estimated total profits over the life of the mine might be those shown by Table 11.2.

Table 11.2   Estimated Mining Profits (Millions of Dollars)—Four States of Nature

		State of Nature			
Action		θ_0'	θ_1'	θ_2'	θ_3'
Renew lease	A_0	-20	-7	5	30
Abandon lease	A_1	0	0	0	0

It would be perfectly possible to consider many more states of nature. Where should one stop? There can be no hard and fast rule, but two points are relevant. It is not wise to enlarge the number of states of nature to the extent that experts cannot assign separate payoffs to different states. Also, the greater the number of states of nature, the more difficult is the analysis of the problem. At present we shall consider only the two states of nature θ_0 and θ_1 with payoffs as shown in Table 11.1.

Later in this chapter we shall be considering the idea of utility, a concept that will be helpful in cases where the estimation of profits or losses in monetary terms is difficult or impossible. In such situations, individuals or groups often have fairly concrete ideas as to the relative worth of outcomes, which they are willing to express in some quantitative form—although not in dollars and cents. Indeed, in view of the obvious difficulties involved in giving the two estimates, $-\$10,000,000$ and $+\$15,000,000$ in the A_0 row of Table 11.1, the present problem might well be attacked in terms of utility measures. However, we defer such analysis.

Whether utility or monetary measures are used, it is convenient to work with losses rather than with profits; furthermore, it is customary to adopt a scale of measurement that assigns zero to the most favorable outcome. Table 11.3 shows Table 11.1 when transformed in this fashion. This procedure eliminates all negative numbers from the succeeding calculations.

Table 11.3   Estimated Mining Losses: Differences from $15,000,000 (Millions of Dollars)

		State of Nature	
		Low-Grade	High-Grade
Action		θ_0	θ_1
Renew lease	A_0	25	0
Abandon lease	A_1	15	15

In effect, it compares the actually realized profit with that which would have been obtained if the optimal decision had been made under the most favorable state of nature. Thus, the "losses" used throughout this chapter are the economist's *opportunity losses*. An opportunity loss of zero implies an optimal decision, and any other entry (which must be positive) indicates that a different action would have resulted in a greater loss. Note that a positive opportunity loss may still mean an over-all profit, for example, a figure of 10 in Table 11.3 would mean an estimated profit of $5 million.

The decision for or against renewal of the lease is an important one to RDC, and must not be made by a flip of a coin. The executives need evidence regarding the probable state of nature. The situation is not unlike that studied previously under hypothesis testing, for instance, in the case where $H_0: \mu \leq \mu_0$ was considered against the alternative $H_1: \mu > \mu_0$. In that situation, to provide evidence for a choice, a random sample was taken. Some analogous evidence-producing procedure is needed here, although formal random sampling is not appropriate. (Why?)

Time is short. A consulting geologist, Dr. C. V. O'Neill, is approached. He is a specialist with experience in pitchblende and carnotite, who possesses a good professional reputation. He agrees to collect a small party, fly to Canada, make a superficial check on the leased property, and report to RDC. He states that his report will be one of the following four statements.

y_0: Ore is definitely high-grade
y_1: Ore is likely to be high-grade
y_2: Ore is likely to be low-grade
y_3: Ore is definitely low-grade

These statements are, of course, couched in terms of average yield. A much more detailed report would be requested following a thorough survey, but Dr. O'Neill customarily uses statements like the foregoing in reporting "quick-and-dirty" judgments.

Dr. O'Neill's work is well known to the RDC executives. He has worked many times for RDC and its competitors. Thus, the executives have experience in evaluating his predictions. They have definite feelings concerning the probability of an O'Neill estimate being correct. These probabilities are summed up in Table 11.4 and refer to brief surveys of the type undertaken here.

Table 11.4 Probability of Receiving a Report Y from Dr O'Neill When θ Is the Actual State of Nature

		State of Nature	
Report		Low-Grade θ_0	High-Grade θ_1
Definitely high-grade	y_0	0.0	0.6
High-grade likely	y_1	0.1	0.2
Low-grade likely	y_2	0.1	0.1
Definitely low-grade	y_3	0.8	0.1

We see that, in general, the executives think well of the geologist's predictive ability. They feel, however, that he is slightly less helpful in evaluating high-grade deposits than otherwise. A tendency away from rose-colored spectacles is suspected. At this point, we should notice that Dr. O'Neill's report is a random variable Y; Table 11.4 shows two probability functions for Y, one for each possible state of nature. The probabilities are conditional. In the first row, first column, we have $f(y_0 \mid \theta_0)$; the probability that Dr. O'Neill will report definitely high-grade pitchblende, given that the deposits are low-grade. What would happen to the probabilities of Table 11.4 if Dr. O'Neill stayed six months in the leased area?

Next, RDC must decide what step it will take when the O'Neill report is received. Suppose he reports "low-grade likely." Should the company then abandon the lease even though the report may be in error? This is a ticklish question. The corporation must adopt a strategy; that is, it must decide which available action to take for each possible form of the report. One intuitively appealing strategy is to renew the lease if the report is "definitely high-grade" or "high-grade likely" and to let it lapse in case the report is "definitely low-grade" or "low-grade likely." This strategy is shown by Table 11.5. We shall call it s_5.

Table 11.5   Strategy s_5: RDC problem

Report	Action
y_0	A_0
y_1	A_0
y_2	A_1
y_3	A_1

In sending the geologist to Canada and receiving his report, the company is conducting an experiment with four outcomes: y_0, y_1, y_2, and y_3. Viewed in this light, a strategy is a function whose domain is the set of all possible outcomes and whose range is the set of all possible actions. Table 11.6 lists all

Table 11.6   Possible Strategies, RDC Problem

Report	Strategy															
	s_0	s_1	s_2	s_3	s_4	s_5	s_6	s_7	s_8	s_9	s_{10}	s_{11}	s_{12}	s_{13}	s_{14}	s_{15}
y_0	A_0	A_0	A_0	A_0	A_1	A_0	A_0	A_0	A_1	A_1	A_1	A_1	A_1	A_1	A_0	A_1
y_1	A_0	A_0	A_0	A_1	A_0	A_0	A_1	A_1	A_0	A_0	A_1	A_1	A_1	A_0	A_1	A_1
y_2	A_0	A_0	A_1	A_0	A_0	A_1	A_0	A_1	A_0	A_1	A_0	A_1	A_0	A_1	A_1	A_1
y_3	A_0	A_1	A_0	A_0	A_0	A_1	A_1	A_0	A_1	A_0	A_0	A_0	A_1	A_1	A_1	A_1

$2^4 = 16$ strategies that RDC may adopt, pending the receipt of Dr. O'Neill's report. How many would be available in the case of three experimental outcomes and five actions? Be sure to understand that, with m outcomes and n actions, there would be n^m strategies available.

Some of these strategies have a strange appearance. Strategies s_{10} and s_{11} lead to actions diametrically opposed to those suggested by the geologist's findings. They seem inappropriate, in view of the evaluation of Dr. O'Neill's ability shown in Table 11.4. Strategies s_0 and s_{15} ignore Dr. O'Neill's report. Their use might be appropriate if the executives had made up their minds on the basis of other evidence—or if they had discovered that he had spent his time at the bar of the Hotel Muskrat in Saskatoon instead of in the Mackenzie fastnesses. Such strategies as s_1, s_5, and s_{14}, appear to be rational, with s_5, as previously stated, having the most intuitive appeal.

In order to compare the desirability of the competing strategies, we shall turn to the concept of expected value, computing the expected loss $E(L)$ for each strategy under each state of nature. Table 11.7 gives detailed computations for s_5 and s_{11} and Table 11.8 is a summary of corresponding results for

Table 11.7 Computation of Expected Losses for s_5 and s_{11}: RDC Problem (Millions of Dollars)

		s_5				s_{11}			
		θ_0		θ_1		θ_0		θ_1	
		Estimated Loss	$f(y \mid \theta_0)$	Estimated Loss	$f(y \mid \theta_1)$	Estimated Loss	$f(y \mid \theta_0)$	Estimated Loss	$f(y \mid \theta_1)$
Action	A_0	25	0.1	0	0.8	25	0.8	0	0.1
	A_1	15	0.9	15	0.2	15	0.2	15	0.9
	$E(L)$	16.0		3.0		23.0		13.5	

$$E(L \mid \theta_0) = 25(0.1) + 15(0.9) = 16.0 \qquad E(L \mid \theta_0) = 25(0.8) + 15(0.2) = 23.0$$
$$E(L \mid \theta_1) = 0(0.8) + 15(0.2) = 3.0 \qquad E(L \mid \theta_1) = 0(0.1) + 15(0.9) = 13.5$$

all strategies. In calculating the expected losses for s_5, the estimated losses are first copied from Table 11.3. Then the accompanying conditional probabilities are obtained as follows. Referring to Table 11.6, we find that s_5 results in A_0, whenever y_0 or y_1 is reported. From Table 11.4, it is seen that y_0 or y_1 will be reported with probability 0.1 when θ_0 is true. Hence $f(y \mid \theta_0)$ is 0.1, the figure entered for $f(y \mid \theta_0)$ in the A_0 row for s_5. The student should check all the remaining conditional probabilities for both s_5 and s_{11}. He should also carry through a computation checking the expected loss for another strategy in Table 11.8. The contents of Table 11.8 are shown graphically in Figure 11.1.

Table 11.8 Summary of Expected Losses for All Strategies, RDC Problem (Millions of Dollars)

State of Nature	Strategy							
	s_0	s_1	s_2	s_3	s_4	s_5	s_6	s_7
θ_0	25.0	17.0	24.0	24.0	25.0	16.0	16.0	23.0
θ_1	0.0	1.5	1.5	3.0	9.0	3.0	4.5	4.5

	s_8	s_9	s_{10}	s_{11}	s_{12}	s_{13}	s_{14}	s_{15}
θ_0	17.0	24.0	24.0	23.0	16.0	16.0	15.0	15.0
θ_1	10.5	10.5	12.0	13.5	13.5	12.0	6.0	15.0

Since the RDC is interested in avoiding losses, it should consider those strategies most desirable for which $E(L \mid \theta_0) = L_0$ and $E(L \mid \theta_1) = L_1$ are both relatively small. Thus, s_1, s_5, s_6, and s_{14} recommend themselves. But if the executives knew that θ_1 (high-grade pitchblende) was going to occur, they would certainly choose s_0. If low-grade ore, θ_0, were certain, either s_{14} or s_{15} would be picked. Notice how helpful Figure 11.1 is in separating reasonably good strategies from obviously bad ones. However, such a vague

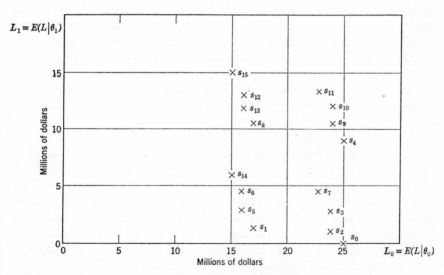

Fig. 11.1. Expected losses for all strategies—RDC problem.

dichotomy is not too helpful for the purposes of decision making. The RDC is seeking a unique strategy, which is, in some sense, optimal. As soon as Dr. O'Neill's report is received, an action will be taken, and this should be the action expected to lead to the smallest losses. It is fairly clear that we have gone about as far as we can go with the apparatus at hand. The next job is to develop new concepts that will prove helpful in dealing with the problem of defining and choosing an optimal strategy.

11.3   ADMISSIBLE STRATEGIES—TWO STATES OF NATURE

We shall first investigate a way of comparing strategies—which we shall think of as identical with the points representing them. We start with a formal definition.

Definition.   Let s_a and s_b be two strategies identified by their coordinates in terms of expected losses, that is, $s_a = (L_{0a}, L_{1a})$; $s_b = (L_{0b}, L_{1b})$. If s_a and s_b are *distinct* strategies such that $L_{0a} \leq L_{0b}$, and $L_{1a} \leq L_{1b}$, then s_a is said to dominate s_b.

Thus, if s_a and s_b are distinct, s_a dominates s_b whenever s_a's expected loss under either state of nature does not exceed the corresponding expected loss for s_b. This implies that s_a lies below s_b and to the left of it on a diagram such as Figure 11.1. Examining that figure, we note that s_8 dominates s_{11}—and, hence, is preferable to s_{11} no matter which state of nature prevails. Estimated dollar losses are the yardstick, and s_{11} will always exceed s_8 in generating these. Also s_{15} is dominated by s_{14}, and s_2 neither dominates s_5 nor is dominated by it. The reader should check Figure 11.1 and discover that, of the 16 strategies, only s_0, s_1, s_5, and s_{14} are dominated by no other strategy.

The set of all undominated strategies in a decision problem is called the set of admissible strategies, W. We have shown that s_0, s_1, s_5, and s_{14} are elements of W and, it appears that W has no other elements. This is not true; there are other strategies available to the RDC. Before discussing W further, we must introduce them.

Suppose that the executives have narrowed the field to s_1 and s_5. One group is battling for s_1, while another faction is holding out for s_5. Eventually both sides are worn down to the compromise point. It is agreed that a single die will be rolled; if an odd number results, s_1 will be adopted; if an even number s_5 will be chosen. Here is a new sort of strategy based on a randomizing procedure. It is called a mixed strategy to distinguish it from the original 16— which are commonly called pure strategies. Let us see if we can locate this new strategy, s_{16}, on Figure 11.1.

This is easy. The die selects s_1 and s_5, each with probability 1/2. The expected losses from s_{16} under θ_0 and θ_1 are

$$L_{0,16} = \frac{1}{2} L_{0,1} + \frac{1}{2} L_{0,5} = \frac{1}{2}(17.0) + \frac{1}{2}(16.0) = 16.5$$

$$L_{1,16} = \frac{1}{2} L_{1,1} + \frac{1}{2} L_{1,5} = \frac{1}{2}(1.5) + \frac{1}{2}(3.0) = 2.25$$

Strategy s_{16} is then represented by the midpoint of the line joining s_1 and s_5—a not unexpected result. Suppose that the randomizing process was weighted so as to choose s_1 when the die showed 1 and s_5 otherwise. The resulting mixed strategy, s_{17}, would be represented by a point 5/6 of the linear distance from s_1 to s_5. The general result is easy to obtain, as is shown in the next paragraph.

Let s_a and s_b be two distinct pure strategies. Let s_m be a mixed strategy generated by a randomizing process which chooses s_a and s_b with probabilities p and $1 - p$, respectively. Then s_m is represented by a point $100(1 - p)$ percent of the linear distance from s_a to s_b. To establish this result, simply refer to Theorem F.1 of Appendix F. In this standard bit of analytic geometry, replace A_1 by s_a, and A_2 by s_b. Define s_m to be that point whose coordinates are

$$(pL_{0a} + [1 - p]L_{0b}, pL_{1a} + [1 - p]L_{1b})$$

Then Theorem F.1 shows that s_m lies on the "join" of s_a and s_b and that the ratio of the distance between s_a and s_m to the distance between s_a and s_b is $1 - p$.

To see how this procedure operates, consider the previously mentioned randomizing process which chooses s_1 with probability 1/6 and s_5 with probability 5/6. Strategy s_{17} will have the coordinates

$$L_{0,17} = \frac{1}{6} L_{0,1} + \frac{5}{6} L_{0,5} = \frac{1}{6}(17.0) + \frac{5}{6}(16.0) = 16.17$$

$$L_{1,17} = \frac{1}{6} L_{1,1} + \frac{5}{6} L_{1,5} = \frac{1}{6}(1.5) + \frac{5}{6}(3.0) = 2.75$$

Furthermore s_{17} is declared to be $100(1 - p) = 83.33$ percent of the distance from s_1 to s_5, as may be easily verified in Figure 11.1.

Again, suppose that a strategy s_{18} was to be employed which randomly chose s_{12} 10 percent of the time and s_{11} the remaining 90 percent. This would not be a very enlightened mixed strategy in view of our discussion of dominance. s_{18} has coordinates:

$$L_{0,18} = \frac{1}{10} L_{0,12} + \frac{9}{10} L_{0,11} = \frac{1}{10}(16.0) + \frac{9}{10}(23.0) = 22.3$$

$$L_{1,18} = \frac{1}{10} L_{1,12} + \frac{9}{10} L_{1,11} = \frac{1}{10}(13.5) + \frac{9}{10}(13.5) = 13.5$$

By which pure strategies is s_{18} dominated?

Also note that, in view of Theorem F.2, any point on the join of two pure strategies s_a and s_b represents a mixed strategy s_m. The generating probability for s_m corresponds to the ratio in which the distance between s_b and s_m stands to the distance between s_a and s_b.

It is now apparent that instead of the 16 pure strategies, shown in Table 11.8 and Figure 11.1, the RDC executives can call on infinitely many strategies. We have shown that all points on all lines joining pairs of pure strategies represent random mixtures of these strategies. A similar proof shows that a random mixture of three pure strategies represents a point lying within the triangle determined by these strategies. Conversely, any point within such a triangle can be shown to give rise to a mixture of three pure strategies, the randomization process being determined by the position of the point within the triangle. We shall now recast Figure 11.1 in such a way as to show mixed as well as pure strategies.

Figure 11.2 is constructed by drawing the

$$\binom{16}{2} = \frac{16 \cdot 15}{2 \cdot 1} = 120$$

joins connecting all possible pairs of pure strategies in Figure 11.1. Any point on these joins or enclosed by them represents a possible pure or mixed strategy for the RDC executives. The set of all such points is called the

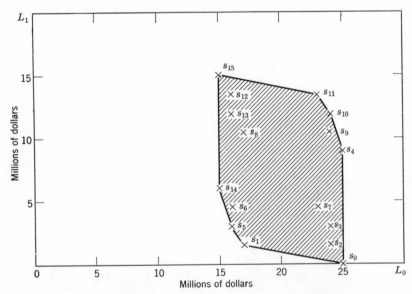

Fig. 11.2. Convex hull of the set of pure strategies—RDC problem.

convex hull of the set of pure strategies and is shown by the shaded area in Figure 11.2. Convex hulls are one special case of an important class of sets: the convex sets. Before proceeding further, Appendix G on convex sets should be studied.

H, the convex hull of the pure strategies, is a closed convex set. Hence it contains its own boundary. This boundary is its border, since the border of its complement is empty. The boundary of the convex hull is then the polygon formed by those pure strategies which are limit points of $E_2 - H$, taken with those joins of these pure strategies which also consist of limit points of $E_2 - H$. (Remember that E_2 is the Euclidean plane; see Appendix G.)

Let us return to the concept of admissible strategies. In terms of pure strategies, we had defined admissible strategies to be those that were not dominated by any other pure strategy. Let us broaden this concept in the natural way. Henceforth an admissible strategy, pure or mixed, will simply be an undominated strategy. Now that we have located the set of all possible strategies as forming the convex hull of the set of pure strategies, let us locate the admissible strategies in Figure 11.2. Any point that has another point of H lying "due south, due west, or generally southwest" of it represents a dominated strategy, and is inadmissible. Thus the set of admissible strategies forms the "southwest" boundary of the convex hull. In Figure 11.2, the set of admissible strategies is composed of s_0, s_1, s_5, s_{14}, all points on the join of s_0 and s_1, all points on the join of s_1 and s_5, and all points on the join of s_5 and s_{14}. Summing up, the set of admissible strategies in a decision problem involving two states of nature is the undominated subset of the boundary of the convex hull of the set of pure strategies.

11.4 MINIMAX EXPECTED LOSS STRATEGIES

In the RDC problem we know that the corporation should adopt one of the admissible strategies. Any other strategy would be dominated by one or more admissible strategies. But which of these admissibles should be adopted? In this section we shall discuss one possible systematic method for making this choice—the principle of minimax expected loss. A pleasant feature of this method is that it requires no information beyond that already discussed. However, it is probably too pessimistic an approach to decision making for across-the-board use. It suspects that the worst possible state of nature will prevail and takes steps to control losses in that case.

Specifically, the minimax expected loss decision principle states that the decision maker should examine each strategy and determine the largest expected loss that can occur if that strategy is used. Then, comparing all strategies, he should adopt one for which the maximum expected loss is as small as possible.

Referring to Table 11.8, we see that of the 16 pure strategies, the ones that minimize the maximum expected loss are s_{14} and s_{15}. Indeed, for any other pure strategy, the expected loss under θ_0, low-grade ore, will exceed $15,000,000. But since this procedure does not take mixed strategies into consideration, it needs to be extended.

From an examination of Figure 11.2, we can see that at any point on the join of s_{14} and s_{15} the expected losses are respectively $15,000,000 under θ_0 and some figure between $6,000,000 and $15,000,000 under θ_1. Thus, the complete set of minimax expected loss strategies is composed of s_{14}, s_{15}, and points on their join.

Look-and-see procedures may be fine for the RDC problem with its two states of nature and limited number of pure strategies, but for more complex problems visual examination would be tedious at best. Even in situations with few pure strategies the visual comparison method will break down when the set of minimax expected loss strategies consists, as it often does, of a single mixed strategy. A geometric procedure, which can be generalized to problems involving n states of nature, is readily available.

Let us consider Figure 11.3. H is the set of all possible strategies. Let j be the 45° half-line drawn through the first quadrant. Its equation is $L_1 - L_0 = 0$. For points lying to the northwest of j we have $L_1 - L_0 > 0$, that is, $L_1 > L_0$. For points lying to the southeast of j, we have $L_1 - L_0 < 0$, that is, $L_1 < L_0$. We wish to determine that set of points of H whose largest coordinate is as small as possible. For points northwest of j, this is L_1; for points southeast of j, it is L_0; for points on j, both coordinates are equal.

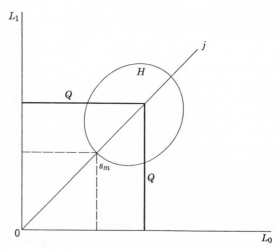

Fig. 11.3. Minimax expected loss strategy.

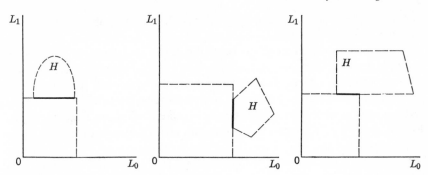

Fig. 11.4. Various minimax expected loss sets.

Now any point on the union of the north and east boundaries of a square based on the origin, the L_0-axis, and the L_1-axis will have the same maximum coordinate. One such set of points is Q, the heavily-lined set in Figure 11.3.

Any point lying to the north or east, or both north and east of Q will have a maximum coordinate (that is, maximum expected loss) greater than the points of Q. Any point lying south or west, or south and west of Q will have a smaller maximum expected loss, and hence will be a more desirable strategy according to the minimax principle. Determine, then, the smallest square based on the origin, the L_0-axis, and the L_1-axis whose boundary contains points of the boundary of H. These points will have a maximum expected loss smaller than all other points of H, hence they will be the desired minimax expected loss strategies for the problem in question. In Figure 11.3, s_m is the sole minimax expected value strategy. Figure 11.4 shows other cases in which the minimax set has a different appearance. In all cases it is easy to find this set. One simply moves up the 45°-line dropping perpendiculars to both axes until tangency with H is obtained. Be sure to understand that the minimax set is usually a subset of the set of all admissible strategies. When is it not? In any case, at least one minimax strategy must be admissible.

In the RDC problem the smallest square to have contact with the set of all possible strategies (see Figure 11.2) is the one whose sides are $L_0 = 15,000,000$ and $L_1 = 15,000,000$. This contains s_{14}, s_{15}, and their join, as we saw intuitively some paragraphs ago, with s_{14} constituting the intersection of the minimax set and the set of admissible strategies. Hence RDC should adopt s_{14} if it is using a minimax decision criterion. Further examples of minimax expected loss strategies will be given in later sections of this chapter.

11.5 BAYES STRATEGIES

The minimax expected loss principle represents one systematic way of resolving the question, "Which admissible strategy should I choose?"

There are other ways of approaching this problem, and we shall now examine one that is widely accepted.

Thomas Bayes was an English clergyman of the 18th century who dabbled in mathematics. After his death, an unpublished probability theorem was found among his effects. This theorem, stated and proved in Chapter 12, gives a systematic way of finding certain conditional probabilities. Since this procedure is closely related to the way expected losses are handled in this section, the set of strategies that we are about to define is called the set of *Bayes strategies*.

It must be specified that, unlike the minimax procedure, selection of a Bayes strategy depends upon the availability of more information than we have thus far assumed. In order to use Bayesian methods we must have some knowledge of the probability that each state of nature will actually obtain. We must have such information prior to the experimenting or sampling phase, for example, sending Dr. O'Neill to Canada. Hence these probabilities are called *a priori* probabilities. Excellent estimates of a priori probabilities may sometimes be obtained; however, it is common in practical situations to work with estimates that leave something to be desired. If no estimates can be made of the a priori probabilities of the several states of nature, then Bayesian procedures will be of no help in making the decision.

Suppose, in the RDC problem, as is very likely, that the Corporation had complete data available on the geology of known Canadian uranium deposits. Suppose these data show that about 75 percent of known Canadian pitchblende is low-grade, with the remainder being high-grade. Then, before Dr. O'Neill is dispatched northward, RDC might well estimate the probabilities of high-grade and low-grade ore respectively as $P(\theta_0) = 3/4$ and $P(\theta_1) = 1/4$. Let us now see how this additional knowledge affects RDC's expected losses.

Consider s_5 whose expected losses are

$$L_0 = E(L \mid \theta_0) = 16 \text{ (millions of dollars)}$$

$$L_1 = E(L \mid \theta_1) = 3 \text{ (millions of dollars)}$$

About three-forths of the time we would expect θ_0 to obtain, with θ_1 occurring otherwise. Hence the expected loss using the a priori probabilities of θ_0 and θ_1 is found to be, for s_5,

$$E(L \mid f(\theta)) = 16\left(\frac{3}{4}\right) + 3\left(\frac{1}{4}\right) = 12.75$$

The symbol "given $f(\theta)$" is used to emphasize that the a priori probabilities are estimated for all possible states of nature, and thus constitute a probability distribution whose domain is the set of states of nature represented as real numbers. For s_{11}, the losses are

$L_0 = 23$ (millions of dollars)   and $L_1 = 13.5$ (millions of dollars)

The corresponding overall expected loss is

$$E(L \mid f(\theta)) = 23\left(\frac{3}{4}\right) + 13.5\left(\frac{1}{4}\right) = 20.625$$

Such an expected loss that combines all states of nature can be found for each of the possible strategies. We shall shortly perform these computations, but first let us formulate the concept of a Bayes strategy.

This is easily done. We have just seen that under the assumption of an a priori probability distribution of the states of nature, a single expected loss may be computed for each strategy. A Bayes strategy is one for which this loss is as small as possible. More succinctly, for a given a priori probability distribution $f(\theta)$ of the states of nature, a Bayes strategy is one that

Table 11.9 Values of $E(L \mid f(\theta))$ for the Pure Strategies of the RDC Problem (Millions of Dollars)

Strategy	s_0	s_1	s_2	s_3	s_4	s_5	s_6	s_7
$E(L \mid f(\theta))$	18.75	13.12	18.38	18.75	21.00	12.75	13.12	18.38

Strategy	s_8	s_9	s_{10}	s_{11}	s_{12}	s_{13}	s_{14}	s_{15}
$E(L \mid f(\theta))$	15.38	20.62	21.00	20.62	15.38	15.00	12.75	15.00

minimizes $E[L \mid f(\theta)]$. In the case we are discussing, where only two states of nature are possible, we shall represent $P(\theta_0)$ by P_0 and $P(\theta_1)$ by $1 - P_0$ to simplify the notation. Hence we are looking for that strategy that will minimize.

$$E[L \mid f(\theta)] = L_0 P_0 + L_1(1 - P_0)$$

Table 11.9 shows the expected losses for the pure strategies in the RDC problem when $P(\theta_0) = 3/4$ and $P(\theta_1) = 1/4$. As far as the pure strategies are concerned, s_5 and s_{14} are minimal. But we need to bring mixed strategies into the picture.

Appendix H should now be studied in order to become familiar with the ideas concerning support and separation discussed there. The three theorems presented are necessary for the development of a more thorough treatment of Bayes strategies. Our conclusions depend upon the following theorem which we prove in the case where there are but two states of nature.

THEOREM.   Every admissible strategy is a Bayes strategy for some a priori probability distribution of the states of nature.

Let H be the convex hull of the set of pure strategies S in a decision problem involving only two states of nature. Let s_a be an admissible strategy; $s_a = (L_{0a}, L_{1a})$ in terms of expected loss coordinates. Define a set T of points as

$$T = \{(L_0, L_1) \mid 0 < L_0 < L_{0a}, 0 < L_1 < L_{1a}\}$$

As is shown in Figure 11.5, T is the set of all points in the first quadrant which dominate s_a—with the boundary removed; that is, T is the set of points lying southwest of s_a and having positive coordinates. We emphasize that T is an open set and that s_a is not an element of T.

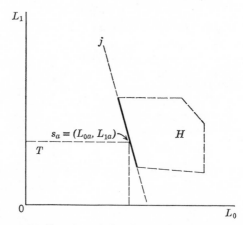

Fig. 11.5. Diagram showing the relation between sets H and T.

Now H, the convex hull is a convex set. Also T, being an open rectangle, must be convex. Since s_a is not in T, $H \cap T = \varnothing$. Then by Theorem H.3, there is a line that separates H and T. Call this line j. It must be that s_a is in j since, otherwise, j would include interior points of H, points of T, or perhaps both, and in none of these cases could it separate H and T.

If j separates H and T, j can contain only boundary points of H; otherwise, points of H would lie on both sides of j. Since j does contain at least one such boundary point, s_a, j supports H. Also, since s_a is in j but $j \cap T = \varnothing$, j cannot have a positive slope. Hence its equation can be written as

$$aL_1 + bL_0 = c \tag{11.1}$$

where a and b cannot have opposite signs. To show this last feature, rewrite the equation of j as

$$L_1 = -\frac{b}{a} L_0 + \frac{c}{a}$$

The slope of j is then $-b/a$, and if this is not to be positive, the signs of a and b must be the same. It follows then that $a + b \neq 0$ under any circumstances. Dividing (11.1) by $a + b$ yields

$$\frac{a}{a + b} L_1 + \frac{b}{a + b} L_0 = \frac{c}{a + b} \tag{11.2}$$

Consider the coefficients of L_1 and L_0 in (11.2).

$$\frac{a}{a + b} \leq 1 \qquad \frac{b}{a + b} \leq 1$$

and

$$\frac{a}{a + b} + \frac{b}{a + b} = 1$$

Let us denote $a/(a + b)$ by P_1, $b/(a + b)$ by P_0, and $c/(a + b)$ by c'. We have shown that for any admissible strategy s_a there exist two positive numbers P_0 and $P_1 = 1 - P_0$ such that the line j

$$(1 - P_0)L_1 + P_0 L_0 = c' \tag{11.3}$$

supports H at s_a. Furthermore, since j separates H from T with H lying above j and to the right,

$$(1 - P_0)L_1 + P_0 L_0 \geq c'$$

for all points (L_0, L_1) in H. Thus, no strategy in H can have a smaller expected loss $E[L \mid f(\theta)]$ than does s_a—given the particular $f(\theta)$ represented by P_0 for θ_0 and $P_1 = 1 - P_0$ for θ_1. This is precisely the statement that s_a is a Bayes strategy when the probability distribution of the two states of nature is as specified.

Using the preceding key theorem, we may easily work out a geometric method for determining the set of all Bayes strategies. Recall that in the minimax solution we first determined the geometrical figure which represented sets of points having their larger coordinate equal. The figure there was part of the boundary of a square. Here we ask: For what sort of figure are the expected losses, $E[L \mid f(\theta)]$, exactly equal—for a fixed $f(\theta)$?

A look at the theorem just proved, and particularly at (11.3), tells that a loss of c' is expected at any point (L_0, L_1) on j when P_0 is fixed. This means that these losses are equal along lines with slope $-P_0/(1 - P_0)$. From the family of lines with this slope, one simply selects the one nearest the origin that contains points of H. $E[L \mid f(\theta)]$ will be minimal for points in the intersection of H and this line. Figure 11.6 illustrates this procedure for the RDC problem with $P_0 = P(\theta_0) = 3/4$; $P_1 = P(\theta_1) = 1/4$ where θ_0 is low-grade ore and θ_1 is high-grade ore. Lines for which the expected loss is constant are also shown. Their equations are

$$\frac{1}{4} L_1 + \frac{3}{4} L_0 = c'$$

and their slopes are

$$-\frac{3}{4} \bigg/ \frac{1}{4} = -3$$

It is apparent that the line j joining s_5 and s_{14} is the line of this family nearest the origin containing points of H. Thus, the set of Bayes strategies is $j \cap H$, that is, the points s_5 and s_{14} together with their join. This is consonant with the preliminary result obtained earlier in this section. To verify our result we show that the line joining s_5 and s_{14} really has slope -3, not -3.0002, for example. The coordinates of s_5 are $(16, 3)$ and of s_{14}, $(15, 6)$. Hence the slope required is

$$\frac{6 - 3}{15 - 16} = \frac{3}{-1} = -3$$

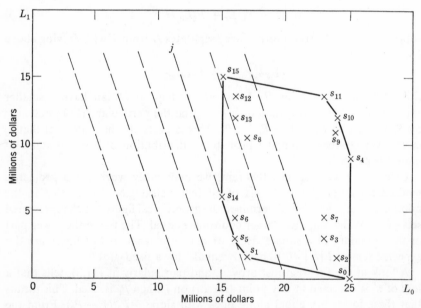

Fig. 11.6. Bayes strategies for the RDC problem.

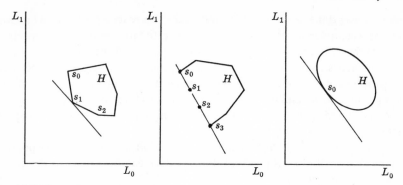

Fig. 11.7. Sets of Bayes strategies.

We are now in a position to show that for a given a priori probability distribution of the states of nature, any Bayes strategy is an admissible strategy. This follows at once since the line with negative slope lying closest to the origin and supporting H must touch H on its southwest flank. We have shown all points there to be admissible. The only exception occurs when either P_0 or P_1 is zero. If P_1 is zero, then j is a vertical line. Refer to Figure 11.6, and suppose that j is vertical. Then the Bayes set is s_{14}, s_{15}, and the points on their join while the admissible set is s_{14}, s_5, s_1, s_0, and the points on the joins of s_{14} and s_5, s_5 and s_1, and s_1 and s_0. However, there will always be a pure Bayes strategy among the admissible strategies, in this case, s_{14}.

Since the set of all Bayes strategies in a decision problem with two states of nature is the intersection $j \cap H$ of the convex hull of the set of pure strategies and one of its supporting lines, further conclusions can be drawn. Since the vertices of H are points of S, the set of pure strategies, there will always exist at least one pure strategy which is a Bayes strategy. Also any mixed Bayes strategy will always be obtainable as a mixture of pure Bayes strategies. To put it another way, the set $j \cap H$ must be either a vertex of H or the union of two vertices and their join. Of course, in this second case additional pure strategies may lie on the join. Figure 11.7 shows several typical situations. In the first and third drawings the set of Bayes strategies is a single pure strategy, while in the second drawing, there are four pure Bayes strategies—plus an infinite number of mixed Bayes strategies on the join of s_0 and s_3.

11.6 UTILITY

In discussing the RDC uranium decision, we mentioned several difficulties that arose. One of the touchiest was the question of estimating future profits or losses as was done in Tables 11.1 and 11.2. The reader probably wondered how the executives managed to place dollar estimates on future prospects as vague as these. If a mining entrepreneur had glanced at these tables, he would have directed strong language at those responsible. Nevertheless, the ideas and procedures have great value even when dollar estimates are unrealistic or impossible to formulate. This happy state of affairs is due to the concept of utility, an idea that allows the evaluation and comparison of prospects under very general conditions.

Suppose a decision is to be made. It may result in one of several possible actions. We shall not assume that dollar values can be affixed to the consequences of these actions.

Definition.   A utility function u is a function whose domain is the set of outcomes in a decision problem, whose range is the set of real numbers, and which satisfies the following two conditions for R_1 and R_2, the consequences of two distinct actions:

(1) $u(R_1) > u(R_2)$ if and only if the decision maker prefers R_1 to R_2.

(2) If R_0 is a mixed result where R_1 and R_2 will occur respectively with probabilities p and $1 - p$, then $u(R_0) = pu(R_1) + (1 - p)u(R_2)$.

The first condition is simple. It states that, if one result is more desirable to the decision maker than another, the function u assigns the larger real number to the more desirable result. The second condition states that the utility of a mixed result may always be computed as a weighted arithmetic mean of its component utilities. The existence of a utility function has been proved by von Neumann and Morgenstern—based on certain quite reasonable assumptions concerning the decision maker's preferences.[1]

Suppose that five-year old Susie Smith has been given an ultimatum by her sitter. "Either go to bed this minute, or I'll paddle you good!" Susie does not consciously assign probabilities to the results of her decision between conformity and defiance; however, if she had studied decision theory, she might do so. Perhaps immediate compliance could be given a utility, for example, of -4. The result of a few minutes of freedom followed by a spanking might be evaluated at -15, in which case Susie would scuttle up the stairs at once.

The actual numbers assigned to the two results are immaterial. We could assign $+1000$ to immediate obedience and $-50,000$ to recalcitrance. It only matters that if the first course of action is preferred to the second, then the first should be assigned the larger utility. Of course if Susie were devouring the contents of the jam jar, she might prefer the spanking to immediate withdrawal.

---

[1] When more than two results are possible, an interval scale must be employed for utility although the unit of measure is still immaterial.

Preferences for different results will vary from person to person. Suppose we propose the following experiment. We shall approach three individuals, one at a time, and offer each of them his choice of three objects: an original by Picasso, a $500 bill, or a cheese sandwich. The three individuals are a shipwrecked sailor, a shoe-shine boy, and the director of the local art museum. Preferences vary.

Not only do preferences for objects change from individual to individual, preferences for the same amount of money vary likewise. Suppose we devise a game whereby the player puts up $1000 to select a card from a deck. If he picks the ace of spades, he receives $520,000. If he does not, he loses his $1000. The expected value of the game is

$$\frac{1}{52}(520,000) + \frac{51}{52}(-1000) = \$9019$$

so that, off the cuff, we should think that any person with $1000 would be willing to play. But this is not true. Consider Joe Doakes with a debt of $1000, long overdue, and creditors about to take legal action. His great-aunt Hattie has just died and left him $1000. Should he play the game? We think most, but not all Joe Doakes, would refuse the opportunity. On the other hand, if his pressing debt were for $10,000, he should almost certainly play. Or perhaps the wealthy Joe Rockeman would not wish to play, since winning would put him in a much higher income bracket.

The relation between utility and money is an interesting one. It is a function of each individual. Nevertheless, patterns are apparent. For example, almost all individuals will assign large negative utility to large losses of money. Also as monetary values become very great, utility functions tend to level out—reflecting the smaller effect of the *second* million dollars on living conditions and aspirations. A typical function connecting utility and money would resemble the one shown in Figure 11.8. The curve passes through the origin, indicating that the individual concerned ascribes no utility to zero dollars. The scale on the vertical axis is arbitrary.

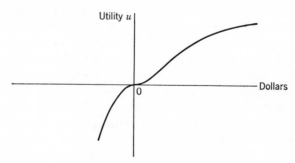

Fig. 11.8. A possible relation between money and utility.

Condition 2 of the definition of a utility function relates to the computation of an expected utility. One of two events must happen, and the a priori probability distribution of these is known. The force of this formula is to allow the calculation of expected utility by exactly the same procedure as is used for expected monetary value—one simply replaces losses by utilities. The expression may be easily generalized; if $R_1, \cdots, R_n$ is a mutually exclusive and exhaustive set of results occurring with probabilities $p_1, \cdots, p_n$, respectively, then the expected utility $u(R_0) = \sum_{i=1}^{n} p_i u(R_i)$ where R_0 is the mixed result.

Scholars have investigated the concept of utility until, at present, a large body of material, both theoretical and applied, is available. In this book we do no more than introduce the concept and a few simple properties. For our purposes, it suffices to know that it is often possible to evaluate results of decisions in terms of these more general units when monetary evaluation is either questionable or impossible. Then an expected utility may be found by a weighted mean procedure exactly parallel to the ordinary expected value computation.

11.7   THE EASY-CALM PROBLEM

The Rasmussen Pharmaceutical Company manufactures a variety of drugs. It is conducting research on a synthetic compound that acts as a specific for reducing high blood pressure. It will be marketed under the name, "Easy-Calm." Pilot plant production is now being instituted, and the drug is ready for controlled tests in animals—according to present government and industry specifications. It has been planned to complete these tests in six months and, if they are successful, to release Easy-Calm immediately to selected physicians. Large-scale production would then be initiated and, unless the physicians' reports were unfavorable, the product would enter the general market in another six months.

However, a committee of the Senate has recently reported favorably on legislation designed to regulate the drug industry more carefully than at present. One provision of the pending bill provides for an elaborate schedule of animal testing before any new drug is released for human usage. If the bill becomes law, present testing procedures in animals will be inadequate. It seems likely that final congressional action on this bill will take place about four to six months from the present time. There is strong opposition to the legislation, and the outcome is far from certain.

The decision concerning how to proceed with Easy-Calm must be made by Taft Hotchkiss, vice-president for research of the Rasmussen Company. To sit back and await congressional developments has been ruled out. There is no guarantee of congressional action, and competing companies are experimenting with similar compounds. Not only would Rasmussen lose its lead in marketing the product but also research and pilot plant facilities would be tied up for an indefinite period of time. Mr. Hotchkiss then has only three actions to consider:

A_0: Commence animal testing as currently required
A_1: Commence animal testing as required under the new bill
A_2: Discontinue all plans for marketing Easy-Calm

Under A_2 the company drops the project and accepts research costs to date as losses. Under A_0 the limited animal testing program, now standard, would be implemented at once. If the pending bill is killed in Congress, this is the best action. Under A_1 the extensive testing program is started immediately. If the bill is killed, this is a considerable extra expense. However, if the bill passes, the Rasmussen Company is far ahead, since if A_0 is adopted, a new animal testing program must be set up in addition to the current one. The states of nature are:

θ_0: Bill fails
θ_1: Bill passes

Mr. Hotchkiss is of a rather cautious disposition. He is not willing to make estimates of dollar profits and losses under the possible actions and states of nature. However, utility seems a reasonable concept to him. After much discussion, he accepts the utility structure given in Table 11.10. Of course, these are opportunity losses. The most promising contingency involves testing by the old standards followed by failure of the bill. Next most desirable to this is testing under the new requirements combined with passage of the

Table 11.10   Estimated Losses in Utility—Easy-Calm Problem

Action		State of Nature	
		Bill Fails θ_0	Bill Passes θ_1
Commence testing, current requirements	A_0	0	15
Commence testing, new requirements	A_1	10	2
Discontinue marketing plans	A_2	5	5

Table 11.11 Probability of Receiving a Report Y from Lobbyist When θ Is the Actual State of Nature

		State of Nature	
		Bill Fails θ_0	Bill Passes θ_1
Report			
Pass	y_0	0.3	0.9
Can't tell	y_1	0.3	0.1
Fail	y_2	0.4	0

bill. Simply giving up the project involves a constant, sizable loss in utility, but this is less disruptive than going ahead with the wrong testing program.

A hurried call is made to the company's Washington lobbyist, who is a fairly inaccurate predictive device when it comes to legislation. He will report either, "Pass," "Fail," or "Can't tell." Based on past performance, the relation between his predictions and actual legislative results is shown in Table 11.11. In the case of bills that pass, the lobbyist almost always has made correct predictions. But in the case of bills that fail, he calls the turn on only about 4 out of 10. Therefore, Mr. Hotchkiss has learned to analyze the lobbyist's ideas closely before acting upon them.

There are $n^m = 3^3$ possible strategies open to Mr. Hotchkiss, as shown in Table 11.12.

Table 11.12 Possible Strategies, Easy-Calm Problem

Strategy

Report	s_0	s_1	s_2	s_3	s_4	s_5	s_6	s_7	s_8	s_9	s_{10}	s_{11}	s_{12}	s_{13}
y_0	A_0	A_0	A_0	A_1	A_0	A_1	A_1	A_1	A_1	A_1	A_2	A_1	A_2	A_2
y_1	A_0	A_0	A_1	A_0	A_1	A_0	A_1	A_1	A_1	A_2	A_1	A_2	A_1	A_2
y_2	A_0	A_1	A_0	A_0	A_1	A_1	A_0	A_1	A_2	A_1	A_1	A_2	A_2	A_1

Report	s_{14}	s_{15}	s_{16}	s_{17}	s_{18}	s_{19}	s_{20}	s_{21}	s_{22}	s_{23}	s_{24}	s_{25}	s_{26}
y_0	A_2	A_2	A_2	A_0	A_2	A_0	A_0	A_0	A_0	A_1	A_1	A_2	A_2
y_1	A_2	A_2	A_0	A_2	A_0	A_2	A_0	A_1	A_2	A_2	A_0	A_0	A_1
y_2	A_2	A_0	A_2	A_2	A_0	A_0	A_2	A_2	A_1	A_0	A_2	A_1	A_0

Table 11.13 gives the expected losses in utility for each state of nature, and Figure 11.9 shows these results graphically.

From Table 11.13 and Figure 11.9, we first can write down the set of admissible strategies. This is composed of s_0, s_{18}, s_3, s_{23}, s_6 and the joins of s_0 and s_{18}, s_{18} and s_3, s_3 and s_{23}, s_{23} and s_6. We note that s_7 and s_8 are dominated by s_6. Which of the admissible strategies should the Rasmussen Company

Table 11.13 Summary of Expected Losses in Utility for All Strategies—Easy-Calm Problem

Strategy

State of Nature	s_0	s_1	s_2	s_3	s_4	s_5	s_6	s_7	s_8	s_9	s_{10}	s_{11}	s_{12}
θ_0	0	4	3	3	7	7	6	10	8	8.5	8.5	6.5	6.5
θ_1	15	15	13.7	3.3	13.7	3.3	2	2	2	2.3	4.7	2.3	4.7

State of Nature	s_{13}	s_{14}	s_{15}	s_{16}	s_{17}	s_{18}	s_{19}	s_{20}	s_{21}	s_{22}	s_{23}	s_{24}	s_{25}	s_{26}
θ_0	7	5	3	3.5	3.5	1.5	1.5	2	5	5.5	4.5	5	5.5	4.5
θ_1	5	5	5	6	14	6	14	15	13.7	14	2.3	3.3	6	4.7

choose? A minimaxer would consider squares based on the origin and the coordinate axes. He would thus select a mixed strategy lying on the join of s_3 and s_{23} quite close to s_3. Let us find its exact coordinates.

The line joining s_3 and s_{23} has the equation

$$L_1 - 3.3 = \frac{2.3 - 3.3}{4.5 - 3}(L_0 - 3)$$

or

$$L_0 + 1.5L_1 = 7.95 \tag{11.4}$$

We need that point on the line (11.4) for which the two coordinates are equal. Setting $L_1 = L_0$, we have

$$2.5L_0 = 7.95$$

$$L_0 = 3.18$$

Hence s_m, the minimax strategy, is given by the point (3.18, 3.18). What does this mean? The coordinates of s_3 and s_{23} are, respectively, (3, 3.3) and

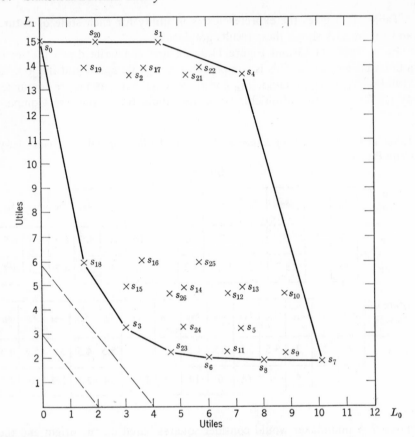

Fig. 11.9. Convex hull of the set of pure strategies—Easy-Calm problem.

(4.5, 2.3). Thus the ratio of the distance between s_3 and s_m to the distance between s_3 and s_{23} is found as

$$\frac{3.3 - 3.18}{3.3 - 2.3} = \frac{0.12}{1} = 0.12$$

by the properties of similar triangles. Hence s_m lies 0.12 of the distance from s_3 to s_{23}. The minimaxer should use a randomizing procedure which selects s_{23}, twelve-hundredths of the time and s_3 eighty-eight-hundredths of the time.

Mr. Hotchkiss is not one who always expects the worst. He feels that the Bayesian criterion is more realistic, and proceeds to employ it. His own considered opinion is that the legislation will probably pass by a close vote; he estimates the probabilities at

$$P_0 = P(\theta_0) = 0.6 \qquad P_1 = P(\theta_1) = 0.4$$

Thus, he is concerned with the family of lines in Figure 11.9 whose equation is

$$0.4L_1 + 0.6L_0 = c'$$

The slope of these lines is $-0.6/0.4 = -3/2$. It is evident that the line of this family nearest the origin which has points in common with the convex hull of the set of pure strategies is the one through s_3. Thus, Mr. Hotchkiss will take action A_1 if the lobbyist's opinion is y_0, and action A_0 if he replies either y_1 or y_2. The Rasmussen Company will thus commence testing under the specifications of the pending bill if the lobbyist says that it will pass. In the case of either a prediction of "Can't tell" or "Fail" from the lobbyist, the Company will continue animal tests according to present specifications.

Note that in this problem the Bayesian and minimax solutions are distinct but not very far apart. In other problems, this may or may not be the case.

*11.8   SEVERAL STATES OF NATURE

In this section we shall not offer a complete analysis of decision problems when more than two states of nature must be taken into account. We shall confine our discussion to how the previous sections can be generalized to handle such cases. Then a problem will be discussed, so that the ideas involved in the generalization may become more concrete.

If several states of nature (for instance, k states) are relevant to a decision problem, it is first necessary to estimate utility or monetary losses for each action under each state of nature. For n actions, there would be nk estimates. If a predicting device is used which has m possible outcomes, one next needs the k probability distributions of these outcomes over the states of nature. There would be n^m strategies available, and it would be necessary to calculate the expected loss for each strategy under each state of nature—a total of kn^m expectations. Then each strategy can be represented as a point in a k-dimensional Euclidean space. Its coordinates are $L_0 = E(L \mid \theta_0), \cdots, L_k = E(L \mid \theta_k)$. Of course, it is pointless to approach the problem geometrically if $k > 3$, since our visual capacities for four or more dimensions are lacking.

These pure strategies have a convex hull which is a k-dimensional set whose faces are analogous to planes in three dimensions. The admissible strategies form the undominated part of the hull's boundary as before—only the set is $k - 1$ dimensional. Minimax strategies are found by considering k-dimensional cubes based on the origin and the coordinate axes. Bayesian strategies are founded by considering $k - 1$ dimensional planes. Points of contact with the boundary of the convex hull give the desired type of strategy in each case. The only difficulty encountered (besides lengthier computation) is the replacement of two-dimensional concepts by the corresponding k-dimensional concepts. To illustrate, we set up, but leave unfinished, the following case.

The Metropolitan Railway provides commuter transportation between the city of Yorkopolis and the suburb of Grandwater. In this suburb huge housing developments have been erected in the last five years. Despite this, there has been no appreciable increase in commuter use of the connecting rail line. Most residents of Grandwater drive to their city jobs—thus contributing to the difficult parking situation in Yorkopolis and to the incredible morning and late-afternoon traffic jams.

A recent transportation study pinpointed Metropolitan's service on the Grandwater line as a horrible example. Ancient and crowded trains, slow schedules, frequent breakdowns, and dirty facilities were mentioned. It was recommended that a local bus line be enfranchised and heavily subsidized to provide nonstop service between Grandwater and Yorkopolis.

Metropolitan's executives were shocked, and six months of hectic activity ensued as the company reevaluated its position. At the end of this period, Metropolitan was considering a complete revamping of its Grandwater line and had obtained pledges of financial support both from Yorkopolis and the federal government. Only two possible plans for change were being given serious consideration. Plan I involved laying additional track, constructing three modern stations with parking facilities in the Grandwater area, purchasing six new locomotives, replacing all coaches, and running frequent nonstop express schedules between Yorkopolis and Grandwater. Plan II also called for the new stations and parking lots; however, its major feature was the scrapping of existing rail facilities and their replacement by a monorail system. Plan III was the continuation of the present operation with no revisions.

Elaborate analyses of costs were submitted for each system and were compared. We shall discuss only certain of the conclusions reached; the details are not directly germane to the decision process. Plan II was clearly the most expensive alternative, both in terms of initial cost and maintenance. However, it was estimated to provide quicker transportation for larger numbers of people than would Plan I. The cost analyses suggested that certain critical points existed in terms of numbers of one-way trips, for instance, on an annual basis. When these were translated into terms of customer potential it was decided to consider three states of nature[2]

θ_0: 15,000 or less regular commuters five years from the present time

θ_1: Between 15,000 and 40,000 regular commuters five years from the present time

θ_2: 40,000 or more regular commuters five years from the present time

[2] A more elaborate analysis might be made by considering θ as a continuous parameter.

Table 11.14 Estimated Losses in Utility—Metropolitan Railway Problem

		State of Nature		
		$\leq 15,000$	$> 15,000$ $< 40,000$	$\geq 40,000$
Action		θ_0	θ_1	θ_2
Plan I	A_0	15	3	5
Plan II	A_1	20	4	0
Plan III	A_2	11	9	7

After considering the three possible actions, namely, the implementation of Plans I, II, and III, the Metropolitan executives decided that the estimates of loss of utility given in Table 11.14 were roughly representative of the situation.

The Metropolitan Railway next decided to obtain an estimate of commuter potential in the Grandwater area. It asked the Regional Development Center to give such an estimate with particular attention to the figures 15,000 and 40,000. The Center's predictive ability was thought by the executives to have the format of Table 11.15. As can be seen, the executives feel that the Center's estimates will usually be on the cautious side.

At this point, we leave the problem. In order to see what decision the Railway should make, one should first write down all of the possible strategies, here $3^3 = 27$. He should then find the expected utility loss for each one under each of the *three* states of nature. The resulting points representing pure strategies will be scattered in the first octant of the three-dimensional space whose axes are L_0, L_1, and L_2. The set will have a three-dimensional convex

Table 11.15 Probability of Receiving a Report Y from Regional Development Center When θ Is the Actual State of Nature

		State of Nature		
		$\leq 15,000$	$> 15,000$ $< 40,000$	$\geq 40,000$
Report		θ_0	θ_1	θ_2
$y \leq 15,000$	y_0	0.9	0.2	0
$15,000 < y < 40,000$	y_1	0.1	0.8	0.4
$y \geq 40,000$	y_2	0	0	0.6

hull. To find the minimax strategies, consider cubes based on the origin and the coordinate axes, picking the point or points just touched by the smallest cube that contacts the hull. To obtain the Bayes strategies, pass planes perpendicular to a fixed line determined by the a priori probabilities, select the one nearest the origin which touches the hull, and use its intersection with the hull.

IMPORTANT TERMS AND CONCEPTS

Action
Admissible strategy
A priori probability distribution .
Bayes strategy
Boundary
Certainty
Convex hull
Convex set
Decision
Dominated strategy
Join
Minimax strategy

Mixed strategy
Opportunity loss
Payoff
Pure strategy
Risk
Separating line
State of nature
Strategy
Supporting line
Uncertainty
Utility

SYMBOLS AND ABBREVIATIONS

θ H
A L_0
Y L_1
s u
S

OFTEN-USED FORMULAS

$$(1 - P_0)L_1 + P_0L_0 = c'$$

$$u(R_0) = pu(R_1) + (1 - p)u(R_2)$$

EXERCISES

1. Distinguish among the terms "certainty," "risk," and "uncertainty" in a decision context.

2. In Table 11.8 check the expected loss computations for s_{14} and s_7. What can you say about dominance between these two strategies?

3. Answer the following questions regarding the RDC problem.
   a. Could a reasonable man ever adopt s_2 as his strategy? Why or why not?
   b. Under what, if any, situation might s_0 be a preferred strategy?
   c. Under what circumstances would s_1 be the preferred strategy?
   d. When should a reasonable man adopt s_{15}, if ever?

4. In the RDC problem, describe a randomizing device that would select a strategy on the join of s_8 and s_{14}, one-fourth of the distance from s_8 to s_{14}.

5. In the RDC problem, state an admissible strategy that is not pure. State a pure strategy that is not admissible. State a mixed strategy that is not admissible.

6. Instead of adopting a minimax expected loss strategy, a decision maker might adopt a strategy which would select the action leading to maximizing the minimum expected loss. Would this strategy be of any use in practical decisions? Discuss.

7. How could you determine the strategy of Problem 6 geometrically? Could your resulting set consist of only one mixed strategy under some circumstances?

8. Must two convex sets in the same plane have a separating line? A common supporting line?

9. Must the convex hull of a set consisting of three points always be a triangular set? When is a set its own convex hull? Is it possible for two different sets to have the same convex hull? Is the empty set the convex hull of any set?

10. Sketch a utility of money function that might be appropriate to a man who:
    a. Was a multimillionaire.
    b. Was about to go bankrupt unless he could raise $100,000 by to-morrow.
    c. Was about to die and wished to leave his fortune to his legal heirs.

    d. Wished to buy a cottage on Walden Pond and lead a meditative, pastoral existence.

11. Assume that the Rasmussen Pharmaceutical Company is willing to consider an additional action in the Easy-Calm problem, namely A_3: Withhold any testing until a decision is reached on the bill. The estimated losses in utility (see Table 11.10) are: for θ_0 and A_3, 4; for θ_1 and A_3, 6. Assume, further, that the estimates of Table 11.11 are unchanged. How many pure strategies may Rasmussen adopt? Calculate the expected losses in utility for each of these strategies.

12. Determine the minimax strategy in Exercise 11.

13. Determine the Bayes strategy in Exercise 11, given the same a priori distribution as Mr. Hotchkiss uses in the text.

14. Determine the Bayes strategy in Exercise 11 if Mr. Hotchkiss used $P_0 = P(\theta_0) = 0.2$; $P_1 = P(\theta_1) = 0.8$.

15. How would the Easy-Calm Problem be changed if the decision makers considered three possibilities: bill passed, bill failed, bill passed in modified form reducing the cost of extra testing by one half.

16. Judy Jones is about to fly to Floridaville for a vacation. She is wondering whether to dress for cold or hot weather—the weather in Floridaville is changeable. She is concerned about two states of nature:

θ_0: Hot in Floridaville
θ_1: Cold in Floridaville

Judy has a limited wardrobe and is faced with a choice between two actions:[3]

A_0: Wear fur coat and boots
A_1: Wear play suit and sandals

Her losses in utility are as follows:

	θ_0	θ_1
A_0	8	0
A_1	2	15

She has at hand a copy of an almanac, which lists probabilities of hot and cold weather in Floridaville on this date. If we let

y_0: "Hot" predicted by almanac
y_1: "Cold" predicted by almanac

---

[3] This single-minded young woman would never wear a fur coat over a play suit.

then Judy feels that the relation between the almanac's prediction and the true state of nature is

	θ_0	θ_1
y_0	0.1	0.7
y_1	0.9	0.3

List all pure strategies open to Judy. Calculate the expected losses in utility for each of them. Determine the set of all admissible strategies.

17. Determine Judy's set of minimax strategies.

18. Determine Judy's set of Bayes' strategies if $P(\theta_0) = P(\theta_1) = 1/2$.

19. The Chocko Candy Company is considering the introduction of a new product—the Mushie-Fudgie bar. If average annual sales of Mushie-Fudgie bars exceed 875,000, the company will realize a nice profit. If the annual figure falls below this level, prospects are not attractive. Hence the company will be concerned with two states of nature:

θ_0: Annual sales > 875,000 bars
θ_1: Annual sales ≤ 875,000 bars

Three actions are possible:

A_0: Do not manufacture Mushie-Fudgies
A_1: Manufacture on a pilot plant basis
A_2: Go to full production at once

Estimated utility losses are:

	θ_0	θ_1
A_0	5	5
A_1	3	2
A_2	0	10

The sales manager of Chocko will predict the success of new products in certain broad categories. Here, relevant to the 875,000 figure:

y_0: Sure-fire success
y_1: Good possibility
y_2: Poor bet

The company thinks well of his predictions—as shown in the table below:

	θ_0	θ_1
y_0	0.6	0
y_1	0.3	0.2
y_2	0.1	0.8

List the various pure strategies open to Chocko. Determine the set of all admissible strategies.

20. Determine the set of minimax strategies in Exercise 19.

21. Determine the set of Bayes strategies in Exercise 19 if $P(\theta_0) = 1/6$, $P(\theta_1) = 5/6$.

22. In the Metropolitan Railway Company problem of Section 11.8, determine the set of all admissible strategies.

23. In Exercise 22, determine the set of all minimax strategies.

24. In Exercise 22, determine the set of all Bayes strategies if $P(\theta_0) = 1/6$, $P(\theta_1) = 1/3$, $P(\theta_2) = 1/2$.

12 Revision of Probabilities in Decision Making

12.1 INTRODUCTION

In the previous chapter we outlined a procedure for making intelligent decisions in certain simple situations. It was discovered that, although a decision maker could systematically delineate the set of admissible strategies, he could not use the criterion of minimum expected loss in utility in a practical problem unless he could write down an additional set of numbers. These we called the *a priori* probability distribution of the states of nature. The purpose of this chapter is to examine the a priori distribution, to develop a systematic method for changing it as additional relevant information appears, and to examine in detail its use in more complex problems.

In this chapter, we pick up a thread that appeared first in Chapter 5. There, we said that the marginal distribution of a random variable Y is the appropriate instrument to use in making probability statements about Y. However, additional information may be available. Suppose X is a second random variable related to Y, and suppose further that x is known. Then probability statements about Y should no longer be based on $h(y)$. The appropriate instrument is now $g_1(y \mid x)$, the conditional distribution of Y given x; g_1 incorporates the additional information. Recall the argument for use of g_1, which is based on the fact that it has a smaller variance than the marginal.

The arguments to be adduced in this chapter are of the same general sort. A decision is to be made, and a probability distribution of the state of nature is to play an important role. As additional relevant information appears, we must now revise the original distribution; that is, in the decision problem its part should now be played by a new distribution—a conditional distribution—the probability distribution of the states of nature dependent on the new information.

12.2 BAYES' THEOREM

This famous theorem is easy to state and prove. Let $B_1, \cdots, B_n$ be a mutually exclusive and exhaustive set of events. Let E be another event that occurs if and only if one of the events B_j has occurred. Let B_i be that event. Then

$$P(B_i \mid E) = \frac{P(B_i)P(E \mid B_i)}{\displaystyle\sum_{j=1}^{n} P(B_j)P(E \mid B_j)} \tag{12.1}$$

To obtain this result we use the general multiplication rule in both its forms:

$$P(B_iE) = P(B_i)P(E \mid B_i) \tag{12.2}$$

$$P(B_iE) = P(E)P(B_i \mid E) \tag{12.3}$$

as well as the fact that because of the exhaustive and mutually exclusive character of the B_j

$$P(E) = \sum_{j=1}^{n} P(B_j)P(E \mid B_j) \tag{12.4}$$

Write (12.3) as

$$P(B_i \mid E) = \frac{P(B_iE)}{P(E)}$$

and substitute (12.2) and (12.4) for numerator and denominator, respectively. The result is (12.1).

Historically, there has been much controversy attached to Bayes' theorem. Some have suspected its mathematical validity—which is not open to question. Others have, with good reason, objected to its use in various problems. The nub of the difficulty is that in order to calculate $P(B_i \mid E)$ one must know the a priori probabilities $P(B_i)$. In many practical situations these quantities are either unavailable or obtainable only as dubious estimates. We shall give some valid and some questionable uses of the theorem.

Pete Paulus has 15 pairs of rolled sox in a bureau drawer. Five are red, four are brown, and six are white. Pairs of the same color are indistinguishable. Two red pairs and one white pair are unwearable because of holes in the toe. Pete selects a pair of sox from the drawer and notes that it is red. What is the probability that it has holes in the toe? We proceed by Bayes' theorem.

B_1: Pair has holes in the toe
B_2: Pair does not have holes in the toe
E: Pair is red

$$P(B_1) = \frac{1}{5}, \qquad P(B_2) = \frac{4}{5}, \qquad P(E \mid B_1) = \frac{2}{3}, \qquad P(E \mid B_2) = \frac{1}{4}$$

Thus

$$P(B_1 \mid E) = \frac{P(B_1)P(E \mid B_1)}{P(B_1)P(E \mid B_1) + P(B_2)P(E \mid B_2)} = \frac{\frac{1}{5} \cdot \frac{2}{3}}{\frac{1}{5} \cdot \frac{2}{3} + \frac{4}{5} \cdot \frac{1}{4}} = \frac{2}{5}$$

In this simple example, note that the effect of Bayes' theorem is one of revising a priori probabilities. Before a pair of sox was selected, the probability of Pete's picking one with holes in the toe was $P(B_1) = 1/5$. But, after the color was seen, it became twice as likely that the pair had holes in the toe because of the greater prevalence of holes in sox of that particular color. Let us examine a closely related problem.

Suppose we make a single change; now the unwearable pairs are one red and two white; then

$$P(B_1) = \frac{1}{5}, \qquad P(B_2) = \frac{4}{5}, \qquad P(E \mid B_1) = \frac{1}{3}, \qquad P(E \mid B_2) = \frac{1}{3}$$

$$P(B_1 \mid E) = \frac{\frac{1}{5} \cdot \frac{1}{3}}{\frac{1}{5} \cdot \frac{1}{3} + \frac{4}{5} \cdot \frac{1}{3}} = \frac{1}{5}$$

Here, the additional information "red" brought about no change in the a priori probability $P(B_1)$. This can only mean one thing: the events must be independent. This is verified by constructing the 2×2 table of probabilities

	E Red	$\bar{E}$ Not Red	
B_1: Holes in toes	$\frac{1}{15}$	$\frac{2}{15}$	$\frac{3}{15}$
B_2: None	$\frac{4}{15}$	$\frac{8}{15}$	$\frac{12}{15}$
	$\frac{5}{15}$	$\frac{10}{15}$	1

and noticing the proportionality between either rows or columns.

A study, conducted by the Bardorff Department Store, of customers paying for purchases by check showed that 40 percent of all forged checks carry the wrong date. On the other hand, only 4 percent of good checks carry the wrong date. If a clerk receives a check and finds that it carries the wrong date, what is the probability that the check is forged if one-tenth of 1 percent of all checks are forged?

B_1: Check forged
B_2: Check not forged
E: Check misdated

$P(B_1) = .001$
$P(B_2) = .999$
$P(E/B_1) = .40$
$P(E/B_2) = .04$

$$P(B_1 \mid E) = \frac{P(B_1)P(E \mid B_1)}{P(B_1)P(E \mid B_1) + P(B_2)P(E \mid B_2)}$$

$$= \frac{(0.001)(0.40)}{(0.001)(0.40) + (0.999)(0.04)} = \frac{0.0004}{0.4036} = 0.0099$$

a higher probability than $P(B_1)$. However it is still unlikely that the check is a forgery.

A production engineer knows "from experience" that when a model CX-12-A hydraulic press is properly adjusted, it will produce aluminum stampings of which, on the average, only 1 in 100 is defective. However, when the press is not properly adjusted, it will produce on the average 30 percent defective stampings. Yesterday the press was adjusted and two trial stampings were made. The engineer feels that there was a 50-50 chance that the press was, in fact, properly adjusted. However, both stampings have been adjudged defective. What is the probability that the machine was not properly adjusted?

B_1: Press properly adjusted
B_2: Press not properly adjusted
E: Two trial stampings defective

We see that $P(B_1) = 0.5$ and $P(B_2) = 0.5$. Furthermore, if we are willing to make the considerable assumption that successive stampings are independent with constant probability of a defective output from stamping to stamping, $P(E \mid B_1)$ and $P(E \mid B_2)$ are binomial.

$$P(E \mid B_1) = \binom{2}{2}(0.01)^2(0.99)^0 = 0.0001$$

$$P(E \mid B_2) = \binom{2}{2}(0.30)^2(0.70)^0 = 0.0900$$

Thus

$$P(B_2 \mid E) = \frac{0.5(0.0900)}{0.5(0.0900) + 0.5(0.0001)} = \frac{0.0900}{0.0901} = 1.000$$

Before the trial stampings were made, the engineer felt that the press was as likely to be properly adjusted as not. But once both pieces of output were shown to be defective, he had to conclude that it was almost impossible that the proper settings had been made.

We emphasize again the dependency of this reasoning on the assumptions of independence and constant probability. In many machines faulty output tends to occur in long sequences. Hence the engineer had best be very sure, when he uses the binomial distribution, to compute the necessary conditional probabilities.

August Rovius is head of the Construction Inspection Section of the Yorkopolis city government. He has three inspection teams under him. Teams A and B are headed by structural engineers; team C by the mayor's brother-in-law. Mr. Rovius receives a hot tip from a trusted source that bribes have been passed to the head of team C.

G_1: Bribes passed to head of team C
G_2: Bribes not passed to head of team C
H: Check shows proper work by team C

A priori, he estimates the probabilities at $P(G_1) = 0.8$, $P(G_2) = 0.2$. He orders a rapid secret check on recent work done by team C, and sets up the conditional probabilities $P(H \mid G_1) = 0.1$, $P(H \mid G_2) = 0.9$. He feels that, if indeed bribes have been passed, then shoddy inspections will have taken place. But if no corruption is really the state of nature, then the team will be doing a competent job. If the investigation indicates no shoddy inspections by team C, what is the revised probability of bribes having been passed to the mayor's brother-in-law?

$$P(G_1 \mid H) = \frac{P(G_1)P(H \mid G_1)}{P(G_1)P(H \mid G_1) + P(G_2)P(H \mid G_2)}$$

$$= \frac{(0.8)(0.1)}{(0.8)(0.1) + (0.2)(0.9)} = 0.308$$

If the investigation does show that team C is performing its duties in an acceptable fashion, the probability of that team's head having been bribed must be drastically reduced. Additional information must not be ignored, rather it must be incorporated into the evidence in some rational way.

12.3 OBJECTIVE AND SUBJECTIVE PROBABILITIES

In Chapter 3 the concept of probability was introduced. Probability distributions are mathematical entities that are interesting both in their own right and in that they are useful in many practical problems. In this context, probability distributions were employed in Chapter 3 as models in cases involving relative frequencies of recurring outcomes in random experiments. We now focus attention upon the use of probabilities as models for situations in which a random experiment may not have been conducted.

As illustrations of this point, consider the examples used to illustrate Bayes' theorem in Section 12.2. The first one concerned Pete Paulus's sox. These were physical objects of identical appearance confined within a drawer. Random selection from the drawer made the situation analogous to the classical relative frequency problems involving cards, coins, and dice, and allowed a standard probability model to be applied with no difficulty. A model used in such a situation is said to be an objective model, and its probabilities are called objective probabilities. In the Pete Paulus problem we used Bayes' theorem to revise an objective probability. But in both the forgery and hydraulic press problems we notice a difference. No random experiment was conducted. In each case historical data were used to estimate the probabilities of later events. There is nothing wrong about such a procedure in many situations; however, it is open to the same objections that beset any problem in prediction. It tacitly assumes that the future will be just like the past as far as all factors relevant to the situation under consideration are concerned. When we use a probability model in the forgery problem we say, in effect, "If the future experience of the Bardorff Department Store regarding forged checks is exactly the same as that store's past experience, then the problem may be considered to be based on a random experiment so that a probability model is appropriate." There are two stages of reasoning here instead of only one as in the Pete Paulus problem. Models involving these two stages of reasoning are called subjective probability models. Incidentally, we should notice that, in the hydraulic press problem where the major feature is a large, substantial machine whose characteristics have been studied by the engineer in question, it is likely that future experience may closely resemble past experience whenever this expert so claims. Presumably he knows his machine.

The last example also employed subjective probabilities. Quite possibly, the reader experienced doubts regarding Mr. Rovius and his bold estimation of probabilities. The chief inspector was not dealing with machines but with that most volatile and treacherous of experimental materials—people! Does it really mean anything when the probability of a bribe being passed to the mayor's brother-in-law is estimated at 0.8? We feel that, although it is not as reliable a figure as a 0.5 probability that a press is operating properly, it still has some meaning. Mr. Rovius is on the scene supervising these men. He knows something about their characters that is worth knowing. But an objection will be made that a character estimate cannot be expressed in quantitative terms. Rather than enter upon a long philosophical argument, we shall merely say that Mr. Rovius was willing to put his conceptual impressions into numerical form—as other executives have been. Since he evaluated $P(G_1) = 0.8$ and $P(G_2) = 0.2$, he feels that the mayor's brother-in-law is more likely to take a bribe than not. Also he would be willing to write down the probabilities of the other two team heads accepting bribes, and the sets of figures could be compared on the same scale. We conclude that even though Mr. Rovius's estimates are not the best data in the world, they are informative and can be used as in the example.

In the case of sox in the drawer, we were dealing with objective probabilities. In a decision problem this would be classified as a case of risk. In the three remaining examples, any decision reached from the given data would be made in an uncertainty situation. The forgery and bribery examples are both essentially the same from this point of view; the difference is in degree, not in kind.

12.4   TWO-ACTION DECISION PROBLEMS

The Slocum Company manufactures a variety of precision tools, in particular the G-106-A micrometer. In recent years the G-106-A work has been sub-contracted by Slocum to a subsidiary, Wilcowitz Industries, with mixed results. Only a final inspection has been done by Slocum, and this involves a set of very severe standards. When a micrometer is judged defective, it must be broken down for scrap at a loss of $12 to the company. The last stage of micrometer production is a complex calibration process. Almost all defective products in the final inspection are so judged because of faulty calibration. Consequently it is now proposed that the calibration process be done at Slocum after the micrometers have been received.

Wilcowitz produces and ships micrometers in standard runs of 800. It is estimated that performing the calibration process at Slocum would add $200 to the cost of producing a single run but would reduce the percentage of defective micrometers in a single run to 2 percent—that is, 16 defective tools out of 800. This is the minimum percentage of defective items that Slocum could expect to obtain.

Let A_1, A_2, and $\tilde{p}$ be defined as follows:

   A_1: Continue present arrangement
   A_2: Perform calibration process at Slocum
   $\tilde{p}$: Population percentage of defective micrometers under present arrangement

We shall try to find a logical basis for the selection of either A_1 or A_2. Table 12.1 summarizes some of the basic information necessary for such a decision.

Table 12.1   Cost Table—Slocum Problem

Percentage of Defective Items under Present Procedures $\tilde{p}$	Prior Probability $P(\tilde{p})$	Costs	
		$c_1 = $ Cost of A_1	$c_2 = $ Cost of A_2
2	0.3	$192	$392
4	0.3	384	392
6	0.2	576	392
8	0.1	768	392
10	0.1	960	392

The probability distributions in the first two columns of Table 12.1 are based on historical evidence. The five percentages in the domain are taken for simplicity; it would have been possible to use ten or more points for the ensuing computations. It was felt that the distribution as shown was a good approximation to reality. The costs in the third column are computed as follows. If there are $\tilde{p}$ percent defective in the shipment of 800 items and action A_1 is taken, the company loses \$12 for each of the 800 $\tilde{p}$ defective micrometers, a total of \$192 when $\tilde{p}$ is 2 percent, etc. On the other hand, if action A_2 is taken, a fixed cost of \$200 per shipment is incurred, and to this must be added \$12 (800) (2%) = \$192.00 for the 2 percent of defective tools still encountered under the proposed procedure. The term "prior probability" used as a heading for column 2 implies another probability distribution—the posterior distribution—which contrasts with it and will be explained later.

On what basis could Slocum choose between A_1 and A_2? The criterion of expected cost per shipment would seem a reasonable one to most of us. Table 12.2 shows the computation of expected cost for each possible action

Table 12.2   Computation of Prior Expected Costs—Slocum Problem

		A_1		A_2
$\tilde{p}$	$P(\tilde{p})$	c_1	$c_1 P(\tilde{p})$	c_2
2%	0.3	\$192	\$57.60	\$392
4	0.3	384	115.20	
6	0.2	576	115.20	
8	0.1	768	76.80	
10	0.1	960	96 00	
			460.80	

under the probability distribution of Table 12.1. Still in anticipation of a posterior distribution, we shall refer to the expected costs computed here as "prior expected costs." The expected cost of A_2 is simply the constant previously computed.

Since Table 12.2 shows an expected cost for continuing the present arrangement of \$68.80 more than for performing the calibration process at Slocum, the company should, indeed, change its procedure—if it accepts the expected value criterion.

The computation of Table 12.2 assumes a probability distribution for $\tilde{p}$. It was stated that this was based upon historical evidence—the experience of the Slocum Company with its subcontractor. What guarantee do we have that future experience will resemble the past? Really none at all—only the idea that, if the same factors which were influential in the past are still operating and if no new important ones have appeared, future results should resemble past results. Any decision based on a prior probability distribution is open to criticism on these grounds. Sometimes the future makes a clean break with the past. However, in some cases the prior distribution will include the decision maker's subjective adjustment of past results in an attempt to overcome this difficulty.

To obtain evidence that is not historical, the Slocum Company decides to sample a new shipment just received from Wilcowitz which consequently could not have been considered in setting up the prior probability distribution. Three micrometers are chosen at random from the shipment, and are inspected. All are judged to be nondefective. Thus, the sample evidence supports the idea that $\tilde{p}$ is small. How small? Let us revise the prior distribution in the light of this sample evidence—thus obtaining the posterior probability distribution of $\tilde{p}$. The sense of the terms "prior" and "posterior" is now clear. Prior refers to a situation obtaining before sampling; posterior implies "after sampling."

Let p be the proportion of defective micrometers in the sample of size three. Assume that the sampling distribution of X, the number of bad micrometers in the sample of size three, is binomial. (Is this a reasonable assumption? Under what conditions?) Then, if $\tilde{p} = 0.02$, since $p = 0$ implies $x = 0$,

$$P(p = 0 \mid \tilde{p} = 0.02) = \binom{3}{0}(0.02)^0(0.98)^3 = 0.9412$$

The other probabilities in column 3 of Table 12.3 are found in the same way.

Table 12.3 The Posterior Probability Distribution—Slocum Problem

$\tilde{p}$	$P(\tilde{p})$	$P(p = 0 \mid \tilde{p})$	$P(p = 0, \tilde{p})$	$P(\tilde{p} \mid p = 0)$
2%	0.3	0.9412	0.2824	0.3266
4	0.3	0.8847	0.2654	0.3069
6	0.2	0.8306	0.1661	0.1921
8	0.1	0.7787	0.0779	0.0901
10	0.1	0.7290	0.0729	0.0843
		$P(p = 0)$	0.8647	1.0000

Table 12.4   Computation of Posterior Expected Costs—Slocum Problem

$\tilde{p}$	$P(\tilde{p} \mid p = 0)$	c_1	A_1 $c_1 P(\tilde{p} \mid p = 0)$	A_2 c_2
2%	0.3266	$192	$62.71	$392
4	0.3069	384	117.85	
6	0.1921	576	110.65	
8	0.0901	768	69.20	
10	0.0843	960	80.93	
			441.34	

In columns 4 and 5, Bayes' theorem is used to find the posterior probabilities $P(\tilde{p} \mid p = 0)$. First, the joint probabilities $P(p = 0, \tilde{p})$ are found by multiplying the marginals in the second column by the conditionals in the third. The joint probabilities are then added to obtain the marginal probability $P(p = 0) = 0.8647$. This total is then divided into the joint probabilities in column 4 to obtain the corresponding conditionals in column 5. The effect of the sampling information has been to raise slightly the probability of the smaller values of $\tilde{p}$, with compensating reductions in the larger values.

The computation just made illustrates the central role of Bayes' theorem in our present topic. Most practical decisions in business, government, and elsewhere are not made on the basis of pure statistical sampling procedures. Most are made of some sort of educated guesswork basis. This involves a roughly outlined probability distribution over the possible states of nature—a prior probability distribution. In cases where statistical sampling procedures are used—and there are many of these cases—decision makers do not exclude from their minds all other relevant information and reach a course of action on the basis of sampling results alone. Of course not. Statistical sampling is but one important contributor of evidence leading to the decision. Bayes' theorem provides a convenient and logical way of combining the sample evidence with all of the nonsampling evidence summed up in the form of the prior distribution. Thus, a decision based on the posterior distribution uses *all available evidence* and, hence, is intuitively attractive to most individuals.

Let us recompute the expected costs of both courses of action, this time employing the posterior distribution (Table 12.4). The action A_2 is still the favored one, although the effect of the sampling information has been to reduce the expected cost of A_1 by $19.46.

12.5   LINEAR COSTS IN TWO-ACTION PROBLEMS

In the problem discussed in the previous section the analysis was simplified by the fact that the cost functions C_1 and C_2 were both linear. C_1, the cost of continuing the present arrangement, is proportional to the number of defective micrometers shipped from Wilcowitz to Slocum. When the percentage of defective tools in a standard shipment of 800 micrometers is shown on the horizontal axis, the slope of the cost function is a constant $96 per 1 percent increase in defectives. It should be noted that since shipments of size 800 are the basis of this problem, the cost function is really discontinuous. $\tilde{p} = 0.359$ is not a possible percentage of defective tools, for example, and hence there is no corresponding point on C_1. C_2, the cost of the proposed new procedure, is represented with the same qualification by a horizontal line, since it is a constant $392. Thus if the Slocum Company is faced with a situation in which the percentage of bad micrometers is a known constant, for instance, p_0, it will choose its action by comparing p_0 with p_b, the abscissa of the point of intersection of the cost lines in Figure 12.1. For our example with $C_1 = 96\tilde{p}$ and $C_2 = 392$,

$$p_b = \frac{392}{96} = 4.08\%$$

If p_0 is less than 4.08 percent, then the company should choose action A_1, or if greater than 4.08 percent, then Slocum should take action A_2. If p_0 is exactly 4.08 percent, the company would be indifferent as to which alternative prevailed. We shall refer to a point such as p_b as a "break-even point."

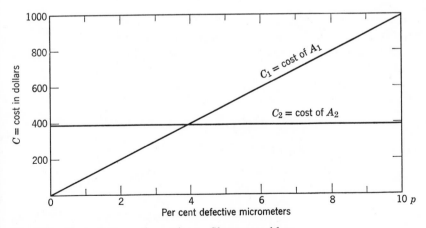

Fig. 12.1. Cost of alternative actions—Slocum problem.

Now the percentage of bad micrometers is not a constant; in fact, we have been using it as a random variable. What effect does this have on Slocum's use of the break-even point? An intuitively attractive procedure is to compute the expected value of the random variable $\tilde{p}$ and to compare it with p_b as before.

$$\text{Take action } A_1 \text{ if } E(\tilde{p}) < p_b$$
$$\text{Take action } A_2 \text{ if } E(\tilde{p}) > p_b \qquad (12.5)$$
$$\text{No preference if } E(\tilde{p}) = p_b$$

Our next task is to justify this decision rule in terms of costs. We shall show that if (12.5) is adopted, the expected cost to Slocum of the decision will be minimized.

Let X be a random variable. In a two-action decision problem based on X, let the costs of the respective actions A_1 and A_2 be

$$C_1 = m_1 X + d_1 \qquad \text{and} \qquad C_2 = m_2 X + d_2$$

such that

$$0 \leq m_2 < m_1 \qquad \text{and} \qquad 0 \leq d_1 < d_2$$

We shall first find x_b, the break-even point; setting $c_1 = c_2$,

$$m_1 x_b + d_1 = m_2 x_b + d_2$$

$$x_b = -\frac{d_1 - d_2}{m_1 - m_2}$$

Its ordinate is

$$c_1 = c_2 = c_b = m_2\left(-\frac{d_1 - d_2}{m_1 - m_2}\right) + d_2 = \frac{-m_2 d_1 + m_2 d_2 + m_1 d_2 - m_2 d_2}{m_1 - m_2}$$

$$c_b = \frac{m_1 d_2 - m_2 d_1}{m_1 - m_2}$$

We notice that, since $d_2 > d_1$ and $m_1 > m_2$, $x_b > 0$ and $c_b > 0$.

It can now be easily shown that whenever $E(X) < x_b$, $E(C_1) < E(C_2)$ as follows:

$$E(X) < x_b = -\frac{d_1 - d_2}{m_1 - m_2}$$

$$(m_1 - m_2)E(X) < d_2 - d_1$$

$$m_1 E(X) + d_1 < m_2 E(X) + d_2$$

$$E(m_1 X + d_1) < E(m_2 X + d_2)$$

$$E(C_1) < E(C)_2$$

Using analogous algebra, it can be shown that when $E(X) > x_b$, $E(C_2) < E(C_1)$.

In the Slocum Company case, $m_1 = 96$, $m_2 = 0$, $d_1 = 0$, $d_2 = 392$. The break-even point can then be found as

$$p_b = -\frac{0 - 392}{96 - 0} = 4.08\%$$

The Company should adopt A_1 whenever $E(\tilde{p}) < 4.08\%$. Using the first two columns of Table 12.1, we find that

$$E(\tilde{p}) = 2(0.3) + 4(0.3) + 6(0.2) + 8(0.1) + 10(0.1)$$

$$= 0.048 = 4.8\%$$

Since $E(\tilde{p}) > p_b$, the company should take action A_2 and perform the calibration process itself.

Be careful *not* to use the expected value criterion developed in this section in cases where costs are not linear. In such cases, expected costs must be computed using the probability distributions under each course of action. $E(C_1)$ and $E(C_2)$ are then compared directly.

12.6   THE COST OF UNCERTAINTY

In Tables 12.2 and 12.4, expected costs were computed in the Slocum problem. It is instructive to repeat these computations in terms of opportunity losses. Referring to each of these tables, we see that A_2 is the best action; the opportunity losses are as summarized in Table 12.5.

Table 12.5   Opportunity Losses—Slocum Problem

$\tilde{p}$	L_1	L_2
2%	$0	$200
4	0	8
6	184	0
8	376	0
10	568	0

Tables 12.6 and 12.7 then show the computations of prior and posterior expected opportunity losses.

There are several points that should be made in connection with Tables 12.6 and 12.7. For one thing, we notice that the expected costs of A_1 and A_2 computed under the prior distribution differed by

$$\$460.80 - \$392.00 = \$68.80$$

Table 12.6   Computation of Prior Expected Opportunity Losses—Slocum Problem

$\tilde{p}$	$P(\tilde{p})$	L_1	$L_1 P(\tilde{p})$	L_2	$L_2 P(\tilde{p})$
		A_1		A_2	
2%	0.3	$0	$0	$200	$60.00
4	0.3	0	0	8	2.40
6	0.2	184	36.80	0	0
8	0.1	376	37.60	0	0
10	0.1	568	56.80	0	0
			131.20		62.40

Table 12.7   Computation of Posterior Expected Opportunity Losses—Slocum Problem

$\tilde{p}$	$P(\tilde{p} \mid p = 0)$	L_1	$L_1 P(\tilde{p} \mid p = 0)$	L_2	$L_2 P(\tilde{p} \mid p = 0)$
		A_1		A_2	
2%	0.3266	$0	$0	$200	$65.32
4	0.3069	0	0	8	2.4552
6	0.1921	184	35.3464	0	0
8	0.0901	376	33.8776	0	0
10	0.0843	568	47.8824	0	0
			117.1064		67.7752

in Table 12.2. Intuitively, this figure should be the same as the difference in expected losses found in Table 12.6. Sure enough,

$$\$131.20 - \$62.40 = \$68.80$$

Similarly, for the posterior distribution, we have from Table 12.4 a difference in costs of

$$\$441.34 - \$392.00 = \$49.34$$

and from Table 12.7 a difference in opportunity losses of

$$\$117.1064 - \$67.7752 = \$49.33$$

The difference in the last decimal is simply rounding error.

There is one further new concept that should be introduced here—the cost of uncertainty. This cost is defined as the expected opportunity loss of the best possible decision. It is clear from Table 12.6 that A_2 is the best decision, hence the cost of uncertainty is \$62.40 under the prior distribution. From Table 12.7 we see that A_2 is again best, and that the cost of uncertainty under the posterior distribution has increased slightly to \$67.78. Since it is possible for the best action under the prior distribution to be the worst under the posterior distribution, there is no special relation between the magnitudes of the costs of uncertainty under the prior and posterior distributions.

If the decision maker possessed perfect information, he could always pick the best decision in the sense that he could minimize his costs and thus reduce his opportunity loss to zero. The cost of uncertainty discussed in the previous paragraph is the penalty that the decision maker must pay as a consequence of his lack of perfect information. Looked at in this light, the cost of uncertainty is the amount that a decision maker should be willing to pay to obtain perfect information—if such information were available. In Section 12.7 we shall develop this idea further, and refer to the expected value of perfect information as a synonym for the cost of uncertainty.

12.7 NORMAL PRIOR DISTRIBUTIONS

In the previous sections of this chapter we have been building up a rationale for dealing with two-action decision problems on the basis of comparative costs or losses. Emphasis has been upon discrete probability distributions; however, the thinking needed in the case of continuous distributions is not very different from that already discussed. We shall now approach those problems in which the prior distribution of the parameter of interest is normal. This material will furnish an important example of the way in which continuous distributions resemble their discrete counterparts in their effect on decisions.

We are interested in a random variable X, which is normally distributed with unknown mean μ and known variance σ^2. In the context of repeated experimentation, μ may also be considered as a random variable; thus μ will be taken as having a normal prior distribution with mean μ_0 and variance σ_0^2.

Suppose that the decision maker is to choose between actions A_1 and A_2 whose costs are

$$A_1: C_1 = m_1\mu + d_1$$
$$A_2: C_2 = m_2\mu + d_2$$

(12.6)

where $0 \leq m_2 < m_1$ and $0 \leq d_1 < d_2$ as in Section 12.5. It was shown there that the break-even point could be found as

$$\mu_b = -\frac{d_1 - d_2}{m_1 - m_2}$$

It was further shown that whenever $E(\mu) > \mu_b$, $E(C_2) < E(C_1)$ so that A_2 was the best choice. Conversely when $E(\mu) < \mu_b$, A_1 was best. Graphically, the situation is as shown in Figure 12.2. Of course, μ_0 may be greater than μ_b, although we shall discuss the case shown in the figure. No complications are introduced if the inequality is reversed.

In the case of a continuous distribution and linear costs the best decision procedure is the comparison of expectation with the break-even point. This

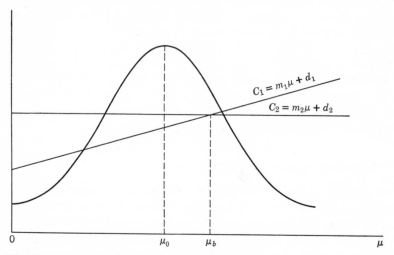

Fig. 12.2. Normal prior distribution with linear costs.

is true because the proof in Section 12.5 applies to continuous as well as discrete variables. We repeat it in terms of the cost functions (12.6). In terms of expectations,

$$E(C_1) = E(m_1\mu + d_1) = m_1 E(\mu) + d_1$$

$$E(C_2) = E(m_2\mu + d_2) = m_2 E(\mu) + d_2$$

so that in order to have $E(C_1) < E(C_2)$,

$$m_1 E(\mu) + d_1 < m_2 E(\mu) + d_2$$

$$[m_1 - m_2]E(\mu) < d_2 - d_1$$

$$E(\mu) < -\frac{d_1 - d_2}{m_1 - m_2} = \mu_b$$

Since the quantity on the right of this equation is the break-even point discussed in Section 12.5, a direct comparison of costs is unnecessary, and the procedure of Section 12.5 is entirely adequate.

Some new ideas may be developed if one is concerned with the cost of uncertainty in a problem involving a continuous prior distribution. Recall that the cost of uncertainty is the expected opportunity loss of the best possible decision—often called the expected value of perfect information. We shall evaluate this quantity in the case of a two-action decision problem with linear costs and a normal prior distribution.

Let the cost functions be as in (12.6). Let the prior distribution of μ be

$$f(\mu) = \frac{1}{\sqrt{2\pi}\,\sigma_0}\, e^{-(\mu-\mu_0)^2/2\sigma_0^2} \qquad -\infty < \mu < \infty$$

Assume that $E(\mu) = \mu_0 < \mu_b$, the break-even point. A_1 would then be the best action, but there remains an expected opportunity loss even for it. With perfect information we would choose A_2 in those cases where A_1 gave an expected opportunity loss and a combined strategy would have no such loss. We should be willing to pay any amount up to the expected opportunity loss associated with A_1 in this situation $[E(\mu) = \mu_0 < \mu_b]$. This loss is equal to the difference in ordinates of the cost lines at μ, namely,

$$C_1 - C_2 = m_1\mu + d_1 - m_2\mu - d_2 = (m_1 - m_2)\mu + (d_1 - d_2)$$
$$= -(m_2 - m_1)\mu - (d_2 - d_1) = -(m_2 - m_1)\mu + (m_2 - m_1)\mu_b$$

Thus, the expected value of perfect information is

$$E_p = \int_{\mu=\mu_b}^{\infty} (c_1 - c_2)f(\mu)\,d\mu$$

$$= -(m_2 - m_1)\int_{\mu_b}^{\infty} \mu f(\mu)\,d\mu + (m_2 - m_1)\mu_b \int_{\mu_b}^{\infty} f(\mu)\,d\mu$$

$$= -\frac{m_2 - m_1}{\sqrt{2\pi}\,\sigma_0}\int_{\mu_b}^{\infty} \mu e^{-(\mu-\mu_0)^2/2\sigma_0^2}\,d\mu + \frac{(m_2 - m_1)\mu_b}{\sqrt{2\pi}\,\sigma_0}\int_{\mu_b}^{\infty} e^{-(\mu-\mu_0)^2/2\sigma_0^2}\,d\mu$$

Let

$$z = \frac{\mu - \mu_0}{\sigma_0} \qquad dz = \frac{d\mu}{\sigma_0} \qquad z_b = \frac{\mu_b - \mu_0}{\sigma_0}$$

$$E_p = -(m_2 - m_1)\left[\frac{\sigma_0}{\sqrt{2\pi}}\int_{z_b}^{\infty} z e^{-z^2/2}\,dz\right.$$

$$\left. + \frac{\mu_0}{\sqrt{2\pi}}\int_{z_b}^{\infty} e^{-z^2/2}\,dz - \frac{\mu_b}{\sqrt{2\pi}}\int_{z_b}^{\infty} e^{-z^2/2}\,dz\right]$$

$$= -(m_2 - m_1)\left[\frac{\sigma_0}{\sqrt{2\pi}}(-e^{-z^2/2})_{z_b}^{\infty} - (\mu_b - \mu_0)P(z > z_b)\right]$$

$$= (m_1 - m_2)\sigma_0\left[\frac{e^{-z_b^2/2}}{\sqrt{2\pi}} - z_b P(z > z_b)\right]$$

Letting $G(z_b)$ stand for the normal loss function,

$$G(z_b) = \frac{e^{-z_b^2/2}}{\sqrt{2\pi}} - z_b P(z > z_b)$$

we obtain the form

$$E_p = (m_1 - m_2)\sigma_0 G(z_b)$$

For convenience in computation, we include in this text Table E.7 which gives a tabulation of this loss function.

If we were to consider the case in which $\mu_0 > \mu_b$, similar algebra would lead us to a result differing only in sign from the one just obtained because of the symmetry of the normal distribution. If we then consider only the absolute values of z_b and the difference $m_1 - m_2$, we may use Table E.7 here also to compute E_p.

$$E_p = |m_1 - m_2| \, \sigma_0 G(|z_b|) \tag{12.7}$$

Let us next examine an example. The Aunt Susie Candy Company manufactures molasses taffy as one of its products. Until the present time, the mixing, cooking, pulling, cutting, and packaging of the taffy have been hand operations. However, because of greatly increased sales during the past year, the company is considering the purchase of machinery that would automate the process of taffy manufacture. It seems likely to the company's management that a saving in labor costs would result from the automatic machinery, but a hard look is being taken before the purchase.

The incremental cost of one labor hour to the Aunt Susie Candy Company is estimated to be $2.50. The useful life of the equipment is estimated at 10 years. The total cost of the machinery, including a complete 10-year service warranty, is $40,000. Thus, if automation will save more than $40,000/$2.50/hr = 16,000 hr, the company will realize a benefit from the new equipment.

To estimate the probable saving to the Aunt Susie Company, a consulting engineer has been employed. He has consulted at length—principally with Annie Stafford who has supervised taffy production for the past six years. He has reached the conclusion that the mean number of hours saved by installation of the equipment is likeliest to be 15,000 hr. He also feels that there is a 50-50 chance that this mean will lie between 12,000 and 18,000 hr. Management, since there is no obvious reason for lack of symmetry in the distribution, has felt justified in assuming a normal prior distribution for the mean number of hours saved. This distribution will have mean of $\mu_0 = $ 15,000 hr. Since a one-tailed probability of 0.25 corresponds to a z value of 0.67 on the unit normal curve, it follows that $0.67\sigma_0 = 3000$ and $\sigma_0 = 4500$ hr.

To reach a decision the company should examine the costs of the two possible actions:

$$A_1 : \text{No change} \qquad A_2 : \text{Automate}$$

The cost functions are simply

$$C_1 = 2.5\mu \qquad C_2 = 40,000$$

yielding $\mu_b = 16,000$ hr as before.

Since $\mu_0 = 15,000 < \mu_b = 16,000$, management should choose A_1 and not purchase the new machinery if it wishes to base its decision on the prior distribution.

Next, we shall find the expected value of perfect information in this problem. Since an opportunity loss is incurred only if the wrong decision is made, we see that if the optimal act A_1 is chosen, the cost function is

$$C_1 - C_2 = 2.5\mu - 40,000 \qquad \mu \geq 16,000 \text{ hr}$$

$$= 0 \qquad\qquad\qquad \mu < 16,000 \text{ hr}$$

The quantity E_p is, then, simply

$$E_p = \int_{16,000}^{\infty} (2.5\mu - 40,000) \, \frac{1}{\sqrt{2\pi}\,(4500)} \, e^{(\mu-15,000)^2/2(4500)^2} \, d\mu$$

which, by (12.7), simplifies to

$$E_p = |m_1 - m_2| \, \sigma_0 G(|z_b|) = |2.5 - 0| \, (4500)(0.2986) = \$3359$$

since

$$|z_b| = \left| \frac{\mu_b - \mu_0}{\sigma_0} \right| = \left| \frac{16,000 - 15,000}{4500} \right| = 0.22$$

and

$$G(0.22) = 0.2986$$

Hence, $E_p = \$3359$. If we had a perfect predictor available, we should be willing to pay \$3359 to use it—but no more. The main reason that E_p is quite large is that z_b is close to zero so that the mean of the prior distribution is near the break-even point in terms of σ_0 as a unit of measure. Consequently, there is more question in the mind of the decision makers than if μ_b and μ_0 were far apart. If z_b were large, it might reflect a case in which the decision makers did not really need much additional information, and the expected value of perfect information would be small. Of course, the difference in slopes is also a factor in such an explanation.

12.8   THE POSTERIOR DISTRIBUTION OF μ—NORMAL CASE

In Table 12.3 we have illustrated the computation of the posterior distribution when the probability distributions involved are discrete. Algebraically the procedure commences with a marginal and a conditional distribution, for instance, $g(z)$ and $g_1(y \mid z)$, multiplies these to obtain the joint distribution

$f(z, y) = g(z)g_1(y \mid z)$, finds the other marginal $h(y)$, and finally divides to arrive at the remaining conditional $h_1(z \mid y)$. When g is considered as a prior probability distribution and g_1 is a sampling distribution contingent on the relevant parameter, then h_1 is the posterior distribution of the parameter; that is, it is the revision of the prior distribution in the light of the sample evidence contained in the first conditional.

Suppose now that we are concerned with a random variable X, which is normally distributed with mean μ and variance σ^2. Suppose further that μ has a prior probability distribution with mean μ_0 and variance σ_0^2. A random sample of size n is selected from the basic random variable. The distribution of the sample mean $\bar{X}$ has been shown in Chapter 8 to be normal with mean μ and variance $\sigma_{\bar{X}} = \sigma^2/n$. We shall now derive the conditional distribution of μ given $\bar{x}$, that is, the posterior distribution of μ.

We commence with the prior and sampling distributions:

$$g(\mu) = \frac{1}{\sqrt{2\pi}\,\sigma_0}\, e^{-(\mu-\mu_0)^2/2\sigma_0^2} \qquad g_1(\bar{x} \mid \mu) = \frac{1}{\sqrt{2\pi}\,\sigma_{\bar{X}}}\, e^{-(\bar{x}-\mu)^2/2\sigma_{\bar{X}}^2}$$

Multiplying these, we obtain the joint distribution:

$$f(\mu, \bar{x}) = \frac{1}{2\pi\sigma_0\sigma_{\bar{X}}}\, e^{-[(\mu-\mu_0)^2/\sigma_0^2 + (\bar{x}-\mu)^2/\sigma_{\bar{X}}^2]/2} \tag{12.8}$$

It is next necessary to find the marginal distribution of $\bar{X}$, $h(\bar{x})$, so that the posterior distribution may be obtained by division:

$$h_1(\mu \mid \bar{x}) = \frac{f(\mu, \bar{x})}{h(\bar{x})}$$

We obtain the marginal by integrating out μ in (12.8).

$$h(\bar{x}) = \frac{1}{2\pi\sigma_0\sigma_{\bar{X}}} \int_{\mu=-\infty}^{\infty} e^{-[(\mu-\mu_0)^2/\sigma_0^2 + (\bar{x}-\mu)^2/\sigma_{\bar{X}}^2]/2}\, d\mu \tag{12.9}$$

Simplifying the exponent,

$$-\frac{1}{2}\left[\frac{(\mu-\mu_0)^2}{\sigma_0^2} + \frac{(\bar{x}-\mu)^2}{\sigma_{\bar{X}}^2}\right]$$

$$= -\frac{1}{2\sigma_0^2\sigma_{\bar{X}}^2}\left[\sigma_{\bar{X}}^2(\mu^2 - 2\mu\mu_0 + \mu_0^2) + \sigma_0^2(\bar{x}^2 - 2\bar{x}\mu + \mu^2)\right]$$

$$= -\frac{1}{2\sigma_0^2\sigma_{\bar{X}}^2}\left[(\sigma_0^2 + \sigma_{\bar{X}}^2)\mu^2 - 2(\sigma_{\bar{X}}^2\mu_0 + \sigma_0^2\bar{x})\mu + (\sigma_{\bar{X}}^2\mu_0^2 + \sigma_0^2\bar{x}^2)\right]$$

$$= -\frac{(\sigma_0^2 + \sigma_{\bar{X}}^2)}{2\sigma_0^2\sigma_{\bar{X}}^2}\left[\mu^2 - 2\frac{(\sigma_{\bar{X}}^2\mu_0 + \sigma_0^2\bar{x})}{\sigma_0^2 + \sigma_{\bar{X}}^2}\mu + \frac{\sigma_{\bar{X}}^2\mu_0^2 + \sigma_0^2\bar{x}^2}{\sigma_0^2 + \sigma_{\bar{X}}^2}\right]$$

Completing the square, we add and subtract the square of half the coefficient of μ

$$= -\frac{(\sigma_0^2 + \sigma_{\bar{x}}^2)}{2\sigma_0^2\sigma_{\bar{x}}^2}\left[\mu - \frac{\sigma_{\bar{x}}^2\mu_0 + \sigma_0^2\bar{x}}{\sigma_0^2 + \sigma_{\bar{x}}^2}\right]^2 + R$$

where R is an expression

$$R = -\frac{(\sigma_0^2 + \sigma_{\bar{x}}^2)}{2\sigma_0^2\sigma_{\bar{x}}^2}\left[-\left(\frac{\sigma_{\bar{x}}^2\mu_0 + \sigma_0^2\bar{x}}{\sigma_0^2 + \sigma_{\bar{x}}^2}\right)^2 + \frac{\sigma_{\bar{x}}^2\mu_0^2 + \sigma_0^2\bar{x}^2}{\sigma_0^2 + \sigma_{\bar{x}}^2}\right]$$

which reduces to

$$R = -\frac{(\bar{x} - \mu_0)^2}{2(\sigma_0^2 + \sigma_{\bar{x}}^2)}$$

Thus, from (12.9),

$$h(\bar{x}) = \frac{1}{2\pi\sigma_0\sigma_{\bar{x}}} e^R \int_{\mu=-\infty}^{\infty} e^{-[(\sigma_0^2+\sigma_{\bar{x}}^2)/2\sigma_0^2\sigma_{\bar{x}}^2][\mu-(\sigma_{\bar{x}}^2\mu_0+\sigma_0^2\bar{x})/(\sigma_0^2+\sigma_{\bar{x}}^2)]^2}\, d\mu$$

Let

$$z = \sqrt{\frac{\sigma_0^2 + \sigma_{\bar{x}}^2}{\sigma_0^2\sigma_{\bar{x}}^2}}\left[\mu - \frac{\sigma_{\bar{x}}^2\mu_0 + \sigma_0^2\bar{x}}{\sigma_0^2 + \sigma_{\bar{x}}^2}\right] \qquad dz = \sqrt{\frac{\sigma_0^2 + \sigma_{\bar{x}}^2}{\sigma_0^2\sigma_{\bar{x}}^2}}\, d\mu$$

Then

$$h(\bar{x}) = \frac{e^R}{\sqrt{2\pi}\sqrt{\sigma_0^2 + \sigma_{\bar{x}}^2}} \cdot \frac{1}{\sqrt{2\pi}}\int_{z=-\infty}^{\infty} e^{-z^2/2}\, dz = \frac{e^R}{\sqrt{2\pi}\sqrt{\sigma_0^2 + \sigma_{\bar{x}}^2}}$$

It only remains to find $h_1(\mu \mid \bar{x})$. To do this most easily, we recall that in evaluating (12.9) we showed that the joint distribution of $\bar{X}$ and μ could be rewritten in a form involving R.

$$f(\mu, \bar{x}) = \frac{1}{2\pi\sigma_0\sigma_{\bar{x}}} e^{-[(\mu-\mu_0)^2/\sigma_0^2+(\bar{x}-\mu)^2/\sigma_{\bar{x}}^2]/2}$$

$$= \frac{e^R}{2\pi\sigma_0\sigma_{\bar{x}}} e^{-[(\sigma_0^2+\sigma_{\bar{x}}^2)/2\sigma_0^2\sigma_{\bar{x}}^2][\mu-(\sigma_{\bar{x}}^2\mu_0+\sigma_0^2\bar{x})/(\sigma_0^2+\sigma_{\bar{x}}^2)]^2}$$

Thus

$$h_1(\mu \mid \bar{x}) = \frac{f(\mu, \bar{x})}{h(\bar{x})} = \frac{\dfrac{e^R}{2\pi\sigma_0\sigma_{\bar{x}}} e^{-[(\sigma_0^2+\sigma_{\bar{x}}^2)/2\sigma_0^2\sigma_{\bar{x}}^2][\mu-(\sigma_{\bar{x}}^2\mu_0+\sigma_0^2\bar{x})/(\sigma_0^2+\sigma_{\bar{x}}^2)]^2}}{\dfrac{e^R}{\sqrt{2\pi}\sqrt{\sigma_0^2 + \sigma_{\bar{x}}^2}}}$$

$$= \frac{1}{\sqrt{2\pi}\sqrt{\dfrac{\sigma_0^2\sigma_{\bar{x}}^2}{\sigma_0^2 + \sigma_{\bar{x}}^2}}} e^{-[\mu-(\sigma_{\bar{x}}^2\mu_0+\sigma_0^2\bar{x})/(\sigma_0^2+\sigma_{\bar{x}}^2)]^2/2[(\sigma_0^2\sigma_{\bar{x}}^2)/(\sigma_0^2+\sigma_{\bar{x}}^2)]}$$

Thus we have shown that the posterior distribution of μ is also normal with mean

$$\mu_1 = \frac{\sigma_{\bar{x}}^2 \mu_0 + \sigma_0^2 \bar{x}}{\sigma_0^2 + \sigma_{\bar{x}}^2} \tag{12.10}$$

and variance

$$\sigma_1^2 = \frac{\sigma_0^2 \sigma_{\bar{x}}^2}{\sigma_0^2 + \sigma_{\bar{x}}^2} \tag{12.11}$$

Thus the mean of the posterior distribution is a weighted mean that combines the mean of the prior distribution and the mean of the sampling distribution, each weighted by the variance of the other. It is clear that, if the variance of the prior distribution is large, the sample mean is weighted heavily, etc.

Furthermore, the variance of the posterior distribution depends only upon the variances of the prior and sampling distributions and is less than either of these quantities.

As a numerical example, consider the case in which the prior distribution of μ is normal with mean 6 and variance 16, while the sampling distribution of $\bar{X}$ is normal, $\bar{x} = 3$, and $\sigma_{\bar{x}}^2 = 4$. We have $\mu_0 = 6$, $\sigma_0^2 = 16$, $\bar{x} = 3$, $\sigma_{\bar{x}}^2 = 4$ so that

$$\mu_1 = \frac{4 \cdot 6 + 16 \cdot 3}{16 + 4} = \frac{72}{20} = 3.6$$

$$\sigma_1^2 = \frac{16 \cdot 4}{16 + 4} = \frac{64}{20} = 3.2$$

As a second example, we return to the Aunt Susie Candy Company whose management has decided to sample labor savings at other candy concerns now using the taffy machinery. In a sample of 20 firms across the nation they discover that, when actual figures are adjusted for number of employees involved and duration of use, $\bar{x} = 17,000$ and $\sigma_{\bar{x}}^2 = 12,100$. This phenomenally consistent result indicates a far better performance than the consulting engineer estimated. Under normal assumptions with $\mu_0 = 15,000$, $\sigma_0 = 4500$, $\bar{x} = 17,000$, and $\sigma_{\bar{x}} = 110$, the following results were then obtained for the posterior distribution:

$$\mu_1 = \frac{12,100 \cdot 15,000 + 20,250,000 \cdot 17,000}{20,250,000 + 12,100} = 16,999 \text{ hr}$$

$$\sigma_1^2 = \frac{20,250,000 \cdot 12,100}{20,250,000 + 12,100} = 12,093 \text{ hr}$$

The fact that the variance of the sampling distribution of $\bar{X}$ was so small compared to the variance of the prior distribution threw all the weight to the former and made the posterior distribution of μ depart almost entirely from the prior. Note also that σ_1^2 is less than both σ_0^2 and $\sigma_{\bar{x}}^2$.

Based on the posterior distribution, management should automate; that is, adopt act A_2, since $\mu_1 > \mu_b$. The moral of the Aunt Susie story is that a decision based on a prior distribution is likely to be a poor one if the prior is unrealistic. Even a very low expected value of perfect information based on the prior does not guarantee against this sort of pitfall, since it is an *expected* value and is computed directly from the prior. It only tells us that in many cases when the prior distribution is as assumed, the long-run expectation is as indicated.

Now let us calculate the expected value of perfect information from the Aunt Susie case, using the posterior distribution. Using σ_1 (which, in this case, approximates $\sigma_{\bar{x}}$),

$$|z_b| = \left| \frac{\mu_b - \mu_1}{\sigma_1} \right| = \left| \frac{16{,}000 - 17{,}000}{110} \right| = +9.1$$

$G(9.1) \approx 0$. Hence

$$E_p = |m_1 - m_2| \, \sigma_1 G(|z_b|)$$
$$= |2.5 - 0| \, (110)(0) \approx 0$$

The sample values are so consistent that management should feel that it has no need of a perfect predictor, since it may consider that it has on hand an approximately perfect one.

Although in this text we do not consider decisions based on more than one sample modifying the prior, the rationale involved in further extension can easily be seen. Since the posterior distribution here was so divergent from the prior, if management put any faith in its consulting engineer, a further sample might be taken as a check. (We assume that experience with automated taffy equipment is sufficiently widespread to allow this.) Then the posterior distribution might be combined with the new sampling distribution giving a "second-stage" posterior distribution as a basis for the final decision.

Of what real use is the cost of uncertainty? This question may be most easily answered by considering E_p as the expected value of perfect information. Not many executives have access to perfect predictors. The most feasible procedure for modifying a current prior distribution is the taking of a sample. It is clear that the information obtainable from a sample is less than per- fect. Hence the decision maker *should not pay as much for any sample as he would for a perfect predictor*. The cost of uncertainty forms an upper limit for possible sampling expenditures.

One of the most important contributions of decision theory to statistics is its approach to the question of whether to sample. It is wasteful to attack a problem through sampling procedures, to spend the money, to do the work, and then find that the information obtained is of insignificant value. By estimating sampling costs *in advance* and comparing these with the expected value of perfect information, one can often gain a useful insight into whether sampling should be used. For example, if $E_p = \$1500$ in a two-action decision problem and if total sampling costs were $6800, it would be better to base one's action on the prior distribution. E_p's usefulness depends on the fact that it can be calculated from the prior distribution, that is, before any sampling is done.

12.9   THE PREPOSTERIOR DISTRIBUTION—NORMAL CASE

In order to investigate more closely the problem of whether to sample before making a decision, we shall introduce the preposterior distribution—or the "preposterous distribution," as some call it. The key idea here relates to the mean of the posterior distribution. Thus far, we have reasoned that with a given prior we draw a sample and combine its information with the prior to obtain the posterior distribution—and, specifically, its mean μ_1. μ_1 is thus a number obtained after sampling. Now, let us shift the point of view and consider μ_1 before any sample is taken. μ_1 is then surely not known. It may have any one of many values depending on which sample actually eventuates. What we are saying is that before the sample is taken, μ_1, the mean of the posterior distribution, is a random variable. Its probability distribution is called the *preposterior distribution*.

Continuing the approach adopted in this chapter, we shall use the normal case to illustrate the algebraic approach, which frequently provides a neat result in continuous problems. Assume that we are faced with the situation described in the second paragraph of Section 12.8 where the prior distribution of μ is normal with mean μ_0 and variance σ_0^2 while the sampling distribution of $\bar{X}$ is also normal with mean μ and variance $\sigma_{\bar{X}}^2$. In this case the preposterior distribution of μ_1 is again normal in form. We shall now prove this and find its mean and variance.

We commence with the joint distribution of $\bar{X}$ and μ given in 12.8.

$$f(\mu, \bar{x}) = \frac{1}{2\pi\sigma_0\sigma_{\bar{X}}} e^{-[(\mu-\mu_0)^2/\sigma_0^2 + (\bar{x}-\mu)^2/\sigma_{\bar{X}}^2]/2} \qquad (12.12)$$

If we had the joint distribution of μ and μ_1 instead of the joint distribution of μ and $\bar{X}$ we could integrate out μ and find the distribution of μ_1 as a marginal. To get $g(\mu, \mu_1)$ we must substitute into (12.12) the value of $\bar{X}$ obtained from (12.10)

$$(\sigma_0^2 + \sigma_{\bar{X}}^2)\mu_1 = \sigma_{\bar{X}}^2\mu_0 + \sigma_0^2\bar{x}$$

$$\bar{x} = \frac{\sigma_0^2 + \sigma_{\bar{X}}^2}{\sigma_0^2}\mu_1 - \frac{\sigma_{\bar{X}}^2}{\sigma_0^2}\mu_0$$

and also multiply (12.12) by the quantity $\dfrac{d\bar{x}}{d\mu}$ [1] which is

$$\frac{d\bar{x}}{d\mu_1} = \frac{\sigma_0^2 + \sigma_{\bar{x}}^2}{\sigma_0^2}$$

(12.12) then becomes

$$g(\mu, \mu_1) = \frac{\sigma_0^2 + \sigma_{\bar{x}}^2}{2\pi\sigma_0^3\sigma_{\bar{x}}}$$

$$\times \exp\left\{-\left\{\frac{[\mu - \mu_0]^2}{\sigma_0^2} + \left[\frac{(\sigma_0^2 + \sigma_{\bar{x}}^2)}{\sigma_0^2}\mu_1 - \frac{\sigma_{\bar{x}}^2}{\sigma_0^2}\mu_0 - \mu\right]^2 \Big/ \sigma_{\bar{x}}^2\right\} \Big/ 2\right\} \quad (12.13)$$

The quantity in the inner braces in (12.13) can be expressed as

$$\frac{(\sigma_0^2 + \sigma_{\bar{x}}^2)}{\sigma_0^2\sigma_{\bar{x}}^2}\left[(\mu - \mu_1)^2 + \frac{\sigma_{\bar{x}}^2}{\sigma_0^2}(\mu_1 - \mu_0)^2\right] \quad (12.14)$$

by completing the square in μ and being reasonably careful about the algebra involved. We can then write (12.13) as

$$g(\mu, \mu_1) = \frac{\sigma_0^2 + \sigma_{\bar{x}}^2}{2\pi\sigma_0^3\sigma_{\bar{x}}}$$

$$\times \exp\left\{-\frac{1}{2}\frac{(\sigma_0^2 + \sigma_{\bar{x}}^2)}{\sigma_0^2\sigma_{\bar{x}}^2}(\mu - \mu_1)^2 - \frac{1}{2}\frac{(\sigma_0^2 + \sigma_{\bar{x}}^2)}{\sigma_0^4}(\mu_1 - \mu_0)^2\right\}$$

so that

$$h(\mu_1) = \frac{\sigma_0^2 + \sigma_{\bar{x}}^2}{2\pi\sigma_0^3\sigma_{\bar{x}}}\exp\left\{-\frac{1}{2}\frac{(\sigma_0^2 + \sigma_{\bar{x}}^2)}{\sigma_0^4}(\mu_1 - \mu_0)^2\right\}$$

$$\times \int_{\mu=-\infty}^{\infty}\exp\left\{-\frac{1}{2}\frac{(\sigma_0^2 + \sigma_{\bar{x}}^2)}{\sigma_0^2\sigma_{\bar{x}}^2}(\mu - \mu_1)^2\right\}d\mu$$

Let

$$z = \sqrt{\frac{\sigma_0^2 + \sigma_{\bar{x}}^2}{\sigma_0^2\sigma_{\bar{x}}^2}}(\mu - \mu_1) \qquad dz = \sqrt{\frac{\sigma_0^2 + \sigma_{\bar{x}}^2}{\sigma_0^2\sigma_{\bar{x}}^2}}\,d\mu$$

$$h(\mu_1) = \frac{(\sigma_0^2 + \sigma_{\bar{x}}^2)\,e^{-\frac{(\sigma_0^2 + \sigma_{\bar{x}}^2)}{2\sigma_0^4}(\mu_1 - \mu_0)^2}}{\sqrt{2\pi}\,\sigma_0^3\sigma_{\bar{x}}\,\sqrt{\dfrac{\sigma_0^2 + \sigma_{\bar{x}}^2}{\sigma_0^2\sigma_{\bar{x}}^2}}}\cdot\frac{1}{\sqrt{2\pi}}\int_{z=-\infty}^{\infty}e^{-z^2/2}\,dz$$

$$= \frac{1}{\sqrt{2\pi}\,\sqrt{\sigma_0^4/(\sigma_0^2 + \sigma_{\bar{x}}^2)}}\,e^{-(\mu_1 - \mu_0)^2/[2\sigma_0^4/(\sigma_0^2 + \sigma_{\bar{x}}^2)]} \quad (12.15)$$

---

[1] See any calculus text which discusses area-preserving transformation of continuous functions.

Thus μ_1 is normally distributed with mean and variance given by

$$E(\mu_1) = \mu_0 \tag{12.16}$$

$$\text{var } (\mu_1) = \frac{\sigma_0{}^4}{\sigma_0{}^2 + \sigma_{\bar{x}}{}^2} \tag{12.17}$$

It should not surprise us that the mean of the preposterior distribution is the same as the mean of the prior distribution. The effect of the sample on the mean μ_1 of the posterior distribution is to move it away from μ_0 in the direction of the sample mean $\bar{x}$. But before the sample is taken, $\bar{x}$ is as likely to be situated y units above μ_0 as it is to lie y units below μ_0. Consequently, in terms of expectations, it could be prophesied that the expected value of μ_1 would, indeed, be μ_0.

On the other hand, the variance of the preposterior distribution cannot be arrived at by intuition. The reader should be particularly careful not to confuse the variance of the preposterior distribution (12.17) with that of the posterior distribution (12.11). Since the preposterior variance may be written as

$$\sigma_0{}^2 \cdot \frac{\sigma_0{}^2}{\sigma_0{}^2 + \sigma_{\bar{x}}{}^2}$$

we see that the second factor is less than unity and that var $(\mu_1) < \sigma_0{}^2$. In other words, as we acquire additional information we reduce variances. Notice, also, that var (μ_1) depends on $\sigma_{\bar{x}}{}^2$. Since we are interested in using this before sampling, either a pilot study must be run to obtain an estimate of this quantity, or an estimate must be obtainable through some other procedure.

We continue the examples of Section 12.8. Given $\mu_0 = 6$, $\sigma_0{}^2 = 16$, and an estimate $\hat{\sigma}_{\bar{x}}{}^2 = 5$. Then $E(\mu_1) = \mu_0 = 6$ and

$$\text{var } (\mu_1) = \frac{(16)^2}{16 + 5} = 12.3$$

For the Aunt Susie Company, we had $\mu_0 = 15{,}000$ and $\sigma_0{}^2 = 20{,}250{,}000$. From a pilot study, an estimate of the population variance is found to be 700,000 in a sample of size 11. Thus, $\sigma_{\bar{x}}{}^2$ is estimated by $\hat{\sigma}_{\bar{x}}{}^2 = 70{,}000$. Hence $E(\mu_1) = \mu_0$ and

$$\text{var } (\mu_1) = \frac{(20{,}250{,}000)^2}{20{,}250{,}000 + 70{,}000} = 20{,}180{,}200$$

A comparison of the mean of the posterior distribution with the break-even point is known to be a valid basis for a decision so it is reasonable to assume that the mean and variance before sampling tell us something about the worthwhileness of sampling. With costs linear,

$$C_1 = m_1\mu + d_1 \qquad C_2 = m_2\mu + d_2$$

the expected value of sample information, E_s, is defined to be

$$E_s = |m_1 - m_2| \sqrt{\operatorname{var}(\mu_1)} G(|z_b'|) \tag{12.18}$$

where $|z_b'| = |\mu_b - \mu_0|/\sqrt{\operatorname{var}\mu_1}$. In other words, the expected value of sample information is computed from the preposterior distribution in exactly the same way in which the expected value of perfect information was computed from either the prior or the posterior distributions. This statement is relevant only to the normal case. We shall, first, compute E_s in the Aunt Susie case and then justify the use of the term "expected value of sample information."

For the numerical data in the Aunt Susie problem, $|m_1 - m_2| = 2.5$,

$$|z_b'| = \left| \frac{16,000 - 15,000}{\sqrt{20,180,200}} \right| = \left| \frac{1000}{4492} \right| = 0.22$$

$$E_s = (2.5)(4492)G(0.22) = (2.5)(4492)(0.2986)$$

$$= \$3304$$

In this example the expected value of sample information turns out to be fairly large. It is expected that considerable additional information will be obtained from sampling. However, reference should be made to the posterior distribution in the Aunt Susie problem to see that, in fact, the sample was valuable, since sample evidence deviated drastically from the prior distribution. It should also be noted that $\$3304 < \$3359$. The expected value of sample information cannot exceed the expected value of perfect information.

Why is E_s called the expected value of sample information? The idea is a simple analog to the expected value of perfect information previously discussed. In Section 12.7 we reasoned that if we chose the wrong alternative we would suffer an opportunity loss equal to the difference of costs of the two alternatives at the true value of μ. Then an expectation was computed based on, for instance, the prior distribution of μ. This quantity was the expected opportunity loss of the wrong decision—the amount that the decision maker should pay to obtain omniscience about the state of nature. Now, as a practical matter, omniscience is a fond hope. Information that it is possible to obtain will be sample information—imperfect information. We have, however, even before sampling a helpful concept—the preposterior distribution. This gives us an indication as to where we shall guess the true value of μ to be after sampling. We then reason as before using the preposterior distribution instead of the prior. If the wrong alternative is chosen, we would suffer an opportunity loss equal to the difference in ordinates of the two cost lines at the true value of μ. When we compute an expected loss based on the preposterior distribution, we find the amount that we should be willing to pay to obtain the sample evidence, since this distribution states, in effect, the expected sample evidence about the true value of μ.

12.10   THE PREPOSTERIOR DISTRIBUTION—DISCRETE CASE

In a problem in which probability distributions are discrete, the concept of expected value of sample information is still valid. The only new procedure is the computation of the preposterior distribution in numerical form. We shall carry out this calculation completely in one problem and then show how it is possible to abbreviate the process.

To get the preposterior distribution in the discrete case we simply compute the value of the parameter conditional on each possible value of the sample statistic. The marginal probabilities of the statistic then form the preposterior distribution of the parameter, since there is a one-to-one correspondence between the possible values of the statistic and the points in the domain of the preposterior distribution. Let us now proceed in Table 12.8 to find the preposterior distribution of $\tilde{p}_1$ for the Slocum problem. The first section of the table repeats Table 12.3 to a large extent.

In Table 12.9 we summarize the preposterior distribution of $\tilde{p}_1$ in the first two columns. In column 3 the costs under c_1 are computed for comparison with column 4. But such a comparison favors c_2 for all values of $\tilde{p}_1$. A moment's consideration shows that this must be the case since all values of $\tilde{p}_1$ are above the break-even point $p_b = 4.08\%$. As a practical matter, this means that no possible value of $\tilde{p}_1$ is small enough so that Slocum would wish to reverse its decision favoring A_2 if a sample were taken. Of course, the cause of this *fait accompli* is that the sample is so small that its evidence must be weighted lightly when it is combined with the prior distribution. We shall carry through computations of the expected value of sample information to illustrate the method, although in a problem where sample evidence cannot result in a change of decision, the expected value of the sample information must be

$$E_s = 0$$

In column 5 of Table 12.9, the costs are subtracted. If any of the entries in this column are negative, this indicates that the decision would be changed for this value of $\tilde{p}_1$; hence, an expected loss would be computed by multiplying the absolute value of each of these negative $c_1 - c_2$ entries by the corresponding figure in the $P(\tilde{p}_1)$ column and adding. This gives the expected value of sample information E_s. In the concluding discrete example this quantity is computed in a nontrivial case.

Table 12.8 The Preposterior Distribution of $\tilde{p}_1$—Slocum Problem

	$\tilde{p}(\%)$	$P(\tilde{p})$	$P(p \mid \tilde{p})$	$P(p, \tilde{p})$	$P(\tilde{p} \mid p)$	$\tilde{p}P(\tilde{p} \mid p)\,(\%)$
	2	0.3	0.9412	0.28236	0.3266	0.6532
	4	0.3	0.8847	0.26541	0.3069	1.2276
$p = 0$	6	0.2	0.8306	0.16612	0.1921	1.1526
	8	0.1	0.7787	0.07787	0.0901	0.7208
	10	0.1	0.7290	0 07290	0.0843	0.8430
			$P(p = 0) = 0.86566$	1.0000		4.5972
	2	0.3	0.0576	0.01728	0.1362	0.2724
	4	0.3	0.1106	0.03318	0.2615	1.0460
$p = 0.33$	6	0.2	0.1590	0.03180	0.2507	1.5042
	8	0.1	0.2031	0.02031	0.1601	1.2808
	10	0.1	0.2430	0.02430	0.1915	1.9150
			$P(p = 1) = 0.12687$	1.0000		6.0184
	2	0.3	0.0012	0.00036	0.0436	0.0872
	4	0.3	0.0046	0 00138	0.1673	0.6692
$p = 0.67$	6	0.2	0.0102	0.00204	0.2474	1.4844
	8	0.1	0.0177	0.00177	0.2145	1.7160
	10	0.1	0.0270	0.00270	0.3273	3.2730
			$P(p = 2) = 0.00825$	1.0001		7.2298
	2	0.3	0.0000	0.00000	0.0000	0.0000
	4	0.3	0.0001	0.00003	0.1364	0.5456
$p = 1.00$	6	0.2	0.0002	0.00004	0.1818	1.0908
	8	0.1	0.0005	0.00005	0.2273	1.8184
	10	0.1	0.0010	0.00010	0.4545	4.5450
			$P(p = 3) = 0.00022$	1.0000		7.9998

Table 12.9 Computation of Expected Value of Sample Information—Slocum Problem

$\tilde{p}_1$	$P(\tilde{p}_1)$	c_1	c_2	$c_1 - c_2$	$(c_1 - c_2)\,P(\tilde{p}_1)$
4.5972%	0.8647	\$441.32	\$392	\$49.32	—
6.0184	0.1269	577.77	392	185.77	—
7.2298	0.0082	694.06	392	302.06	—
7.9998	0.0002	767.98	392	375.98	—

Two other comments regarding samples are in order. We have just seen, in the Slocum case, that no sample of size three could possibly result in a value of $\tilde{p}_1$ that would call for a reversal of a decision based on the prior distribution. In the Aunt Susie case, where normal distributions were assumed, it was always possible for the sample to reverse the decision based on the prior, since unlikely extreme values may occur—and did in Section 12.8. This should suggest that an assumption of normality regarding the prior distribution is critical.

An important problem in decision theory follows from this discussion. Given that the expected value of sample information, for samples of size n_0, exceeds the costs of sampling, is n_0 in any sense optimal? Would not $n_0 + 10$ perhaps yield a larger difference between E_s and the costs of sampling? In general, as sample size increases, the costs of sampling rise, since a part of these costs are proportional to the number of items in the sample. On the other hand, as sample size increases, information obtained increases. We would expect that an optimum point would exist below and above which E_s minus sampling costs would diminish. Such is indeed the case in a number of situations, but we do not intend to do more than call attention to the problem of the best sample size.

12.11   CONCLUDING EXAMPLES

Wynn-Door Incorporated is a small company specializing in millwork—windows, doors, shelving, balusters, baseboards—any sort of home woodwork. Its largest selling items are doors of various sizes. Barney Sill, the owner of Wynn-Door, has been bothered in recent months by the number of finished doors that are not claimed by the customers who ordered them. These doors are not a total loss since most of them can be reworked to fit the specifications of other customers. However, storage costs are involved in addition to the reworking costs so that Mr. Sill estimates his losses on unclaimed doors at about $4.20 per door.

At present Wynn-Door charges a nominal down payment of $5.00 on all orders. Mr. Sill, in his exasperation, is considering instituting a policy of charging a down payment of half the selling price on all orders for doors. On the basis of yearly average sales of 1500 doors, he estimates that the introduction of such a policy would cost him about $1200 in goodwill—this, of course, above the cost of the doors themselves.

His records on unclaimed doors are not very complete. For the last several years he has not been directly concerned with the operation of the mill. Therefore, his prior distribution of $\tilde{p}$, the population percentage of unclaimed doors per year, leaves something to be desired. It is shown in Table 12.10 along with the expected costs based upon it.

Table 12.10   Expected Prior Costs—Wynn-Door Problem

			A_1	A_2
$\tilde{p}$	$P(\tilde{p})$	c_1	$c_1 P(\tilde{p})$	c_2
10%	0.1	$630	$63.00	$1200
15	0 2	945	189.00	
20	0.5	1260	630.00	
25	0.1	1575	157.50	
30	0.1	1890	189.00	
			1228.50	

Mr. Sill is thus considering two possible actions:

A_1: Continue present policy
A_2: Increase down payment to half price

His cost functions are

$$C_1 = 63\tilde{p} \qquad C_2 = 1200$$

Thus, the break-even point is $p_b = 1200/63 = 19.03\%$. Since

$$E(\tilde{p}) = 10(0.1) + 15(0.2) + 20(0.5) + 25(0.1) + 30(0.1)$$
$$= 1.0 + 3.0 + 10.0 + 2.5 + 3.0 = 19.5\%$$

we have $E(\tilde{p}) > p_b$, so that A_2, increase down payment, is the preferable action.

Let us next find the expected value of perfect information, a quantity that has been shown relevant to the decision to sample or not to sample. We compute prior expected opportunity losses in Table 12.11. E_p, the cost of uncertainty, is thus the smaller of the expected losses, $108. Mr. Sill should not pay more than $108 for sampling. We shortly obtain a better estimate by computing the expected value of sample information. Note that Table 12.11 confirms, as it must, the decision just taken on the basis of the prior distribution. Note also that $136.50 - 108.00 = $1228.50 - 1200.00 = $28.50.

Although Mr. Sill wishes to reach a decision in a hurry, he decides to wait until ten doors are sold, treating these as a random sample, and checking the percentage unclaimed. To compute the expected value of sample information we might determine the complete preposterior distribution of $\tilde{p}_1 = E(\tilde{p})$ as in Table 12.8 and then find E_s as in Table 12.9. But the eleven possible values of p would lead to eleven values of $\tilde{p}_1$ and a fair amount of computation.

Table 12.11 Expected Prior Opportunity Losses—Wynn-Door Problem

| $\tilde{p}$ | $P(\tilde{p})$ | A_1 | | A_2 | |
		L_1	$L_1P(\tilde{p})$	L_2	$L_2P(\tilde{p})$
10%	0.1	$0	$0	$570	$57
15	0.2	0	0	255	51
20	0.5	60	30.00	0	0
25	0.1	375	37.50	0	0
30	0.1	690	69.00	0	0
			136.50		108

Table 12.12 Abbreviated Preposterior Distribution of $\tilde{p}_1$—Wynn-Door Problem

	$\tilde{p}(\%)$	$P(\tilde{p})$	$P(p\mid\tilde{p})$	$P(p,\tilde{p})$	$P(\tilde{p}\mid p)$	$\tilde{p}P(\tilde{p}\mid p)\;(\%)$
	10	0.1	0.3487	0.03487	0.2556	2.5560
	15	0.2	0.1969	0.03938	0.2887	4.3305
$p = 0$	20	0.5	0.1074	0.05370	0.3937	7.8740
	25	0.1	0.0563	0.00563	0.0413	1.0325
	30	0.1	0.0282	0.00282	0.0207	0.6210
				0.13640	1.0000	16.4140
	10	0.1	0.3874	0.03874	0.1417	1.4170
	15	0.2	0.3474	0.06948	0.2542	3.8130
$p = 0.1$	20	0.5	0.2684	0.13420	0.4911	9.8220
	25	0.1	0.1877	0 01877	0.0687	1.7175
	30	0.1	0.1211	0.01211	0.0443	1.3290
				0.27330	1.0000	18.0985
	10	0.1	0.1937	0.01937	0.0699	0.6990
	15	0.2	0.2759	0.05518	0.1992	2.9880
$p = 0.2$	20	0.5	0.3020	0.15100	0.5450	10.9000
	25	0.1	0.2816	0.02816	0.1016	2.5400
	30	0.1	0.2335	0.02335	0.0843	2.5290
				0.27706	1.0000	19.6560

What if the sample size were 50 or 500? It seems worthwhile to develop an abbreviated method of finding E_s.

This is not hard to do. For all values of $\tilde{p}_1$ which are greater than the break-even point $p_b = 19.03$ percent, A_2 will be the best action, and its cost will be the constant $1200. Therefore, we need only to enumerate the individual values of $\tilde{p}_1$ up to p_b, and the remaining computations can be lumped together. Tables 12.12 and 12.13 contain the necessary arithmetic.

Table 12.12 shows that $\tilde{p}_1$ first exceeds $p_b = 19.03$ percent when $p = 0.2$. Thus in Table 12.13 the marginal probabilities above $p = 0.2$ (or $\tilde{p}_1$ above

Table 12.13   Expected Value of Sample Information—Wynn-Door Problem

$\tilde{p}_1$	$P(\tilde{p}_1)$	c_1	c_2	$c_1 - c_2$	$|c_1 - c_2|\, P(\tilde{p}_1)$
16.4140%	0.1364	$1034.08	$1200	−$165.92	$22.63
18.0985	0.2733	1140.20	1200	−59.80	16.34
$> p_b = 19.03$	0.5903	—	1200	>0	—
					38.97

19.03 percent) are classed together. For any value of $\tilde{p}_1 > 19.03$, the decision to adopt A_2 and increase the down payment would stand, as the sample evidence would only confirm the decision based on the prior distribution. In such cases, the sample information would have no value to Mr. Sill. Only if the sample leads to a reversal of the decision based on the prior distribution— that is, only if $\tilde{p}_1 < 19.03$—is the sample information worth obtaining. We compute the expected value of sample information in the last column of Table 12.13 by using only the first two rows and obtain $E_s = \$38.97$.

Since Mr. Sill thinks that the cost of actually obtaining a sample of 10 doors will be only about $10.00 (10 new orders for doors should certainly turn up within a week) he decides to take the sample. When this is done, it is found that exactly 1 out of 10 doors is unclaimed. Thus $p = 0.1$, and the posterior distribution $P(\tilde{p} \mid p)$ is that of Table 12.12, column 5, across from $p = 0.1$. Table 12.14 gives the computation of expected posterior costs. Based on these costs, we see that the best action is A_1—continue the present procedure. Of course, the computations of Table 12.14 would not be needed in practice since, based on the posterior distribution with $p = 0.1$, we have already shown in Table 12.12 that the expected value $\tilde{p}_1$ is less than the break-even value p_b.

Because the values $E(\tilde{p})$ (based on the prior distribution) and $\tilde{p}_1$ (based on the posterior) are both close to the break-even point, Mr. Sill should

Table 12.14   Expected Posterior Costs—Wynn-Door Problem

		A_1		A_2
$\tilde{p}$	$P(\tilde{p} \mid p)$	c_1	$c_1 P(\tilde{p} \mid p)$	c_2
10%	0.1417	$630	$89.27	$1200
15	0.2542	945	240.22	
20	0.4911	1260	618.79	
25	0.0687	1575	108.20	
30	0.0443	1890	83.73	
			1140.21	

not be too confident that the decision that he reached was optimal. He would do well to examine another sample from his current door operations—perhaps paying more attention to the idea of a random sample—and to combine its information with that of the first and second columns of Table 12.14 to obtain a new posterior distribution and, hence, a new basis for his decision. In general, many decisions can benefit from a recurring review summed up in the development of some new posterior distribution.

We close this discussion of the Wynn-Door problem with Table 12.15, which computes expected opportunity losses based on the posterior distribution. It can be seen that the difference in expectations checks with that of Table 12.14—as, of course, it must.

$$\$145.59 - 85.80 = \$1200.00 - 1140.21 = \$59.79$$

Table 12.15   Expected Posterior Opportunity Losses—Wynn-Door Problem

		A_1		A_2	
$\tilde{p}$	$P(\tilde{p} \mid p)$	L_1	$L_1 P(\tilde{p} \mid p)$	L_2	$L_2 P(\tilde{p} \mid p)$
10%	0.1417	$0	$0	$570	$80.77
15	0.2542	0	0	255	64.82
20	0.4911	60	29.47	0	0
25	0.0687	375	25.76	0	0
30	0.0443	690	30.57	0	0
	1.0000		85.80		145.59

As a final illustration of two-action decisions where sampling and non-sampling information may be profitably combined, let us consider a problem faced by the Rosselini Rifle Company. One of its products is a 22-caliber rifle that enjoys great popularity among the youth of the nation. However, there has recently been customer dissatisfaction with its gunsight. This standard sight is numbered Gunsight 80-D and is, indeed, not overly accurate. Rosselini is considering replacing it by the more accurate 93-B sight. Use of the 93-B sight would increase the cost of each rifle to Rosselini by $1. Because of close competition, it would not be feasible to raise the selling price of the rifles. Thus the question is: Would the improved sight result in an increase in sales sufficient to offset the cost increase?

In any case, it is not planned either to increase or diminish the sales effort. Present sales average 50,000 rifles annually. Profit per rifle is estimated at $3.00 (tax aspects of the Rosselini problem will not be considered here). Thus the company would benefit from adopting the 93-B gunsight if its mean annual sales, μ, were greater than 75,000 rifles after the change. This break-even point is given by

$$50,000(\$3) = \mu_b(\$2)$$

$$\mu_b = 75,000$$

since the $1 increase in costs would leave $2 profit after the change. The question is, then: Would the adoption of the new gunsight increase rifle sales by more than 25,000 on an average annual basis?

Let the possible choices be:

A_1: Change to the 93-B sight

A_2: Continue the 80-D sight

Instead of cost functions, it is convenient to work here with profit functions. If the present profit on a 22-caliber rifle is $3, then the profit function under A_2 is

$$F_2 = 50,000(3) = 150,000$$

while under A_1 it is

$$F_1 = 2\mu$$

giving $\mu_b = 75,000$ as before. Note that dealing with profits instead of costs will reverse some of the previous reasoning.

Rosselini's sales manager was consulted concerning the possible effects of introducing the more accurate gunsight. After discussion he was willing to estimate that the most likely average number of yearly sales would be 80,000, and that there was a 50-50 chance that the number would be between 74,000 and 86,000. Based on these rough estimates, the Rosselini Company's prior distribution of μ was obtained as follows: first, normality was assumed, then μ_0 was taken as 80,000, and finally σ_0 was computed from $0.67\sigma_0 = 6000$ as $\sigma_0 = 9000$.

Since $\mu_0 > \mu_b$, the company should surely adopt A_1 and change to the 93-B gunsight if the prior distribution is to be the determining factor. The cost of uncertainty, computed from (12.7), is given by

$$E_p = 2(9000)G(0.56) = 2(9000)(0.1799) = \$3238.20$$

since

$$|z_b| = \left| \frac{\mu_b - \mu_0}{\sigma_0} \right| = \left| \frac{75,000 - 80,000}{9000} \right| = |-0.56| = 0.56$$

The rather sizable cost of uncertainty is caused primarily by the large size of the sales manager's estimate of σ_0. His estimate of μ is not very reliable; hence the company should be willing to pay a little more than \$3200 for a perfect sales predictor, if such were available.

Of course, it is *not* available. However, the company was interested in obtaining further information before making a decision. The preposterior distribution of μ_1 has a normal form with mean $\mu_0 = 80,000$ and, from (12.17), variance:

$$\text{var}\,(\mu_1) = \frac{(9000)^4}{(9000)^2 + \sigma_{\bar{x}}{}^2}$$

A rough estimate of $\sigma_{\bar{x}}{}^2$ was needed. Rosselini had sales data on a similar sight modification that it had made on a more powerful rifle a number of years before. Based on a random sample of six years of such data, and with modifications to allow for the larger number of sales in the 22 category, it seemed reasonable to estimate $\sigma_{\bar{x}} = 5000$, making the standard deviation of the preposterior distribution equal to

$$\sqrt{\text{var}\,\mu_1} = \frac{(9000)^2}{\sqrt{(9000)^2 + (5000)^2}} = 7868$$

'The expected value of sample information is then found from the preposterior distribution in the same way as the expected value of perfect information is found from the prior distribution.

$$E_s = 2(7868)G(0.64) = 2(7868)(0.1580) = \$2486.29$$

since

$$|z_b{}'| = \left| \frac{75,000 - 80,000}{7868} \right| = |-0.64| = 0.64$$

Now the Rosselini Company recognized the difficulty of obtaining random sampling information from the real population of interest, that is, future yearly sales. But since management was conservative in product modification, it decided to adopt a compromise. It chose a set of representative outlets in several cities and placed models with the new sight on sale there for two consecutive years. The sales figures for the set of outlets were compiled, modified, and formed into estimates of $\bar{x}$ and $\sigma_{\bar{x}}$ based on a sample of size two from the population of yearly sales. The figures obtained were $\bar{x} = 70,000$, $\sigma_{\bar{x}} = 4000$.

The posterior distribution of μ was then found to have mean

$$\mu_1 = \frac{(4000)^2 80,000 + (9000)^2 70,000}{(9000)^2 + (4000)^2} = 71,649$$

and variance

$$\sigma_1{}^2 = \frac{(9000)^2 (4000)^2}{(9000)^2 + (4000)^2} = 13,360,825$$

or standard deviation $\sigma_1 = 3655$.

Since $\mu_1 = 71,649$ rifles was less than the break-even point $\mu_b = 75,000$ rifles, Rosselini decided not to introduce the more expensive gunsight. The evidence failed to suggest that the use of the 93-B sight would improve sales sufficiently to cover the additional costs.

The analysis presented in the Rosselini case is open to criticism at several points. What are these points, and why might they be criticized?

IMPORTANT TERMS AND CONCEPTS

Bayes' theorem
Break-even point
Cost
  Expected
  Of uncertainty
Expected value
  Of perfect information
  Of sample information
Linear cost function

Loss
  Expected opportunity
  Opportunity
Probability
  Objective
  Subjective
Probability distribution
  Posterior
  Preposterior
  Prior
Two-action decision problem

SYMBOLS AND ABBREVIATIONS

A_1	$\tilde{p}$	σ_0
A_2	p	μ_1
C_1	p_b	σ_1
C_2	μ	$E(\tilde{p})$
c_1	$\bar{x}$	$E(\mu)$
c_2	μ_b	$E(\mu_1)$
L_1	μ_0	var (μ_1)
L_2		

OFTEN-USED FORMULAS

$$P(B_i \mid E) = \frac{P(B_i)P(E \mid B_i)}{\sum_{j=1}^{n} P(B_j)P(E \mid B_j)}$$

If $C_1 = m_1 X + d_1$ and $C_2 = m_2 X + d_2$

then $x_b = -\dfrac{d_1 - d_2}{m_1 - m_2}$ $C_b = \dfrac{m_1 d_2 - m_2 d_1}{m_1 - m_2}$

$$E_p = |m_1 - m_2|\, \sigma_0 G(|z_b|)$$

where $z_b = \dfrac{\mu_b - \mu_0}{\sigma_0}$

$$\mu_1 = \frac{\sigma_{\bar{x}}^2 \mu_0 + \sigma_0^2 \bar{x}}{\sigma_0^2 + \sigma_{\bar{x}}^2} \; ; \qquad \sigma_1^2 = \frac{\sigma_0^2 \sigma_{\bar{x}}^2}{\sigma_0^2 + \sigma_{\bar{x}}^2}$$

$$E(\mu_1) = \mu_0; \qquad \text{var} \,(\mu_1) = \frac{\sigma_0^4}{\sigma_0^2 + \sigma_{\bar{x}}^2}$$

$$E_s = |m_1 - m_2|\, \sqrt{\text{var} \,(\mu_1)}\; G(|z_b'|)$$

where $z_b' = \dfrac{\mu_b - \mu_0}{\sqrt{\text{var} \,(\mu_1)}}$

EXERCISES

1. Two boxes, B_1 and B_2, contain red and white tickets in different proportions. Box B_1 contains 15 white and 30 red tickets, while B_2 contains 20 white and 40 red tickets. One box is chosen at random and a ticket is removed. It is white. What is the probability that B_1 was selected?

2. Suppose that in Exercise 1 a sample of two tickets was chosen at random (without replacement) from a randomly selected box. If the tickets were one white and one red, what is the probability that box B_1 was selected?

3. The Landschmidt Corporation owns three plants which we shall designate as Albany plant, Denver plant, and Houston plant. These plants have, respectively, 100, 150, and 200 employees in the age bracket from 35 to 45 years. Of these employees, respectively, 30 percent, 60 percent, and 25 percent have worked for the company long enough to have standard benefits accruing to their heirs in case of death. Assuming that all workers in this age bracket are equally likely to die, what is the probability that if a Denver plant worker in the 35 to 45 age bracket dies, his heirs receive standard death benefits?

4. The string section of the Chugville Symphony Orchestra is composed of 12 first violins, 10 second violins, 8 violas, 8 violincellos, and 6 double basses. In this orchestra there are only two types of players: average players, who play 1 sour note per 100, and poor players, who play 1 sour note per 25. There are 4 poor players among the first violins, 8 among the second violins, 2 among the violas, 1 among the cellos, and 4 among the basses. During the orchestra's performance of Brahms' Fourth Symphony, a horrid sour note is heard, emanating from the cellos. What is the probability that it originated with one of the average players?

5. Of 100 persons attending a meeting to discuss the construction of a community fall-out shelter, 60 are Republicans, 30 are Democrats, and 10 are Radicals. There are 30 Republicans, 5 Democrats, and 1 Radical who are known to favor the project—the rest are opposed. An unidentified person arises from the group to speak in favor of constructing the shelter. What is the probability that he is a Democrat?

6. A selected group of 50 common stocks contains 25 industrials, 10 railroads, and 15 utilities. On January 2, 20 industrials, 5 railroads, and 3 utilities rose; the rest fell. If a single stock is picked at random from the group and is discovered to have fallen on January 2, what is the probability that it is a railroad issue?

7. A vase V_1 contains 7 white and 4 red marbles. A second vase V_2 contains 3 white and 9 red marbles. Two marbles are transferred from V_1 to V_2, and then one marble is selected from V_2 and found to be red. What is the probability that both of the transferred marbles were red?

8. The Sultan of Bangaloo has been captured by a band of rebellious conspirators consisting of 12 janissaries, 6 mercenaries, 3 dignitaries, and 4 secretaries. They argue all day as to what to do with His Highness. There are 5 janissaries, 3 mercenaries, 2 dignitaries, and 1 secretary who favor chopping off his ears; 6 janissaries, 3 mercenaries, 1 dignitary, and no secretaries favor chopping off his head; the rest wish to release him unharmed. To reach a decision, 62 clam shells are placed in a pot, 61 of these being blank, and one marked with a letter X. The person drawing the marked shell will be allowed to go to the tent in which the Sultan is held captive and proceed as he wishes. Dignitaries are allowed 4 draws, janissaries 3, secretaries 2, and mercenaries 1. Eventually, the Sultan is found in a badly decapitated condition. Assuming that no one cheated, what is the probability that a janissary drew the marked clamshell?

9. In the Bardorff Department Store problem (Section 12.2), find the probability that the misdated check is not forged, given that one-tenth of 1 percent of all checks are forged. Show that this number plus $P(B_1 \mid E) = 1$.

10. Describe a decision from your own experience that was made on the basis of a subjective prior probability distribution.

11. In the Slocum problem (Section 12.4), suppose that the prior probability distribution was:

$\tilde{p}$	$P(\tilde{p})$
2%	0.1
4	0.2
6	0.3
8	0.3
10	0.1

Suppose, also, that the cost functions were as originally given.
a. Use the expected value criterion to reach a decision favoring either A_1 or A_2.
b. Compute the posterior distribution of $\tilde{p}$ given no defective micrometers in a random sample of three.
c. Use the expected value criterion to reconsider the previous decision in the light of the posterior distribution.

12. a. In Exercise 11, compute the expected value of perfect information based on the prior distribution.

b. Also compute the expected value of sample information—calculating only as much of the preposterior distribution as is necessary.

13. King Hammurabi of Babylon was once engaged in a large-scale building project involving a ziggurat and several temples. He needed 1 million high-quality mud bricks. The standard Babylonian process produced 5 percent defective bricks. However, it was reported that a better process had been developed at the nearby city of Warka which produced only 2 percent defective bricks. The loss accruing to Hammurabi from one defective brick, when converted into modern terms, was approximately $0.03. The king's chief artisan was consulted and asked to assign probabilities to likely percentages of defective bricks—using the Warka process. The chief artisan's prior distribution was thus

$\tilde{p}$	$P(\tilde{p})$
2	0.400
3	0.300
4	0.200
5	0.050
6	0.025
7	0.025

a. Reach a decision as to which process Hammurabi should use on the basis of the chief artisan's prior distribution.
b. What is the expected value to Hammurabi of perfect information using the prior distribution?
c. Compute the preposterior distribution of $\tilde{p}_1$ in this problem.
d. What is the expected value of the sample information of part *b* to Hammurabi?
e. Hammurabi, a shrewd old solon who knows that all that glitters isn't necessarily mud, sends a trusty minion to Warka who returns with 50 guaranteed Warka process bricks. Under testing, 5 are found to be defective. Compute Hammurabi's posterior distribution under binomial assumptions, and reach a revised decision as to which process should be used.

14. In Exercise 13, assume that Hammurabi reevaluates the cost of a defective brick at 2.5¢.

a. Set up new cost functions and reach a decision on the basis of expected costs using the prior distribution.
b. Calculate expected opportunity losses and reach a decision on their comparison.

   c. Check your results in parts *a* and *b* to show that the difference in expected costs equals the difference in expected losses.

15. In Exercise 14 use the posterior distribution:
   a. To reach a decision on the basis of expected costs.
   b. To reach a decision on the basis of expected opportunity losses.

16. Derive formula (12.7) for the case in which $E(\mu) = \mu_0 > \mu_b$.

17. In the Aunt Susie Candy Company problem (Section 12.7), assume that the consulting engineer had estimated that the mean number of hours saved is most likely to be 15,250 hours, with a 50-50 chance that this average would lie between 13,250 and 17,250 hours.
   a. Reach a decision to automate or not to automate, based on the expected value criterion and the prior distribution.
   b. Calculate the cost of uncertainty based upon the prior distribution.
   c. Find the preposterior distribution of μ for an estimated $\sigma_{\bar{x}}^2$ of 3 million.
   d. Find the expected value of sample information.
   e. Given a sample with $\bar{x} = 16,500$ and $\sigma_{\bar{x}}^2 = 3$ million, find the posterior distribution of μ.
   f. Reach a decision to automate or not to automate, based on the expected value criterion and the posterior distribution.
   g. Calculate the cost of uncertainty based on the posterior distribution.

18. Transtonic, Inc. was a newly organized firm attempting to enter the small computer market—which, at that time, was split between three large manufacturers of computers. Transtonic's engineering division had produced a preliminary model that would compete with current machines, but would not sweep the field. As almost all projected business would be in terms of rentals, the daily rental price of the new computer was the key figure. This would almost certainly have to be about $100 per day.

   Two of Transtonic's executives were formerly with National Wiretube Associates, one of the most important manufacturers of computers. On the basis of that company's experience, Transtonic felt that the firm could realize profits with a discounted present value of $40 for each day's rental during the initial year of sales.

   Now the costs of going into production with the preliminary model were estimated at $2,000,000. If a rental volume of $2,000,000/$40/day = 50,000 days was not attained during the first sales year, it was felt that the operation would wind up in the red. The sales department had compiled a list of 25,000 businesses and other groups which, it felt, represented essentially all of its potential customers in the small computer field. The break-even point was, then, 50,000/25,000 = 2 rental days per potential customer during the first year.

The sales department was presented with this analysis and asked for an estimate of average rental days during the first year, based on its own list. After much comment on blue-sky predictions, the department came up with an average of 1.8 rental days per potential customer as the most likely figure. However, it was felt that there was a 50-50 chance that the figure might be as low as 1.0 or as high as 2.6 rental days per year.

    a. Determine the prior distribution of μ, the first-year's average rental days per potential customer, and reach a decision to produce the computer or not, on the basis of the prior distribution.

    b. Determine the cost of uncertainty based on the prior distribution.

19. Because of the vague nature of the sales department's estimate in Exercise 18, it was felt necessary to take a random sample from the list of 25,000 potential customers. $n = 25$ was chosen, and representatives of 25 randomly selected firms were given a day's introduction to the preliminary model.

    a. Before this was done, the Transtonic executives estimated the variance of a sample of 25 firms at 0.09 (rental days per potential customer). What is the preposterior distribution of μ? What is the expected value of sample information?

    b. The actual sample gave an estimate of 2.3 rental days per potential customer with a variance of 0.04. Find the posterior distribution of μ. What is the cost of uncertainty based on the posterior distribution?

    c. Should Transtonic produce its new computer?

20. The West Yorkopolis Community Association is endeavoring to finance a private swimming club. Construction of a pool and ancillary facilities will cost $35,000 initially. Maintenance will be covered from annual dues, but construction costs must be covered by an entrance fee, which has been set at $250 per family. Thus, 140 families must join the club to cover the construction costs.

    West Yorkopolis has 3500 families, and no outsiders are eligible. Thus a break-even point of $p_b = 140/3500 = 4\%$ is critical. The Splasharound Pool Company, during negotiation with the Association, estimated the percentage of families joining according to the following prior distribution.

$\tilde{p}$	$P(\tilde{p})$
1%	0.01
2	0.05
3	0.16
4	0.18
5	0.48
6	0.12

a. Use the expected value criterion to reach a decision to sign or not to sign a construction contract with Splasharound.

b. Find the cost of uncertainty based on the prior.

21. The Community Association in Exercise 20 is suspicious of Splasharound's rosy picture and decides to take a random sample of six families and check as to whether they will become members.

a. Compute the preposterior distribution of $\tilde{p}_1$, the percentage of swimming club member families in West Yorkopolis.

b. Find the expected value of sample information in this case.

22. In the random sample of Exercise 21, one family appears likely to join the swimming club. Determine the posterior distribution of the percentage of member families. Reach a decision to sign or not to sign with Splasharound on the basis of the posterior distribution. Should the Association actually act on the basis of the posterior distribution? Discuss.

23. In the case where $g(\mu)$ and $g_1(\bar{x} \mid \mu)$ are both normally distributed, prove that $E_p \geq E_s$ when E_p is based on the prior.

13 Descriptive Measures of Bivariate Distributions

13.1 INTRODUCTION

Suppose that, in connection with an advertising campaign for a luxury product, we need to estimate the incomes of readers of a magazine that circulates widely among upper-income families. Income data are regarded as confidential and are difficult to obtain. Therefore, we would like to estimate income from some other variable that is more readily available but that bears a close relationship to income. For families living in owner-occupied dwellings, assessed value of the dwelling might be such a variable, while for families living in a rented dwelling, monthly rental could serve the purpose. Suppose we restrict ourselves to families living in owner-occupied dwellings. We wish to estimate annual family income Y from assessed value of the family dwelling X. In order to estimate Y from X, we need to know the joint probability distribution of the two variables. From this joint distribution, we can derive the conditional distribution of family income, Y, given the assessed value of the family dwelling, x. This conditional distribution will help us to make probability statements about family income from a knowledge of the assessed value of the family dwelling. We will have gained something from these calculations if they reduce the degree of our uncertainty about family income. This degree of uncertainty is measured by the variance of the conditional probability distribution of family income.

If we had not decided to seek information on a variable that we thought closely related to income, we would have had to base our estimates on the marginal probability distribution of incomes. Our measure of uncertainty in this case would be the variance of the marginal distribution. When we introduced information on the assessed value of the family dwelling, we base our estimates of income, Y, on the conditional distribution of Y given the assessed value of the family dwelling, x. Our measure of uncertainty becomes the variance of this conditional distribution. For each possible value of X

there is a different conditional distribution. If, on the average, the variance of the conditional distribution of Y given x is less than the variance of the marginal distribution of Y, then information about X reduces the degree of uncertainty about Y. In this chapter we shall consider the computation and comparison of descriptive measures of marginal and conditional probability distributions.

We shall also introduce a new idea. In choosing to use information on the assessed value of the family dwelling to help in estimating family income, we thought that these variables were "closely related." What do we mean by this? In mathematics—or in science—when we study the relationship between two variables, we study the behavior of one variable as the other changes; that is, we see if the two variables vary together. In a probabilistic sense, we do the same thing in statistics; as one variable changes, we can examine the behavior of either the conditional probability distribution of the other variable or of its moments. In either case, we are studying related changes in the two variables, and we must introduce the idea of "correlation," a measure of the way in which two random variables vary together.

It is clear that we shall be dealing with joint probability distributions of two random variables. We suggest a review of Chapter 5 to make sure that the concepts of joint, marginal, and conditional probability distributions are understood, since these ideas will be of fundamental importance in what follows.

13.2   THE COMPARISON OF DESCRIPTIVE MEASURES FOR MARGINAL AND CONDITIONAL DISTRIBUTIONS

To introduce some of the basic ideas of this chapter more specifically, let us consider an example. Let X be the pre-tax income from salaries, and Y, the pre-tax income from other sources of 5000 middle-management men. The joint distribution of these two variables can be represented by the model

$$f(x, y) = \frac{1}{256} \qquad 10 < x < 26 \qquad 2 < y < x$$

Both X and Y are in thousands of dollars. Suppose, now, that we want to estimate pre-tax income from other sources for a middle-management man picked at random from the 5000 studied. If we cannot use information about pre-tax income from salaries as auxiliary information, then our estimate will have to be based on the marginal distribution of Y, the variable that we want to estimate. To obtain this distribution, we must "integrate out" x in $f(x, y)$. When we draw a sketch, we will see that the range of integration for x depends on y. If y is between 2 and 10, x can take any value between 10 and 26, whereas, if y is between 10 and 26, x can take any value between y and

26. We have, then,

$$h(y) = \int_{10}^{26} \frac{1}{256} \, dx = \frac{1}{16} \qquad 2 < y \le 10$$

$$h(y) = \int_{y}^{26} \frac{1}{256} \, dx = \frac{26 - y}{256} \qquad 10 < y < 26$$

Having obtained $h(y)$, we can make our estimate. The form of this estimate depends on its purpose, and we shall assume that the mean is satisfactory. Our estimate of y is

$$E(Y) = \frac{1}{16} \int_2^{10} y \, dy + \frac{1}{256} \int_{10}^{26} y(26 - y) \, dy = 3 + \frac{23}{3} = \frac{32}{3}$$

Without information about pre-tax income from salary, we would estimate that the pretax income from other sources for a middle-management man, picked at random from the 5000 studied, would be about \$10,700. The variance of $h(y)$ is a measure of our uncertainty concerning this estimate. We compute the variance in steps:

$$E(Y^2) = \frac{1}{16} \int_2^{10} y^2 \, dy + \frac{1}{256} \int_{10}^{26} y^2(26 - y) \, dy = \frac{62}{3} + \frac{374}{3} = \frac{436}{3}$$

$$\sigma_Y{}^2 = E(Y^2) - [E(Y)]^2 = \frac{436}{3} - \left(\frac{32}{3}\right)^2 = \frac{284}{9}$$

If information about X, pre-tax income from salaries, is available, we should base our estimate of Y on the conditional distribution of Y given x. When we apply the methods of Chapter 5, we obtain

$$g_1(y \mid x) = \frac{f(x, y)}{g(x)} = \frac{1/256}{(x - 2)/256} = \frac{1}{x - 2} \qquad 2 < y < x$$

Since the conditional distribution of Y given x depends on x, there is reason to hope that information about X is useful in estimating Y. Conditional probability distributions have descriptive measures just as do other distributions. Here, we are interested in the mean and variance of $f(y \mid x)$. We shall indicate these measures by $E(Y \mid x)$ and $\sigma^2(Y \mid x)$ and refer to them as the conditional mean and conditional variance of Y given x. When we apply the usual definitions,

$$E(Y \mid x) = \int_2^x \frac{y}{x - 2} \, dy = \frac{1}{2} \frac{x^2 - 4}{x - 2} = \frac{1}{2}(x + 2)$$

$$E(Y^2 \mid x) = \int_2^x \frac{y^2}{x - 2} \, dy = \frac{1}{3} \frac{x^3 - 8}{x - 2} = \frac{1}{3}(x^2 + 2x + 4)$$

$$\sigma^2(Y \mid x) = \frac{1}{3}(x^2 + 2x + 4) - \frac{1}{4}(x + 2)^2 = \frac{1}{12}(x - 2)^2$$

Given the pre-tax income from salary, X, the estimated pre-tax income from other sources is a linear function of pre-tax income from salary. For example, suppose we have a middle-management man whose pre-tax salary was $12,000. In this case, $x = 12$, and

$$E(Y \mid x = 12) = \frac{1}{2}(12 + 2) = 7$$

Our estimate of his pre-tax income from other sources is $7000. Our measure of uncertainty, the variance, depends on X, the pre-tax income from salaries (in thousands of dollars). If $x = 12$, then

$$\sigma^2(Y \mid x = 12) = \frac{1}{12}(12 - 2)^2 = \frac{100}{12}$$

Without information about pre-tax income from salaries, our measure of uncertainty, σ_Y^2, was 284/9. Hence, when $x = 12$, information about X produces a smaller degree of uncertainty than no information about X.

To make a general statement about the reduction in the degree of uncertainty, we must consider the fact that X is a random variable. We must compute the expected value of $\sigma^2(Y \mid x)$ by taking into account the marginal probability distribution of X. We are "averaging" over X, and we denote this operation by the symbol $E_X[\sigma^2(Y \mid x)]$. Thus

$$E_X[\sigma^2(Y \mid x)] = \int_{-\infty}^{\infty} \sigma^2(y \mid x) f(x) \, dx$$

$$= \frac{1}{12} \int_{10}^{26} (x - 2)^2 \frac{(x - 2)}{256} \, dx = \frac{1}{12(256)} \int_{8}^{24} u^3 \, du = \frac{80}{3}$$

if we let $u = x - 2$.

When information about X is used, on the average, our measure of uncertainty is 80/3; when information about X is not used, it is 284/9. Hence, information about X reduces the measure of uncertainty by

$$\frac{284/9 - 80/3}{284/9} = \frac{44}{284} = 0.155$$

or 15.5 percent. In Figure 13.1 we compare the marginal distribution of pre-tax income from other sources, Y, with the conditional distribution of this variable given that pre-tax income from salaries is $12,000. This figure shows how information about X shifts the mean of the conditional distribution of Y away from the mean of the marginal distribution and how the "spread" of the distribution of Y is reduced when information about X is available.

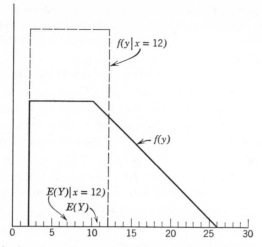

Fig. 13.1. Marginal and conditional distributions of pre-tax income from sources other than salaries.

The conditional expected value of Y varies in a reasonable way with X in the sense that, as pre-tax income from salaries increases, pre-tax income from other sources also increases. To examine this relationship more closely, note that the marginal distribution of X is given by

$$g(x) = \frac{x - 2}{256} \qquad 10 < x < 26$$

From this, we compute

$$E(X) = \int_{10}^{26} x\, \frac{x - 2}{256}\, dx = \frac{58}{3}$$

We have already computed

$$E(Y) = \frac{32}{3}$$

With these marginal expected values, we can rewrite the deviation of the conditional mean from the marginal mean as

$$E(Y \mid x) - E(Y) = \frac{x + 2}{2} - \frac{32}{3} = \frac{x + 2 - 64/3}{2}$$

$$= \frac{x - 58/3}{2} = \frac{x - E(X)}{2}$$

We see that, as X deviates from its expected value in a given direction, the conditional expected value of Y deviates from the marginal expected value of Y in the same direction. If pre-tax income from salaries is above average, we would expect pre-tax income from other sources to be above average, while below average pre-tax income from salaries leads to the expectation of below average pre-tax income from other sources. It is in this sense that the two variables are related.

To summarize, the preceding analysis has introduced the following ideas.

1. If we are faced with the problem of estimating the value of a random variable, Y, we can consider the possibility of using the value of another random variable, X, as auxiliary information. In order to use this information, we must consider the joint distribution of the two random variables.

2. Without information about the value of X, our estimate of the value of Y must be based on the marginal distribution of Y. One estimate of y would be the mean of this marginal distribution, and the measure of our uncertainty about the estimate would be the variance of the marginal distribution.

3. With information about the value of X, our estimate of the value of Y will be based on the conditional distribution of Y given x. Our estimate will be the mean of this conditional distribution, and our measure of uncertainty will be its variance.

4. Auxiliary information about X will be useful in estimating Y if the conditional expected value of Y given x depends in some way on the value of X and if, on the average, the variance of the conditional distribution of Y given x is less than the variance of the marginal distribution of Y.

Suppose now that we consider the joint distribution of the same two variables, pre-tax income from salaries and pre-tax income from other sources, for college professors. This (very hypothetical) distribution is

$$f(x, y) = \frac{3}{40,000} (x - 5)(25 - x) \qquad 5 < x < 25 \qquad 0 < y < 10$$

The derived marginal and conditional distributions are.

$$h(y) = \frac{1}{10} \qquad 0 < y < 10$$

$$g(x) = \frac{3}{4000} (x - 5)(25 - x) \qquad 5 < x < 25$$

$$g_1(y \mid x) = \frac{1}{10} \qquad 0 < y < 10$$

We see, here, that the marginal and conditional distributions of Y are the same. Any conclusion drawn from the conditional distribution could be drawn from the marginal distribution, and information about X is of no help in estimating Y. We learned in Chapter 5 that X and Y are independent random variables if the marginal distribution of Y is the same as the conditional distribution of Y given x. We see, then, that if the auxiliary variable, X, is independent of the variable we are trying to estimate, Y, then X is of no use in estimating Y. For these methods to be useful, X and Y must be *interdependent*, not *independent*.

13.3   THE BIVARIATE NORMAL DISTRIBUTION

In applications, the most important bivariate probability distribution is the bivariate normal, which was introduced in Section 5.8. In its most general form, it is given by

$$
f(x, y) = \frac{1}{2\pi\sigma_X\sigma_Y\sqrt{1 - \rho^2}} \exp\left\{\frac{-1}{2(1 - \rho^2)}\left[\left(\frac{x - \mu_X}{\sigma_X}\right)^2\right.\right.
$$

$$
\left.\left. - 2\rho\left(\frac{x - \mu_X}{\sigma_X}\right)\left(\frac{y - \mu_Y}{\sigma_Y}\right) + \left(\frac{y - \mu_Y}{\sigma_Y}\right)^2\right]\right] \tag{13.1}
$$

$$
-\infty < x < \infty \qquad -\infty < y < \infty
$$

As in Chapter 5, we shall simplify this function by introducing the new variables

$$
u = \frac{x - \mu_X}{\sigma_X} \qquad v = \frac{y - \mu_Y}{\sigma_Y}
$$

The joint, marginal, and conditional distributions of the new variables were derived in Chapter 5, and we repeat them here. The joint distribution is

$$
f(u, v) = \frac{1}{2\pi\sqrt{1 - \rho^2}} e^{-(u^2 - 2\rho uv + v^2)/2(1 - \rho^2)} \qquad -\infty < u, v < \infty \tag{13.2}
$$

the two marginal distributions are

$$
g(u) = \frac{1}{\sqrt{2\pi}} e^{-u^2/2} \qquad -\infty < u < \infty \tag{13.3}
$$

$$
h(v) = \frac{1}{\sqrt{2\pi}} e^{-v^2/2} \qquad -\infty < v < \infty \tag{13.4}
$$

and the two conditional distributions are

$$
g_1(v \mid u) = \frac{1}{\sqrt{1 - \rho^2}\sqrt{2\pi}} e^{-(v - \rho u)^2/2(1 - \rho^2)} \qquad -\infty < v < \infty \tag{13.5}
$$

$$
h_1(u \mid v) = \frac{1}{\sqrt{1 - \rho^2}\sqrt{2\pi}} e^{-(u - \rho v)^2/2(1 - \rho^2)} \qquad -\infty < u < \infty \tag{13.6}
$$

The marginal and conditional distributions are symmetric in the sense that the marginal distribution of V can be obtained from that of U by changing the letter u to the letter v, and the conditional distribution of U given v can be obtained from the conditional distribution of V given u in the same way. Hence, it will suffice to consider the marginal and conditional distributions of only one of the variables, for example, U.

Since the marginal distribution of U in (13.3) is just the standardized normal distribution, we know without calculation that

$$E(U) = 0 \quad \text{and} \quad \sigma_U{}^2 = 1 \tag{13.7}$$

And by examining the conditional distribution of U given V shown in (13.6), we see that this is the distribution of a normally distributed random variable with mean ρv and standard deviation $\sqrt{1 - \rho^2}$.[1] This gives, without calculation,

$$E(U \mid v) = \rho v$$
$$\sigma^2(U \mid v) = 1 - \rho^2 \tag{13.8}$$

The mean is a linear function of v, and the variance is independent of v. Hence,

$$E_V[\sigma^2(U \mid v)] = 1 - \rho^2.$$

The interpretation of our results for the bivariate normal distribution will be easier if we first put them in terms of X and Y rather than in terms of U and V. For the marginal mean and variance,

$$E(U) = E\left(\frac{X - \mu_X}{\sigma_X}\right) = \frac{1}{\sigma_X} E(X) - \frac{1}{\sigma_X} \mu_X = 0$$

or

$$E(X) = \mu_X$$

$$\sigma_U{}^2 = E\left(\frac{X - \mu_X}{\sigma_X}\right)^2 = \frac{1}{\sigma_X{}^2}[E(X^2) - 2\mu_X E(X) + \mu_X{}^2]$$

$$= \frac{1}{\sigma_X{}^2}[E(X^2) - \mu_X{}^2] = 1$$

since

$$E(X^2) - \mu_X{}^2 = E(X^2) - [E(X)]^2 = \sigma_X{}^2$$

The same kind of argument, applied to the conditional mean and variance,

---

[1] See the discussion of the mean and variance of the normal distribution in Chapter 6.

gives

$$E(U \mid v) = E\left(\frac{X - \mu_X}{\sigma_X} \,\bigg|\, \frac{y - \mu_Y}{\sigma_Y}\right) = \rho v = \rho\left(\frac{y - \mu_Y}{\sigma_Y}\right)$$

$$\frac{1}{\sigma_X}\left[E\left(X \,\bigg|\, \frac{y - \mu_Y}{\sigma_Y}\right)\right] - \frac{1}{\sigma_X}\mu_X = \frac{1}{\sigma_Y}(\rho y - \rho \mu_Y)$$

$$E\left(X \,\bigg|\, \frac{y - \mu_Y}{\sigma_Y}\right) = \mu_X + \rho\frac{\sigma_X}{\sigma_Y}(y - \mu_Y)$$

If we are given $(y - \mu_Y)/\sigma_Y$ and know μ_Y and σ_Y we are, essentially, given y, so we can write

$$E(X \mid y) = \mu_X + \rho\frac{\sigma_X}{\sigma_Y}(y - \mu_Y) \tag{13.9}$$

By a lengthy but very similar argument, we can show that

$$\sigma^2(X \mid y) = \sigma_X{}^2(1 - \rho^2) \tag{13.10}$$

Formulas (13.9) and (13.10) apply, of course, only to the bivariate normal distribution.

13.4   USE OF THE BIVARIATE NORMAL

In the preceding section, we have obtained the expected value and the variance of the marginal and conditional distributions of one of the two variables in a bivariate normal distribution. By interchanging symbols we easily obtain the results for the second variable. We summarize our results in (13.11)

$$E(X) = \mu_X \qquad\qquad E(Y) = \mu_Y$$

$$E(X^2) - [E(X)]^2 = \sigma_X{}^2 \qquad\qquad E(Y^2) - [E(Y)]^2 = \sigma_Y{}^2$$

$$E(X \mid y) = \mu_X + \rho\frac{\sigma_X}{\sigma_Y}(y - \mu_Y) \quad E(Y \mid x) = \mu_Y + \rho\frac{\sigma_Y}{\sigma_X}(x - \mu_X) \tag{13.11}$$

$$\sigma^2(X \mid y) = \sigma_X{}^2(1 - \rho^2) \qquad\qquad \sigma^2(Y \mid x) = \sigma_Y{}^2(1 - \rho^2)$$

As an illustration of the use of these results, suppose that we are interested in predicting a student's numerical grade in elementary statistics on the basis of his score in a mathematics aptitude test and that we are willing to assume that the joint distribution of these two variables can be approximated by the bivariate normal distribution given by (13.1). We shall designate score in the aptitude test by X and numerical grade in elementary statistics by Y, and we shall assume that the parameters in (13.1) are:

$$\mu_X = 600 \qquad \sigma_X = 50 \qquad \mu_Y = 85 \qquad \sigma_Y = 5 \qquad \rho = 0.8$$

Since we are interested in predicting Y from X, we can write

$$E(Y \mid x) = \mu_Y + \rho \frac{\sigma_Y}{\sigma_X}(x - \mu_X) = 85 + 0.8\left(\frac{5}{50}\right)(x - 600)$$

$$= 37 + 0.08x$$

$$\sigma^2(Y \mid x) = \sigma_Y^2(1 - \rho^2) = 25(1 - 0.64) = 9$$

From $E(Y \mid x)$, we see that the expected grade in statistics increases as the score in the mathematics aptitude test increases and that the variance of the conditional distribution of Y given x is less than that of the marginal distribution of Y. Use of information about mathematics aptitude score in predicting numerical grade in statistics reduces our measure of uncertainty, the variance of the appropriate probability distribution of Y, by

$$\frac{25 - 9}{25} = \frac{16}{25} = 0.64$$

or 64 percent. The fact that $\rho^2 = 0.64$ and that the use of information about X to predict Y reduces the measure of uncertainty by 64 percent is not a coincidence when X and Y have the bivariate normal probability distribution. We can see this from the results given in (13.11). If we do not use information about X, then the measure of uncertainty is σ_Y^2; when we use information about X, this measure is reduced to $\sigma^2(Y \mid x) = \sigma_Y^2(1 - \rho^2)$. The reduction in variance expressed as a proportion of σ_Y^2 is

$$\frac{\sigma_Y^2 - \sigma_Y^2(1 - \rho^2)}{\sigma_Y^2} = \rho^2$$

We can say that, in the bivariate normal probability distribution, ρ^2 is the proportion by which $\sigma^2(Y \mid x)$ differs from σ_Y^2 and by which $\sigma^2(X \mid y)$ differs from σ_X^2. The quantity ρ^2 has the same interpretation when X is being predicted from Y as it does when Y is being predicted from X.

The usefulness of the reduction in uncertainty will become clear if we illustrate with a specific numerical example. Suppose we want to predict a certain student's grade in elementary statistics. Because this grade is a random variable, we admit at the outset that we cannot expect to predict it "on the nose." We decide, instead, to state a range of possible grades and to give odds that the student's grade will lie within the stated range. Furthermore, we want the range to be as narrow as possible for any given set of odds. In the case of the bivariate normal distribution, the range will be as narrow as possible if we center it on the mean of the distribution of grades. The odds that we give are quite arbitrary; the greater the odds, the greater the range. Suppose we set the odds at 19 to 1; that is, we want to state a range centered on the mean of the distribution of grades such that the chances are 95 percent (19 out of 20) that the grade of the student we have in mind will fall in this range. If the distribution of grades is normal, the range would be given by the mean plus or minus 1.96 times the standard deviation. Knowing nothing about this student's aptitude score, we would have to base our range on the marginal distribution of grades.

$$95 \text{ Percent Range} = 85 \pm 1.96(5) = 85 \pm 9.8$$

that is, we will give odds of 19 to 1 that the grade of this particular student will be between 75.2 and 94.8. This is the best we can do knowing nothing about his mathematics aptitude score.

Suppose, however, that this particular student is very good at mathematics, his mathematics aptitude score being 700. His aptitude for mathematics should be of some help to him in statistics. In this case the conditional distribution of grades, given mathematics aptitude score, is normal with a mean of

$$E(Y \mid x = 700) = 37 + 0.08(700) = 37 + 56 = 93$$

and a variance of

$$\sigma^2(Y \mid x = 700) = 9$$

We can now base our range on a normal probability distribution with a mean of 93 and a standard deviation of 3:

$$95 \text{ Percent Range} = 93 \pm 1.96(3) = 93 \pm 5.9$$

Knowing his mathematics aptitude score, we are now willing to give odds of 19 to 1 that his grade will be between 87.1 and 98.9. Two things have happened to the range. First, the center has shifted upward to take account of the fact that this student's mathematics aptitude score is above average. Second, the width has been narrowed from $94.8 - 75.2 = 19.6$ to $98.9 - 87.1 = 11.8$ grade points. In this sense, information about the student's mathematics aptitude score has made us less uncertain about his grade in statistics.

13.5 THE CORRELATION RATIO

In the preceding sections, we have implicitly introduced a measure of association between two random variables. In each of the examples we have computed the proportion by which, on the average, the variance of the conditional distribution of the variable being predicted differed from the variance of the marginal distribution. This proportion is the ratio of the difference between the two variances divided by the variance of the marginal distribution, and it is called the *correlation ratio*.

Definition 13.1. If X and Y are random variables, $g_1(y \mid x)$ the conditional distribution of Y given x, $h(y)$ the marginal distribution of Y, and $g(x)$ the marginal distribution of X, then the *correlation ratio of Y on X* is denoted by the symbol $\eta^2(Y \cdot X)$ and defined by

$$\eta^2(Y \cdot X) = 1 - \frac{E_X[\sigma^2(Y \mid x)]}{\sigma_Y^2} \tag{13.12}$$

where $\sigma^2(Y \mid x)$ is the variance of $g_1(y \mid x)$ and σ_Y^2 is the variance of $h(y)$. The numerator of the ratio in (13.12) is given by

$$E_X[\sigma^2(Y \mid x)] = \sum_{x=-\infty}^{\infty} \sigma^2(Y \mid x)g(x)$$

if X is discrete, and by

$$E_X[\sigma^2(Y \mid x)] = \int_{-\infty}^{\infty} \sigma^2(Y \mid x)g(x)\,dx$$

if X is continuous. $\eta^2(Y \cdot X)$ is not defined if σ_Y^2 is zero.

The correlation ratio of Y on X may be thought of as a measure of the reduction in uncertainty obtained by using $E(Y \mid x)$ as a prediction of Y instead of $E(Y)$. If the ratio is large, the reduction in uncertainty is large, and there is something to be gained by taking X into account; if the ratio is small, the reduction in uncertainty is small, and there is not much to be gained by taking X into account. What is meant by "large" and "small" in this case is a matter for personal judgment. Since variances are never negative, the correlation ratio cannot exceed unity. Also it can be shown that $E_X[\sigma^2(Y \mid x)]$ cannot exceed σ_Y^2. Hence, the correlation ratio must lie between zero and unity.

13.6   LINEAR PREDICTION

Other measures of association between two random variables arise in connection with the theory of *linear prediction*. Suppose that X and Y are discrete random variables whose joint distribution is $f(x, y)$ and that we want to predict Y from an equation of the form:

$$Y_p = \alpha + \beta X \tag{13.13}$$

where the subscript p means "predicted." [2] We are using a linear equation

[2] We specify that X and Y are discrete in order to simplify the mathematics. Our final results will be unaffected by this assumption.

in X as a prediction of Y. The error that we make in our prediction is measured by the difference $Y - Y_p$, that is, by $Y - \alpha - \beta X$. When we take into account the probabilistic behavior of both X and Y, we want our average squared error to be as small as possible. We can choose any values we wish for α and β, so we will choose these values in such a way that this average squared error,

$$E[(Y - \alpha - \beta X)^2] = \sum \sum (y - \alpha - \beta x)^2 f(x, y) \qquad (13.14)$$

is as small as possible. The sums in (13.14) are understood to be taken over all values of X and Y in the domain of $f(x, y)$.

If the quantity to be minimized in (13.14) were only a function of one variable, we could differentiate with respect to this variable, set the derivative equal to zero, and solve for the variable. We have two variables to find, α and β, but we do essentially the same thing.[3] We differentiate (13.14) with respect to α, treating β as a constant, and set the derivative equal to zero. Then we differentiate (13.14) with respect to β, treating α as a constant, and set the derivative equal to zero. We will have two equations in two unknowns; all we have to do is solve them for α and β. The derivative of (13.14) with respect to α when β is treated as a constant is called the *partial derivative with respect to α*. It is denoted by the symbol:

$$\frac{\partial}{\partial \alpha} E[(Y - \alpha - \beta X)^2]$$

Similarly, the derivative with respect to β when α is treated as a constant is called the *partial derivative with respect to β* and is denoted by

$$\frac{\partial}{\partial \beta} E[(Y - \alpha - \beta X)^2]$$

Partial derivatives were used in Section 9.4.

Now (13.14) is a sum, and the derivative of a sum is the sum of the derivatives of the quantities that make up the sum. When we take the partial derivative of (13.14) with respect to α and set it equal to zero, we obtain

$$\frac{\partial}{\partial \alpha} E[(Y - \alpha - \beta X)^2] = -2 \sum \sum (y - \alpha - \beta x) f(x, y) = 0$$

This quantity will be equal to zero if the double sum is equal to zero, so we can divide out "-2." Thus

$$\sum \sum y f(x, y) - \alpha \sum \sum f(x, y) - \beta \sum \sum x f(x, y) = 0$$

---

[3] More strictly, the vanishing of the first partial derivative is a necessary but not sufficient condition for a relative maximum or minimum.

Since $f(x, y)$ is a probability distribution, $\sum \sum f(x, y) = 1$ and the other sums are, respectively, the means of Y and X. Hence

$$E(Y) = \alpha + \beta E(X) \tag{13.15}$$

Next, we differentiate (partially, remember) with respect to β.

$$\frac{\partial}{\partial \beta} E[(Y - \alpha - \beta X)^2] = -2 \sum \sum x(y - \alpha - \beta x) f(x, y) = 0$$

Again we can divide by the "-2," so that

$$\sum \sum xy f(x, y) - \alpha \sum \sum x f(x, y) - \beta \sum \sum x^2 f(x, y) = 0$$

or

$$E(XY) = \alpha E(X) + \beta E(X^2) \tag{13.16}$$

The quantities $E(Y)$, $E(X)$, $E(XY)$, and $E(X^2)$ can be computed if we know $f(x, y)$, so (13.15) and (13.16) constitute a system of two linear equations in two unknowns, α and β.[4] In matrix notation, we can write this system as

$$\begin{bmatrix} E(Y) \\ E(XY) \end{bmatrix} = \begin{bmatrix} 1 & E(X) \\ E(X) & E(X^2) \end{bmatrix} \begin{bmatrix} \alpha \\ \beta \end{bmatrix} \tag{13.17}$$

We wish to find α and β. Suppose we multiply each side of (13.17) by the matrix

$$\begin{bmatrix} 1 & E(X) \\ E(X) & E(X^2) \end{bmatrix}^{-1}$$

and then exchange sides. Since any matrix times its inverse is the unit matrix,

$$\begin{bmatrix} \alpha \\ \beta \end{bmatrix} = \begin{bmatrix} 1 & E(X) \\ E(X) & E(X^2) \end{bmatrix}^{-1} \begin{bmatrix} E(Y) \\ E(XY) \end{bmatrix} \tag{13.18}$$

The inverse of a two-by-two matrix is easy to compute. Suppose

$$A = \begin{bmatrix} a & b \\ c & d \end{bmatrix}$$

The inverse of A is

$$A^{-1} = \frac{1}{ad - bc} \begin{bmatrix} d & -b \\ -c & a \end{bmatrix}$$

---

[4] The reader who is unfamiliar with vectors and matrices may skip the rest of this paragraph and the next two paragraphs. α and β may be obtained by solving (13.15) and (13.16) by elimination and substitution. The use of matrices may seem unnecessary in this problem, but in more difficult problems their use greatly facilitates the calculations involved.

The reader should check this by multiplying A by A^{-1} and showing that this product is the unit matrix. For us,

$$\begin{bmatrix} 1 & E(X) \\ E(X) & E(X^2) \end{bmatrix}^{-1} = \frac{1}{E(X^2) - E^2(X)} \begin{bmatrix} E(X^2) & -E(X) \\ -E(X) & 1 \end{bmatrix}$$

but

$$E(X^2) - E^2(X) = \sigma_X^2$$

and

$$\begin{bmatrix} 1 & E(X) \\ E(X) & E(X^2) \end{bmatrix}^{-1} = \frac{1}{\sigma_X^2} \begin{bmatrix} E(X^2) & -E(X) \\ -E(X) & 1 \end{bmatrix} \qquad (13.19)$$

When we apply (13.19) to (13.18) and do the necessary arithmetic, we obtain the values of α and β which minimize $E[(Y - \alpha - \beta X)^2]$.

$$\alpha = \frac{E(X^2)E(Y) - E(X)E(XY)}{\sigma_X^2}$$

$$\qquad (13.20)$$

$$\beta = \frac{E(XY) - E(X)E(Y)}{\sigma_X^2}$$

From the computational point of view, it is easiest to compute β from the formula given in (13.20) and then to find α from a rearranged form of (13.15):

$$\alpha = E(Y) - \beta E(X)$$

This method of computing α and β is called the method of "least squares" because we have chosen α and β so as to minimize the average squared error in prediction.

As an illustration of the application of these results, let us return to our example of the sources of income of middle-management men. For this example, we know that

$$f(x, y) = \frac{1}{256} \qquad 10 < x < 26 \qquad 2 < y < x$$

let's do the following:

$$h(y) = \begin{cases} \dfrac{1}{16} & 2 < y \le 10 \\[2mm] \dfrac{1}{256}(26 - y) & 10 < y < 26 \end{cases}$$

$$g(x) = \frac{1}{256}(x - 2) \qquad 10 < x < 26$$

There is no need to illustrate the computation of

$$E(X) = \frac{58}{3} \qquad E(X^2) = \frac{1180}{3} \qquad E(Y) = \frac{32}{3} \qquad \sigma_X^2 = \frac{176}{9}$$

but for $E(XY)$.

$$E(XY) = \int_{-\infty}^{\infty} \int_{-\infty}^{\infty} xyf(x, y)\, dy\, dx$$

$$= \frac{1}{256} \int_{10}^{26} \int_{2}^{x} xy\, dy\, dx = \frac{1}{256} \int_{10}^{26} x \left[\int_{2}^{x} y\, dy \right] dx$$

$$= \frac{1}{256} \int_{10}^{26} x \left(\frac{x^2 - 4}{2} \right) dx = \frac{1}{512} \int_{10}^{26} (x^3 - 4x)\, dx = 216$$

When we substitute our computed quantities into (13.17),

$$\begin{bmatrix} \dfrac{32}{3} \\[2mm] 216 \end{bmatrix} = \begin{bmatrix} 1 & \dfrac{58}{3} \\[2mm] \dfrac{58}{3} & \dfrac{1180}{3} \end{bmatrix} \begin{bmatrix} \alpha \\[2mm] \beta \end{bmatrix}$$

In order to solve this system, we use (13.19) to compute the inverse of the matrix on the right.

$$\begin{bmatrix} 1 & \dfrac{58}{3} \\[2mm] \dfrac{58}{3} & \dfrac{1180}{3} \end{bmatrix}^{-1} = \frac{9}{176} \begin{bmatrix} \dfrac{1180}{3} & -\dfrac{58}{3} \\[2mm] -\dfrac{58}{3} & \dfrac{3}{3} \end{bmatrix} = \frac{3}{176} \begin{bmatrix} 1180 & -58 \\[2mm] -58 & 3 \end{bmatrix}$$

Thus, setting $216 = 648/3$ to simplify the calculation,

$$\begin{bmatrix} \alpha \\ \beta \end{bmatrix} = \frac{3}{176} \begin{bmatrix} 1180 & -58 \\ -58 & 3 \end{bmatrix} \begin{bmatrix} 32 \\ 648 \end{bmatrix} \frac{1}{3} = \frac{1}{176} \begin{bmatrix} 176 \\ 88 \end{bmatrix} = \begin{bmatrix} 1 \\ 1/2 \end{bmatrix}$$

Our predicting equation is

$$Y_p = 1 + \tfrac{1}{2} X$$

Notice that this predicting equation is the same as $E(Y \mid x)$. This result is quite general; whenever $E(Y \mid x)$ is a linear function of X, the linear predicting equation whose coefficients are obtained by the method of least squares will be the same as $E(Y \mid x)$.

The equation given by (13.13) is called the *least-squares regression equation of Y on X*, and the constant β, which is its slope, is called the *least-squares regression coefficient*. As we have said, the term "least-squares" arises from the fact that we minimized the expected value of the squared error in prediction. The term "regression" was first used by the English scientist, Sir Francis Galton (1822–1911), who noticed that tall fathers tended to have tall sons and short fathers short sons. Although there is nothing remarkable in this observation, he also noticed that the sons of both tall and short fathers tended to have heights that were closer to average than did their fathers. He called this phenomenon "regression toward the mean," and he named the line describing it graphically the "regression line." Galton is considered the originator of many of the concepts of this section.

13.7   THE COEFFICIENT OF DETERMINATION

The regression coefficient, β, is a measure of the "sensitivity" of Y_p to changes in X. The numerator in the formula for β given by (13.20) depends on both X and Y and is a measure of the way in which the expected value of one variable changes as the other variable changes. It is in units of X times units of Y. The denominator is in the square of the units of X. Hence, the units of β are units of Y per unit of X. The numerator of β is called the *covariance of X and Y*. It was introduced in Chapter 7.

Definition 13.2.   If X and Y are random variables, their covariance is

$$\text{cov}\,(X,\ Y) = E[X - E(X)][Y - E(Y)] \tag{13.21}$$

A more convenient form of the covariance was given in (7.14). This was

$$\text{cov}\,(X,\ Y) = E(XY) - E(X)E(Y)$$

If X and Y are independent, their covariance will be zero, since $E(XY)$, in that case, can easily be shown to equal $E(X)E(Y)$.

By examining the covariance as defined by (13.21), we can see how the nature of the relationship between X and Y determines at least the sign of the covariance. Suppose, first, that large values of X tend to be associated with large values of Y and small values of X with small values of Y. That is, when X exceeds its expected value, Y tends to exceed its expected value, and when X is less than its expected value, Y tends also to be less than its expected value. Under these circumstances, $X - E(X)$ and $Y - E(Y)$ will tend to have the same sign, and the expected value of their product will be positive. On the other hand, if large values of X tend to be associated with small values of Y and small values of X with large values of Y, then $X - E(X)$ and $Y - E(Y)$

will tend to have opposite signs so that the expected value of their product is negative. Hence, a positive covariance implies a tendency for Y to increase as X increases so that β in the regression equation should be positive, and a negative covariance implies a tendency for Y to decrease as X increases so that β should be negative. If X and Y are independent, there is no tendency for Y to vary with X so that the product of $X - E(X)$ and $Y - E(Y)$ will sometimes be positive and at other times be negative. On the average these positive and negative values will cancel each other so that the covariance of X and Y is zero. When X and Y are independent, the regression equation should predict the same value of Y for every value of X, and β should be zero.

If, instead of computing the slope of the least-squares regression line of Y on X, we had computed the slope of the least-squares regression line of X on Y, we would find it to be equal to the covariance of X and Y divided by the variance of Y. Thus, the slopes of both least-squares regression lines depend directly on the covariance. Since variances are never negative, both slopes will have the same sign as the covariance. The product of the slopes of the two regression lines is called the *coefficient of determination*, but this coefficient is easier to interpret if we arrive at it in another way.

We can predict Y either by using (13.13), which is based on information about X, or by using the expected value of the marginal distribution of Y, which makes no use of such information. If we use the regression equation, our average squared error in prediction is $E[(Y - \alpha - \beta X)^2]$, whereas if we use the expected value of the marginal distribution of Y, our average squared error is $\sigma_Y{}^2$. The complement of the ratio of these two quantities would be a measure of the reduction of error obtained if the regression equation, instead of the mean of the marginal distribution, were used as a prediction. Before developing this measure however, we had better put $E[(Y - \alpha - \beta X)^2]$ into more tractable terms. By squaring, substituting for α, and performing some judicious algebra, one can show that

$$E[(Y - \alpha - \beta X)^2] = \sigma_Y{}^2 - \beta^2 \sigma_X{}^2 \tag{13.22}$$

We seek the complement of the ratio of $E[(Y - \alpha - \beta X)^2]$ to $\sigma_Y{}^2$. We shall call this quantity ρ^2. (The ρ that appears in the bivariate normal distribution is a special case of this ρ, as we shall see shortly.) Now

$$\rho^2 = 1 - \frac{E[(Y - \alpha - \beta X)^2]}{\sigma_Y{}^2} = 1 - \frac{\sigma_Y{}^2 - \beta^2 \sigma_X{}^2}{\sigma_Y{}^2} = \frac{\beta^2 \sigma_X{}^2}{\sigma_Y{}^2} \tag{13.23}$$

But, from the second equation of (13.20),

$$\beta = \frac{\operatorname{cov}(X, Y)}{\sigma_X{}^2} \tag{13.24}$$

and (13.23) can be written as

$$\rho^2 = \frac{[\text{cov}(X, Y)]^2}{\sigma_X{}^2 \sigma_Y{}^2} \tag{13.25}$$

The β given by (13.24) is the slope of the least-squares regression line of Y on X. To avoid confusion, we shall sometimes use a more descriptive notation: $\beta(y . x)$. Similarly, $\beta(x . y)$ is the slope of the least-squares regression line of X on Y. The notation $\alpha(y . x)$ and $\alpha(x . y)$ will also unambiguously identify the regression line to which the constant α belongs. Analogously to (13.24), we can write

$$\beta(y . x) = \frac{\text{cov}(X, Y)}{\sigma_X{}^2} \qquad \beta(x . y) = \frac{\text{cov}(X, Y)}{\sigma_Y{}^2}$$

Our measure of improvement, ρ^2, is the product of these two quantities, but it has a more meaningful interpretation. If we predict Y from the least-squares regression line of Y on X instead of predicting the expected value of the marginal distribution of Y, or if we predict X from the least-squares regression line of X on Y instead of predicting the expected value of the marginal distribution of X, we will reduce our average squared error by the proportion ρ^2. This implies that ρ^2 must be a number between zero and unity, a fact that can be easily deduced from our results. Suppose, first, that we could predict Y from the regression line without error. Then $Y - \alpha - \beta X$ would be zero for all values of X so that $E[(Y - \alpha - \beta X)^2]$ would be identically zero. From (13.23) we see that ρ^2 would be unity. If, on the other hand, X and Y were independent, the covariance and hence $\beta(y . x)$ would be zero. If $\beta(y . x)$ is zero, we can see from (13.15) that $\alpha(y . x)$ will be the same as $E(Y)$. Under these circumstances $E[(Y - \alpha - \beta X)^2]$ would be the same as $\sigma_Y{}^2$, and (13.23) tells us that ρ^2 would be zero. The larger the value of ρ^2, the more we stand to gain by using the regression line as a prediction instead of the expected value of the marginal distribution. The symbol ρ^2 is called the coefficient of determination. Its square root, ρ, is called the *coefficient of correlation* and is given the same sign as the covariance or as β.

Definition 13.3. If X and Y are random variables with standard deviations σ_X and σ_Y, respectively, and covariance cov (X, Y), the coefficient of correlation of X and Y is denoted by the symbol ρ and defined by

$$\rho = \frac{\text{cov}(X, Y)}{\sigma_X \sigma_Y}$$

The square of ρ is called the coefficient of determination.

For our source of income example,

$$\text{cov}(X, Y) = E(XY) - E(X)E(Y) = 216 - \frac{58}{3} \cdot \frac{32}{3} = \frac{88}{9}$$

The covariance is positive, which means that when X, income from salaries, is above average, Y, income from other sources, tends to be above average. If we want to estimate income from salaries using income from other sources as an auxiliary variable, we must compute

$$\beta(x \cdot y) = \frac{\text{cov}(X, Y)}{\sigma_Y^2} = \frac{88/9}{284/9} = \frac{22}{71}$$

The constant in the predicting equation, which we shall denote by $\alpha(x \cdot y)$, can be obtained by interchanging X and Y in (13.15) above and solving for α.

$$E(X) = \alpha(x \cdot y) + \beta(x \cdot y)E(Y)$$

$$\frac{58}{3} = \alpha(x \cdot y) + \left(\frac{22}{71}\right)\left(\frac{32}{3}\right)$$

$$\alpha(x \cdot y) = \frac{58}{3} - \left(\frac{22}{71}\right)\left(\frac{32}{3}\right) = \frac{1138}{71}$$

Our predicting equation is

$$X_p = \frac{1138}{71} + \frac{22}{71} Y$$

The coefficient of determination, ρ^2, is, from (13.25)

$$\rho^2 = \frac{[\text{cov}(X, Y)]^2}{\sigma_X^2 \sigma_Y^2} = \frac{(88/9)^2}{(176/9)(284/9)} = \frac{(88)^2}{(176)(284)} = 0.155$$

Where information about one variable is used to estimate the other in our linear regression equation instead of using the marginal probability distribution of the variable being estimated, the average squared error is reduced by 15.5 percent.

One further point needs discussion. We have described two methods for predicting one random variable from a knowledge of another. To be specific, let us suppose that we want to use information about X to make a prediction of Y. On one hand, we could use the conditional probability distribution of Y given x as a basis for making probability statements about Y. In particular, we could predict $E(Y \mid x)$. In this case, the correlation ratio, $\eta^2(Y \cdot X)$, would tell us the proportion by which we would reduce our average squared error by using $E(Y \mid x)$ as a prediction instead of $E(Y)$. On the other hand, we could use the theory of linear prediction to find the best linear function of X to use as a prediction of Y. The best linear function is that *linear* function of X which minimizes average squared error in prediction. The coefficient of determination, ρ^2, tells us the proportion by which we will reduce our average squared error if we use this linear function as a prediction instead of $E(Y)$.

Now, if $E(Y \mid x)$ is a linear function of X, as is the case in our income example, the linear function arrived at by the use of the theory of linear prediction will be precisely $E(Y \mid x)$. In this case, the correlation ratio and the coefficient of determination will be the same number (0.155). If, however, $E(Y \mid x)$ is not a linear function of X, the correlation ratio will be larger than the coefficient of determination. From this we can conclude that the average squared error in prediction using $E(Y \mid x)$ will always be equal to or less than the average squared error in prediction using a regression line. In this sense, predictions made using $E(Y \mid x)$ are always at least as good as those made using the theory of linear prediction.

If this is so, why not always use $E(Y \mid x)$ as a prediction? Why bother at all with a theory of linear prediction? There are two reasons. First, in practice, we do not always know $f(x, y)$; all that we may have is a sample of observations on Y for various values of X. We may be willing to assume that a linear function of X will provide an approximation to $E(Y \mid x)$ which will give better predictions of Y than would be possible if we were to use the average of the sample values of Y. If we are willing to make this assumption, we can apply the theory of linear prediction to the sample in order to obtain the predicting equation. This procedure will be discussed more completely in Chapter 14. Second, $E(Y \mid x)$ may be a very complicated function of X. If this is true, and we want to make predictions of Y quickly, without too much calculation, and over fairly narrow ranges of x, a linear function of X may give predictions that are good enough for our purposes. In this case, the linear function is regarded as a "first approximation" to $E(Y \mid x)$. By adding terms in X^2, X^3, and higher powers of X, we may get better approximations to $E(Y \mid x)$, but the improvement in accuracy is often not worth the additional labor of calculation.

13.8 LINEAR PREDICTION AND THE BIVARIATE NORMAL

Now, let us apply linear prediction to the problem of predicting a student's numerical grade in statistics from his mathematics aptitude score. It will be recalled that the joint distribution in this problem was a bivariate normal. All of the necessary quantities except $E(XY)$ were computed in Section 13.4, when we approached this problem from a different point of view. It will be easiest to compute $E(XY)$ if we first transform the variables to u and v, as we did in Section 13.4, and computing $E(UV)$.

$$u = \frac{x - \mu_X}{\sigma_X} \qquad v = \frac{y - \mu_Y}{\sigma_Y}$$

Applying the definition of $E(UV)$ to the joint probability distribution in (13.2),

$$E(UV) = \int_{-\infty}^{\infty} \int_{-\infty}^{\infty} uv f(u, v) \, dv \, du$$

$$= \int_{-\infty}^{\infty} \int_{-\infty}^{\infty} uv g(u) g(v \mid u) \, dv \, du$$

$$= \int_{-\infty}^{\infty} u g(u) \left[\int_{-\infty}^{\infty} v g(v \mid u) \, dv \right] du$$

$$= \int_{-\infty}^{\infty} u g(u) E(v \mid u) \, du = \int_{-\infty}^{\infty} u g(u) \, \rho u \, du$$

$$= \rho \int_{-\infty}^{\infty} u^2 g(u) \, du = \rho E(u^2) = \rho \cdot 1 = \rho$$

Now, we can introduce the definitions of u and v:

$$E(UV) = E\left[\left(\frac{X - \mu_X}{\sigma_X} \right) \left(\frac{Y - \mu_Y}{\sigma_Y} \right) \right]$$

$$= \frac{1}{\sigma_X \sigma_Y} E(XY - \mu_X Y - \mu_Y X + \mu_X \mu_Y)$$

$$= \frac{1}{\sigma_X \sigma_Y} [E(XY) - \mu_X E(Y) - \mu_Y E(X) + \mu_X \mu_Y]$$

$$= \frac{1}{\sigma_X \sigma_Y} [E(XY) - \mu_X \mu_Y] = \rho$$

Hence

$$E(XY) = \rho \sigma_X \sigma_Y + \mu_X \mu_Y$$

We can obtain general expressions for the two regression equations by computing $\beta(y \cdot x)$ and $\beta(x \cdot y)$ from their definitions in terms of the covariance rather than by using matrix inversion. For the covariance

$$\text{cov}\,(X, Y) = E(XY) - E(X)E(Y)$$

$$= \rho \sigma_X \sigma_Y + \mu_X \mu_Y - \mu_X \mu_Y = \rho \sigma_X \sigma_Y$$

Then

$$\beta(y \cdot x) = \frac{\text{cov}(X, Y)}{\sigma_X^2} = \frac{\rho\sigma_X\sigma_Y}{\sigma_X^2} = \frac{\rho\sigma_Y}{\sigma_X}$$

$$\beta(x \cdot y) = \frac{\text{cov}(X, Y)}{\sigma_Y^2} = \frac{\rho\sigma_X\sigma_Y}{\sigma_Y^2} = \frac{\rho\sigma_X}{\sigma_Y}$$

and

$$\alpha(y \cdot x) = E(Y) - \beta(y \cdot x)E(X) = \mu_Y - \frac{\rho\sigma_Y}{\sigma_X}\mu_X$$

$$\alpha(x \cdot y) = E(X) - \beta(x \cdot y)E(Y) = \mu_X - \frac{\rho\sigma_X}{\sigma_Y}\mu_Y$$

Therefore, the two regression equations are

$$Y_p = \alpha(y \cdot x) + \beta(y \cdot x)X = \left[\mu_Y - \frac{\rho\sigma_Y}{\sigma_X}\mu_X\right] + \frac{\rho\sigma_Y}{\sigma_X}X$$

$$X_p = \alpha(x \cdot y) + \beta(x \cdot y)Y = \left[\mu_X - \frac{\rho\sigma_X}{\sigma_Y}\mu_Y\right] + \frac{\rho\sigma_X}{\sigma_Y}Y$$

Application of Definition 13.3 will show that the coefficient of correlation between X and Y is ρ.

The basic quantities for the mathematics aptitude and grade in statistics example are

$$\mu_X = 600 \qquad \sigma_X = 50 \qquad \mu_Y = 85 \qquad \sigma_Y = 5 \qquad \rho = 0.8$$

With these, we compute

$$\text{cov}(X, Y) = \rho\sigma_X\sigma_Y = 0.8(50)(5) = 200$$

$$\beta(y \cdot x) = \frac{\rho\sigma_Y}{\sigma_X} = 0.8\frac{5}{50} = 0.08$$

$$\beta(x \cdot y) = \frac{\rho\sigma_X}{\sigma_Y} = 0.8\frac{50}{5} = 8$$

$$\alpha(y \cdot x) = \mu_Y - \beta(y \cdot x)\mu_X = 85 - 0.08(600) = 85 - 48 = 37$$

$$\alpha(x \cdot y) = \mu_X - \beta(x \cdot y)\mu_Y = 600 - 8(85) = 600 - 680 = -80$$

Thus, the two regression equations are

$$Y_p = 37 + 0.08X$$

$$X_p = -80 + 8Y$$

We can use (13.22) to compute the average squared error in prediction for each regression equation:

$$E[(Y - \alpha(y . x) - \beta(y . x)X)^2] = \sigma_Y^2 - \beta^2(y . x)\sigma_X^2$$
$$= 25 - 0.0064(2500) = 9$$
$$E[(X - \alpha(x . y) - \beta(x . y)Y)^2] = \sigma_X^2 - \beta^2(x . y)\sigma_Y^2$$
$$= 2500 - 64(25) = 900.$$

If we did not know a student's mathematics aptitude score, we would predict his grade in statistics as μ_Y, or 85. Our average squared error in prediction would be σ_Y^2, or 25. If we knew his aptitude score, we would predict his grade in statistics by using Y_p, and our average squared error in prediction would be 9. Using aptitude score as an auxiliary variable reduces our average squared error by 64 percent. If our problem is to estimate a student's mathematics aptitude score from a knowledge of his grade in statistics, we can make similar interpretations of the regression equation for X_p and its average squared error. Inspection of these results reveals that the application of linear prediction to a situation in which the variables have a bivariate normal distribution yields identically the same $E(Y \mid x)$, $\sigma^2(Y \mid x)$, and ρ^2 as those obtained when we started with knowledge that the joint distribution was the bivariate normal. We shall see in Chapter 14 how these ideas can be applied to sample evidence.

IMPORTANT TERMS AND CONCEPTS

Bivariate normal distribution
Coefficient of correlation
Coefficient of determination
Conditional distribution
Correlation ratio
Covariance

Independence
Least squares
Linear prediction
Marginal distribution
Partial derivative
Regression line

SYMBOLS AND ABBREVIATIONS

σ_X^2
σ_Y^2
$E(Y \mid x)$
$\sigma^2(Y \mid x)$

ρ
η^2
A^{-1}

α
β
cov (X, Y)

OFTEN-USED FORMULAS

$$f(x, y) = \frac{1}{2\pi\sigma_X\sigma_Y\sqrt{1 - \rho^2}}$$

$$\times \exp\left\{\frac{-1}{2(1 - \rho^2)}\left[\left(\frac{x - \mu_X}{\sigma_X}\right)^2 - 2\rho\left(\frac{x - \mu_X}{\sigma_X}\right)\left(\frac{y - \mu_Y}{\sigma_Y}\right) + \left(\frac{y - \mu_Y}{\sigma_Y}\right)^2\right]\right\}$$

$$\text{cov}(X, Y) = E(XY) - E(X)E(Y)$$

$$E(Y \mid x) = \mu_Y + \rho\frac{\sigma_Y}{\sigma_X}(x - \mu_X)$$

$$\sigma^2(Y \mid x) = \sigma_Y^2(1 - \rho^2)$$

$$\begin{bmatrix} E(Y) \\ E(XY) \end{bmatrix} = \begin{bmatrix} 1 & E(X) \\ E(X) & E(X^2) \end{bmatrix}\begin{bmatrix} \alpha \\ \beta \end{bmatrix}$$

$$\beta = \frac{E(XY) - E(X)E(Y)}{\sigma_X^2} \qquad \alpha = E(Y) - \beta E(X)$$

$$\rho^2 = \frac{[\text{cov}(X, Y)]^2}{\sigma_X^2\sigma_Y^2}$$

EXERCISES

1. Describe the coefficient of correlation in terms of moments. How large and how small may it be? As the covariance of X and Y decreases, how does the coefficient of correlation change?

2. For the probability distribution

$$f(x, y) = \frac{3}{8}x \qquad 0 < y < x \qquad 0 < x < 2$$

find the following quantities:
a. Covariance of X and Y.
b. Coefficient of correlation of X and Y.
c. Locus of the means of the conditional distributions of Y given x.
d. Variance of the conditional distribution of Y given x.

3. For the probability distribution

$$f(x, y) = e^{-x-y} \qquad x > 0 \qquad y > 0$$

find the following quantities:

a. cov (X, Y) c. $E(Y \mid x)$
b. ρ d. $\sigma^2(Y \mid x)$

4. For the probability distribution

$$f(x, y) = 24y(1 - x - y) \qquad 0 < x < 1 \qquad 0 < y < 1 - x$$

compute:

a. cov (X, Y) c. $E(Y \mid x)$
b. ρ d. $\sigma^2(Y \mid x)$

5. Find the correlation ratio for the probability distribution of
   a. Exercise 2   c. Exercise 4
   b. Exercise 3

6. Describe in detail the meaning of the correlation ratio you have found in
   a. Exercise 5a   c. Exercise 5c
   b. Exercise 5b

7. Use the theory of linear prediction to obtain the regression line of Y on X for the probability distribution of:
   a. Exercise 2
   b. Exercise 3
   c. Exercise 4

8. Given that X and Y have a bivariate normal distribution with the following parameters:

$$\mu_X = 10 \qquad \mu_Y = 4 \qquad \sigma_X = 2 \qquad \sigma_Y = 5 \qquad \text{cov } (X, Y) = 6$$

   a. Find the correlation coefficient of X and Y.
   b. Find the regression equation of Y on X.

9. If X and Y have a bivariate normal distribution with the following parameters:

$$\mu_X = 50 \qquad \mu_Y = 60 \qquad \sigma_X = 20 \qquad \sigma_Y = 20 \qquad \text{cov } (X, Y) = -100$$

   a. Find the correlation coefficient of X and Y.
   b. Find the coefficient of determination of X and Y.
   c. Find the regression equation of Y on X.
   d. Find the regression equation of X on Y.

10. For the distribution of Exercise 8, find:
    a. The probability that Y will be between 7 and 12 when no information is available about X.
    b. The probability that Y will be between 7 and 12 when X is known to be 6.

c. What do you conclude from a comparison of your answers to parts *a* and *b*?

11. For the distribution of Exercise 9, find:
    a. The variance of Y given that X is 45.
    b. The variance of X given that Y is 45.
    c. What, if anything, can you conclude from a comparison of your answers to parts *a* and *b*?

12. Given that the joint distribution of X and Y is
$$f(x, y) = x + y \qquad 0 \le x \le 1 \qquad 0 \le y \le 1$$
    If $E(Y \mid x)$ is used instead of $E(Y)$ as a predictor of Y, what percentage reduction in uncertainty is obtained?

13. If the theory of linear prediction is used to predict Y in the situation described in Exercise 12, what percentage reduction in uncertainty is obtained?

14. Suppose that instead of using a linear function
$$Y_p = \alpha + \beta X$$
    to predict Y for a given x, we decided to use a quadratic function
$$Y_p = \alpha + \beta X + \gamma X^2$$
    If we employed the least-squares criterion, derive the set of equations whose solutions would give the best estimates of α, β, and γ.

15. Given the joint probability distribution shown in Exercise 11 of Chapter 5
    a. Find the regression function $E(Y \mid x)$.
    b. Find the best linear predictor $Y_p = \alpha + \beta X$.
    c. Calculate and interpret the correlation ratio $\eta^2(Y . X)$.

16. Given the joint probability distribution shown in Exercise 12 in Chapter 5,
    a. Find the regression function $E(Y \mid x)$.
    b. Compute the correlation ratio $\eta^2(Y . X)$.
    c. Explain why $\eta^2(Y . X)$ has the value you found in part *b*.
    d. If you computed ρ in this exercise, what value would it have?

17. The number of purchase orders X received on a weekday morning at the A. T. Biswock Company has a Poisson distribution with mean 5 orders. It has also been observed that Y, the number of purchase orders received on a weekday morning for items not in stock, has the distribution
$$g_1(y \mid x) = \binom{x}{y}(0.1)^y(0.9)^{x-y} \qquad y = 0, \cdots, x$$
    Use the theory of linear prediction to find the least-squares regression line for predicting number of purchase orders for out of stock items from number of purchase orders.

18. Let X be the retail price of a dozen grade A large-size eggs at the Uptown Grocery. Let Y be the sales volume (number of dozens sold) on Tuesday for such eggs. A study has shown that the joint distribution of X and Y is closely approximated by the model

$$f(x, y) = \frac{1000}{9} xy^{-2} \qquad \$0.50 < x < \$0.70 \qquad 10 < y < 40$$

a. Find the regression function $E(Y \mid x)$.
b. What is the best prediction you can make based on part *a* for Tuesday sales of large-size eggs at the Uptown Grocery selling at $0.65 per dozen?
c. Calculate and interpret the correlation ratio in this exercise.

19. Use the theory of linear prediction in Exercise 18 to
a. Obtain the best *linear* prediction for Tuesday sales of large-size eggs selling at $0.65 per dozen.
b. Calculate and interpret the coefficient of determination for the prediction procedure of part *a*.

20. Suppose that the owner of the Uptown Grocery was examining his records for the month and noticed that 30 dozen eggs had been sold on Tuesday, May 18. He had no record of the selling price on that date at hand.
a. Obtain the best linear prediction of the retail price of eggs on May 18.
b. Calculate and determine the coefficient of determination for the prediction procedure in part *a*.

14 Regression and Correlation

14.1 INTRODUCTION

Suppose you were asked to estimate the weight of a person whom you had never seen. What would you do? If there were time, you would want to ask several questions: What sex? What age? What race? Why is the estimate needed? How precise must it be? If you had to make room for this person in an overcrowded lifeboat, you would have to make a wild guess. If, on the other hand, you were designing a space capsule in which this person was to ride to the moon, you would want many questions answered before you made your estimate. Is this person a young Ph.D. in geology? Is it an experienced test pilot in his middle thirties? Or is it an American housewife who has won the trip by finishing a soap jingle in 25 words or less? The answers to these questions are important because you want to reduce the possible range of error by making the estimate for a population that is as homogeneous as possible with respect to weight. In technical terms, you would prefer estimating the value of an observation drawn at random from the conditional distribution of weight given race, sex, age, stature, and as many other relevant variables as possible to estimating the value of an observation drawn at random from the marginal distribution of weight averaged over these other relevant variables.

In this chapter we shall study a way of estimating the value of one random variable given the values of other, supposedly relevant, variables. The estimate will be based on a simple random sample of observations taken on the variable being estimated (the *dependent* variable) and the variables on which the estimate is to be based (the *independent* variables).[1] For simplicity, we shall

---

[1] The terms "dependent" variable and "independent" variable are used in a very special way. In this context dependent variable means that the value of the variable being estimated *depends* on the values of the variables on which the estimate is based. The term independent variable, on the other hand, means that the variables so designated can vary in a somewhat arbitrary manner. Strictly speaking, the term "independent" implies that the values of these variables are preassigned and that the value of the dependent variable results, at least in part, from this preassignment.

assume in this chapter only one independent variable, but the procedures we develop can easily be extended to include more than one.

To be more specific, suppose that we have been asked to estimate the weight of a white male college freshman and that we are to be told his height. We are also allowed to make a small preliminary study. In this case, we might select a simple random sample of white male freshmen. We would measure the height and weight of each freshman in the sample and try to base our estimate of the weight of the unknown freshman on some sort of relationship between heights and weights of white male freshmen in our simple random sample.

If this is our procedure, we are basing it on several unstated assumptions. We are assuming, first, that height is a relevant variable; that is, that the conditional probability distribution of weight given height is different from the marginal probability distribution of weight alone, so that information about height is useful in estimating weight. Second, we are assuming that the expected value of weight given height is a function of height that is simple enough to be estimated with reasonable accuracy from a relatively small random sample of heights and weights. Third, we are assuming that height and weight are related because they are both characteristics of the same individual. We measured the height *and* the weight of each freshman in our sample; we did not measure the heights of some freshmen and the weights of others. The individual possessing the related characteristics in this case— a freshman possessing height and weight—is called the "unit of association." This unit of association links the dependent and the independent variables. As we shall see when we discuss the limitations of the procedures developed in this chapter, this link can sometimes be rather tenuous so that uncritical application of the procedures can lead to ridiculous conclusions.

As we continue to develop the estimating procedure, we shall make other assumptions. Although the sample data may suggest the nature of the relationship between height and the expected value of weight given height, we shall have to assume the functional form of this relationship. Here, we shall assume either that this form is linear or that there is a linear relationship between some function, such as the logarithm or reciprocal, of the expected value of weight given height and some function of height. This linear relationship is postulated by the investigator; it may be suggested by the data, but it is not derived from them. Finally, we shall assume that the individual deviations of the actual weights from their conditional expected values are independent, that is, that the error made in estimating one freshman's weight from his height is independent of the error made in estimating another freshman's weight from his height.

In developing our estimating method, we can set five objectives. In terms of the problem of estimating weight from height, they are:

1. *To estimate the parameters in a linear equation relating the dependent and independent variables.* If we designate weight by Y and height by X and postulate a linear relationship between height and the expected value of weight given height, we want to obtain estimates of the quantities α and β in

$$E(Y \mid x) = \alpha + \beta x \qquad (14.1)$$

2. *To obtain measures of the sampling error in the estimates of α and β.* Since α and β are estimated from a simple random sample of heights and weights, these estimates will vary from sample to sample. Hence, they can be regarded as random variables. They have a joint probability distribution which describes their probabilistic behavior. Our measures of sampling error will be estimates of the variances of the estimates of α and β from sample to sample.

3. *To estimate the variance of the conditional probability distribution of weight given height.* Our estimating equation, (14.1), provides an estimate of the *average* weight for white male freshmen of a given height. Actual weights will vary about this average. When we are given the height of a particular freshman and asked to estimate his weight, the best we can do is to make a probability statement. We would base this statement on $E(Y \mid x)$, which we would compute from our sample estimate of (14.1), and $\sigma^2(Y \mid x)$, which we must also estimate from the sample.

4. *To obtain a measure of the improvement—in terms of reduction in estimating error—when a sample estimate of* (14.1) *is used to estimate weight from height instead of using a sample estimate of $E(Y)$ to estimate weight with no knowledge of height.* If we were asked to estimate weight with no knowledge of height, we would estimate $E(Y)$ and σ_Y^2 from our sample and make a probability statement based on these estimates. If we were allowed to use information about height, we would estimate $E(Y \mid x)$ and $\sigma^2(Y \mid x)$ from our sample and make a probability statement based on these estimates. If our estimate of $\sigma^2(Y \mid x)$ is smaller than our estimate of σ_Y^2, the second procedure would appear to be better than the first because there is less uncertainty in it. Our measure of improvement will tell us how much better. Similar measures have already been discussed in Chapter 13.

5. *To test the degree of dependence of weight on height.* If height and weight are independent, then information about height is of no use in estimating weight, and there would be no point in going through the analysis we have outlined. Hence, before using our results to make estimates, we want to test the null hypothesis that height and weight are independent. If we cannot reject this hypothesis, we had better look for a new variable that is not independent of weight. If we can reject it, however, we can use our estimating procedure with some degree of confidence.

We shall consider each of these objectives in the remaining sections of this chapter.

The computational procedures employed in the analysis depend on what is assumed concerning the way in which the data have been generated. Ordinarily, we distinguish three situations.

1. Items (units of association) are drawn at random from the population, and the values of X and Y are determined for each. Here, X and Y are both random variables as in our height-weight example. We draw freshmen at random and observe both the height and the weight of each. Our computational procedures will depend on what is assumed about the *joint* distribution of height and weight. This type of analysis is called *correlation* analysis.

2. Values of x are preassigned. Items having these preassigned values of x are drawn at random from the population, and the value of Y is determined for each. Here, only Y is a random variable. This might be the case, for example, if we wanted to determine the effect on total production cost (Y) of the size of a production run (X). We would decide in advance on the sizes of the production runs in which we were interested. We would make several runs of each size and compute the total production cost of each. Here, our computational procedures will depend on what is assumed about the *conditional* distribution of Y given x. The analysis, in this case, is called *regression* analysis.

3. We are unwilling to make any assumption about the joint distribution of X and Y, which we must do in correlation; nor are we willing to make any assumption about the conditional distribution of Y given x, which is required in regression. Although we are unwilling to assume the form of either of these distributions, we might be willing to predict Y from X using a linear equation. In this case, we would have to base our predicting equation on our observations and find the equation that best fits them. One way of finding this equation is by the method of "least squares." If we are unwilling to make any assumptions concerning the underlying probability distributions, we cannot make any probability statements about Y even after we have determined the predicting equation. If, however, we assume that X and Y have the bivariate normal probability distribution or that the conditional distribution of Y given x is normal, then the computational procedures of both correlation analysis and regression analysis reduce to the method of least squares. It is for this reason that this method is of interest to us.

It is clear that we shall be concerned with the problem of drawing inferences from samples about the joint and conditional probability distributions of two or more random variables. The theory of joint and conditional probability distributions is given in Chapter 5, and descriptive measures appropriate for them appear in Chapters 7 and 13. In this chapter we shall use some elementary matrix algebra, a brief review of which will be found in Appendix D.

14.2 COMPUTING THE CONSTANTS OF THE ESTIMATING EQUATION BY THE METHOD OF LEAST SQUARES

Suppose that we have available the heights and weights of a random sample of 10 white male college freshmen and that we are to use these data as a basis for estimating the weight of a white male freshman who is not in the sample from his height. Table 14.1 shows hypothetical but typical data.[2] They are

Table 14.1   Heights in Inches x and Weights in Pounds y of a Random Sample of Ten White Male College Freshmen

Freshman Number i	Height in Inches x	Weight in Pounds y
1	63.5	122
2	64.2	137
3	66.3	145
4	67.7	154
5	68.2	142
6	68.6	161
7	69.4	147
8	70.3	174
9	71.5	180
10	72.3	166

Source. Hypothetical.

given in increasing order of height. Table 14.1 seems to indicate a rough relationship between height and weight. This indication will become somewhat stronger if we examine the data graphically. We shall let the vertical axis of our graph represent weight and the horizontal axis represent height, so that the height x and the weight y of each freshman determine a point

[2] Actually, they are not typical; they are more closely related than heights and weights usually are.

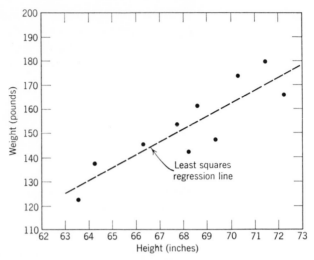

Fig. 14.1. Scatter diagram and least-squares regression line for height-weight data in Table 14.1.

(x, y) on the graph. Such a graph is called a "scatter diagram." The scatter diagram for the data in Table 14.1 is shown in Figure 14.1. This figure shows no clear functional relationship between height and weight. The points are truly "scattered." Yet, looking at the graph, we would say that, as height increases, weight tends to increase. While we cannot hope to estimate weight "on the nose" from a knowledge of height, we should be able to make a better estimate of weight, knowing height, than we could without it. The problem is: How do we utilize information about height in order to estimate weight?

If we are unwilling to make any assumptions about probability distributions, one way of utilizing this information is in an equation that expresses the estimated weight as a function of the observed height. The simplest such equation is linear

$$\hat{y}_x = a + bx$$

where the symbol $\hat{y}_x$ indicates an estimate of Y that is based on x.[3] The problem now becomes one of drawing a straight line on Figure 14.1 in such a way as to obtain estimates which are "best" from some point of view. One commonly accepted definition of the "best" line is that which would minimize the average squared error in estimation *for the observations we have.* (We are making no probability assumptions, remember.) Consider the height,

---

[3] We use the symbols a and b here to indicate that these are numbers computed from other numbers. They are neither parameters nor estimates of parameters. They have no *statistical* meaning at all.

x_i, and the weight, y_i, of the ith freshman in our sample. With our linear estimating equation, we would estimate this freshman's weight from his height as $a + bx_i$. His actual weight is y_i, so that our error in estimation, e_i, is

$$e_i = y_i - (a + bx_i)$$

Minimizing the average squared error in estimation for a sample of finite size is equivalent to minimizing the sum of the squares of the estimating errors. Our problem is to find values of a and b that minimize

$$\theta = \sum_{i=1}^{n} [y_i - (a + bx_i)]^2$$

This is precisely the same problem that we considered in Section 13.6.

We find the first partial derivatives of θ with respect to a and b. We set both partial derivatives equal to zero and solve the resulting pair of equations for a and b, obtaining

$$\begin{cases} \sum y = na + b \sum x \\ \sum xy = a \sum x + b \sum x^2 \end{cases} \tag{14.2}$$

In matrix form, the solution to this pair of equations is

$$\begin{bmatrix} a \\ b \end{bmatrix} = \frac{1}{n^2 s_x^2} \begin{bmatrix} \sum x^2 & -\sum x \\ -\sum x & n \end{bmatrix} \begin{bmatrix} \sum y \\ \sum xy \end{bmatrix}$$

where, the symbol

$$s_x^2 = \frac{1}{n} [\sum x^2 - \bar{x} \sum x]$$

is used to save space rather than because of its statistical meaning.

In Table 14.2 we show the calculations necessary in order to apply (14.2) to our height-weight example. We see that our estimating equation is

$$\hat{y}_x = -213.98 + 5.38x \tag{14.3}$$

We have sketched this equation as a dashed line in Figure 14.1.

Because we have made no assumptions concerning the probability distributions of height and weight, we can give only a limited interpretation of the result expressed in (14.3). Strictly speaking, all we can say is that (14.3) minimizes the average squared error in estimation *for the sample of observations that we have on hand.*

Because the sample is a random one, we hope that it is representative of the population from which it is drawn. If this is true, then (14.3) should provide estimates of weight for freshmen not in the sample that are about as accurate as the estimates that it provides for those included.

In spite of this caution, it is reasonable to ask if the results make sense in the light of what we know—or think we know—about heights and weights. The slope of the line is given by the constant, b. In this case b is positive,

Table 14.2 Computations Required for Obtaining a Least-Squares Estimating Equation from the Data in Table 14.1

a. Preliminary Computations

Column 1 i	Column 2 x_i	Column 3 y_i	Column 4 x_i^2 (Col. 2)²	Column 5 x_iy_i (Col. 2 × Col. 3)	Column 6[a] y_i^2 (Col. 3)²
1	63.5	122	4032.25	7747.0	14884
2	64.2	137	4121.64	8795.4	18769
3	66.3	145	4395.69	9613.5	21025
4	67.7	154	4583.29	10425.8	23716
5	68.2	142	4651.24	9684.4	20164
6	68.6	161	4705.96	11044.6	25921
7	69.4	147	4816.36	10201.8	21609
8	70.3	174	4942.09	12232.2	30276
9	71.5	180	5112.25	12870.0	32400
10	72.3	166	5227.29	12001.8	27556
Totals	682.0	1528	46588.06	104616.5	236320

b. Matrix Computations

1.
$$\begin{bmatrix} \sum y \\ \sum xy \end{bmatrix} = \begin{bmatrix} n & \sum x \\ \sum x & \sum x^2 \end{bmatrix} \begin{bmatrix} a \\ b \end{bmatrix}$$

$$\begin{bmatrix} 1528 \\ 104616.5 \end{bmatrix} = \begin{bmatrix} 10 & 682 \\ 682 & 46588.06 \end{bmatrix} \begin{bmatrix} a \\ b \end{bmatrix} = M \begin{bmatrix} a \\ b \end{bmatrix}$$

2. $n \sum x^2 - (\sum x)^2 = 10(46588.06) - (682)^2 = 756.6$

3.
$$M^{-1} = \begin{bmatrix} 10 & 682 \\ 682 & 46588.06 \end{bmatrix}^{-1} = \frac{1}{756.6} \begin{bmatrix} 46588.06 & -682 \\ -682 & 10 \end{bmatrix}$$

4.
$$M^{-1} \begin{bmatrix} 1528 \\ 104616.5 \end{bmatrix} = \frac{1}{756.6} \begin{bmatrix} -1618973.20 \\ 4069.00 \end{bmatrix} = \begin{bmatrix} -213.98 \\ 5.38 \end{bmatrix} = \begin{bmatrix} a \\ b \end{bmatrix}$$

5. $y_x = -213.98 + 5.38x$

---

[a] The entries in this column are not needed in computing a and b. They will be used, however, for later calculations.

indicating that, as height increases, the estimated weight increases. This makes sense, although some people are tall and thin and others are short and fat. In general, however, we would say that tall people will weigh more than similarly proportioned short people. The numerical value of b is 5.38. Since the units of $\hat{y}_x$ are pounds of estimated weight and the units of x are in inches of observed height, the units of b must be pounds of estimated weight per inch of observed height. This means that the *estimated* weights of two freshmen whose observed heights differ by 1 in. will differ by 5.38 lb. It does *not* mean that a freshman who grows 1 in. in height will gain about 5 lb in weight. Loosely speaking, we could say that a difference of 1 in. in height is associated with a difference of 5.38 lb in estimated weight. Although we cannot be sure of the precise numerical magnitude, this number seems more reasonable than, for instance, 53.8 lb/in. or 0.538 lb/in.

The constant a is the y-intercept of our least-squares estimating equation. The numerical magnitude of a in (14.3) is -213.98, which implies that we would estimate the weight of a freshman of zero height as -213.98 lb. This result is nonsensical, but is no more so than the question it answers. In practice, we should never have to estimate the weight of a male freshman who is zero inches tall. The regression equation given by (14.3) is based on a study of the heights and weights of a random sample of boys in their late teens whose heights ranged roughly between 63 and 73 in. If the equation provides reasonably good estimates of the weights of boys in this age-height class, this is all we can expect of it. If we want to estimate the weights of individuals not in this class, then we should take a new random sample of individuals typical of those whose weights we want to estimate and construct a new estimating question.

The problem of interpreting the constant a in (14.3) indicates a limitation of the procedures discussed in this chapter. They are generally valid only over a finite range of possible values for the independent variables. Extrapolation beyond this range will often lead to ridiculous conclusions. We shall return to this problem in the concluding section of this chapter.

*14.3   ESTIMATING THE PARAMETERS OF A REGRESSION LINE BY THE METHOD OF MAXIMUM LIKELIHOOD[4]

As we have seen, the method of least squares is of limited usefulness because it involves no probabilistic assumptions about the population from which

---

[4] This section consists of a justification of the method of least squares as an estimating procedure when the dependent variable is assumed to be conditionally normally distributed. The important results of this section will be restated later, so that the reader who is primarily interested in applications need not read this section. He can go directly to Section 14.5.

the sample is drawn. In this case, we cannot make probability inferences about this population. In order to obtain results that are useful in a statistical sense, we shall have to make assumptions about the probability distributions of the dependent and independent variables.

If we are willing to assume either that the joint distribution of X and Y is approximately bivariate normal or that the conditional distribution of Y given x is approximately normal with a mean that is a linear function of x and a variance that is independent of x, the method of maximum likelihood estimation gives the same results as the method of least squares. There is a net gain, however, because our probability assumptions permit us to make statistical statements about the population from which the sample was drawn. In this section we shall show that the method of maximum likelihood estimation leads to the method of least squares when we assume:

1. That the values taken on by x are predetermined.

2. That the conditional distribution of Y given x is normal with a mean that is a linear function of x and a variance that is independent of x.

3. That successive values of $[Y - E(Y \mid x)]$ are independent.

This is the simplest case that can be treated by the method of maximum likelihood. As we have indicated in the introduction to this chapter, the analysis of this case is called *regression* analysis.

Suppose, then, that we are interested only in certain specific values of x and that, given one of these values of x, Y is a normally distributed random variable with

$$E(Y \mid x) = \alpha + \beta x$$

and variance (14.4)

$$\sigma^2(Y \mid x)$$

The first equation in (14.4) is called the regression equation. We take n pairs of observations, $(x_1, y_1; x_2, y_2; \cdots ; x_n, y_n)$, using only the values of x in which we are interested. The symbol x might represent the number of items produced in a single "run" of a production process, and Y might be the total cost of the units produced in the run. Here, we can control x but we cannot control Y. Our problem is to use the observations to obtain estimates of α, β, and σ in (14.4). We assume that our observations are a random sample from the population of production runs in which we are interested. In practice, we would have to be very careful to take our observations in such a way that this assumption was met. We would not, for example, make the production runs in increasing or decreasing order of size. We would determine the sizes of the runs in advance and number the runs in either increasing or decreasing order of size. Then, using a table of random numbers, we would arrange the run numbers in random order. This would assure that the production workers do not get practice by making consecutive runs of the same size and that the effect of machine wear on cost is not concentrated on either the large runs or the small runs.

Under the assumptions that we have made,

$$f(y_i \mid x_i) = \frac{1}{\sigma(Y \mid x)\sqrt{2\pi}}\, e^{-[y_i-(\alpha+\beta x_i)]^2/2\sigma^2(Y\mid x)}$$

$$i = 1, 2, \cdots, n$$

and the likelihood function of our sample is

$$L = \prod_{i=1}^{n} \frac{1}{\sigma(Y \mid x)\sqrt{2\pi}}\, e^{-[y_i-(\alpha+\beta x_i)]^2/2\sigma^2(Y\mid x)}$$

$$= [2\pi\sigma^2(Y \mid x)]^{-n/2} e^{-\sum_{i=1}^{n}[y_i-(\alpha+\beta x_i)]^2/2\sigma^2(Y\mid x)}$$

If we use the method of maximum likelihood estimation, we choose those values of α, β, and σ which maximize L—or, equivalently, its natural logarithm for our particular sample of observations.

Thus

$$\ln L = -\frac{n}{2} \ln 2\pi\sigma^2(Y \mid x) - \frac{1}{2\sigma^2(Y \mid x)} \sum [y - (\alpha + \beta x)]^2$$

where subscripts and limits of summation have been omitted. We take partial derivatives of $\ln L$ with respect to α, β, and σ, set these partial derivatives equal to zero, and solve for our maximum likelihood estimates.

$$\frac{\partial \ln L}{\partial \alpha} = \frac{1}{\sigma^2(Y \mid x)} \sum [y - (\alpha + \beta x)]$$

$$\frac{\partial \ln L}{\partial \beta} = \frac{1}{\sigma^2(Y \mid x)} \sum x[y - (\alpha + \beta x)]$$

$$\frac{\partial \ln L}{\partial \sigma(Y \mid x)} = -\frac{n}{\sigma(Y \mid x)} + \frac{1}{\sigma^3(Y \mid x)} \sum [y - (\alpha + \beta x)]^2$$

When these partial derivatives are set equal to zero, the resulting equations are:

$$\sum y = n\hat{\alpha} + \hat{\beta} \sum x$$
$$\sum xy = \hat{\alpha} \sum x + \hat{\beta} \sum x^2 \tag{14.5}$$

$$s^2(Y \mid x) = \frac{1}{n} \sum [y - (\hat{\alpha} + \hat{\beta} x)]^2 \tag{14.6}$$

We use the notation $s^2(Y \mid x)$ because (14.6) looks something like a sample variance and because we are saving the symbol $\hat{\sigma}^2(Y \mid x)$ for something else.

When we compare (14.5) with (14.2), we see that, except for the symbols $\hat{\alpha}$ and $\hat{\beta}$ instead of a and b, the equations for obtaining maximum likelihood estimates of α and β are identical with the equations for computing a and b by least squares. In addition, the estimate of σ will permit us to make approximate probability statements about Y given particular values of X. We shall consider a numerical application of these results after we investigate the bias and sampling variability of our estimates of α, β, and $\sigma(Y \mid x)$.

*14.4   THE BIAS AND SAMPLING VARIABILITY OF MAXIMUM LIKELIHOOD ESTIMATES IN REGRESSION ANALYSIS[5]

Our estimates of α, β, and $\sigma^2(Y \mid x)$, which we derived in Section 14.3, depend on sample observations and will vary from sample to sample. Therefore, for simple random samples, we can regard $\hat{\alpha}$, $\hat{\beta}$, and $s^2(Y \mid x)$ as random variables. They have a joint probability distribution and, if we are going to use our sample estimates to make probability statements about the population from which the sample is drawn, then we should investigate the expected values and the variances and covariances of these estimates. In this section we shall show that, under the assumptions of the preceding section, $\hat{\alpha}$ and $\hat{\beta}$ are unbiased estimates of α and β. We shall also show the variances and the covariance of $\hat{\alpha}$ and $\hat{\beta}$, although we shall not derive them. We shall state without proof that $s^2(Y \mid x)$ is a biased estimator of $\sigma^2(Y \mid x)$ and give a correction factor that adjusts for this bias. In Section 14.5 we shall apply the results of this and the previous section to a numerical example.

If the pair of linear equations in (14.5) is solved for $\hat{\alpha}$ and $\hat{\beta}$, we obtain

$$\hat{\alpha} = \frac{\sum x^2 \sum y - \sum x \sum xy}{n \sum x^2 - (\sum x)^2}$$

$$\hat{\beta} = \frac{n \sum xy - \sum x \sum y}{n \sum x^2 - (\sum x)^2}$$

(14.7)

In this analysis, the values assumed by x are predetermined, so that x is not a random variable. The variable, Y, however, is a random variable whose expected value is determined by the value of x associated with particular values of Y. Hence, both $\hat{\alpha}$ and $\hat{\beta}$ are linear functions of random variables. Their expected values, therefore, are linear functions of the expected values of these random variables and easy to calculate. For $\hat{\alpha}$,

$$E(\hat{\alpha}) = \frac{\sum x^2 \sum E(Y \mid x) - \sum x \sum xE(Y \mid x)}{n \sum x^2 - (\sum x)^2}$$

(14.8)

---

[5] The important results of this and the previous section are summarized in the next section. The reader who is primarily interested in applications can go directly to Section 14.5.

The argument that follows will be easier to see if we consider only the numerator of (14.8). The denominator, remember, is not a random variable. When we take expected values in the numerator,

$$\sum x^2 \sum E(Y \mid x) - \sum x \sum xE(Y \mid x)$$

$$= \sum x^2 \sum (\alpha + \beta x) - \sum x \sum (\alpha x + \beta x^2)$$

$$= \sum x^2 [n\alpha + \beta \sum x] - \alpha (\sum x)^2 - \beta \sum x \sum x^2$$

$$= \alpha [n \sum x^2 - (\sum x)^2]$$

When we divide this result by the denominator of (14.8) we see that

$$E(\hat{\alpha}) = \alpha$$

A similar argument applied to the second equation of (14.7) will show that

$$E(\hat{\beta}) = \beta$$

Hence, $\hat{\alpha}$ is an unbiased estimator of α, and $\hat{\beta}$ is an unbiased estimator of β.

Because $\hat{\alpha}$ and $\hat{\beta}$ are linear functions of independent random variables, their variances are linear combinations of the variances of these independent random variables. We could derive these variances, as well as the covariance of $\hat{\alpha}$ and $\hat{\beta}$, but, unless we resort to matrix algebra of a sort that is too advanced for this text, these derivations are lengthy. Hence, we will simply state the results.

$$\sigma^2(\hat{\alpha}) = \frac{\sigma^2(Y \mid x) \sum x^2}{n \sum x^2 - (\sum x)^2}$$

$$\sigma^2(\hat{\beta}) = \frac{n\sigma^2(Y \mid x)}{n \sum x^2 - (\sum x)^2}$$

$$\mathrm{cov}\,(\hat{\alpha}, \hat{\beta}) = -\frac{\sigma^2(Y \mid x) \sum x}{n \sum x^2 - (\sum x)^2}$$

Under our assumption that the conditional distribution of Y given x is normal with mean $\alpha + \beta x$ and variance $\sigma^2(Y \mid x)$, the sample estimates $\hat{\alpha}$ and $\hat{\beta}$ will be random variables having the bivariate normal distribution (Chapter 5, Section 5.8). The correlation coefficient, ρ, in this particular bivariate normal distribution is

$$\rho(\hat{\alpha}, \hat{\beta}) = -\frac{\sum x}{\sqrt{n \sum x^2}}$$

The variances and covariances of jointly distributed random variables are often presented in matrix form. This matrix is called the "variance-co-variance" matrix.

Definition.   If $X_1, \cdots, X_n$ are random variables, the variance-covariance matrix of $X_1, \cdots, X_n$ is denoted by the symbol $V(X_1, \cdots, X_n)$ and given by

$$V(X_1, \cdots, X_n) = \begin{bmatrix} \sigma^2(X_1) & \text{cov } (X_1, X_2) & \cdots & \text{cov } (X_1, X_n) \\ \text{cov } (X_2, X_1) & \sigma^2(X_2) & \cdots & \text{cov } (X_2, X_n) \\ \cdots & \cdots & \cdots & \cdots \\ \text{cov } (X_n, X_1) & \text{cov } (X_n, X_2) & \cdots & \sigma^2(X_n) \end{bmatrix}$$

Since

$$\text{cov } (X_i, X_j) = \text{cov } (X_j, X_i),$$

$V(X_1, \cdots, X_n)$ is a symmetric matrix.

If we write out the variance-covariance matrix of $\hat{\alpha}$ and $\hat{\beta}$,

$$V(\hat{\alpha}, \hat{\beta}) = \begin{bmatrix} \sigma^2(\hat{\alpha}) & \text{cov } (\hat{\alpha}, \hat{\beta}) \\ \text{cov } (\hat{\alpha}, \hat{\beta}) & \sigma^2(\hat{\beta}) \end{bmatrix} = \frac{\sigma^2(Y \mid x)}{n^2 s_x^2} \begin{bmatrix} \sum x^2 & -\sum x \\ -\sum x & n \end{bmatrix} \quad (14.9)$$

where s_x^2 is given in Section 14.2. Now, in computing $\hat{\alpha}$ and $\hat{\beta}$, we had to invert a matrix. Let us call this matrix M. Then

$$M = \begin{bmatrix} n & \sum x \\ \sum x & \sum x^2 \end{bmatrix}$$

From M, we compute

$$M^{-1} = \frac{1}{n^2 s_x^2} \begin{bmatrix} \sum x^2 & -\sum x \\ -\sum x & n \end{bmatrix} \quad (14.10)$$

If we compare the matrix in (14.10) with the variance-covariance matrix of $\hat{\alpha}$ and $\hat{\beta}$ given in (14.9) we see that

$$V(\hat{\alpha}, \hat{\beta}) = \sigma^2(Y \mid x)M^{-1}$$

Once we have an estimate of $\sigma^2(Y \mid x)$, we can estimate the elements of $V(\hat{\alpha}, \hat{\beta})$ very easily if we have solved the pair of equations in (14.5) above by matrix inversion. We are thus led naturally to a consideration of the bias in our estimate, $s^2(Y \mid x)$, of $\sigma^2(Y \mid x)$. This estimate is given by (14.6).

In Chapter 9 we learned that the sample variance,

$$s^2 = \frac{1}{n} \sum (x - \bar{x})^2$$

is a biased estimator of the universe variance, σ^2. There, we also saw that

$$E(S^2) = \frac{(n-1)\sigma^2}{n}$$

This suggested

$$\hat{\sigma}^2 = \frac{ns^2}{n-1} = \frac{1}{n-1} \sum (x - \bar{x})^2$$

as an unbiased estimator of σ^2.

A similar bias is present in our estimate, $s^2(Y \mid x)$, given by (14.6). In this case, it may be shown that

$$E[S^2(Y \mid x)] = \frac{(n-2)\sigma^2(Y \mid x)}{n}$$

which suggests

$$\hat{\sigma}^2(Y \mid x) = \frac{ns^2(Y \mid x)}{n-2} = \frac{1}{n-2} \sum [y - (\hat{\alpha} + \hat{\beta}x)]^2$$

as an unbiased estimator of $\sigma^2(Y \mid x)$. In what follows, we shall usually replace $\sigma^2(Y \mid x)$ by its estimate $\hat{\sigma}^2(Y \mid x)$.

In this and the preceding section, we have considered the case where the values of x are known numbers and the values of Y are normally distributed random variables with means $\alpha + \beta x$ and variances $\sigma^2(Y \mid x)$. The variance is independent of x. This describes a laboratorylike situation in which the experimenter controls one variable and observes another. Situations of this kind are relatively rare in business or in the social sciences. Ideally, the economist might wish to vary family income and to observe what happens to food expenditures while holding other socioeconomic factors constant. Unfortunately, he cannot do this. Instead, he must divide the population into groups that are relatively homogeneous with respect to the socio-economic factors he considers important. From a particular socioeconomic group he selects families at random and observes both family income and food expenditures. Here, both the dependent variable (food expenditures) and the independent variable (family income) are random variables. This situation requires a somewhat different form of statistical treatment than the situation in which the independent variable is subject to control. Yet, if the two variables have the bivariate normal distribution, the net result is about the same as in the case we have examined. The equations for estimating α, β, and $\sigma^2(Y \mid x)$ are the same, and a sample estimate of $V(\hat{\alpha}, \hat{\beta})$ can be used to establish confidence intervals for α and β. In the next section we shall consider a numerical example of each type of problem.

14.5 ESTIMATING PARAMETERS AND STATING CONFIDENCE INTERVALS IN REGRESSION ANALYSIS

As we have seen in Section 14.2, the method of least squares is of limited usefulness in making estimates or predictions because it does not require any probability assumptions. To obtain statistically useful results, we must introduce probability assumptions. In the simple situations that we shall consider, these assumptions will involve the normal distribution. In this section, we shall consider two examples in which it seems reasonable to assume that the normal distribution enters some aspect of the situation, and we shall show how this assumption permits us to make probability statements.

The Wearing Bearing Company makes ball bearings. In order to make bearings of a particular size and hardness, it is necessary to adjust several of the machines on which the bearings are processed. The cost of setting the machines does not depend on the number of bearings that are to be made. It is economical, therefore, to produce a large number of bearings of one size and hardness, once the machines have been adjusted. There are also certain other costs, such as overhead, which do not vary with the number of bearings produced. Therefore, the total cost of producing bearings is made up of two parts: fixed and variable costs. In addition, there is a third component of total cost, which is neither fixed nor directly dependent on the number of bearings produced. It arises from a variety of causes. Orders from different customers may require different amounts of paper work. A machine might break down in the middle of a run. Variations in raw material quality may cause minor variations in cost. This third component of cost seems to be completely random; since it is the sum of a large number of small variations, it is reasonable to assume that it is approximately normally distributed.

In order to set prices, Wearing Bearing wants to estimate total production costs. It sells bearings in multiples of 2000. Orders in excess of 10,000 bearings are so rare as to be unheard of. The statistician for the company decides to estimate a total cost function for a bearing that has stock number 6684—the company's best seller for years. To do so, he plans a controlled experiment. He makes 10 production runs, two each of 2000, 4000, 6000, 8000, and 10,000 bearings. Before each production run, the machines are taken down and reset. The statistician realizes that he had better not make the runs in either increasing or decreasing order of lot size. (Lot size is a term meaning the number of items made in one production run.) This would tend to concentrate the effects of tool wear on the lot sizes that were run last, increasing cost because of the necessity of rework. The systematic effect of tool wear would be "confounded" with the effect of systematic variation in lot size. (Confounded is a statistical term meaning that the effects of two or more experimental factors are so intermixed that they cannot be measured separately.) Therefore, the statistician randomizes the order in which different lot sizes are made.

Since this statistician knows his business, he has in mind a mathematical model of the process by which his experimental data will be generated. He assumes that total production cost comprises three components: a fixed component, one that varies directly with lot size, and a random one. If Y is the total cost of a production run and x is lot size in thousands of bearings, the model the statistician has in mind is

$$Y = \alpha + \beta x + \epsilon \qquad (14.11)$$

This implies that the nonrandom component of total production cost is a linear function of lot size. He also assumes that ϵ is a normally distributed random variable with a mean of zero and a constant variance and that values of ϵ in successive production runs are independent.

Under these assumptions, for a fixed lot size (x times 1000), total cost, Y, is a normally distributed random variable whose mean and variance are given by

$$E(Y \mid x) = \alpha + \beta x \qquad \text{and} \qquad \sigma^2(Y \mid x)$$

The variance of Y when x is held constant is the same for all values of x. If the statistician can estimate α, β, and $\sigma^2(Y \mid x)$, he can make probability statements about the total production costs of runs of the lot sizes he has studied. If he is willing to assume that the assumptions of (14.11) are valid for lot sizes other than the ones he has studied in his controlled experiment, then he can also make probability statements about total production costs for these other lot sizes.

It turns out that our statistician has made some convenient assumptions, since he can use the method of least squares described in Section 14.2 to obtain estimates of α and β which are unbiased, and from his experimental data he can obtain estimates of the variances of the sampling distributions of his estimates of α and β. The estimates, $\hat{\alpha}$ and $\hat{\beta}$, of α and β can be obtained by solving the following pair of simultaneous linear equations:

$$\sum y = \hat{\alpha} n + \hat{\beta} \sum x \qquad (14.12)$$

$$\sum xy = \hat{\alpha} \sum x + \hat{\beta} \sum x^2$$

Here, n is the number of production runs in the controlled experiment. If we solve (14.12) by matrix inversion, we shall require the inverse of M, the matrix of coefficients of $\hat{\alpha}$ and $\hat{\beta}$ in (14.12). Then

$$M = \begin{bmatrix} n & \sum x \\ \sum x & \sum x^2 \end{bmatrix}$$

and

$$M^{-1} = \frac{1}{n^2 s_x^2} \begin{bmatrix} \sum x^2 & -\sum x \\ -\sum x & n \end{bmatrix}$$

where

$$s_x^2 = \frac{1}{n} [\sum x^2 - \bar{x} \sum x]$$

The solution of (14.12) by matrix inversion is worth the trouble because the elements of M^{-1} are useful in estimating the variances of the sampling distributions of $\hat{\alpha}$ and $\hat{\beta}$.

One possible estimate of $\sigma^2(Y \mid x)$ is the following:

$$s^2(Y \mid x) = \frac{1}{n} \sum [y - (\hat{\alpha} + \hat{\beta}x)]^2$$

Compare this with

$$s_y^2 = \frac{1}{n} \sum (y - \bar{y})^2$$

The second expression is the definition for the variance of the y values (total production costs) observed in the experiment. The first expression looks somewhat like the second except that instead of $\bar{y}$ we have $\hat{\alpha} + \hat{\beta}x$. It is natural, therefore, to compute the variance of Y about the sample estimate of the mean value of Y, allowing this mean to change as x changes

The first expression turns out to be a biased estimator of $\sigma^2(Y \mid x)$. An unbiased estimate is given by

$$\hat{\sigma}^2(Y \mid x) = \frac{1}{n-2} \sum [y - (\hat{\alpha} + \hat{\beta}x)]^2$$

However, an equivalent form is

$$\hat{\sigma}^2(Y \mid x) = \frac{1}{n-2} [\sum y^2 - \hat{\alpha} \sum y - \hat{\beta} \sum xy],$$

which is easier to compute.

The data obtained by the statistician of the Wearing Bearing Company are given in Table 14.3. The steps required to compute $\hat{\alpha}$, $\hat{\beta}$, and $\hat{\sigma}^2(Y \mid x)$ from the data in Table 14.3 are given in Table 14.4.

Table 14.3 Experimental Results of the Wearing Bearing Company's Controlled Production Cost Experiment

Production Run Number i	Lot Size (Thousands of Bearings) x_i	Total Production Cost ($) y_i
1	8	463
2	10	501
3	8	449
4	4	374
5	6	421
6	2	322
7	2	341
8	10	494
9	6	429
10	4	391

Table 14.4 Computation of $\hat{\alpha}$, $\hat{\beta}$, and $\hat{\sigma}^2(Y \mid x)$ from the Wearing Bearing Company's Experimental Data

a. Preliminary Computations

Column 1 i	Column 2 x_i	Column 3 y_i	Column 4 x_i^2 (Col. 2)^2	Column 5 $x_i y_i$ (Col. 2 × Col. 3)	Column 6 y_i^2 (Col. 3)^2
1	8	463	64	3704	214,369
2	10	501	100	5010	251,001
3	8	449	64	3592	201,601
4	4	374	16	1496	139,876
5	6	421	36	2526	177,241
6	2	322	4	644	103,684
7	2	341	4	682	116,281
8	10	494	100	4940	244,036
9	6	429	36	2574	184,041
10	4	391	16	1564	152,881
Total	60	4185	440	26,732	1,785,011

b. Computation of Estimates

1. Equations (14.12) in matrix form:

$$\begin{bmatrix} 4185 \\ 26732 \end{bmatrix} = \begin{bmatrix} 10 & 60 \\ 60 & 440 \end{bmatrix} \begin{bmatrix} \hat{\alpha} \\ \hat{\beta} \end{bmatrix}$$

2.
$$M = \begin{bmatrix} 10 & 60 \\ 60 & 440 \end{bmatrix}$$

$$n^2 s^2 = n \sum x^2 - \left(\sum x \right)^2 = 10(440) - (60)^2 = 800$$

3.
$$\begin{bmatrix} \hat{\alpha} \\ \hat{\beta} \end{bmatrix} = M^{-1} \begin{bmatrix} \sum y \\ \sum xy \end{bmatrix} = \frac{1}{800} \begin{bmatrix} 440 & -60 \\ -60 & 10 \end{bmatrix} \begin{bmatrix} 4185 \\ 26732 \end{bmatrix}$$

$$\frac{1}{800} \begin{bmatrix} 237480 \\ 16220 \end{bmatrix} = \begin{bmatrix} 296.850 \\ 20.275 \end{bmatrix}$$

4. Regression equation:

$$\hat{E}(Y \mid x) = \hat{\alpha} + \hat{\beta}x = 296.850 + 20.275x$$

5. $\sum y^2 - \hat{\alpha} \sum y - \hat{\beta} \sum xy = 1785011 - 296.850(4185) - 20.275(26732)$
$$= 702.45$$

6. $\hat{\sigma}^2(Y \mid x) = \dfrac{1}{n-2} \left[\sum y^2 - \hat{\alpha} \sum y - \hat{\beta} \sum xy \right] = \dfrac{1}{8}(702.45) = 87.81$

7. $\hat{\sigma}(Y \mid x) = \sqrt{87.81} = 9.37$

The statistician has now obtained parameter estimates for his model. Specifically, he has a cost estimating equation,

$$\hat{E}(Y \mid x) = 296.850 + 20.275x \qquad (14.13)$$

where the caret on E indicates that it is an estimated expected value. He also has an estimate of the variance of actual cost about the estimated cost obtained from (14.13),

$$\hat{\sigma}^2(Y \mid x) = 87.81$$

A more useful measure would be the standard deviation of actual cost measured about the cost estimated from (14.13),

$$\hat{\sigma}(Y \mid x) = \$9.37 \qquad (14.14)$$

Equation 14.13 is called the regression equation, and $\hat{\sigma}(Y \mid x)$ is called the (estimated) "standard error" of the estimate.

Statistically and in terms of the cost of producing ball bearings, what do these results mean? Their statistical and practical meaning is contained in the assumptions the statistician made in constructing his model. He has assumed that total production cost is made up of three components: a fixed component, a component that varies linearly with lot size (for lots of the sizes in which he is interested), and a random component. The results of his controlled experiment suggest a fixed cost of about $297 per production run. He must be careful, however, in interpreting the variable cost component. His results indicate a variable cost of about $20 per 1000 bearings produced, but in planning his controlled experiment, the statistician indicated that he was interested only in certain fixed lot sizes which varied in units of 2000 bearings. (14.13) provides an estimate of the average total cost of producing a lot of x thousand bearings, and in the experiment x was allowed to assume values of 2, 4, 6, 8, and 10 and no others. If the statistician is interested in only these values of x, then (14.13) tells him that, if he moves from one acceptable lot size to the next larger or smaller acceptable one, *average* total production cost will differ by slightly more than $40. This implies that it makes no sense to draw a regression line on a scatter diagram as in Figure 14.1. This would be true if, for example, the bearings are most economically produced in "batches" of 2000 each and batches of less than 2000 require special processing. On the other hand, if the statistician chose the lot sizes as representative of a range in which he was interested and if he is willing to assume that, except for random variation, total production cost is a linear function of lot size for any size between 2000 and 10,000 bearings, then it makes sense to draw a regression line on a scatter diagram. In this case, the parameter estimates, $\hat{\alpha}$ and $\hat{\beta}$, in (14.13) can be given a more flexible interpretation. This equation can now be regarded as the locus of *average* total production cost for lot sizes of between 2000 and 10,000 bearings. Actual total production cost will vary about this average. The equation says that the average fixed cost for lot sizes in this range is about $297. It does *not* say that the average cost of producing *no* ball bearings is $297 because the experiment did not include production runs of no ball bearings, and the statistician has made no assumptions about runs of this size.[6] (14.13) also says that, as lot size varies, so does average total production cost in such a way that a difference of 1000 bearings will be accompanied by a difference in the same direction of about $20 in average total production cost.

The statistician, then, may regard (14.13) as either a continuous function or as a convenient way of expressing five estimated averages. In either case, he has constructed a useful device for both estimating and controlling production costs. Suppose, for example, that Wearing Bearing receives an order for 6000 Number 6684 bearings. By setting x equal to 6 in (14.13), the statistician can obtain an estimate of the average total cost of a production run of 6000 bearings.

$$\hat{E}(Y \mid x = 6) = 296.850 + 20.275(6) = \$418.50$$

This means that if a large number of production runs of 6000 bearings each were made and total production costs were averaged, the estimated average total production cost per run would be $418.50. The statistician must next take account of random variation about this average. He has assumed that actual total production cost is a normally distributed random variable with an estimated mean which can be computed from (14.13)—in this case $418.50—and with an estimated standard deviation of $9.37, which is indicated by (14.14). Because the standard deviation is estimated from a sample, the statistician must base probability statements about total cost on the t distribution rather than on the normal distribution. The theory required to determine the appropriate number of degrees of freedom in the case of regression analysis is too complicated for this text, but we can use the following rule of thumb:

> *The number of degrees of freedom appropriate when the t distribution is used to draw inferences in regression analysis is equal to the number of observations from which the regression equation was estimated minus the number of parameters in the regression equation which were estimated from these observations.*

---

[6] It is possible, although hardly likely, that the data from the statistician's experiment could have produced a negative $\hat{\alpha}$, implying a negative fixed cost. If this occurred, the statistician would have to check his results very carefully and examine the conditions under which the experiment was run. A negative $\hat{\alpha}$ makes no sense in this problem and would indicate that something was seriously wrong.

The Wearing Bearing cost-estimating equation was obtained from 10 observations. Two parameters, α and β, were estimated. Hence, the statistician must use a t distribution based on 8 degrees of freedom. Suppose he wants to estimate the range within which total production cost would fall 95 percent of the time in runs of 6000 bearings. That is, he wants to estimate the range of the middle 95 percent of the total production costs per run of a large number of runs of 6000 bearings each. With 8 degrees of freedom, the appropriate value of t is 2.306. This means that $\hat{E}(Y \mid x = 6) \pm 2.306 \hat{\sigma}(Y \mid x)$ will give a range within which total production cost should fall 95 percent of the time for a production run of 6000 Number 6684 bearings.[7] Thus

$$\hat{E}(Y \mid x = 6) \pm 2.306 \hat{\sigma}(Y \mid x) = 418.50 \pm 2.306(9.37) = 418.50 \pm 21.61$$

If this procedure was used in a large number of production runs of 6000 bearings, 95 percent of the time the total cost of the production run would lie within the interval obtained. We give estimates to the nearest dollar because that is the accuracy to which the experimental data were recorded.

If the statistician regards (14.13) as a continuous function when $2 \leq x \leq 10$ and if he must make estimates of the type just illustrated as a matter of routine and for various lot sizes, he could save himself computation by making a chart such as Figure 14.2. From this chart we can read the estimated range within which total production cost will fall 95 percent of the time for any lot size between 2000 and 10,000 bearings. It was constructed by computing the lower and upper limits for both 2000 and 10,000 bearings and connecting the two lower and the two upper limits by straight lines. For runs of 2000 and 10,000 bearings, respectively,

$$\hat{E}(Y \mid x = 2) \pm 2.306 \hat{\sigma}(Y \mid x) = 337.40 \pm 21.61$$

$$\hat{E}(Y \mid x = 10) \pm 2.306 \hat{\sigma}(Y \mid x) = 499.60 \pm 21.61$$

These results imply the following confidence intervals:

$$C\{316 \leq y \leq 359 \mid x = 2\} = 0.95$$

$$C\{478 \leq y \leq 521 \mid x = 10\} = 0.95$$

With the aid of Figure 14.2, similar statements can be made for other lot sizes without computation. Recall from footnote 7 that the ranges given in this figure are only approximate.

Figure 14.2 can serve as a cost-control device as well as an estimating device. Suppose, for example, that a run of 5000 Number 6684 bearings cost $430. According to Figure 14.2, a cost in excess of $420 will occur in only

---

[7] Strictly speaking, this range is only approximate because it does not take full account of the random variation in $\hat{\alpha}$ and $\hat{\beta}$.

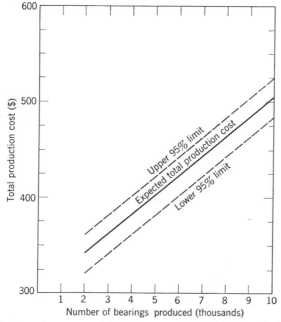

Fig. 14.2. Estimated upper and lower 95 percent probability limits for total production cost of production runs between 2000 and 10,000 bearings, Wearing Bearing Company catalogue Number 6684.

about 2.5 percent of production runs of 5000 Number 6684 bearings. Is this one of those times, or is there an assignable cause? Perhaps some of the costs of another run were mistakenly assigned to this run. Perhaps one of the machines is breaking down frequently. Perhaps inspection procedures are shoddy. Without checking, of course, there is no way of telling why costs on this run were high. Figure 14.2 has called attention to the fact that something might be wrong; it is up to management to track down the cause.

The statistician must face one more fact before he puts away his slide rule and his t table. His estimates of α and β are based on a sample. If he were to run a second experiment using the same lot sizes, he would obtain slightly different results because of the random variation in costs. These different experimental results would produce different estimates of α and β. His estimates are really random variables. How good they are as parameter estimates depends on their probability distributions. What can the statistician say about the probability distributions of $\hat{\alpha}$ and $\hat{\beta}$?

If his assumptions are valid, he can say quite a lot. He is assuming that total production cost, Y, is a normally distributed random variable whose variance, $\sigma^2(Y \mid x)$, is the same for all x and whose mean is a linear function of x. Under these assumptions, $\hat{\alpha}$ and $\hat{\beta}$ are unbiased estimates of α and β. That is,

$$E(\hat{\alpha}) = \alpha \qquad E(\hat{\beta}) = \beta$$

Furthermore, $\hat{\alpha}$ and $\hat{\beta}$ are each normally distributed. Since they are computed from the same sample, they are not independent, except under special circumstances. The statistician can use his experimental results to obtain estimates of the variance of $\hat{\alpha}$, the variance of $\hat{\beta}$, and the covariance of $\hat{\alpha}$ and $\hat{\beta}$. The covariance, remember, is a measure of the way in which $\hat{\alpha}$ and $\hat{\beta}$ vary together.

As mentioned in Section 14.4, when a statistician wants to describe the way in which several random variables vary, he uses the "variance-covariance" matrix, V. The variance-covariance matrix for $\hat{\alpha}$ and $\hat{\beta}$ is given by (14.9) in Section 14.4. If we introduce $\hat{\sigma}^2(Y \mid x)$ as our unbiased estimate of the conditional variance and employ matrix M, the variance-covariance matrix for $\hat{\alpha}$ and $\hat{\beta}$ is simply

$$\hat{V}(\hat{\alpha}, \hat{\beta}) = \hat{\sigma}^2(Y \mid x)M^{-1} \tag{14.15}$$

For the Wearing Bearing problem,

$$\hat{V}(\hat{\alpha}, \hat{\beta}) = 87.81 \begin{bmatrix} 0.5500 & -0.0750 \\ -0.0750 & 0.0125 \end{bmatrix} = \begin{bmatrix} 48.30 & -6.59 \\ -6.59 & 1.10 \end{bmatrix}$$

For our purposes, all we need from this matrix are $\hat{\sigma}^2(\hat{\alpha})$ and $\hat{\sigma}^2(\hat{\beta})$. These are given by the entries along the main diagonal.

$$\hat{\sigma}^2(\hat{\alpha}) = 48.30 \qquad \hat{\sigma}(\hat{\alpha}) = 6.95$$

$$\hat{\sigma}^2(\hat{\beta}) = 1.10 \qquad \hat{\sigma}(\hat{\beta}) = 1.05$$

The statistician can now use these results to state confidence intervals for α and β. Since the variances are estimated, he must use the t distribution, applying the rule of thumb about degrees of freedom. To establish 95 percent confidence intervals, he computes

$$\hat{\alpha} \pm 2.306\hat{\sigma}(\hat{\alpha}) = 296.850 \pm 2.306(6.95) = 296.850 \pm 16.027$$

$$\hat{\beta} \pm 2.306\hat{\sigma}(\hat{\beta}) = 20.275 \pm 2.306(1.05) = 20.275 \pm 2.421$$

From this, he can write

$$C\{280.8 \le \alpha \le 312.9\} = 0.95$$

$$C\{17.9 \le \beta \le 22.7\} = 0.95$$

These results do *not* mean that the probability is 0.95 that α lies between 280.8 and 312.9 and the probability is 0.95 that β lies between 17.9 and 22.7. They mean that, if the statistician were to run many experiments under the same conditions as those described, computing 95 percent confidence intervals from his experimental results just as these have been computed, then 95 percent of the intervals he computes for α will contain α and 95 percent of the intervals he computes for β will contain β. The *intervals* are random variables; α and β are fixed parameters.

14.6   ESTIMATING PARAMETERS AND STATING CONFIDENCE INTERVALS IN CORRELATION ANALYSIS

The Physical Education Department at Ironclad University is worried about the condition of its freshmen. The Director of Physical Education wants to establish weight standards for male freshmen. He recognizes that he will have to take height into account, and perhaps other physical characteristics. Before setting his standards, the director decides to investigate his raw material. What is the average weight for freshmen of a given height, and how do the weights of individual freshmen vary about this average?

Ironclad is deemphasizing athletics, and the department has a small budget. Therefore, the director decides to do a small-scale study on his own. Using a table of random numbers, he draws from his files on recent freshman classes the records of ten freshmen. We have already seen his data; the heights and weights of these ten freshmen were given in Table 14.1. What inferences can he draw from his sample?

The director recognizes that in his sample both height and weight are random variables. His experience indicates that it is reasonable to assume that height is approximately a normally distributed random variable and that, for freshman of a given height, weight is also approximately normally distributed. He assumes that average weight is a linear function of height and that the variance of the weights of freshmen of a given height does not depend on height. To put this in mathematical terms, the director decides to designate weight by Y and height by X. He is then assuming that X is a normal random variable with mean $E(X) = \mu_X$ and variance $\sigma^2(X) = \sigma_X{}^2$, and that the conditional distribution of Y given x is normal with mean $E(Y \mid x) = \alpha + \beta x$ and variance $\sigma^2(Y \mid x)$ where $\sigma^2(Y \mid x)$ does not depend on X. These assumptions imply that the marginal distribution of Y is normal with[8]

$$E(Y) = \mu_Y$$
$$\sigma_Y{}^2 \geq \sigma^2(Y \mid x)$$

The director has lots of things to estimate from his sample, but he does not need any new theory in order to do the estimating. He can use the theory of Chapter 9 plus that used up to now in this chapter.

[8] See Sections 5.8, 13.3, 13.4, and 13.7.

Before we do any estimating, however, let us see whether the mathematical model assumed by the director differs from that used by the statistician for Wearing Bearing. There is only one important difference, namely, in what is assumed about the independent variable.

The statistician was able to assume that the independent variable was predetermined rather than random. A value of x (lot size in the case of Wearing Bearing) was preassigned, and a value of Y (total production cost) was observed. There, it made no sense to talk about the probability distribution of X or a marginal distribution of Y. The statistician was interested in estimating cost for known lot sizes. He designed his experiment in order to do this. Because he did not pick lot sizes at random, we cannot use his sample results to make probability statements about lot size.

The director, on the other hand, is assuming that the independent variable is a random variable. He has picked freshmen (units of association) at random and observed two variables, height and weight, for each unit of association. Therefore, it makes sense to talk about the probability distribution of height and the marginal distribution of weight. The director is interested in estimating weight from height. He could as easily use his data to obtain an equation for estimating height from weight, thus reversing the roles of the dependent and independent variables. But it would be impossible for the statistician to use his data with the roles of the variables reversed.

In spite of this important difference, the same estimating procedures can be applied to both. In addition, we can use the procedures of Chapter 9 to estimate the parameters of the probability distribution of height and the marginal distribution of weight. The necessary preliminary calculations have been made in Table 14.2, part a, and $\hat{\alpha}$, $\hat{\beta}$, and M^{-1} have been computed in Table 14.2, part b. Table 14.5 gives the remaining calculations of parameter estimates and their standard errors.

Table 14.6 shows the calculation of 95 percent confidence intervals for α, β, μ_X, and μ_Y. The confidence intervals for α and β are based on 8 degrees of freedom, while the confidence intervals for μ_X and μ_Y are based on 9 degrees of freedom. With all of these results, what can the Director of Physical Education conclude about the heights and weights of his freshmen?

First, he has an estimating equation:

$$\hat{E}(Y \mid x) = -213.99 + 5.38x \tag{14.16}$$

With this equation, he can estimate the average weight for freshmen of a given height. This equation indicates that average weight increases as height increases. Because both X and Y are random variables whose distributions are assumed known, the slope $\hat{\beta}$ of the estimating equation can be given a statistical interpretation. If we pick pairs of freshmen at random whose heights differ by 1 in., then, on the average, their weights will differ by

Table 14.5 Calculation of Parameter Estimates from the Numerical Results in Table 14.2

---

1. $\hat{\alpha}$, $\hat{\beta}$, and M^{-1}, taken directly from Table 14.2:

$$\hat{\alpha} = -213.99, \qquad \hat{\beta} = 5.38$$

$$M^{-1} = \frac{1}{756.6} \begin{bmatrix} 46588.06 & -682 \\ -682 & 10 \end{bmatrix}$$

2. $s^2(Y \mid x)$, $\hat{\sigma}^2(Y \mid x)$, and $\hat{\sigma}(Y \mid x)$:

$$\sum y^2 - \hat{\alpha} \sum y - \hat{\beta} \sum xy = 236320 - 213.99(1528)$$

$$- 5.38(104616.5) = 459.95$$

$$s^2(Y \mid x) = \frac{1}{10}(459.95) = 45.995; \; \hat{\sigma}^2(Y \mid x) = \frac{1}{8}(459.95) = 57.49$$

$$\hat{\sigma}(Y \mid x) = \sqrt{57.49} = 7.58$$

3. $\hat{V}(\hat{\alpha}, \hat{\beta})$, $\hat{\sigma}(\hat{\alpha})$, and $\hat{\sigma}(\hat{\beta})$:

$$\hat{V}(\hat{\alpha}, \hat{\beta}) = \hat{\sigma}^2(Y \mid x)M^{-1} = \frac{57.49}{756.6} \begin{bmatrix} 46588.06 & -682 \\ -682 & 10 \end{bmatrix}$$

$$= \begin{bmatrix} 3540 & -51.82 \\ -51.82 & 0.76 \end{bmatrix}$$

$$\hat{\sigma}(\hat{\alpha}) = \sqrt{3540} = 59.50; \; \hat{\sigma}(\hat{\beta}) = \sqrt{0.76} = 0.87$$

4. Parameter estimates for marginal distributions of X and Y:

$$\bar{x} = \frac{1}{10}(682) = 68.2: \qquad \bar{y} = \frac{1}{10}(1528) = 152.8$$

$$s_x^2 = \frac{1}{10}[46588.06 - 68.2(682)] = 7.566$$

$$s_y^2 = \frac{1}{10}[236320 - 152.8(1528)] = 284.16$$

$$\hat{\sigma}_X^2 = \frac{1}{9}(75.66) = 8.41; \qquad \hat{\sigma}_Y^2 = \frac{1}{9}(2841.6) = 315.7$$

$$\hat{\sigma}_X = \sqrt{8.41} = 2.90; \qquad \hat{\sigma}_Y = \sqrt{315.7} = 17.8$$

$$\hat{\sigma}_{\bar{X}}^2 = \frac{1}{10}(8.41) = 0.841; \qquad \hat{\sigma}_{\bar{Y}}^2 = \frac{1}{10}(315.7) = 31.57$$

$$\hat{\sigma}_{\bar{X}} = \sqrt{0.841} = 0.917; \qquad \hat{\sigma}_{\bar{Y}} = \sqrt{31.57} = 5.62$$

Table 14.6   Computation of 95 Percent Confidence Intervals for α, β, μ_X and μ_Y from the Numerical Results in Table 14.5

1.	$\hat{\alpha} \pm 2.306 \hat{\sigma}(\hat{\alpha}) = -213.99 \pm 2.306(59.50) = -213.99 \pm 137.21$
	$C\{-351.20 \le \alpha \le -76.78\} = 0.95$
2.	$\hat{\beta} \pm 2.306 \hat{\sigma}(\hat{\beta}) = 5.38 \pm 2.306(0.87) = 5.38 \pm 2.01$
	$C\{3.37 \le \beta \le 7.39\} = 0.95$
3	$\bar{x} \pm 2.262 \hat{\sigma}_{\bar{x}} = 68.2 \pm 2.262(0.917) = 68.2 \pm 2.1$
	$C\{66.1 \le \mu_X \le 70.3\} = 0.95$
4.	$\bar{y} \pm 2.262 \hat{\sigma}_{\bar{y}} = 152.8 \pm 2.262(5.62) = 152.8 \pm 12.7$
	$C\{140.1 \le \mu_Y \le 165.5\} = 0.95$

an estimated 5.38 lb. When both the dependent and the independent variables are random variables, the slope of the estimating equation can be interpreted in two ways. It is the difference in the average value of the dependent variable per unit difference in the independent variable, and it is also the average difference in the dependent variable per unit difference in the independent variable. The second interpretation implies an averaging over both the dependent and the independent variables. When the independent variable is not regarded as a random variable, averaging is impossible because we have no probability weights. Hence, when the independent variable is predetermined rather than random, the slope of the regression line can be interpreted only as the difference in the average value of the dependent variable per unit difference in the independent variable.

In interpreting slopes of regression lines, we must be careful to avoid confusing a difference *among* units of association with a change *within* a unit of association. As we have suggested earlier in Section 14.2, the value of $\hat{\beta}$ of 5.38 lb of weight per 1 in. of height does *not* mean that, on the average, a freshman's weight will change by about 5.38 lb if his height changes by 1 in. Estimating the effect on weight of a change in height of an individual freshman could not be done by our model which assumes that successive observations are independent. Successive observations of the weight and height of the same individual are not independent. The model required would have to take account of this dependence.

We discussed the problem of the y intercept in Section 14.2. Unless the dependent variable was observed when the independent variable was at or near zero or unless the investigator is willing to assume that his regression line describes what happens there, the y intercept should not be interpreted as the expected value of the dependent variable when the independent variable is zero. The regression line should be regarded as invalid outside of the range of values observed in the independent variable.

Second, the director has an estimate of the variance of the weights of individual freshmen of a given height about the estimated average weight of freshman of the given height.

$$\hat{\sigma}^2(Y \mid x) = 57.49$$

For the director's purposes, the standard error of estimate is more useful.

$$\hat{\sigma}(Y \mid x) = 7.58$$

He can use his estimating equation (14.16) and this standard error to draw conclusions about the weights of freshmen of various heights. For example, suppose he observes a freshman who cannot do "chin ups." The boy looks a little flabby. Perhaps he is overweight. He is 69 in. tall; he weighs 175 lb. What is the probability that a male freshman at Ironclad who is 69 in. tall would weigh 175 lb or more? Since the variance was estimated, the director has to use the t distribution in order to answer this question. Since he is going to use (14.16) to estimate the average weight, he computes the number of degrees of freedom by deducting two from the number of observations. He first computes

$$\hat{E}(Y \mid x = 69) = -213.99 + 5.38(69) = 157.23$$

Next, he finds

$$t = \frac{175 - 157.23}{7.58} = 2.344$$

Entering his table of t with 8 degrees of freedom, the director sees that less than 2.5 percent of the time ($t = 2.306$) would a freshman who is 69 in. tall weigh 175 lb or more. He decides that this particular freshman is overweight and imposes a strict regimen of exercise and no between-meal eating.

The director can use his regression equation and standard error of estimate as a control device just as did the statistician at Wearing Bearing. Suppose he decides that if a freshman's weight falls within the estimated range of the middle 90 percent of the weights of freshmen having the same height, he is "normal." If the freshman's weight falls outside this range, some corrective action must be taken. The director can then construct a weight control chart somewhat like the Wearing Bearing Company's cost control chart. Such a chart is shown in Figure 14.3. Deducing its method of construction is left to the reader as an exercise. Again, as mentioned in footnote 7, the ranges implied by the chart are only approximate.

Third, the Director can use his estimates to draw inferences about the marginal distributions of height and of weight. Suppose that he needs a

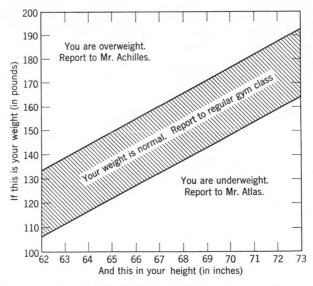

Fig. 14.3. Ironclad University freshmen weight-control chart (men).

center for the freshman basketball team. He would like the center to be 72 in. tall or taller. What proportion of his male freshmen can he expect to have the required height? From his sample, he has estimated that the mean height of his male freshmen is 68.2 in. and that the standard deviation of heights is 2.9 in. He is assuming that heights are approximately normal; hence he can use the t distribution. Since the variance of heights is computed about a sample mean rather than a sample regression equation, the methods of Chapter 9 apply. The director deducts one from the number of observations to obtain the number of degrees of freedom. Then

$$t = \frac{72 - 68.2}{2.9} = 1.31$$

and he enters the t table with 9 degrees of freedom. From the table, the director concludes that somewhere between 10 and 15 percent of his male freshmen will be 72 in. tall or taller. In a similar way, he can use his estimates of the mean and variance of the marginal distribution of weight to draw conclusions about the weights of his freshmen without regard to their heights.

There are other conclusions about the heights and weights of the male freshmen which the director could draw from his sample and calculations. One of these involves a measure of the degree of interdependence between height and weight. This concept is important enough, however, to deserve a separate section.

14.7 MEASURES OF ASSOCIATION AND INTERDEPENDENCE: THE COEFFICIENTS OF DETERMINATION AND CORRELATION

We are still at Ironclad University. Suppose that the Director of Physical Education has received an application for coxswain on the freshman crew from a male freshman whose height and weight he does not know. If he wants to estimate the weight of this freshman, the director must use estimates which pertain to the marginal distribution of weights. In order to establish a 95 percent confidence interval for this freshman's weight, the director would use methods like those in Chapter 9. The mean of his sample of weights is 152.8 lb, and the estimated standard deviation of the weight of all male freshmen is 17.8 lb. This estimate is based on 9 degrees of freedom. Hence, using the t distribution, the director would compute

$$\bar{y} \pm 2.262 \hat{\sigma}_Y = 152.8 \pm 2.262(17.8) = 152.8 \pm 40.3$$

and say that he is 95 percent confident that this particular freshman's weight is somewhere between 112.5 and 193.1 lb. This does not tell him very much about the usefulness of this freshman as a potential coxswain. Suppose, however, that this freshman mentions in his application that he is 64 in. tall. Now the director can use the methods developed in the previous section. He computes

$$\hat{E}(Y \mid x = 64) = -213.99 + 5.38(64) = 130.33$$

$$\hat{E}(Y \mid x = 64) \pm 2.306 \hat{\sigma}(Y \mid x) = 130.33 \pm 2.306(7.58) = 130.33 \pm 17.48$$

He can now say that he is 95 percent confident that the weight of the applicant is somewhere between 112.8 and 147.8 lb. Without information about height, the director's 95 percent confidence interval is about 80 lb wide; with information about height, it is only about 35 lb wide. Information about height seems to be useful in estimating weight. Furthermore, this result seems to indicate that height and weight vary together. In Chapter 13 we discussed the coefficients of determination ρ^2 and correlation ρ, which describe the way in which two random variables vary together. These quantities can also be interpreted as measures of the usefulness of one variable in predicting another. Our discussion in Chapter 13 was in terms of the universe, and we defined the coefficient of determination by

$$\rho^2 = \frac{\sigma_Y^2 - \sigma^2(Y \mid x)}{\sigma_Y^2} = 1 - \frac{\sigma^2(Y \mid x)}{\sigma_Y^2} \qquad (14.17)$$

Also the coefficient of correlation was defined as the square root of ρ^2. In the present section we are interested in the sample counterparts, specifically in two pairs of coefficients: the first, estimates of the universe coefficients based on sample evidence; and the second, coefficients within the sample itself.

When the Director of Physical Education estimated the weight of his potential coxswain without knowing his height, the width of the confidence interval was determined by $\hat{\sigma}_Y{}^2$. When the height of the freshman was introduced, the width of the confidence interval was determined by $\hat{\sigma}^2(Y \mid x)$. If $\hat{\sigma}^2(Y \mid x)$ is small relative to $\hat{\sigma}_Y{}^2$, we can conclude that information about height is useful in estimating weight. Because $\hat{\sigma}^2(Y \mid x)$ is measured about a linear regression equation, the complement of the ratio of $\hat{\sigma}^2(Y \mid x)$ to $\hat{\sigma}_Y{}^2$ is an estimate of ρ^2. We can write

$$\hat{\rho}^2 = 1 - \frac{\hat{\sigma}^2(Y \mid x)}{\hat{\sigma}_Y{}^2}$$

This is a *sample estimate* of the universe value of ρ^2. We shall use R^2 to represent the coefficient of determination considered as a random variable in relation to all possible samples of size n. A value of R^2 *for a particular sample* is indicated by the symbol r^2 and is computed by using sample variances instead of estimated universe variances.

$$r^2 = 1 - \frac{s^2(Y \mid x)}{s_y{}^2}$$

In statistical work, r^2 is usually computed; $\hat{\rho}^2$ seldom.

For the freshman height-weight data, we have, from Table 14.5,

$$\hat{\rho}^2 = 1 - \frac{57.49}{315.7} = 1 - 0.1821 = 0.8179$$

$$r^2 = 1 - \frac{45.995}{284.16} = 1 - 0.1619 = 0.8381$$

The interpretations of these numbers are very similar to those of ρ^2 and ρ. As we recall from Chapter 13, $\sigma_Y{}^2$ and $\sigma^2(Y \mid x)$ are measures of the variances of estimating errors from the universe mean and the universe regression line. Hence, as we see in (14.17), ρ^2 gives the proportion by which the variance of the estimating errors is reduced if the universe regression equation is used in combination with height to estimate individual weights instead of using the mean of all weights. The quantity $\hat{\rho}^2$ is a sample estimate of this quantity. If we have to estimate the weights of freshmen who were not in the sample, we estimate that we would reduce the variance of our estimating errors by 82 percent if we use the sample regression equation in combination with height instead of using the sample mean. This indicates that it is a good idea to use the regression equation if we can. The statistic r^2, on the other hand, applies only to the sample. If we estimate only the weights of the freshmen in the sample, we will reduce the variance of our estimating errors by 84 percent if we use the sample regression equation in combination with height instead of using the sample mean.

The three measures ρ^2, $\hat{\rho}^2$, and r^2 can be given a slightly different interpretation. We shall illustrate it with r^2, although the idea extends easily to ρ^2 and $\hat{\rho}^2$, and, for brevity and generality, we shall speak in terms of y, a general dependent variable. The variance of y about $\bar{y}$ can be split into two parts. One is the variance of $\hat{E}(Y \mid x)$ about $\bar{y}$, and the other is the variance of y about $\hat{E}(Y \mid x)$. The proof of this fact would interrupt the continuity of the explanation, so we shall defer it to the next section. Now, we can write as a mathematical identity

$$(y - \bar{y}) = [y - \hat{E}(Y \mid x)] + [\hat{E}(Y \mid x) - \bar{y}]$$

As a consequence of the proof in the next section, we can square each of these terms and sum to obtain, after dividing by n,

$$\frac{1}{n} \sum (y - \bar{y})^2 = \frac{1}{n} \sum [y - \hat{E}(Y \mid x)]^2 + \frac{1}{n} \sum [\hat{E}(Y \mid x) - \bar{y}]^2 \quad (14.18)$$

The expression on the left is merely $s_y{}^2$, and the first term on the right is $s^2(Y \mid x)$ in a slightly disguised form. The disguise is easily penetrated, however, since $\hat{E}(Y \mid x) = \hat{\alpha} + \hat{\beta}x$. The second term on the right, which we shall call $s_{\hat{E}}{}^2$, is the variance of $\hat{E}(Y \mid x)$ about $\bar{y}$, a measure of that portion of the total variance in y which is explained by the regression equation. The first term on the right, $s^2(Y \mid x)$, is that portion of the total variance in y which is not explained by the regression equation. In words and symbols:

$$\text{Total variance in } y = s_y{}^2$$
$$\text{Unexplained variance in } y = s^2(Y \mid x)$$
$$\text{Explained variance in } y = s_{\hat{E}}{}^2$$

Equation (14.18) now becomes

$$\text{Total variance} = \text{unexplained variance} + \text{explained variance,}$$

which we can write in symbols as

$$s_y{}^2 = s^2(Y \mid x) + s_{\hat{E}}{}^2$$

Solving for $s_{\hat{E}}{}^2$,

$$s_{\hat{E}}{}^2 = s_y{}^2 - s^2(Y \mid x)$$

After dividing by $s_y{}^2$, we get

$$\frac{s_{\hat{E}}{}^2}{s_y{}^2} = 1 - \frac{s^2(Y \mid x)}{s_y{}^2} = r^2$$

In words, again,

$$r^2 = \frac{\text{explained variance in } y}{\text{total variance in } y}$$

This means that r^2 can be interpreted as the proportion of the total variance in y that is "explained" by the regression equation. For our sample of heights and weights, we would say that about 84 percent of the variance of weights (in the sample, remember) is so explained. The partitioning of the total variance in weights is illustrated graphically in Figure 14.4.

From either interpretation of the coefficient of determination, we can deduce its minimum and maximum possible values. The smallest value is

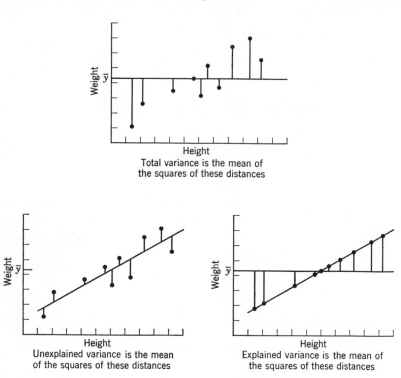

Fig. 14.4. Partitioning the total variance in weights (scales omitted).

zero, which means that no reduction in error variance is possible using the regression equation and that none of the variance in y is explained by the regression equation. In this case, the regression line is horizontal and intercepts the y axis at $\bar{y}$. The largest possible value for the coefficient of determination is unity, which means that error variance can be completely eliminated by using the regression line and that all of the variance in y is explained by the regression equation. In this case, the regression line will have a nonzero slope, and all of the points in the sample scatter diagram will lie on it.

The square root of the coefficient of determination is the coefficient of correlation. The appropriate symbols are $\hat{\rho}$ for the sample estimate of ρ, R for the random variable, and r for the sample coefficient of correlation. Since a square root can be either positive or negative, we attach to $\hat{\rho}$ and r the sign of $\hat{\beta}$, just as in Chapter 13 we attached the sign of β to ρ. Hence, the coefficient of correlation tells us a little more about the nature of the relationship between the two variables in question. The sign tells us whether both variables tend to increase and decrease together (positive coefficient of correlation) or whether one variable tends to increase when the other decreases (negative coefficient of correlation). For our height-weight data,

$$\hat{\rho} = 0.9044 \qquad r = 0.9155$$

The signs are positive, indicating that both variables tend to increase or decrease together. The squares have already been interpreted as coefficients of determination. Whether we regard these numbers as representing a high or a low correlation is a matter for judgment based on experience with similar kinds of data. Our correlation is extremely high for height-weight data. A study of the heights and weights of roughly 100,000 white male Selective Service examinees who were between the ages of 18 and 19 in 1943 yielded a coefficient of correlation of 0.4770.[9] On the other hand, in the physical sciences coefficients of correlation of 0.99 or higher are quite common.

The numerical values of the coefficients of determination and correlation do not depend on which variable is regarded as dependent. That is, if the Director of Physical Education had decided to estimate height from weight instead of weight from height, he would have obtained the same values for $\hat{\rho}^2$ and r^2. This would indicate that weight is as useful in estimating height as height is in estimating weight. This symmetrical property of the coefficients of determination and correlation means that it makes no sense to calculate them if the roles of the two variables in question cannot be reversed, that is, unless both the dependent and the independent variables are considered to be random. Thus, it makes no sense to calculate coefficients of determination and correlation in the Wearing Bearing example. The calculation of the coefficient of determination requires division by the variance of the marginal distribution of the dependent variable. The dependent variable will not have a marginal distribution unless the independent variable is assumed to have a probability distribution and, in order to have a probability distribution, the independent variable must be regarded as a random variable.

---

[9] B. D. Karpinos, "Weight-Height Standards Based on World War II Experience," *Journal of the American Statistical Association*, June, 1958, pp. 409–419. The coefficient of correlation in this article is based on the regression equation.

$$\log \text{weight} = \alpha + \beta \ (\text{height})$$

In the next section we give the promised proof that the total variance in y about $\bar{y}$ can be split into two parts. An understanding of this proof is not required in any later sections of this book. Hence, the reader who is not interested in the mathematical justification of our assertion can go directly to Section 14.9, where we face the fact that samples can sometimes mislead us.

*14.8   A PROOF THAT THE VARIANCE OF THE DEPENDENT VARIABLE CAN BE PARTITIONED

In (14.18) we wrote

$$\frac{1}{n}\sum(y - \bar{y})^2 = \frac{1}{n}\sum[y - \hat{E}(Y \mid x)]^2 + \frac{1}{n}\sum[\hat{E}(Y \mid x) - \bar{y}]^2$$

In this section we shall prove an equivalent statement, namely,

$$\sum(y - \bar{y})^2 = \sum(y - \hat{\alpha} - \hat{\beta}x)^2 + \sum(\hat{\alpha} + \hat{\beta}x - \bar{y})^2 \qquad (14.19)$$

but, before doing so, we shall obtain a few lemmas which make the proof easier.

LEMMA 1:

$$\hat{\alpha} = \bar{y} - \hat{\beta}\bar{x}$$

This follows directly from the first of the pair of equations in (14.12) when we divide both sides by n and rearrange.

LEMMA 2:

$$\sum(y - \bar{y})(x - \bar{x}) = \sum xy - \bar{x}\sum y$$

Proof.

$$\sum(y - \bar{y})(x - \bar{x}) = \sum(xy - \bar{x}y - \bar{y}x + \bar{x}\bar{y})$$
$$= \sum xy - \bar{x}\sum y - \bar{y}\sum x + n\bar{x}\bar{y}$$

Now

$$n\bar{x} = \sum x$$

Hence

$$\sum xy - \bar{x}\sum y - \bar{y}\sum x + n\bar{x}\bar{y} = \sum xy - \bar{x}\sum y - \bar{y}\sum x + \bar{y}\sum x$$
$$= \sum xy - \bar{x}\sum y$$

LEMMA 3:

$$\sum(x - \bar{x})^2 = \sum x^2 - \bar{x}\sum x$$

Proof.

$$\sum(x - \bar{x})^2 = \sum(x^2 - 2x\bar{x} + \bar{x}^2) = \sum x^2 - 2\bar{x}\sum x + n\bar{x}^2$$

Using the same fact that we used in Lemma 2,

$$\sum x^2 - 2\bar{x}\sum x + n\bar{x}^2 = \sum x^2 - 2\bar{x}\sum x + \bar{x}\sum x = \sum x^2 - \bar{x}\sum x$$

LEMMA 4:

$$\hat{\beta} = \sum (y - \bar{y})(x - \bar{x})/\sum (x - \bar{x})^2$$

Proof.   From (14.7),

$$\hat{\beta} = [n \sum xy - \sum x \sum y]/[n \sum x^2 - (\sum x)^2]$$

Divide numerator and denominator by n, obtaining

$$\hat{\beta} = [\sum xy - \bar{x} \sum y]/[\sum x^2 - \bar{x} \sum x]$$

When we apply Lemma 2 to the numerator and Lemma 3 to the denominator, Lemma 4 follows.

Now, we can prove (14.19). Applying Lemma 1 and then Lemma 4 to the first term on the right of (14.19) gives

$$\sum (y - \hat{\alpha} - \hat{\beta}x)^2 = \sum [(y - \bar{y}) - \hat{\beta}(x - \bar{x})]^2$$

$$= \sum (y - \bar{y})^2 - 2\hat{\beta} \sum (y - \bar{y})(x - \bar{x}) + \hat{\beta}^2 \sum (x - \bar{x})^2$$

$$= \sum (y - \bar{y})^2 - 2 \frac{[\sum (y - \bar{y})(x - \bar{x})]^2}{\sum (x - \bar{x})^2}$$

$$+ \frac{[\sum (y - \bar{y})(x - \bar{x})]^2}{\sum (x - \bar{x})^2}$$

$$= \sum (y - \bar{y})^2 - \hat{\beta}^2 \sum (x - \bar{x})^2$$

Next, apply Lemma 1 to the second term on the right of (14.19):

$$\sum (\hat{\alpha} + \hat{\beta}x - \bar{y})^2 = \sum [\hat{\beta}(x - \bar{x})]^2 = \hat{\beta}^2 \sum (x - \bar{x})^2$$

When we add these two results,

$$\sum (y - \hat{\alpha} - \hat{\beta}x)^2 + \sum (\hat{\alpha} + \hat{\beta}x - \bar{y})^2$$

$$= \sum (y - \bar{y})^2 - \hat{\beta}^2 \sum (x - \bar{x})^2 + \hat{\beta}^2 \sum (x - \bar{x})^2 = \sum (y - \bar{y})^2$$

This proves (14.19).

14.9   TESTS OF HYPOTHESES IN CORRELATION
AND REGRESSION ANALYSIS

Suppose that, in the universe of male freshmen, height and weight are independent. In this case, if we could take a very large simple random sample, say of 100,000 paired observations, the scatter diagram would have roughly an elliptical shape with the points densely clustered near the center and becoming sparser away from it. The axes of the ellipse would lie parallel to the

x and y axes, and the regression line (if weight were the dependent variable) would coincide with the axis parallel to the x axis. Both the slope of the regression line and the coefficient of correlation would be approximately zero. Now, imagine that our sample of ten observations is actually a subsample of this very large sample. Since we have picked ten points at random from a scatter of 100,000 points, the vagaries of random sampling could have led us to the ten points that we actually chose and to the fallacious conclusion that heights and weights are related. If heights and weights are actually unrelated, the chances of obtaining a coefficient of correlation as large as ours or larger are rather slim. It could occur, however, and we have to decide whether, in fact, it did occur.

If we could take all possible different simple random samples of ten points from the scatter of 100,000 points and compute r for each, we would find that r would vary from sample to sample. Sometimes it is positive and sometimes negative. It is close to zero most of the time but sometimes close to unity. If we then constructed a frequency distribution of these sample values of r, we would have a good approximation to its sampling distribution. Now, the numerical value of r does not depend on the units in which the variables are measured. If we converted the heights in our sample from inches to centimeters and the weights from pounds to kilograms, the sample value of r would be unaffected. This means that the sampling distribution of R, whose construction we have just described, applies in *any* situation in which sample values of R are computed from simple random samples of ten paired observations drawn from a population in which there is no correlation. Therefore, we can use this sampling distribution—or one that is derived from it—to test the null hypothesis that there is no correlation in the universe from which a simple random sample of ten paired observations has been drawn. In this way, we can guard against the mistake of concluding that two variables are linearly related when, in fact, they are not.

It turns out that, when a sample of n paired observations has been drawn from a universe in which there is no correlation, the quantity

$$t = R\sqrt{\frac{n-2}{1-R^2}} \qquad (14.20)$$

is a random variable whose probability distribution is the t distribution with $n-2$ degrees of freedom.[10] Hence, we can test the null hypothesis that $\rho = 0$ using the t distribution as the sampling distribution of $(R - 0)/\hat{\sigma}_R$.

---

[10] The test applied here, in previous form, is $t = (R - \rho)/\hat{\sigma}_R$ where

$$\hat{\sigma}_R = \sqrt{(1 - R^2)/(n - 2)}$$

This test is invalid, however, for any hypothesized value of ρ other than zero.

The alternative hypothesis depends on the question we wanted to answer when we collected the data. If the question is, "Is there a linear relationship with non-zero slope?" then the alternative hypothesis is $\rho \neq 0$ because our question has not specified that ρ have a particular sign. If, on the other hand, the question is, "Does the dependent variable tend to increase as the independent variable increases?" then the alternative hypothesis is $\rho > 0$ because our question has specified that ρ be positive.

"Can I really conclude that, in the universe of male freshmen at Ironclad, weight tends to increase as height increases?" asks the Director of Physical Education as he looks at his scatter diagram. That depends on whether he is willing to run the risk of saying that weight tends to increase as height increases when, in fact, height and weight are independent. Let us calculate t from (14.20) and see what conclusions we can draw.

$$t = 0.9155\sqrt{\frac{8}{1 - 0.8381}} = 0.9155\sqrt{49.41} = 6.435$$

When we look up values for t with 8 degrees of freedom, we see that 6.435 is so big that it is not even on our table. Less than 1 time in 1000 would we get a value of t as big as 6.435 or bigger if the sample of heights and weights were really drawn from a universe in which they were uncorrelated. Either something very unusual has happened, or heights and weights are positively correlated. Unless the director is a very conservative man, he can conclude that with his freshmen weight tends to increase as height increases.

The correlation in the Ironclad University sample is so strong that it is not very useful as an example, so let us change the scene to Honeydew Junior College, where the director's female counterpart is contemplating a scatter diagram showing the heights and weights of 11 female freshmen. The sample coefficient of correlation is 0.60. "Are their heights and weights really related?" she asks. Again, the answer depends on the risk that she is willing to take of saying that heights and weights are related when, in fact, in the universe of female freshmen at Honeydew they are not. Two variables are related if the universe coefficient of correlation is not zero. A sample coefficient of correlation of -0.60 is just as strong an indication of a relationship as a sample coefficient of correlation of $+0.60$. To the gym teacher, therefore, the relevant alternative hypotheses are:

$$H_0: \rho = 0$$

$$H_1: \rho \neq 0$$

Suppose the teacher is willing to run a 5 percent risk of accepting H_1 when H_0 is true. We have a two-sided alternative to the null hypothesis, a 5 percent risk of Type I error, and 9 degrees of freedom. From the t table, we see that if t is less than -2.262 or greater than $+2.262$, we should reject H_0; otherwise, we cannot reject H_0. Now, we calculate t:

$$t = 0.60\sqrt{\frac{9}{1 - 0.36}} = 2.25$$

On the basis of her sample evidence, the teacher cannot conclude that the heights and weights of her freshmen are linearly related—assuming, of course, that the freshman class is so large that a sample of 11 girls does not represent any substantial portion of it.

As we have indicated, when the independent variable cannot be regarded as a random variable, it is senseless to compute a coefficient of correlation or to test hypotheses concerning it. We can, however, ask questions concerning the nature of the regression equation. For an example, let us return to the Wearing Bearing Company.

The cost accountant at Wearing Bearing asserts that the average variable production cost per run for Number 6684 bearings should not exceed $18 per 1000 bearings. The statistician's cost-estimating equation,

$$\hat{E}(Y \mid x) = 296.850 + 20.275x$$

indicates an average variable cost per production run of slightly over $20 per 1000 bearings. The accountant claims that this means that variable costs on this bearing are too high. Is his claim justified?

The accountant is basing his claim on the fact that $\hat{\beta}$ is 20.275 when his cost figures indicate that it should be closer to 18. Now $\hat{\beta}$ is an estimate of a universe parameter, β. It is a normally distributed variable with a mean of β and a standard deviation of $\sigma(\hat{\beta})$. Deciding on the truth of the accountant's claim reduces to the question: Is β less than or equal to 18, or is β greater than 18? The burden of proof should be on the accountant to show that costs are too high because the company does not want to introduce cost-cutting procedures, disrupting production, unless it must. At Wearing Bearing it is more serious to cut costs when they do not have to be cut than it is not to cut them when they should be cut. For this reason, we set up the following pair of hypotheses:

$$H_0: \beta \le 18 \qquad H_1: \beta > 18$$

The statistician and the accountant agree that a 5 percent risk of taking unnecessary steps to cut costs is satisfactory. In Section 14.5 we obtained a sample estimate of $\sigma(\hat{\beta})$. It was

$$\hat{\sigma}(\hat{\beta}) = 1.05$$

This estimate is based on 8 degrees of freedom. (Remember our rule of thumb.) Since $\hat{\sigma}(\hat{\beta})$ is estimated, we must test our hypothesis using the t distribution. Now, if a $\hat{\beta}$ of 20.275 is significantly greater than 18, it is certainly significantly greater than any value less than 18. Hence, we can use the sampling distribution which obtains when β is 18 to represent all possibilities under H_0. We compute t just as we did in Chapter 9:

$$t = \frac{\hat{\beta} - \beta}{\hat{\sigma}(\hat{\beta})} = \frac{20.275 - 18}{1.05} = 2.167$$

We have a one-sided alternative hypothesis and a risk of Type I error of 5 percent. The t distribution for 8 degrees of freedom shows a critical value of t of 1.860. Our value of t exceeds this value. If H_0 were true in the sense that β is exactly 18, we would get a value of t as big as our value or bigger less than 5 percent of the time. This is smaller than the risk of Type I error that we are willing to tolerate. Therefore, we reject H_0 and conclude that variable production costs on this bearing are too high. The accountant appears to be right.

14.10   SOME LIMITATIONS AND CAUTIONS

Like all statistical methods, those of this chapter should be used only after careful thought shows that they are appropriate. Much of the theory of correlation and regression is simple and generalizes easily; yet its application leads to computations, numerical tables, and graphs which give the impression of being extremely scientific. However, before applying any technique, it is necessary to match its underlying assumptions to the physical realities of the problem. After the technique has been applied and numerical results are available, the assumptions must be examined again to see if apparently obvious conclusions are really justified. What are some of the important assumptions which should be questioned and what are some of the common pitfalls which should be avoided in correlation and regression analysis?

The Unit of Association

The unit of association links the dependent and independent variables. We assume that the height and weight *of the same individual* are related, that lot size and total production cost *for the same production run* are related. The reasons for the association in these two cases are intuitively clear, although a written explanation might be lengthy. In other cases, the connection between the variables is tenuous at best. It is tempting, for example, to assume that two events are related because they occur either at the same time or place or at points in time or space which are close to each other. Next month's sales are related to this month's sales. Spring rainfall in a certain county in a certain year is related to the production of truck crops in the same county in the same year. These are fairly reasonable links. But is it reasonable to link the number of automobile registrations in California with the number of divorces in New York, for example, just because they happen to occur at the same time? The theory might be amusing, but it would not be convincing. The theoretical reasons for relating two aspects of the same unit of association must be carefully considered.

The Form of the Regression Equation

Although a study of the data may suggest it, the functional form of the regression equation is postulated by the investigator. He must be guided by practical and theoretical considerations; not the least of these is the quantity of data and the computing equipment available. The statistician with a thousand observations on each of 50 variables and an electronic digital computer has more flexibility than does the statistician who has ten observations on each of two variables and a slide rule. At a more elementary level, we have considered the problem of estimating the parameters of a linear regression equation which connects a dependent variable and one independent variable. It may be that there are other relevant independent variables which could be added to the regression equation in order to improve its use as an estimating device. For example, in estimating the weight of a male freshman, we might want to include in the regression equation the weight of his father. If we designate weight by Y, height by X, and weight of father by Z, our new regression equation would become

$$E(Y \mid x, z) = \alpha + \beta x + \gamma z$$

Before doing this, however, we have to consider the reasonableness of linking weight of father to weight of son and the availability of the information. If father's weight is difficult to observe, there is little point in including it.

Another consideration is that the relationship among the variables might not be linear. Suppose, for example, that we wanted to estimate the time that it takes for a falling body to traverse various distances. Distance, s, is the controlled variable, and time, T, is the dependent variable. If we were to estimate the parameters of a regression equation of the linear form

$$E(T \mid s) = \alpha + \beta s$$

we would obtain estimates of α and β which would give reasonably good estimates of T, provided that the range of s was not too great. However, the nonlinear equation

$$E(T \mid s) = \gamma + \delta\sqrt{s}$$

would give much better estimates of T over much wider ranges of s. We could make this equation linear by defining

$$u = \sqrt{s}$$

Since s (and, hence, u) is a controlled variable, we can apply the theory of this chapter to estimate the parameters of the linear regression equation:

$$E(T \mid s) = \gamma + \delta u$$

This suggests that when the assumption of linearity of the regression equation is open to question, it is sometimes possible to transform one or both variables in such a way that the resulting equation is linear in the new variables. Such a transformation may not be possible, however.

When we transform variables, we have to be careful about probability assumptions, particularly if we transform the dependent variable. If, for example, we transform the dependent variable Y to a new dependent variable $Z = \log Y$ and use a regression equation of the form

$$E(Z \mid x) = \alpha + \beta x$$

obtaining estimates of α and β by the methods of this chapter, we are saying that *log* Y rather than Y is a normal random variable. Such an assumption could make a great deal of theoretical sense, but we must remember that our transformation implies, among other things, that Y can never be negative and that values of Y greater than twice the expected value of Y are as likely to occur as values of Y less than one half the expected value of Y. Transforming the dependent variable implies the assumption that the transformed rather than the original dependent variable is normally distributed.

In actual practice, particularly in business problems, regression analysis is a matter of "cut and try." Different independent variables and different transformations of both dependent and independent variables are tested in various combinations until the regression equation that best "fits" the data is obtained. This equation may involve assumptions about the process generating the data which are different from those that led to the investigation in the first place. When this happens, there are at least two things that we should do. First, we should ask ourselves if the assumptions implicit in the final regression equation make good theoretical sense. Second, we should estimate the parameters in a similar regression equation applied to new data and compare the estimates. Often this is impossible because new data cannot be obtained. If this is the case, a reasonable substitute procedure is to fit the regression equation to a subsample of the original data and then test the ability of this equation to estimate data points not in the subsample. The "cut and try" method of regression analysis is a way of constructing a theory about the process generating the data. The theory should be tested with new data.

Independence

A theoretical model which can be said to underlie both correlation and regression analysis is

$$Y = \alpha + \beta x + \epsilon$$

In this model, ϵ is assumed to be a normally distributed random variable with a mean of zero and a variance which is the same for all values of x. It is further assumed that, in successive observations on Y, successive values of ϵ are independent. In collecting the data, every effort should be made to see that this assumption is met, since its violation can lead to many complications including bias in the estimates of α and β. When possible, units of association should be selected at random in correlation analysis. In regression analysis, the order in which increasing or decreasing values of x are observed should be randomized. In business and economic problems where the unit of association is a point in time or a time interval, there is some danger that this assumption is not met because observations of economic variables taken at successive points in time are usually not independent. In this case, one can either hope that the assumption is met or transform the data so that it is more likely to be met.[11] There are tests of this assumption which can be applied in regression analysis, but they are too advanced for this text.

Conclusions Based on the Numerical Magnitude of the Correlation Coefficient

A large correlation coefficient does not necessarily indicate that a linear relationship exists between the variables. It is possible that a Type I error has been made in the test of the null hypothesis described in the previous section. A simple check of this possibility can be deduced from a formula for r which we have not considered. It is

$$r = \frac{\sum (x - \bar{x})(y - \bar{y})}{ns_x s_y} \tag{14.21}$$

Suppose that in the sample there is one pair of observations, (x, y), which has the property that both $(x - \bar{x})$ and $(y - \bar{y})$ are very large. The presence

---

[11] If successive observations are not independent, for example, the differences between them might be independent.

of this pair increases the value of the numerator in the formula for r and, of course, the value of R. If the hypothesis that ρ is zero can be rejected with this extreme pair omitted, the investigator can conclude that his sample evidence indicates that the two variables in question are linearly related. Another test is to convert the x and y values to ranks and to compute r for the ranks. If the hypothesis that $\rho = 0$ in the universe of ranks can be rejected, the investigator can also conclude that his sample evidence indicates a relationship. In this latter case, the relationship may not be linear but monotonic.

Even when no extreme pairs are present, a large coefficient of correlation can be misleading. Suppose, for example, that an economist is interested in the relationship between the number of marriages and the number of new housing starts. He picks several counties at random and for each records the number of marriages in 1967 and the number of new housing starts in 1969. If the economist correlates marriages and new housing starts using the rather complicated unit of association implied, he will probably get a high coefficient of correlation. Part of this, of course, is due to the fact that couples do buy houses after they have been married for a year or two. But another part of the correlation is attributable to the fact that both the number of marriages and the number of new housing starts in a county are related to the total population. Total population appears in disguised form as part of both the dependent and independent variables. There are several ways to take account of this fact in the analysis, but a discussion of them would take us too far afield.

A coefficient of correlation which is small in absolute value, on the other hand, need not indicate no relationship between the variables. It may be that a high correlation exists when the variables are transformed. This is a good reason for drawing a scatter diagram before doing the numerical analysis. The diagram and some careful thought about the process generating the data may suggest a transformation that leads to a higher correlation coefficient than would be obtained otherwise.

Finally, even a large coefficient of correlation may not be large enough for our purposes if we want to make very reliable estimates. Reliability is determined by $\sigma^2(Y \mid x)$, while the coefficient of correlation depends upon the ratio of $\sigma^2(Y \mid x)$ to $\sigma_Y{}^2$. Hence, if we are concerned with reliability, we must look at $\hat{\sigma}(Y \mid x)$ rather than at r. In using a regression equation to make estimates, we compute $\hat{E}(Y \mid x) \pm t\hat{\sigma}(Y \mid x)$, where t depends on the level of confidence desired and on the number of observations. If this interval is too wide for our purposes, then we must somehow reduce $\hat{\sigma}(Y \mid x)$. We can sometimes do this by adding another independent variable to the regression equation. This variable, of course, should be related in some way (preferably linear) to the dependent variable.

Extrapolation and Interpolation

As suggested earlier, use of the regression equation to make estimates of the dependent variable when the independent variable lies beyond the range over which it varied in the sample is often unwise. This procedure is called *extrapolation*. It is an unwise procedure, especially when the regression equation is thought of as a linear approximation to a more complicated relationship. Usually, linear approximations give satisfactory estimates only over relatively narrow ranges of variation of the independent variable. Regression analysis is often used as an exploratory tool when not much is known about relationships among variables and the investigator is either testing a tentative theory or searching for a better one. Generally, the only circumstance under which estimates can be made with some degree of confidence for values of the dependent variable outside of the range studied is when the form of the regression line is determined by a well-established theory, and the order of magnitude of the parameters is verifiable in other studies. There are often situations, especially business or military situations, in which we must extrapolate. An estimate is needed in a hurry, and additional observations are either too expensive or impossible to obtain in the time available. In this case, of course, we do the best we can, fully aware that we may be painfully wrong.

Interpolation between successive observed values of the independent variable also can lead to errors. This is especially true when the values of the independent variable have been chosen in advance. In the Wearing Bearing example we provided an illustration of the danger of interpolation. If bearings are made in batches of 2000 and if odd-sized batches require special processing, then a cost-estimating equation based on lot sizes which are multiples of 2000 will not give good estimates of the cost of producing bearings in lot sizes which are not.

Causal Inferences

Cause is not a fact; it is a postulate. It cannot be proved by an experiment, and our ideas about it are changing continually. Since before the time of Aristotle, philosophers have debated the definition of cause and its experimental verification. We cannot settle this debate here, but we can certainly assert that no correlation analysis will prove cause. In order to show that the event x is "the cause" of the event y, we must first show that the occurrence of the event x is both necessary and sufficient for the occurrence of y. When x occurs, y occurs; when x does not occur, y does not occur. If x is a necessary condition for y, then x and y are said to stand in a "producer-product" relationship. Correlation analysis cannot even show that two variables stand in such a relationship. If the correlation between x and y is not a matter of pure chance, it may be due to the fact that x is a producer of y, that y is a producer of x, or that a third variable, z, is a producer of both x and y. A producer-product relationship is a theoretical construct. Correlation analysis can only show that a theory is tenable; it cannot show that it is true.

IMPORTANT TERMS AND CONCEPTS

Coefficient of correlation
Coefficient of determination
Confidence interval
Correlation analysis
Extrapolation
Interpolation
Inverse
Linear relationship
Mathematical model
Matrix
Method of least squares
Parameter estimate
Regression analysis
Scatter diagram

Slope
Test of hypothesis
Unit of association
Variable
  Dependent
  Independent
  Predetermined
Variance
  Explained
  Total
  Unexplained
Variance-covariance matrix
y-Intercept

SYMBOLS AND ABBREVIATIONS

α
β
$\hat{\alpha}$
$\hat{\beta}$
a
b
$E(Y \mid x)$
$\hat{y}_x$
$\sigma^2(Y \mid x)$
$\hat{\sigma}^2(Y \mid x)$

$\sigma^2(\hat{\alpha})$
$\sigma^2(\hat{\beta})$
$V(\hat{\alpha}, \hat{\beta})$
M
M^{-1}
s_y^2
$s^2(Y \mid x)$
ρ
$\hat{\rho}$
R
r

OFTEN-USED FORMULAS

$$E(Y \mid x) = \alpha + \beta x$$

$$\begin{bmatrix} a & b \\ c & d \end{bmatrix}^{-1} = \frac{1}{ad - bc} \begin{bmatrix} d & -b \\ -b & a \end{bmatrix}$$

$$s_x^2 = \frac{1}{n} [\sum x^2 - \bar{x} \sum x]$$

$$\hat{\alpha} = \frac{\sum x^2 \sum y - \sum x \sum xy}{n \sum x^2 - (\sum x)^2}$$

$$\hat{\beta} = \frac{n \sum xy - \sum x \sum y}{n \sum x^2 - (\sum x)^2}$$

$$\sigma^2(\hat{\alpha}) = \frac{\sigma^2(Y \mid x) \sum x^2}{n \sum x^2 - (\sum x)^2}$$

$$\sigma^2(\hat{\beta}) = \frac{n\sigma^2(Y \mid x)}{n \sum x^2 - (\sum x)^2}$$

$$\operatorname{cov}(\hat{\alpha}, \hat{\beta}) = \frac{-\sigma^2(Y \mid x) \sum x}{n \sum x^2 - (\sum x)^2}$$

$$V(\hat{\alpha}, \hat{\beta}) = \begin{bmatrix} \sigma^2(\hat{\alpha}) & \operatorname{cov}(\hat{\alpha}, \hat{\beta}) \\ \operatorname{cov}(\hat{\alpha}, \hat{\beta}) & \sigma^2(\hat{\beta}) \end{bmatrix} = \sigma^2(Y \mid x)M^{-1}$$

$$M = \begin{bmatrix} n & \sum x \\ \sum x & \sum x^2 \end{bmatrix}$$

$$\hat{\sigma}^2(Y \mid x) = \frac{1}{n-2} (\sum y^2 - \hat{\alpha} \sum y - \hat{\beta} \sum xy)$$

$$\hat{\rho}^2 = 1 - \frac{\hat{\sigma}^2(Y \mid x)}{\hat{\sigma}_Y^2}$$

$$s_y^2 = \frac{1}{n} (\sum y^2 - \bar{y} \sum y)$$

$$s^2(Y \mid x) = \frac{1}{n} (\sum y^2 - \hat{\alpha} \sum y - \hat{\beta} \sum xy)$$

$$r^2 = 1 - \frac{s^2(Y \mid x)}{s_y^2}$$

$$t = R\sqrt{\frac{n-2}{1-R^2}}$$

EXERCISES

1. The systems of equations given below are of the form:

$$\begin{bmatrix} \sum y \\ \sum xy \end{bmatrix} = \begin{bmatrix} n & \sum x \\ \sum x & \sum x^2 \end{bmatrix} \begin{bmatrix} a \\ b \end{bmatrix}$$

Compute the inverses of the square matrices on the right and check your answers by matrix multiplication.

a.
$$\begin{bmatrix} 1000 \\ 25{,}000 \end{bmatrix} = \begin{bmatrix} 500 & 3000 \\ 3000 & 100{,}000 \end{bmatrix} \begin{bmatrix} a \\ b \end{bmatrix}$$

$X =$ number of castings ordered, $10 \le x \le 50$; and $Y =$ average unit cost of the order in dollars per casting.

b.
$$\begin{bmatrix} 300 \\ 3360 \end{bmatrix} = \begin{bmatrix} 15 & 50 \\ 50 & 500 \end{bmatrix} \begin{bmatrix} a \\ b \end{bmatrix}$$

$X =$ average number of calls per day (for salesmen), $6 \le x \le 14$; and $Y =$ average weekly number of sales.

c.
$$\begin{bmatrix} 2000 \\ 11{,}800 \end{bmatrix} = \begin{bmatrix} 100 & 500 \\ 500 & 4400 \end{bmatrix} \begin{bmatrix} a \\ b \end{bmatrix}$$

$X =$ advertising expenses in \$100 units, $1 \le x \le 10$; and $Y =$ sales in \$1000 units.

d.
$$\begin{bmatrix} 187 \\ 15{,}125 \end{bmatrix} = \begin{bmatrix} 11 & 880 \\ 880 & 81{,}500 \end{bmatrix} \begin{bmatrix} a \\ b \end{bmatrix}$$

$X =$ family annual income in \$100 units, $40 \le x \le 120$; and $Y =$ family annual food expenditures in \$100 units.

2. Using the inverses that you computed in Exercise 1, solve the equations— obtaining a and b.

3. What are the basic assumptions underlying
   a. Estimation of the parameters of a linear model by least squares.
   b. Regression analysis.
   c. Correlation analysis.
   d. Estimation of the parameters of a linear model by maximum likelihood.

4. Given the following data, where $X =$ age of astronaut and $Y =$ number

of space flights engaged in before retirement, for two astronauts chosen at random:

x	y
30	3
40	2

a. Find the regression line of number of space flights on age of astronaut.
b. Find the coefficient of correlation between X and Y.
c. Why does this coefficient have the value you calculated? State a general explanatory theorem.

5. Is it possible for a variance-covariance matrix to have a negative entry? If so, what does this imply about the relationship of X and Y?

6. If the regression equation of Y on x has the form:

$$\hat{y}_x = 8 + 15x$$

Explain the exact meaning of:
a. The number 8.
b. The number 15.

7. If, in addition, the standard error of estimate for the equation of Exercise 6 is given by $s^2(Y \mid x) = 25$ and the variance of y is $s_y^2 = 49$, interpret these quantities and compute the coefficient of correlation between X and Y.

8. Using the information given in Exercises 6 and 7:
a. Estimate the probability that Y will lie between 30 and 40, given that x is 2.
b. Estimate the probability that Y will lie between 175 and 185, given that x is 10.
c. Under what circumstances would you be unwilling to use either or both of these estimates?

9. a. Let x_i and y_i, $i = 1, \cdots, n$ be a set of bivariate observations on n units of association. If 10 is added to each of the x_i and 5 is subtracted from each of the y_i, how is the original coefficient of correlation affected?
b. If each x_i is multiplied by 10 and each y_i divided by 5, how is the original coefficient of correlation affected?

10. The following data show X, age of home in years, and Y, assessed valuation of home in thousands of dollars, for six randomly chosen homes in a large housing development.

x	3	6	2	5	1	8
y	7	5	7	4	10	7

    a. What is your best prediction of the assessed valuation of a seventh home in this development which is four years old?

    b. Set a 90 percent confidence interval for your prediction in part *a*.

    c. What is the exact meaning of the confidence interval you have computed in part *b*?

11. a. Compute the coefficient of correlation between X and Y in Exercise 10.

    b. At the 0.05 level of significance, is it likely that there is a significant association between age of home and its assessed valuation in this large development?

12. The RBC Corporation manufactures ammonia products. During the first eight days of operation of its new plant, the following output (in thousands of gallons) was observed:

Day	1	2	3	4	5	6	7	8
Output	12	14	17	16	19	14	18	18

    a. Is a correlation model or a regression model appropriate for analyzing these data?

    b. Set 95 percent confidence limits for the slope of the regression line in the population.

    c. Test the hypothesis that the slope of the population's regression line is really zero. Use $\alpha = 0.05$.

    d. Describe the population from which these observations could be considered a sample.

13. The following data relate $X =$ number of persons entering store in hundreds to $Y =$ total sales volume in thousands of dollars on seven Saturdays at the Mammoth Discount House.

x	3	5	8	5	2	1	6
y	6	7	10	8	7	4	8

    a. What is your best estimate of total sales volume on a Saturday if information about the number of persons entering the store is not available?

    b. Set 99 percent confidence limits for your prediction in part *a*.

    c. What is your best estimate of total sales volume on a Saturday when 400 persons entered the store?

    d. Set 99 percent confidence limits for your prediction in part *c*.

14. a. In Exercise 13, what percentage of the variance in total sales volume was explained by the number of persons entering the Mammoth Discount House on Saturday?

   b. What is your best estimate of the population's correlation coefficient between total sales volume and number of persons entering the Mammoth Discount House on Saturday?

   c. In part b, state exactly which population it is whose correlation coefficient you are estimating.

15. Describe exactly what is meant by each of the following terms:

   a. The regression line of Y on X.
   b. The sampling distribution of R.
   c. The standard error of estimate.
   d. The sampling distribution of $\hat{\beta}$.

16. Consider the following set of data relating U = millions of dollars spent in exploratory drilling from 1950 to 1968 and V = millions of dollars profit before taxes in 1969 for 15 oil companies.

u	3	16	1	7	2	17	20	4	24	2	5	5	1	10	2
v	1	7	2	9	4	3	2	1	2	3	5	6	2	8	2

   a. Plot these data in a scatter diagram.
   b. Would you be willing to fit a linear function to these data? Why or why not?
   c. Would analysis of these data involve correlation analysis or regression analysis?
   d. What is your best prediction for the 1969 profits of a sixteenth oil company which spent 12 millions of dollars on exploratory drilling between 1950 and 1968?
   e. Set a 90 percent confidence interval for your estimate in part d.

17. Among other appropriate courses, Sylvia's Secretarial School offers a six-week course in typing. The director of the school is interested in predicting the typing speed of a student who has just completed the course from the typing speed of the student at the end of the first week of the course. The director selects a random sample of ten beginning students. At the end of the first week and at the end of the sixth week they are timed in typing a standard short business letter. The results are given at top of the facing page.

   a. Which of the two types of models (regression or correlation) is appropriate to this problem and why? Discuss briefly.

Student	Time in Minutes	
	At End of Week 1 x	At End of Week 6 y
A	9.0	4.6
B	10.8	5.4
C	11.8	5.5
D	13.0	7.8
E	12.8	6.4
F	12.0	7.4
G	12.6	6.2
H	11.8	5.4
I	8.0	3.4
J	11.6	6.2

b. Plot the data in the form of a scatter diagram, being sure to identify the scales properly. On the basis of the diagram, do you think an estimating equation of the form $E(Y \mid x) = \alpha + \beta x$ is appropriate here? Why or why not?

c. Using the data given:
   (1) Estimate the parameters α and β in a linear equation from which time at the end of the course can be estimated from time at the end of the first week of the course. Show all work. (Ignore your answer to part b if necessary.)
   (2) Interpret your parameter estimates specifically in terms of this problem.
   (3) State and interpret a 90 percent confidence interval for β.

d. On the basis of the evidence in the sample, would you be willing to use the results of your analysis to predict the time to type a standard business letter at the end of the course from a similar time after the first week of the course? Why or why not?

18. The time required for an operator to set up a piece of complicated metal-working machinery depends on the experience and training of the operator on the machine. A large company producing metal products has arranged a training program for its machinists to learn to set up and operate a new type of metal lathe. The training period lasts ten weeks. A new group enters the training program every week so that, after the program has been operating for ten weeks, there will be a group (or class) of machinists in each week of the training period. The training director is interested in estimating set-up time from the number of weeks of training. He selects two machinists at random from each of the ten classes (20

machinists in all) and measures their set-up time on a typical job for the lathe. His observations are given below.

Week of Training w	$\dfrac{1}{w}$ x	Set-up Times (Minutes)	
		Machinist 1[a] y	Machinist 2[a] y
1	1.00	9.5	10.2
2	0.50	9.0	6.4
3	0.33	5.5	7.1
4	0.25	5.8	6.8
5	0.20	6.6	5.3
6	0.17	5.5	7.3
7	0.14	5.2	5.4
8	0.12	4.9	7.6
9	0.11'	5.9	4.2
10	0.10	4.5	6.3

[a] A *different* pair of machinists is observed each week of training.

a. The training director cannot decide which of these two models is the best to use:

Model A: $Y = \alpha_A + \beta_A w + e_A$

Model B: $Y = \alpha_B + \beta_B x + e_B,$ where $x = \dfrac{1}{w}$

He is willing to assume that the residual, either e_A or e_B, is normally distributed with a mean of zero and a variance that is the same for all values of the independent variable. Draw two scatter diagrams: one of Y against w and one of Y against x. (Remember, there are two values of Y for every w and every x.) On the basis of your scatter diagrams, which model do you suggest and why?

b. The training director selects model B. Obtain estimates of α_B, β_B, and $\sigma^2(Y \mid x)$ for this model. The following quantities may be useful in your calculations:

$$\sum x = 5.84 \qquad \sum y = 129.0 \qquad \sum x^2 = 3.0928$$
$$\sum xy = 44.439 \qquad \sum y^2 = 882.34$$

Give 95 percent confidence intervals for α_B and β_B, and write the estimated variance-covariance matrix of $\hat{\alpha}$ and $\hat{\beta}$.

c. It is asserted that model B is a more "reasonable" model than model A because model A implies that a machinist with no experience (or training) could set up the lathe in a finite expected time, while a machinist with much experience (and training) will set up the lathe in a negative expected time. Model B, on the other hand, implies that a machinist with no experience cannot set up the lathe and that the set-up time for a machinist with a great deal of experience (and training) approaches a finite lower limit of α_B.

(1) Do you agree with this assertion? Why or why not?

(2) If you agree, would you be willing to use model B to estimate the set-up time for a machinist with 15 weeks of training? Why or why not?

(3) If you disagree with the assertion, would you be willing to use model A to estimate the set-up time for a machinist with 15 weeks of training? Why or why not?

d. Suppose that the study had been made by observing the set-up times for the same two machinists during each week of their ten-week training period. Which of the assumptions, if any, necessary for the use of either model A or model B has not been met? Why not?

e. A machinist in his fifth week of training set up the lathe in four minutes. On the basis of the results of the study would you say he was:

(1) Within the normal range of variation for a machinist with five weeks of training?

(2) Unusually slow for a machinist with five weeks of training?

(3) Unusually fast for a machinist with five weeks of training?

Support your answer with a statistical test, being sure to state clearly the null hypothesis and its alternative.

f. Would you be willing to compute the coefficient of correlation between set-up time and the number of weeks of training? Why or why not?

19. Prove that $E(\hat{\beta}) = \beta$.

20. Starting from (14.21), show that the sample correlation coefficient can be written in the useful computational form

$$r = \frac{n \sum xy - \sum x \sum y}{\sqrt{n \sum x^2 - (\sum x)^2} \sqrt{n \sum y^2 - (\sum y)^2}}$$

21. Show that the sample coefficient of determination can be written in the form

$$r^2 = \frac{[\sum (x - \bar{x})(y - \bar{y})]^2}{\sum (x - \bar{x})^2 \cdot \sum (y - \bar{y})^2}$$

22. Prove Schwartz' inequality—that for real numbers $a_1, \cdots, a_n$ and $b_1, \cdots, b_n$

$$\sum a_i^2 \sum b_i^2 \geq [\sum a_i b_i]^2$$

23. Use the result of Exercise 22 to prove that the sample correlation coefficient must lie in the closed interval from -1 to $+1$.

15 The Analysis of Time Series

15.1 INTRODUCTION

A time series has been defined as a sequence of measurements arranged in chronological order. Such a definition requires amplification. For example, a mere lapse of time does not, in itself, create a time series. There is a lapse of time between the dropping of a weight and the moment that it hits the floor, but this in itself does not give rise to a time series. A time series must describe the changes occurring in a variable over time. It constitutes a summary of the effect of the factors bearing on the data being studied. It does not consist only of numbers and dates but, rather, pictures a continuum of change. Passage of time occurs in nearly every set of statistical data; yet in studies outside the time series field the time element is eliminated or minimized. Wages examined in the analysis of a frequency distribution may cover a day, a week, or a year, but the time element is not considered important.

A time series must reveal factors that are operating before there is any significance in applying statistical measures. A listing of the number of United States senators from 1912 to 1958 inclusive would be a time series although not a very interesting one. The number of senators was constant at 96 throughout that period. On the other hand, the number of United States senators from 1787 to the present year would form a more interesting time series, since changes would reflect the addition of new states, which, in turn, would show the results of westward expansion and growth coupled with political maneuvering.

Two factors complicate time-series analysis. First, the problem of homogeneity is even more acute than in the analysis of spatial data; and second, changes through time are not usually the result of a single independent influence.

Homogeneous data, it will be remembered, cannot be divided on the basis of characteristics other than the one under investigation into subgroups which yield significant differences for the characteristic studied. Thus, in a homogeneous series, the items classified under a particular heading must not differ significantly through time. For example, in the field of vital statistics there should be little classification difference between data on cancer of a given type in 1970 and 1900. But, we know this is not true. There has been such an improvement in diagnosis that many persons classified as non-cancerous in 1900 would now be classified as having the disease. A situation such as this greatly complicates the analysis of time series. It is difficult, if not impossible, to determine how much of the change through time is attributable to a "real" change in the prevalence of cancer and how much to improvement in the techniques of diagnosis. If there is not a quantitative method available for making the series homogeneous, the only approach is to analyze the data as though they were homogeneous and then to use judgment in modifying the generalizations found.

Changes through time are not usually the result of a single independent force, even though the series is homogeneous. Our basic objective in studying a characteristic over time is to secure a better understanding of how, and if possible why, changes occur with the passage of time. At a minimum we shall describe these changes. At a higher level, we hope to explain them and, perhaps, predict future changes. The characteristic that interests us is the dependent variable, and we attempt to construct a function that incorporates the various relevant independent variables. A simple approach to the problem is to employ the single independent variable of time itself by stating $y = f(x)$ where x is time, a variable whose domain covers the period for which we have data, and y is the characteristic of interest. Later we shall introduce other independent variables.

15.2 TWO SIMPLE MODELS

A common question in business is "What was the average increase in sales between two dates?" Consider the series of Table 15.1, showing the sales of the Smith and Jones Department Store. The student will quickly see that the average increase in the series is $(400,000 - 200,000)/10 = \$20,000$ per year, but he should have reservations about the utility of the result. If sales in 1967 had been \$600,000 or \$100,000, the same average would have been obtained. The calculation depends solely upon the initial and terminal values. The average figure of \$20,000 simply tells us that, if the series had increased by constant annual amounts between 1960 and 1970, it would have increased by \$20,000 each year. If we had stopped the series in 1969, the average increase would have been \$16,667. With most series it is possible for the politician, business manager, or labor leader to color discussions by choosing his own initial and terminal dates.

Table 15.1 Annual Sales of the Smith and Jones Department Store, 1960 to 1970

Year	Sales ($1000)	Annual Percentage Change
1960	200	—
1961	250	+25.0
1962	250	0.0
1963	225	−10.0
1964	275	+22.2
1965	300	+9.1
1966	250	−16.7
1967	350	+40.0
1968	325	−7.1
1969	350	+7.7
1970	400	+14.3

If we wish to describe the Smith and Jones series by a model based on the arithmetic mean yearly increase, we could use

$$f(x) = 200,000 + 20,000x \qquad 0 \le x \le 10$$
$$x = 0 \text{ in } 1960 \qquad (15.1)$$
$$x = 10 \text{ in } 1970$$

Figure 15.1 shows this function. Notice the transformation that has been performed on x in order to make the arithmetic simpler. Any linear transformation could have been used, and we shall consider several other useful ones later. The student should note that $f(x)$ is not a probability distribution.

A second common question in business is "What was the average percentage increase in sales?" Once more we shall use the Smith and Jones data, the annual percentage changes being given in Table 15.1. Now an arithmetic mean of these values will be misleading if by "average percentage change" we mean the percentage applied as a constant rate that could be substituted for the different rates actually experienced and yet yield the same terminal figure. The correct rate can easily be derived, however.

Let $n + 1$ be the number of periods in a time series represented by one item for each period. Let r_i be the rate at which the time series changes from the ith period to the $i + 1$st, $i = 1, \cdots, n$. Let J_i be the datum for the ith period. For the second period, we may write the datum as

$$J_2 = J_1 + r_1 J_1 = J_1(1 + r_1)$$

For the third period,

$$J_3 = J_2 + r_2 J_2 = J_2(1 + r_2) = J_1(1 + r_1)(1 + r_2)$$

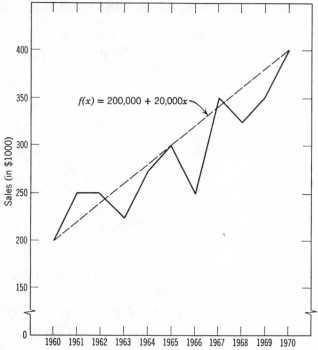

Fig. 15.1. Annual sales of the Smith and Jones Department Store, 1960–1970.

Continuing this process, we obtain for the final datum

$$J_{n+1} = J_n + r_n J_n = J_1(1 + r_1) \cdots (1 + r_n)$$

$$J_{n+1} = J_1 \prod_{i=1}^{n} (1 + r_i) \tag{15.2}$$

Now we wish to obtain the constant rate r which will cause J_1 to change to J_{n+1} over the same period of time. This relationship is obtained from (15.2) by setting $r_1 = \cdots = r_n = r$; it is the well-known compound interest formula

$$J_{n+1} = J_1(1 + r)^n \tag{15.3}$$

Equating (15.2) and (15.3) gives

$$(1 + r)^n = \prod_{i=1}^{n} (1 + r_i)$$

$$1 + r = \left[\prod_{i=1}^{n} (1 + r_i) \right]^{1/n} \tag{15.4}$$

$$\log (1 + r) = \frac{1}{n} \log \prod_{i=1}^{n} (1 + r_i) = \frac{1}{n} \sum_{i=1}^{n} \log (1 + r_i)$$

$$r = \text{antilog} \left[\frac{1}{n} \sum_{i=1}^{n} \log (1 + r_i) \right] - 1 \tag{15.5}$$

A computationally more convenient form may be developed by noting from (15.2) that

$$\prod_{i=1}^{n} (1 + r_i) = \frac{J_{n+1}}{J_1}$$

from which

$$\sum_{i=1}^{n} \log (1 + r_i) = \log J_{n+1} - \log J_1$$

We may then write (15.5) in a form depending only upon the initial and terminal items of data:

$$r = \text{antilog} \left[\frac{1}{n} (\log J_{n+1} - \log J_1) \right] - 1 \qquad (15.6)$$

For the Smith and Jones data, the constant rate of increase is found to be

$$r = \text{antilog} \left[\frac{1}{10} (\log 400 - \log 200) \right] - 1$$

$$= \text{antilog } 0.0301 - 1$$

$$= 1.072 - 1 = 0.072$$

The average annual change in the series is a 7.2 percent increase.

If we wish to represent the series by a model based upon a constant rate of change, the compound interest model

$$f(x) = \$200,000(1.072)^x \qquad 0 \le x \le 10$$
$$x = 0 \text{ in } 1960 \qquad (15.7)$$
$$x = 10 \text{ in } 1970$$

would be appropriate. By taking logarithms, this function could be rewritten as the linear one

$$g(x) = \log f(x) = 5.3010 + 0.0301x \qquad 0 \le x \le 10$$
$$x = 0 \text{ in } 1960 \qquad (15.8)$$
$$x = 10 \text{ in } 1970$$

If the $f(x)$ axis is given a logarithmic scale, then the function (15.7) graphs as a straight line. Such a graph is referred to as a semilogarithmic graph. The calculation of the average percentage increase in the series above simply asks for a straight line on such a chart joining the first value with the last. The extent to which this line is descriptive of the way in which the series actually changes is shown by the amount of dispersion of the original data about the line. Figure 15.2 presents the Smith and Jones data along with the model (15.7).

The constant rate of increase for a time series may easily be related to an average which we have not mentioned before—the geometric mean. Given

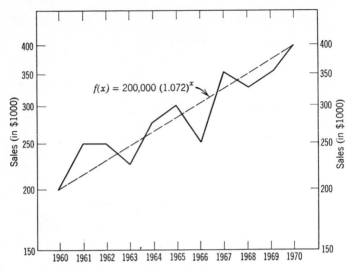

$f(x) = 200{,}000\,(1.072)^x$

Fig. 15.2. Annual sales of the Smith and Jones Department Store, 1960–1970. Semilogarithmic scale.

a set of positive items y_i, $i = 1, \cdots, n$, their geometric mean, y_G, is defined to be

$$y_G = \sqrt[n]{\prod_{i=1}^{n} y_i} \qquad (15.9)$$

If one or more y_i are zero or negative, the geometric mean is not defined. Looking at (15.4), we see that r, the constant rate of increase, is one less than the geometric mean of the quantities $1 + r_i$, called the relatives of the series. The average percentage change, r, may be either positive or negative, but the geometric mean of the relatives, $1 + r$, must be positive. Obviously, if J_{n+1} is greater than J_1, the series is increasing, and r will be positive; if, however, J_{n+1} is less than J_1, the series is decreasing, and r will be negative.

The fact that the average percentage change is dependent on only the initial and terminal values of a time series means that the calculation can be made even if all the intermediate values are missing. Given that the population of Pennsylvania was 9,631,000 in 1930 and 11,343,000 in 1960, what was the average percentage change per decade? The solution is simply the value of r that satisfies

$$1 + r = \sqrt[3]{\frac{11{,}343{,}000}{9{,}631{,}000}}$$

or

$$r = 0.056 = 5.6 \text{ percent per decade}$$

What was the average percentage change per year? Familiarity with the principle of compounding should convince the student that the result is less than 5.6/10 = 0.56 percent. The answer is found from

$$1 + r = \sqrt[3]{\frac{11,343,000}{9,631,000}}$$

to be

$$r = 0.0055 = 0.55 \text{ percent per year}$$

From Table 15.1 several properties of time series can be deduced.

1. The arithmetic mean of the percentage changes is larger than the geometric mean of these changes.

2. Equal percentage increases and decreases do not balance each other.

3. The sequence of percentage changes has no effect upon the terminal value.

Property 1 is very general; the arithmetic mean of a set of positive real numbers is always greater than the geometric mean except in the limiting case where all items are identical.[1] In this limiting case, the arithmetic and geometric means are obviously equal as are the median and mode. The arithmetic mean of the annual percentage changes in Table 15.1 is 1.0845 − 1 = 8.45 percent in contrast to the 7.2 percent derived from the geometric mean of relatives.

Referring to the sales figures for 1967, 1968, and 1969 shown in Table 15.1, we see that the decline of 7.1 percent between 1967 and 1968 was exactly counteracted in 1969. However, an increase of 7.7 percent was required to bring this about because the base upon which the increase was calculated was lower than that upon which decrease was figured. Suppose the increase had come first. If the values in 1967 and 1969 were equal, which percentage change would have been greater? The answer is apparent if we examine the years 1960 to 1963. During this period there was one 25 percent increase, one 10 percent decrease, and one year of no change. No matter what the order of these changes, the terminal value is the same since

$$\$200,000(1.25)(1.00)(0.90) = \$200,000(1.00)(0.90)(1.25) = \text{etc.}$$

After all, multiplication is commutative.

The points raised in the last two paragraphs are consequences of the use of (15.7) or (15.8), based on the geometric mean of relatives, as a model for a time series. Both these models and (15.1), which uses the arithmetic mean

---

[1] A proof is given in M. G. Kendall, *The Advanced Theory of Statistics*, Vol. I, Hafner, New York, pg. 33.

amount of change, reflect only the initial and terminal items and consequently may be of limited utility. We shall now proceed to other ways of describing time series in terms of time as the single independent variable.

15.3   APPLICATION OF LEAST SQUARES TO TIME SERIES

Both models discussed in the preceding section are linear, one using the dependent variable in its original form and the other employing a logarithmic transformation. As indicated in the discussion, both are based on only two values—the first and the last. It is possible to retain the linear form of the models, but to determine the constants by other methods. One such method is the method of least squares. The theoretical justification for least squares when time is the independent variable is rather dubious, but we shall postpone that discussion.

The form of the first model was

$$f(x) = a + bx \qquad (15.10)$$

the same as that in Section 14.2: $\hat{y}_x = a + bx$. Letting y equal the observed values of the dependent variable and $\hat{y}$ the estimates obtained from (15.10), we can solve the familiar simultaneous equations (15.11) for a and b.

$$\sum y = na + b \sum x$$
$$\sum xy = a \sum x + b \sum x^2 \qquad (15.11)$$

However, our arithmetic will be considerably simplified if we first use a linear transformation of the time variable to make $\sum x = 0$. One such transformation which is convenient for an odd number of observations is given in Table 15.2. The result is a simple solution

$$a = \frac{\sum y}{n} = \bar{y} \qquad b = \frac{\sum xy}{\sum x^2} \qquad (15.12)$$

Calculations of these coefficients in the Smith and Jones example are also shown in Table 15.2.

The method of least squares can also be applied to a logarithmic equation. The reader can easily verify that the constants of the equation

$$\log \hat{y} = a + bx$$

would be obtained from

$$a = \frac{\sum \log y}{n} \qquad b = \frac{\sum x \log y}{\sum x^2} \qquad (15.13)$$

Table 15.2   Calculation of a Linear Time-Series Model by the Method of Least Squares, Smith and Jones Data

Year	y Sales (\$1000)	x	x^2	xy	$\hat{y}$	$y - \hat{y}$
1960	200	−5	25	−1000	205	−5
1961	250	−4	16	−1000	221	+29
1962	250	−3	9	−750	238	+12
1963	225	−2	4	−450	255	−30
1964	275	−1	1	−275	272	+3
1965	300	0	0	0	289	+11
1966	250	+1	1	+250	305	−55
1967	350	+2	4	+700	322	+28
1968	325	+3	9	+975	339	−14
1969	350	+4	16	+1400	356	−6
1970	400	+5	25	+2000	373	+27
	3175	0	110	1850		

$$a = \frac{\sum y}{n} = \frac{3175}{11} = 288.6$$

$$b = \frac{\sum xy}{\sum x^2} = \frac{1850}{110} = 16.8$$

$$\hat{y} = 288.6 + 16.8x; \quad -5 \leq x \leq +5$$

$$x = -5 \text{ in } 1960$$

$$x = 0 \text{ in } 1965$$

provided that $\sum x = 0$. The method is illustrated in Table 15.3 where the previous 1970 figure is omitted to show one desirable method of transforming x when there is an even number of observations.

So far in this chapter, the same data[2] have been described by four different models. Two of them show the series as increasing by constant amounts and the other two as increasing by constant percentages. Within the first pair, one presents the annual amount of increase as \$20,000 while the other shows \$16,800. Within the second pair, one gives the change as 7.2 percent per year while the second estimates antilog $0.0252 - 1 = 6.0$ percent.

Not only do the various models yield different summary descriptions but they also yield different calculated values for the dependent variable in any

---

[2] The results of the least-squares logarithmic model using 1970 data are employed in the ensuing comparison.

Table 15.3   Calculation of a Logarithmic Linear Time-Series Model by the Method of Least Squares, Smith and Jones Data[a]

Year	y Sales ($1000)	$\log y$	x	x^2	$x \log y$	$\log \hat{y}$	$\hat{y}$
1960	200	2.3010	−9	81	−20.7090	2.3302	214
1961	250	2.3979	−7	49	−16.7853	2.3538	226
1962	250	2.3979	−5	25	−11.9895	2.3774	238
1963	225	2.3522	−3	9	−7.0566	2.4010	252
1964	275	2.4393	−1	1	−2.4393	2.4246	266
1965	300	2.4771	+1	1	+2.4771	2.4481	281
1966	250	2.3979	+3	9	+7.1937	2.4718	296
1967	350	2.5441	+5	25	+12.7205	2.4953	313
1968	325	2.5119	+7	49	+17.5833	2.5189	330
1969	350	2.5441	+9	81	+22.8969	2.5425	349
		24.3634		330	3.8918		

$$a = \frac{\sum \log y}{n} = \frac{24.3634}{10} = 2.43634$$

$$b = \frac{\sum x \log y}{\sum x^2} = \frac{3.8918}{330} = 0.01179$$

$$\log \hat{y} = 2.43634 + 0.01179x; \qquad -9 \leq x \leq +9$$
$$x = -9 \text{ in } 1960$$
$$x = 0 \text{ in } 1964\tfrac{1}{2}$$

[a] If the 1970 figure of 400 is included, the resulting equation is
$$\log \hat{y} = 2.45141 + 0.02522x; \quad -5 \leq x \leq +5, \quad x = -5 \text{ in } 1960$$
$$x = 0 \text{ in } 1965.$$

particular year.[3] For example, the calculated values for 1967 are $340,000 (15.1), $325,000 (15.8), $322,000 (Table 15.2), and $318,000 (Table 15.3 including 1970). The first is closer to the actual figure, but other models would be closer for other dates. The model using least squares and the original data would have the smallest sum of squared differences, but that is not impressive since it is the criterion imposed by the method. Why squared deviations? Why not fourth powers or absolute values of deviations? And why the original data rather than the logarithms? The answer must go back

[3] The models of Section 15.2, of course, yield the same results for the initial and terminal values.

to assumptions concerning the relationship between the variables, the nature of the data employed, and the purpose of the model.

What interpretation can we give to the value of sales computed from one of the models? When we considered correlation and regression in Chapter 14, the calculated value of the dependent variable was an estimate, given a specific value for the independent variable. Then, making certain assumptions, we established confidence intervals for our estimates. But the situation for a time series, particularly when time is the independent variable, is quite different.

As we recall, correlation is addressed to problems in which both dependent and independent variables are random; regression to problems in which only the dependent variable is random. Certainly we are not dealing with a correlation situation here. Time is not a random variable; the observations are made at stated intervals, determined in advance or simply dictated by availability.

Are we, then, dealing with a regression problem? It depends on the assumptions that we are willing to make. Is there a probability distribution of Smith and Jones sales values for the year 1967? In a study of gravity we might give an affirmative answer to a similar question: "Is there a probability distribution for the speed of a falling body two seconds after it has been dropped from the top of a tall building?" Elementary physics gives a model for predicting the dependent variable (speed) given that the independent variable (elapsed time) is two seconds. The result will vary slightly from trial to trial and thus will possess a probability distribution. We start there with a random experiment.

In the case of the Smith and Jones Department Store, it is much more difficult to visualize sales as the result of a random experiment. How can the experiment possibly be repeated? Is it possible to make two or more observations for the same value of the independent variable? Only if we can transform time into an experimental context divorced from an historical one. In the gravity problem, repeated observations for $x = 2$ would be possible because the experiment could be repeated with $x = 0$ identified as the instant of drop. Unless an equivalent view of the economic phenomenon with repeated experiments can be defended, we cannot consider the dependent variable to be a random variable. Therefore, use of least squares in our present problem must rest on a pragmatic basis and not on any probability assumptions.[4] The basis usually presented is that the line should be as close to the observations as possible, and arbitrarily we stipulate that the squared deviations should be minimized.

---

[4] Recall that least squares was shown to be appropriate in Chapter 14 if the conditional distributions were normal. Here, since we have rejected the existence of a conditional distribution, it is meaningless to discuss its form.

It is possible to think of sales for a particular year as a random variable by focusing attention on the forces responsible for them.[5] In that approach we may visualize a joint probability distribution with sales as the dependent variable and the factors that "produce" the sales as independent variables. This leads to a quite different approach to the problem with time no longer the independent variable; we shall consider it in Chapter 16. We now examine other models with time as the only independent variable.

15.4 MOVING AVERAGE MODELS

Although we are attempting to discern systematic movement in time series, actual economic data generally present an uneven appearance. Several methods that can be employed to remove this irregularity are based upon the idea of a moving average. They are simple to use and, more important, they involve no assumptions about the form of the function used to represent the series. We have already seen that in dealing with economic series it is often difficult to justify any assumption about functional form.

Let (x_i, y_i), $i = 1, \cdots, n$ be the time series of concern, where x_i is the point in time representing the ith period and where y_i is the corresponding observation. Let p be a positive integer; then $2p + 1$ is an odd number. We shall first wish to average over sets containing an odd number of observations. For the given time series, we define the moving average series of period $2p + 1$ by

$$(x_i, z_i), i = p + 1, \cdots, n - p$$

$$z_i = \frac{\displaystyle\sum_{k=-p}^{p} y_{i+k}}{2p + 1} \qquad (15.14)$$

For example, when $2p + 1 = 5$, $p = 2$, and $p + 1 = 3$. Then the first term of the moving average series is (x_3, z_3) where z_3 is the arithmetic mean of the first five observations.

The reason for averaging over an odd number of observations is our desire to have the abscissae of the resulting points equal to those of terms of the original series. This is desirable if we are to have the z_i used in computations based on the time periods of the original series—as is often the case. Sometimes, however, it will be necessary to work with a moving average series of period $2p$ as in Section 15.6 when we must average over twelve months in order to create a seasonal index.

---

[5] The phrase "are responsible for them" could set off a long philosophic argument. As indicated in Chapter 14, statistical methods will not show causation; we simply choose what seem to be likely candidates as independent variables.

In such a case, one intuitively reasonable way to make the abscissae of the moving average series coincide with those of the original series is to proceed in two steps. First, compute the moving average series of period $2p$. The abscissae of this series are located halfway between those of the original series. Then an average in pairs will yield the final series whose abscissae are the same as the original. Calling the final moving average series (x_i, z_i'), we may write it as

$$(x_i, z_i'), i = p + 1, \cdots, n - p$$

where

$$z_i' = \frac{z_{(2i-1)/2} + z_{(2i+1)/2}}{2}$$

and

$$z_{(2i-1)/2} = \frac{\sum_{k=-p}^{p-1} y_{i+k}}{2p}$$

(15.15)

We shall illustrate (15.15) in Section 15.6; here we shall smooth the Smith and Jones series of Table 15.1 using first a three-year and then a five-year moving average. Figure 15.3 shows these series visually. Note that the

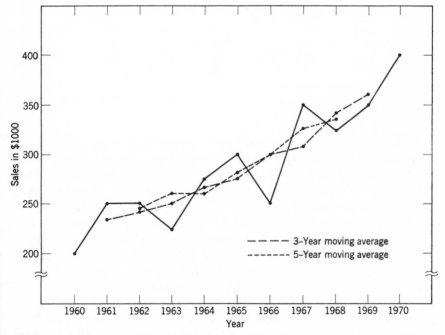

Fig. 15.3. Three- and five-year moving averages of Smith and Jones data.

computations may be considerably simplified if one sees that

$$z_i = z_{i-1} + \frac{y_{i+p} - y_{i-p-1}}{2p + 1} \qquad (15.16)$$

For the second entry in the five-year moving average column in Table 15.4 we obtain

$$260 = 240 + \frac{300 - 200}{5}$$

as an illustration of (15.16).

Table 15.4   Three- and Five-Year Moving Averages of Smith and Jones Data

Year	Sales ($1000)	Three-Year Moving Average	Five-Year Moving Average
1960	200		
1961	250	233	
1962	250	242	240
1963	225	250	260
1964	275	267	260
1965	300	275	280
1966	250	300	300
1967	350	308	315
1968	325	342	335
1969	350	358	
1970	400		

The reader will note that the five-year moving average is slightly smoother than the three-year moving average. Both, however, seem to give reasonable representations of the growth of the series. One obvious difficulty is the loss of data at each end of the fitted series. If we average over $2p + 1$ periods, then we lose p points at each end of the series—a total of $2p$ in all. This may be a serious matter when one is averaging a skimpy set of data and needs to use a fairly large p. On the other hand, there is a theoretical justification for the use of a moving average; it is equivalent to fitting lines to sets of $2p + 1$ observations by the method of least squares.

A refinement upon the moving average procedure introduces weights. If one is primarily interested in describing the current behavior of a time series, it is reasonable to think that the most recent observation contains the most valuable information. Thus, one would weight each observation more heavily than its predecessor. For example, in updating a five-month moving average of company sales in order to describe current activity, one might weight the most recent observation by 5 and its forerunners by 4, 3, 2, and 1 as we move to the left on the time scale. Or we could use any other sequence of weights which increase with time and which we felt reflected the contribution of each observation to the forthcoming prediction.

A well-known method of describing time series for prediction purposes that relates to weighted moving averages is called exponential smoothing. In addition to weighting recent observations most heavily, it has another advantage. It computes one summary figure for each period, and uses only this and the new observation to determine the next point in the smoothed series. Thus, in computerized operations, for example, it is not necessary to tie up memory by storing previous observations. The weighting system used is essentially arbitrary. However, once it has been accepted, it can be shown that the method minimizes the weighted sum of the squared residuals about the model.

Suppose that we had just observed y_i, the observation representing the most recent time period, using a five-period moving average. Suppose further that at the same point in the process we lost our past observations $y_1, \cdots, y_{i-1}$ and the moving averages $z_3, \cdots, z_{i-4}$ as well. We have only the last moving average figure z_{i-3}. How can we update the moving average, that is, what function of z_{i-3} and y_i should be used to estimate z_{i-2}?

If we had not lost our data, we would use (15.16) and compute

$$z_{i-2} = z_{i-3} + \frac{y_i - y_{i-5}}{5}$$

However, we no longer know y_{i-5}. Our best estimate of this quantity—in fact our only estimate—is z_{i-3}. Hence, we estimate

$$\hat{z}_{i-2} = z_{i-3} + \frac{y_i - z_{i-3}}{5}$$

$$= \frac{y_i}{5} + \frac{4z_{i-3}}{5}$$

This expression demonstrates the central idea of exponential smoothing: in computing a new estimate $\hat{z}$, if the weight α is given to the most recent observation, then the complementary weight $1 - \alpha$ must be given to the previous average. We shall, however, make one change.

The preceding discussion develops exponential smoothing from a weighted average procedure. In practice, exponential smoothing stands on its own feet. An initial figure may be a weighted average, but thereafter we only find a z representing all previous data and modify it by a new observation to give a new z. The change is that we shall place the new z at the same point in time as our new observation y. After all, it is our summary figure computed after we obtain this observation. Thus the general expression for a new prediction is usually written

$$\hat{z}_i = \alpha y_i + (1 - \alpha)\hat{z}_{i-1} \tag{15.17}$$

To see why the process is called exponential smoothing, let us work backward to an initial value $\hat{z}_0$.

$$\hat{z}_i = \alpha y_i + (1 - \alpha)[\alpha y_{i-1} + (1 - \alpha)\hat{z}_{i-2}]$$
$$= \alpha y_i + \alpha(1 - \alpha)y_{i-1} + (1 - \alpha)^2[\alpha y_{i-2} + (1 - \alpha)\hat{z}_{i-3}]$$
$$= \alpha y_i + \alpha(1 - \alpha)y_{i-1} + \alpha(1 - \alpha)^2 y_{i-2} + \alpha(1 - \alpha)^3 y_{i-3}$$
$$+ \cdots + (1 - \alpha)^i \hat{z}_0$$

or

$$\hat{z}_i = \alpha \sum_{j=0}^{i-1} (1 - \alpha)^j y_{i-j} + (1 - \alpha)^i \hat{z}_0$$

where $\hat{z}_0$ is an initial weighted average or arbitrary value and the process has gone on for i periods. If our smoothing constant is $\alpha = 0.4$, then in order of recency the observations have weights

$$\alpha(1 - \alpha)^0 = \alpha = 0.400$$
$$\alpha(1 - \alpha)^1 = \alpha(1 - \alpha) = 0.2400$$
$$\alpha(1 - \alpha)^2 = 0.1440$$
$$\alpha(1 - \alpha)^3 = 0.0864$$

etc.

Table 15.5 Exponential Smoothing of Motorcycle Production Data, B. K. Thornton Company

Year	Number of Motorcycles Produced y_i	$\alpha y_i = 0.4 y_i$	$\hat{z}_i$	$(1 - \alpha)\hat{z}_i = 0.6\hat{z}_i$
1961			$\hat{z}_0 = 3200$	1920
1962	3200	1280	3200	1920
1963	3000	1200	3120	1872
1964	3400	1360	3232	1939
1965	3800	1520	3459	2075
1966	4600	1840	3915	2349
1967	4100	1640	3989	2393
1968	4800	1920	4313	2587
1969	3700	1480	4067	2440
1970	4800	1920	4360	

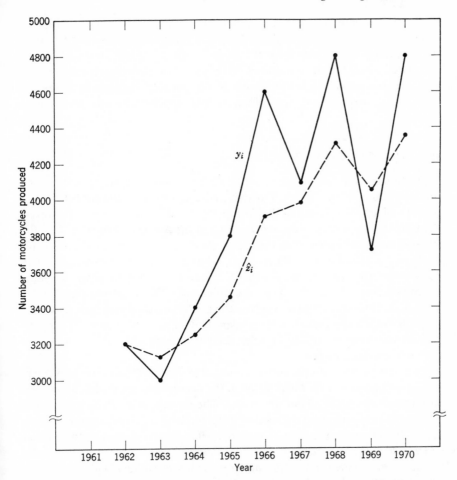

Fig. 15.4. Exponentially smoothed motorcycle production data, B. K. Thornton Company.

The weights decline steadily in a geometric series, and in the continuous case (which we shall not examine) the analog is an exponential function—hence the name, exponential smoothing.

Let us illustrate exponential smoothing using production data, shown in Table 15.5, from the B. K. Thornton Company, a motorcycle manufacturer, with an α of 0.4 and a $\hat{z}_0$ of 3200. The data and the smoothed function z_i are also shown in Figure 15.4.

The exponentially smoothed series is seen to form a reasonably stable model for this set of data. It is less regular than an unweighted moving average would be. If the purpose is prediction, exponential smoothing must be considered superior to the unweighted average. It is more sensitive to recent developments—particularly when α is fairly large. It should be noted that z_i cannot be calculated for the period to be predicted; only z_{i-k} can be calculated where k is the number of periods between the most recent observation and the period to be predicted. If the purpose is to study long-term movements, exponential smoothing is not superior to the unweighted average.

15.5   THE CLASSICAL MODEL

Inspection of the last column of Table 15.2 raises questions concerning interpretation of the figures. Do they indicate errors in the model? If the model's object is to describe the data perfectly, the answer is yes. However, the initially announced objective was to find the average change or, in more general terms, to summarize the series. Assuming that the model of Table 15.2 does a satisfactory summary job, what does the $+29$ associated with 1961 mean? It means that sales in 1961 were $29,000 more than the figure computed from the model. Why the difference? For some reason, sales in 1961 were unusually good and, given the model, much better than they were in 1966 despite the fact that both years had sales of $250,000. The model provides a changing frame of reference in precisely the same way as our earlier regression models.

Thus the purpose of time-series models is to show the long-term movement of the series—called its *trend*. Short-term fluctuations may then be studied in terms of deviations from the model. The deviations in Table 15.2 reflect periods of prosperity and depression if the model is a good description of the trend. In summary, the method employed in time-series analysis, when time is treated as the independent variable, involves the construction of a trend model against which short-run fluctuations may be studied. This is the heart of the so-called *classical model*.

The classical model assumes that different factors are influencing the dependent variable, even though we restrict ourselves to the single independent variable, time. This approach asserts that each factor exerts its influence within a certain span of time. The various time spans are studied individually and described separately. The forces operative within each are thus grouped together for study. The number of these sets of forces to be studied depends upon the nature of the series, but most economic time series can be conveniently divided into four sets which reveal themselves in four types of movement: (1) trend, (2) seasonal variation, (3) cyclical fluctuation, and (4) residual movement. If we believe that there are other components of importance, such as long cycles, in a particular series, these should also be introduced. Our discussion will be limited to the four identified.

The *trend* of a series is an identifiable movement occurring over a long period of time, usually 25 years or more. Two factors are especially important in their effect on the trend of most economic series: population changes and technological progress. Ninety years ago one would have thought that an increase in population would be accompanied by an increase in the number of buggies. Technological progress, however—in this case the invention of a preferable substitute—so predominated over the influence of population growth that the number of buggies rapidly declined as the substitute product became popular. Here a declining trend was evidence of progress. Generally speaking, however, a rising trend in a productive, distributive, or consumption series is indicative of technological improvements and growth. Such improvements have made it possible for real national income to rise more rapidly than population throughout most of American history. The influence of population and of technological improvements may often be segregated by transforming a given series into per capita values. The underlying movement of per capita data would then indicate the influence of technological change, assuming that these two factors were the only major ones present.

Climate and custom are the two dominating factors in *seasonal variation.* Custom is frequently associated with climate as, for example, in June weddings. Yet custom and climate are not always associated in the same way; Christmas is celebrated with snowflakes in the northern hemisphere and with surfboarding in the southern. Custom and climate repeat themselves annually in a given locality, and seasonal variation consequently tends to follow a pattern within each year.

Cyclical fluctuation is a periodic movement with a period (from one peak to the next) of from two years to as much as 15 or 20. Although in cycles one might expect to find the duration of expansion equalling that of contraction, this is not usually true. Cyclical fluctuation does not conform to any pattern; it varies both in timing and in amplitude. The forces inducing cyclical movements are a major concern of those interested in economic conditions, but there is no unanimity of belief as to their causes. They have been attributed to factors as divergent as sunspots and mass psychological forces swinging between optimism and pessimism. Many hold the position of Wesley C. Mitchell that there is no simple explanation and that business cycles are the result of many varied factors.

Trend, seasonal variation, and cyclical fluctuation are usually modeled by continuous functions. Actual data, however, do not show such smoothness so that other factors must also be operating. There are erratic movements in nearly every time series—movements unrelated to trend, cycle, and seasonal pattern. Such movements are called *residual.* They are attributable to chance or to nonpredictable factors such as floods, wars, pestilences, and the like.

The classical model assumes that the effects of the four sets of factors are additive. Let the time series of concern be given by the set of data (x_i, y_i), $i = 1, \cdots, n$. We shall represent the components of y_i resulting from trend, seasonal variation, cyclical fluctuation, and residual movement respectively by t_i, s_i, c_i, and r_i. The model is then

$$y_i = t_i + s_i + c_i + r_i \qquad i = 1, \cdots, n \qquad (15.18)$$

The problem is to decompose the observations y_i into these four components. If the data have been collected for subdivisions of a year (weeks, months, quarters, etc.), it is first customary to remove the seasonal factor. This is done by developing seasonal indices. If the series has m observations per year, we will represent the jth seasonal index by a_j, $j = 1, \cdots, m$. Dividing by the appropriate seasonal index gives $y_i' = y_i/a_j$, the deseasonalized data composed only of trend, cycle, and residual. The seasonal effect is then found by subtracting

$$s_i = y_i - y_i'$$

If one is working with annual data, $y_i' = y_i$.

Next we fit a trend function to the deseasonalized data y_i' and obtain its ordinates t_i at the points x_i. The quantity

$$y_i'' = y_i' - t_i$$

then represents the effects of cyclical and residual movements. Finally, we obtain a representation of the cycle from the y_i'' and determine the residual movement by subtraction.

In summary

$$y_i'' = c_i + r_i$$

$$y_i' - t_i = c_i + r_i$$

$$y_i' = t_i + c_i + r_i$$

$$y_i - s_i = t_i + c_i + r_i$$

$$y_i = t_i + s_i + c_i + r_i$$

As has been previously mentioned, if the investigator considers that other sets of factors should be considered and is willing to assume that their effects are also additive, they may also be included in the model.

Central to this model are assumptions concerning the nature of the trend component. Indeed, once a representation of trend has been decided upon, studies of seasonal and cyclical effects are carried out in terms of deviations from it. Assumptions about trend are thus basic to studies of any component of the series. The models of Sections 15.2 and 15.3 make strong assumptions—namely, that the trend component is increasing on the average either by constant amounts or by a constant percentage. Also, in two of the models, the least-squares criterion was adopted to give a definition of the best fitting line.

The reader should note that (15.18) expresses the results of trend, seasonal variation, cyclical fluctuation, and residual movement in absolute units at a particular point in time. General descriptions of the seasonal and cyclical components are usually expressed in percentage terms and must be converted before use in (15.18).

These are by no means the only possible assumptions. Indeed, most people would think it unrealistic to assume a linear trend, with or without a logarithmic transformation for a long period. We could assume that the percentage change in the trend was gradually decreasing, or increasing in the early part of the series and thereafter decreasing, or any other form we thought appropriate. Given the functional form, the method of least squares is only one way to estimate the model's parameters.

If we were attempting to extrapolate a trend line, we should probably consider the upper and lower limits of the trend model as well as the existence or nonexistence of reversals. Recall that in Chapter 14 we were reluctant to use regression equations for extrapolation; in that case, contrary to the present one, we were dealing with probability distributions that had a theoretical justification. Whether theoretically justified or not, one aim of time-series analysis is the prediction of future values of the dependent variable. The subjective appraisal of the model should certainly consider the real world counterparts of its various properties. Although there is no objective test available, one might be dubious about predicting very far into the future with a model that has no upper limit or with one that had a reversal prior to the date for which the prediction was desired. Any linear model with an increasing trend has no upper limit; this is reason enough to doubt its appropriateness for most economic time series.

Let us suppose that we wish to describe the U.S. Gross National Product from 1923 to 1957. The period is sufficiently long to establish a trend function, but what properties should the function possess? Even before that, what data should we use—GNP in current or constant dollars? Assuming that we wish to examine the effect of population and technological change, we should remove the influence of price fluctuations from the series. It is then said to be in "constant dollars"; in Section 15.9 we shall discuss the adjustment of a series for price changes.

Should we be satisfied with GNP, or is GNP per capita a better series to study? The answer depends on our purpose. If we are primarily interested in the change in total economic activity, we would employ GNP itself. Assuming this to be our purpose (notice that we are accepting the definition of GNP and the accuracy of the data without any discussion at all—should we?), we must select what we think are desirable properties of the trend curve. Many economists prefer to study the percentage changes in such a series, rather than the dollar changes because of the huge differences in the level of the series over a long time interval.

The adoption of such a view suggests a logarithmic transformation, but does not necessarily imply a linear trend. A trend increasing by decreasing percentages might be thought appropriate. What about reversals? We could stipulate whatever properties are desired and permit the data to generate the coefficients using either least squares or another criterion. For this particular problem we might accept a linear trend fitted to the logarithms of the data. For the period covered this is as satisfactory as a more complex function.

Just what data should be employed? If the least-squares method is used, different data will yield different coefficients. Should we use figures for every year, average annual figures for groups of years, annual figures at selected intervals, etc.? If the results are similar regardless of the data and if the observations fall reasonably close to the trend model without prolonged periods where all observations are on the same side, the trend model would seem satisfactory as a historical description. How should one choose among alternatives if the results are dissimilar?

Using the method of least squares with annual averages for five-year periods, the trend equation computed for the United States GNP is

$$\hat{y} = 227.9(1.183)^x \qquad -3 \leq x \leq 3$$

$$x = -3 \text{ in } 1925 \qquad\qquad (15.19)$$

$$x = 0 \text{ in } 1940$$

y is GNP in billions of 1954 dollars

What is the proper interpretation of the constants in this equation if it is a satisfactory description of the series?

The figure 227.9 is the calculated trend value of GNP in 1940. It is not the estimate of actual GNP, but the estimate of the contribution of trend. This 227.9 billion is the estimate of the level that had been realized by the long-run factors at that particular point in time. It was not established by the 1940 level of GNP alone, but by all the values used in computing (15.19). The same interpretation would be applied to any other value computed from (15.19). The figure 1.183 indicates that the trend is increasing by 18.3 percent every five years.

Next, let us turn to cycles in GNP for the portion of this period after the Second World War. Since prosperity and depression are defined as levels of activity above and below trend, we must be satisfied that the trend equation is a good base from which to measure deviations. Annual GNP figures for 1946 to 1957 are presented in Table 15.6 along with trend calculated from (15.19) and the deviations from those ordinates. Note the succession of negative deviations from 1947 to 1950 followed by positive deviations, with the exception of 1954. The first would be classified as a period of recession and the latter as a period of prosperity.

Table 15.6   Basic Data for a Study of Cycles in GNP, 1946 to 1957

Year	GNP (in Billions of 1954 Dollars) y_i	Trend (15.19) t_i	Deviation $y_i - t_i$
1946	282.5	278.7	+3.8
1947	282.3	288.3	−6.0
1948	293.1	298.1	−5.0
1949	292.7	308.3	−15.6
1950	318.1	318.8	−0.7
1951	341.8	329.8	+12.0
1952	353.5	341.2	+12.3
1953	369.0	352.8	+16.2
1954	363.1	364.9	−1.8
1955	392.7	377.4	+15.3
1956	402.2	390.2	+12.0
1957	407.0	403.6	+3.4

Source for GNP. Historical Statistics, Colonial Times to 1957, Tables F87–103.

As we have seen, the moving average is a quite different approach. It makes no assumptions about the form of the trend function, but it does assume that the cycles within a particular series are rather constant in duration. Table 15.7 illustrates this approach with a five-year moving average. Since every figure in the moving average column is based on five annual figures, the column would be devoid of cyclical fluctuations if our assumption of a five-year cycle were correct. If this assumption were invalid, the moving average would still contain cyclical elements, and deviations from the moving average would not measure cyclical phenomena very well. There is some similarity between the deviations in Tables 15.6 and 15.7, but disagreements are also much in evidence.

Table 15.7   Alternative Approach to Study of GNP Cycles, 1946 to 1957

Year	GNP (in Billions of 1954 Dollars) y_i	Five-Year Moving Average[a] z_i	Deviation $y_i - z_i$
1946	282.5	298.0	−15.5
1947	282.3	292.9	−10.6
1948	293.1	293.7	−0.6
1949	292.7	305.6	−12.9
1950	318.1	319.8	−1.7
1951	341.8	335.0	+6.8
1952	353.5	349.1	+4.4
1953	369.0	364.0	+5.0
1954	363.1	376.1	−13.0
1955	392.7	386.8	+5.9
1956	402.2	—	—
1957	407.0	—	—

[a] Five-year moving averages for the first two years were obtained from data not presented in the table.

15.6   STATISTICAL DESCRIPTION OF SEASONAL VARIATIONS

If the data presented for analysis pertain to periods of less than one year, the amount of variability will usually be greater than the variability in annual data for the same series. The increased fluctuation is the result of seasonal and irregular factors. Those fluctuations that repeat themselves each year are evidence of seasonal forces, and we wish to consider ways of measuring them at this time.

With annual data, the appropriate reference figure was the trend ordinate. Deviations from that reference point were the result of cyclical or irregular components, or both. The appropriate reference figure for the study of seasonal variations must clearly include not only the trend but also the cyclical and irregular components.

Inspection of the quarterly profits after taxes of electrical utilities (Table 15.8) shows considerable variability from quarter to quarter.[6] The next three columns show the composition of z_i', a moving average of period 4 ($p = 2$). Note that, while the $z_{(2i-1)/2}$ values of 757 and 781 are placed at June 30 and

---

[6] The principles developed in this section can also be applied to monthly, weekly, or daily data.

Table 15.8 Computation of Four-Quarter Moving Average of Profits After Taxes for Utility Companies, 1949 to 1958; of y_i/z_i' Values; and Profits Adjusted for Seasonal Variation

Quarter	Profits after Taxes—Electric Utilities ($1,000,000) y_i	Four Quarter Moving Total $z_{(2i-1)/2}$	Sum by Pairs $z_{(2i-1)/2}+z_{(2i+1)/2}$	Moving Average z_i'	Original Data ÷ Moving Average y_i/z_i'	Seasonal Index a_j	Profits after Taxes—Adjusted for Seasonal Factors $y_i'_j=y_i/a_j$
1949							
1st	206		—	—	—	1.149	179.3
2nd	180	—	—	—	—	0.956	188.3
3rd	175	757	1538	192	0.911	0.898	194.9
4th	196	781	1594	199	0.985	0.997	196.6
1950							
1st	230	813	1622	203	1.133	1.149	200.2
2nd	212	809	1633	204	1.039	0.956	221.8
3rd	171	824	1649	206	0.830	0.898	190.4
4th	211	825	1635	204	1.034	0.997	211.6
1951							
1st	231	810	1620	202	1.144	1.149	201.0
2nd	197	810	1625	203	0.970	0.956	206.1
3rd	171	815	1664	208	0.822	0.898	190.4
4th	216	849	1721	215	1.005	0.997	216.6
1952							
1st	265	872	1783	223	1.188	1.149	230.6
2nd	220	911	1859	232	0.948	0.956	230.1
3rd	210	948	1924	240	0.875	0.898	233.9
4th	253	976	1979	247	1.024	0.997	253.8
1953							
1st	293	1003	2027	253	1.158	1.149	255.0
2nd	247	1024	2055	257	0.961	0.956	258.4
3rd	231	1031	2090	261	0.885	0.898	257.2
4th	260	1059	2137	267	0.974	0.997	260.8
1954							
1st	321	1078	2189	274	1.172	1.149	279.4
2nd	266	1111	2250	281	0.947	0.956	278.2
3rd	264	1139	2298	287	0.920	0.898	294.0
4th	288	1159	2344	293	0.983	0.997	288.9
1955							
1st	341	1185	2391	299	1.140	1.149	296.8
2nd	292	1206	2449	306	0.954	0.956	305.4
3rd	285	1243	2517	315	0.905	0.898	317.4
4th	325	1274	2575	322	1.009	0.997	326.0
1956							
1st	372	1301	2618	327	1.138	1.149	323.8
2nd	319	1317	2643	330	0.967	0.956	333.7
3rd	301	1326	2673	334	0.901	0.898	335.2
4th	334	1347	2702	338	0.988	0.997	335.0
1957							
1st	393	1355	2735	342	1.149	1.149	342.0
2nd	327	1380	2783	348	0.940	0.956	342.1
3rd	326	1403	2834	354	0.921	0.898	363.0
4th	357	1431	2884	360	0.992	0.997	358.1
1958							
1st	421	1453	2937	367	1.147	1.149	366.4
2nd	349	1484	3001	375	0.931	0.956	365.1
3rd	357	1517	—	—	—	0.898	397.6
4th	390	—	—	—	—	0.997	391.2

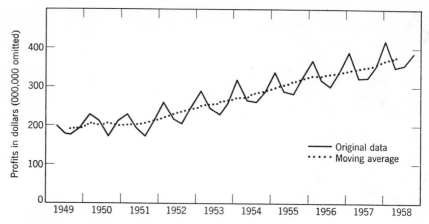

Fig. 15.5. Profits after taxes—electrical utilities.

September 30 respectively, both $y_i = 175$ and $z_i' = 192$ are placed at August 15, the midpoint of the third quarter. y_i and z_i' are plotted in Figure 15.5. Notice the smoothness of the moving average and its lack of seasonal variation.

If the seasonal pattern is at all constant from year to year, it will probably be on a percentage deviation basis rather than in absolute terms. In the fifth column of Table 15.8 we see the original data y_i expressed as a relative of the moving average z_i'; for example, profits in the third quarter of 1949 were 91 percent of the moving average for that period. If the seasonal pattern is constant and if the moving average contains all the nonseasonal factors, the y_i/z_i' values for any particular quarter would be the same year after year. They are presented in Table 15.9 and Figure 15.6. Some variability is apparent. If we are willing to assume a constant seasonal pattern, this variability must result from the failure of the moving average to measure the nonseasonal components properly.

The moving average will satisfactorily reflect trend and, except for turning points, cyclical fluctuations. Residual movements will appear in it only if they persist; short-run residuals will not be included. Despite this failure of the moving average to describe the nonseasonal elements completely, the one element that is constant in all y_i/z_i' values for a particular quarter is the seasonal variation. Nonseasonal elements should sometimes produce higher values and sometimes lower ones. Our objective is to ascertain this constant element; there are a number of methods of doing this, of which we are presenting only one.

In Table 15.9 we have shown the y_i/z_i' values for each quarter and have taken the mean of the middle three. The central core of items should be the

Table 15.9 Computation of Seasonal Indices, Profits After Taxes—Electric Utilities

| Quarter | y_i/z_i' Values | | | | | | | | | | Mean of Middle Three | Seasonal Indexes, Adjusted |
	1949 (1)	1950 (2)	1951 (3)	1952 (4)	1953 (5)	1954 (6)	1955 (7)	1956 (8)	1957 (9)	1958 (10)	(11)	(12)
First	—	1 1.133	4 1.144	9 1.188	7 1.158	8 1.172	3 1.140	2 1.138	6 1.149	5 1.147	1.147	1.149
Second	—	9 1.039	8 0.970	4 0.948	6 0.961	.3 0.947	5 0.954	7 0.967	2 0.940	1 0.931	0.954	0.956
Third	7 0.911	2 0.830	1 0.822	3 0.875	4 0.885	8 0.920	6 0.905	5 0.901	9 0.921	—	0.897	0.898
Fourth	3 0.985	9 1.034	6 1.005	8 1.024	1 0.974	2 0.983	7 1.009	4 0.988	5 0.992	—	0.995	0.997
											3.994	4.000

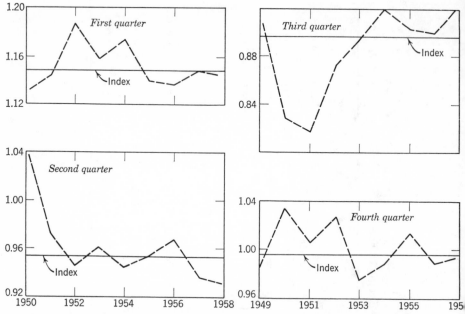

Fig. 15.6. y_i/z_i' values of profits after taxes—electric utilities by quarters.

ones least disturbed by nonseasonal factors. Since we wish to interpret seasonal indices in terms of percentage deviations, the final column of Table 15.9 shows these means adjusted to an average value of 1.0. Only after such an adjustment can we interpret the seasonal index for the first quarter in terms of a 14.9 percent deviation. This adjustment is particularly important when the average value is markedly different from 1.0.

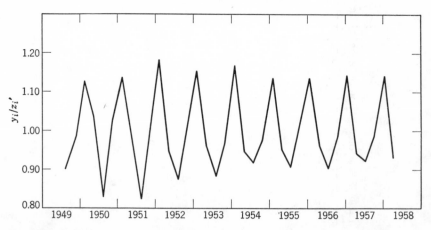

Fig. 15.7. y_i/z_i' values of profits after taxes—electrical utilities, 1949 to 1958.

The seasonal indices a_j are plotted as solid lines on Figure 15.6 in order to show the pattern of the deviations over time. The y_i/z_i' values should fall above and below the computed index and should not demonstrate a systematic change over time. The third quarter seems to have increased in relative importance in recent years, and the graph raises some doubts concerning the appropriateness of using a constant pattern. If the evidence for several of the quarters indicated that the relative importance of the different periods was changing, it might be advisable to determine different seasonal indices for each year, a procedure known as obtaining moving seasonal indices (the technique will not be discussed here).[7] The seasonal pattern for this problem is shown graphically in Figure 15.8.

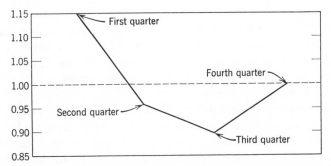

Fig. 15.8. Seasonal indices of profits after taxes—electric utilities.

Seasonal indices serve two main purposes: (1) adjusting historical data in order to study cycle, or trend, or both, and (2) planning future operations or predicting future results. For the first purpose we take the original data and remove the seasonal component. For the second we introduce the seasonal factor in order to obtain an estimate of the original data to be expected.

The final column of Table 15.8 illustrates the adjustment of the original data for seasonal factors. Each was computed by dividing y_i, the actual profit after taxes, by a_j, the seasonal index for the appropriate quarter. For example, the $206 million profit for the first quarter of 1949 is considered the result after seasonal forces brought about a 14.9 percent increase over what profit would have been if all forces except seasonal had been operative. Therefore, 206 divided by 1.149, yielding 179.3, is the estimate of profits (after taxes) produced by trend, cycle, and irregular factors. The difference, 26.7, is

---

[7] The longer the period covered, the less likely it is that a constant seasonal index is appropriate. For most economic series, a minimum of five years is needed to find a typical pattern, but anything in excess of ten years is suspect in terms of constancy.

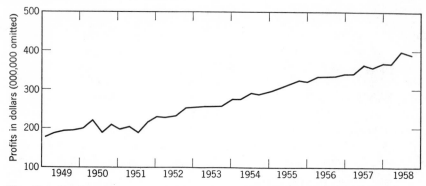

Fig. 15.9. Profits after taxes—electric utilities adjusted for seasonal variation.

attributed to the seasonal force. Note that for all quarters except the first, seasonal forces are viewed as negative. Figure 15.9 shows profits after taxes, adjusted for the seasonal element. It is a much smoother line than the original data, but not as smooth as the moving average which contains practically no residual component.

The use of seasonal indices in predictions reverses the procedure. Here, with more or less confidence, one starts with a figure that includes everything except the seasonal factor. Suppose, for example, that one were to estimate that trend, cycle, and irregular forces were to place profits after taxes at $510 million for the second quarter of 1966. Seasonal forces would be expected to decrease this figure by 4.4 percent (seasonal index of 0.956), yielding an estimate of $488 million.

15.7 ADDITIVE DECOMPOSITION OF TIME SERIES

We are now ready to isolate each time-series component, that is, to apply the model of (15.18). We shall use the electric utility data to illustrate the method although they do not appear to have a sizable cyclical component, and they represent a period too short to give a description of trend in which one has much confidence. The seasonal effect has already been determined, and we now turn to the combined effects of trend, cycle, and residual as given in the last column of Table 15.8. As has previously been mentioned, cyclical fluctuations must be studied as deviations from trend, so we next need a trend model.

An examination of Figure 15.9 assures us that a linear function is appropriate. Working from the last column of Table 15.8, using December 30, 1953 as the origin, coding February 15, 1954 as +1, and letting $y_i' = y_i/a_j$

we find[8]

$$a = \frac{\sum y'}{n} = \frac{11,016.3}{40} = 275.4$$

$$b = \frac{\sum xy'}{\sum x^2} = \frac{58,488.7}{21,320} = 2.743$$

so that the trend function is

$$t = 275.4 + 2.743x$$

The third column of Table 15.10 shows the ordinates of the trend function for the various quarters, and the fourth column, obtained by computing $y_i' - t_i$, represents the combined effects of cyclical and residual forces. A graph of this column is given in Figure 15.10.

Obvious peaks occur near the end of 1949 and at the end of 1958. An obvious trough is seen at the end of 1951. This suggests the presence of an eight-year cycle with peaks in 1950 and 1958. It is characterized by an initial sharp decline and then a slow rise to the next peak accompanied by many irregular movements. Notice that from our 10-year sample of data it is impossible to tell whether or not such a cyclical movement is really characteristic of the whole series. We would need at least 30 years of data before we could reach any such conclusion.

One way of removing an eight-year cycle from a set of data is to calculate an eight-year moving average. We would do this if we had a larger set of data initially, but for utility profits we would lose $p = 16$ points at each end of the series and thus be left with only 8 points—a relatively worthless result. For the sake of illustration we will instead assume a three-year cycle with additional peaks in 1952 and 1955 and troughs between. The evidence for the existence of these short cycles is tenuous, but we wish to illustrate the method. Calculation of a moving average with $p = 6$ is again done following (15.15). Since trend has already been removed, if only a three-year cycle were present in $c_i + r_i$, z_i' would represent this cycle. Assuming that this is true, the final column represents the residual movements r_i. They are also graphed in Figure 15.10; the fact that the residual pattern follows the movement of the $c_i + r_i$ series so closely shows that, as we suspected, a three-year cycle is not an important component of this series.

The additivity of our model is exhibited in Tables 15.8 and 15.10. For example, in the last quarter of 1950

$$t_i + s_i + c_i + r_i = 206.8 - 0.6 - 1.2 + 6.0 = 211.0 = y_i$$

---

[8] Many statisticians would prefer to determine the trend equation from annual data instead of from the quarterly data as we have done here.

Table 15.10 Further Decomposition of Utility Data

Year	x_i	$y_i' = t_i + c_i + r_i$	t_i	$y_i'' = c_i + r_i$	z_i'	r_i
1949	−39	179.3	168.4	10.9		
	−37	188.3	173.9	14.4		
	−35	194.9	179.4	15.5		
	−33	196.6	184.9	11.7		
1950	−31	200.2	190.4	9.8		
	−29	221.8	195.9	25.9		
	−27	190.4	201.3	−11.9	0.5	−12.4
	−25	211.6	206.8	4.8	−1.2	6.0
1951	−23	201.0	212.3	−11.3	−3.4	−7.9
	−21	206.1	217.8	−11.7	−4.8	−6.9
	−19	190.4	223.3	−32.9	−5.6	−27.3
	−17	216.6	228.8	−12.2	−7.2	−5.0
1952	−15	230.6	234.3	−3.7	−8.4	4.7
	−13	230.1	239.7	−9.6	−9.0	−0.6
	−11	233.9	245.2	−11.3	−9.2	−2.1
	−9	253.8	250.7	3.1	−8.4	11.5
1953	−7	255.0	256.2	−1.2	−6.5	5.3
	−5	258.4	261.7	−3.3	−4.6	1.3
	−3	257.2	267.2	−10.0	−4.4	−5.6
	−1	260.8	272.7	−11.9	−4.0	−7.9
1954	1	279.4	278.1	1.3	−2.8	4.1
	3	278.2	283.6	−5.4	−1.8	−3.6
	5	294.0	289.1	4.9	−1.4	6.3
	7	288.9	294.6	−5.7	−0.9	−4.8
1955	9	296.8	300.1	−3.3	0.0	−3.3
	11	305.4	305.6	−0.2	0.8	−1.0
	13	317.4	311.1	6.3	1.0	5.3
	15	326.0	316.5	9.5	0.8	8.7
1956	17	323.8	322.0	1.8	0.8	1.0
	19	333.7	327.5	6.2	1.2	5.0
	21	335.2	333.0	2.2	1.4	0.8
	23	335.0	338.5	−3.5	1.4	−4.9
1957	25	342.0	344.0	−2.0	1.7	−3.7
	27	342.1	349.5	−7.4	2.2	−9.6
	29	363.0	354.9	8.1		
	31	358.1	360.4	−2.3		
1958	33	366.4	365.9	0.5		
	35	365.1	371.4	−6.3		
	37	397.6	376.9	20.7		
	39	391.2	382.4	8.8		

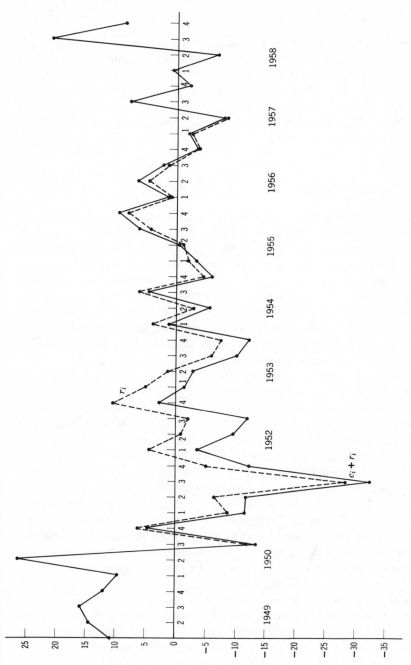

Fig. 15.10. Cyclical and residual components of data representing profits after taxes of electrical utilities.

For some purposes, it is more meaningful to examine the several components of a time series in terms of percentages of a relevant base. In the last quarter of 1949, it is more informative to know that the combined effects of seasonal variation, cyclical fluctuation and residual movement were less than 7 percent of trend, than to know the numerical values of the components themselves. The three other components are usually expressed in relative form as percentages of trend.

15.8   INDEX NUMBERS

An index number is often considered as synonymous with an indicator; for example, the number of persons employed might be considered an index of economic activity. It is certainly possible to define an index number in this way, but such an approach is so general that it would encompass all measurements. We shall impose two restrictions on our definition because these establish a set for which there are some rather unique problems and whose elements are frequently useful in the analysis of business. For our purposes, index numbers are summary figures for sets of observations arrived at by either averaging ratios or taking the ratio of averages. Thus the index number is addressed to a relative comparison between sets of items.

In order for an index number to have utility there must be a rational basis for combining the various characteristics. It might be difficult to justify an index number in which the characteristics to be combined were rainfall, newspaper circulation, number of strike outs, and teachers' salaries. It would, however, still be an index number. If, on the other hand, all characteristics referred to various aspects of economic well-being, it would seem reasonable to average them in some way. If the index number is to have utility, the individual relatives should represent the same types of comparisons. Typically, each relative will be computed by comparing the measurement of a specific phenomenon at two points in time, and the same two points will be employed for all of the relatives that are to be combined. It is for this reason that index numbers are discussed here under the subject of time series, but they are also appropriate in comparisons with respect to geographic locations at the same point in time.

Before investigating the construction of a specific index, it might be well to present the general structure of index number construction. As is true in any research investigation, the problem must be defined precisely so that one can identify the appropriate universe and the relevant characteristic. In most cases the entire universe will not be studied, but a sample will be selected and information collected on the relevant characteristics for at least two time and space coordinates. Then, depending upon the problem, either time or space will be held constant. The information to this point is indicated by Table 15.11.

Table 15.11 Basic Data Format for any Index Number

	Value of Characteristic	
Sample Element Number	Time and Space Coordinate No. 1	Time and Space Coordinate No. 2
1	x_{11}	x_{12}
2	x_{21}	x_{22}
.	.	.
.	.	.
.	.	.

The observations x_{ij} are then combined into an index number either by averaging the ratios of the coordinates of each sample item or by taking the ratio of the aggregated coordinates, as will shortly be discussed. Since construction of an index number is an averaging process, dispersion is of some significance. If there is little dispersion among individual relatives, almost all methods of computation will yield similar results. But if there is a great deal of dispersion, the average may be quite unrepresentative.

There are many methods of constructing index numbers. We shall consider several common methods, but our list is very incomplete. The reader should be particularly conscious of the interpretation associated with each method; the proper method is the one that has an interpretation appropriate for the problem at hand. If all of the information required for that method is not available, the researcher either adopts a compromise, secures the needed data, or throws up his hands in despair—a situation not unique to index numbers.

In considering methods of constructing index numbers, we shall study a price-index problem. Most of the important problems will be encountered. We shall define a rather vague problem. If we were to define it well, only one method would be appropriate, and we want to consider several. Our question is "How much change was there in the price of retail food for home use in the Philadelphia area between 1950 and 1962?" The universe consists of all food products sold in the Philadelphia area; for example, bread, milk, sugar, fruit, meat, etc.—a list too long to enumerate. Note how much larger it would become if we were to consider the many variants of quality and size available even within a single retail outlet, and then multiply that by the number of different types of outlets. This is a problem where sampling must be employed. In most instances the sample selected will not be a probability sample, but a judgment sample chosen to the best of the ability of the researcher that he hopes will be representative of the universe. In order to reduce the arithmetic we shall limit our sample to four items. Price is the relevant characteristic, but we would have to collect prices at the appropriate retail outlets for quality and size specifications that apply to whatever group we had in mind when we said "home use." Assuming that these questions have been answered satisfactorily, we shall employ the data of Table 15.12.

Table 15.12   Food Prices in the Philadelphia Area, 1950 and 1962

| | Price (P) | | Price Relative |
Product	P_{50}	P_{62}	P_{62}/P_{50}
Bread (loaf)	0.15	0.21	1.400
Milk (quart)	0.25	0.28	1.120
Sugar (5 lb)	0.64	0.56	0.875
Butter (1 lb)	0.90	0.81	0.900
	1.94	1.86	4.295

Inspection of the individual price relatives shows that these four items experienced diverse price movements between 1950 and 1962. Bread and milk both increased, but by different percentages, whereas sugar and butter both declined. Various methods might yield radically different summary statistics in such a case. Each method assigns weights, consciously or unconsciously, to the individual items. Heavy weight to bread will produce a high index, while heavy weight to sugar and butter will show that the "average" price declined.

The most obvious average of relatives is probably the arithmetic mean. The unweighted arithmetic mean of relatives for our data is

$$\frac{\sum (P_{62}/P_{50})}{n} = \frac{4.295}{4} = 1.074$$

A second method, the unweighted relative of aggregates, compares the total of the prices for 1962 with the total for 1950. The result,

$$\frac{\sum P_{62}}{\sum P_{50}} = \frac{1.86}{1.94} = 0.959$$

is quite different from that obtained by the first method although both are called "unweighted."

The crux of the difference between the two methods is most easily seen by asking what would cost $100(1.074 - 1.000) = 7.4$ percent more and what would cost $100(1.000 - 0.959) = 4.1$ percent less. If one had established a market basket in 1950 by spending the same amount of money (perhaps $1) for each of the four products and then purchased the same quantities of those products in 1962, it would have cost 7.4 percent more in 1962 that it did in 1950. This can be observed by inspecting column 3 of Table 15.12. Bread, instead of costing $1 in 1962, would cost $1.40; milk $1.12 instead of $1, etc.; and the entire market basket would cost $4.295 instead of $4, an increase of 7.4 percent.

The quantities in the market basket of the second method are obvious: one loaf of bread, one quart of milk, one 5-lb bag of sugar, and one pound of butter; or more generally, one unit of each item. This method (unweighted relative of aggregates) is dominated by the high-priced items. In this instance the two products with the highest prices (butter and sugar) both declined, thus explaining the decline in the index.

If either of these market baskets is acceptable for the problem to be considered, the method yielding that market basket is appropriate; if not, some other weighting scheme should be employed. Each of the methods cited has undesirable properties that are not obvious. The unweighted relative of aggregates yields different answers when the units for which the prices are quoted are changed. The unweighted arithmetic mean of relatives employs a different weighting scheme if the base year is changed.

Considering first the unweighted relative of aggregates, what would be the result if the prices of milk in half-gallon containers were quoted as 50 cents and 56 cents in the two respective years? The weight given to each product is indicated by the price itself, and that given to milk would therefore be increased. Since the relative for milk is 1.120 (higher than the index of 0.959 in which milk was quoted in quarts), the index will be increased; the result in this case would be 0.977. A somewhat similar phenomenon occurs in the Dow-Jones Stock Average[9] every time there is a stock spilt. The indices are based on price per share so that the relative weight given the stock which has been split will be decreased, since the price per share afterwards is less than it was prior to the split.

Turning to the weighting scheme of the unweighted arithmetic mean of relatives, assume that the prices of the four products in 1970 return to the same values as 1950. Our earlier discussion[10] indicated that an increase

[9] The Dow-Jones is not an index, according to our definition, but is simply the arithmetic mean price per share for the stocks included. In order to make successive observations comparable, certain changes must be introduced in the calculations. These techniques are not of concern to us at this point.

[10] See Section 15.2.

of 7.4 percent would be more than offset by a subsequent decrease of that amount. In order to achieve a precise balancing, the subsequent relative would be given by 1/1.074 or a decline of 6.9 percent. An unweighted arithmetic mean of relatives for 1970 using 1962 as a base would be 0.965, a decline of only 3.5 percent. Obviously, if we had posed the question how do prices in 1950 compare with those of 1962, our index again would have been 0.965 and not the reciprocal of the answer to the first question. This is quite general: when the base year is changed the weighting scheme of the unweighted arithmetic mean of relatives is changed, and the results of the two calculations are not arithmetically consistent.

If, on the other hand, we were to compute an unweighted geometric mean of relatives for our data the result would be 1.054, as shown in Table 15.13. This result is arithmetically consistent in the sense that, if we make

Table 15.13   Calculation of the Unweighted Geometric Mean of Relatives

Product	P_{62}/P_{50}	$\log (P_{62}/P_{50})$
Bread	1.400	0.1461
Milk	1.120	0.0492
Sugar	0.875	9.9420–10
Butter	0.900	9.9542–10
		20.0915–20

$$\text{Log unweighted } x_G = \frac{\sum [\log (P_{62}/P_{50})]}{n}$$

$$= \frac{0.0915}{4}$$

$$= 0.0229$$

$$\text{Unweighted } x_G = 1.054$$

1962 the base year and compute the index for 1950, the result will be the reciprocal of 1.054. Unfortunately, the weighting scheme used for the unweighted geometric mean is somewhat abstract; equal weight is not given to each relative but to its logarithm. Consequently the interpretation of the result cannot be made in terms of a specific market basket.

The weights employed in the three methods discussed have not been based on data obtained from an investigation. Suppose a survey revealed that a typical urban family of four consumed five loaves of bread, ten quarts of milk, 1/2 of a five-pound bag of sugar and two pounds of butter per week. If the index is designed to measure change in food prices for such a family, weights based on such information would be preferable to weights chosen without reference to it. An easy way of posing this question is to ask how much more (or less) it would cost to purchase the designated market basket in 1962 than in 1950. Table 15.14 presents the calculations needed. The index computed is called a weighted relative of aggregates.

Table 15.14 Calculation of a Price Index Based upon a Known Consumption Pattern

Product	P_{50}	P_{62}	Consumption (Q)	$P_{50}Q$	$P_{62}Q$
Bread	0.15	0.21	5	0.75	1.05
Milk	0.25	0.28	10	2.50	2.80
Sugar	0.64	0.56	$\frac{1}{2}$	0.32	0.28
Butter	0.90	0.81	2	1.80	1.62
				5.37	5.75

$$\text{Weighted Relative of Aggregates} = \frac{\sum(P_{62}Q)}{\sum(P_{50}Q)} = \frac{5.75}{5.37} = 1.071$$

The weights applied in this calculation are shown by $P_{50}Q$. Milk, which increased by 12 percent is given the most weight; butter, which decreased in price, is given the next, etc. As a matter of fact, the calculation can be made by using relative weights based on amount of money spent on the product in a certain period and applying these weights to the individual relatives. The advantage of this approach is that no absolute figures are required. This is useful when one is working in an area where data are confidential or when a single item is used as representative of a large set.

Consider the case of the food index. One item might be a particular kind of cereal. The appropriate weight given to that item might be the amount spent on all cereals or, since the weighting scheme would be determined from a sample of families, the weight would be designated more accurately as the estimated percentage of food expenditures allocated to cereals. The weights for other items would be determined in the same way.

This method can be expressed as $\sum[PQ(P_{62}/P_{50})]/\sum(PQ)$ and identified as a weighted arithmetic mean of relatives. It should be obvious that it will also yield 1.071.

Before leaving the calculation of a price index, the implication of constant weights should be made explicit. A price index is designed to measure only changes in price, not changes in the "cost of living." Tastes do not remain constant over time; new products are introduced and old products fall into disuse. These changes are not reflected in a price index. Nor does a price index reflect changes in consumption that accompany increases in income or changes in consumption that are the result of price changes. The price index measures only changes in prices; other variables are held constant to the extent possible.

15.9   ADDITIONAL TOPICS

Most of us have heard our parents refer to the days when "a dollar would buy a dollar's worth of merchandise." They are, of course, referring to the phenomenon of inflation or decreasing purchasing power of money. As a consequence of this phenomenon, businessmen and economists are frequently interested in separating time series expressed in monetary terms into two factors. These can be identified as the "real" component (that is, changes in the level of goods, services, or both) and the price component. The combined effect of the two yields a "value" series expressed as price × quantity (or simply PQ). If we wish to express only the quantity aspect of the series, a division of value by price would seem appropriate. In practice, we choose a price index as the "deflator," taking care to choose one that is relevant for the series under consideration.

This approach is not restricted to the removal of price effects from a time series. In fact, in earlier sections of this chapter we have suggested similar operations for other purposes. In studying economic well-being, we often express our figures on a per capita basis. The total series reflects changes in individual well-being and changes in population. We remove the latter by dividing by population. In the present problem, we attempt to remove the effect of price by dividing by price. An analogous problem was the removal of the seasonal factor in a time series. This was again accomplished by division— in that case by the seasonal index.

Returning to the Smith and Jones Department Store illustration, how much did the fluctuations in sales reflect price changes and how much changes in amount of goods sold? Using a price index for department stores as an appropriate deflator, the fourth column of Table 15.15 shows an estimate of the fluctuations in the amount of goods sold. Since the price index is computed with a base year of 1950, the figures in this column could be interpreted as the valuation that would have been placed on the goods if those quantities had been sold in 1950. The usual terminology is "constant 1950 dollars."[11]

Between 1960 and 1970, sales of Smith and Jones increased by $100[(400 - 200) \div 200] = 100$ percent, and prices increased by

$$100[(1.32 - 1.00) \div 1.00] = 32 \text{ percent}$$

[11] In Section 15.5, the Gross National Product series has been adjusted in a similar manner, but to "constant 1954 dollars."

Table 15.15 Sales of the Smith and Jones Department Store Adjusted for Price Changes, 1960 to 1970

Year	Sales ($1000)	Department Store Price Index	Sales Adjusted for Price Changes ($1000)
1960	200	1.00	200
1961	250	1.03	243
1962	250	1.04	240
1963	225	1.06	212
1964	275	1.06	259
1965	300	1.09	275
1966	250	1.13	221
1967	350	1.17	299
1968	325	1.22	266
1969	350	1.27	275
1970	400	1.32	303

The estimate of the gain in physical volume of goods sold, as shown in column 4, is only $100[(303 - 200) \div 200] = 52$ percent in contrast to 68 percent, the difference between 100 percent and 32 percent. The answer could be immediately calculated from the statement that a price times a quantity is equal to a value. When changed to indices the equality no longer holds because of the various systems of weights applied to the different indices. Despite this fact, the best estimating procedure available is often the approximation VI/PI. Substituting into this estimator,

$$\frac{2.00}{1.32} = 1.52$$

If a series of indices over time is desired, it is possible to compute all of them on the same base period or to change the base period with successive calculations. When the latter procedure is followed, the resulting indices are called link relatives. The reader has encountered such indices in his reading; for example, "average hourly wages rose 2.5 percent last year; department store sales were down 4 percent last week; employment in April was 2 percent higher than the preceding April." Each figure is compared to what is believed to be the relevant preceding figure. The last example indicates a recognition that there may be a seasonal pattern in the series and that comparison should be made with the same month of the preceding year rather than the preceding month of the same year.

Quite frequently, link relatives are employed because data are not available from precisely the same elements for every time period. Typically in such a situation, elements supply data for the present and preceding periods. As a consequence the individual links can be computed, but no continuous series is provided. A series of link relatives, however, can be transformed into a series with a common base by simple arithmetic. This process is referred to as *chaining* and is illustrated in Table 15.16.

Table 15.16   Chain Index of Production in Widget Industry, 1960 to 1970 on 1964 Base

Year	Link Relative	Chain Index	Calculation of Chain Index
1960	106.2	96.2	(97.5 ÷ 1.013)
1961	101.3	97.5	(95.9 ÷ 0.984)
1962	98.4	95.9	(99.5 ÷ 1.037)
1963	103.7	99.5	(100.0 ÷ 1.005)
1964	100.5	100.0	
1965	97.6	97.6	(100.0 × 0.976)
1966	104.5	102.0	(97.6 × 1.045)
1967	102.0	104.0	(102.0 × 1.02)
1968	95.3	99.1	(104.0 × 0.953)
1969	106.7	105.7	(99.1 × 1.067)
1970	102.8	108.7	(105.7 × 1.028)

Caution should be exercised in the interpretation of the chain index. It is easy to lose sight of the fact that the original links were probably computed with different weighting schemes. The process of chaining does not introduce a constant weighting scheme, but simply gives a continuous time series. If the more successful firms continue to report, and the less successful ones are "drop-outs," the chain obviously has a built-in bias. Periodic censuses may provide a basis for estimating its size.

A process similar to chaining is that of splicing two or more series. As time passes, one may decide that a more current base period is desirable. During the past few decades, most government agencies have shifted from a 1935–1939 base to a 1947–1949 base, and later to 1957–1959. In such instances, the values of the old series must all be restated on the new base period. This is accomplished in precisely the manner indicated in Table 15.16 for 1963, except that new values are required for many periods.

IMPORTANT TERMS AND CONCEPTS

Base period
Chain index
Classical model
Cyclical fluctuations
Deflation
Deseasonalized data
Extrapolation
Geometric mean
Index number
Irregular component
Linear trend
   To logarithms
   To original data
Link relative
Method of least squares
Moving average
Parabola

Percentage change
Price index
Quantity index
Rate of change
Relative
Seasonal variation
Seasonal index
Semilogarithmic scale
Time series
Trend
Unweighted indices
   Arithmetic mean of relatives
   Geometric mean of relatives
   Relative of aggregates
Value series
Weighted indices

SYMBOLS AND ABBREVIATIONS

y_i
z_i
z_i'
a_j
$\hat{y}$

$1 + r$
P_1
P_0
x_G

OFTEN-USED FORMULAS

$$\hat{y} = a + bx \quad \text{if} \quad \sum x = 0$$

$$a = \frac{\sum y}{n} \qquad b = \frac{\sum xy}{\sum x^2}$$

$$\log \hat{y} = a + bx \qquad \text{if} \quad \sum x = 0$$

$$a = \frac{\sum \log y}{n} \qquad b = \frac{\sum x \log y}{\sum x^2}$$

$$1 + r = \sqrt{\frac{J_{n+1}}{J_1}} = \sqrt{\prod_{i=1}^{n} (1 + r_i)}$$

$$x_G = \sqrt{\prod_{i=1}^{n} x_i}$$

$$z_i = \sum_{k=-p}^{p} \frac{y_{i+k}}{2p + 1}$$

$$\hat{z}_i = \alpha y_i + (1 - \alpha)\hat{z}_{i-1}$$

$$y_i = t_i + s_i + c_i + r_i$$

$$\sum (P_1/P_0)/n = \text{unweighted arithmetic mean of relatives}$$

$$\sqrt[n]{\prod (P_1/P_0)} = \text{antilog } \{[\sum \log (P_1/P_0)]/n\}$$
$$= \text{unweighted geometric mean of relatives}$$

$$\sum P_1/\sum P_0 = \text{unweighted relative of aggregates}$$

$$\sum (w \times P_1/P_0)/\sum w = \text{weighted arithmetic mean of relatives}$$

EXERCISES

1. Define a time series.

2. Explain how the same set of data might be treated by one person as a time series and by another as a frequency distribution. Give an original example.

3. Observe the following data.

Number of United States Life Insurance Companies

1900	84
1910	284
1920	335
1930	438
1940	444
1950	649
1960	1440

Source. Life Insurance Fact Book, 1964, p. 99.

a. Do you think that a linear equation fitted to either the original data or the logarithms of the original data would be appropriate for describing the trend of this series? Why?

b. Using the method of least squares, determine the constants of a linear equation fitted to the logarithms of the data.

c. Explain precisely in terms of this problem the meaning of the constants of your equation in part *b*.

d. Would your answer in part *b* have been the same if you had used all of the annual data between 1900 and 1960? Why?

e. Would you be willing to use your trend line to estimate the number of United States Life Insurance Companies in 1980? Why?

4. The number of United States Life Insurance Companies in the decade between 1950 and 1959 is given below

1950	649	1955	1107
1951	679	1956	1191
1952	730	1957	1273
1953	832	1958	1365
1954	917	1959	1425

Source. Life Insurance Fact Book, 1964, p. 99.

a. Using your results from Exercise 3, do you see any evidence of a cyclical pattern within this decade? Explain.

b. What is the best way to describe the rate of change during this decade? (Make the necessary calculations.)

5. Obtain from the library the estimate of GNP for the most recent year available.

a. What has been the average annual percentage rate of change since 1957?

b. Should your calculation in part *a* have been based on current dollars or constant dollars? Why?

c. Suppose that you wished to compute the average percentage rate of change in GNP between two quarters. Should you use estimates adjusted for seasonal variations? Why?

6. a. The arithmetic mean height of boys in the graduating class of Delchow High School is given on the next page.

Year	Arithmetic Mean Height (in Inches)
1953	67.16
1954	67.08
1955	68.03
1956	68.53
1957	67.84
1958	68.15
1959	68.24
1960	68.43
1961	68.30
1962	67.89
1963	68.17
1964	68.25

1. Is this a time series? Why?
2. What type of analysis would you recommend for this series?

b. Additional information is available for boys in the Delchow School System for the year 1964.

Class	Arithmetic Mean Height (in Inches)
Senior	68.22
Junior	66.32
Sophomore	64.05
Freshman	62.18
Eighth grade	60.61

Is this a time series? Why?

7. The table indicates the size of the United States civilian labor force at five-year intervals.

Year	Millions in Labor Force
1925	45
1930	51
1935	53
1940	56
1945	54
1950	63
1955	66

Source. United States Department of Commerce, Bureau of the Census.

a. Fit a trend line to the above labor force data.

b. Compute the trend ordinate for 1952 and interpret it specifically in terms of this problem.

c. Suppose that part *b* had asked for 1958. Would your answer have been any different (except for the number)? Why?

8. a. Use the data of Exercise 7 to illustrate the method of exponential smoothing. Use an initial z_i' value of 45 million and $\alpha = 0.3$. Obtain a $\hat{z}_i$ value for each of the seven years for which observations are given.

b. Repeat part *a* using $\alpha = 0.1$.

c. Which of these two values of α do you consider more appropriate in this particular context? Why?

9. a. Determine the constants of a linear model fitted to the logarithms of the following data by the method of least squares. The data are paired 12 month moving averages for the receipts of a grocery chain.

Date	Moving Average (in $100,000)
August 1940	1.2
August 1945	1.5
August 1950	2.3
August 1955	2.9
August 1960	3.9

b. For the period 1945 to 1955 a constant seasonal pattern was determined. The monthly indices ranged from a high of 130 in December to a low of 80 in August. Since August was the lowest month, the August moving averages should not have been used in determining the trend equation. Discuss.

c. Assume that the trend line established is appropriate. If receipts in August 1948 were $160,000, how would you allocate this sum to the different time series components (that is, trend, cycle, seasonal, and residual)?

10. Explain briefly the features that distinguish the following time-series components:

a. Trend and cycle.

b. Cycle and seasonal.

c. Seasonal and residual.

11. a. Using monthly or quarterly data for a particular series, determine a constant seasonal pattern for the series. (You should have between 5 and 10 years of data.)

    b. Do you think that constant seasonal indices are appropriate for this series? Why?

12. The following table gives the consumption of electric power in the United States.

Year	Consumption in Billion Kilowatt-Hours
1910	30
1920	48
1930	113
1940	195
1950	450
1960	831

    a. What was the average amount of increase per decade in the above series between 1910 and 1960?

    b. What was the average percentage increase per decade between 1910 and 1960?

    c. Do you think the figures that you calculated in parts *a* and *b* are typical for the series? Discuss.

    d. Fit a linear trend line to the logarithms of the above data by the method of least squares.

    e. Interpret the meaning of the constants of the trend equation specifically in terms of this problem.

    f. Is the answer to part *b* consistent with the slope implicit in part *d*? Why or why not?

    g. In 1932 the consumption of electric power was 100 billion kilowatt-hours. Compute and interpret both the absolute cyclical residual and the relative cyclical residual for 1932.

13. The data are the number of automobiles sold by the Valey Rudentino Corp. (top of facing page).

    a. Determine constant seasonal indices for each of the four quarters.

    b. Do you think constant seasonal indices should be employed in this problem? Why or why not?

    c. Assuming that constant seasonal indices are appropriate, adjust the quarterly sales figures between 1950 and 1955 for seasonal variation.

    d. Assume that the trend in sales for the Valey Rudentino Corp. can be described by the following equation:

$$\hat{y} = 200 + 25x$$

$$x = 0 \text{ in second quarter of 1950}$$

$$x = +5 \text{ in second quarter of 1955}$$

Year	Quarter	Number of Automobiles Sold
1950	1st	152
	2nd	277
	3rd	203
	4th	174
1951	1st	205
	2nd	363
	3rd	255
	4th	182
1952	1st	171
	2nd	325
	3rd	233
	4th	180
1953	1st	202
	2nd	396
	3rd	274
	4th	238
1954	1st	212
	2nd	350
	3rd	246
	4th	208
1955	1st	241
	2nd	453
	3rd	362
	4th	355

Do you see any evidence of cycles in the data between 1950 and 1955? What basis do you have for your answer?

14. Using the data of Exercise 13, compute
   a. A nine-quarter moving average of the $c_i + r_i$ values with which you terminated Exercise 13.
   b. The series of residuals r_i with the nine-quarter cycle removed.
   c. An exponentially smoothed series calculated from the original data with $\alpha = 0.4$. Use $\hat{z}_0 = 200$ automobiles.
   d. An exponentially smoothed series calculated from the deseasonalized data with $\alpha = 0.4$. Use $\hat{z}_0 = 200$ automobiles.
   e. Explain what use, if any, might be made of each of these series, and interpret the meaning of the last figure in each. Use the initial value given in part *d* if necessary.

15. The following table shows the semiannual number of deposits in savings accounts made at the Majestic National Bank over a ten-year period.

Year	Half	Number	Year	Half	Number
1960	1	3022	1965	1	2813
	2	2933		2	2692
1961	1	3286	1966	1	2701
	2	3152		2	2620
1962	1	3540	1967	1	2749
	2	3422		2	2688
1963	1	3116	1968	1	2956
	2	3045		2	2879
1964	1	3081	1969	1	3147
	2	2976		2	3022

a. Determine a constant seasonal index for each half year.
b. Fit a linear trend to the deseasonalized data.
c. Compute the combined cyclical and residual components for the series.
d. Does there appear to be a sizable cyclical component in these data? If so, how could it be isolated? Do not perform any computations, but assume that 30 years' data are available and that the pattern seen here is typical.
e. If instead of assuming a linear trend for these observations, we had assumed a parabolic one, what effect would this have had upon our cyclical analysis in part *d*?

16. Given the following data for a particular country. Did the increase in the physical volume of imports exceed the increase in the physical volume of exports? What assumptions underlie the necessary calculations?

Year	Imports (Billion $)	Import Price Index (1950 = 100)	Exports (Billion $)	Export Price Index (1950 = 100)
1959	1.0	150	1.5	180
1963	1.5	200	2.0	200

17. The prices of three consumer products and the quantities consumed per week in 1955 and in 1964 are shown on the following page.

	1955		1964	
Product	Price ($)	Quantity	Price ($)	Quantity
A (in quarts)	0.20	10	0.30	8
B (in pounds)	0.40	5	0.80	4
C (in dozens)	0.50	2	0.60	3

a. Calculate the weighted arithmetic mean of relatives price index for 1964 on 1955 as a base, using base-year weights.
b. Interpret your answer to part *a* specifically in terms of this problem.
c. Would any other indices be generally satisfactory for these data? Discuss.

18. Observe the following series of price indices (base year 1957), computed by the relative of aggregates method and 1957 weights.

Year	Price Index
1955	110
1956	95
1957	100
1958	92
1959	105
1960	120

a. Compute a new series of price indices with 1958 as the base year.
b. Interpret specifically the meaning of your new index for 1956.

19. The following are stock-market indicators: Dow-Jones Industrial Average, Standard and Poor's Composite Common Stock Index, and SEC Common Stock Index.
a. How do the three methods differ?
b. How do the three series compare in movement over the past three years?
c. Does your answer in part *a* explain any differences in part *b*?

20. Link relatives for employment in a certain industry are shown below.

Year	Link Relative
1966	107
1967	85
1968	115
1969	110
1970	102
1971	94

    a. Construct a chain index for employment in this industry, using 1968 as the base year.

    b. Interpret clearly the meaning of both the link relative and the chain index for 1967.

21. Suppose that a school official wishes to construct a monthly series of student price indices for your school. Outline, in detail, the steps you would recommend that he follow in establishing such a series. Be sure to cover all phases of the research and all decisions that must be made.

22. Obtain population figures for your home town from 1920 to date.

    a. Would it be necessary to use all figures available in determining the trend in population for your community? Why?

    b. Would it be advisable? Why?

    c. Using the data that you think should be used and the model that you think most appropriate, determine the trend in population for your hometown.

23. Between 1930 and 1960 the total income of a certain midwestern town increased by 500 percent. During the same period prices rose by 200 percent, and population tripled.

    a. What was the average annual percentage change in "real" income per capita?

    b. What was the corresponding change per decade?

24. The following trend equation, fitted to monthly data, was established for output of the J. J. Holt Candy Co.

$$\hat{y} = 87.2 + 1.2x \qquad -10 \le x \le 10$$

y is monthly output in thousands of pounds

$x = 0$ in July 1954

$x = +10$ in July 1964

Other information available:

          January seasonal index: $a_1 = 1.05$

          February seasonal index: $a_2 = 0.90$

    a. Actual production in January 1961 was 121,250 lb. The y_i/z_i' value for January 1961 was 91. Calculate the contribution of each time series component for January 1961.

    b. Production in February 1961 was 110,500 lb. Did production, when adjusted for seasonal variation, decrease between January and February?

16 Econometric Models

16.1 INTRODUCTION

Two of the more important aims of any science are prediction and the understanding of the relations among the important variables with which the science is concerned. These are really two aspects of the same thing, since—in principle, at least—our predictions should improve with our understanding of the underlying relationships among variables. Yet, when the immediate goal of an investigation is prediction and we know little about the underlying mechanisms, we are often forced to use crude models and approximate methods.

The time-series models of the previous chapter are a case in point. There, we used time as an explanatory variable, giving little thought to the mechanism generating the series. Because of their limited use of sophisticated ideas, the models of the previous chapter are sometimes called "naive." They were borrowed largely from astronomy, where the use of time as an explanatory variable is more appropriate. The mathematical models of astronomy are based on the laws of motion governing a system of dispersed masses. Since these laws are usually expressed as velocities and accelerations (derivatives with respect to time), it is natural to use time as the independent variable in the equations describing the behavior of the system. If the state of such a system—the positions, velocities, and accelerations of the masses that constitute it—is known at one point of time, it is known for all time, provided that the system is allowed to operate undisturbed. Although mathematical models of such systems are used with remarkable success in astronomy, their uncritical use in business and economics is unjustified. We are continually interfering with the operation of our economic system, and if we want to control it or to predict its behavior under different policies, we must understand the relations among the many economic and noneconomic variables involved. In order to improve our understanding of these relations, we construct mathematical models and test them empirically. The word *econometrics* is used to describe the measurement of economic variables and the formulation and testing of mathematical models of their interrelationships. In this chapter we shall consider a few of the simpler problems and methods of econometrics. Our main purpose is to indicate some of the difficulties in the empirical study of economic relations.

Since we shall be studying relationships among variables, our basic methods will be regression and correlation. We shall be concerned primarily with correlation because we have little opportunity to control variables in an economic system solely for the purpose of measuring an economic relationship.

Two general classes of difficulties arise when we try to apply the ideas of correlation to economic relationships. First, there are difficulties of model formulation. Although economic theory may specify some of the variables to be included in a mathematical model, it is usually of little help in deciding on the mathematical forms—linear, exponential, logarithmic, etc.—of the equations. The econometrician must decide this for himself, making the equations economically plausible and, at the same time, taking into account the statistical problems of parameter estimation. Also, many economic variables, such as price and quantity in a market, are simultaneously determined. In an equation expressing a relationship among such variables, there is often no justification for singling out one of them as "dependent."

Second, there are statistical difficulties. The assumptions made in Chapter 14 are often not valid in the data available to the econometrician. In Chapter 14, we considered a model of the form

$$Y_i = \alpha + \beta X_i + \epsilon_i \qquad i = 1, \cdots, n$$

and assumed that ϵ_i was a random variable independent of X_i and that successive values of ϵ_i were also independent. When the observations are successive over time, as they often are in econometrics, the latter assumption may not be met; and when both X_i and Y_i are closely related to other economic variables not included in the equation, the former assumption is not met. Besides, observations on economic variables are often subject to error. An equation relating error-free values of economic variables will not express the relationship among the same variables subject to error. Estimates of the parameters in such equations will, therefore, be biased.

Many economic relationships involve more than two variables. Therefore, in the next section we shall sketch an extension of the ideas of Chapter 14 to linear equations containing two or more independent variables. This extension is called multiple regression or multiple correlation. In the following sections, we consider a few of the problems that must be faced in econometrics and show how some of the simpler ones are solved.

16.2   METHODS OF MULTIPLE REGRESSION AND CORRELATION

Suppose that we want to estimate the parameters $\alpha_0, \alpha_1, \cdots, \alpha_r$ in a linear equation relating a "dependent" variable Y to r "independent" variables, $X_1, \cdots, X_r$.

$$Y = \alpha_0 + \alpha_1 X_1 + \alpha_2 X_2 + \cdots + \alpha_r X_r + \epsilon \tag{16.1}$$

Here, ϵ is a random variable. We have multiple regression if the X's are fixed in advance and multiple correlation if the X's are regarded as random variables. If successive values of ϵ are independent, normally distributed and uncorrelated with successive values of $X_1, \cdots, X_r$, and if the values of $X_1, \cdots, X_r$ are either fixed in advance or have the multivariate normal probability distribution, then the method of maximum likelihood yields the same estimates as the method of least squares. We shall assume that this is true. Specifically, we shall assume that

$$E(Y \mid X_1, \cdots, X_r) = \alpha_0 + \alpha_1 X_1 + \cdots + \alpha_r X_r \tag{16.2}$$

$$\sigma^2(Y \mid X_1, \cdots, X_r) = \sigma_\epsilon^2 = \sigma^2$$

Let $Y_i, X_{1i}, X_{2i}, \cdots, X_{ri}, i = 1, \cdots, n$, be n independent sets of observations on the variables $Y, X_1, X_2, \cdots, X_r$. We want to choose estimates, $\alpha_0, \alpha_1, \cdots, \alpha_r$, of the parameters $\alpha_0, \alpha_1, \cdots, \alpha_r$ in such a way that the sum of squares

$$\theta = \sum_{i=1}^{n} (Y_i - \alpha_0 - \alpha_1 X_{1i} - \cdots - \alpha_r X_{ri})^2 \tag{16.3}$$

is a minimum. We proceed as we did in Chapter 14, differentiating θ with respect to $\alpha_0, \alpha_1, \cdots, \alpha_r$, setting the derivatives equal to zero, and solving the resulting system of equations for the estimates.[1] We obtain, first, the system:

$$\frac{\partial \theta}{\partial \alpha_0} = -2 \sum_{i=1}^{n} (Y_i - \hat{\alpha}_0 - \hat{\alpha}_1 X_{1i} - \cdots - \hat{\alpha}_r X_{ri}) = 0$$

$$\frac{\partial \theta}{\partial \alpha_1} = -2 \sum_{i=1}^{n} X_{1i}(Y_i - \hat{\alpha}_0 - \hat{\alpha}_1 X_{1i} - \cdots - \hat{\alpha}_r X_{ri}) = 0 \tag{16.4}$$

$$\cdots\cdots\cdots\cdots\cdots\cdots\cdots\cdots\cdots\cdots\cdots\cdots\cdots$$

$$\frac{\partial \theta}{\partial \alpha_r} = -2 \sum_{i=1}^{n} X_{ri}(Y_i - \hat{\alpha}_0 - \hat{\alpha}_1 X_{1i} - \cdots - \hat{\alpha}_r X_{ri}) = 0$$

[1] Again this is only a necessary condition.

When we divide out the -2, sum, and rearrange, the result, omitting the subscript i, is

$$\sum Y = \hat{\alpha}_0 n + \hat{\alpha}_1 \sum X_1 + \hat{\alpha}_2 \sum X_2 + \cdots + \hat{\alpha}_r \sum X_r$$

$$\sum X_1 Y = \hat{\alpha}_0 \sum X_1 + \hat{\alpha}_1 \sum X_1^2 + \hat{\alpha}_2 \sum X_1 X_2 + \cdots + \hat{\alpha}_r \sum X_1 X_r$$

$$\sum X_2 Y = \hat{\alpha}_0 \sum X_2 + \hat{\alpha}_1 \sum X_1 X_2 + \hat{\alpha}_2 \sum X_2^2 + \cdots + \hat{\alpha}_r \sum X_2 X_r \quad (16.5)$$

$$\cdots \cdots \cdots \cdots \cdots \cdots \cdots \cdots \cdots \cdots \cdots \cdots \cdots \cdots \cdots$$

$$\sum X_r Y = \hat{\alpha}_0 \sum X_r + \hat{\alpha}_1 \sum X_1 X_r + \hat{\alpha}_2 \sum X_2 X_r + \cdots + \hat{\alpha}_r \sum X_r^2$$

The system (16.5) will be expressed more succinctly if we define the vectors Y^* and $\hat{\alpha}^*$ and the matrix X^* as

$$Y^* = \begin{bmatrix} Y_1 \\ Y_2 \\ \cdots \\ Y_n \end{bmatrix} \qquad \hat{\alpha}^* = \begin{bmatrix} \hat{\alpha}_0 \\ \hat{\alpha}_1 \\ \cdots \\ \hat{\alpha}_r \end{bmatrix}$$

$$X^* = \begin{bmatrix} 1 & X_{11} & X_{21} & \cdots & X_{r1} \\ 1 & X_{12} & X_{22} & \cdots & X_{r2} \\ \cdots & \cdots & \cdots & \cdots & \cdots \\ 1 & X_{1n} & X_{2n} & \cdots & X_{rn} \end{bmatrix}$$

The transpose of a vector or a matrix is indicated by the superscript T.[2] Then (16.5) can be written as

$$X^{*T}Y^* = (X^{*T}X^*)\hat{\alpha}^* \quad (16.6)$$

If one multiplies each side of this equation by $(X^{*T}X^*)^{-1}$ on the left, then

$$\hat{\alpha}^* = (X^{*T}X^*)^{-1}X^{*T}Y^* \quad (16.7)$$

We shall illustrate the application of these results after giving formulas for estimates of σ^2 and of the variance-covariance matrix, $V(\hat{\alpha}_0, \hat{\alpha}_1, \cdots, \hat{\alpha}_r)$. These are

$$\hat{\sigma}^2 = \frac{1}{n - (r + 1)} [\sum Y^2 - \hat{\alpha}_0 \sum Y - \hat{\alpha}_1 \sum X_1 Y - \cdots - \hat{\alpha}_r \sum X_r Y] \quad (16.8)$$

and

$$\hat{V}(\hat{\alpha}_0, \hat{\alpha}_1, \cdots, \hat{\alpha}_r) = \hat{\sigma}^2 (X^{*T}X^*)^{-1} \quad (16.9)$$

Comparison with Chapter 14 will show that (16.7), (16.8), and (16.9), are extensions of the formulas in the earlier chapter. The comparison will be

---

[2] If A is a matrix, A^T may be obtained from A by writing the columns of A as the rows of A^T.

made easier if we write

$$X^{*T}X^* = M = \begin{bmatrix} n & \sum X_1 & \sum X_2 & \cdots & \sum X_r \\ \sum X_1 & \sum X_1^2 & \sum X_1 X_2 & \cdots & \sum X_1 X_r \\ \sum X_2 & \sum X_1 X_2 & \sum X_2^2 & \cdots & \sum X_2 X_r \\ \cdots & \cdots & \cdots & \cdots & \cdots \\ \sum X_r & \sum X_1 X_r & \sum X_2 X_r & \cdots & \sum X_r^2 \end{bmatrix} \quad (16.10)$$

From here on, we shall use M instead of the more complicated symbol $X^{*T}X^*$.

As an example, suppose that we are interested in studying the relationship among personal consumption expenditures Y, disposable personal income X_1, and population X_2. We postulate a linear relationship,

$$Y = \alpha_0 + \alpha_1 X_1 + \alpha_2 X_2 + \epsilon \quad (16.11)$$

where ϵ is a normally distributed random variable. The problem is to estimate the parameters α_0, α_1, and α_2 from whatever data are available. A useful source is *Business Statistics*, a biennial publication of the United States Department of Commerce. From the 1963 edition we obtain the data given in Table 16.1. Since we are not interested in the effects of price changes, we

Table 16.1   Total Personal Consumption Expenditures (Y), Total Disposable Personal Income (X_1) in Billions of 1954 Dollars, and Total United States Population (X_2) in Millions of Persons, 1953 to 1962

Year	Y[a]	X_1[b]	X_2[c]
1953	235	254	160
1954	238	257	163
1955	256	275	166
1956	264	290	169
1957	271	295	172
1958	273	296	175
1959	289	311	178
1960	298	318	181
1961	304	327	184
1962	318	341	187

[a] *Source. Business Statistics, 1963 Biennial Edition*, U.S. Department of Commerce, 1963, p. 6.
[b] Ibid., p. 7, corrected to 1954 dollars.
[c] Ibid., p. 65.

have put the money figures into 1954 dollars. The consumption figures Y are given in 1954 dollars in *Business Statistics*, but the disposable income figures X_1 had first to be adjusted by dividing by the Consumers Price Index with $1954 = 100$. Next, we must compute sums and sums of squares and cross products. With these, we can determine the matrix M and its inverse. This work is shown in Table 16.2. Finally, (16.7), (16.8), and (16.9) are applied

Table 16.2   Computation of Parameter Estimates from Data in Table 16.1

$$\sum Y = 2746 \qquad \sum X_1 = 2964 \qquad \sum X_2 = 1735$$

$$\sum Y^2 = 760936 \qquad \sum X_1 Y = 821058 \qquad \sum X_2 Y = 478675$$

$$\sum X_1^2 = 885986 \qquad \sum X_1 X_2 = 516582 \qquad \sum X_2^2 = 301765$$

$$M = \begin{bmatrix} 10 & 2964 & 1735 \\ 2964 & 885986 & 516582 \\ 1735 & 516582 & 301765 \end{bmatrix}$$

$$M^{-1} = \begin{bmatrix} 430.33620676 & 1.57398988 & -5.16868477 \\ 1.57398988 & 0.00635740 & -0.01993270 \\ -5.16868477 & -0.01993270 & 0.06384287 \end{bmatrix}$$

$$\begin{bmatrix} \hat{\alpha}_0 \\ \hat{\alpha}_1 \\ \hat{\alpha}_2 \end{bmatrix} = M^{-1} \begin{bmatrix} 2746 \\ 821058 \\ 478675 \end{bmatrix} = \begin{bmatrix} -80.2305 \\ 0.6852 \\ 0.8746 \end{bmatrix}$$

$$\hat{\sigma}^2 = \frac{1}{10-3} [\sum Y^2 - \hat{\alpha}_0 \sum Y - \hat{\alpha}_1 \sum X_1 Y - \hat{\alpha}_2 \sum X_2 Y] = 3.8839$$

$$\hat{V} = \hat{\sigma}^2 \cdot M^{-1} = \begin{bmatrix} 1671.3828 & 6.1133 & -20.0747 \\ 6.1133 & 0.0249 & -0.0773 \\ -20.0747 & -0.0773 & 0.2478 \end{bmatrix}$$

to obtain estimates of the parameters of (16.11) and their variances and covariances. Our estimate is

$$Y = -80.2305 + 0.6852 X_1 + 0.8746 X_2 + \epsilon$$

Before discussing the sampling variances of the parameter estimates, let us consider their economic meaning. The constant term, $\hat{\alpha}_0 = -80.2305$, is meaningless. It implies that if disposable income and population were both zero, consumption expenditures would be negative. Zero values of disposable income and population were not observed, and in the conclusion to Chapter 14 we indicated the dangers of extrapolating beyond observed ranges of independent variables. The estimate $\hat{\alpha}_1 = 0.6852$ means that, population remaining constant, we would expect a change of a billion dollars in disposable income to be accompanied by a change in the same direction of about \$0.685 billion in consumption expenditures, both measured in 1954 dollars. This, of course, is an estimate of the marginal propensity to consume. Since the function (16.11) is linear, we would conclude that, population remaining constant, about 69 percent of additional increments of income will be consumed with about 31 percent being saved. The parameter estimate $\hat{\alpha}_2 = 0.8746$ means that, disposable income remaining constant, a change of one million in population will produce, on the average, a change in the same direction of about \$0.875 billion in consumption expenditures.

The estimated sampling variances of the parameter estimates are given by the entries in Table 16.2 on the main diagonal of $\hat{V}$. Taking square roots, we have

$$\hat{\sigma}(\hat{\alpha}_0) = \sqrt{1671.3828} = 40.8826$$

$$\hat{\sigma}(\hat{\alpha}_1) = \sqrt{0.0249} = 0.1578$$

$$\hat{\sigma}(\hat{\alpha}_2) = \sqrt{0.2478} = 0.4979$$

To see whether the parameter estimates differ significantly from zero, we perform a t test, as in Chapter 14. We should give some thought to the economic meaning of the parameters, however, before formulating null hypotheses and their alternatives. Since α_0 is economically meaningless, we cannot formulate meaningful hypotheses concerning it. We really do not care whether its sample estimate differs significantly from zero. On the other hand, we would expect increases in either disposable income or population to be accompanied by an increase in consumption. Hence, if the result is to have economic meaning, $\hat{\alpha}_1$ and $\hat{\alpha}_2$ should both be significantly greater than zero. Since we like to show meaningful results by the rejection of the null hypothesis, we shall test $H_0^{(1)}: \alpha_1 \leq 0$ against $H_1^{(1)}: \alpha_1 > 0$ and $H_0^{(2)}: \alpha_2 \leq 0$ against $H_1^{(2)}: \alpha_2 > 0$. Arbitrarily, we shall set the risk of Type I error at 0.05. For $\hat{\alpha}_1$,

$$t = \frac{0.6852}{0.1578} = 4.34$$

and, for $\hat{\alpha}_2$,

$$t = \frac{0.8746}{0.4979} = 1.76$$

We have 7 degrees of freedom in both cases. The critical value of t is 1.895 Hence, only $\hat{\alpha}_1$ is significantly greater than zero.

Before concluding that population has no effect on consumption, however, we should remember the possibility of a Type II error. Moreover, during the period 1953 to 1962 both population and disposable income were increasing. Hence, the two "independent" variables in (16.11) are correlated.[3] We shall see later that correlation among the independent variables in a linear regression equation tends to increase the estimated sampling variance of the parameter estimates.

To summarize the results, we write them as an econometrician might, using more suggestive symbols and showing estimated standard errors in parentheses below the parameter estimates. We use the symbol C for consumption expenditures, Y_D for disposable income, and P for population.

$$C = -80.23 + 0.6852 Y_D + 0.8746P + \epsilon$$
$$\quad\;\;(40.88)\quad\;(0.1578)\quad\;(0.4979)$$

Because $\hat{\alpha}_2$ turned out not to be significantly greater than zero, we might consider a regression equation of the form:

$$C = \beta_0 + \beta_1 Y_D + U$$

where U is a random variable with zero mean and with successive values independent. U is also uncorrelated with Y_D. The preliminary calculations have already been made in Table 16.2. We must solve the system:

$$\begin{bmatrix} 2746 \\ 821058 \end{bmatrix} = \begin{bmatrix} 10 & 2964 \\ 2964 & 885986 \end{bmatrix} \begin{bmatrix} \hat{\beta}_0 \\ \hat{\beta}_1 \end{bmatrix}$$

From this, we compute

$$M^{-1} = \begin{bmatrix} 10 & 2964 \\ 2964 & 885986 \end{bmatrix}^{-1} = \begin{bmatrix} 11.88222199 & -0.03975109 \\ -0.03975109 & 0.00013411 \end{bmatrix}$$

Hence

$$\begin{bmatrix} \hat{\beta}_0 \\ \hat{\beta}_1 \end{bmatrix} = M^{-1} \begin{bmatrix} 2746 \\ 821058 \end{bmatrix} = \begin{bmatrix} -9.3659 \\ 0.9580 \end{bmatrix}$$

Further

$$\hat{\sigma}_U{}^2 = \frac{1}{10-2} [760936 + 9.3659(2746) - 0.9580(821058)]$$

$$= 10.1497$$

so that

$$\hat{V} = \hat{\sigma}_U{}^2 \cdot M^{-1} = \begin{bmatrix} 120.6008 & -0.4035 \\ -0.4035 & 0.0014 \end{bmatrix}$$

---

[3] Calculations from Table 16.2 show that the coefficient of correlation is $r = 0.9894$.

Taking square roots of the elements on the main diagonal of $\hat{V}$,

$$\hat{\sigma}(\hat{\beta}_0) = 10.9818$$
$$\hat{\sigma}(\hat{\beta}_1) = 0.0374$$

As in the original regression equation, the constant term, β_0, makes little economic sense. $\hat{\beta}_1$ is more than 25 times its own standard error. The appropriate null hypothesis is $H_0:\beta_1 \leq 0$, which is tested against the alternative $H_1:\beta_1 > 0$. With 8 degrees of freedom and a 5 percent risk of Type I error, the critical value of t is 1.860; thus, $\hat{\beta}_1$ is significantly greater than zero. Actually, $\hat{\beta}_1$ is probably much too large, since it implies that about 96 percent of additional increments of income are consumed. The earlier figure of about 69 percent is much more reasonable. Nonetheless, we summarize the result with

$$C = -9.3659 + 0.9580 Y_D + U$$
$$(10.98) \qquad (0.0374)$$

16.3   ECONOMETRIC PROBLEMS ARISING FROM THE MATHEMATICAL MODEL

In elementary courses, the functional relationships of economics, such as supply and demand curves, cost curves, and the consumption function, are usually drawn as smooth curves. Economists, however, are seldom so bold as to write equations for these curves. If we were to plot observed cost, for instance, as a function of observed output for a particular firm in each of several years, we would find that the plotted points do not lie along a smooth curve. With luck, they might be closely scattered about a curve, but we could not specify even the general form of its equation. In fact, there might be many different functions which fit the data equally well. This apparent discrepancy between observation and theory does not seem to disturb most economists. Economic relationships change over time, and measurements of economic variables are notoriously inexact. We can expect nothing better than a scatter of points about some smooth curve. It is left to the econometrician to specify the equation describing the economic relationship and to take account of errors in measurement and of other sources of variation in the data. In doing so, he faces statistical problems in addition to the difficulties of economic theory.

Consider, first, the problem of specifying an economic relationship. Suppose, for example, that we want to study the demand for a certain product. To simplify the problem, suppose that the product is homogeneous and is sold in one competitive market so that there is only one price prevailing at any one time. What variables do we include? We are studying demand, so we would like to make demand the dependent variable. Yet, we cannot observe demand; we can observe only the quantity sold. We can also observe the price at which a given quantity is sold. The demand curves in elementary textbooks are usually negatively sloping, smooth curves, which express quantity as a function of price. The quantity associated with a given price is the quantity that would be sold if it were made available at that price. A market in action, however, contains not only buyers—or would-be buyers— who determine demand, but also sellers—or would-be sellers—who determine supply. The supply curve is usually drawn as a positively sloping, smooth curve expressing quantity as a function of price. Here, the quantity associated with a given price is the quantity that would be offered on the market if that price prevailed. The actual price and quantity sold are determined by the intersection of the demand and supply curves; hence, price and quantity lie on two curves simultaneously. If these points appear to be closely scattered about a smooth curve, is the curve a demand curve, a supply curve, or a composite? What, if anything, can we do to isolate the demand curve?

Before even specifying all of the variables to be included in the demand relationship and its functional form, we have met one of the really difficult problems of econometrics. It is called the problem of *identification* because we must somehow identify a relationship perceived in the data as the one in which we are interested.

Three possible situations are illustrated with exaggerated simplicity in Figures 16.1. In Figure 16.1a, the demand curve remains fixed and the supply curve shifts so that the observations lie along the fixed demand curve. The reverse is true in Figure 16.1b; the observations lie along the fixed supply curve. In Figure 16.1c, both curves shift about while the observations are made, and the curve traced out is neither a demand nor a supply curve. In the "real world" of econometrics, of course, things are not as simple as in Figure 16.1. Both demand and supply curves shift over time. If the demand curve is relatively more stable than the supply curve, then the observations tend to be scattered about the demand curve, and we have a means of identifying the relationship perceived in the data as an approximation to the demand curve. This is probably the simplest solution to the identification problem, and it was solved in this way in early econometric studies of the demand for agricultural products, where it is safe to assume that supply is more variable than demand.

We can obtain other clues to the solution of the identification problem by considering a simple mathematical model of the market. Let

$$D_t = \text{Quantity demanded at time } t$$
$$S_t = \text{Quantity supplied at time } t$$
$$P_t = \text{Market price at time } t$$

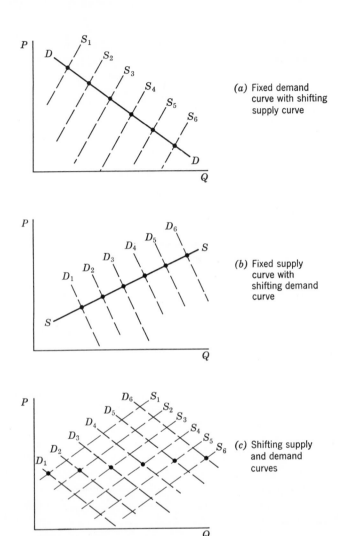

Fig. 16.1. Three possible situations in the identification of a demand relationship. (a) Fixed demand curve with shifting supply curve. (b) Fixed supply curve with shifting demand curve. (c) Shifting supply and demand curves.

We shall assume that both the supply and demand curves are linear and shall allow for random shifts in the curves by introducing random "disturbance" terms, u_t, v_t, and w_t, into the equations. Our model is

$$\text{Model I} \begin{cases} D_t = \alpha + \beta P_t + u_t \\ S_t = \gamma + \delta P_t + v_t \\ D_t = S_t + w_t \end{cases}$$

The last equation says that, except for random disturbances, supply and demand are equal. By substitution of the third equation into the second,

$$D_t = \gamma + \delta P_t + (v_t + w_t)$$

When we compare this with the first equation in Model I, we see that they are statistically indistinguishable. The same variables are involved, and the two equations are of the same form. In fact, if we multiply the first equation by a constant, C_1, and the derived equation by another constant, C_2, add, and rearrange:

$$D_t = \frac{C_1\alpha + C_2\gamma}{C_1 + C_2} + \frac{C_1\beta + C_2\delta}{C_1 + C_2} P_t + \frac{C_1 u_t + C_2(v_t + w_t)}{C_1 + C_2}$$

which is an equation of precisely the same form. If we determine the constants in the regression equation which relates quantity and price, have we estimated α and β, γ and δ, or the "mongrel" coefficients in the linear combination of the derived equation and the demand equation? Statistically, we have no way of knowing.

Here, we have one clue to the solution of the problem of identification. The problem arises because the variables in the relationship with which we are concerned also occur in other economic relationships. Any mathematical model of the mechanism generating the observations must, therefore, consist of more than one equation. If all equations are linear, as they are in this simple model, then we shall be unable to identify a particular equation in the system if it is possible to obtain an equation involving the same variables by taking linear combinations of other equations in the system. If it is not possible to do this, then we can identify our economic relationship. Hence, we can achieve identification by the manner in which we construct the mathematical model. One way to do this is to introduce variables into the other equations in the system which are not in the equation in which we are interested. However, these variables must make economic sense; they cannot be arbitrarily chosen.

It is useful to think of the variables in an economic relationship as being of two types: those generated by the mechanism under study and those generated outside of this mechanism. In our simple model both price and quantity were determined simultaneously by the market. Such variables are called *endogenous*, and a mathematical model of an economic mechanism should contain at least as many equations as there are endogenous variables. Variables generated outside of the mechanism but influencing the endogenous variables are called *exogenous*. The supply of an agricultural commodity is partially determined by weather conditions during the growing season, for example. Such variables as rainfall and temperature are not determined by the market; they are clearly exogenous. The supply of an agricultural commodity may also be influenced by its price in the previous year. Because this price is not influenced by the operation of the market in the current year, it is exogenous. In general, endogenous variables are determined by both exogenous and other endogenous variables, whereas exogenous variables partially determine endogenous variables but are not, in turn, influenced by them.

The distinction between endogenous and exogenous variables, unfortunately, is not always clear. The demand for a consumer product, for example, is partially determined by consumer incomes and the prices of competing products. Consumer incomes are partially determined by the prices of all products, including the product in question, and the price of this product influences the prices of others. Hence, strictly speaking, consumer incomes and the prices of other products are endogenous variables in a complete model of the market. Yet, the market for this product may have a negligible influence on consumer incomes and other prices. In this case, these variables could safely be treated as exogenous.

Since exogenous variables do not have to be "explained" by the model, they can be used to identify an econometric relationship without the necessity of adding equations to the model. In the extreme case, we would have one endogenous variable and one or more exogenous variables. The model would consist of one completely identified equation with the endogenous variable acting as dependent variable and the exogenous variables as independent variables. Usually, however, the model will contain more than one endogenous variable and several exogenous variables. There will be an equation for each endogenous variable, and identification of the individual equations will be achieved by the inclusion and exclusion of certain variables.

As a simple example, let us change Model I so as to identify both the supply and demand equations. Suppose that demand, D_t, is a function only of current price, P_t, while supply depends only on the price in the previous period P_{t-1}. This means that, except for random disturbances, the quantity brought to market is determined in advance, and the market mechanism determines only the price at which the market will be cleared. In the original formulation, Model I, we made the quantity demanded, D_t, dependent on current price. Model II (below), reverses this dependence. Ignoring random disturbances and indicating dependence by arrows, Model II implies:

$$P_{t-1} \rightarrow S_t = D_t \rightarrow P_t$$

Introducing random disturbances, we write Model II as

$$\text{Model II} \begin{cases} P_t = \alpha' + \beta' D_t + v_t' \\ S_t = \gamma' + \delta' P_{t-1} + U_t' \\ D_t = S_t + w_t' \end{cases}$$

We have marked the coefficients and the random disturbances with a prime to indicate that they are not the same as those in Model I. By rearranging slightly, we can reduce our model to two equations. First,

$$D_t = -\frac{\alpha'}{\beta'} + \frac{P_t}{\beta'} - \frac{v_t'}{\beta'}$$

or, introducing new symbols whose definitions are obvious,

$$D_t = \alpha'' + \beta'' P_t + v_t''$$

Second, the supply equation can be combined with the equation requiring that the market be cleared to give

$$D_t = \gamma' + \delta' P_{t-1} + U_t' + w_t'$$

Since there is a different independent variable in each of these equations both are identified. The model contains one exogenous variable, P_{t-1}, and two endogenous variables, D_t and P_t.

The definition of endogenous variables implies that their values are determined simultaneously by the economic mechanism under study. When two or more endogenous variables appear in one equation, none of them can be uniquely specified as *the* dependent variable. This means that "ordinary" least squares, the method illustrated in Section 16.2, cannot be used to estimate the parameters in a linear equation containing one or more "independent" endogenous variables. This is a statistical problem, however, and we shall discuss it briefly in Section 16.5.

We have yet to specify the mathematical form of our economic relationship. Since economic theory usually does little more than suggest the variables to be included and the signs of partial derivatives, such practical considerations as the data available and the ease with which parameters can be estimated often determine the form of the equation. The parameters of linear equations are easiest to estimate by least squares. Therefore, the econometrician, when he can, specifies an equation that is linear or that can be made linear by suitable transformations such as those shown in Table 16.3.

Table 16.3 Several Common Transformations in Econometrics

Original Equation	Transformation	Linearized Equation
$Y_i = \alpha + \beta\left[\dfrac{1}{X_i}\right] + U_i$	$Z_i = \dfrac{1}{X_i}$	$Y_i = \alpha + \beta Z_i + U_i$
$Y_i = \alpha e^{\beta X_i} U_i$	$W_i = \log_e Y_i$	$W_i = A + \beta X_i + v_i$
	$A = \log_e \alpha$	
	$v_i = \log_e U_i$	
$Y_i = \alpha X_i^{\beta} U_i$	$W_i = \log_e Y_i$	$W_i = A + \beta Z_i + v_i$
	$Z_i = \log_e X_i$	
	$v_i = \log_e U_i$	
	$A = \log_e \alpha$	

Notice that in the second and third equations, we have assumed that the original error term, U_i, is multiplicative so that a logarithmic transformation makes the transformed error term, v_i, additive. The probability distribution of the transformed error term will not be the same as that of the original error term, and our method of parameter estimation in the transformed equation will depend on what is assumed about the distribution of v_i. Usually, the application of the method of least squares to the transformed equation will not yield the same estimates as would be obtained if it were applied to the original equations.

In Appendix B it is shown that, under certain conditions, a function, $y = f(x)$, can be represented by a MacLaurin series,

$$y = f(0) + xf^{(1)}(0) + \frac{x^2}{2!}f^{(2)}(0) + \cdots + \frac{x^n}{n!}f^{(n)}(0) + \cdots$$

where $f^{(n)}(0)$ denotes the nth derivative of $f(x)$ evaluated at $x = 0$. This suggests that a complicated economic relationship between two variables, x and y, might be approximated by a polynomial of finite degree plus an error term:

$$y_i = \alpha_0 + \alpha_1 x_i + \alpha_2 x_i^2 + \cdots + \alpha_n x_i^n + U_i$$

To do so implies that we regard derivatives of order higher than the nth as negligible when evaluated at $x = 0$; their total effect is contained in the error term, U_i. This approximation can be linearized by defining $z_{ni} = x_i^n$. Then

$$y_i = \alpha_0 + \alpha_1 z_{1i} + \alpha_2 z_{2i} + \cdots + \alpha_n z_{ni} + U_i$$

We must warn against going to extremes, however. If we have $n + 1$ pairs of observations (x_i, y_i), $i = 1, \cdots, n + 1$, then the method of least squares will determine the values of $\alpha_0, \cdots, \alpha_n$ in such a way that U_i is identically zero for every i. The measure of variance will be zero, but we shall have no degrees of freedom in the measure either, since we have used them all up in the parameters. The variances of the parameter estimates will be of the form $0/0$ which is indeterminate. We want the function to fit the data well; at the same time, we want the function to be simple. In practice, in econometrics, polynomial approximations seldom involve higher powers of x than the second or third.

Finally, the form of the equation may be partially dictated by what is assumed about the probability distribution of U_i and about the degree of interdependence among successive values of the U_i. This is a statistical problem, however, and we shall take it up in the next section.

There is one final problem in econometric model formulation known as the problem of *aggregation*. Economic theory often begins with the behavior of the individual consumer or the individual firm and builds by addition or aggregation. Total demand is the sum of individual demands. Total cost in an industry is the sum of the total costs of the firms in the industry. Since the econometrician often can observe only aggregates, he must be aware that the sum of functions of a given form need not be a function of the same form.

Suppose, for example, that we want to study the relationship between total cost in an industry, y, and total output, x. Let y_{it} be the total cost of the ith firm in the tth time period, and let x_{it} be the corresponding output. If the cost functions for the individual firms are linear, with the same parameters for all firms,

$$y_{it} = \alpha + \beta x_{it} + U_{it} \qquad i = 1, \cdots, n \qquad t = 1, \cdots, T$$

then aggregation over firms produces a function of the same form:

$$\sum_{i=1}^{n} y_{it} = n\alpha + \beta \sum_{i=1}^{n} x_{it} + \sum_{i=1}^{n} U_{it}$$

If we let

$$y_t = \sum_{i=1}^{n} y_{it} \qquad \text{and} \qquad x_t = \sum_{i=1}^{n} x_{it}$$

be total industry cost in the tth time period, and the corresponding total output, then

$$y_t = n\alpha + \beta x_t + U_t$$

where

$$U_t = \sum_{i=1}^{n} U_{it}$$

The aggregate cost function is of the same form as the individual cost functions. If the individual cost functions are quadratic, however,

$$y_{it} = \alpha + \beta x_{it} + \gamma x_{it}^2 + U_{it}$$

we run into difficulty when we aggregate. Summing and using the definitions of the aggregates gives

$$y_t = n\alpha + \beta x_t + \gamma \sum_{i=1}^{n} x_{it}^2 + U_t$$

The variance of the individual outputs is

$$\sigma_t^2(x) = \frac{1}{n} \sum_{i=1}^{n} x_{it}^2 - \left(\frac{x_t}{n}\right)^2$$

so we can write

$$\sum_{i=1}^{n} x_{it}^2 = n\sigma_t^2(x) + \frac{x_t^2}{n}$$

Our aggregate cost function now becomes

$$y_t = n\alpha + \beta x_t + \frac{1}{n} \gamma x_t^2 + n\gamma\sigma_t^2(x) + U_t$$

which is not of the same form as the individual cost functions. The aggregate cost function depends on both total output and the variance of the individual outputs. In general, the aggregation of individual linear functions produces no difficulty, provided that the coefficients are the same in all functions; the sum of the functions is the function of the sums. When we aggregate non-linear functions, however, this is no longer true.

In this section we have sketched three of the problems of model formulation in econometrics: the problems of specification, identification, and aggregation. The problem of specification has to do with specifying both the variables that appear in an econometric relationship and its functional form. When the econometric relationship of interest is but a single relationship in a larger model which describes the simultaneous determination of more than one economic variable, we must be able to identify a relationship perceived among specified variables as the one in which we are interested. This is the problem of identification. Finally, if we begin our theoretical analysis with a function describing the behavior of individual economic entities and add these to obtain a function describing the behavior of the group, it is only in very special circumstances that the sum of the functions in the individual variables is a function of the same form in the sums (aggregates) of the individual variables. Aggregation may require descriptive measures, such as the variance or geometric mean of the individual variables, which are not ordinarily available to the econometrician.

16.4   STATISTICAL PROBLEMS RELATED TO DISTURBANCE TERMS

As we have suggested, the econometrician is often forced to work with models in which the assumptions of ordinary regression and correlation are not met. His observations are subject to error. The "random" disturbance term, which he includes in the model to account for variation not otherwise explained, may not be completely random and may be correlated with the "independent" variables. The independent variables may themselves be highly interrelated and may also be the "dependent" variables in other equations in the model. In these situations, the assumptions of ordinary regression and correlation are not met, so that the econometrician must modify his model, his methods of parameter estimation, or both.

Let us consider, first, the random disturbance term, which is included in most econometric models. It is there for the very practical reason that the relationships between observed values of economic variables are not in the form of simple continuous functions, and these irregularities must be accounted for in the model. The econometrician usually "explains" the disturbance term in one or more of the following ways.

First, the disturbance term may be truly random. Economic data are generated by the activities of human beings, who individually are notoriously unpredictable in their behavior. Econometric models are models of relationships among averages or totals. Random deviations from these relationships are to be expected and are, in fact, the reason why statistical techniques must be used in econometrics. If the disturbance term is truly random—that is, if the values of U are independent of one another and of the independent variables—then the methods of Chapter 14 and their extensions apply.

Second, we have already mentioned the problem of specification. Econometric models are sometimes regarded as simple approximations to more complicated relationships. The actual functional form may be different from the model, and variables may be omitted. The disturbance term may not be random in the usual sense. It may be correlated with some of the independent variables, and its successive values may be correlated with one another. Suppose, for example, that we are interested in the relationship between annual family income, Y, and annual family expenditures for food, F, and that our model takes the form

$$F_i = \alpha + \beta Y_i + U_i \qquad i = 1, \cdots, n$$

where we have observed the income and food expenditures of a sample of n families. In addition to being dependent on income, family food expenditures depend on family size. Typically, the income of the head of the family reaches its maximum some time after the children are grown up and have families of their own. Hence, even within a given socioeconomic group, larger incomes tend to be associated with smaller families and smaller food expenditures. If family size is not held constant, positive values of U will be associated with small incomes and negative values with large incomes. The value of β estimated from the available data will be smaller than the value of β in the equation describing the relationship between food expenditures and income, ignoring the effect of family size. Because of the relationship between family size and family income, values of U_i are correlated (negatively) with values of Y_i. This results in a biased estimate of β. The difficulty can be corrected, of course, by including family size as an independent variable in the model. As we shall see, the correlation between family size and family income will be troublesome. This situation is common in econometrics; the cure for one ailment brings on another and, sometimes, worse ailment.

Third, the random disturbance term is included because observations on economic variables are subject to error. As long as only the dependent variable is subject to error, there is no statistical difficulty, but if the independent variables are also, least-squares estimates of the parameters of the model may be biased.

Consider the linear model relating the error-free variables X and Y,

$$\text{Model III:} \qquad Y = \alpha + \beta X + U$$

where U is a random disturbance term, which has been included because of the vagaries of human behavior. If, instead of the error-free variable Y, we observe $y = Y + v$, and if we observe X without error, we can write

$$y - v = \alpha + \beta X + U$$

$$\text{Model IV:} \qquad y = \alpha + \beta X + (U + v)$$

Assume that U and v have means of zero and variances $\sigma_U{}^2$ and $\sigma_v{}^2$, that U and v are uncorrelated with each other and with X and Y, and that successive values of both U and v are independent. If we fit Model III by least squares, using a sample of n observations, our parameter estimates become:

$$\hat{\alpha} = \frac{\sum X^2 \sum Y - \sum X \sum XY}{n \sum X^2 - (\sum X)^2}$$

$$\hat{\beta} = \frac{n \sum XY - \sum X \sum Y}{n \sum X^2 - (\sum X)^2}$$

Only the numerators of these expressions are random variables because X is error-free. When we take expected values, we obtain for the numerator of $\hat{\alpha}$:

$$E[\sum X^2 \sum Y - \sum X \sum XY]$$
$$= \sum X^2 E[\sum (\alpha + \beta X + U)] - \sum XE[\sum X(\alpha + \beta X + U)]$$
$$= n\alpha \sum X^2 + \beta \sum X^2 \sum X + \sum X^2 E(\sum U)$$
$$- \alpha(\sum X)^2 - \beta \sum X \sum X^2 - \sum XE(\sum XU)$$

Since U has mean zero and is uncorrelated with X, the expected values of the terms involving U are both zero, so that

$$E[\sum X^2 \sum Y - \sum X \sum XY] = \alpha[n \sum X^2 - (\sum X)^2]$$

The coefficient of α in this expression is the same as the denominator of $\hat{\alpha}$. Hence

$$E(\hat{\alpha}) = \alpha$$

By a similar argument, we can show that

$$E(\hat{\beta}) = \beta$$

If Model III applies, $\hat{\alpha}$ and $\hat{\beta}$ are unbiased. If Model IV applies, the only change will be the substitution of $U + v$ for U in the derivation, so that $\hat{\alpha}$ and $\hat{\beta}$ are unbiased in Model IV also. Any error in Y changes the conditional variance of Y given X. For Model III,

$$\sigma^2(Y \mid X) = \sigma_U{}^2$$

while for Model IV,

$$\sigma^2(y \mid X) = \sigma^2_{u+v} = \sigma_u{}^2 + \sigma_v{}^2$$

because U and v are independent. Since $\sigma^2(\hat{\alpha})$ and $\sigma^2(\hat{\beta})$ are proportional to $\sigma^2(Y \mid X)$ in Model III and to $\sigma^2(y \mid X)$ in Model IV, $\hat{\alpha}$ and $\hat{\beta}$ will have larger sampling variances in Model IV than in Model III.

If X is subject to errors in measurement, estimates of α and β will no longer be unbiased. Suppose that Model III describes the relationship between the error-free variables, X and Y, but that we observe $x = X + w$ instead of X and that values of w are mutually independent. The introduction of error in Y will not change the result, so we shall assume, for simplicity, that Y is error-free. The denominators of the expressions for $\hat{\alpha}$ and $\hat{\beta}$ will contain x instead of X. Assume that w has a mean of zero and a variance $\sigma_w{}^2$ and is uncorrelated with X and U, and define,

$$\sigma_X{}^2 = \frac{1}{n}\left[\sum X^2 - \frac{1}{n}(\sum X)^2\right]$$

Then

$$n \sum X^2 - (\sum X)^2 = n^2 \sigma_X{}^2$$

We can write

$$n \sum x^2 - (\sum x)^2 = n \sum (X + w)^2 - [\sum (X + w)]^2$$
$$= n \sum X^2 + 2n \sum Xw + n \sum w^2 - (\sum X)^2$$
$$- 2 \sum X \sum w - (\sum w)^2$$
$$= n^2 \sigma_X^2 + 2[n \sum Xw - \sum X \sum w] + n \sum w^2 - (\sum w)^2$$

The middle term vanishes because X and w are independent. When we take expected values,

$$E[n \sum x^2 - (\sum x)^2] = n^2 \sigma_X^2 + n(n - 1)\sigma_w^2$$

again because X and w are independent and

$$E(\sum w^2) = n\sigma_w^2 = E[(\sum w)^2]$$

When values of w are mutually independent, the expression for $E(\hat{\alpha})$ is somewhat complicated. For $\hat{\beta}$,

$$\hat{\beta} = \frac{n \sum xY - \sum x \sum Y}{n \sum x^2 - (\sum x)^2}$$

When n is large, both numerator and denominator will be approximately equal to their expected values. We have already derived the expected value of the denominator. For the numerator,

$$E(\sum xY) = E[\sum (X + w)(\alpha + \beta X + U)]$$
$$= \alpha \sum X + \beta \sum X^2 + E(\sum UX)$$
$$+ \alpha E(\sum w) + \beta E(\sum Xw) + E(\sum Uw)$$
$$= \alpha \sum X + \beta \sum X^2$$
$$E[\sum x \sum Y] = E[\sum (X + w) \sum (\alpha + \beta X + U)]$$
$$= n\alpha \sum X + \beta(\sum X)^2 + \sum XE(\sum U) + n\alpha E(\sum w)$$
$$+ \beta \sum XE(\sum w) + E[(\sum U)(\sum w)]$$
$$= n\alpha \sum X + \beta(\sum X)^2$$

Hence

$$E[n \sum x Y - \sum x \sum Y] = \beta[n \sum X^2 - (\sum X)^2] = \beta n^2 \sigma_X^2$$

so that, for large n,

$$E(\hat{\beta}) = \frac{\beta n^2 \sigma_X^2}{n^2 \sigma_X^2 + n(n - 1)\sigma_w^2} = \frac{\beta}{1 + \dfrac{n - 1}{n} \dfrac{\sigma_w^2}{\sigma_X^2}}$$

On the average, $\hat{\beta}$ will tend to understate β. This bias increases as n increases because $(n-1)\sigma_w^2/n\sigma_X^2$ approaches σ_w^2/σ_X^2 from below as n increases. Also, the larger the relative error in measurements of X the greater is the expected degree of understatement in estimating β. If the ratio σ_w^2/σ_X^2 is known, an unbiased estimate of β can be obtained quite simply. It is

$$\tilde{\beta} = \left(1 + \frac{n-1}{n}\frac{\sigma_w^2}{\sigma_X^2}\right)\hat{\beta}$$

However, this ratio is seldom known even approximately.

In econometrics, as in any discipline, we must keep the purpose of the study firmly in mind. If the purpose is to obtain unbiased estimates of the "true" relationship between the error-free variables, X and Y, then the errors in the observed variables will give trouble unless we are willing to make stringent assumptions about the errors of measurement and their variances. If, however, the purpose is to predict the observed value of $y = Y + v$ from the observed value of $x = X + w$ using a linear regression equation, then the linear regression of y on x will give an unbiased prediction, and ordinary least squares will be the appropriate procedure. Similarly, if the disturbance term has been included because the postulated linear relationship between the variables is regarded as an approximation to the "true" relationship, then ordinary least-squares regression will give unbiased predictions of the dependent variable provided that there is no extrapolation. We must distinguish between the problem of prediction and the problem of estimating an underlying functional relationship. In one case, we want to minimize the error in predicting the dependent variable; in the other, we want to minimize the error in estimating the parameters of the model.

Throughout the discussion we have emphasized the assumption that successive values of the disturbance term are uncorrelated. When the observations are in the form of time series, this may not be true. If we denote the time of the observation by a subscript, t, and our model is of the form:

$$Y_t = \alpha + \beta X_t + U_t \qquad t = 1, \cdots, T$$

then U_t may be correlated with U_{t-1} and, in general, with U_{t-k}. When this is true, we say that we have "autocorrelation" or "serial correlation." In the presence of autocorrelation, least-squares estimates of α and β will be unbiased but will have larger variances than if there were no autocorrelation. These variances can be reduced, however, if we are willing to make assumptions concerning the nature of the autocorrelation. In addition, the application of ordinary least squares in the presence of autocorrelation can produce a serious understatement of the variance of Y_t about the regression line. This means that estimates of the variances of $\hat{\alpha}$ and $\hat{\beta}$ will tend to be smaller than these variances actually are.

As we have suggested, if we are willing to make assumptions about the nature of the autocorrelation, we can do something about the problem. Suppose, for example, that we assume that

$$U_t = \lambda U_{t-1} + \epsilon_t$$

where successive values of the random variable ϵ_t are independent and normally distributed with mean zero and variance σ^2. This implies that a proportion, λ, of the disturbance in period $t - 1$ is carried over to period t, and a new disturbance, ϵ_t, is added. In order to have the effect of a disturbance "die out" in the long run, we must assume that the absolute value of λ is less than unity. In the long run, the correlation between U_t and U_{t-1} tends to λ.

Assume that we know the value of λ. Then

$$Y_t - \lambda Y_{t-1} = \alpha + \beta X_t + U_t - \lambda \alpha - \lambda \beta X_{t-1} - \lambda U_{t-1}$$
$$= \alpha + \beta X_t + \lambda U_{t-1} + \epsilon_t - \lambda \alpha - \lambda \beta X_{t-1} - \lambda U_{t-1}$$
$$= \alpha(1 - \lambda) + \beta(X_t - \lambda X_{t-1}) + \epsilon_t$$

Because of our assumptions about ϵ_t, the assumptions of Chapter 14 apply to the linear regression relating the variables $Z_t = Y_t - \lambda Y_{t-1}$ and $w_t = X_t - \lambda X_{t-1}$. If we know λ, we can obtain unbiased estimates of α and β. We can derive estimates of their variances from the fact that β is the same in both the relationship between X_t and Y_t and that between w_t and Z_t, and

$$\sigma^2(\hat{\alpha}) = \frac{\sigma^2[\hat{\alpha}(1-\lambda)]}{(1 - \lambda)^2}$$

Under most circumstances, we do not know the value of λ, but we can estimate it in the following way. We begin by fitting an equation of the form

$$Y_t = \alpha + \beta X_t + U_t$$

by the usual least-squares procedure. Next we estimate U_t by

$$\hat{U}_t = Y_t - \hat{\alpha}^{(1)} - \hat{\beta}^{(1)} X_t$$

where the superscript (1) implies that $\hat{\alpha}^{(1)}$ and $\hat{\beta}^{(1)}$ are initial estimates of α and β. Then, applying least squares to the model, $U_t = \lambda U_{t-1} + \epsilon_t$, we obtain as an estimate of λ,

$$\hat{\lambda} = \frac{\displaystyle\sum_{t=2}^{T} \hat{U}_t \hat{U}_{t-1}}{\displaystyle\sum_{t=2}^{T} \hat{U}_{t-1}^2}$$

Finally, we can estimate the regression coefficients in

$$Z_t = \alpha(1 - \lambda) + \beta w_t + \epsilon_t \qquad t = 2, \cdots, T$$

We shall illustrate this procedure with the example of the regression of consumption on disposable income presented earlier. We have already computed initial estimates of α and β obtaining the regression equation,

$$C_t = -9.3659 + 0.9580 Y_{D_t} + U_t$$

Table 16.4   Calculation of $\hat{U}_t$ and $\hat{\lambda}$

Year t	Actual C_t	Computed $\hat{C}_t$	$\hat{U}_t = C_t - \hat{C}_t$
1953	235	233.98	1.02
1954	238	236.85	1.15
1955	256	254.10	1.90
1956	264	268.47	−4.47
1957	271	273.26	−2.26
1958	273	274.22	−1.22
1959	289	288.59	0.41
1960	298	295.29	2.71
1961	304	303.92	0.08
1962	318	317.33	0.67

$$\sum_{t=1954}^{1963} \hat{U}_t \hat{U}_{t-1} = 8.6057; \quad \sum_{t=1954}^{1963} \hat{U}_{t-1}^2 = 40.0684;$$

$$\hat{\lambda} = 0.2148$$

We can use this equation to estimate U_t. The calculation of $\hat{U}_t$ and $\hat{\lambda}$ is shown in Table 16.4. The next step is to compute values of Z_t and w_t and the estimated parameters in the regression equation which relates them. Finally, we compute $\sigma^2[\hat{\alpha}(1 - \hat{\lambda})]$ and $\sigma^2(\hat{\beta})$ and adjust $\sigma^2[\hat{\alpha}(1 - \hat{\lambda})]$ to $\sigma^2(\hat{\alpha})$. These steps are illustrated in Tables 16.5 and 16.6. The final result is

$$C_t = -12.3045 + 0.9674 Y_{D_t} + U_t$$
$$(9.0067) \qquad (0.0300)$$

The earlier estimate of this relationship was

$$C_t = -9.366 + 0.958 Y_{D_t} + U_t$$
$$(10.98) \qquad (0.0374)$$

Table 16.5 Values of Z_t and w_t

Year t	$Z_t = C_t - \hat{\lambda} C_{t-1}$	$w_t = Y_{D_t} - \hat{\lambda} Y_{D_{t-1}}$
1954	187.5	202.4
1955	204.9	219.8
1956	209.0	230.9
1957	214.3	232.7
1958	214.8	232.6
1959	230.4	247.4
1960	235.9	251.2
1961	240.0	258.7
1962	252.7	270.8

$$\Sigma Z = 1989.5; \quad \Sigma w = 2146.5$$

$$\Sigma Z^2 = 443075.05 \quad \Sigma Z w = 477853.41$$

$$\Sigma w^2 = 515411.19$$

Table 16.6 Calculation of Estimated Parameters and Sampling Variances

$$M = \begin{bmatrix} 9.00 & 2146.50 \\ 2146.50 & 515411.19 \end{bmatrix}$$

$$M^{-1} = \begin{bmatrix} 16.49925093 & -0.06871337 \\ -0.06871337 & 0.00028811 \end{bmatrix}$$

$$\begin{bmatrix} \hat{\alpha}(1 - \hat{\lambda}) \\ \hat{\beta} \end{bmatrix} = M^{-1} \begin{bmatrix} 1989.50 \\ 477853.41 \end{bmatrix} = \begin{bmatrix} -9.6615 \\ 0.9674 \end{bmatrix}$$

$$\hat{\sigma}_\epsilon^2 = \frac{1}{9 - 2} [443075.05 + 9.6615(1989.50) - 0.9674(477853.41)] = 3.0308$$

$$\hat{V} = \hat{\sigma}_\epsilon^2 M^{-1} = \begin{bmatrix} 50.0061 & -0.2083 \\ -0.2083 & 0.0009 \end{bmatrix}$$

$$\hat{\sigma}^2(\hat{\alpha}) = \frac{50.0061}{[1 - 0.2148]^2} = 81.1129$$

$$\hat{\sigma}(\hat{\alpha}) = \sqrt{81.1129} = 9.0067; \quad \hat{\sigma}(\hat{\beta}) = \sqrt{0.0009} = 0.0300$$

$$\hat{\alpha} = -\frac{9.6615}{1 - 0.2148} = -12.3045$$

The two estimates are strikingly similar and, in fact, the estimated standard errors of the parameter estimates are slightly smaller when the possibility of autocorrelation is taken into account than when it is not.[4] This result suggests that there is no autocorrelation.

16.5 OTHER STATISTICAL PROBLEMS IN ECONOMETRICS

So much for the difficulties connected with the random disturbance term; let us turn to other problems. When the model is linear and contains more than one "independent" variable, the intercorrelation of these variables will tend to increase the variances of the parameter estimates. The simplest case involves two independent variables. Suppose the model has the form:

$$Y_t = \alpha + \beta_1 X_{1t} + \beta_2 X_{2t} + U_t \qquad t = 1, \cdots, T$$

Define the variances of X_{1t} and X_{2t} by

$$S_1^2 = \frac{1}{T} \sum_{t=1}^{T} (X_{1t} - \bar{X}_1)^2 = \frac{1}{T^2} [T \sum X_{1t}^2 - (\sum X_{1t})^2]$$

$$S_2^2 = \frac{1}{T} \sum_{t=1}^{T} (X_{2t} - \bar{X}_2)^2 = \frac{1}{T^2} [T \sum X_{2t}^2 - (\sum X_{2t})^2]$$

and their covariance by

$$S_{12} = \frac{1}{T} \sum_{t=1}^{T} (X_{1t} - \bar{X}_1)(X_{2t} - \bar{X}_2) = \frac{1}{T^2} [T \sum X_{1t} X_{2t} - (\sum X_{1t})(\sum X_{2t})]$$

If r is the coefficient of correlation between X_{1t} and X_{2t}, then

$$S_{12} = r S_1 S_2$$

For simplicity in what follows, we shall omit limits of summation and the subscript t. To obtain estimates of α, β_1, and β_2, we must solve the system:

$$\sum Y = \alpha T + \beta_1 \sum X_1 + \beta_2 \sum X_2$$

$$\sum X_1 Y = \alpha \sum X_1 + \beta_1 \sum X_1^2 + \beta_2 \sum X_1 X_2$$

$$\sum X_2 Y = \alpha \sum X_2 + \beta_1 \sum X_1 X_2 + \beta_2 \sum X_2^2$$

---

[4] When the work is carried to ten significant figures, the estimated standard errors of the parameter estimates are slightly larger when the possibility of autocorrelation is taken into account. The difference is negligible, however.

$$\acute{\sigma}(\acute{\alpha}) = 11.8748 \quad \text{and} \quad \acute{\sigma}(\acute{\beta}) = 0.0400$$

A statistical test for autocorrelation, too complicated to discuss here, shows none.

This will require the inversion of the matrix:

$$M = \begin{bmatrix} T & \sum X_1 & \sum X_2 \\ \sum X_1 & \sum X_1^2 & \sum X_1 X_2 \\ \sum X_2 & \sum X_1 X_2 & \sum X_2^2 \end{bmatrix}$$

The expression for the inverse of M is unwieldy, but every term in it will be divided by the determinant of M which can be written as

$$D = T \sum X_1^2 \sum X_2^2 + 2 \sum X_1 \sum X_2 \sum X_1 X_2$$
$$- \sum X_1^2 (\sum X_2)^2 - (\sum X_1)^2 \sum X_2^2 - T(\sum X_1 X_2)^2$$

A little algebraic manipulation will show that

$$D = \frac{1}{T} [T \sum X_1^2 - (\sum X_1)^2][T \sum X_2^2 - (\sum X_2)^2]$$
$$- \frac{1}{T} [T \sum X_1 X_2 - (\sum X_1)(\sum X_2)]^2$$
$$= \frac{1}{T} (T^2 S_1^2)(T^2 S_2^2) - \frac{1}{T} (T^2 S_{12})^2$$
$$= T^3 S_1^2 S_2^2 - T^3 S_{12}^2$$
$$= T^3 S_1^2 S_2^2 (1 - r^2)$$

We see that the greater the correlation between X_1 and X_2, the smaller the value of D. Since we are dividing by D, a value of r^2 close to unity will tend to make the elements of M^{-1} very large. Now, the variance-covariance matrix of the estimates of α, β_1, and β_2 is obtained by multiplying the matrix M^{-1} by $\sigma^2(Y \mid X_1, X_2)$. Hence, when X_1 and X_2 are highly correlated, estimates of the parameters in the linear regression equation relating Y, X_1, and X_2 will have large variances, although the estimates themselves will be unbiased.

When the "independent" variables in a linear regression equation correlate highly, we say that there is *multicollinearity*. This word comes from the geometrical interpretation of the situation. When we are fitting a linear equation relating Y to X_1 and X_2, we begin with a scatter of points, (Y_t, X_{1t}, X_{2t}), $t = 1, \cdots, T$, in three dimensions. The regression equation represents a plane passing through this scatter of points. For simplicity, suppose that

$$Y_t = \alpha + \beta_1 X_{1t} + \beta_2 X_{2t}$$

that is, there is no error term. Y_t is completely determined by X_1 and X_2. All points (Y_t, X_{1t}, X_{2t}) will lie on the plane given by the equation. If X_1 and X_2 are independent, then the points will tend to be widely scattered over the plane. Suppose, next, that X_1 and X_2 are perfectly correlated and related by the equation

$$X_{2t} = \gamma + \delta X_{1t}$$

In three dimensions, this is the equation of a plane parallel to the Y axis and passing through a line $X_2 = \gamma + \delta X_1$ in the (X_1, X_2) plane. Our points (Y_t, X_{1t}, X_{2t}) will now lie on a line which is the intersection of the two planes

$$Y = \alpha + \beta_1 X_1 + \beta_2 X_2$$

and

$$0 = \gamma + \delta X_1 - X_2$$

But this line could just as easily be determined by the intersection of two other planes and, in fact, we can pass an infinite number of planes through the line determined by our two. We will be unable to determine the "plane of best fit" because there are infinitely many such planes. In this case, r would be unity and the matrix M would have no inverse. Geometrically, we are in difficulty because there is more than one linear relationship among our variables. The points tend to lie along more than one plane. Unfortunately, like so many problems in econometrics, there is not much we can do about multicollinearity. It implies that the model has not completely specified the relationships among variables and that what is required is a model consisting of more than one equation.

This brings us to the final problem of this chapter: the estimation of parameters in an equation which is part of a larger model. If all of the variables, except one, are exogenous, there is no special problem. We can compute the regression of the endogenous variable on the exogenous variables.

The statistical difficulty of simultaneous equation systems is illustrated by the following simple (and completely identified) two equation model:

$$Y_{1t} = \alpha_1 + \beta_1 Y_{2t} + \gamma_1 X_{1t} + U_{1t}$$

$$Y_{2t} = \alpha_2 + \beta_2 Y_{1t} + \gamma_2 X_{2t} + U_{2t}$$

We assume that U_1 and U_2 are independent of each other and of X_1 and X_2, and that

$$E(U_{1t}) = E(U_{2t}) = 0$$

$$E(U_{1t}U_{1, t+S}) = \begin{cases} 0, & S \neq 0 \\ \sigma_1{}^2, & S = 0 \end{cases}$$

$$E(U_{2t}U_{2, t+S}) = \begin{cases} 0, & S \neq 0 \\ \sigma_2{}^2, & S = 0 \end{cases}$$

Y_1 and Y_2 are endogenous variables, and X_1 and X_2 are exogenous variables. When we solve the system for Y_1 and Y_2 in terms of X_1 and X_2,

$$Y_{1t} = \frac{1}{1 - \beta_1\beta_2} [\alpha_1 + \beta_1\alpha_2 + \gamma_1 X_{1t} + \beta_1\gamma_2 X_{2t} + U_{1t} + \beta_1 U_{2t}]$$

$$Y_{2t} = \frac{1}{1 - \beta_1\beta_2} [\beta_2\alpha_1 + \alpha_2 + \beta_2\gamma_1 X_{1t} + \gamma_2 X_{2t} + \beta_2 U_{1t} + U_{2t}]$$

We have expressed the endogenous variables in terms of the exogenous variables. In econometric terms, we have put the model into "reduced form." If we are interested in predicting Y_{1t} and Y_{2t} from X_{1t} and X_{2t}, we can do so with the reduced form, writing it as

$$Y_{1t} = \pi_{10} + \pi_{11} X_{1t} + \pi_{12} X_{2t} + v_{1t}$$

$$Y_{2t} = \pi_{20} + \pi_{21} X_{1t} + \pi_{22} X_{2t} + v_{2t}$$

No statistical difficulty arises in estimating the parameters π_{ij}, $i = 1, 2$; $j = 0, 1, 2$, because the necessary assumptions are met.

However, if we are interested in estimating the parameters of the original model, a difficulty arises. It is clear from the reduced form that Y_{2t} is correlated with U_{1t} and that Y_{1t} is correlated with U_{2t}. In each equation, one of the "independent" variables is correlated with the disturbance term. As we have seen, when this happens, the ordinary least-squares parameter estimates are biased, and the bias does not decrease with increasing sample size.

Several ways of dealing with this difficulty have been proposed. One of the simplest is called the method of "two-stage" least squares. This method yields parameter estimates which are consistent; that is, the bias approaches zero as the sample size increases. As the name implies, the procedure is broken into two stages. First, a linear regression equation is fitted for each endogenous variable using all of the exogenous variables as independent variables. For the ith endogenous variable we would have, assuming r exogenous variables,

$$\hat{Y}_{it} = \pi_{i0} + \hat{\pi}_{i1} X_{1t} + \hat{\pi}_{i2} X_{2t} + \cdots + \hat{\pi}_{ir} X_{rt}$$

Then, instead of using the observed values of the endogenous variables, the values computed from the regression equations are used as the "independent" variables in the equations in the original model. Thus, if we wanted to estimate the parameters α_1, β_1, and γ_1 in the first equation in the two-equation model, we would begin by computing the regression of Y_2 on X_1 and X_2 because Y_2 appears as an "independent" variable in the first equation. We would obtain a regression equation:

$$\hat{Y}_{2t} = \hat{\pi}_{20} + \hat{\pi}_{21} X_{1t} + \hat{\pi}_{22} X_{2t}$$

Then using $\hat{Y}_{2t}$ instead of Y_{2t}, we would apply least squares to the original equation

$$Y_{1t} = \alpha_1 + \beta_1 \hat{Y}_{2t} + \gamma_1 X_{1t} + U_{1t}$$

Notice that the *observed* values of Y_{1t} and the *computed* values of $\hat{Y}_{2t}$ are used here. Loosely speaking, the effect of two-stage least squares in this case is to "purify" Y_{2t} of its partial dependence on the random disturbance term, U_{1t}. Notice, finally, that if we are interested in estimating the parameters of only one equation in a simultaneous system, all we need to specify is the form of this equation and all of the exogenous variables in the system. The remaining equations need not be completely specified.

To illustrate the procedure, let us return to the problem of the consumption function in slightly different form. Let C_t be personal consumption expenditures in time period t, and let Y_t be gross national product in the same time period. We want to estimate the parameters, α and β of the linear consumption function:

$$C_t = \alpha + \beta Y_t + U_t$$

We know from our study of economics that gross national product is the sum of (1) personal consumption expenditures, (2) gross private domestic investment, (3) net exports of goods and services, and (4) government purchases of goods and services. Since net exports are small in magnitude, we shall include them in the random disturbance term of some other equation in the system and shall treat gross private domestic investment I_t, and

Table 16.7   Gross National Product Y_t, Personal Consumption Expenditures C_t, Gross Private Domestic Investment I_t, and Government Purchases of Goods and Services G_t, in Billions of 1954 Dollars, 1953 to 1962

Year t	Y_t	C_t	I_t	G_t
1953	369	235	51	84
1954	363	238	49	75
1955	393	256	62	73
1956	401	264	62	72
1957	409	271	58	76
1958	401	273	49	79
1959	429	289	62	80
1960	440	298	60	80
1961	448	304	58	84
1962	475	318	65	90

Source: Business Statistics, 1963, p. 6.

government purchases of goods and services, G_t, as exogenous. The basic data are given in Table 16.7.

First, we compute the coefficients in the regression equation expressing Y_t as a linear function of I_t and G_t. We omit the calculations because we illustrated the method earlier. The resulting regression equation is

$$\hat{Y}_t = -78.0580 + 3.7854I_t + 3.4404G_t$$

Next, using this equation, we compute $\hat{Y}_t$ for the years 1953 to 1962. $\hat{Y}_t$ and Y_t are shown in Table 16.8 where we have rounded $\hat{Y}_t$ to three significant

Table 16.8   Actual and Estimated Y_t

Year	$Y_t{}^a$	$\hat{Y}_t{}^b$	$C_t{}^a$
1953	369	404	235
1954	363	365	238
1955	393	408	256
1956	401	404	264
1957	409	403	271
1958	401	379	273
1959	429	432	289
1960	440	424	298
1961	448	430	304
1962	475	478	318

[a] *Source.* From Table 16.7.
[b] *Source.* Computed from

$$\hat{Y}_t = -78.0580 + 3.7854I_t + 3.4404G_t$$

and rounded to three significant digits

$$\Sigma\, C_t = 2746 \qquad \Sigma\, \hat{Y}_t = 4127$$
$$\Sigma\, C_t^2 = 760936 \qquad \Sigma\, C_t \hat{Y}_t = 1139518$$
$$\Sigma\, \hat{Y}_t^2 = 1711955$$

digits. In this table we also give the sums and products necessary to estimate the parameters in the regression of C_t on $\hat{Y}_t$. Again, since the procedure has already been illustrated, we shall not show the calculations. Standard errors of the parameter estimates are computed in the usual way. The final regression equation is

$$\hat{C}_t = -20.16 + 0.7142\,\hat{Y}_t$$
$$\quad\ (77.44) \qquad (0.0592)$$

This is our estimate of the consumption function. The estimate takes into account the fact that Y_t is an endogenous variable. The marginal propensity to consume given by this equation, $\hat{\beta} = 0.7142$, cannot be compared with our earlier marginal propensities to consume. The earlier estimates were of the proportion of additional increments of personal disposable income to be consumed, whereas the present estimate is of the proportion of additional increments of gross national product to be consumed.

Finally, if we ignore the fact that Y_t is endogenous, and compute the regression of C_t on Y_t, we find

$$\hat{C}_t = -45.77 + 0.7761\,Y_t$$
$$\quad\quad (3.91) \quad\quad (0.0094)$$

This equation is quite similar to the previous one. The difference between the two estimates of the marginal propensity to consume is well within the limits expected from sampling fluctuations. The smaller standard errors in the second equation are deceptive; it would be a lucky econometrician indeed who could regard gross national product as an exogenous variable.

IMPORTANT TERMS AND CONCEPTS

Aggregation	Multicollinearity
Autocorrelation	Multiple correlation
Disturbance term	Multiple regression
Econometrics	Reduced form
Endogenous variable	Serial correlation
Errors in measurement	Simultaneous equation system
Exogenous variable	Specification
Identification	Two-stage least squares

SYMBOLS

α	$\hat{V}$
β	$\sigma(\hat{\alpha})$
γ	$\sigma(\hat{\beta})$
σ^2	D_t
X^T	S_t
X^{-1}	P_t
M	$\hat{\alpha}$
ϵ	$\hat{\beta}$
V	C_t

OFTEN-USED FORMULAS

$$E(Y \mid X_1, \cdots, X_r) = \alpha_0 + \alpha_1 X_1 + \alpha_2 X_2 + \cdots + \alpha_r X_r$$

$$\sum Y = \hat{\alpha}_0 n + \hat{\alpha}_1 \sum X_1 + \hat{\alpha}_2 \sum X_2 + \cdots + \hat{\alpha}_r \sum X_r$$

$$\sum X_1 Y = \hat{\alpha}_0 \sum X_1 + \hat{\alpha}_1 \sum X_1^2 + \hat{\alpha}_2 \sum X_1 X_2 + \cdots + \hat{\alpha}_r \sum X_1 X_r$$

$$\sum X_2 Y = \hat{\alpha}_0 \sum X_2 + \hat{\alpha}_1 \sum X_1 X_2 + \hat{\alpha}_2 \sum X_2^2 + \cdots + \hat{\alpha}_r \sum X_2 X_r$$

$$\cdots\cdots\cdots\cdots\cdots\cdots\cdots\cdots\cdots\cdots\cdots\cdots\cdots\cdots\cdots$$

$$\sum X_r Y = \hat{\alpha}_0 \sum X_r + \hat{\alpha}_1 \sum X_1 X_r + \hat{\alpha}_2 \sum X_2 X_r + \cdots + \hat{\alpha}_r \sum X_r^2$$

$$M = \begin{bmatrix} n & \sum X_1 & \sum X_2 & \cdots & \sum X_r \\ \sum X_1 & \sum X_1^2 & \sum X_1 X_2 & \cdots & \sum X_1 X_r \\ \sum X_2 & \sum X_1 X_2 & \sum X_2^2 & \cdots & \sum X_2 X_r \\ \cdots & \cdots & \cdots & \cdots & \cdots \\ \sum X_r & \sum X_1 X_r & \sum X_2 X_r & \cdots & \sum X_r^2 \end{bmatrix}$$

$$X^* = \begin{bmatrix} 1 & X_{11} & X_{21} & \cdots & X_{r1} \\ 1 & X_{12} & X_{22} & \cdots & X_{r2} \\ \cdots & \cdots & \cdots & \cdots & \cdots \\ 1 & X_{1n} & X_{2n} & \cdots & X_{rn} \end{bmatrix}$$

$$Y^* = \begin{bmatrix} Y_1 \\ Y_2 \\ \cdots \\ Y_n \end{bmatrix} \qquad \hat{\alpha}^* = \begin{bmatrix} \hat{\alpha}_0 \\ \hat{\alpha}_1 \\ \cdots \\ \hat{\alpha}_r \end{bmatrix}$$

$$X^{*T} Y^* = M\hat{\alpha}^*$$

$$\hat{\alpha}^* = M^{-1} X^{*T} Y^*$$

$$\hat{\sigma}^2 = \frac{1}{n - (r + 1)} \left[\sum Y^2 - \hat{\alpha}_0 \sum Y - \hat{\alpha}_1 \sum X_1 Y - \cdots - \hat{\alpha}_r \sum X_r Y \right]$$

$$\hat{V}(\hat{\alpha}_0, \hat{\alpha}_1, \cdots, \hat{\alpha}_r) = \hat{\sigma}^2 M^{-1}$$

Autocorrelation:

$$Y_t = \alpha + \beta X_t + U_t$$

$$U_t = \lambda U_{t-1} + \epsilon_t$$

Fit the model by ordinary least squares, obtaining

$$\hat{Y}_t = \hat{\alpha}^{(1)} + \hat{\beta}^{(1)}X_t, \qquad t = 1, \cdots, T$$

$$\hat{U}_t = Y_t - \hat{\alpha}^{(1)} - \hat{\beta}^{(1)}X_t, \qquad t = 1, \cdots, T$$

$$\hat{\lambda} = \sum_{t=2}^{T} \hat{U}_t \hat{U}_{t-1} \Big/ \sum_{t=2}^{T} \hat{U}_{t-1}^2$$

$$\hat{Z}_t = Y_t - \hat{\lambda}Y_{t-1}; \qquad \hat{w}_t = X_t - \hat{\lambda}X_{t-1}$$

$$Z_t = \alpha(1 - \lambda) + \beta w_t + \epsilon_t$$

EXERCISES

1. The data shown are expenditures for new plant and equipment by manufacturing industries Y_t, and total sales of manufacturing industries in the previous two years X_{t-1} and X_{t-2} for the period 1953 to 1962.

	Billions of Dollars		
Year	New Plant and Equipment Expenditures[a] Y_t	Sales Previous Year[b] X_{t-1}	Sales Two Years Previous[b] X_{t-2}
1953	11.9	274	268
1954	11.0	294	274
1955	11.4	282	294
1956	15.0	316	282
1957	16.0	332	316
1958	11.4	341	332
1959	12.1	314	341
1960	14.5	356	314
1961	13.7	365	356
1962	14.7	368	365

[a] *Source.* Computed from quarterly averages in *Business Statistics*, 1963, p. 9.
[b] *Source.* Computed from monthly averages given in ibid., p. 22.

a. Determine the parameters in the regression equation relating Y to X_{t-1} and X_{t-2}. Write the equation, and indicate the estimated standard errors of the parameter estimates.

b. Formulate a meaningful hypothesis concerning one of the regression coefficients and test this hypothesis. Be sure to indicate whether the hypothesis is one-sided or two-sided.

c. Do you think multicollinearity is a problem here? Why or why not?

2. In the following econometric models, X denotes an exogenous variable, Y an endogenous variable, and ϵ a random disturbance term. In each model, determine whether the parameters of the first equation could be unambiguously estimated if the necessary data were available.

$$\text{Model I:} \begin{cases} Y_1 = \alpha_1 + \beta_{12} Y_2 + \gamma_{11} X_1 + \epsilon_1 \\ Y_3 = \alpha_3 + \beta_{31} Y_1 + \beta_{32} Y_2 + \epsilon_3 \\ Y_2 = Y_1 + Y_3 \end{cases}$$

$$\text{Model II:} \begin{cases} Y_1 = \alpha_1 + \beta_{12} Y_2 + \gamma_{11} X_1 + \gamma_{12} X_2 + \epsilon_1 \\ Y_3 = \alpha_2 + \beta_{32} Y_2 + \gamma_{33} X_3 + \epsilon_3 \\ Y_2 = Y_1 + Y_3 \end{cases}$$

$$\text{Model III:} \begin{cases} Y_1 = \alpha_1 + \beta_{12} Y_2 + \beta_{13} Y_3 + \gamma_{11} X_1 + \epsilon_1 \\ Y_2 = \alpha_2 + \beta_{23} Y_3 + \gamma_{22} X_2 + \epsilon_2 \\ Y_3 = \alpha_3 + \gamma_{33} X_3 + \epsilon_3 \end{cases}$$

3. An econometrician is interested in constructing a model of investment in new plant and equipment in a certain consumer-goods industry. He knows that, in this industry, decisions to invest in new plant and equipment are based on (1) sales forecasts for the current year, and (2) depreciation on the existing plant and equipment. He is willing to assume that sales in the current year depend on disposable income for both the current and the previous year. Using whatever symbols seem appropriate and linear equations:

a. Write an investment equation and a sales forecasting equation.

b. Identify the endogenous and exogenous variables in each equation.

c. Indicate what additional equations would be necessary in order to complete the model.

4. In each of the following equations, Y denotes the dependent variable, X_i the ith independent variable, and ϵ a disturbance term. Transform the variables so that the resulting equation is linear.

a. $Y = \alpha X_1^{\beta_1} X_2^{\beta_2} \epsilon$

b. $Y = \alpha e^{\beta_1 X_1 + \beta_2 X_2 + \epsilon}$

c. $Y = \dfrac{k C X_1^{\alpha} X_2^{\beta} \epsilon}{1 + C X_1^{\alpha} X_2^{\beta} \epsilon}$ (assume that k is known)

d. $\dfrac{Y + \epsilon}{X} = \alpha + \beta X$

5. An econometrician has developed a model of the form:

$$Y = (\alpha + \beta X)^\delta$$

where α, β, and δ are unknown parameters. He is willing to approximate this function by a second degree polynomial plus an error term

$$Y = a + bX + cX^2 + \epsilon$$

   a. If the polynomial represents the first three terms in the MacLaurin series expansion of $Y = (\alpha + \beta X)^\delta$, what is the relationship between a, b, and c and the parameters α, β, and δ?

   b. Given estimates of the parameters a, b, and c, how would you use them to obtain estimates of α, β, and δ?

6. Farmers growing a certain crop save a portion of the crop each year as seed for the following year. The crop that the farmer plants each year depends on the seed that he has available and the market price for the crop prevailing in the previous year. The yield in any year depends on the amount planted and rainfall during the growing season. Assume that there are N farmers in a region, all exposed to the same prices and rainfall, and assume that the relationships indicated above are linear.

   a. Write an equation for the ith farmer, describing the dependence of the current year's crop on last year's crop, last year's prices, and current rainfall.

   b. Under what conditions would a similar equation prevail for the total crop in the region? Write the equation.

7. In econometrics it is often reasonable to assume that the error in measuring X is proportional to X. That is, if x is the measured value and X is the true value, we can write

$$x = X(1 + \delta)$$

where δ has zero mean and variance σ^2, and successive values of δ are independent. Statistical collection agencies often publish estimates of σ^2 along with x. Assume that σ^2 is known without error and is the same for all X. You wish to estimate the regression coefficient, β, in the equation relating error-free variables:

$$Y = \alpha + \beta X + \epsilon$$

Y is measured without error, but, instead of X, we measure $x = X(1 + \delta)$. If β is estimated by fitting the regression of Y on x:

a. For large samples, what is $E(\hat{\beta})$?

b. How would you correct for bias?

8. In our discussion of autocorrelated disturbances, we set up the model:

$$u_t = \lambda u_{t-1} + \epsilon_t$$

where the ϵ_t are independent with zero mean and variance σ^2. Assume that $-1 < \lambda < 1$ and that $u_0 = \epsilon_0$ is the initial disturbance. Then

$$u_t = \lambda^t \epsilon_0 + \lambda^{t-1} \epsilon_1 + \cdots + \lambda \epsilon_{t-1} + \epsilon_t$$

Show that, when t is large:

a. $E(u_t{}^2) \approx \sigma^2/(1 - \lambda^2)$
b. $E(u_t u_{t-1}) \approx \lambda \sigma^2/(1 - \lambda^2)$
c. The coefficient of correlation between u_t and u_{t-1} tends to λ.

9. The data shown are end-of-year inventories Y_t and annual sales X_t in the retail trade from 1953 to 1962.

	Billions of Dollars	
Year	End-of-Year Inventories[a] Y_t	Annual Sales[b] X_t
1953	21.5	169.2
1954	20.9	169.2
1955	22.8	183.6
1956	23.4	189.6
1957	24.6	200.4
1958	24.3	200.4
1959	25.5	216.0
1960	27.2	219.6
1961	26.9	218.4
1962	27.4	225.2

[a] *Source. Business Statistics*, 1963, p. 23.
[b] *Source.* Computed from monthly averages given in ibid., p. 22.

a. Assume that the disturbance term, u_t, in the equation relating inventories and sales,

$$Y_t = \alpha + \beta X_t + u_t$$

is correlated with u_{t-1}. Estimate the value of λ in the equation relating u_t and u_{t-1},

$$u_t = \lambda u_{t-1} + \epsilon_t$$

b. Using the value of λ that you computed above, estimate α and β (along with the standard errors of the estimates) in the equation relating inventories and sales.

c. Compare your initial estimates of α and β with your final estimates. Do you think autocorrelation is a serious problem here? Why or why not?

10. An economist is interested in studying the relationship between new plant and equipment expenditures in nondurable goods manufacturing

Year	I_t[a]	S_t[b]	Billions of Dollars C_t[c]	I_{t-1}[a]	C_{t-1}[c]	Z_t[d]
1953	6.24	145.7	232.6	6.00	219.8	82.4
1954	5.96	147.5	238.0	6.24	232.6	76.3
1955	6.00	159.1	256.9	5.96	238.0	76.7
1956	7.32	166.9	269.9	6.00	256.9	81.9
1957	7.92	170.6	285.2	7.32	269.9	91.4
1958	5.96	166.2	293.2	7.92	285.2	94.7
1959	6.28	182.8	313.5	5.96	293.2	96.4
1960	7.28	188.8	328.2	6.28	313.5	102.6
1961	7.40	194.2	336.8	7.28	328.2	112.3
1962	7.64	204.7	355.4	7.40	336.8	120.8

Sources:
[a] Computed from quarterly averages given in *Business Statistics*, 1963, p. 9.
[b] Computed from monthly averages given in ibid., p. 22.
[c] Ibid., p. 3.
[d] Computed from separate figures given in ibid., p. 4.

industries and certain other variables. He has developed a model in which the following two equations appear:

$$I_t = \alpha_1 + \beta_{11}S_t + \beta_{12}I_{t-1} + \epsilon_{1t}$$
$$S_t = \alpha_2 + \beta_{21}C_t + \beta_{22}C_{t-1} + \epsilon_{2t}$$

where

I_t = new plant and equipment expenditures by nondurable goods manufacturing industries in year t.

S_t = sales by nondurable goods manufacturing industries in year t.

C_t = Personal consumption expenditures in year t.

In the complete model, there is one additional exogenous variable,

Z_t = Net exports of goods and service in year t + government purchases of goods and services in year t.

The economist is willing to assume that the disturbances ϵ_{1t} and ϵ_{2t} are independent and not autocorrelated. There are three endogenous variables, I_t, S_t, and C_t, in the above equations, and there are three exogenous variables in the model, I_{t-1}, C_{t-1}, and Z_t. The data are given for the years 1953 to 1962. Use the method of two-stage least squares to estimate the parameters (and their standard errors) in both equations. Discuss the economic sense of these estimates.

APPENDIX A The Number e

One of the most important limits in mathematics is the real number

$$e = \lim_{y \to 0} (1 + y)^{1/y}$$

It is not difficult to prove that the function $(1 + y)^{1/y}$ actually does approach a limiting value as y nears zero; however, such a proof requires mathematical techniques that are beyond the scope of this text. Consequently, we shall only give an indication of the behavior of the function under these circumstances.

Suppose we assign to y a sequence of numbers that approach zero and compute the corresponding values of

$$(1 + y)^{1/y}$$

For one such sequence we find, using logarithms,

y	1	$\frac{1}{2}$	$\frac{1}{4}$	$\frac{1}{8}$	$\frac{1}{16}$	$\frac{1}{32}$	$\frac{1}{64}$
$(1 + y)^{1/y}$	2.00	2.25	2.44	2.57	2.64	2.68	2.70

The values for $(1 + y)^{1/y}$ seem to be steadying down toward some value. It has been shown that as $y \to 0$, $(1 + y)^{1/y}$ does, indeed, approach a fixed value. This limit is approximately 2.7183, and is customarily denoted by e.

By letting $z = 1/y$, we see that the limit may be written in a different form,

$$e = \lim_{z \to \infty} \left(1 + \frac{1}{z}\right)^z$$

The number e is an extremely important constant in mathematics. One of its uses is as a base for natural logarithms. It occurs frequently in statistics.

632

The MacLaurin Series Expansion

It is a well-known fact that many functions can be represented in the form of infinite series. For instance, consider the function $1/(1 - y)$. If a division is performed, we have immediately

$$\frac{1}{1 - y} = 1 + y + y^2 + \cdots = \sum_{n=0}^{\infty} y^n$$

Suppose that a function $f(y)$ has an infinite series expansion. Then

$$f(y) = a_0 + a_1 y + a_2 y^2 + \cdots + a_n y^n + \cdots = \sum_{n=0}^{\infty} a_n y^n$$

Finding the correct series is simply a matter of evaluating the constants $a_0, \cdots, a_n, \cdots$. Let $y = 0$. Then

$$a_0 = f(0)$$

Take the first derivative:

$$f'(y) = a_1 + 2a_2 y + 3a_3 y^2 + \cdots + na_n y^{n-1} + \cdots$$

Let $y = 0$ again, and we obtain $f'(0) = a_1$

$$a_1 = f'(0)$$

Repeating the process at length, we find that

$$a_2 = \frac{f''(0)}{2} \qquad a_3 = \frac{f'''(0)}{6} \qquad a_4 = \frac{f^{iv}(0)}{24}$$

and, in general,

$$a_n = \frac{f^n(0)}{n!}$$

We have thus shown how to find the so-called MacLaurin series expansion of a function. In cases where no such expansion exists, the technique of computing the coefficients will break down. We have shown that

$$f(y) = f(0) + f'(0)y + \frac{f''(0)}{2!}y^2 + \cdots + \frac{f^n(0)}{n!}y^n + \cdots$$

or in more concise form,

$$f(y) = \sum_{n=0}^{\infty} \frac{f^n(0)}{n!} y^n$$

We shall need to know the MacLaurin series expansion of the function e^y; for this function:

$$f(y) = e^y \qquad f(0) = 1$$
$$f'(y) = e^y \qquad f'(0) = 1$$
$$\cdots \qquad \cdots$$
$$f^n(y) = e^y \qquad f^n(0) = 1$$

Then

$$f(y) = 1 + 1 \cdot \frac{y}{1!} + 1 \cdot \frac{y^2}{2!} + \cdots + 1 \cdot \frac{y^n}{n!} + \cdots = \sum_{n=0}^{\infty} \frac{y^n}{n!}$$

This series expansion is used at several places in this text.

As another example, let us find the MacLaurin series expansion of the function $\ln(1 + y)$. We merely differentiate repeatedly, set $y = 0$ to find the coefficients, and substitute in the formula.

$$f(y) = \ln(1 + y) \qquad f(0) = 0$$
$$f'(y) = \frac{1}{1 + y} = (1 + y)^{-1} \qquad f'(0) = 1$$
$$f''(y) = -1(1 + y)^{-2} \qquad f''(0) = -1$$
$$f'''(y) = 2(1 + y)^{-3} \qquad f'''(0) = 2$$
$$f^{iv}(y) = -6(1 + y)^{-4} \qquad f^{iv}(0) = -6$$

Thus

$$f(y) = \ln(1 + y) = 0 + 1 \cdot y + \left(-\frac{1}{2}\right)y^2 + \left(\frac{2}{6}\right)y^3 + \left(\frac{-6}{24}\right)y^4 + \cdots$$

$$= y - \frac{y^2}{2} + \frac{y^3}{3} - \frac{y^4}{4} + \cdots + (-1)^{n+1}\frac{y^n}{n} + \cdots$$

is the required expansion.

APPENDIX C Multiple Integration

The student is acquainted with the process of integration where a function of one variable is of concern. The process can be easily generalized to functions of several variables. The result is called *multiple integration,* and any good calculus text will serve as a satisfactory reference. We shall discuss the evaluation of multiple integrals in a brief and rather mechanical fashion. This will provide a minimal background for understanding the appropriate textual material; however, supplementary reading is highly desirable. We commence with double integration.

A definite double integral is a symbol of the form:

$$\int_x \int_y f(x, y)\, dy\, dx$$

As with any definite integral, the symbol represents a real number. In calculus courses it is proved that such an expression may be evaluated by integrating the variables one at a time. Conventionally, these integrations are performed from the inside out, as in the examples that follow. An important point to remember is that an integration always takes place with respect to one variable: the one indicated by the differential symbol. While that process is going on, all other variables must be held constant. Thus, the operations and formulas of single integration are entirely adequate for double integration.

As an example, let us evaluate the double integral

$$\int_{x=0}^{1} \int_{y=2}^{4} x^2 y\, dy\, dx = \int_{x=0}^{1} \left[x^2 \int_{y=2}^{4} y\, dy \right] dx = \int_{x=0}^{1} x^2 \left[\frac{y^2}{2} \right]_2^4 dx$$

$$= \int_0^1 x^2 (8 - 2)\, dx = 6 \int_0^1 x^2\, dx = 6 \left[\frac{x^3}{3} \right]_0^1 = 6 \cdot \frac{1}{3} = 2$$

Geometrically, this problem is equivalent to finding the volume lying below

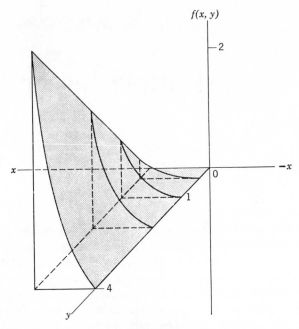

Fig. C.1. Volume as a double integral; $f(x, y) = x^2 y$.

the surface $f(x, y) = x^2 y$ and above the rectangle in the xy plane bounded by the four lines $x = 0$, $x = 1$, $y = 2$, and $y = 4$. Figure C.1 shows this volume. Let us take another example.

$$\int_{x=1}^{2} \int_{y=0}^{x} (x - y)\, dy\, dx = \int_{x=1}^{2} \left[\int_{y=0}^{x} (x - y)\, dy \right] dx$$

$$= \int_{x=1}^{2} \left[x \int_{y=0}^{x} dy - \int_{y=0}^{x} y\, dy \right] dx$$

$$= \int_{x=1}^{2} \left[x \left(y \right)_{y=0}^{x} - \left(\frac{y^2}{2} \right)_{y=0}^{x} \right] dx = \int_{x=1}^{2} \left[x^2 - \frac{x^2}{2} \right] dx$$

$$= \frac{1}{2} \int_{x=1}^{2} x^2\, dx = \frac{1}{2} \left[\frac{x^3}{3} \right]_{1}^{2} = \frac{1}{2} \cdot \frac{7}{3} = \frac{7}{6}$$

A corresponding geometrical problem would ask for the volume under the surface $f(x, y) = x - y$ and lying above the trapezoid in the xy plane bounded by the lines $y = 0$, $y = x$, $x = 1$, and $x = 2$. Figure C.2 shows this volume.

As a last example of double integration, we shall find the volume lying under the surface $f(x, y) = e^{-x-y}$ and above the first quadrant.

$$V = \int_{x=0}^{\infty} \int_{y=0}^{\infty} e^{-x-y} \, dy \, dx = \int_{x=0}^{\infty} \left[e^{-x} \int_{y=0}^{\infty} e^{-y} \, dy \right] dx$$

$$= \int_{x=0}^{\infty} \left[e^{-x} \left(-e^{-y} \right)_{0}^{\infty} \right] dx = \int_{x=0}^{\infty} [e^{-x}(-(-1))] \, dx$$

$$= \int_{x=0}^{\infty} e^{-x} \, dx = \left[-e^{-x} \right]_{0}^{\infty} = 0 - 1(-1) = 1$$

Figure C.3 exhibits this volume—or rather a portion of it. The thin wedge extending to infinity over the first quadrant is cut away.

The process that we have been describing can be easily extended to more than two variables. We can, in fact, say that a definite multiple integral is an expression of the form:

$$\int_{x_1} \cdots \int_{x_n} f(x_1, \cdots, x_n) \, dx_n \cdots dx_1$$

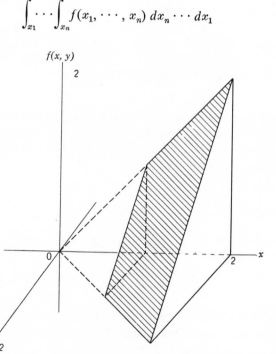

Fig. C.2. Volume as a double integral; $f(x, y) = x - y$.

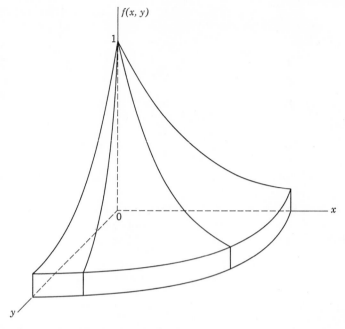

Fig. C.3. Volume as a double integral; $f(x, y) = e^{-x-y}$.

It is proved in calculus courses that such an expression may be evaluated by integrating out the variables, one at a time, as with double integration. Conventionally, the integration is performed from the inside out, as illustrated in the examples that follow.

$$\int_{x_1=0}^{4} \int_{x_2=0}^{3} \int_{x_3=-1}^{1} dx_3\, dx_2\, dx_1 = \int_{x_1=0}^{4} \int_{x_2=0}^{3} \left[\int_{x_3=-1}^{1} dx_3 \right] dx_2\, dx_1$$

$$= \int_{x_1=0}^{4} \int_{x_2=0}^{3} 2\, dx_2\, dx_1 = 2 \int_{x_1=0}^{4} \left[\int_{x_2=0}^{3} dx_2 \right] dx_1$$

$$= 2 \int_{x_1=0}^{4} 3\, dx_1 = 6 \int_{x_1=0}^{4} dx_1 = 24$$

In such expressions, the limits may, of course, be functions of the variables remaining at any stage of the operation; for example, we next evaluate

$$\frac{8}{9} \int_{x_1=0}^{1} \int_{x_2=0}^{x_1} \int_{x_3=-x_1}^{x_1+x_2} (x_1 + x_2 + x_3)\, dx_3\, dx_2\, dx_1$$

Remembering that when a given variable is being integrated out, all others are held fixed, we find that

$$\int_{x_3=-x_1}^{x_1+x_2} (x_1 + x_2 + x_3)\, dx_3 = \left[(x_1 + x_2)x_3 + \frac{x_3^2}{2} \right]_{x_3=-x_1}^{x_1+x_2}$$

$$= x_1^2 + 2x_1x_2 + x_2^2 + \frac{x_1^2}{2} + x_1x_2$$

$$+ \frac{x_2^2}{2} + x_1^2 + x_1x_2 - \frac{x_1^2}{2}$$

$$= 2x_1^2 + 4x_1x_2 + \frac{3}{2} x_2^2$$

Next we integrate out x_2.

$$\int_{x_2=0}^{x_1} \left[2x_1^2 + 4x_1x_2 + \frac{3}{2} x_2^2 \right] dx_2 = \left[2x_1^2 x_2 + 2x_1 x_2^2 + \frac{x_2^3}{2} \right]_{x_2=0}^{x_1}$$

$$= 2x_1^3 + 2x_1^3 + \frac{x_1^3}{2} = \frac{9}{2} x_1^3$$

The final integration concerns x_1, the only remaining variable.

$$\frac{8}{9} \int_{x_1=0}^{1} \frac{9}{2} x_1^3\, dx_1 = \frac{8}{9} \cdot \frac{9}{2} \left[\frac{x_1^4}{4} \right]_0^1 = 4 \cdot \frac{1}{4} = 1$$

In the discussion of double integration it has been mentioned that the volume bounded by various surfaces can be expressed as a double integral. In general, multiple integrals can represent volumes; however, when more than two variables are involved, the volumes are more than three dimensional. This explains why diagrams are omitted in the current illustrations.

APPENDIX D Review of Some Matrix Operations

In this brief review of matrices, we assume that most of us have some notion of the way in which the mathematician looks at matrices. He regards matrices as symbolic representations of linear transformations on vector spaces and, from the properties of these he derives the algebraic laws of matrices. Then any set of elements having the properties of a vector space will obey these laws under linear transformation. Aside from the aesthetic appeal of this algebra, it has great practical use, since many aspects of the physical world seem to have properties like those of vector spaces, and many computational problems can be reformulated in such a way that they can be solved by matrix algebra. Here, we shall be concerned with those aspects of matrix algebra which can help us to solve computational problems, so we shall merely state these algebraic laws without proof and illustrate them with one or two numerical examples. Only the rules for matrix multiplication and matrix inversion are used here, but this appendix provides a background in the matrix operations which are used in correlation and regression analysis.

Definition. A matrix is a rectangular arrangement of symbols, usually enclosed in either square brackets or parentheses. It is usually designated by a capital Roman or italic letter, and the symbols which are its entries are often designated by lower case Roman or italic letters with two subscripts. The first subscript indicates the *row* and the second subscript indicates the *column* in which the symbol appears. Rows run horizontally; columns run vertically. Symbolically, the matrix A with m rows and n columns would be written as

$$
A = \begin{bmatrix}
a_{11} & a_{12} & a_{13} & \cdots & a_{1n} \\
a_{21} & a_{22} & a_{23} & \cdots & a_{2n} \\
\cdots & \cdots & \cdots & \cdots & \cdots \\
a_{m1} & a_{m2} & a_{m3} & \cdots & a_{mn}
\end{bmatrix}
$$

Typical matrices used in correlation and regression analysis are

$$X = \begin{bmatrix} 1 & 1 \\ 1 & 3 \\ 1 & 2 \\ 1 & 5 \\ 1 & 4 \end{bmatrix}, \qquad y = \begin{bmatrix} 6 \\ 9 \\ 6 \\ 14 \\ 10 \end{bmatrix}$$

A matrix like y above consists of one column. It is called a *column vector*. Vectors are usually designated by lower case Roman letters. The *transpose* of a matrix is a new matrix derived by writing the *rows* of the original as the *columns* of the new matrix. Transposes will be indicated by the letter T, thus:

$$X^T = \begin{bmatrix} 1 & 1 & 1 & 1 & 1 \\ 1 & 3 & 2 & 5 & 4 \end{bmatrix} \qquad y^T = [6, 9, 6, 14, 10]$$

The matrix y^T consists of only one row and is called a *row vector*.

Addition and Subtraction of Matrices

Mathematically speaking, two matrices may be added or subtracted provided only that they both have the same number of rows and the same number of columns. In practice, however, matrices are not added or subtracted unless the operation makes sense. This means that the units in which the matrix elements are measured either must be the same or make sense when added. Thus, we would be very unlikely to add a matrix describing the batting performance of baseball players to a matrix describing the behavior of stock market prices even if both matrices have the same number of rows and the same number of columns. Provided the necessary conditions are met, however, we add or subtract matrices by adding or subtracting elements whose row and column locations are the same. Thus, if

$$A = \begin{bmatrix} 3 & 2 & 1 \\ 4 & 7 & 5 \end{bmatrix}, \qquad B = \begin{bmatrix} 4 & 1 & 2 \\ 1 & 6 & 3 \end{bmatrix},$$

then

$$A + B = \begin{bmatrix} 7 & 3 & 3 \\ 5 & 13 & 8 \end{bmatrix}, \qquad A - B = \begin{bmatrix} -1 & 1 & -1 \\ 3 & 1 & 2 \end{bmatrix}.$$

Multiplication of a Matrix by a Scalar

In statistics, we sometimes have to multiply a matrix by a number. In matrix algebra, a number standing alone is called a *scalar*. To multiply a matrix by a scalar, we simply multiply every element in the matrix by the scalar. If we multiply the matrices A and B above by 2 and 0.3, respectively, we get

$$2A = \begin{bmatrix} 6 & 4 & 2 \\ 8 & 14 & 10 \end{bmatrix} \qquad 0.3B = \begin{bmatrix} 1.2 & 0.3 & 0.6 \\ 0.3 & 1.8 & 0.9 \end{bmatrix}$$

Multiplication of Two Matrices

In matrix multiplication, order is important; the matrix product CD is not necessarily the same as the matrix product DC. In fact, the computational possibility of CD in no way guarantees the computational possibility of DC. In order for the product CD to exist, the number of columns in C must be the same as the number of rows in D. If this is true, then the matrix product CD will be another matrix. It will have as many rows as C and as many columns as D. The matrix element which lies at the intersection of the ith row and the jth column of CD is obtained by multiplying the elements in the ith row of C by the corresponding elements in the jth column of D and adding these products. Suppose

$$C = \begin{bmatrix} 1 & 3 & 2 \\ 2 & 2 & 4 \end{bmatrix}, \qquad D = \begin{bmatrix} 4 & 5 \\ 1 & 2 \\ 3 & 1 \end{bmatrix}$$

Then

$$CD = \begin{bmatrix} 1 & 3 & 2 \\ 2 & 2 & 4 \end{bmatrix} \begin{bmatrix} 4 & 5 \\ 1 & 2 \\ 3 & 1 \end{bmatrix}$$

(1st *row* of C × 1st *column* of D)   (1st *row* of C × 2nd *column* of D)

$$= \begin{bmatrix} 1 \times 4 + 3 \times 1 + 2 \times 3 & 1 \times 5 + 3 \times 2 + 2 \times 1 \\ 2 \times 4 + 2 \times 1 + 4 \times 3 & 2 \times 5 + 2 \times 2 + 4 \times 1 \end{bmatrix}$$

(2nd *row* of C × 1st *column* of D)   (2nd *row* of C × 2nd *column* of D)

$$= \begin{bmatrix} 4 + 3 + 6 & 5 + 6 + 2 \\ 8 + 2 + 12 & 10 + 4 + 4 \end{bmatrix} = \begin{bmatrix} 13 & 13 \\ 22 & 18 \end{bmatrix}$$

Notice that C has two rows and three columns and D has three rows and two columns. The number of columns of C is the same as the number of rows of D so that multiplication is possible. (Is multiplication possible with the matrices A and B that we considered when we discussed addition and subtraction?) Notice, further, that the product, CD, has two rows and two columns. The number of rows of CD is the same as that of C and the number of columns of

CD is the same as that of D. In this case, it is also possible to form the matrix product DC:

$$DC = \begin{bmatrix} 4 & 5 \\ 1 & 2 \\ 3 & 1 \end{bmatrix} \begin{bmatrix} 1 & 3 & 2 \\ 2 & 2 & 4 \end{bmatrix}$$

$$= \begin{bmatrix} 4 \times 1 + 5 \times 2 & 4 \times 3 + 5 \times 2 & 4 \times 2 + 5 \times 4 \\ 1 \times 1 + 2 \times 2 & 1 \times 3 + 2 \times 2 & 1 \times 2 + 2 \times 4 \\ 3 \times 1 + 1 \times 2 & 3 \times 3 + 1 \times 2 & 3 \times 2 + 1 \times 4 \end{bmatrix}$$

$$= \begin{bmatrix} 4 + 10 & 12 + 10 & 8 + 20 \\ 1 + 4 & 3 + 4 & 2 + 8 \\ 3 + 2 & 9 + 2 & 6 + 4 \end{bmatrix} = \begin{bmatrix} 14 & 22 & 28 \\ 5 & 7 & 10 \\ 5 & 11 & 10 \end{bmatrix}$$

The number of rows and the number of columns of a matrix are called its *dimensions*. A matrix that has three rows and five columns, for example, is called a 3×5 matrix. The number of rows is always written first. Using dimensions makes it easy to check on the possibility of matrix multiplication and to determine the dimensions of the product. If, for example, we wish to multiply a 3×5 matrix by a 5×2 matrix, we "cancel" the fives and see that the result is a 3×2 matrix. But with the same matrices, if we tried to take the product in the reverse order, we would be multiplying a 5×2 by a 3×5 and no cancellation of the inner digits can occur. This shows that the operation is impossible.

In correlation and regression analysis we make some use of the transposes of products. The transpose of a product of two matrices is the product of the transposes of the two matrices *multiplied in reverse order*. That is

$$(AB)^T = B^T A^T$$

To see this, suppose

$$A = \begin{bmatrix} 1 & 2 \\ 3 & 4 \end{bmatrix}, \quad B = \begin{bmatrix} 1 & 3 & 1 \\ 2 & 1 & 1 \end{bmatrix}$$

Then

$$AB = \begin{bmatrix} 1 & 2 \\ 3 & 4 \end{bmatrix} \begin{bmatrix} 1 & 3 & 1 \\ 2 & 1 & 1 \end{bmatrix} = \begin{bmatrix} 5 & 5 & 3 \\ 11 & 13 & 7 \end{bmatrix}$$

So that

$$(AB)^T = \begin{bmatrix} 5 & 11 \\ 5 & 13 \\ 3 & 7 \end{bmatrix}$$

On the other hand

$$B^T A^T = \begin{bmatrix} 1 & 2 \\ 3 & 1 \\ 1 & 1 \end{bmatrix} \begin{bmatrix} 1 & 3 \\ 2 & 4 \end{bmatrix} = \begin{bmatrix} 5 & 11 \\ 5 & 13 \\ 3 & 7 \end{bmatrix} = [AB]^T$$

A matrix that is equal to its transpose is called *symmetric*. Can you prove that $(A'A)$ is symmetric?

Identity Matrix

An identity matrix is one that acts in matrix multiplication in the same way as the number 1 acts in the multiplication of real numbers. Multiplication of a matrix by an identity leaves the original matrix unchanged. An identity matrix is always square; that is, it has as many rows as it has columns. It consists of ones written along the main diagonal and zeros elsewhere. (The main diagonal of a matrix consists of the first element of the first row, the second element of the second row, the third element of the third row, and so on.) Identity matrices are usually denoted by the symbol I. A 3×3 identity matrix would be written as

$$I = \begin{bmatrix} 1 & 0 & 0 \\ 0 & 1 & 0 \\ 0 & 0 & 1 \end{bmatrix}$$

From the rules of matrix multiplication, it is clear that an identity matrix which appears on the left of another matrix by which it is to be multiplied must have as many rows and columns as the second matrix has rows. If the identity matrix appears on the right, it must have as many rows and columns as the matrix by which it is to be multiplied has columns. An example will make this clear.

$$A = \begin{bmatrix} 3 & 2 & 1 \\ 4 & 7 & 5 \end{bmatrix}$$

then

$$IA = \begin{bmatrix} 1 & 0 \\ 0 & 1 \end{bmatrix} \begin{bmatrix} 3 & 2 & 1 \\ 4 & 7 & 5 \end{bmatrix} = \begin{bmatrix} 3 & 2 & 1 \\ 4 & 7 & 5 \end{bmatrix} = A$$

and

$$AI = \begin{bmatrix} 3 & 2 & 1 \\ 4 & 7 & 5 \end{bmatrix} \begin{bmatrix} 1 & 0 & 0 \\ 0 & 1 & 0 \\ 0 & 0 & 1 \end{bmatrix} = \begin{bmatrix} 3 & 2 & 1 \\ 4 & 7 & 5 \end{bmatrix} = A$$

In most of our work, we shall be dealing with square matrices so that the dimensions of an identity matrix will not depend on the order of multiplication. (Why is this a property of square matrices?)

Inverse of a Matrix

In ordinary algebra, the fact that every real number except zero has a reciprocal permits us to solve linear algebraic equations. Thus, the solution of the linear equation in one unknown,

$$ax = b \qquad a \neq 0$$

is

$$x = \frac{1}{a} \cdot b = \frac{b}{a} \qquad a \neq 0$$

We solved this equation by multiplying it by the reciprocal of a. That is, we utilized the fact that

$$\frac{1}{a} \cdot a = 1 \qquad a \neq 0$$

The reciprocal of a when multiplied by a is equal to unity. Unity is the "identity" element for the real numbers when ordinary multiplication is being considered.

Under certain conditions, some square matrices have "reciprocals" that act on matrices in much the same way as the reciprocals of real numbers act on those numbers. A matrix times its reciprocal is equal to the identity matrix. The reciprocal of the matrix A is usually called the *inverse* of the matrix and denoted by the symbol A^{-1}. Hence, we can write

$$A \cdot A^{-1} = A^{-1} \cdot A = I$$

if A^{-1} exists. In order for A^{-1} to exist, A must be a square matrix and its rows (or columns) must be linearly independent. This means that it must be impossible to obtain any row of A by a process of multiplying the other rows of A by scalars and adding them. For example, if

$$A = \begin{bmatrix} 1 & 3 \\ 2 & 6 \end{bmatrix}$$

A has no inverse because the second row of A is twice the first row. Again, if

$$B = \begin{bmatrix} 1 & 3 & 2 \\ 4 & 5 & 1 \\ 2 & -1 & -3 \end{bmatrix}$$

then B has no inverse because the second row is equal to twice the first row plus the last row. Ordinarily, we do not apply a test for linear independence of the rows; we assume that the inverse of a square matrix exists and discover that it does not only when we try to compute it. In this text, the inverses of the matrices with which we deal will exist.

To compute the inverse of the 2 × 2 matrix

$$A = \begin{bmatrix} a & b \\ c & d \end{bmatrix}$$

use

$$A^{-1} = \frac{1}{ad - bc} \begin{bmatrix} d & -b \\ -c & a \end{bmatrix}$$

With 2 × 2 matrices, we soon discover whether the inverse exists. If the quantity $ad - bc$ is equal to zero, the necessary division is impossible, and the matrix has no inverse. For example, if

$$A = \begin{bmatrix} 1 & 3 \\ 2 & 6 \end{bmatrix}$$

then

$$ad - bc = 1 \times 6 - 3 \times 2 = 6 - 6 = 0.$$

On the other hand, suppose

$$A = \begin{bmatrix} 2 & 3 \\ 2 & 6 \end{bmatrix}$$

Then

$$ad - bc = 2 \times 6 - 3 \times 2 = 12 - 6 = 6,$$

and

$$A^{-1} = \frac{1}{6} \begin{bmatrix} 6 & -3 \\ -2 & 2 \end{bmatrix} = \begin{bmatrix} 1 & -\dfrac{1}{2} \\ -\dfrac{1}{3} & \dfrac{1}{3} \end{bmatrix}$$

After computing an inverse, it is always a good idea to check it by multiplication. For our example,

$$AA^{-1} = \begin{bmatrix} 2 & 3 \\ 2 & 6 \end{bmatrix} \begin{bmatrix} 1 & -\dfrac{1}{2} \\ -\dfrac{1}{3} & \dfrac{1}{3} \end{bmatrix}$$

$$= \begin{bmatrix} 2 \times 1 - 3 \times \dfrac{1}{3} & -2 \times \dfrac{1}{2} + 3 \times \dfrac{1}{3} \\ 2 \times 1 - 6 \times \dfrac{1}{3} & -2 \times \dfrac{1}{2} + 6 \times \dfrac{1}{3} \end{bmatrix} = \begin{bmatrix} 1 & 0 \\ 0 & 1 \end{bmatrix}$$

There are many ways to compute the inverses of matrices that are larger than 2 × 2. One of the easiest is based on the following fact. If we reduce a matrix to the identity matrix by multiplying the rows by constants and adding them and, at the same time, perform exactly the same operations on the rows of the identity matrix, we reduce the identity matrix to the inverse of the original matrix. This is not as complicated as it sounds. Consider the matrix whose inverse we have just computed. We write it and the identity matrix side by side and, by multiplying rows by constants and adding them, we reduce the original matrix to the identity matrix. We perform exactly the same operations on the identity matrix (see Table D.1). In the last box of the table under the identity matrix we have the inverse of the original matrix.

Table D.1

Line	Original	Identity	Operation
1	2 3	1 0	Line 3 = line 1
2	2 6	0 1	Line 4 = line 2 − line 1
3	2 3	1 0	Line 5 = line 3 − line 4
4	0 3	−1 1	Line 6 = line 4
5	2 0	2 −1	Line 7 = $\frac{1}{2}$ line 5
6	0 3	−1 1	Line 8 = $\frac{1}{3}$ line 6
7	1 0	1 $-\frac{1}{2}$	Finished
8	0 1	$-\frac{1}{3}$ $\frac{1}{3}$	

Next, suppose that we apply the same kind of process to a 3 × 3 matrix (see Table D.2). Let

$$A = \begin{bmatrix} 1 & 2 & 1 \\ 2 & 1 & 2 \\ 1 & 1 & 2 \end{bmatrix}$$

According to our calculations

$$A^{-1} = \begin{bmatrix} 0 & 1 & -1 \\ \dfrac{2}{3} & -\dfrac{1}{3} & 0 \\ -\dfrac{1}{3} & -\dfrac{1}{3} & 1 \end{bmatrix}$$

Table D.2

Line	Original			Identity			Operation
1	1	2	1	1	0	0	Line 4 = line 1
2	2	1	2	0	1	0	Line 5 = line 2 − 2 line 1
3	1	1	2	0	0	1	Line 6 = line 3 − line 1
4	1	2	1	1	0	0	Line 7 = line 4
5	0	−3	0	−2	1	0	Line 8 = $-\frac{1}{3}$ line 5
6	0	−1	1	−1	0	1	Line 9 = line 6 − $\frac{1}{3}$ line 5
7	1	2	1	1	0	0	Line 10 = line 7 − 2 line 8 − line 9
8	0	1	0	$\frac{2}{3}$	$-\frac{1}{3}$	0	Line 11 = line 8
9	0	0	1	$-\frac{1}{3}$	$-\frac{1}{3}$	1	Line 12 = line 9
10	1	0	0	0	1	−1	
11	0	1	0	$\frac{2}{3}$	$-\frac{1}{3}$	0	Finished
12	0	0	1	$-\frac{1}{3}$	$-\frac{1}{3}$	1	

but we had better check it;

$$AA^{-1} = \begin{bmatrix} 1 & 2 & 1 \\ 2 & 1 & 2 \\ 1 & 1 & 2 \end{bmatrix} \begin{bmatrix} 0 & 1 & -1 \\ \dfrac{2}{3} & -\dfrac{1}{3} & 0 \\ -\dfrac{1}{3} & -\dfrac{1}{3} & 1 \end{bmatrix} = \begin{bmatrix} 1 & 0 & 0 \\ 0 & 1 & 0 \\ 0 & 0 & 1 \end{bmatrix}$$

The actual multiplication is left to the reader as an exercise.

Table E.1 Common Logarithms of Numbers and Proportional Parts

	0	1	2	3	4	5	6	7	8	9	Proportional Parts								
											1	2	3	4	5	6	7	8	9
10	0000	0043	0086	0128	0170	0212	0253	0294	0334	0374	4	8	12	17	21	25	29	33	37
11	0414	0453	0492	0531	0569	0607	0645	0682	0719	0755	4	8	11	15	19	23	26	30	34
12	0792	0828	0864	0899	0934	0969	1004	1038	1072	1106	3	7	10	14	17	21	24	28	31
13	1139	1173	1206	1239	1271	1303	1335	1367	1399	1430	3	6	10	13	16	19	23	26	29
14	1461	1492	1523	1553	1584	1614	1644	1673	1703	1732	3	6	9	12	15	18	21	24	27
15	1761	1790	1818	1847	1875	1903	1931	1959	1987	2014	3	6	8	11	14	17	20	22	25
16	2041	2068	2095	2122	2148	2175	2201	2227	2253	2279	3	5	8	11	13	16	18	21	24
17	2304	2330	2355	2380	2405	2430	2455	2480	2504	2529	2	5	7	10	12	15	17	20	22
18	2553	2577	2601	2625	2648	2672	2695	2718	2742	2765	2	5	7	9	12	14	16	19	21
19	2788	2810	2833	2856	2878	2900	2923	2945	2967	2989	2	4	7	9	11	13	16	18	20
20	3010	3032	3054	3075	3096	3118	3139	3160	3181	3201	2	4	6	8	11	13	15	17	19
21	3222	3243	3263	3284	3304	3324	3345	3365	3385	3404	2	4	6	8	10	12	14	16	18
22	3424	3444	3464	3483	3502	3522	3541	3560	3579	3598	2	4	6	8	10	12	14	15	17
23	3617	3636	3655	3674	3692	3711	3729	3747	3766	3784	2	4	6	7	9	11	13	15	17
24	3802	3820	3838	3856	3874	3892	3909	3927	3945	3962	2	4	5	7	9	11	12	14	16
25	3979	3997	4014	4031	4048	4065	4082	4099	4116	4133	2	3	5	7	9	10	12	14	15
26	4150	4166	4183	4200	4216	4232	4249	4265	4281	4298	2	3	5	7	8	10	11	13	15
27	4314	4330	4346	4362	4378	4393	4409	4425	4440	4456	2	3	5	6	8	9	11	13	14
28	4472	4487	4502	4518	4533	4548	4564	4579	4594	4609	2	3	5	6	8	9	11	12	14
29	4624	4639	4654	4669	4683	4698	4713	4728	4742	4757	1	3	4	6	7	9	10	12	13
30	4771	4786	4800	4814	4829	4843	4857	4871	4886	4900	1	3	4	6	7	9	10	11	13
31	4914	4928	4942	4955	4969	4983	4997	5011	5024	5038	1	3	4	6	7	8	10	11	12
32	5051	5065	5079	5092	5105	5119	5132	5145	5159	5172	1	3	4	5	7	8	9	11	12
33	5185	5198	5211	5224	5237	5250	5263	5276	5289	5302	1	3	4	5	6	8	9	10	12
34	5315	5328	5340	5353	5366	5378	5391	5403	5416	5428	1	3	4	5	6	8	9	10	11
35	5441	5453	5465	5478	5490	5502	5514	5527	5539	5551	1	2	4	5	6	7	9	10	11
36	5563	5575	5587	5599	5611	5623	5635	5647	5658	5670	1	2	4	5	6	7	8	10	11
37	5682	5694	5705	5717	5729	5740	5752	5763	5775	5786	1	2	3	5	6	7	8	9	10
38	5798	5809	5821	5832	5843	5855	5866	5877	5888	5899	1	2	3	5	6	7	8	9	10
39	5911	5922	5933	5944	5955	5966	5977	5988	5999	6010	1	2	3	4	5	7	8	9	10
40	6021	6031	6042	6053	6064	6075	6085	6096	6107	6117	1	2	3	4	5	6	8	9	10

Table E.1 (*continued*)

	0	1	2	3	4	5	6	7	8	9	Proportional Parts								
											1	2	3	4	5	6	7	8	9
41	6128	6138	6149	6160	6170	6180	6191	6201	6212	6222	1	2	3	4	5	6	7	8	9
42	6232	6243	6253	6263	6274	6284	6294	6304	6314	6325	1	2	3	4	5	6	7	8	9
43	6335	6345	6355	6365	6375	6385	6395	6405	6415	6425	1	2	3	4	5	6	7	8	9
44	6435	6444	6454	6464	6474	6484	6493	6503	6513	6522	1	2	3	4	5	6	7	8	9
45	6532	6542	6551	6561	6571	6580	6590	6599	6609	6618	1	2	3	4	5	6	7	8	9
46	6628	6637	6646	6656	6665	6675	6684	6693	6702	6712	1	2	3	4	5	6	7	7	8
47	6721	6730	6739	6749	6758	6767	6776	6785	6794	6803	1	2	3	4	5	5	6	7	8
48	6812	6821	6830	6839	6848	6857	6866	6875	6884	6893	1	2	3	4	4	5	6	7	8
49	6902	6911	6920	6928	6937	6946	6955	6964	6972	6981	1	2	3	4	4	5	6	7	8
50	6990	6998	7007	7016	7024	7033	7042	7050	7059	7067	1	2	3	3	4	5	6	7	8
51	7076	7084	7093	7101	7110	7118	7126	7135	7143	7152	1	2	3	3	4	5	6	7	8
52	7160	7168	7177	7185	7193	7202	7210	7218	7226	7235	1	2	2	3	4	5	6	7	7
53	7243	7251	7259	7267	7275	7284	7292	7300	7308	7316	1	2	2	3	4	5	6	6	7
54	7324	7332	7340	7348	7356	7364	7372	7380	7388	7396	1	2	2	3	4	5	6	6	7
55	7404	7412	7419	7427	7435	7443	7451	7459	7466	7474	1	2	2	3	4	5	5	6	7
56	7482	7490	7497	7505	7513	7520	7528	7536	7543	7551	1	2	2	3	4	5	5	6	7
57	7559	7566	7574	7582	7589	7597	7604	7612	7619	7627	1	2	2	3	4	5	5	6	7
58	7634	7642	7649	7657	7664	7672	7679	7686	7694	7701	1	1	2	3	4	4	5	6	7
59	7709	7716	7723	7731	7738	7745	7752	7760	7767	7774	1	1	2	3	4	4	5	6	7
60	7782	7789	7796	7803	7810	7818	7825	7832	7839	7846	1	1	2	3	4	4	5	6	6
61	7853	7860	7868	7875	7882	7889	7896	7903	7910	7917	1	1	2	3	4	4	5	6	6
62	7924	7931	7938	7945	7952	7959	7966	7973	7980	7987	1	1	2	3	3	4	5	6	6
63	7993	8000	8007	8014	8021	8028	8035	8041	8048	8055	1	1	2	3	3	4	5	5	6
64	8062	8069	8075	8082	8089	8096	8102	8109	8116	8122	1	1	2	3	3	4	5	5	6
65	8129	8136	8142	8149	8156	8162	8169	8176	8182	8189	1	1	2	3	3	4	5	5	6
66	8195	8202	8209	8215	8222	8228	8235	8241	8248	8254	1	1	2	3	3	4	5	5	6
67	8261	8267	8274	8280	8287	8293	8299	8306	8312	8319	1	1	2	3	3	4	5	5	6
68	8325	8331	8338	8344	8351	8357	8363	8370	8376	8382	1	1	2	3	3	4	4	5	6
69	8388	8395	8401	8407	8414	8420	8426	8432	8439	8445	1	1	2	2	3	4	4	5	6
70	8451	8457	8463	8470	8476	8482	8488	8494	8500	8506	1	1	2	2	3	4	4	5	6
71	8513	8519	8525	8531	8537	8543	8549	8555	8561	8567	1	1	2	2	3	4	4	5	5

Table E.1 *(continued)*

	0	1	2	3	4	5	6	7	8	9	Proportional Parts								
											1	2	3	4	5	6	7	8	9
72	8573	8579	8585	8591	8597	8603	8609	8615	8621	8627	1	1	2	2	3	4	4	5	5
73	8633	8639	8645	8651	8657	8663	8669	8675	8681	8686	1	1	2	2	3	4	4	5	5
74	8692	8698	8704	8710	8716	8722	8727	8733	8739	8745	1	1	2	2	3	4	4	5	5
75	8751	8756	8762	8768	8774	8779	8785	8791	8797	8802	1	1	2	2	3	3	4	5	5
76	8808	8814	8820	8825	8831	8837	8842	8848	8854	8859	1	1	2	2	3	3	4	5	5
77	8865	8871	8876	8882	8887	8893	8899	8904	8910	8915	1	1	2	2	3	3	4	4	5
78	8921	8927	8932	8938	8943	8949	8954	8960	8965	8971	1	1	2	2	3	3	4	4	5
79	8976	8982	8987	8993	8998	9004	9009	9015	9020	9025	1	1	2	2	3	3	4	4	5
80	9031	9036	9042	9047	9053	9058	9063	9069	9074	9079	1	1	2	2	3	3	4	4	5
81	9085	9090	9096	9101	9106	9112	9117	9122	9128	9133	1	1	2	2	3	3	4	4	5
82	9138	9143	9149	9154	9159	9165	9170	9175	9180	9186	1	1	2	2	3	3	4	4	5
83	9191	9196	9201	9206	9212	9217	9222	9227	9232	9238	1	1	2	2	3	3	4	4	5
84	9243	9248	9253	9258	9263	9269	9274	9279	9284	9289	1	1	2	2	3	3	4	4	5
85	9294	9299	9304	9309	9315	9320	9325	9330	9335	9340	1	1	2	2	3	3	4	4	5
86	9345	9350	9355	9360	9365	9370	9375	9380	9385	9390	1	1	2	2	3	3	4	4	5
87	9395	9400	9405	9410	9415	9420	9425	9430	9435	9440	0	1	1	2	2	3	3	4	4
88	9445	9450	9455	9460	9465	9469	9474	9479	9484	9489	0	1	1	2	2	3	3	4	4
89	9494	9499	9504	9509	9513	9518	9523	9528	9533	9538	0	1	1	2	2	3	3	4	4
90	9542	9547	9552	9557	9562	9566	9571	9576	9581	9586	0	1	1	2	2	3	3	4	4
91	9590	9595	9600	9605	9609	9614	9619	9624	9628	9633	0	1	1	2	2	3	3	4	4
92	9638	9643	9647	9652	9657	9661	9666	9671	9675	9680	0	1	1	2	2	3	3	4	4
93	9685	9689	9694	9699	9703	9708	9713	9717	9722	9727	0	1	1	2	2	3	3	4	4
94	9731	9736	9741	9745	9750	9754	9759	9763	9768	9773	0	1	1	2	2	3	3	4	4
95	9777	9782	9786	9791	9795	9800	9805	9809	9814	9818	0	1	1	2	2	3	3	4	4
96	9823	9827	9832	9836	9841	9845	9850	9854	9859	9863	0	1	1	2	2	3	3	4	4
97	9868	9872	9877	9881	9886	9890	9894	9899	9903	9908	0	1	1	2	2	3	3	4	4
98	9912	9917	9921	9926	9930	9934	9939	9943	9948	9952	0	1	1	2	2	3	3	4	4
99	9956	9961	9965	9969	9974	9978	9983	9987	9991	9996	0	1	1	2	2	3	3	3	4

Table E.2 Exponential Functions

x	e^x	e^{-x}	x	e^x	e^{-x}
0.00	1.000	1.000	3.00	20.086	0.050
0.10	1.105	0.905	3.10	22.198	0.045
0.20	1.221	0.819	3.20	24.533	0.041
0.30	1.350	0.741	3.30	27.113	0.037
0.40	1.492	0.670	3.40	29.964	0.033
0.50	1.649	0.607	3.50	33.115	0.030
0.60	1.822	0.549	3.60	36.598	0.027
0.70	2.014	0.497	3.70	40.447	0.025
0.80	2.226	0.449	3.80	44.701	0.022
0.90	2.460	0.407	3.90	49.402	0.020
1.00	2.718	0.368	4.00	54.598	0.018
1.10	3.004	0.333	4.10	60.340	0.017
1.20	3.320	0.301	4.20	66.686	0.015
1.30	3.669	0.273	4.30	73.700	0.014
1.40	4.055	0.247	4.40	81.451	0.012
1.50	4.482	0.223	4.50	90.017	0.011
1.60	4.953	0.202	4.60	99.484	0.010
1.70	5.474	0.183	4.70	109.95	0.009
1.80	6.050	0.165	4.80	121.51	0.008
1.90	6.686	0.150	4.90	134.29	0.007
2.00	7.389	0.135	5.00	148.41	0.007
2.10	8.166	0.122	5.10	164.02	0.006
2.20	9.025	0.111	5.20	181.27	0.006
2.30	9.974	0.100	5.30	200.34	0.005
2.40	11.023	0.091	5.40	221.41	0.005
2.50	12.182	0.082	5.50	244.69	0.004
2.60	13.464	0.074	5.60	270.43	0.004
2.70	14.880	0.067	5.70	298.87	0.003
2.80	16.445	0.061	5.80	330.30	0.003
2.90	18.174	0.055	5.90	365.04	0.003
3.00	20.086	0.050	6.00	403.43	0.002

Table E.3 Table of Areas of the Unit Normal Distribution Between the Maximum Ordinate and Values of Z (Factor 10^{-5} Omitted)

z	0.00	0.01	0.02	0.03	0.04	0.05	0.06	0.07	0.08	0.09
0.0	00000	00399	00798	01197	01595	01994	02392	02790	03188	03586
0.1	03983	04380	04776	05172	05567	05962	06356	06749	07142	07535
0.2	07926	08317	08706	09095	09483	09871	10257	10642	11026	11409
0.3	11791	12172	12552	12930	13307	13683	14058	14431	14803	15173
0.4	15542	15910	16276	16640	17003	17364	17724	18082	18439	18793
0.5	19146	19497	19847	20194	20540	20884	21226	21566	21904	22240
0.6	22575	22907	23237	23565	23891	24215	24537	24857	25175	25490
0.7	25804	26115	26424	26730	27035	27337	27637	27935	28230	28524
0.8	28814	29103	29389	29673	29955	30234	30511	30785	31057	31327
0.9	31594	31859	32121	32381	32639	32894	33147	33398	33646	33891
1.0	34134	34375	34614	34850	35083	35314	35543	35769	35993	36214
1.1	36433	36650	36864	37076	37286	37493	37698	37900	38100	38298
1.2	38493	38686	38877	39065	39251	39435	39617	39796	39973	40147
1.3	40320	40490	40658	40824	40988	41149	41309	41466	41621	41774
1.4	41924	42073	42220	42364	42507	42647	42786	42922	43056	43189
1.5	43319	43448	43574	43699	43822	43943	44062	44179	44295	44408
1.6	44520	44630	44738	44845	44950	45053	45154	45254	45352	45449
1.7	45543	45637	45728	45818	45907	45994	46080	46164	46246	46327
1.8	46407	46485	46562	46638	46712	46784	46856	46926	46995	47062
1.9	47128	47193	47257	47320	47381	47441	47500	47558	47615	47670
2.0	47725	47778	47831	47882	47932	47982	48030	48077	48124	48169
2.1	48214	48257	48300	48341	48382	48422	48461	48500	48537	48574
2.2	48610	48645	48679	48713	48745	48778	48809	48840	48870	48899
2.3	48928	48956	48983	49010	49036	49061	49086	49111	49134	49158
2.4	49180	49202	49224	49245	49266	49286	49305	49324	49343	49361
2.5	49377	49396	49413	49430	49446	49461	49477	49492	49506	49520
2.6	49534	49547	49560	49573	49585	49598	49609	49621	49632	49643
2.7	49653	49664	49674	49683	49693	49702	49711	49720	49728	49736
2.8	49744	49752	49760	49767	49774	49781	49788	49795	49801	49807
2.9	49813	49819	49825	49831	49836	49841	49846	49851	49856	49861
3.0	49865	49869	49874	49878	49882	49886	49889	49893	49897	49900
3.1	49903	49906	49910	49913	49916	49918	49921	49924	49926	49929
3.2	49931	49934	49936	49938	49940	49942	49944	49946	49948	49950
3.3	49952	49953	49955	49957	49958	49960	49961	49962	49964	49965
3.4	49966	49968	49969	49970	49971	49972	49973	49974	49975	49976
3.5	49977	49978	49978	49979	49980	49981	49981	49982	49983	49983
3.6	49984	49985	49985	49986	49986	49987	49987	49988	49988	49989
3.7	49989	49990	49990	49990	49991	49991	49992	49992	49992	49992
3.8	49993	49993	49993	49994	49994	49994	49994	49995	49995	49995
3.9	49995	49995	49996	49996	49996	49996	49996	49996	49997	49997
4.0	49997	49997	49997	49997	49997	49997	49998	49998	49998	49998

Table E.4 Random Digits

39 65 76 45 45	19 90 69 64 61	20 26 36 31 62	58 24 97 14 97	95 06 70 99 00
73 71 23 70 90	65 97 60 12 11	31 56 34 19 19	47 83 75 51 33	30 62 38 20 46
72 20 47 33 84	51 67 47 97 19	98 40 07 17 66	23 05 09 51 80	59 78 11 52 49
75 17 25 69 17	17 95 21 78 58	24 33 45 77 48	69 81 84 09 29	93 22 70 45 80
37 48 79 88 74	63 52 06 34 30	01 31 60 10 27	35 07 79 71 53	28 99 52 01 41
02 89 08 16 94	85 53 83 29 95	56 27 09 24 43	21 78 55 09 82	72 61 88 73 61
87 18 15 70 07	37 79 49 12 38	48 13 93 55 96	41 92 45 71 51	09 18 25 58 94
98 83 71 70 15	89 09 39 59 24	00 06 41 41 20	14 36 59 25 47	54 45 17 24 89
10 08 58 07 04	76 62 16 48 68	58 76 17 14 86	59 53 11 52 21	66 04 18 72 87
47 90 56 37 31	71 82 13 50 41	27 55 10 24 92	28 04 67 53 44	95 23 00 84 47
93 05 31 03 07	34 18 04 52 35	74 13 39 35 22	68 95 23 92 35	36 63 70 35 33
21 89 11 47 99	11 20 99 45 18	76 51 94 84 86	13 79 93 37 55	98 16 04 41 67
95 18 94 06 97	27 37 83 28 71	79 57 95 13 91	09 61 87 25 21	56 20 11 32 44
97 08 31 55 73	10 65 81 92 59	77 31 61 95 46	20 44 90 32 64	26 99 76 75 63
69 26 88 86 13	59 71 74 17 32	48 38 75 93 29	73 37 32 04 05	60 82 29 20 25
41 47 10 25 03	87 63 93 95 17	81 83 83 04 49	77 45 85 50 51	79 88 01 97 30
91 94 14 63 62	08 61 74 51 69	92 79 43 89 79	29 18 94 51 23	14 85 11 47 23
80 06 54 18 47	08 52 85 08 40	48 40 35 94 22	72 65 71 08 86	50 03 42 99 36
67 72 77 63 99	89 85 84 46 06	64 71 06 21 66	89 37 20 70 01	61 65 70 22 12
59 40 24 13 75	42 29 72 23 19	06 94 76 10 08	81 30 15 39 14	81 83 17 16 33
63 62 06 34 41	79 53 36 02 95	94 61 09 43 62	20 21 14 68 86	84 95 48 46 45
78 47 23 53 90	79 93 96 38 63	34 85 52 05 09	85 43 01 72 73	14 93 87 81 40
87 68 62 15 43	97 48 72 66 48	53 16 71 13 81	59 97 50 99 52	24 62 20 42 31
47 60 92 10 77	26 97 05 73 51	88 46 38 03 58	72 68 49 29 31	75 70 16 08 24
56 88 87 59 41	06 87 37 78 48	65 88 69 58 39	88 02 84 27 83	85 81 56 39 38
22 17 68 65 84	87 02 22 57 51	68 69 80 95 44	11 29 01 95 80	49 34 35 86 47
19 36 27 59 46	39 77 32 77 09	79 57 92 36 59	89 74 39 82 15	08 58 94 34 74
16 77 23 02 77	28 06 24 25 93	22 45 44 84 11	87 80 61 65 31	09 71 91 74 25
78 43 76 71 61	97 67 63 99 61	80 45 67 93 82	59 73 19 85 23	53 33 65 97 21
03 28 28 26 08	69 30 16 09 05	53 58 47 70 93	66 56 45 65 79	45 56 20 19 47
04 31 17 21 56	33 73 99 19 87	26 72 39 27 67	53 77 57 68 93	60 61 97 22 61
61 06 98 03 91	87 14 77 43 96	43 00 65 98 50	45 60 33 01 07	98 99 46 50 47
23 68 35 26 00	99 53 93 61 28	52 70 05 48 34	56 65 05 61 86	90 92 10 70 80
15 39 25 70 99	93 86 52 77 65	15 33 59 05 28	22 87 26 07 47	86 96 98 29 06
58 71 96 30 24	18 46 23 34 27	85 13 99 24 44	49 18 09 79 49	74 16 32 23 02
93 22 53 64 39	07 10 63 76 35	87 03 04 79 88	08 13 13 85 51	55 34 57 72 69
78 76 58 54 74	92 38 70 96 92	52 06 79 79 45	82 63 18 27 44	69 66 92 19 09
61 81 31 96 82	00 57 25 60 59	46 72 60 18 77	55 66 12 62 11	08 99 55 64 57
42 88 07 10 05	24 98 65 63 21	47 21 61 88 32	27 80 30 21 60	10 92 35 36 12
77 94 30 05 39	28 10 99 00 27	12 73 73 99 12	49 99 57 94 82	96 88 57 17 91

Table E.5 Common Logarithms of Factorials 1–100

n	Log $n!$	n	Log $n!$
1	0.00000	51	66.19065
2	0.30103	52	67.90665
3	0.77815	53	69.63092
4	1.38021	54	71.36332
5	2.07918	55	73.10368
6	2.85733	56	74.85187
7	3.70243	57	76.60774
8	4.60552	58	78.37117
9	5.55976	59	80.14202
10	6.55976	60	81.92017
11	7.60116	61	83.70550
12	8.68034	62	85.49790
13	9.79428	63	87.29724
14	10.94041	64	89.10342
15	12.11650	65	90.91633
16	13.32062	66	92.73587
17	14.55107	67	94.56195
18	15.80634	68	96.39446
19	17.08509	69	98.23331
20	18.38612	70	100.07841
21	19.70834	71	101.92966
22	21.05077	72	103.78700
23	22.41249	73	105.65032
24	23.79271	74	107.51955
25	25.19065	75	109.39461
26	26.60562	76	111.27543
27	28.03698	77	113.16192
28	29.48414	78	115.05401
29	30.94654	79	116.95164
30	32.42366	80	118.85473
31	33.91502	81	120.76321
32	35.42017	82	122.67703
33	36.93869	83	124.59610
34	38.47016	84	126.52038
35	40.01423	85	128.44980
36	41.57054	86	130.38430
37	43.13874	87	132.32382
38	44.71852	88	134.26830
39	46.30959	89	136.21769
40	47.91165	90	138.17194
41	49.52443	91	140.13098
42	51.14768	92	142.09477
43	52.78115	93	144.06325
44	54.42460	94	146.03638
45	56.07781	95	148.01410
46	57.74057	96	149.99637
47	59.41267	97	151.98314
48	61.09391	98	153.97437
49	62.78410	99	155.97000
50	64.48307	100	157.97000

Table E.6 Percentage Points of the t Distribution with m Degrees of Freedom (Two-Tailed Probabilities)[a]

							Percentage Point								
m	0.9	0.8	0.7	0.6	0.5	0.4	0.3	0.2	0.1	0.05	0.02	0.01	0.001
1	0.158	0.325	0.510	0.727	1.000	1.376	1.963	3.078	6.314	12.706	31.821	63.657	636.619
2	0.142	0.289	0.445	0.617	0.816	1.061	1.386	1.886	2.920	4.303	6.965	9.925	31.598
3	0.137	0.277	0.424	0.584	0.765	0.978	1.250	1.638	2.353	3.182	4.541	5.841	12.941
4	0.134	0.271	0.414	0.569	0.741	0.941	1.190	1.533	2.132	2.776	3.747	4.604	8.610
5	0.132	0.267	0.408	0.559	0.727	0.920	1.156	1.476	2.015	2.571	3.365	4.032	6.859
6	0.131	0.265	0.404	0.553	0.718	0.906	1.134	1.440	1.943	2.447	3.143	3.707	5.959
7	0.130	0.263	0.402	0.549	0.711	0.896	1.119	1.415	1.895	2.365	2.998	3.499	5.405
8	0.130	0.262	0.399	0.546	0.706	0.889	1.108	1.397	1.860	2.306	2.896	3.355	5.041
9	0.129	0.261	0.398	0.543	0.703	0.883	1.100	1.383	1.833	2.262	2.821	3.250	4.781
10	0.129	0.260	0.397	0.542	0.700	0.879	1.093	1.372	1.812	2.228	2.764	3.169	4.587
11	0.129	0.260	0.396	0.540	0.697	0.876	1.088	1.363	1.796	2.201	2.718	3.106	4.437
12	0.128	0.259	0.395	0.539	0.695	0.873	1.083	1.356	1.782	2.179	2.681	3.055	4.318
13	0.128	0.259	0.394	0.538	0.694	0.870	1.079	1.350	1.771	2.160	2.650	3.012	4.221
14	0.128	0.258	0.393	0.537	0.692	0.868	1.076	1.345	1.761	2.145	2.624	2.977	4.140
15	0.128	0.258	0.393	0.536	0.691	0.866	1.074	1.341	1.753	2.131	2.602	2.947	4.073

16	0.128	0.258	0.392	0.535	0.690	0.865	1.071	1.337	1.746	2.120	2.583	2.921	4.015
17	0.128	0.257	0.392	0.534	0.689	0.863	1.069	1.333	1.740	2.110	2.567	2.898	3.965
18	0.127	0.257	0.392	0.534	0.688	0.862	1.067	1.330	1.734	2.101	2.552	2.878	3.922
19	0.127	0.257	0.391	0.533	0.688	0.861	1.066	1.328	1.729	2.093	2.539	2.861	3.883
20	0.127	0.257	0.391	0.533	0.687	0.860	1.064	1.325	1.725	2.086	2.528	2.845	3.850
21	0.127	0.257	0.391	0.532	0.686	0.859	1.063	1.323	1.721	2.080	2.518	2.831	3.819
22	0.127	0.256	0.390	0.532	0.686	0.858	1.061	1.321	1.717	2.074	2.508	2.819	3.792
23	0.127	0.256	0.390	0.532	0.685	0.858	1.060	1.319	1.714	2.069	2.500	2.807	3.767
24	0.127	0.256	0.390	0.531	0.685	0.857	1.059	1.318	1.711	2.064	2.492	2.797	3.745
25	0.127	0.256	0.390	0.531	0.684	0.856	1.058	1.316	1.708	2.060	2.485	2.787	3.725
26	0.127	0.256	0.390	0.531	0.684	0.856	1.058	1.315	1.706	2.056	2.479	2.779	3.707
27	0.127	0.256	0.389	0.531	0.684	0.855	1.057	1.314	1.703	2.052	2.473	2.771	3.690
28	0.127	0.256	0.389	0.530	0.683	0.855	1.056	1.313	1.701	2.048	2.467	2.763	3.674
29	0.127	0.256	0.389	0.530	0.683	0.854	1.055	1.311	1.699	2.045	2.462	2.756	3.659
30	0.127	0.256	0.389	0.530	0.683	0.854	1.055	1.310	1.697	2.042	2.457	2.750	3.646
40	0.126	0.255	0.388	0.529	0.681	0.851	1.050	1.303	1.684	2.021	2.423	2.704	3.551
60	0.126	0.254	0.387	0.527	0.679	0.848	1.046	1.296	1.671	2.000	2.390	2.660	3.460
120	0.126	0.254	0.386	0.526	0.677	0.845	1.041	1.289	1.658	1.980	2.358	2.617	3.373
∞	0.126	0.253	0.385	0.524	0.674	0.842	1.036	1.282	1.645	1.960	2.326	2.576	3.291

a This table is taken by consent from *Statistical Tables for Biological, Agricultural, and Medical Research*, by Prof. R. A. Fisher and F. Yates, published by Oliver and Boyd, Edinburgh.

Table E.7 Unit Normal Loss Integral $G(|u|)^a$

u	0.00	0.01	0.02	0.03	0.04	0.05	0.06	0.07	0.08	0.09
0.0	0.3989	0.3940	0.3890	0.3841	0.3793	0.3744	0.3697	0.3649	0.3602	0.3556
0.1	0.3509	0.3464	0.3418	0.3373	0.3328	0.3284	0.3240	0.3197	0.3154	0.3111
0.2	0.3069	0.3027	0.2986	0.2944	0.2904	0.2863	0.2824	0.2784	0.2745	0.2706
0.3	0.2668	0.2630	0.2592	0.2555	0.2518	0.2481	0.2445	0.2409	0.2374	0.2339
0.4	0.2304	0.2270	0.2236	0.2203	0.2169	0.2137	0.2104	0.2072	0.2040	0.2009
0.5	0.1978	0.1947	0.1917	0.1887	0.1857	0.1828	0.1799	0.1771	0.1742	0.1714
0.6	0.1687	0.1659	0.1633	0.1606	0.1580	0.1554	0.1528	0.1503	0.1478	0.1453
0.7	0.1429	0.1405	0.1381	0.1358	0.1334	0.1312	0.1289	0.1267	0.1245	0.1223
0.8	0.1202	0.1181	0.1160	0.1140	0.1120	0.1100	0.1080	0.1061	0.1042	0.1023
0.9	0.1004	0.09860	0.09680	0.09503	0.09328	0.09156	0.08986	0.08819	0.08654	0.08491
1.0	0.08332	0.08174	0.08019	0.07866	0.07716	0.07568	0.07422	0.07279	0.07138	0.06999
1.1	0.06862	0.06727	0.06595	0.06465	0.06336	0.06210	0.06086	0.05964	0.05844	0.05726
1.2	0.05610	0.05496	0.05384	0.05274	0.05165	0.05059	0.04954	0.04851	0.04750	0.04650
1.3	0.04553	0.04457	0.04363	0.04270	0.04179	0.04090	0.04002	0.03916	0.03831	0.03748
1.4	0.03667	0.03587	0.03508	0.03431	0.03356	0.03281	0.03208	0.03137	0.03067	0.02998
1.5	0.02931	0.02865	0.02800	0.02736	0.02674	0.02612	0.02552	0.02494	0.02436	0.02380
1.6	0.02324	0.02270	0.02217	0.02165	0.02114	0.02064	0.02015	0.01967	0.01920	0.01874
1.7	0.01829	0.01785	0.01742	0.01699	0.01658	0.01617	0.01578	0.01539	0.01501	0.01464
1.8	0.01428	0.01392	0.01357	0.01323	0.01290	0.01257	0.01226	0.01195	0.01164	0.01134
1.9	0.01105	0.01077	0.01049	0.01022	0.0^29957	0.0^29698	0.0^29445	0.0^29198	0.0^28957	0.0^28721
2.0	0.0^28491	0.0^28266	0.0^28046	0.0^27832	0.0^27623	0.0^27418	0.0^27219	0.0^27024	0.0^26835	0.0^26649
2.1	0.0^26468	0.0^26292	0.0^26120	0.0^25952	0.0^25788	0.0^25628	0.0^25472	0.0^25320	0.0^25172	0.0^25028
2.2	0.0^24887	0.0^24750	0.0^24616	0.0^24486	0.0^24358	0.0^24235	0.0^24114	0.0^23996	0.0^23882	0.0^23770
2.3	0.0^23662	0.0^23556	0.0^23453	0.0^23352	0.0^23255	0.0^23159	0.0^23067	0.0^22977	0.0^22889	0.0^22804
2.4	0.0^22720	0.0^22640	0.0^22561	0.0^22484	0.0^22410	0.0^22337	0.0^22267	0.0^22199	0.0^22132	0.0^22067

2.6	0.0^21464	0.0^21418	0.0^21373	0.0^21330	0.0^21288	0.0^21247	0.0^21207	0.0^21169	0.0^21132	0.0^21095
2.7	0.0^21060	0.0^21026	0.0^39928	0.0^39607	0.0^39295	0.0^38992	0.0^38699	0.0^38414	0.0^38138	0.0^37870
2.8	0.0^37611	0.0^37359	0.0^37115	0.0^36879	0.0^36650	0.0^36428	0.0^36213	0.0^36004	0.0^35802	0.0^35606
2.9	0.0^35417	0.0^35233	0.0^35055	0.0^34883	0.0^34716	0.0^34555	0.0^34398	0.0^34247	0.0^34101	0.0^33959
3.0	0.0^33822	0.0^33689	0.0^33560	0.0^33436	0.0^33316	0.0^33199	0.0^33087	0.0^32978	0.0^32873	0.0^32771
3.1	0.0^32673	0.0^32577	0.0^32485	0.0^32396	0.0^32311	0.0^32227	0.0^32147	0.0^32070	0.0^31995	0.0^31922
3.2	0.0^31852	0.0^31785	0.0^31720	0.0^31657	0.0^31596	0.0^31537	0.0^31480	0.0^31426	0.0^31373	0.0^31322
3.3	0.0^31273	0.0^31225	0.0^31179	0.0^31135	0.0^31093	0.0^31051	0.0^31012	0.0^49734	0.0^49365	0.0^49009
3.4	0.0^48666	0.0^48335	0.0^48016	0.0^47709	0.0^47413	0.0^47127	0.0^46852	0.0^46587	0.0^46331	0.0^46085
3.5	0.0^45848	0.0^45620	0.0^45400	0.0^45188	0.0^44984	0.0^44788	0.0^44599	0.0^44417	0.0^44242	0.0^44073
3.6	0.0^43911	0.0^43755	0.0^43605	0.0^43460	0.0^43321	0.0^43188	0.0^43059	0.0^42935	0.0^42816	0.0^42702
3.7	0.0^42592	0.0^42486	0.0^42385	0.0^42287	0.0^42193	0.0^42103	0.0^42016	0.0^41933	0.0^41853	0.0^41776
3.8	0.0^41702	0.0^41632	0.0^41563	0.0^41498	0.0^41435	0.0^41375	0.0^41317	0.0^41262	0.0^41208	0.0^41157
3.9	0.0^41108	0.0^41061	0.0^41016	0.0^59723	0.0^59307	0.0^58908	0.0^58525	0.0^58158	0.0^57806	0.0^57469
4.0	0.0^57145	0.0^56835	0.0^56538	0.0^56253	0.0^55980	0.0^55718	0.0^55468	0.0^55227	0.0^54997	0.0^54777
4.1	0.0^54566	0.0^54364	0.0^54170	0.0^53985	0.0^53807	0.0^53637	0.0^53475	0.0^53319	0.0^53170	0.0^53027
4.2	0.0^52891	0.0^52760	0.0^52635	0.0^52516	0.0^52402	0.0^52292	0.0^52188	0.0^52088	0.0^51992	0.0^51901
4.3	0.0^51814	0.0^51730	0.0^51650	0.0^51574	0.0^51501	0.0^51431	0.0^51365	0.0^51301	0.0^51241	0.0^51183
4.4	0.0^51127	0.0^51074	0.0^51024	0.0^69756	0.0^69296	0.0^68857	0.0^68437	0.0^68037	0.0^67655	0.0^67290
4.5	0.0^66942	0.0^66610	0.0^66294	0.0^65992	0.0^65704	0.0^65429	0.0^65167	0.0^64917	0.0^64679	0.0^64452
4.6	0.0^64236	0.0^64029	0.0^63833	0.0^63645	0.0^63467	0.0^63297	0.0^63135	0.0^62981	0.0^62834	0.0^62694
4.7	0.0^62560	0.0^62433	0.0^62313	0.0^62197	0.0^62088	0.0^61984	0.0^61884	0.0^61790	0.0^61700	0.0^61615
4.8	0.0^61533	0.0^61456	0.0^61382	0.0^61312	0.0^61246	0.0^61182	0.0^61122	0.0^61065	0.0^61011	0.0^79588
4.9	0.0^79096	0.0^78629	0.0^78185	0.0^77763	0.0^77362	0.0^76982	0.0^76620	0.0^76276	0.0^75950	0.0^75640

$$G(-u) = u + G(u)$$

Examples: $G(3.57) = 0.0^44417 = 0.00004417$
$G(-3.57) = 3.57004417$

[a] Reproduced by permission from R. Schlaifer, *Probability and Statistics For Business Decisions*, McGraw-Hill Book Co., New York, 1959.

Point of Division
of an Interval

In this appendix we give certain standard results from analytic geometry which are helpful in the study of mixed strategies and in convexity problems. We shall refer to the union of two points and the line segment connecting them as the "join" of the two points.

THEOREM F.1. Consider the points $A_1(x_1, y_1)$ and $A_2(x_2, y_2)$. Let p be a real number such that $0 \leq p \leq 1$. Then the point $A[px_1 + (1-p)x_2, py_1 + (1-p)y_2]$ lies on the join of A_1 and A_2. Furthermore, the ratio of the distance between A_1 and A to the distance between A_1 and A_2 is $1 - p$.

Proof. We shall first show that A lies on the line determined by A_1 and A_2. The equation of this line is

$$y - y_1 = \frac{y_2 - y_1}{x_2 - x_1}(x - x_1)$$

Substituting the coordinates of A gives

$$py_1 + (1-p)y_2 - y_1 = \frac{y_2 - y_1}{x_2 - x_1}(px_1 + [1-p]x_2 - x_1)$$

$$(1-p)(y_2 - y_1) = \frac{y_2 - y_1}{x_2 - x_1}(1-p)(x_2 - x_1)$$

Since all factors cancel, the expression is an identity, and A does lie on the line determined by A_1 and A_2. Furthermore, A must lie on the join of A_1 and A_2, since if $x_1 \leq x_2$,

$$x_1 = px_1 + (1-p)x_1 \leq px_1 + (1-p)x_2 \leq px_2 + (1-p)x_2 = x_2$$

with a similar relation holding for y.

It remains to show that the ratio of the distance between A_1 and A to the distance between A_1 and A_2 is $1 - p$.

The distance between A_1 and A is

$$\sqrt{(x_1 - px_1 - (1 - p)x_2)^2 + (y_1 - py_1 - (1 - p)y_2)^2}$$
$$= \sqrt{(1 - p)^2(x_1 - x_2)^2 + (1 - p)^2(y_1 - y_2)^2}$$
$$= (1 - p)\sqrt{(x_1 - x_2)^2 + (y_1 - y_2)^2}$$

But this last radical is the distance between A_1 and A_2, so that the theorem is established.

We need the converse also.

THEOREM F.2. Let A_1 and A_2 be as in Theorem F.1. Let A be any point on the join of A_1 and A_2. Then there is a real number w such that $0 \leq w \leq 1$ for which the coordinates of A may be written as

$$A[wx_1 + (1 - w)x_2, wy_1 + (1 - w)y_2]$$

Proof. Let the distance between A_1 and A_2 be c. Let A divide the join of A_1 and A_2 into two parts such that the distances A_1A and AA_2 are, respectively, $(1 - w)c$ and wc. Then, surely, $0 \leq w \leq 1$. Let θ be the inclination of the line determined by A_1 and A_2 as shown in Figure F.1. Then

$$\sin \theta = \frac{y_2 - y_1}{c} = \frac{y - y_1}{(1 - w)c}$$
$$(1 - w)(y_2 - y_1) = y - y_1$$
$$y = wy_1 + (1 - w)y_2$$

and

$$\cos \theta = \frac{x_2 - x_1}{c} = \frac{x - x_1}{(1 - w)c}$$
$$(1 - w)(x_2 - x_1) = x - x_1$$
$$x = wx_1 + (1 - w)x_2$$

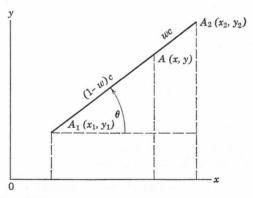

Fig. F.1. Geometry of Theorem F.2.

APPENDIX G Convex Sets

It is not the purpose of this appendix to discuss convex sets in a general way. In Chapter 11, we place almost all emphasis upon decisions involving only two states of nature; consequently the material on convex sets presented here is restricted to subsets of E_2, the Euclidean plane. Elements of such sets will be called points and will be represented in the usual Cartesian system. We shall first introduce a few basic ideas, then discuss convexity, and finally prove some theorems that will be useful in Chapter 11.

Let S be a subset of E_2. Let s and t be elements of S. We write $S \subseteq E_2$; $s \in S$, $t \in S$. The symbol $d(st)$ will be used to represent the distance between s and t.

Definition G.1. s is defined to be a limit point of S if and only if, given any real number $N > 0$, there is some other point $t \in S$ such that $d(st) < N$.

This idea is a very important concept in much mathematical development. Intuitively, a limit point of S is seen to be a point which has points of S arbitrarily close to it. The limit point itself may be a point of S or it may not. For example, if we consider all points in the plane for which $x > 1$, then the point $(1, 2)$ is a limit point of S, but does not itself belong to S. The point $(6, 6)$ belongs to S and is a limit point of S.

If we consider the set consisting of the four points $(0, 0)$, $(1, 5)$, $(-1, 3)$, and $(8, 7)$, we see that it has no limit points at all. If we examine the set of all points (x, y) such that

$$x^2 + y^2 \leq r^2$$

for some real number r, we see that every point of this set is also a limit point of the set and that the set has no other limit points.

Definition G.2. A set is called closed if and only if it contains all its limit points.

Definition G.3. A set is called open if and only if it is the complement of a closed set.

As an illustration, consider the previously mentioned set of all (x, y) such that $x^2 + y^2 \leq r^2$. It is closed. Its complement, the set of all (x, y) such that $x^2 + y^2 > r^2$, is open. Or examine the set of points (x, y) such that $x \leq 5$. It is closed and its complement, the set for which $x > 5$, is open. The set of (x, y) for which $x^2 + y^2 = r^2$ is closed and its complement is open. The set consisting of the four points $(0, 0)$, $(1, 5)$, $(-1, 3)$, and $(8, 7)$ is closed. It has no limit points; hence, it contains all its limit points. It is interesting to notice that E_2, the whole plane, contains all its limit points and is therefore closed. Its complement, $E_2 - E_2 = \varnothing$, is the null set, and this must be an open set. However, the null set has no limit points and thus is a closed set by virtue of containing them all. Thus its complement, $E_2 - \varnothing = E_2$, is open! The whole plane and the null set are the only subsets of E_2 which are both open and closed.

Definition G.4. S^0, the interior of S, is the union of all open sets contained in S.

Definition G.5. The border of S is the set $S - S^0$.

Definition G.6. The boundary of S is the union of the border of S and the border of its complement $E_2 - S$.

Suppose that we consider the closed set $x^2 + y^2 \leq r^2$. Its border is $x^2 + y^2 = r^2$. The border of its complement is $\varnothing$. Hence the boundary of the original set is the circle $x^2 + y^2 = r^2$ itself. Or consider the set consisting of the four points $(0, 0)$, $(1, 5)$, $(-1, 3)$, and $(8, 7)$. Its border consists of the same four points. The border of its complement is again null; hence the boundary of this set equals the set itself.

Since closed sets contain their own borders, and open sets have null sets as borders, it follows that the boundary of any closed set is a subset of the set, while open sets do not contain their boundaries. We note that the set $x^2 + y^2 = r^2$, discussed in the preceding paragraph, is the boundary of each of the following sets: $x^2 + y^2 \leq r^2$, $x^2 + y^2 < r^2$, $x^2 + y^2 > r^2$, and $x^2 + y^2 \geq r^2$.

We shall shortly need to work with the concept of a half-plane. Let j be a line lying in E_2. The set of points lying on one side of j is called an open half-plane. The union of this set and j is called a closed half-plane. The line j is the boundary of both the open and the closed half-planes. If the equation of j is $ax + by = c$, then in one of the open half-planes formed by j the relation $ax + by < c$ will hold true while, in the other, $ax + by > c$ will obtain. If difficulties arise in connection with this notion, try a few numerical examples. We are now in a position to begin a discussion of convex sets.

Definition G.7.   A set C is called convex if and only if every point on the join of any two points in C belongs to C. More formally, let $A_1(x_1, y_1)$ and $A_2(x_2, y_2)$ be points of C. Then C is a convex set if and only if, for all w such that $0 \leq w \leq 1$, $A(wx_1 + [1 - w]x_2, wy_1 + [1 - w]y_2)$ is in C.

There are many examples of convex sets. Note that the first line of Figure G.1 exhibits sets in E_2 that are convex. Those in the second line are not. The first item in row one indicates that all of the points within and on a circle form a convex set, while the last item in row two shows that the circle, by itself, is not convex. Comparison of the fifth item of each row brings out the fact that although one point alone constitutes a convex set, a set of discrete points is never convex.

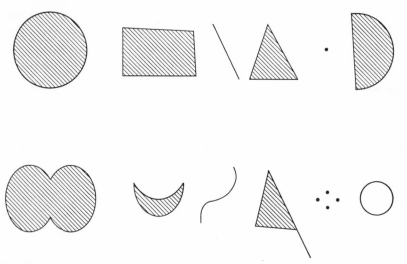

Fig. G.1. Convex and nonconvex sets in the plane.

It is evident also that a half-plane, whether closed or open, is a convex set. Surely if any two points in a half-plane are selected, all points on the join are in that half-plane. We now prove a preliminary theorem.

THEOREM G.1.   The intersection of two convex sets is again a convex set.

Proof.   Let C_1 and C_2 be convex sets. Let s and t be points in $C_1 \cap C_2$. Let u be a point on the join of s and t. Then, since $s \in C_1$ and $t \in C_1$, $u \in C_1$ by the convexity of C_1. Similarly, $s \in C_2$ and $t \in C_2$ giving $u \in C_2$. Hence $u \in C_1$ and $u \in C_2$ so that $u \in C_1 \cap C_2$. This establishes the fact that every point on the join of any two points in $C_1 \cap C_2$ lies in that intersection—

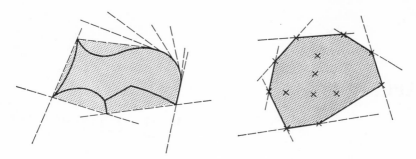

Fig. G.2. Convex hulls of two sets in E_2.

which proves the theorem. The relation can easily be generalized to apply to any number of convex sets.

Definition G.8. Let S be any subset of E_2. H, the convex hull of S in E_2, is the intersection of all closed half-planes containing S as a subset.

Figure G.2 shows two illustrations of a convex hull, the first for a set with an irregularly curved boundary and the second for a set of discrete points. It is next necessary to show that a convex hull is really a convex set—a point that appears reasonable but needs proof. Also there are many other convex sets that contain S. What are the distinctive features of H? Theorem G.2 deals with these points.

THEOREM G.2. *H, the convex hull of the set S, is a convex set such that $S \subseteq H$. Furthermore, if C is any convex set such that $S \subseteq C$, then $H \subseteq C$.*

Proof. First, we prove that $H \supseteq S$. Let $Q = \{Q_i\}$ be the set of all closed half-planes containing S. Then, since $S \subseteq Q_i$ for each value of i, $S \subseteq \cap Q_i = H$. Thus, any set is a subset of its convex hull.

Next, we show that H is really a convex set. This follows easily from the extension of Theorem G.1. H is defined as the intersection of a set of half-planes, each of which is convex. The intersection of a set of convex sets is again convex, so H is convex.

Finally, we shall prove the minimum nature of H, that it is the "smallest" convex set containing S. Let C be a convex set containing S. Let $h \in H$. h is then, by definition, an element of all closed half-planes containing S. It then must be an element of every closed half-plane containing C, since $S \subseteq C$. Hence, $h \in H_c$, the convex hull of C. But, since C is convex, $H_c = C$, so that $h \in C$. We have thus shown that any point in H is also a point of C, which establishes the relation $H \subseteq C$.

APPENDIX H Supporting and Separating Lines

In this appendix we shall develop a few simple concepts that are useful in the discussion of Bayes strategies given in Chapter 11. Sets here are two-dimensional.

Definition H.1. A set is said to be bounded provided that it is a subset of some circle interior of finite radius.

Definition H.2. A line j is called a supporting line of a set S at the boundary point b provided that no two points of S are on opposite sides of j and that b is an element of $j \cap B$ where B is the boundary of S.

Definition H.3. The line j is said to separate the sets S_1 and S_2 provided that all points of S_1 lie either on j or on one side of it, while all points of S_2 lie on the other side.

Figure H.1 illustrates the ideas incorporated in these three definitions. In the first panel, S_1 and S_2 are bounded sets separated by j_1; j_2 is a supporting line of S_2; j_1 supports both S_1 and S_2. In the second panel, S_3 and S_4 are

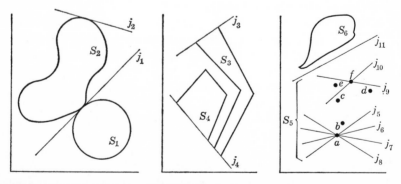

Fig. H.1. Bounded sets, supporting lines and separating lines.

bounded sets; j_3 supports S_3 and j_4 supports both S_3 and S_4. There is no line that separates S_3 and S_4. In the third panel, S_5 is a set consisting of the six discrete points: a, b, c, d, e, and f. The lines j_5, j_6, j_7, j_8, and j_9 are all supporting lines of S_5, but j_{10} is not. Why? Is S_5 bounded? Also j_{11} separates S_5 and S_6.

THEOREM H.1. Let S be a bounded set and j a line; then there is a supporting line of S which is parallel to j.

Proof. CASE I. All points of S lie on the same side of j. In this case, select a point s in B, the boundary of S, such that the perpendicular distance from s to j is as small as possible. Draw a line j_1 through s parallel to j. We shall show that j_1 is a supporting line of S.

1. No point of S could lie on the same side of j_1, as does j, or the perpendicular distance from it to j would be less than the perpendicular distance from s to j. Hence no two points of S are on opposite sides of j_1.

2. $s \in B$ by definition.
3. $s \in j_1$ by construction.

Thus the theorem is proved in Case I by simply verifying the statements in the definition of a supporting line. (See Figure H.2.)

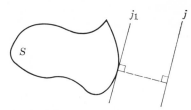

Fig. H.2. Existence of a parallel supporting line.

Proof. CASE II. Some points of S lie on each side of j. Since S is bounded, $S \subseteq G$, where G is some circle interior of finite radius. Since G is of finite radius, we can choose a line j_2 which does not intersect G and is parallel to j. The line j_2 then cannot intersect S. Using Case I, determine the point s and the line j_1 such that the perpendicular distance from s to j_2 is minimal and j_1 parallel to j_2. The line j_1 is then a supporting line of S which is parallel to j_2 and hence to j.

THEOREM H.2. Let b be a boundary point of the convex set C. Then there exists a supporting line j of C which contains b.

Proof. A rigorous proof of this point will not be given; however, it is apparent that if b belongs to a linear subset of the boundary of C, the line containing that subset is a supporting line of C. If b does not belong to a linear subset of the boundary of C, then the boundary is curvilinear in the neighborhood of b, and the tangent line at b supports C.

THEOREM H.3. Let C_1 and C_2 be two convex sets such that $C_1 \cap C_2 = \varnothing$. Then there is a line j which separates C_1 and C_2.

Proof. CASE I. When C_1 and C_2 are closed.

In this case we determine two points c_1 and c_2 such that $d(c_1 c_2)$ is as small as possible. Consider j_1, the perpendicular bisector of the join of c_1 and c_2. We shall show that it can be used as j, the separating line.

Now, even though convex sets are not necessarily bounded, we may proceed as in Theorem H.1. There is a supporting line of C_1 parallel to j_1 which passes through c_1, since c_1 is the point of C_1 lying closest to j_1. Also there is a supporting line of C_2 through c_2 parallel to j_1. Hence there are no points of either C_1 or C_2 between these two parallel supporting lines. The line j_1 is then a separating line j for C_1 and C_2.

Proof. CASE II. When at least one of C_1, C_2 is open.

Form the closed sets C_1' and C_2' by taking the union of C_1 and C_2 with their respective boundaries. If $C_1' \cap C_2' = \varnothing$, determine a minimal join and use its perpendicular bisector, as before.

In the remaining situations, the boundaries of C_1' and C_2' will intersect. We shall describe the results (see Figure H.3) without attempting any

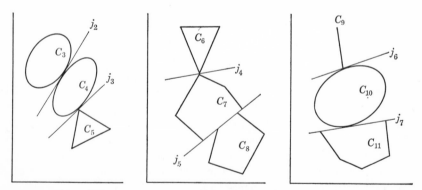

Fig. H.3. Some separating lines for convex sets.

formal proof. The student should consider various combinations of the C_i as being open while others are closed. A distinction should be made between situations such as j_5 separating C_7 and C_8 and j_4 separating C_6 and C_7. The first is a unique separating line, the second is not. Which of j_2, j_3, j_6 are unique separating lines?

Answers to Selected Exercises

Chapter 1

3. c. (1) Inductive
   (2) Descriptive
   (3) Descriptive
   (4) Inductive
   (5) Descriptive

However, students can defend other answers.

6. Among other possible answers, students might give the following:
   All persons who were employed by Hubertus since the corporation was founded.
   All persons who were employed by Hubertus since the corporation was founded and who participated in any pension plan during the time that they were so employed.
   Present employees of Hubertus participating in the present pension plan.

Chapter 2

1. A student will usually give the following answers:

a. Variable	d. Attribute
b. Attribute	e. Variable
c. Attribute	f. Variable

However, others are possible—depending upon the way in which the data are treated.

6. In any homogeneous population, stratification is of no use. A simple random sample would be as good as a stratified random sample and also easier to select.

11. a. No. Valuable results can often be obtained from samples much smaller than 1000.

b. This is a bad procedure. The data for the whole United States may not be homogeneous with respect to an east–west classification.

c. The person who answers the phone might not know if the television set is on or off. Since he is at the phone, he may not know the actual program being watched. The number of persons in the family is not necessarily the same as the number of viewers.

16. No. The population may not be homogenous with respect to education, skills, and other factors.

18. Yes. Tables should always be set up and considered in the initial stage of a research project to make sure that the right data are collected and that these can be properly analyzed.

21. a. All owners of listed telephones in San Francisco. The universe that should have been used was all owners of TV sets in San Franscico.

b. No, not necessarily. Viewers in San Francisco may not follow national patterns.

25. a. Pupils in the Lower Fenwick schools.

b. No. Some parents have more than one child.

c. No. The board should have studied voters, not parents. The study would probably be biased in favor of the assessment.

26. a. Yes. A decrease in union work force for large firms as opposed to small and medium.

b. Yes. It could be so based.

c. Yes. Data do not really vary by size of firm to any extent. They vary by type of industry. Differences in numbers of firms in these industries cause the balancing out observed in the first table.

Chapter 3

2. a. *T, U, W, X, Y*
   b. *B*
   c. {4}

5. a. 5040

7. 12

8. a. 359,300
   b. 1.281×10^{14}

11. a. 40,320
    b. 1152
    c. 2880
    d. 1/14
    e. 1/35

13. 19,958,400

14. 1/3

19. b. (1) 0.167   (6) 0.178
    (2) 0.156   (7) 0
    (3) 0.130   (8) 0.051
    (4) 0.121   (9) 0.823
    (5) 0.026

23. 24/95

25. 1/6

26. 0.373

Chapter 4

1. b. (1) $\{1/3, 2/3\}$
    (2) $\{-0.25, 0.50, 0.75\}$
    (3) $\{0, 1, 2, 3, 4, 5\}$
    (4) $\{1/8\}$
    (5) $\{0 \leq f(x) \leq 3\}$

5. a. The infinitely many expressions: $A, AB, AAB, AAAB, \cdots$ where A is the event "no shell" and B is the event "shell." Note that this holds only if the cylinder is spun after each trial.
  b. Yes.

6. 1/2

8. 0.299

11. 148

12. 5/18

15. a. Yes, if one is willing to assume that truck arrivals are independent with constant probability of marring from trial to trial.
  c. $1 - 3125 \times 10^{-10} \approx 1$
  d. $3125 \times 10^{-10} \approx 0$
  e. 0.9988
  h. 90

18. 0.002 under the Poisson assumptions. These seem rather unreasonable here.

20. a. Poisson model probably satisfactory.
  b. 0.0498
  c. 0.1494
  d. 0.004998

22. a. 0.0635
    b. 0.2503
25. a. 5/24

$$F(x) = \begin{cases} 0 & x < 2 \\ (x^2 + 3x - 10)/18 & 2 \leq x \leq 4 \\ 1 & x > 4 \end{cases}$$

c. as above

27. 0.368
30. b. 0.788
32. a. 0.894; 0.500
    b. 15.54 oz
35. 0.691

Chapter 5

2. a. 1/2
   b. 0
   c. 0
   d. 1/2
   e. 5/8
3. a. $k = 4$
   b. 0
   c. $1 - e^{-4} = 0.9817$
   d. 1/2
5. $\dbinom{26}{3}\dbinom{26}{3} / \dbinom{52}{6} = 0.33; 0.386$
7. 0.0574
9. 0.135
12. a. $P(Y = 2 \mid X = 1) = 1/3,$ $P(Y = 2 \mid 2) = 3/7,$
       $P(Y = 3 \mid X = 1) = 0,$ $P(Y = 3 \mid 2) = 0,$
       $P(Y = 4 \mid X = 1) = 2/3,$ $P(Y = 4 \mid 2) = 4/7,$
                          $P(Y = 2 \mid 3) = 3/8$
                          $P(Y = 3 \mid 3) = 0$
                          $P(Y = 4 \mid 3) = 5/8$
    b. $P(Y = 2) = 7/18$
       $P(Y = 3) = 0$
       $P(Y = 4) = 11/18$
    c. $P(X = 1) = 3/18,\ P(Y = 1) = 7/18$
       $(3/18)(7/18) \neq 1/18$ so X and Y are dependent random variables.

15. a. $e^{-4} = 0.0183$
    b. $1 - e^{-10} = 0.99995$
    c. 0.981
    d. 0
17. a. 0.0772
    b. 0.9807
18. a. $g(x) = 1/4 \qquad x = 1, 2, 3, 4$

    b. $h(y) = \binom{5}{y}\left(\frac{1}{2}\right)^5 \qquad y = 0, 1, 2, 3, 4, 5$

    c. $f(x, y) = \binom{5}{y}\left(\frac{1}{2}\right)^7 \qquad x = 1, 2, 3, 4 \quad y = 0, 1, 2, 3, 4, 5$

    d. $g(y \mid x) = h(y)$, See b.
    e. $h(x \mid y) = g(x)$, See a.
19. a. 0.0078
    b. 0.0312
    c. 0.234
    d. 0.0312
    e. 0.0312
    f. Yes, $g(x) = h(x \mid y)$
    g. 0.156

Chapter 6

2. a. Equal positive and negative deviations about a central value are given equal weight in μ_2. In μ_2', equal deviations about zero are given equal weight, but zero may not be a central value.
   b. μ_1 would be a particularly bad measure of dispersion since it always equals zero.

7. a. 2
   b. 2, 2

10. a. 0
    b. Symmetry about the mean
    c. 80, 80
    d. Yes, because of b

11. a. $\mu = 5/3, \sigma = \sqrt{2}/3$
    c. Not a probability distribution
    d. $\mu = 45/128, \sigma = \sqrt{391}/128$

13. a. 2
    b. If the experiment is repeated many times, then μ is the expected number of heads that would appear.
    c. (1) Used to measure dispersion
    d. Parameters
    e. 6; it could occur.

15. a. 1, 1
    c. μ_3 would be greater than zero since the distribution is skewed to the right.

17. a. 1/2, 1

20. a. 1/2
    b. 2/3
    d. $f(x) = 0, x < 0; f(x) = x^2, 0 \le x \le 1; f(x) = 1, x > 1$

21. a. Mode equals the mean
    b. Median equals the mean
    c. 15.87 percent; 99.38 percent
    d. 69.12 in.

25. a. 17
    b. 18
    c. 19

26. a. 13.8
    b. 14
    c. 14

29. a. $30,800
    b. $32,667
    c. $15,400,000
    d. No. Half the firms, not half the payroll.

31. a. Median expected to be between 160 and 175 lb.
    b. Positively skewed.

34. a. Not if workers with high wage rates worked more (or less) than 38 hours during the week in question; not if the midpoint assumption is poor.
    b. Half the workers received an hourly wage rate of $2.43 or more during the week in question.

37. Using eight classes with class interval 10 dollars and classes 90 — 99.9, 100 — 109.99, etc.
    d. $125.33
    e. $119.99
    f. $21.98
    g. $125.60
    i. $119.98

39. a. $13,000
    b. $4,136
    c. 0.43

40. a. 6
    b. 2.31
    c. 0.12

43. a. 0.13, 0.84
    b. No, each establishment should be weighted by its sales.
    c. More uniform for shoe repair establishments. The coefficients of variation are 0.161 for tailors and 0.151 for shoe repairmen.

44. a. 40.135, 2.949, 0.07
    b. Numerator measures dispersion. Denominator measures central tendency. The coefficient of variation itself measures variation relative to the mean.
    c. 40.18
    d. The mean and median are fairly close since the distribution is not very skewed.

Chapter 7

1. $(1 - 70\theta)^{-1}$

3. $3(e^{3+\theta} - 1)/(e^3 - 1)(3 + \theta)$

6. $2^{-n}/(1 + e^\theta)^n$

7. $n/2, n/4$

9. a. Continuous uniform distribution, $b = 2, a = 0$
   c. Poisson distribution, $\lambda = 2$
   e. Binomial distribution, $p = 2/3, n = n$

10. a. 2, 2
    b. $\dfrac{2}{3}n, \dfrac{2}{9}n$

11. Both random variables have the same distribution: Poisson with parameter a.

14. 1/2, 1/2, 1/12, 1/12, 0

17. a. No
    b. 4/225

19. a. Yes
    b. 0

Chapter 8

2. a. The first distribution involves the incomes of all lawyers in the United States in that year. Call its mean μ and its standard deviation σ. It will be positively skewed.

b. The second distribution involves the incomes of the 300 randomly selected lawyers. Its mean is probably near μ and its standard deviation near σ; however, each of these statistics may be larger or smaller than its parameter. This distribution is probably positively skewed but may not be.

c. The third distribution involves the means of all possible samples of size 300 selected from the incomes of all United States lawyers that year. Its mean is μ. Its standard deviation is very close to $\sigma/\sqrt{n}$. If the population was infinite, it would be exactly equal to $\sigma/\sqrt{n}$. It is approximately normal, hence nearly symmetric.

3. If the first name is chosen at random, the sample will be a probability sample but not a simple random sample. If the first name is not chosen at random, the sample will be a judgment sample.

5. a. No, because of bias.
   b. Occasionally a judgment sample may be better for some purposes.
   c. Random sampling is the simplest form of probability sampling; that is, it is the simplest form of sampling for which an exact measure of reliability is available.

7. a. $(1 - p + pe^\theta)^{4n}$
   b. $4np$

9. Normal with mean a and variance b^2

11. 0.13591

13. $(1 - \theta)^{-2}, 2$

16. a. $\mu_{\bar{x}} = \mu = \$125.60$ $\sigma_{\bar{x}} = \sigma/\sqrt{9} = \$7.47$
    c. Usually different from the results of a because of sampling error.
    d. $\mu_1 = 0$; various answers for the others.
    e. $\mu_1' = \mu$ the mean; $\mu_2 = \sigma^2$, the variance.
    f. The results will be different from those of a but relatively close to them. Variation is caused by sampling error since in d we based our estimate on five samples instead of all samples.

18. a. 96 percent
    b. 4 percent
    c. 0.77182, 0.88866
    d. From \$7919.40 to \$8280.60
    e. 63,504, which is impossible

20. a. Agree. The probabilities are 0.0062 and 0.00009

22. a. 0.00798
    d. Option (2) is much simpler.

24. a. 0.0082
    b. 0.0082

25. 0.01500

Chapter 9

2. b. An interval estimate must be based on a random sample.

5. a. $66.00
   b. $58.70 to $73.30

7. a. $\bar{x} = \$9,800$
   b. Unbiased
   c. The estimated population standard deviation is $2000.
   d. Slightly biased; if c is answered $2002.50, this estimate is unbiased.
   e. 0.0375
   f. Unbiased
   g. All past and present guests at the hotel.

9. $(x_1 + x_2)/1000$

11. $\hat{\sigma} = \sqrt{\sum_{i=1}^{n}(x_i - 41)^2/n}$

13. a. -5.64 to -2.36

15. a. 9.15 percent to 20.85 percent

17. His resources are sufficient only if he interprets "practically certain" as referring to a confidence level of 92 percent.

19. a. 74.05 to 95.95
    b. 73.39 to 96.61

21. a. 3.315 to 3.345 in.
    b. Since the process is out of control, it should be shut down. The entire set up should be thoroughly checked.
    c. 0.8413
    d. 0.2266

23. a. 0.663 to 0.737

Chapter 10

4. a. Reject $H_0: \mu = 28$ in favor of $H_1: \mu > 28$ at the 0.05 level. Sample $z = 11.11$.

6. Reject $H_0: \mu = 72$ in favor of $H_1: \mu \neq 72$ at the 0.05 level. Sample $t_9 = 9$.

8. Reject $H_0:\mu = 560$ in favor of $H_1:\mu > 560$ at the 0.01 level. Sample $t_4 = 4$. Hence conclude that it is likely that the average number of customers does exceed 560.

10. a. Accept $H_0:\mu = 2.5000$. The region of acceptance is 2.4972 in. $\leq \bar{x} \leq 2.5028$ in.

12. a. Reject $H_1:\pi > 5$ percent in favor of $H_0:\pi = 5$ percent. Hence conclude that the shipment is likely to contain 5 percent or less defective bulbs.
    c. 0.8159.

14. a. Accept $H_0:\mu = 116$ since $\bar{x} = 117 < 117.48$. Conclude that the officials should not assume that the average IQ at Ironclad is higher than the average for all United States college students.

17. Accept $H_0:\pi_A - \pi_B = 0$ against $H_1:\pi_A - \pi_B < 0$ since $p_A - p_B = -0.02 > -0.0321$. Conclude percentage unemployed not likely to be higher in area B.

19. b. Reject $H_0:\pi_1 - \pi_2 = 0$ in favor of $H_1:\pi_1 - \pi_2 \neq 0$ since $p_1 - p_2 = 0.05 > 0.0492$. Conclude that the stores do differ in proportion of items returned.

23. a. Accept $H_0:\pi_B - \pi_L = 0$ as against $H_1:\pi_B - \pi_L \neq 0$ since $p_B - p_L = 0.08 < 0.0813$. Conclude that the percentage favoring more mathematics probably did not differ between these types of schools.

24. a. Accept $H_0:\pi_A - \pi_B = 0$ as against $H_1:\pi_A - \pi_B < 0$ since $p_A - p_B = -0.044 > -0.074$. Conclude that there is probably no difference in percentage of families with incomes over \$8000 between the two cities.

25. a. Accept $H_0:\pi = 0.10$ as against $H_1:\pi > 0.10$ since $p = 0.11 < 0.17$. Hence accept the lot.
    b. 0, 0.9382
    c. 0.319

Chapter 11

2. Neither strategy dominates the other.

4. One possible procedure is to draw one card at random from a standard deck selecting s_{14} if it is a spade and otherwise selecting s_8.

8. No. No.

9. No, it might be a line segment. If not a line, then it is a triangular set. Whenever the set is closed and convex. Yes, two different sets may have the same convex hull. The empty set is its own convex hull.

16. There are four pure strategies: s_0, s_1, s_2, s_3. The respective expected losses are:

$$s_0: (8.0, 0.0)$$
$$s_1: (2.6, 4.5)$$
$$s_2: (7.4, 10.5)$$
$$s_3: (2.0, 15.0)$$

The admissible strategies are s_0, s_1, and s_3 along with the joins $s_0 s_1$ and $s_1 s_3$.

17. The minimax set consists of the single point $(40/11, 40/11)$.

18. The Bayes set consists of the single point $(2.6, 4.5)$.

19. The admissible strategies are $s_{14}: (0, 10)$, $s_{20}: (0.3, 3.6)$, $s_{17}: (1.2, 2)$, all mixed strategies on the join of s_{14} and s_{20}, and all mixed strategies on the join of s_{20} and s_{17}.

20. $(1.2, 2.0)$, $(2.0, 2.0)$, and all mixed strategies on their join.

21. $(1.2, 2.0)$ is the unique Bayes strategy.

24. $(11.9, 5.0, 0.0)$ is the unique Bayes strategy.

Chapter 12

1. $1/2$

3. $3/5$

5. $5/36$

7. $66/535$

9. 0.9901

11. a. $E(\tilde{p}) = 6.2$ percent $> p_b = 4.08$ percent; company should take action A_2 and perform the calibration process at Slocum.

   b. $\text{P}(\tilde{p} = 2\% \mid p = 0) = 0.1138$
   $\text{P}(\tilde{p} = 4\% \mid p = 0) = 0.2140$
   $\text{P}(\tilde{p} = 6\% \mid p = 0) = 0.3014$
   $\text{P}(\tilde{p} = 8\% \mid p = 0) = 0.2826$
   $\text{P}(\tilde{p} = 10\% \mid p = 0) = 0.0882$

   c. $E(\tilde{p}) = 6.03$ percent $> p_b = 4.08$ percent; company should take action A_2 and perform the calibration process at Slocum.

12. a. $E_p = \$21.60$.
   b. $E_s = 0$.

17. a. Since $\mu_0 = 15,250 < \mu_b = 16,000$; decide A_1, and do not purchase the new machinery.
   b. $\$2147.25$

    c. Normal with mean 15,250 hr and variance 6,750,000 hr².

    d. $1757.54

    e. Normal with mean 16,188 hr and variance 2,250,000 hr².

    f. Since $\mu_1 = 16,188 > \mu_b = 16,000$ hr, decide A_2 and purchase the machinery.

    g. $1264.88

21. a.

$\tilde{p}_1$	$P\,(\tilde{p}_1)$
4.35	0.7635
4.66	0.2091
4.87	0.0256
5.03	0.0017
5.15	0.0001
5.27	0.0000
	1.0000

    b. $E_s = 0$.

22.

$\tilde{p}$	$P\,(\tilde{p}\,|\,p = 1/6)$
1	0.0027
2	0.0259
3	0.1183
4	0.1685
5	0.5329
6	0.1516

Since $E(\tilde{p}) = 4.658$ percent $> p_b = 4$ percent, action A_2 should be taken and the contract signed. The association should never even compute the posterior distribution since it is clear from the preposterior that no outcome of a sample of size six can reverse the decision based on the prior.

Chapter 13

2. a. 3/40

   b. $\sqrt{57}/19$

   c. $x/2$

   d. $x^2/12$

4. a. $-1/75$

   b. $-\sqrt{6}/6$

   c. $(1 - x)/2$

   d. $(1 - x)^2/20$

5. a. 3/19

7. a. $y_p = x/2$

9. a. $-1/4$
   b. $1/16$
   c. $y_p = -x/4 + 145/2$
   d. $x_p = -y/4 + 65$

11. a. 375
    b. 375
    c. The variance about the first regression line, measured in a vertical direction, is equal to the variance about the second regression line, measured in a horizontal direction.

17. $y_p = +x/10$

18. a. $E(y \mid x) = (40/3) \ln 4 = 18.48.$
    b. 18.48 (or 18 dozen eggs)
    c. 0

19. a. $y_p = (40/3) \ln 4 = 18.48$ (or 18 dozen).
    b. 0

20. a. $x_p = \$0.61$
    b. 0

Chapter 14

2. a. $a = 25/41, b = 19/82$
   c. $a = 290/19, b = 18/19$

4. a. $y = -x/10 + 6$
   b. -1

5. Yes. Increases in x are associated with decreases in y.

6. a. 8 is the ordinate of the regression line when $x = 0$. If $x = 0$ lies within the range of the data, then 8 is our best estimate of $E(Y \mid x = 0)$.
   b. 15 is the slope of the regression line. Within the range of the data it is the average change in y per unit change in x.

7. 25 is our best estimate of the variance in Y which is not associated with changes in X. 49 is our best estimate of the variance in Y including that portion associated with changes in X. 0.70.

10. a. \$6742
    b. \$2713 to \$10,771

11. a. -0.57
    b. It is not likely that a significant association exists since $t_4 = 1.39 < 2.776$. Accept H_0: $\rho = 0$.

13. a. $7143
    b. $4530 to $9756
    c. $6944
    d. $3516 to $10,372

14. a. 83 percent
    b. 0.89

18. b. $a = 5.0250$, $b = 4.8799$, $\hat{\sigma}^2(Y \mid x) = 0.9587$

$$\hat{V}(\hat{\alpha}, \hat{\beta}) = \begin{bmatrix} 0.1068 & -0.2017 \\ -0.2017 & 0.6909 \end{bmatrix}$$

Confidence limits, for α: 4.34 to 5.71

for β: 3.13 to 6.63.

e. Test $H_0: E(Y \mid x) = 6$ versus $H_1: E(Y \mid x) \neq 6$. With $\alpha = 0.05$, accept H_0, and conclude that this machinist is within the normal range of variation.

f. No, x is preassigned.

Chapter 15

3. a. Fit to the logarithms of the data. This plot is approximately linear.
   b. $a = 2.5945$, $b = 0.1622$

$$\log \hat{y} = 2.5945 + 0.1622x$$

d. No. The cyclical and residual factors would have made the resulting equation different but hopefully not too different.
e. Very dangerous. Make such a prediction only if forced to do so. Qualify it carefully.

6. a. (1) Yes, if data are to be analyzed for changes over time; no, if data are treated as a sample, and time is not considered.
   (2) Analysis recommended should be consistent with part (1).
   b. No. The observations are taken at the same point in time.

7. a. $\hat{y} = 55.43 + 3.14x$

$$x = 0 \text{ in } 1940 \qquad x = -3 \text{ in } 1925$$

b. 62.94 millions
c. Be a bit more cautious in such an extrapolation. However, six-tenths of a time unit is not an unreasonable period for an extrapolation.

9. a. $a = 0.3341$, $b = 0.1310$

$$\log \hat{y} = 0.3341 + 0.1310x$$
$$x = 0 \text{ in } 1950, \text{ and } x = -2 \text{ in } 1940$$

b. It would have been more usual to use a month whose seasonal index was approximately one. The trend ordinates all tend to be low when the lowest month is used.

c. Trend: \$191,300; seasonal: $-$ \$38,260, cyclical and residual: \$6960.

12. a. 160.2 billions of kilowatt hours

b. 94.3 percent

d. $\log \hat{y} = 2.179 + 0.148x$

$$x = -5 \text{ in } 1910, \text{ and } x = 5 \text{ in } 1960$$

e. The intercept estimates the consumption of electric power in the United States in 1935 as 151 billion kilowatt-hr. The slope estimates the consumption of electric power as increasing by about 98 percent per ten-year period.

g. -23 billion kilowatt-hr; -0.187

16. The increase in the physical volume of exports, 0.17 billions of 1950 dollars, was greater than the increase in the physical volume of imports, 0.08 billions of 1950 dollars. We assume that the two price indices are appropriate for the respective series, and that the physical volume per dollar is approximately the same in each case.

18. a.

1955	120	1958	100
1956	103	1959	114
1957	109	1960	130

b. Prices in 1956 were on the average 103 percent of prices in 1958 for a constant group of products and fixed quantities of those products. The quantities were those quantities appropriate in 1957.

20. a.

1965	95	1969	110
1966	102	1970	112
1967	87	1971	105
1968	100		

b. Employment in 1967 was 85 percent of employment in the base year and 87 percent of employment in 1968.

23. a. 1.3 percent decrease

b. 12.6 percent decrease

24. a. Trend: 95,000 lb

Seasonal: 5,774 lb

Cyclical plus residual: 20,476 lb

b. No. Compare 115,476 lb with 122,778 lb.

Chapter 16

1. a. $Y_t = 4.3432 + 0.0567X_{t-1} - 0.304X_{t-2} + \epsilon$

$\quad\quad\quad\quad\quad (0.0270) \quad\quad\quad (0.0267)$

b. The regression coefficient for last year's sales should be positive. High sales suggest high future sales and larger new plant and equipment expenditures. Since calculated $t_7 = 2.10 >$ tabulated $t_7 (0.05) = 1.895$, we conclude that last year's sales have a significant effect on the current year's new plant and equipment expenditures.

c. Yes. X_{t-1} and X_{t-2} would usually be highly correlated. For these data the sample correlation coefficient is 0.8250.

3. a. $I_t = \alpha_1 + \beta \hat{S}_t + \delta K_{t-1}$
$\hat{S}_t = \alpha_2 + \gamma_{21} Y_t + \gamma_{22} Y_{t-1}$

b. $I_t =$ investment in the current year.
$\hat{S}_t =$ forecast sales for the current year.
$K_{t-1} =$ stock of existing plant and equipment at end of previous year.
$Y_t, Y_{t-1} =$ current and previous year's disposable income
K_{t-1} and Y_{t-1} are exogenous; the others are endogenous.

c. We need an equation for Y_t.

5. a. $a = \alpha^\delta;$ $\qquad b = \delta \alpha^{\delta-1} \beta;$ $\qquad c = \delta(\delta - 1)\alpha^{\delta-2}\beta^2$
$\epsilon =$ remainder term plus error

b. Solve the equations of part a simultaneously obtaining

$$\delta = b^2/(b^2 - ac); \qquad \log \alpha = (\log a)/\delta;$$
$$\beta = b/\delta\alpha^{\delta-1}$$

In practice, this device will sometimes lead to unreasonable estimates.

7. a. Let $n^2 \sigma_X{}^2 = n \sum X^2 - (\sum X)^2$, then

$$E(\hat{\beta}) = \frac{\beta}{1 + (n - 1/n^2)(\sigma^2 \sum X^2/\sigma_X{}^2)}$$

b. If σ^2 is known, then an unbiased estimate of β would be

$$\beta^* = \left[1 + \frac{n-1}{n^2} \frac{\sigma^2 \sum X^2}{\sigma_X{}^2}\right]\hat{\beta}$$

9. a. The initial estimate of the regression equation is
$$Y_t = 2.4727 + 0.11035 X_t + U_t$$
yielding $\hat{\lambda} = -0.0736$.

b. The regression of Z_t on w_t is estimated by
$$Z_t = 1.8014 + 0.1141 w_t + \epsilon_t$$
$$(4.4649) \quad (0.0205)$$

Hence the new estimate of the regression of Y_t on X_t is
$$Y_t = 1.6779 + 0.1141 X_t + U_t$$
$$(4.1588) \quad (0.0205)$$

c. Autocorrelation does not seem to be a serious problem. $\hat{\lambda}$ is small, and the two estimates of β do not differ by very much.

Bibliography

Business and Economic Statistics

Chao, L. C., *Statistics: Methods and Analyses*, McGraw-Hill, New York, 1969.

Croxton, F. E., Cowden, D. J., and Bolch, B. W., *Practical Business Statistics*, Prentice-Hall, Englewood Cliffs, N.J., 1969.

Fox, K. A., *Intermediate Economic Statistics*, Wiley, New York, 1968.

Merrett, A. J. and Bannock, G., *Business Economics and Statistics*, Prentice-Hall, Englewood Cliffs, N.J., 1962.

Merrill, W. C. and Fox, K. A., *Introduction to Economic Statistics*, Wiley, New York, 1970.

Neter, J. and Wasserman, W., *Fundamental Statistics for Business and Economics*, Allyn and Bacon, Boston, 1966.

Richmond, S. B., *Statistical Analysis*, Ronald, New York, 1964.

Schlaifer, R., *Probability and Statistics for Business Decisions*, McGraw-Hill, New York, 1959.

Sasaki, K., *Statistics for Modern Business Decision Making*, Wadsworth, Belmont, Calif., 1968.

Applied Statistics

Bailey, D. E., *Probability and Statistics*, Wiley, New York, 1971.

Dixon, W. J. and Massey, F. J., *Introduction to Statistical Analysis*, McGraw-Hill, New York, 1969.

Freund, J. E., *Modern Elementary Statistics*, Prentice-Hall, Englewood Cliffs, N.J., 1960.

Fryer, H. C., *Concepts and Methods of Experimental Statistics*, Allyn and Bacon, Boston, 1966.

Hughes, A. and Grawoig, D., *Statistics: A Foundation for Analysis*, Addison-Wesley, Reading, Mass., 1971.

Snedecor, G. W., *Statistical Methods*, Iowa State Press, Ames, Iowa, 1957.

Steel, R. G. D. and Torrie, J. H., *Principles and Procedures of Statistics*, McGraw-Hill, New York, 1960.

Wonnacott, T. H. and Wonnacott, R. J., *Introductory Statistics*, Wiley, New York, 1969.

Yale, G. U. and Kendall, M. G., *An Introduction to the Theory of Statistics*, Hafner, New York, 1950.

Sampling

Cochran, W. G., *Sampling Techniques*, Wiley, New York, 1953.

Deming, W. E., *Some Theory of Sampling*, Wiley, New York, 1950.

Hansen, M. H., Hurwitz, W. N., and Madow, W. G., *Sample Survey Methods and Theory*, Wiley, New York, 1953.

Raj, D., *Sampling Theory*, McGraw-Hill, New York, 1968.

Probability Theory

Drake, A. W., *Fundamentals of Applied Probability Theory*, McGraw-Hill, New York, 1967.

Feller, W., *An Introduction to Probability Theory and Its Applications*, Vol. I, Wiley, New York, 1968.

Goldberg, S., *Probability, An Introduction*, Prentice-Hall, Englewood Cliffs, N.J., 1964.

Guenther, W. C., *Concepts of Probability*, McGraw-Hill, New York, 1968.

Hodges, J. L. and Lehmann, E. L., *Elements of Finite Probability*, Holden-Day, San Francisco, 1964.

Parzen, E., *Modern Probability Theory and Its Applications*, Wiley, New York, 1960.

Wadsworth, G. P. and Bryan, J. G., *Introduction to Probability and Random Variables*, McGraw-Hill, New York, 1960.

Elementary Mathematical Statistics

Birnbaum, Z. W., *Introduction to Probability and Mathematical Statistics*, Harper, New York, 1962.

Brunk, H. D., *An Introduction to Mathematical Statistics*, Ginn, Boston, 1960.

Dwass, M., *Probability and Statistics*, Benjamin, New York, 1970.

Fraser, D. A. S., *Statistics: An Introduction*, Wiley, New York, 1958.

Freund, J. E., *Mathematical Statistics*, Prentice-Hall, Englewood Cliffs, N.J., 1962.

Hoel, P. G., *Introduction to Mathematical Statistics*, Wiley, New York, 1971.

Hogg, R. V. and Craig, A. T., *Introduction to Mathematical Statistics*, Macmillan, New York, 1970.

Meyer, P. L., *Introductory Probability and Statistical Applications*, Addison-Wesley, Reading, Mass., 1970.

Mood, A. M. and Graybill, F. A., *Introduction to the Theory of Statistics*, McGraw-Hill, New York, 1963.

Tucker, H. G., *An Introduction to Probability and Mathematical Statistics*, Academic Press, New York, 1962.

Several Advanced Texts

Anderson, T. W., *An Introduction to Multivariate Statistical Analysis*, Wiley, New York, 1958.

Johnston, J., *Econometric Methods*, McGraw-Hill, New York, 1963.

Kendall, M. G. and Stuart, A., *The Advanced Theory of Statistics*, Griffin, London, 1966.

Lehmann, E. L., *Testing Statistical Hypotheses*, Wiley, New York, 1959.

Morrison, D. F., *Multivariate Statistical Methods*, McGraw-Hill, New York, 1967.

Raiffa, H. and Schlaifer, R., *Applied Statistical Decision Theory*, Harvard, Boston, 1961.

Wilks, S. S., *Mathematical Statistics*, Wiley, New York, 1962.

Index

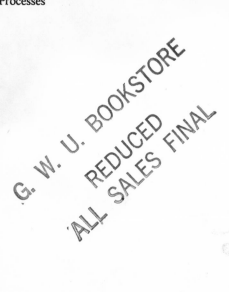